Global Marketplace for Private Health Insurance

Global Marketplace for Private Health Insurance

Strength in Numbers

Editors

Alexander S. Preker, Peter Zweifel,
and **Onno P. Schellekens**

THE WORLD BANK
Washington, D.C.

1818 H Street, NW
Washington, D.C. 20433
Telephone: 202-473-1000
Internet: www.worldbank.org
E-mail: feedback@worldbank.org

1 2 3 4 13 12 11 10

ISBN: 978-0-8213-7507-5
e-ISBN: 978-0-8213-7677-5
DOI: 10.1596/978-0-8213-7507-5

Library of Congress Cataloging-in-Publication Data

Global marketplace for private health insurance : strength in numbers / Alexander S. Preker, Peter Zweifel, and Onno P. Schellekens, eds.
p. cm.—(Health, nutrition and population series)
Includes bibliographical references and index.
ISBN-13: 978-0-8213-7507-5 (alk. paper); e-ISBN: 978-0-8213-7677-5
1. Insurance, Health—Economic aspects—Developing countries. I. Preker, Alexander S., 1951– II. Zweifel, Peter. 1946– III. Schellekens, Onno P., 1964– IV. World Bank.
[DNLM: 1. Insurance, Health—economics. 2. Health Expenditures. 3. Models, Econometric. 4. Private Sector. 5. World Health. W 100 G562 2008]
RA413.5.D44G56 2008368.38'2--dc22

2008008388

Contents

BOXES

FIGURES

TABLES

Foreword

The development challenges of addressing health problems in low- and middle-income countries are daunting but not insurmountable. There are now known and affordable interventions to deal with many aspects of the HIV/AIDS crisis as well as the continued challenge posed by malaria and other major infectious diseases.

Unfortunately, the cost to individual households is unpredictable and can impoverish even middle-income families who are often not insured. Thus, achieving the health-related Millennium Development Goals (MDGs) will require mobilization of substantial additional financial resources for the health sector, improved management of financial risk and better spending of existing scarce resources, in addition to addressing the intersectoral and other key determinants of illness.

Significant resources are already being mobilized through both governments and donors. There is a tremendous opportunity to leverage this public sector engagement with additional private sector resources. As demonstrated in this volume, private voluntary health insurance already plays an important and growing role in this story.

Three major development objectives of health insurance in low- and middle-income countries are highlighted in this volume: securing sustainable financing for health care providers that serve the health needs of vulnerable populations; providing financial protection against the impoverishing cost of illness; and reducing social exclusion from organized health financing and delivery systems. Private health insurance schemes can address the needs of the poor and other vulnerable populations with appropriate combinations of subsidies, risk pooling, household savings, and user charges. The authors of this book argue in favor of a *multipillar* approach to health care financing in low- and middle-income countries that combines these instruments in addressing the underlying development objectives described above, while putting a strong emphasis on private voluntary health insurance. In this way, private means can make a significant contribution to public ends.

Lars H. Thunell
Executive Vice President
International Finance
Corporation (IFC)

Bert Koenders
Minister for Development
Cooperation
Netherlands

Preface

Developing countries face an enormous challenge balancing competing demands for scarce resources available to the public sector. Mobilizing financial resources for the health sector at a time of global economic turmoil is even more daunting. More than 100 million of the poor have already fallen back into poverty as a result of the financial crisis. Millions more are at risk of following them. It is precisely at such a time—when the poorest and most vulnerable groups are at greatest risk—that new and innovative financing mechanisms are most needed.

The research for this volume shows that private voluntary health insurance (PVHI) can contribute to social goals like other forms of health insurance. When properly designed and coupled with subsidies, it contributes to the well-being of poor and middle-class households, not just the rich. And it can contribute to development goals such as improved access to health care, better financial protection against the cost of illness, and reduced social exclusion.

The world of technical experts and policy wonks is divided into two camps. One vilifies private voluntary health insurance as an evil to be avoided at all cost. Its constituency claims that such insurance leads to overconsumption of care, escalating costs, shunting of scarce resources away from the poor, cream skimming, adverse selection, moral hazard, and an inequitable, U.S.-styled health care system.

But for others private insurance is the answer to many intractable problems. They claim that private insurance coverage provides access to care when needed without the long waiting lists, low-quality care, and rudeness often suffered by households using public services provided by Ministries of Health. Besides, these PVHI proponents assert, many of the problems observed in private health insurance are equally true for social health insurance and subsidized or free access to government-provided health services.

In a world of improved knowledge about the causes and potential solutions to poor health and illness—but limited resources—there is no shortage of anecdotal personal experience to substantiate the arguments on both sides of this debate. Some people may have been refused coverage by an insurance plan or perceive unjust premium increases. Or they may have seen a sick relative wait for hours in the emergency room of a public hospital before being examined by the attending physician only to be sent home without treatment.

Such divergent views on the role of the state and the private sector in health care financing and health insurance are central to debate on health reform in many countries. Barack Obama has put his presidency on the line by pledging to expand insurance coverage to all Americans during his first term in office.

For decades, many middle-income countries have struggled with this same challenge.

New and innovative approaches to health insurance are also emerging in South Asia and Africa. At a Conference on Healthcare Systems in Africa (2008), Bert Koenders, Minister for Development Cooperation of the Netherlands, stressed that health insurance is becoming a new paradigm for reaching the Millennium Development Goals in low-income countries. In Nigeria, private health maintenance organizations (HMOs) are used to provide health insurance coverage for the population. The National Health Insurance Scheme in Ghana has reached almost 70 percent population coverage through nongovernmental District Mutual Health Organizations. In Rwanda, community-level health insurance has reached coverage rates higher than 80 percent in some areas. These are a few of the many examples provided in this book that challenge common myths about the limited potential role for private voluntary health insurance in development.

Global Marketplace for Private Health Insurance: Strength in Numbers is the fourth volume in a series of in-depth reviews on the role of health care financing in improving access for low-income populations to needed care, protecting them from the impoverishing effects of illness, and addressing the important issues of social exclusion in government financed programs. In an earlier volume, *Health Financing for Poor People: Resource Mobilization and Risk Sharing*, the editors Alexander S. Preker and Guy Carrin presented work from a World Bank review of the role of community financing schemes in reaching the poor in outlying rural areas or inner city slums. Most community financing schemes have evolved under severe economic constraints, political instability, and lack of good governance. Government taxation capacity is usually weak in poor countries, formal mechanisms of social protection for vulnerable populations absent, and government oversight of the informal health sector lacking.

In this context of extreme public sector failure, community involvement in the financing of health care provides a critical though insufficient first step in the long march toward improved access to health care by the poor and social protection against the cost of illness. Though not a panacea, community financing can complement weak government involvement in health care financing and risk management related to the cost of illness. Based on an extensive survey of the literature, the main strengths of community financing schemes are the degree of outreach penetration achieved through community participation, their contribution to financial protection against illness, and their increase in access to health care for low-income rural and informal sector workers. Some of their main weaknesses are the low level of revenues that can be mobilized from poor communities, the frequent exclusion of the very poorest from participation in such schemes without some form of subsidy, the small size of the risk pool, the limited management capacity in rural and low-income contexts, and their isolation from the more comprehensive benefits that are often available through more formal health financing mechanisms and provider networks. Many of these observations are also true for private voluntary health insurance.

In another related work, *Social Reinsurance: A New Approach to Sustainable Community Health Financing,* the editors David M. Dror and Alexander S. Preker detail the use of community rather than individual risk-rated reinsurance as a way of addressing some of the known weaknesses of community financing schemes. The authors of this volume show how standard techniques of reinsurance, used for a long time in other branches of insurance, can be applied to microinsurance in health care. This is especially relevant in situations in which the underlying risk pool is too small to protect the schemes against the expected expenditure variance. In this context, the reinsurance provides a "virtual" expansion of the risk pool without undermining the social capital underpinning participation by rural and urban informal sector workers in such small community-based schemes.

In the third volume, *Private Voluntary Health Insurance in Development: Friend or Foe,* the editors Alexander S. Preker, Richard M. Scheffler, and Mark C. Bassett present work from a World Bank review of the present and potential future roles of private voluntary health insurance in low- and middle-income countries. The research was designed specifically to explore health care financing challenges faced at low-income levels such as in the Africa and South Asia Regions, but the review also draws upon important lessons learned elsewhere in the world and should therefore also be of interest to a broader readership.

Lessons learned from these earlier reviews provide an important backdrop for the empirical review of case studies on private voluntary health insurance presented in this volume. Notably, there are close parallels between community financing and private health insurance. Both are nongovernmental but often have important interfaces with government programs through subsidies and shared provider networks. Both rely on voluntary membership. Membership is small unless the effective risk pool is enlarged through reinsurance or federation with other schemes. Both depend on trust. Their members must have confidence that their contribution paid today will lead to benefits when needed tomorrow. Both are vulnerable to insurance market failure such as adverse selection, cream skimming, moral hazard, and the free-rider phenomenon.

But there are also some important differences. Community financing schemes emerged largely due to governments' inability to reach rural poor and urban informal sector workers. In this context—for lack of better solutions—small communities such as rice growers, fishermen, carpenters, and other trades people started their own programs, often linked with rural loans, savings, and microinsurance programs. Many have benefited from donor involvement during the early start up phase. The populations served are usually poor. The benefits package they can offer is constrained by their limited resources unless they receive a government or donor subsidy.

Private voluntary health insurance schemes were often set up by large enterprises. Such programs were seen as fostering a "self-help" attitude by encouraging employees to pay in advance for the health care benefits that they would receive later. It was hoped that access to health care would cut illness-related absenteeism and improve labor productivity. The populations served are usually formal sector workers. The benefits provided are often generous compared with those provided by community financing schemes and publicly financed government programs. Whereas community financing schemes tend to be not for profit, many private voluntary health insurance schemes are for profit.

Success in improving access and financial protection through community and private voluntary health insurance have led many countries to attempt to make membership compulsory and to offer subsidized insurance through the public sector. Arguments in favor of this approach include the potential for achieving higher population coverage and broadening the risk pool by collecting at source from formally employed workers. This important topic will be the focus of a forthcoming review of *Scaling Up Affordable Health Insurance,* edited by Alexander S. Preker, Onno P. Schellekens, Marianne Lindner, and Dov Chernichovsky.

Some countries have tried to "leap frog" both private and public insurance by introducing legislation to give the population at large access to a free government-subsidized National Health Service. For several reasons, however, few low- and middle-income countries have succeeded in securing universal access through this approach. First, at low income levels, weak taxation capacity limits the fiscal space available for health and other segments of the public sector. Second, there is a lack of trust in government-run programs into which the population is asked to pay today for benefits that may or may not be available tomorrow due to shifting priorities and volatile resource flows. Finally, public subsidies often do not reach the poor when programs are designed to provide care for everyone. The resulting underfinanced and low-quality publicly financed health services leave the poor and other households without adequate care and exposed to severe financial risk at the time of illness.

How scarce money is spent in the public sector probably has a greater impact on the services available to the poor than the presence or absence of private and government-run mandatory health insurance. This is the topic of four other past reviews: *Spending Wisely: Buying Health Services for the Poor,* edited by Alexander S. Preker and John C. Langenbrunner; *Public Ends: Private Means,* edited by Alexander S. Preker, Xingzhu Liu, Edit V. Velényi, and Enis Baris; *The Corporatization of Public Hospitals,* edited by Alexander S. Preker and April Harding; and *Private Participation in Health* Services, edited by April Harding and Alexander S. Preker. These four reviews emphasize the important role that markets and nongovernmental providers play in improving value for money spent not only by the public sector but also the range of services available through mandates with private health insurance companies.

In all cases, strong public policies and government involvement are needed to secure an efficient and equitable system of health care financing. But state involvement by itself is not sufficient. The editors and authors contributing to the review presented in this volume argue a strong case for giving private health insurance greater attention than it has received in the past. It is an important instrument—together with other financing mechanisms—for achieving fiscally sustainable access to needed health services, financial protection against the impoverishing cost of illness, and health insurance coverage for certain social groups that are often excluded from access to publicly provided health care.

This volume, *Global Marketplace for Private Voluntary Health Insurance: Strength in Numbers,* builds on the story presented in *Private Health Insurance in Development: Friend or Foe.* That first volume on private health insurance in developing countries was divided into three parts: (1) Economic Underpinnings, (2) Empirical Evidence, from global trends in OECD and developing countries, and (3) From Theory to Practice, on the evolution of the health insurance industry, regulatory issues, and feasibility of expanding private health insurance in low- and middle-income countries. This second volume is also divided into three parts: (1) Empirical and Economic Underpinnings of private health insurance in low- and middle-income countries; (2) Evidence from the Past; and (3) Opportunities for the Future.

In the Introduction, chapter 1, "Strength in Numbers," Alexander S. Preker and Onno P. Schellekens summarize the key health financing challenges in the Africa Region and low-income countries in other regions, policy options for reform, methodology for the study on private voluntary health insurance, and key findings from this study. They emphasize the need to combine several instruments to achieve three major development objectives in health care financing: (1) sustainable access to needed health care; (2) greater financial protection against the impoverishing cost of illness; and (3) reduction in social exclusion from organized health financing instruments. These instruments include subsidies, insurance, savings, and user charges. Few organizational and institutional arrangements include all four of these instruments under a single system.

The authors argue in favor of a *multipillar approach* to health care financing in low- and middle-income countries, which would include an important private voluntary health insurance component (community- and private enterprise-based programs).

Part 1 Empirical and Economic Underpinnings

In chapter 2, "Six Regions: One Story," Denis Drechsler and Johannes P. Jütting review the current status of private health insurance in low- and middle-income countries and its significance for national health systems in the future.

The authors observe that PVHI involving prepayment and risk sharing plays a small but rising role in the developing world. Although coverage rates are generally below 10 percent of the population, this share is growing in a number of countries (for example, South Africa, Uruguay, and Lebanon). Various factors contribute to this development: growing dissatisfaction with public health care, liberalization of markets, and increased international trade in the insurance industry. Economic growth in these countries is allowing stronger and more diversified consumer demand. Consumer demand is expected to put pressure on the supply side of the system to increase choices and improve the quality of health care coverage.

Growth in PVHI presents both opportunities and threats to health care systems in developing countries. If PVHI is carefully managed and adapted to local needs and preferences, it can be a valuable complement to existing health care financing options. In particular, nonprofit group–based insurance schemes could become an important pillar of health care financing, especially for individuals who would otherwise be left outside a country's health insurance system. However, PVHI could also undermine the objective of universal coverage. Opening up markets for private health insurance without an appropriate regulatory framework might widen inequalities in access to health care: it may lead to cost escalation, a deterioration in public services, a reduction in the provision of preventive health care, and a widening of the rich-poor divide in a country's medical system. Given these risks, the crucial challenge for policy makers is to develop a regulatory framework that is adapted to a country's institutional capacities and which, at the same time, sets the rules and standards in which PVHI can efficiently operate and develop.

In chapter 3, "From Theory to Practice," Peter Zweifel reviews the empirical evidence of private voluntary health insurance against the theoretical groundwork laid out by Mark V. Pauly and Peter Zweifel in *Private Voluntary Health Insurance in Development: Friend or Foe?* edited by Alexander S. Preker, Richard M. Scheffler, and Mark C. Bassett. Zweifel and Pauly draw not only on the received theory of demand for insurance, but also on industrial organization to assess the potential of voluntary private health insurance in low-income countries. Moreover, barriers to entry (as an example) crucially depend on institutional detail that varies between countries and about which the authors knew little. For this reason, their theoretical predictions and conclusions were in need of empirical verification. The economic theory of demand for insurance was pioneered by K.J. Arrow more than forty years ago. Early work by E.B. Keeler, J.P. Newhouse, and C.E. Phelps on demand for health insurance dates to about thirty years ago. Empirical evidence concerning the determinants of health insurance demand has been slow to accumulate outside the United States. Whether and to what extent such demand is met also depends on supply, namely, the behavior of insurers. Here, the gaps in knowledge are even more glaring. Although the behavior of U.S. for-profit insurers has been studied extensively, much less is know about various forms of health insurance in developing countries. For example, why do consumers in some settings in developing counties opt for community-based health insurance even when care is freely available in public hospitals and clinics? This chapter is a first attempt to test some longstanding theories about private voluntary health insurance against an emerging body of empirical information.

Part 2 Evidence from the Past

Part 2 presents six country case studies in which existing household survey data allowed analysis of the role of private health insurance in financing health care. The authors that contributed to this section of the book analyzed the impact of private health insurance in countries that have such programs on financial protection against the cost of illness, insurance coverage, nonmedical consumption, access to health care, and labor markets.

In chapters 4 to 9, the authors look at what has worked and what has not worked in terms of the impact private voluntary health insurance on several outcome and process indicators. They use a range of quantitative analysis of micro-level household survey data and qualitative analysis of key policy, management, organizational, and institutional determinants of good outcomes. The analyses indicate that private health insurance can contribute, in a positive way, to: (1) providing financial protection against the cost of illness; (2) expanding coverage and including a wide range of client groups; (3) increasing disposable income and smoothing household consumption; (4) increasing access to affordable health care; and (5) improving labor market participation.

In chapter 4, Ricardo Bitrán and Rodrigo Muñoz review the role of voluntary health insurance (VHI) in Chile, focusing on the determinants of enrolment and its impact on access to care and financial protection, based on household data from the CASEN 2000 national socioeconomic survey (MIDEPLAN 2000). The results may help decision makers assess the potential role of VHI in low- and middle-income countries as a policy tool for improving access to services and financial protection. First, the authors examine household VHI enrolment decisions. Second, they evaluate the impact of VHI on access to health services. Third, they use a financial protection indicator based on the stability of nonmedical consumption to evaluate the performance of VHI. The findings show that enrolment in VHI is positively correlated with health risk, income, and education. Also, access to health care is better and financially more equitable among households with mandatory or voluntary health insurance than among uninsured households. What is more, nonmedical consumption appears substantially more stable among insured households. These results highlight the importance of mandatory and VHI schemes in developing countries. A main policy challenge is achieving enrolment for the poor, especially in the informal sector.

In chapter 5, Heba Nassar and Sameh El-Saharty review the role of private health insurance in the Arab Republic of Egypt. With its significant progress in health status, Egypt has caught up with other economically comparable countries. Demand for health services will continue to grow, however, due to Egypt's demographic and health transitions and other challenges confronting the health system. Health expenditure has been outpacing economic growth and is therefore unsustainable, given the modest medium-term economic growth projections. Social health insurance coverage is inequitable, covering less than half the population, and the health spending burden on households has increased. Public expenditures on health are inefficient, as exemplified by the sector's fragmented organization, low bed occupancy rate, and lack of performance-based payments to public providers. The VHI market is underdeveloped, covering only 5 percent of the population, and is concentrated (96 percent) in the hands of professional syndicates. This chapter examines the impact of voluntary health insurance on financial protection, consumption smoothing, access to health care, and labor market productivity; and the determinants of enrolment with VHI. According to their econometric analysis, the authors find that VHI could increase workers' financial protection and that Egypt's people might not object to sharing in its cost for better quality health services and access to them.

In chapter 6, Michael Thiede and Vimbayi Mutyambizi review the role of private health insurance in South Africa. More than 10 years after the first democratic elections, the provision of health services in South Africa is still characterized by extreme inequities. This chapter focuses on the levels of financial protection in the public and private sectors of the South African health system and analyzes the determinants of health services utilization. The chapter provides an overview of the context within which the health sector operates. It further sketches the peculiar structure of the private sector, namely the medical schemes environment. Extreme socioeconomic inequality is identified as the main determinant of differences in financial vulnerability through analysis of financial protection and financial vulnerability at different income levels between the public and private sectors (the medical schemes environment) on the basis of a national survey The chapter examines health services utilization, based on another national household survey. These results reflect the dichotomy of the South African health system and reemphasize the role of socioeconomic status as reflected in education and household wealth. Today, VHI in the form of medical scheme membership is an option only for the better off. The chapter briefly addresses the government's health reform agenda to conclude that the proposed steps ought to be accompanied by efforts to investigate insurance options for lower socioeconomic strata.

In chapter 7, Siripen Supakankunti reviews the role of private health insurance in Thailand. Universal health care coverage began in Thailand late in 2002, so its full effects are not yet known. The analyses done for this study confirm that private health insurance can improve access to health care for the insured. However, services are unlikely to cost less. The coexistence of universal coverage heavily influences a person's decision to apply for voluntary private health insurance, it was also found. As a supplementary scheme, private health insurance looks attractive to some Thais, mainly the better off. Unless PVHI becomes widely affordable, however, its impact on the kingdom as a whole does not seem promising. This chapter examines the roles of private health insurance that affect access to health care of people in Thailand. It starts with a descriptive review of the relative importance of voluntary private health insurance vis-à-vis the public scheme. The second part covers quantitative aspects. It was found that private health insurance still has a promising future as the Thai economy prospers even though its share in the whole industry is relatively small, especially under the present circumstances of the implementation of the Universal Coverage (UC) scheme, both for the status of private health insurance as a supplementary scheme, and the impacts of the scheme.

In chapter 8, Anna Cederberg Heard and Ajay Mahal review the role of private health insurance in Turkey. PVHI coverage in Turkey, though still small, has been growing rapidly. This growth has occurred in an environment where, despite significant coverage by social insurance schemes, government financing, and insurance for the poor, between 10 percent and 30 percent of the population is uninsured. Out-of-pocket (OOP) payments account for 28 percent of all spending on health. In this chapter, the role of private insurance in influencing access to health care and OOP health spending is examined. Using data from a large household health care utilization and expenditure survey for Turkey, a two-part model (for example, Yip and Berman 2001) is estimated to assess the impact of private health insurance on health care utilization and expenditures. The main finding is that private health insurance has increased utilization of outpatient care, and possibly inpatient care, controlling for other confounders. However, private insurance is associated with increased spending on outpatient care, indicating that it has done more to increase access to high-end private care than to provide protection against the financial risk from illness. The chapter concludes with policy implications and highlights potential areas where an expansion of private insurance may contribute to enhanced utilization and financial risk protection against catastrophic illness.

In chapter 9, M. Kate Bundorf and Mark V. Pauly review the role of private health insurance for low-income populations in the United States. Protection from the financial risk associated with uncertain future spending on health care is an important theoretical rationale for the purchase of health insurance, but relatively little empirical research has been devoted to this benefit. In this chapter, the relationship between the purchase of private health insurance, and variation in out-of-pocket spending on health care in the United States is examined. The estimates presented suggest that an important benefit of private health insurance is the extent to which it provides protection from financial risk, particularly for low-income individuals. In a country where a significant part of the population still does not have full access to health insurance and basic care, the results of this study have significant policy implications.

Part 3 Opportunities for the Future

Part 3 presents six case studies of countries in which existing data on ability and willingness to pay and other variables allowed the authors to construct economic models of the potential role of private health insurance. In the settings examined, PVHI coverage currently plays a minor role but, if the facilitating environment is made more favorable, it might become more significant in the future.

In chapters 10 to 15, the authors look forward to what might happen in terms of financial protection, access to affordable care, fiscal sustainability, labor market effects, and other economic variables if private voluntary health insurance were to play a bigger or smaller role in the future than it now does or did in the past. These case studies use financial modeling of future revenue and expenditure flows (2005–15). In most cases, existing information on willingness and ability to pay indicates considerable growth potential for private voluntary health insurance in most low- and middle-income countries, in parallel to growth in state subsidies for the health sector and government-run mandatory health insurance.

In chapter 10, Teh-wei Hu and Xiao-hua Ying review the current and growing role of private health insurance in China. Despite China's rapid economic growth during the past decade, health insurance coverage has not improved in either urban or rural areas. Between 1993 and 2003, the proportion of urban residents without health insurance rose from 27 percent to 50 percent. In rural areas, 79 percent of the population did not have health insurance in 2003. The Chinese government has not been able to play a major role in providing public health insurance. Although the government has recently increased some public funding for health care, private health insurance may also play an important role by allotting private financial resources for these services. In the coming few years, at least an additional 2.6 million urban individuals, are projected to enroll in China's private health insurance. Since China's entry into the World Trade Organization (WTO) in 2001, foreign insurance companies have been very actively exploring the Chinese private health insurance market. The Chinese government needs to develop an effective regulatory system to ensure that private financial resources will be used efficiently to achieve the intended goal of health insurance coverage for all.

In chapter 11, Bernard F. Couttolenc and Alexandre C. Nicolella review the current and growing role of private health insurance in Brazil. Voluntary health insurance has been a feature of the Brazilian health system for many years. It covers more than 40 million people through a diversified set of contractual and coverage arrangements. The private health care sector expanded rapidly in the 1980s and early 1990s while the public sector was undergoing reform to ensure free access to care for all. Macroeconomic difficulties and restrictive legislation passed at the end of the 1990s reduced the growth rate and the prospects of the VHI sector in recent years. This chapter assesses the impact of VHI on the financial protection of households against disease, on access to health care, and on the labor market, as well as the long-run prospects of the sector under different scenarios. VHI sustainability and expansion are shown to depend in a major way on economic growth through its impact on employers' revenue, household income, and employment (especially in the formal sector), and on a relaxation of some restrictive legislation.

In chapter 12, Peter A. Berman, Rajeev Ahuja, and Vijaysekar Kalavakonda review the current and growing role of private health insurance in India. The private voluntary health insurance market in India is large and growing. If barriers to the development of this market are removed and the estimated potential is tapped, private health insurance can finance a much higher part of India's total health care spending by 2016. Realization of this potential will, however, bring risks as well as benefits, and success will depend on appropriate government activities and policies. After a brief overview of issues and problems in health care financing in India, the current situation with private voluntary insurance is briefly reviewed and the potential size of the PVHI market in the current environment is estimated. Projections are made for health insurance and health care costs in 2006, 2011, and 2016 under alternate scenarios of medical inflation. Some broad conclusions and policy implications are drawn in the final section.

In chapter 13, Obinna Onwujekwe and Edit V. Velényi review the current and growing role of private voluntary health insurance in Nigeria. The feasibility of PVHI in southeast Nigeria was assessed, using a pretested questionnaire to find out whether households and companies would be willing to pay for it. Most said they would, but budget constraint differences are marked. Smaller firms, rural dwellers, and poorer socioeconomic status groups are less willing than bigger firms, urbanites, and better-off socioeconomic groups. PVHI appears to be a feasible method of paying for health care in southeast Nigeria. However, PVHI could fail if equity issues are not addressed, according to the authors. Preliminary results from a more recent experience with subsidizing the premiums of the poor in Niger suggest that such a program would confer considerable benefits to the poor in terms of both financial protection and improved access to quality health services.

In chapter 14, Maks Tajnikar and Petra Došenovič Bonča review the current and growing role of private health insurance in Slovenia. The scope and size of the voluntary health insurance market in Slovenia is determined largely by the features of the compulsory health insurance, which provides near-universal coverage and comprehensive benefits. Because the system does not cover the full price of health care services, copayments of between 5 and 75 percent of the price of a service are also required. To provide full coverage of the copayment, the predominant form of VHI was introduced, in 1992. Since then, this type of voluntary health insurance has undergone changes. In 2003, its role was seriously debated, and proposals were made for its elimination and the transfer of premiums paid for full copayment coverage to compulsory health insurance. In 2005, it was eventually decided not to change the general system of health insurance and to reform VHI for full copayment coverage according to the principle of intergenerational mutuality, to declare it in the public interest of Slovenia, and to implement a system of risk-equalization schemes.

In chapter 15, Kee Taig Jung reviews the current and growing role of private health insurance in the Republic of Korea. Until 2000, the introduction of a national health insurance (NHI) in Korea in a little over 10 years was often cited as a miracle. Then, the financial distress of the NHI damaged not only the reputation of health services but also the trust of the Korean people in the social security of health care. In response, the private health insurance market expanded to 40 percent of the total NHI reimbursements, making it one of the world's largest such markets. It is surprising that the Korean insurance market reached this size without offering any comprehensive major medical coverage. All the PVHI products are supplementary or complementary to the national health insurance. The PVHI market grew more than 20 percent a year from 1996 to 2004. Most products sold cover specific diseases like cancer or 4 to 10 other critical illnesses and pay fixed amounts instead of covering a patient's actual bills. In this evaluation study, empirical analysis was performed to find factors that affect enrolment in PVHI, moral hazard, adverse selection, and financial protection. Age, gender, and chronic illnesses were found to affect enrolment in PVHI. Moral hazard was found in outpatient but not in inpatient care. Having PVHI improved financial protection. People with fixed-payment insurance had higher financial protection than those with indemnity type. The success and viability of the Korean health care system will depend on the development of linkages between public and private payers.

In 2007, *Healthy Development: The World Bank Strategy for Health, Nutrition, and Population Results* emphasized a need for the international development community to support health services and financing with the private sector and civil society, in addition to the public sector. In 2008, International Finance Corporation (IFC), with assistance from the Bill & Melinda Gates Foundation and McKinsey&Company, formulated a Private Health Sector Strategy on *The Business of Health in Africa.*

The resulting US$1 billion Health in Africa (HiA) Initiative aims to provide small- and medium-sized health businesses with better access to (a) affordable capital (equity and credit); (b) a strong business environment and investment climate; and (c) shared knowledge about what works and what does not work on the ground.

Global Marketplace for Private Health Insurance: Strength in Numbers contributes to this agenda by reviewing the global experience on private voluntary health insurance and providing new ideas and opportunities for countries that are at an earlier stage in their health systems development path

September 2009

Alexander S. Preker
Peter Zweifel
Onno P. Schellekens

Acknowledgments

This project would not have been possible without the support of Richard M. Scheffler (University of California, Berkeley). Peter Zweifel (University of Zurich) and Mark V. Pauly (Wharton School, University of Pennsylvania) were a driving force behind exploring the economic underpinnings of private health insurance in low-income countries. The resulting volume was edited by Alexander S. Preker, Peter Zweifel, and Onno P. Schellekens.

The study was supported by the Honorable Thomas Sackville, executive director of the International Federation of Health Plans (iFHP); Pauline Ramprasad and Benedict Boullet of the World Bank Staff Exchange Program (SEP); and Valerie Gooding, Dean Holden, Peter Jones, Fergus Kee, and Bob Watson of the British United Provident Association (BUPA), which seconded Mark C. Basset to the Bank for two years.

Important support was also provided by management from across the World Bank Group—the World Bank, International Finance Corporation (IFC), and World Bank Institute (WBI). Notable encouragement was provided by several managers: Alexandre Abrantes, Guy Ellena, Eva Jarawan, Rodney Lester, Antony Thompson, and Marilou Uy. Scott Douglas Featherston from International Finance Corporation (IFC) provided valuable guidance on the implications of private health insurance for capital investment in developing countries. John Page, chief economist, Africa Region, chaired the internal review meetings and provided invaluable insights on linking this review of voluntary health insurance to the Bank's broader development agenda.

Financial and in-kind sponsorship was provided by the World Bank, IFC, WBI, iFHP, BlueCross BlueShield Massachusetts, BUPA, Kaiser Foundation Health Plan, United Health Care, the Health Insurance Fund for Africa, Merck, Novartis, Pfizer, PharmAccess, the Canadian International Development Agency (CIDA), and the U.S. Agency for International Development.

The editors are grateful to the authors whose collective contribution made this volume possible. These contributors are: Peter A. Berman, Ricardo Bitrán, M. Kate Bundorff, Anna Cederberg Heard, Bernard F. Couttolenc, Denis Drechsler, Teh-wei Hu, Johannes P. Jütting, Vijaysekar Kalavakonda, Ajay Mahal, Rodrigo Muñoz, Vimbayi Mutyambizi, Heba Nassar, Obinna Onwujekwe, Mark V. Pauly, Sameh El-Saharty, Siripen Supakankunti, Michael Thiede, Edit V. Velényi, and Xiao-hua Ying.

Two steering groups provided technical guidance. Members of the Economic Steering Group included: Mark Pauly, Richard Scheffler, and Peter Zweifel. Members of the Industry Consultative Group included Ladi Awosika (chief executive officer, Total Health Trust Ltd., Nigeria), Macdonald Chaora (chief executive,

CIMAS, Zimbabwe), Robert Crane (vice president, Kaiser), Kabelo Ebineng (managing director, Botswana Public Officers Medical Aide Scheme and Pula Medical Aide Scheme, Botswana); George Halvorson (chief executive officer, Kaiser), Cleve Killingsworth (chief executive officer, BlueCross BlueShield Massachusetts), Bafana Nkosi (chief executive officer, Bonitas Medical Fund, South Africa), Nimish Parekh, (chief executive officer, United Health Care, India); Penny Tlhabi (chief executive officer, Board of Healthcare Funders Southern Africa).

The U.S. Federal Employee Benefit Program (Anne Easton and staff members Bryant Cook, Ed de Harde, Michael Garth, and Vince Smithers) provided practical insights. The following organizations provided technical advice: America's Health Insurance Plans (Diana Dennet and Charles Stellar), Bill & Melinda Gates Foundation (Daniel Kress and Sheryl Scott), BlueCross and BlueShield Massachusetts (Bruce Butler, Debra Devaux, Edward Esposito, Allen Maltz, Harold Picken, John Sheinbaum, Laura Zirpolo Stout, Karen Thompson-Yancey, and Carole Waite, the BlueCross and BlueShield Association (Paul Danao), BUPA (Mark Bassett, Nicholas Beazley, Fergus Kee, and Martin O'Rouke), Health Insurance Fund for Africa (Christopher van der Vorm), Dutch Ministry of Foreign Affairs (Aaltje-de Roos) Fernbow Consulting (Roger Bowie), Investment Fund for Africa (Max Coppoolse), Kaiser (Fish Brown and Herman Weil), PharmAccess (Onno P. Schellekens and Marianne Lindner), and United Health Care (Gregory Arms).

Among the international organizations consulted were the Organisation for Economic Co-operation and Development, iFHP, the International Labour Organization, the World Health Organization, the Association of Health Insurance Plans, and Association Internationale de la Mutualité.

Thanks go to the following reviewers: Cristian C. Baeza, Enis Baris, Peter A. Berman, Paolo Belli, Mukesh Chawla, Rafael Cortez, Agnes Couffinhal, Jose Pablo Gomez-Meza, Birgit Hansl, April Harding, Loraine Hawkins, Vijaysekar Kalavakonda, Gerard Martin la Forgia, John C. Langenbrunner, Oscar Picazo, Firas Raad, Yee Mun Sin, Sameh El-Saharty, and Agnes Soucat.

Other Bank staff members who contributed insights during various stages of the review include Pablo Gottrett, Dominic Haazen, Richard Hinz, Rodney Lester, Emmett Moriarty, Mead Over, Ok Pannenborg, Eric de Roodenbeke, George Schieber, Nicole Tapay, Robert Taylor, and Adam Wagstaff. External reviewers included May Cheng, Alan Fairbank, Bill Hsiao, Pere Iben, Xingzhu Liu, Philip Musgrove, Haluk Ozari, Jim Rice, and Mehtap Tatar.

Mohamed Diaw assisted in trust fund management. Jim Surges and Allison Hedges helped organize the Wharton school consultations. Caroline Ly, Maria Cox, and Kathleen A. Lynch provided invaluable help with editing and text processing.

Abbreviations and Acronyms

AIDS	acquired immune deficiency syndrome
ALOS	average length of stay
ANS	Agência Nacional de Saúde Suplementar, National Agency for Private Health ("Supplementary") Insurance, Brazil
CBI	community-based insurance
CGHS	Central Government Health Scheme, India
CIRC	China Insurance Regulation Commission
CIS	Clinical Information System
CMS	Council of Medical Schemes, South Africa
CVM	contingent valuation method
DHS	Demographic and Health Survey
DOH	Department of Health, South Africa
DRG	diagnosis-related group
EAP	East Asia and Pacific Region, World Bank
ECA	Eastern Europe and Central Asia Region, World Bank
EHHUES	Egypt Household Health Utilization and Expenditures Survey
EIMIC	Egyptian International Medical Insurance Company
EISA	Egyptian Insurance Supervisory Agency
ESIS	Employee State Insurance Scheme, India
EU	European Union
FMIS	Fund Management Information System
FONASA	Fondo Nacional de Salud, National Health Fund, Chile
GIS	Government Insurance Scheme, China
GNI	gross national income
GDP	gross domestic product
GNP	gross national product
HCE	health care expenditure
HIC	highly indebted country
HIF	Health Insurance Fund for Africa
HMO	health maintenance organization
HSRI	Health Systems Research Institute, Thailand
ILO	International Labour Organization
IRDA	Insurance Regulatory and Development Authority, India
ISAPRE	Institucione de Salud Previsional, Private Health Insurance Scheme, Chile
LCR	Latin America and Caribbean Region, World Bank
LIC	low-income country
LIS	Labor Insurance Scheme, China
LSMS	Living Standard Measurement Survey
MC	managed care

MDG	Millennium Development Goal
MENA	Middle East and North Africa Region
MHI	mutual health insurance
MOFE	Ministry of Finance and Economy, Republic of Korea
MOH	Ministry of Health
MOHP	Ministry of Health and Population, Arab Republic of Egypt
MOHW	Ministry of Health and Welfare, Republic of Korea
MOPH	Ministry of Public Health, Arab Republic of Egypt
MSA	medical savings account
NCAER	National Council for Applied Economic Research, India
NCMS	New Cooperative Medical Services, China
NGO	nongovernmental organization
NHA	National Health Account
NHIC	National Health Insurance Corporation
NHIS	National Health Insurance Scheme, Nigeria
NHRPL	National Health Reference Price List, South Africa
NHS	National Health Service
NMC	nonmedical consumption
NSSO	National Sample Survey Organisation, India
OECD	Organisation for Economic Co-operation and Development
OOP	out of pocket
OOPS	out-of-pocket spending
ORT	Organisation for Educational Resources and Technological Training
PHI	private health insurance
PMB	prescribed minimum benefit
PPO	preferred provider organization
PVHI	private voluntary health insurance
PVO	private voluntary organization
REF	Risk Equalization Fund, South Africa
SAR	South Asia Region, World Bank
SARS	severe acute respiratory syndrome
SES	socioeconomic status
SHI	social health insurance
SRP	Social Risk Pool, China
SSA	Sub-Saharan Africa Region, World Bank
SSI	social security insurance
SUS	Sistema Unificado de Saúde, Unified Health System, Brazil
THE	total health expenditure
VAT	value-added tax
VHI	voluntary health insurance
WHO	World Health Organization
WTO	World Trade Organization
WTP	willingness to pay

CHAPTER 1

Introduction: Strength in Numbers

Alexander S. Preker, Onno P. Schellekens, and Marianne Lindner

To achieve the health-related Millennium Development Goals (MDGs), significant additional financial resources will have to be mobilized for the health sector (box 1.1). Management of financial risk, and spending of scarce resources will also have to be made more effective, in addition to addressing the intersectoral determinants of illness (Preker 2003; and Preker et al. 2003).

Additional resources could be mobilized by increasing the share of government funding allocated to the health sector (WHO 2000; World Bank 1993, 1997, 2007a, 2007b). But expanding fiscal space has significant negative macroeconomic repercussions that could damage long-term spending on health. Increasing the relative share of resources allocated to the health sector also means giving up public expenditure on other programs, some of which contribute significantly to overall gains in health. In most low- and middle-income countries, economic growth and government taxation capacity put an upper binding constraint on the funds that can be spent on health care through the public sector (Preker, Langenbrunner, and Suzuki 2002). Many countries are therefore exploring ways to achieve public ends through private means (Harding and Preker, eds. 2003; Preker et al., eds. 2007).

INTRODUCTION

This chapter reviews the recent role of private voluntary health insurance (PVHI) as one of several sources of funding for health, expanding on work described in *Private Voluntary Health Insurance in Development: Friend or Foe,* edited by Alexander S. Preker, Richard M. Scheffler, and Mark C. Bassett (2007). The *multipillar approach* to health care financing in low- and middle-income countries put forward in this chapter includes an important PVHI component and a targeted premium subsidy for the poor to make such insurance programs affordable to them. Large sums of money now used by governments and donors as supply subsidies to specialized providers of vertical programs could be better spent if channeled through a mechanism like insurance that improves targeting of subsidies for the poor and improves financial risk management.

A summary of the main global health financing challenges to which PVHI must contribute is provided in this chapter. The summary is followed by a discussion of policy design issues related to institutional arrangements, the demand

BOX 1.1 THE GLOBAL HEALTH FINANCING CHALLENGE

Addressing the health challenge in low- and middle-income countries has become a major goal for the international development community and for individual countries. Since the turn of the millennium, donors have spent billions of dollars trying to help countries "jump-start," "scale up," and "leapfrog" the slow development path that characterized the latter part of the 20th century. Much of this money is now at risk of being wasted supporting unsustainable health systems.

Global health spending in 2006 was around $3.5 trillion, about 10 percent of global gross domestic product (GDP). Of those resources, about $380 billion, 12 percent, was spent in low- and middle-income countries. If current spending patterns are maintained, developing countries will face annual increases of between 2 and 3 percent in health care expenditure needs (or pressures) from demographic trends alone (World Bank 2007a). Even well-meaning and socially oriented governments and donors find it hard to keep up with such expenditure pressures from the health sector.

Developing countries account for 84 percent of the global population and 90 percent of the global disease burden, but only 12 percent of global health spending (see table).

Regions and income	*Per capita GDP ($US)*	*Per capita health expenditures ($US)*	*Per capita health expenditures (PPP)*	*Total health expenditures (% GDP)*	*Public (% total health expenditures)*	*Out-of-pocket (% total health expenditures)*	*External (% total health expenditures)*	*Social Security (% total health expenditures)*	*Life expectancy at birth (years)*	*Under-5 mortality rate (per 1,000 live births)*
East Asia and Pacific	1,457	64	251	4.4	39.8	51.1	0.5	17.6	70	37
Eastern Europe and Central Asia	3,801	250	547	6.6	67.8	26.4	1.1	40.5	69	34
Latin America and the Caribbean	3,777	273	892	7.3	51.2	36.2	0.4	17.9	72	31
Middle East and North Africa	1,833	103	307	5.7	49.1	46.1	1.2	11.9	69	55
South Asia	611	27	84	4.6	18.8	76.1	1.5	0.9	63	92
Sub-Saharan Africa	732	45	102	6.3	41.8	26.2	6.8	1.4	46	168
Sub-Saharan Africa[a]	462	21	58	4.7	43.6	46.8	15.0	0.9	46	168
Low-income countries	533	24	79	4.7	23.9	70.0	5.4	1.1	59	122
Lower middle-income countries	1,681	91	365	5.4	47.3	42.8	0.5	14.4	70	42
Upper middle-income countries	5,193	342	676	6.6	57.8	30.2	0.7	32.2	69	28
High-income countries	33,929	3,810	3,637	11.2	60.4	14.9	0.0	26.0	79	7
High-income countries[b]	31,243	2,778	2,527	8.8	76.0	16.6	0.0	39.3	79	7

Source: World Bank 2007a.
Note: Population-weighted 2004 data.
a. SSA, GDP, and health spending data excluding South Africa.
b. Highly indebted countries (HICs) GDP and health spending data excluding the United States.

The global population is projected to grow to 7.5 billion by 2020. Most of this growth is expected to occur in developing countries parallel to an epidemiological shift to noncommunicable diseases (NCDs) and injuries, which have very different needs in terms of financing of prevention and curative services. Many low-income countries still do not attain the minimum levels of per capita health expenditure needed to address the most pressing health challenges and recommended by the international development community (ILO 2007; WHO 2000; and World Bank 1993, 1997, 2007a, 2007b.).

Poor households and poor countries bear the largest burden of illness and have the least financial protection against health shocks. There are significant inequities in both households' contributions toward financing health care and in their access to publicly financed health services (large reliance on regressive user charges and pro-rich benefit incidence of spending). The public share of total health expenditure is 29 percent in low-income countries, 42 percent in lower-middle-income countries, 56 percent in upper-middle-income countries, and 65 percent in high-income countries.

Paradoxically, the poorer the country, the larger is the amount of out-of-pocket spending and the lower is the level of financial protection against health shocks (Dror and Preker, eds. 2002): 93 percent in low-income countries; 85 percent in middle-income countries; and 56 percent in high-income countries. It is unfortunate that out-of-pocket expenditure—the most inequitable source of health financing—predominates in low- and middle-income countries. Government-mandated public health insurance programs account for only some 2 percent of total spending on health in low-income countries, 15 percent in lower-middle income countries, and 30 percent in upper-middle-income and high-income countries.

Despite the massive increases in donor assistance during recent years, external sources of financing for the health sector account for only 8 percent of total health spending in low-income countries and less than 1 percent in middle-income countries. There are, however, exceptions to this trend: external sources account for a much higher share in some countries. In 12 Sub-Saharan African countries, for instance, external sources finance more than 30 percent of total health expenditures. In a few rare, post-conflict counties the external share has reached 90 percent.

High donor dependence in some countries is both a blessing and curse, with external donor assistance being characterized by a crowding out of domestic sources (*fungibility*), variability over time (*volatility*), and poor targeting of vulnerable groups. Billions of dollars are now at risk of being wasted and having little impact. This dismal prospect is due to a failure of current health financing arrangements to ensure that the large flows of external donor funds effectively target vulnerable populations, that the government secures value for money from these additional resources, and that these external resources do not cause major distortionary effects on the scarce and already vulnerable domestic resources in low- and middle-income countries.

for private voluntary health insurance, the supply of such insurance, and market equilibrium issues. Policymakers' difficult choices in expanding health insurance coverage to larger segments of the population are then highlighted.

To address both equity and efficiency concerns, a new paradigm for financing health care in lower- and middle-income countries is proposed in this chapter. Recent research suggests that financing of health care in low- and middle-income countries might be more effective if countries and donors replaced the traditional direct subsidies to providers with demand-side subsidies to patients or financial intermediaries like health insurance (Schellekens et al. 2007). The chapter ends by summarizing some of the implementation challenges facing countries that venture down the health insurance path.

POLICY DESIGN

What "makes" or "breaks" a health insurance reform is often more closely related to the political economy of the reform process than to strengths and flaws in the underlying policy design. Nonetheless, policy design does matter. A number of fatal flaws can be avoided in terms of the role that health insurance plays in the overall structure of financing health care and the basic economics of insurance, including the demand for insurance, the supply of insurance, and health insurance market equilibrium.

Multipillar Framework for Financing Health Care

The literature on health care financing is marred by definitional problems that have led to a great deal of confusion and contributed to futile ideological arguments. Although health systems have been stereotyped as belonging to either a U.K.-styled National Heath Service model, German-styled "sickness fund" model, or U.S.-styled private health insurance model, this portrayal of health care financing is an oversimplification of the trade-off between competition and solidarity-based approaches (Chinitz, Warsem, and Preker 1997). Notions of solidarity, social health insurance, social protection and universality, and other values-laden terms will be avoided in this volume.

In reality most countries use a combination of voluntary and mandatory mechanisms through both pubic and private financing agents (figure 1.1). PVHI is one of the several components of a *multipillar* system for financing health care.

FIGURE 1.1 Strength in Numbers under a Multipillar Approach

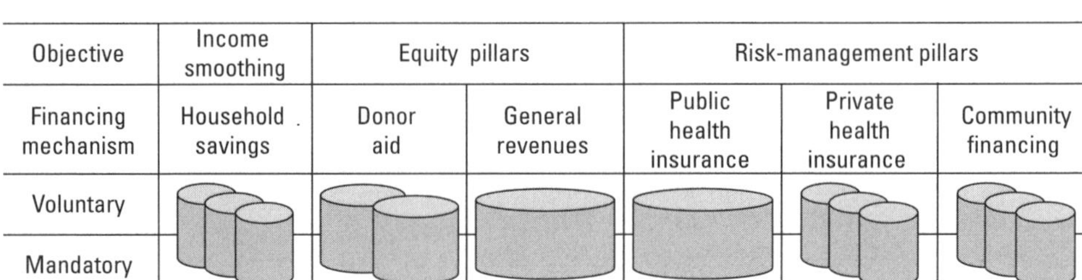

Source: Adapted from Preker, Scheffler, and Bassett, eds. 2007.

Some combination of these four dimensions are better at smoothing income across the lifecycle. Others are better at achieving equity objectives. Still others are better at managing financial risk. More complex health financing systems combine these various dimensions to optimize achievement of the underlying policy objectives (Preker, Scheffler, and Bassett, eds. 2007).

Health care risks are complex, influenced in part by genetics and the lifestyle of individuals and household and in part by external factors such as diseases, environmental factors, and specific external events. Some heath risks are predictable (preexisting diseases or identified predisposition). Some health risks are less predictable (a biological event, accident, or access to effective care).

Insurance is a mechanism for financing health risks by combining sufficient loss-exposure units to make the loss predictable. Health insurance allows the cost of treating a health event to be spread over a group of individuals or households.

It is in this context that PVHI is evolving in many developing countries. PVHI provides one of several critical components of a multipillar system for financing health care that includes direct household contributions, subsidies, and insurance to achieve the objectives of household income smoothing, equity, and risk management (box 1.2). Although PVHI can also be used to address issues of income redistribution and lifetime income smoothing, it is most effective at dealing with the cost of unpredictable health risks.

BOX 1.2 TYPES OF PRIVATE VOLUNTARY HEALTH INSURANCE

The OECD has developed a typology of the roles or functions of PVHI: duplicative, substitutive, supplemental, or complementary (Bassett and Kane 2007). These forms of PVHI often have very different policy objectives, institutional arrangements and impact.

Primary PVHI

Primary PVHI is private insurance that gives individuals who do not have access to public health insurance their only available access to basic health coverage. Individuals might lack access to public health insurance because there is none, or because individuals are not eligible to public health insurance coverage, or because, though entitled to public coverage, they have opted out. There are two subtypes of primary PVHI:

- *Principal primary PVHI* is private insurance for health costs that is an individual's only available access to coverage when there is no social security scheme. It can include employers' compulsory schemes if coverage is privately insured or self-insured.
- *Substitute primary PVHI* is private insurance for health costs that substitutes for coverage that would, if it existed, be provided by social insurance or publicly financed insurance or employers' schemes.

Duplicate PVHI

Duplicate PVHI is private insurance that offers coverage for health services already included under public health insurance. Duplicate health insurance provides an alternative to the public coverage, although it does not exempt individuals from contributing to public health insurance. Although duplicate PVHI offers access to the same medical services as the public scheme, it gives access to different providers or levels of service. Duplicate PVHI might, for example, give the insured access to fast or privileged coverage by bypassing queues in the public system, access to care without going through a referral or gatekeeper system, choice of doctor, hospital, or other health provider, and access to private health facilities not accessible through public insurance when the full cost of the service is paid by private insurance.

Complementary PVHI

Complementary PVHI is private insurance that pays for benefits already covered under an existing health insurance program. It is used to pay for all or part of the residual costs not otherwise reimbursed (for example, copayments). It is sometimes referred to as "gap" insurance.

Supplementary PVHI

Supplementary PVHI is private health insurance that provides coverage for health services not covered by the public scheme. Depending on the country, it may include luxury care, elective care, long-term care, dental care, pharmaceuticals, rehabilitation, alternative or complementary medicine, or superior hotel and amenity hospital services (even when other portions of the service (such as the medical component) are covered by the public system).

Demand for Private Voluntary Health Insurance

Because insurance offers potentially large welfare gains, including protection against unexpected, large shocks to consumption or wealth, efforts to furnish it in low-income countries are well justified (Pauly et al. 2006).

The high out-of-pocket expenditure by low-income households in most developing countries provides a "prima facie" case that insurance is both desirable and "affordable" if it can be offered at relatively moderate *loading cost* (administrative costs, losses due to fraud and abuse, profit and transaction cost of meeting regulatory requirements). Figure 1.2 shows that the share of out-of-pocket on health care is greater at low-income levels in every part of the world.

Risk-averse populations that might, if uninsured, be forced to make large out-of-pocket payments would gain by protecting themselves from rare but very high medical expenses if such insurance was offered at affordable premiums (Pauly 2007). Lowering the number of people experiencing serious financial hardship and barriers to access at the time of illness would also confer aggregate societal welfare gains.

Demand for private voluntary health insurance is not only concentrated in the highest-income groups. It extends to lower-income groups as well (Pauly, Blavin,

FIGURE 1.2 Low-Income Countries Have Less Insurance Coverage than High-Income Countries

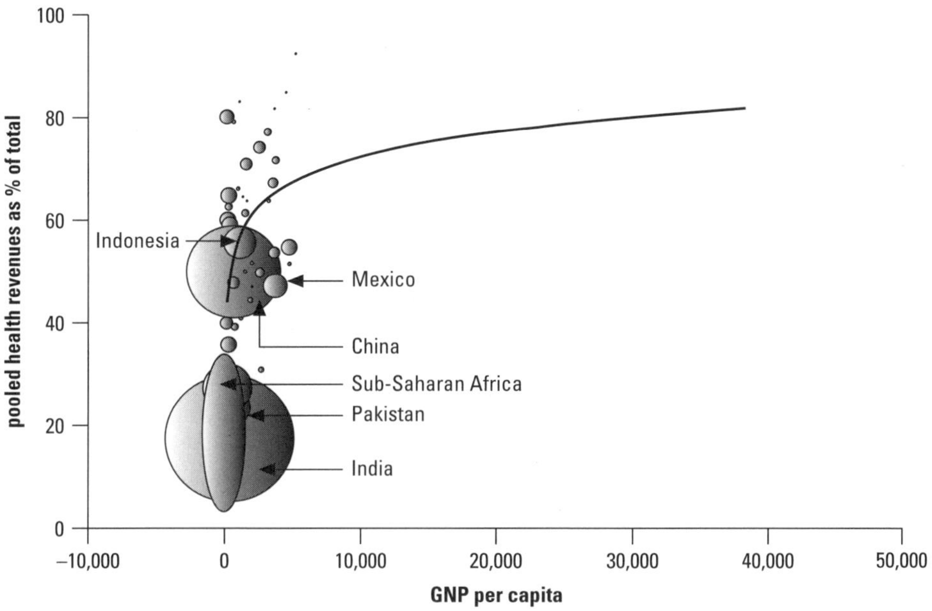

Source: Preker and Carrin, 2004.

Note: The share of the world's 1.3 billion people living on less than US$1 a day is indicated by the size of the bubbles.

and Meghan 2008). Demand for health insurance among lower-income groups appears to exist for two reasons: first, the risk (even if small) of being exposed to high out-of-pocket payment poses a considerable threat to many households; second, the variance of potential out-of-pocket spending is sufficiently large that many households would be willing to pay more than the expected value of the benefits to avoid exposure to the upper extreme in expenditures. Insurance plans should therefore be able to charge premiums that would cover the cost of expected benefits and the loading cost.

In most countries, low-income populations account for the greatest share of out-of-pocket expenditure. Because the expected out-of-pocket expense varies with income, making such insurance affordable to low-income populations in a voluntary market will require market segmentation. In this way, lower-income people pay lower premiums based on their below-average spending and setting premiums in relation to average expense across all other income groups.

As an indicator of the feasibility of introducing such insurance in low- and middle-income contexts, Pauly, Blavin, and Meghan (2008) suggest using the amount people would be willing to pay for insurance beyond the expected value of benefits and comparing this "risk premium" (as part of the total premium) with the administrative expense share of insurance premiums. In many countries, this risk premium (expressed as a percentage of expected benefits for full coverage insurance) was in the range of the expected administrative expense that markets could generate. This formula is especially apt in the case of insurance that would pay for some care and comprehensive insurance covering hospital, physician, and drug expenses. The authors also found that the risk premium for stand-alone drug insurance is relatively low, even though spending on drugs constitutes a large share of total out-of-pocket spending. These findings suggest that comprehensive insurance (rather than a hospitalization-only or a drugs-only policy) might be the most feasible way of achieving good financial protection.

Based on this research, it can be predicted that risk-averse households will voluntarily purchase health insurance if the associated expenses are smaller than the "risk premium" they would be willing to pay. That risk premium depends on the variance of the losses the insurance will cover and on the extent of a household's risk aversion. If the variance of the losses is small or if the loading cost is high, there will be little demand for insurance.

The implication is that a voluntary health insurance market is most likely to emerge when three conditions hold: (1) there is a risk of high out-of-pocket payments relative to income or wealth; (2) insurance firms can offer different households premiums that are close to the individual household's expected value of out-of-pocket medical spending; and (3) loading costs are moderate.

Supply of Private Voluntary Health Insurance

Private voluntary health insurance already exists and is growing globally (Drechsler and Jütting 2007), especially in the Latin America and Caribbean Region and in the East Asia and Pacific Region. Yet growth in the global marketplace has been slower than what would be predicted based on the above analysis of demand.

Earlier research (Zweifel, Krey, and Tagli 2007) identified three factors that restrain the growth of private voluntary health insurance: inadequate demand because of low risk aversion or misperception, regulatory restrictions in supply (or regulation-induced death spirals), and high administrative costs. Five factors that contribute to constraints in supply include: benefits package creep, risk-selection effort, loading cost, vertical integration between insurers and health care providers, and market concentration.

Benefits package creep. Private health insurers in developing countries are forced to offer comprehensive benefits packages that are not affordable at the premium that can be collected from low-income populations without a significant premium subsidy. Donor money is often used to pay providers direct subsidies for some of the more expensive vertical programs such as HIV/AIDS and malaria. This vertical funding contributes to a perceived marginalization of the benefits package that can be provided through private voluntary programs. The more comprehensive benefits packages provided in industrial countries are still used as a competitive benchmark.

Risk-selection effort. Risk selection is greater in low- and middle-income countries than in industrial countries because regulators in the developing world often prefer fully uniform premiums, which induce maximum effort at cream skimming. Another reason such mechanisms are little used in developing countries is the lack of institutional capacity to introduce risk-adjustment mechanisms, which are designed to neutralize health insurers' incentive to select favorable risks. Such mechanisms are difficult to manage even in industrial countries.

Loading cost. The loading cost on premiums is high in low- and middle-income countries compared with the competitive benchmark because of higher levels of fraud, abuse, and overregulation. Many countries have significant regulation-induced impediments that make it very difficult to offer private health insurance at affordable rates. The rationale often given is that government-run mandatory health insurance should be the preferred mechanism. But so far mandatory health insurance has not played a large role in financial protection at low-income levels.

Vertical integration. The degree of vertical integration between insurers and health care providers is less at low-income levels than in industrial countries. Such vertical integration is often part of the development path toward expanded private insurance coverage. Once again, community financing may have a competitive advantage in this respect because the behavior of community insurers is less likely to hurt their reputation with health care providers. Moreover, community insurers do not have to deal with provider cartels.

Market concentration. Finally, the degree of market concentration (fewer firms) in the private health insurance market is higher in low- and middle-income countries than in industrial countries because of high barriers to entry.

At a minimum, this analysis suggests a need for a change in focus in the design of private voluntary health insurance in developing countries. Several possibilities have been tried successfully in different contexts:

- Limiting the benefits package to what is really affordable under private voluntary health insurance
- Using donor and government subsidies to support the premium of poorer household rather than giving the money directly to providers
- Addressing market failure such as adverse selection, cream skimming, and moral hazard
- Limiting policy-oriented regulatory barriers
- Enforcing antitrust regulations to break up both provider and health insurance cartels
- Breaking up market concentration by lowering barriers to entry for new firms.

Market Equilibrium

Governments in low- and middle-income countries often intervene aggressively to prevent or address market imperfections such as adverse selection, moral hazard, cream skimming, fraud, and abuse in the private sector. Yet heavy-handed use of regulation, subsidies, and public production (government-run mandatory health insurance) seriously disrupts the market equilibrium for private voluntary health insurance (Zweifel and Pauly 2007).

Three different contexts lead to markedly different market equilibrium in private voluntary health insurance: no regulation and no subsidies, minimal regulation but some subsidies, and regulation and subsidies.

No regulation, no subsidies. In an unregulated and unsubsidized market, on the demand side, potential purchasers are individuals who expect they might choose to spend out of pocket on medical services or products in the near future (say, the next 12 months). The maximum out-of-pocket spending contemplated by such individuals sets a lower bound to the premium they can "afford." For many people, even those with moderate incomes in developing countries, this maximum feasible out-of-pocket payment might well exceed the premium an insurer would have to charge to cover its benefits and administrative costs.

Those who could afford no substantial out-of-pocket payment (and who therefore would not make such a payment) are thus excluded from the set of potential unsubsidized private voluntary health insurance purchasers. Such individuals need a subsidy if they are to obtain insurance voluntarily. The "nonpoor" segment of the population would demand such insurance to mitigate the risk of catastrophic expenses.

On the supply side, premiums must be nearly equal to consumers' expected expenses (or benefits, given the provisions of coverage and experience)—that is, of a reasonably modest loading cost. Sufficiently low loading costs may be feasible on average. But premiums tailored to each buyer's expected expenses are also needed. Such differential premiums are generally the outcome in competitive markets as long as asymmetry of information operates to the detriment of insurance suppliers.

When out-of-pocket expenses vary greatly with income, as in many developing countries, lower-income people with lower expected expenses must have lower premiums than higher-income people (minimal adverse selection). Also, insurance use by lower-income people must not expand to the level of use by higher-income people when insurance coverage becomes available (minimal moral hazard). Although the existence of income-related adverse selection or moral hazard does not preclude the emergence of insurance, it does limit the scope of coverage.

The other necessary condition on the supply side for emergence of private voluntary health insurance is the capacity of financial infrastructure, property rights, and contract law to support insurance policies. At a minimum, insurers must be seen to collect premiums and use them to pay benefits according to the language in the insurance contract. The actual mechanics of these transactions depend on the nature of the insurance contract and the familiarity of the population with transactions that require time to be fulfilled. Consumers who are familiar with borrowing and lending in capital markets will be best situated to understand insurance contracts.

Minimal regulation but some subsidies for the poor. An alternative approach would be to pay a means-tested subsidy sufficient to close the gap between the competitive, risk-based premium of reference policies (usually with rather modest benefits) and a maximum contribution deemed politically acceptable—for example, 10 percent of personal income. This alternative has the advantage of minimizing regulation while empowering consumers, rich and poor. Its downside is that government must explicitly commit funds to the financing of health insurance for the poor. Middle- and upper-class taxpayers may seek to benefit from this public expenditure for subsidization of health care access, which may cause the expenditure to explode. Therefore, policy suggestions are made in recognition of the importance of differences among institutions.

But both subsidies and taxation can also have negative effects. Taxation inhibits the full growth of a market. Governments often seek to redistribute income and wealth through health insurance by forcing the rich and low-risk individuals to join the risk pool and pay excess contributions that can subsidize the insurance of the poor and high-risk individuals. This strategy is inconsistent with competition, because each insurer has an incentive to offer rich consumers, low-risk consumers, or both, a slightly better deal until everyone again pays a risk-based premium.

Regulations and subsidies. Market equilibrium is often seriously disturbed by government efforts, some well meaning and others not, to regulate, subsidize, and tax private voluntary health insurance. Safeguard regulation to enforce or to standardize contracts is needed as is regulation to prevent arbitrary and capricious decisions by insurers. But stringent regulation of reserves or premiums (beyond disclosure) may do more harm than good. A few examples of the potential negative impact of regulatory interventions follow.

Insurers may occasionally find that total claims are unusually high. Requiring insurers to attract enough capital to reduce the potential for this occurrence to (almost) zero will mean higher premiums for consumers, but more dependable coverage. When capital markets and premium setting are in their infancy, offering consumers less-than-guaranteed insurance may be preferable if the alternative is no insurance or absolutely reliable insurance but at a premium so high that few people buy it.

When loading costs become very high, fewer people, especially in low-income countries, are willing to purchase health insurance. Government typically reacts by forcing at least a portion of the population into a compulsory risk pool. Thus, government can be viewed as the supplier of regulation, while consumers (and more often, insurers) are demanders of regulation. In this market for regulation, government usually does not take into account the efficiency losses it imposes on the remainder of the economy, thereby creating a negative externality. The equilibrium outcome likely entails excessively intense health insurance regulation.

In conclusion, the available empirical evidence suggests that a market equilibrium is possible for private voluntary health insurance in developing countries. Determining the optimal degree of regulation, subsidies, and taxes of health insurance is important, because "excessive" public policy intervention will undermine the viability of such programs.

The *optimal amount of regulation* can be defined as the equilibrium that would result if government as the supplier of regulation took into account regulation's full social (marginal) cost. Because government is unlikely to levy an internalizing (Pigou) tax on itself, demand for regulation should be kept as small as possible. This goal calls for mitigation of the consequences of any insolvency—for example, by means of a guarantee fund to be built up by (private) health insurers.

A NEW PARADIGM FOR FINANCING HEALTH CARE

As is evident from the high reliance on out-of-pocket expenditure, most donor- and government-funded programs in low- and middle-income countries have failed to achieve the risk-management and income-smoothing objectives through such a mechanism alone. As a result, almost all of them already rely on a *multipillar* system for financing health care (figure 1.3). Under such a sys-

FIGURE 1.3 Multipillar System for Financing Health Care

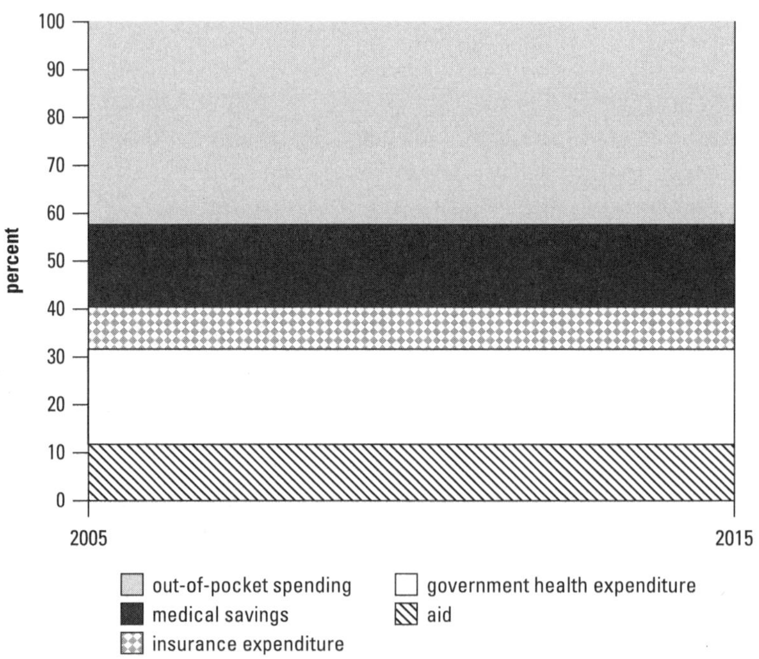

Source: Authors.

FIGURE 1.4 Changes in Financing Mechanisms, 2005–15

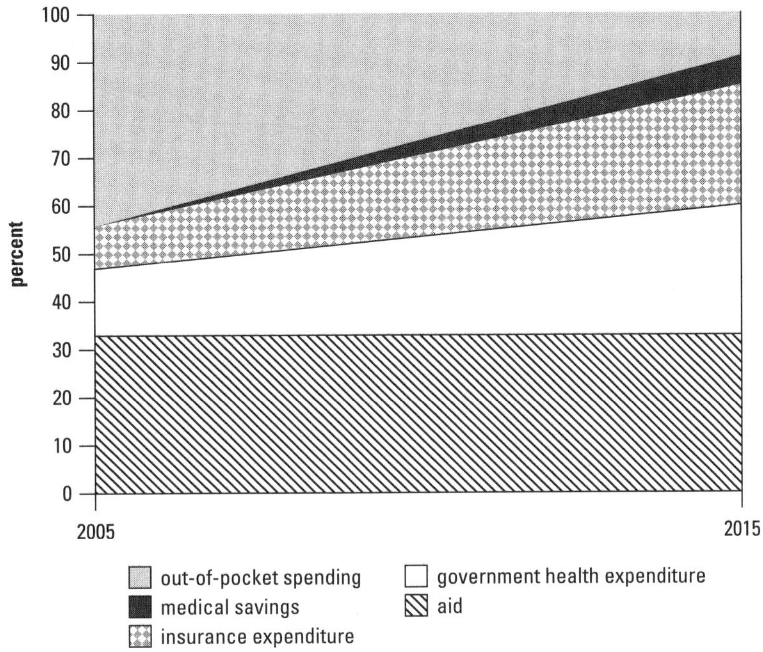

Source: Authors.

tem, donor and government funding tend to be spent on mandatory program whereas the direct household and savings components tend to be voluntary. Insurance falls somewhere in between. The general trend observed in most low- and middle-income countries is to increase government spending and/or insurance coverage over the next few years parallel to a reduction in the relative share of out-of-pocket spending (figure 1.4).

Demand-Side rather than Supply-Side Subsidies

Two alternative approaches underpin recent efforts to expand coverage through insurance-based mechanisms (Pauly et al. 2007). Under one approach, health insurance is introduced for a small part of the population that can afford to pay and from whom employers can easily collect payroll taxes at source, usually civil servants and formal sector workers. The poor and low-income informal sector workers continue to be covered through access to subsidized public hospitals and ambulatory clinics. Although at first sight this policy option would appear to be pro-rich, because only the formally employed who can afford to pay can join the program, in reality it frees up public money that can then be used to subsidize care for the poor and informal sector workers who may not have the

FIGURE 1.5 Shift Traditional Subsidies to Cover Premiums for the Poor, 2005–15

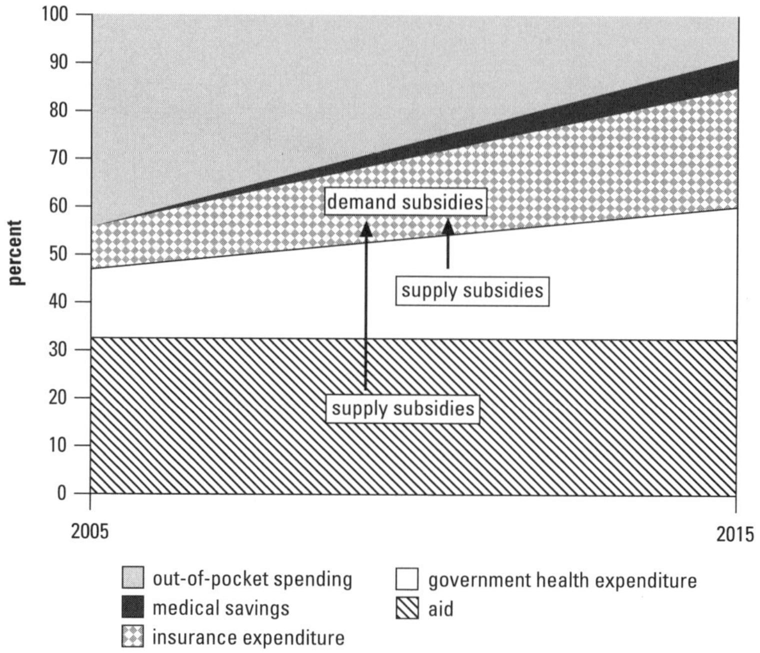

Source: Authors.

means to pay themselves. It therefore allows indirect targeting of the limited government finances available to the Ministry of Health.

Under another approach, health insurance is introduced for a broader segment of the population by applying a demand-driven approach, involving paying for or subsidizing the premium of the poor and low-income informal sector workers (patient-based subsidization). This allows a more rapid expansion of coverage, by using resources that are freed up from the contributing part of the population to subsidize the premium of the poor and low-income informal sector workers rather than their service providers (figure 1.5). This approach offers the advantage of allowing more direct targeting of poor households than the supply-side subsidies described in the previous example (Schellekens et al. 2007).

The world of health financing is locked into two camps: proponents of a government-financed National Health Service and proponents of an insurance-based system. The first system is generally financed through taxation. The second system is often financed through voluntary or mandatory health insurance payments. Citizen demand for risk protection is a common motivation for both. Demand for public insurance may also be motivated by externalities such as care for contagious diseases or the altruistic and paternalistic ones that reflect consensus about the health and health care of fellow citizens.

The use of the tax system generates economic distortion or "excess burden" compared with private voluntary health insurance. This observation may be especially relevant for developing countries with poorly administered tax systems or small shares of the economy in the formal sector. The reason for economic distortion is both that incomes are low and that tax-collected funds are costly and therefore scarce. In this sense, private voluntary health insurance, which will generate less distortion, is less costly. The emergence of private voluntary health insurance is therefore not only a desirable alternative to public provision but also an unavoidable one. Private voluntary health insurance may be the desirable instrument when public insurance is too costly to be efficient.

Employment-based insurance chosen voluntarily responds to worker perception of coverage and cost savings associated with group insurance. Compared with public provision or group insurance, individual insurance can allow each person to get exactly the insurance he or she demands, but the administrative cost will be high. In contrast, group insurance will generally have lower administrative cost but less perfect tailoring to individual desires. The relative costs and benefits of each of these alternatives determine which system is more viable in a given context.

As described above, the alternative to full public provision is subsidization of private insurance. This strategy can tap private willingness to pay and still achieve equity and efficiency goals if coupled with appropriate premium subsidies for the poor and measures to avoid known effects of insurance failure. Because people value insurance, they are willing to make at least a small private payment that can be matched with a public subsidy. These household contributions lower the needed level of public subsidies, which can then be spread more widely.

Insurance for Catastrophic Risk rather than Subsidies for Low-Cost Care

Insurance allows countries to use resources in a better way. It gives providers a more sustainable source of funding and protects households from economic shocks at the time of illness. Insurance helps channel household expenditure on health care through a more efficient and effective financing mechanism than direct out-of-pocket payments. It may also increase the total funding envelope allocated to health care through an insurance effect (households paying for insurance will still buy some services directly due to limits on the benefits covered under the benefits package). In low-income countries, there will still not be enough resources to go around even with insurance. Difficult decisions are therefore needed about which benefits to include and which not to include under health insurance.

One way to look at this challenge is to reexamine the frequency and cost of treating medical events. One approach is to cover high-frequency events associated with relatively low-cost interventions (basic package). During recent years many low- and middle-income countries have introduced publicly financed health care systems that offer the whole population such benefits through public providers.

FIGURE 1.6 Subsidize Cost of Basic Package for Everyone

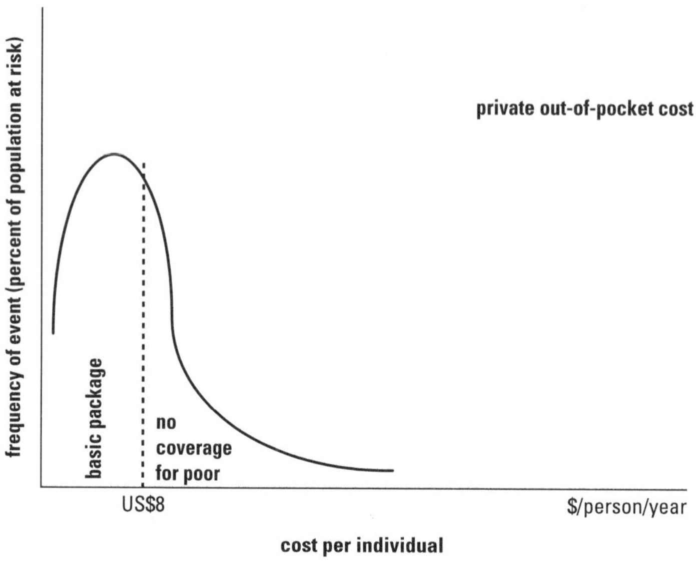

Source: Authors.

Under this approach everyone has access in principle to what is considered an essential package of basic services (figure 1.6). The resulting services are often underfunded when offered to the whole population, and less-frequent but more expensive or life-threatening conditions have to be excluded from the benefits package. As a result, in reality under this approach the population, including the poor, end up paying out of pocket for a large share of their health care even though in principle they are offered universal access to care.

The alternative approach, as suggested above, is to let households that can afford it cover the high-frequency and low-cost interventions themselves. This frees up significant public and donor funds that can then be used to subsidize the premium of risk-sharing mechanisms, especially in the case of the poor and vulnerable populations (figure 1.7). People's willingness and ability to pay for health care—even among the poor—is far greater than their governments' capacity to mobilize revenues through formal taxation mechanisms. In much of Sub-Saharan Africa and Asia, the relative share of health expenditures financed directly through households can run as high as 80 percent of total expenditures.

Households are already paying for their health care under the existing system. Therefore, instead of tying up public resources on care that households are both willing and able to pay for themselves, why not target public funds on public health interventions with large externalities and on health insurance premiums for the poor to give them access to more expensive, unaffordable care?

FIGURE 1.7 Subsidize Expanded Insurance Benefits for the Poor

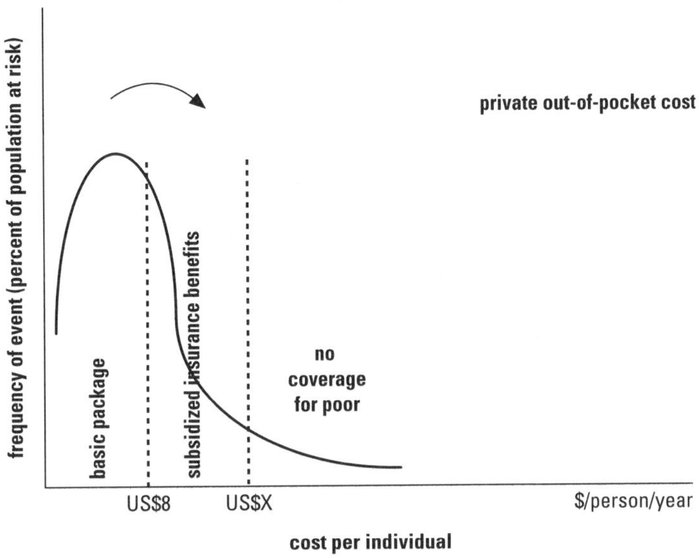

Source: Authors.

Some very expensive care such as the treatment for HIV/AIDS or expensive treatment for malaria and other priority public health programs will be too costly to include in the expanded insurance benefits under such a system without additional subsidies. The current approach for dealing with this problem is to leave it to governments and the international donor community to cover their costs through direct supply-side subsidies that finance free public services for the poor or expensive vertical parallel programs (Smith 2007). Programs like the Global Fund to Fight AIDS, Tuberculosis, and Malaria (Global Fund), the United States President's Emergency Plan for AIDS Relief, President's Malaria Initiative (PMI), and the World Bank spend billions of dollars each year covering the cost of some of these items that are include in the tail end of the distribution curve. Usually this money is spent on supply-side subsidies to providers that specialize in offering services to address conditions like HIV/AIDS, malaria, and other priority public health interventions.

An alternative approach would be for donors and government to channel these additional earmarked resources through health insurance programs that would cover the tail end of the distribution curve (figure 1.8). Under this approach, these programs could benefit from risk-mitigation mechanisms and be better integrated into the overall health system. Funding for the current vertical programs could be integrated under health insurance schemes in an actuarially sound manner as a supplemental or reinsurance pillar (Schellekens et al. 2007).

This approach would allow the donor agencies to continue to earmark their funding for the targeted programs for which their constituents have given their

FIGURE 1.8 Add Supplemental Insurance Coverage for Infrequent High-Cost Events

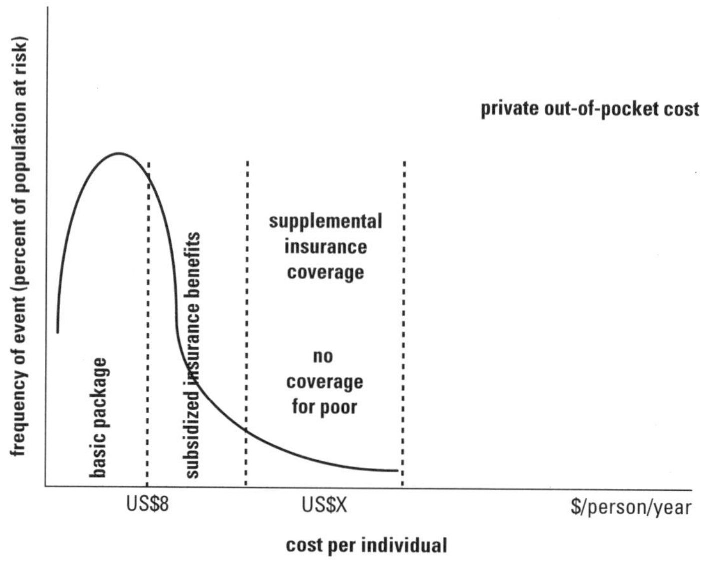

Source: Authors.

money, while benefiting from a more refined spending mechanism and targeting of the poor rather than the current direct supply-side subsidies to providers. It also has the added benefit of allowing better integration of care and more comprehensive quality assurance and care management, thus contributing to a general strengthening of the health system. By including prevention and health promotion activities under the insurance package and by becoming much more active in quality assurance and care management, it will be possible to reduce the incidence and prevalence of both these diseases themselves, and also expensive associated complications (figure 1.9). Members will also be more willing to contribute to a scheme that provides such benefits.

Looked at in a different way, health insurance programs designed in this way will allow a better matching of risk with appropriate financing instruments (figure 1.10). High-frequency conditions associated with low-cost interventions—considered uninsurable risks in technical terms—can be financed through direct household contributions or a demand-side subsidy from governments and donors. Less-frequent conditions associated with higher-cost interventions—considered insurable risks in technical terms—can be covered by insurance and reinsurance (or supplemental insurance) with governments and donors channeling a premium subsidy through existing insurance programs.

Under a *multipillar* approach, individual and household consumption of the basic package of services for high-frequency, low-cost care is close to the average cost per person of such services because everyone uses the services every year.

FIGURE 1.9 Shift Frequency Curve Downward by Improved Care Management and Prevention

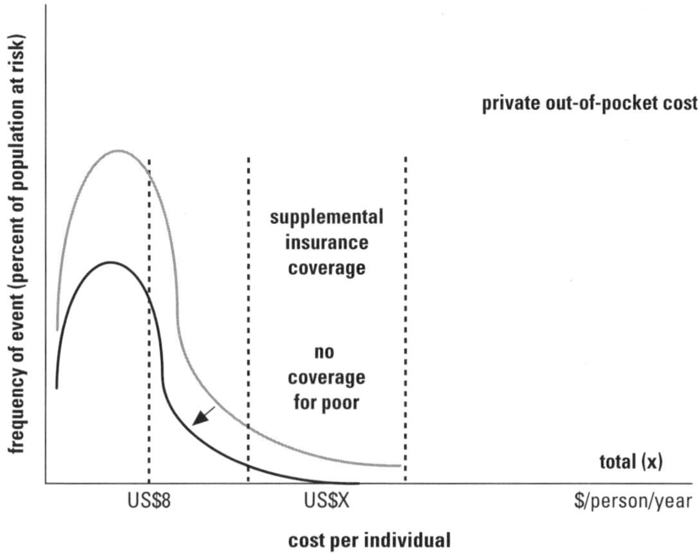

Source: Authors.

FIGURE 1.10 Match Variance and Risk with Instruments

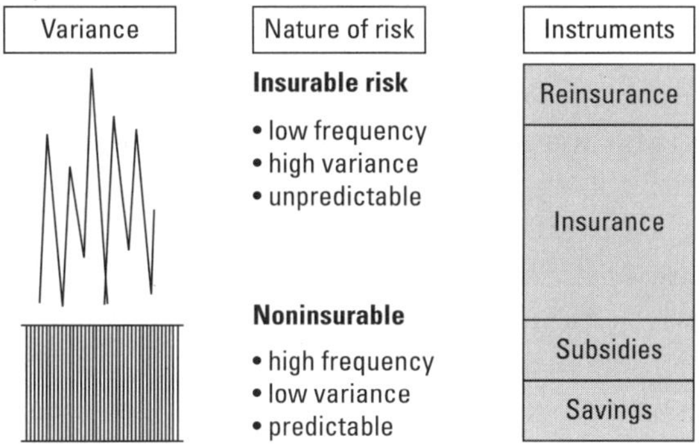

Source: Authors.

But since individual and household consumption of low-frequency, high-cost care will not happen every year, the insurance benefits package can be set to include health care that is much more expensive then the average cost of a car.

There is now good evidence that if subsidies were given to poor households rather than to providers, they would be used on health services that serve the poor rather than the rich. Such subsidy transfers could take the form of vouchers to buy care directly or premium subsidies so that the poor can have access to the same type of health insurance as the rich. A viable health insurance program requires that everyone pays an actuarially sound premium (Cichon et al. 1999). This does not necessarily exclude the poor if there is a partial or full subsidy for their premiums. The advantage of this approach is that the poor can then choose the services they feel meet their needs, and service providers will be paid accordingly, thereby achieving both equity and efficiency objectives.

Households—even the poor—are insurable. Health insurance involves some transfer of resources from rich to poor, healthy to sick, and gainfully employed to inactive. Households in low-income settings understand the nature of such transfers and are willing to contribute small amounts of money today if it secures benefits needed tomorrow. Current systems for financing health care in most low- and middle-income countries deprive the poor of such financial protection against the cost of illness.

IMPLEMENTATION CHALLENGES

Because many private voluntary health insurance programs are still small with low population-coverage and restricted outreach, governments, health care providers, and donors can help the emerging marketplace develop by working closely with the schemes in supporting a scaling up of their operations (Awosika 2007; Bowie and Adams 2007; Schellekens et al. 2007).

For their part, private voluntary health insurance schemes need to reinforce their institutional, managerial, and administrative capacities. Of particular importance is the strengthening expertise in, and establishing mechanisms for, fund management, premium setting, risk management, cost control, eligibility determination, claims management, fraud and abuse detection and control, communications, marketing, and quality assurance. Given recent advances and the drop in the cost of information technology, access to effective electronic management tools is a critical part of strengthening the capacity of the emerging private health insurance marketplace.

Governments can help by: ensuring that reliable information is available that will allow consumers to make informed choices about the cost and benefits of available health insurance programs; focusing mainly on market facilitating and fiduciary safeguard regulations while enforcing quality standards among providers; providing targeted premium subsidies for low-income populations that would not otherwise be able to join the schemes and covering the cost of expensive services that have a public goods nature (for example, medical education and population-based public health programs); and ensuring that patients have access to catastrophic coverage for events that go beyond the affordable level of benefits that can reasonably be provided by private voluntary health insurance programs.

Donor could do much more to assist the emerging health insurance marketplace by channeling a greater share of development assistance through health insurance systems and providing funding for technical assistance to the health insurance programs themselves and to governments and providers that have to adapt their practices to the emerging health insurance marketplace.

Summarized below are several implementation challenges that need to be addressed as private voluntary health insurance grows in developing countries (Preker, Scheffler, and Bassett, eds. 2007). A first set of implementation challenges relates to the political process of reform. The underlying motives for health financing reform are a complex array of political and social factors in addition to the usual economic and technical considerations about improving equity and efficiency. There are usually subtle ideological agendas.

Health insurance reforms are often part of a broader attempt to rebalance the roles of state and nongovernmental actors in a society. The fact that there are almost always both winners and losers is an inherent part of any reform that involves redistribution from one part of society to another. Health insurance reforms always involve such redistribution in terms of transfer of financial resources from the better-off to the less well-off, from healthy individuals who contribute but do not collect benefits to the less healthy who need benefits, and from the actively employed who can contribute part of their income to inactive segments of the population who may need temporary to medium-term cross-subsidies.

Health insurance reforms also involve major changes in the institutional, organizational, and management arrangements for handling significant financial resource flows through the health sector. Managing money means brokering power. Such reforms threaten established stakeholders who controlled financial resources under the old system and give power to the new set of actors who will run the health insurance system. Not surprisingly, such reforms often provoke strong resistance from the established bureaucracy.

A second set of challenges relates to behavior of the three core health care financing functions at low-income levels: revenue collection, financial risk management, and spending of resources on providers.

In the case of effectiveness of revenue collection, private voluntary health insurance schemes face the following challenges: securing a stable enrolment, deciding the range of choice offered to members, setting the premium at affordable levels, and handling premium subsidies that policy makers may impose. Effective financial risk management poses the challenges of securing a sufficiently large risk pool through direct membership or reinsurance mechanisms and handling any risk equalization that policy makers may impose. For effective resource allocation and purchasing, schemes must decide which members to target, what services to include in the benefits package, and which providers to use. Then they must negotiate affordable prices, select workable payment mechanisms, and deal with an array of issues related to determination of eligibility and claims management.

A third set of challenges relates to the institutional environment of health insurance funds at low-income levels. Often institutional capacity is weak, the underlying legal framework is incomplete, administrative procedures are rigid, and informal customs and practices are difficult to change (Fuenzalida-Puelma, Kalavakonda, and Cáceres 2007). As discussed earlier in this chapter, governments are sometimes tempted to overcompensate for some of these weakness by clamping down and over regulating the private health insurance market rather than securing facilitating, safeguard and fiduciary regulations (Harrington 2007).

A fourth set of challenges relates to the organizational structure of health insurance funds at low-income levels. In countries with many small, community-based funds, there is a problem in the scale and scope of insurance coverage and in the benefits that can be provided. Although in theory many government-run health insurance programs have the status of semi-autonomous agencies, they often suffer from the same rigid hierarchical incentive structures as state-owned and -run national health services. This is especially true in countries where the insurance schemes have acquired extensive networks of their own providers, thereby undermining the benefits of a purchaser-provider split. Multiple employment-based funds benefit from competitive pressures but suffer from all the shortcomings of fragmented risk pools and purchasing arrangements, including insurance market failure, high administration costs, and information asymmetry (Smith et al. 2005).

A fifth set of challenges relates to the management characteristics of health insurance funds at low-income levels. Management capacity is often weak in terms of stewardship, governance, line management, and client services. In addition, management skills in mandatory insurance are scarce. Health insurers as multiplicitous agents for the government, health services, and providers have to serve many masters at the same time (Preker and Langenbrunner 2005). This leads to conflicting incentive and reward structures. Finally, the management tools needed to deliver a health insurance program are often lacking in terms of effective IT, communications, and other systems needed for effective financial management, human resources management, tracking of health information, and utilization reviews, to name just a few.

Too often health insurance funds focus almost exclusively on signing up contributing members, collecting premiums, and managing the claims-settlement process. For the functioning and viability of the insurance program, smoothly executing these activities is important—but insufficient in itself. Top-performing health insurance programs today spend an increasing amount of time on strategic purchasing of quality care, care management, and healthy lifestyle promotion among their members (Preker 2005).

Effective ways of dealing with these issues are illustrated by the case studies in this book and discussed in greater detail in the previous volume and by other authors (Awosika 2007; Bowie and Adams 2007; and Schellekens et al. 2007).

Conclusion

Over time, governments in many developing countries have introduced publicly funded and publicly managed national health services run by their Ministries of Health. Either they provide and finance services directly, or they compel third-party entities (employers, sickness funds) to finance public and private providers of care. This system has had some success. Millions of people in low- and middle-income countries today have access to limited government-run and -financed health services.

But it is increasingly recognized that governments cannot by themselves assume the entire challenge of providing adequate financial protection for their citizens and access to needed care. This failure by government to secure both a sustainable source of funding for providers and financial protection for the population shows up starkly in the form of private out-of-pocket spending on health care in settings where "universal access" to government-run and -financed health services is, in principle, available to the population. There are many reasons for this government failure. Among the most commonly cited are lack of funding to hire adequate staff and pay for needed medical interventions, low clinical and consumer quality, and poor client responsiveness through publicly mandated programs (Preker and Carrin 2004).

These and other observations highlight that, although government intervention is needed, public financing of health care at low-income levels is usually insufficient for sustainable funding to protect people, especially the poor, against illness-induced financial hardship and catastrophe. That is why many countries now favor a *multipillar approach* to health care financing in low- and middle-income countries. And one of these pillars is a strong private voluntary health insurance component and a partial premium subsidy to make such programs affordable even for the poor.

REFERENCES

Awosika, L. 2007. "Opportunities and Constraints in Management Practices in Sub-Saharan Africa." In *Private Voluntary Health Insurance in Development: Friend or Foe,* ed. A.S. Preker, R.M. Scheffler, and M.C. Bassett, 297–307. Washington, DC: World Bank.

Bassett, M.C., and V.M. Kane. 2007. "Review of the Literature on Voluntary Health Insurance." In *Private Voluntary Health Insurance in Development: Friend or Foe,* ed. A.S. Preker, R.M. Scheffler, and M.C. Bassett, 335–98. Washington, DC: World Bank.

Bowie, R., and G. Adams 2007. "Financial and Management Best Practice in Private Voluntary Health Insurance. " In *Private Voluntary Health Insurance in Development: Friend or Foe,* ed. A.S. Preker, R.M. Scheffler, and M.C. Bassett, 267–96. Washington, DC: World Bank.

Cichon, M., W. Newbrander, H. Yamabana, A. Weber, C. Normand, D.M. Dror, and A.S. Preker. 1999. *Modelling in Health Care Finance: A Compendium of Quantitative Techniques for Health Care Financing.* Geneva: International Labour Office /ISSA.

Chinitz D., J. Wasem, and A.S. Preker. 1997. "Balancing Competition and Solidarity in Health Care Financing." In *Critical Challenges for Health Care Reform in Europe,* ed. R.B. Saltman, J. Figueras, and C. Sakallarides, 55–77. Copenhagen: World Health Organization/ European Observatory on Health Care Reform.

Drechsler, D., and J.P. Jütting. 2007. "Scope, Limitations, and Policy Response," In *Private Voluntary Health Insurance in Development: Friend or Foe,* ed. A.S. Preker, R.M. Scheffler, and M.C. Bassett, 181–209. Washington, DC: World Bank.

Dror, D.M., and A.S. Preker, eds. 2002. *Social Reinsurance: A New Approach to Sustainable Community Health Financing*. Washington DC/Geneva: World Bank/International Labour Office.

Fuenzalida-Puelma, H.L., V. Kalavakonda, and M. Cáceres. 2007. "Financial and Other Regulatory Challenges in Low-Income Countries, " In *Private Voluntary Health Insurance in Development: Friend or Foe,* ed. A.S. Preker, R.M. Scheffler, and M.C. Bassett, 325–34. Washington, DC: World Bank.

Harding, A., and A.S. Preker, eds. 2003. "Private Participation in Health Services." Health, Nutrition, and Population (HNP) Series, World Bank, Washington, DC.

Harrington, S.E. 2007. "Facilitating and Safeguarding Regulations in Advanced Market Economies." In *Private Voluntary Health Insurance in Development: Friend or Foe,* ed. A.S. Preker, R.M. Scheffler, and M.C. Bassett, 309–24. Washington, DC: World Bank.

ILO (International Labour Office). 2007. *Social Health Protection: An ILO Strategy Towards Universal Access to Health Care.* Geneva: ILO.

Pauly, M.V. 2007. "Insights on Demand for Private Voluntary Health Insurance in Less Developed Countries, " In *Private Voluntary Health Insurance in Development: Friend or Foe,* ed. A.S. Preker, R.M. Scheffler, and M.C. Bassett, 23–54. Washington, DC: World Bank.

Pauly, M.V., F.E. Blavin, and S. Meghan. 2008. "Is There a Market for Voluntary Health Insurance in Developing Countries?" NBER Working Paper No. W14095, National Bureau for Economic Research (NBER), Cambridge, MA.

Pauly, M.V., P. Zweifel, R.M. Scheffler, A.S. Preker, and M.C. Bassett 2006. "Private Health Insurance in Developing Countries." *Health Affairs* 25 (2): 369–79.

Preker, A.S. 2003. "Expenditure Gaps and Development Traps." HNP Discussion Paper, World Bank, Washington, DC.

Preker, A.S. 2005. "Managing Scarcity through Strategic Purchasing of Health Care." In *Spending Wisely: Buying Health Services for the Poor,* ed. A.S. Preker and J.C. Langenbrunner, 23–46. Washington, DC: World Bank.

Preker, A.S. and J.C. Langenbrunner, eds. 2005. *Spending Wisely: Buying Health Services for the Poor.* Washington, DC: World Bank.

Preker, A.S., J.C. Langenbrunner, and E. Suzuki. 2002. "The Global Expenditure Gap: Securing Financial Protection and Access to Health Care for the Poor." HNP Discussion Paper, World Bank, Washington, DC.

Preker, A.S., X. Liu, E.V. Velényi, and E. Baris, eds. 2007. *Public Ends, Private Means: Strategic Purchasing of Value for Money in Health Care.* Washington, DC: World Bank.

Preker A.S., R.M. Scheffler, and M.C. Bassett, eds. 2007. *Private Voluntary Health Insurance in Development: Friend or Foe.* Washington, DC: World Bank.

Preker A.S., E. Suzuki, F. Bustero, A. Soucat, and J.C. Langenbrunner. 2003. "Costing Accelerated Progress Towards Achieving the Millennium Development Goals." HNP Discussion Paper, World Bank, Washington, DC.

Schellekens, O.P, M.E. Lindner, J.M.A. Lange, and J. Van der Gaag. 2007. "A New Paradigm for Increased Access to Healthcare in Africa." Issues Brief, International Finance Corporation (IFC), Washington, DC.

Smith, P. 2007. "Provision of a Public Benefit Package alongside Private Voluntary Health Insurance." In *Private Voluntary Health Insurance in Development: Friend or Foe,* ed. A.S. Preker, R.M. Scheffler, and M.C. Bassett, 147–67. Washington, DC: World Bank.

Smith, P.C., A.S. Preker, D.W. Light, and S. Richards. 2005. "Role of Markets and Competition." In *Purchasing to Improve Health Systems Performance,* ed. J. Figueras, R. Robinson, and E. Jakubowski, 102–21. Buckingham, UK: Open University Press.

WHO (World Health Organization). 2000. *The World Health Report 2000—Health Systems: Measuring Performance.* Geneva: World Health Organization.

World Bank. 1993. *World Development Report 1993: Investing in Health.* New York, NY: Oxford University Press.

———. 1997. *Sector Strategy for HNP 1997.* Washington, DC: World Bank.

———. 2007a. *Health Financing Revisited: A Practitioner's Guide.* Washington, DC: World Bank.

———. 2007b. *Healthy Development: World Bank Strategy for Health, Nutrition and Population Results.* Washington, DC: World Bank.

Zweifel, P., B.B. Krey, and M. Tagli. 2007. "Supply of Private Voluntary Health Insurance in Low-Income Countries." In *Private Voluntary Health Insurance in Development: Friend or Foe,* ed. A.S. Preker, R.M. Scheffler, and M.C. Bassett, 55–113. Washington, DC: World Bank.

Zweifel, P., and M.V. Pauly 2007. "Market Outcomes, Regulation, and Policy Recommendations." In *Private Voluntary Health Insurance in Development: Friend or Foe,* ed. A.S. Preker, R.M. Scheffler, and M.C. Bassett, 115–45. Washington, DC: World Bank.

PART 1

Empirical and Economic Underpinnings

CHAPTER 2

Six Regions, One Story

Denis Drechsler and Johannes P. Jütting

Private health insurance (PHI) in low- and middle-income countries and its significance for national health systems has three major characteristics. First, PHI involving prepayment and risk sharing plays a marginal role in the developing world. Coverage rates are generally below 10 percent of the population. Private risk-sharing programs have wider significance in only a small number of countries (for example, South Africa, Uruguay, and Lebanon). Second, the importance of PHI in financing health care is rising in many countries. Various factors contribute to this development: growing dissatisfaction with public health care, liberalization of markets and increased international trade in the insurance industry, as well as overall economic growth, allowing higher and more diversified consumer demand. Consumer demand is expected to put pressure on the supply side of the system to increase choices and improve the quality of health care coverage. Third, the development of PHI presents both opportunities and threats to health care systems in developing countries. If PHI is carefully managed and adapted to local needs and preferences, it can be a valuable complement to existing health financing options. In particular, nonprofit group–based insurance schemes could become an important pillar of health care financing, especially for individuals who would otherwise be left outside a country's health insurance system. Opening up markets for private health insurance without an appropriate regulatory framework might widen inequalities in access to health care: it may lead to cost escalation, a deterioration in public services, a reduction in the provision of preventive health care, and a widening of the rich-poor divide in a country's medical system. Given these risks, the crucial challenge for policy makers is to develop a regulatory framework that is adapted to a country's institutional capacities and which, at the same time, sets the rules and standards in which PHI can efficiently operate and develop.

INTRODUCTION

Health care financing continues to be a key challenge in many low- and middle-income countries. Despite various efforts to improve the health situation in the developing world, many countries are still far from achieving "universal health coverage."[1] Worldwide, 1.3 billion people do not have access to effective and affordable health care, including drugs, surgeries, and other medical interventions

(Preker et al. 2002: 22). As documented by the World Health Organization (WHO 2000: 7), low- and middle-income countries bear 93 percent of the world's disease burden, yet account for merely 18 percent of world income and 11 percent of global health spending. Poor health drastically impedes a country's social and economic development. Besides directly impairing people's well-being (for example, reduced life expectancy, high infant mortality, spread of infectious diseases), poor health also lowers the productivity of labor and menaces the entire economy (WHO 2001a). Estimates for Botswana, for example, suggest that the economy will be between 33 percent and 40 percent smaller by 2010 due to the impact of AIDS (HSRC 2003).

To a large extent, health problems of low- and middle-income countries stem from financial and institutional deficiencies. According to estimates by the Commission on Macroeconomics and Health (WHO 2001a), around US$34 per year is needed to cover an individual's essential interventions. In 2002, only about 15 percent of all low-income countries[2] reached this amount. For private expenditure on health, the number drops to a little over 6 percent (WHO 2005). The situation is equally worrisome as regards public provision of health care. In low-income countries, universal health coverage would require public spending of around 12 percent of GNP to meet the international development goals (Gupta et al. 2001: 19). Such levels are far from being realized; in only three low-income countries (Timor-Leste, Lesotho, and São Tomé and Principe) does public health care spending exceed 5 percent of national income (WHO 2005). To expand health coverage, pooling resources by bundling available funds and spreading the risk of illness and heath care cost thus seems indispensable.

Low- and middle-income countries rarely have the financial means and institutional capacity to provide state-based social health insurance. A large percentage of health spending consequently comes directly out of patients' pockets. According to WHO (2004) data, out-of-pocket (OOP) payments account for a third of total health care spending in two thirds of all low-income countries. *Catastrophic health costs* (payments exceeding 40 percent of a household's capacity to pay) occur in many countries and drastically increase the risk of impoverishment; especially adding in the indirect costs of health expenditure resulting from illness-associated loss of productive capital (Xu et al. 2003). In view of these perils, a main focus of the current debate on health reform emphasizes the need "to move away from excessive reliance on out-of-pocket payment as a source of health financing" (Bennett and Gilson 2001: 1).

Problem Setting

Given the limitations of a public health care system, private health insurance (PHI)[3] offers a potential alternative to insure against the cost of illness. As indicated by the WHO (2000: xviii), private schemes can serve as "a preparatory process of consolidating small pools into larger ones" to eventually achieve universal coverage. This is what happened in many industrialized countries, where universal (social) insurance emerged out of private risk-sharing programs (for example, Germany and Sweden [Sekhri and Savedoff 2005: 129]).

The relative importance of health care financing through private risk-sharing entities is surprisingly similar across the world (figure 2.1). With the exception of low-income countries, PHI exists in nearly the same share of middle- and high-income countries. Similar observations apply for an increase in the relative importance of private health insurance because the share of countries in which contributions exceed 5, 10, and 20 percent of total health care spending are equally alike. At the same time, figure 2.1 also highlights that few countries cover large parts of their health care expenses through PHI: in only six countries do payments to private risk-sharing programs exceed 20 percent of total health expenditure (THE). The contribution of PHI toward universal health coverage is thus still very limited.

Yet, this picture may gradually change as insurance markets in developing countries are burgeoning. Measured as premium volume, the insurance industry in low- and middle-income countries grew more than twice as fast as in industrialized economies between 1998 and 2003 (10.2 percent as compared with 2.6 percent in the life insurance sector and 7.7 percent as compared with 4.7 percent in the non–life insurance sector, respectively[4]). This development has been particularly strong in Asia and Eastern Europe where the industry expanded by 10.5 percent and 13 percent between 1998 and 2003 (Swiss Re 2004b: 15).

FIGURE 2.1 Private Health Insurance in WHO Countries

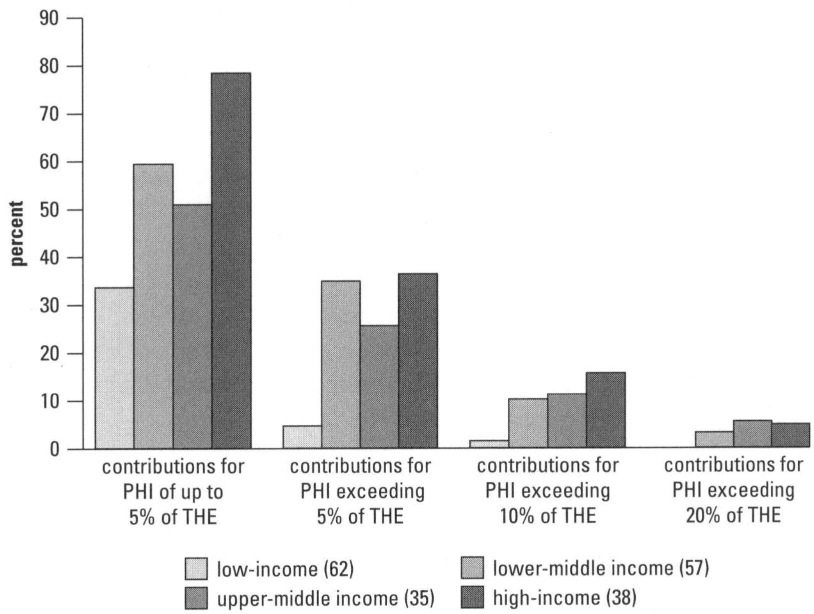

Source: Authors' calculations based on WHO 2005.

Note: Existence of PHI and volume of contributions are measured as share of private spending on prepaid risk-sharing programs relative to THE. The number of countries in each income group is given in parentheses in the key.

Although growth rates have recently dropped below their long-term average, analysts still see a large development potential for the insurance industry in low- and, especially, middle-income countries. The overall development may be even more dynamic than indicated in these numbers. Available data often only capture the revenue of commercial providers, and consequently are missing other forms of insurance contracts that may be particularly important in the developing world (for example, nonprofit or community-based programs). Considering the general growth trend of insurance markets, PHI can be expected to gain importance in low- and middle-income countries.

Nevertheless, it is essential to note that low- and middle-income countries compose a very heterogeneous group. Particularly striking is the large disparity of expenditure for insurance premiums among individual countries, ranging from per capita values of US$1,064 in Barbados to US$3 in Bangladesh. Similarly, *insurance penetration* (premium income relative to gross domestic product, GDP) varies from 0.5 percent in Saudi Arabia to 15.9 percent in South Africa, which indeed is the highest penetration rate in the world (Swiss Re 2004a: 21).

Chapter Structure and Data

Although PHI is becoming increasingly important to finance health care in low- and middle-income countries (Sekhri and Savedoff 2005), little is known about its impact on health care coverage. This chapter presents an analysis of characteristics of private health insurance in the developing world and evaluates its significance for national health systems. Regrettably, data on health care financing are scarce, especially in the context of low- and middle-income countries that sometimes fail to collect information in a systematic and comprehensive fashion. To overcome this problem, various data sources are employed, including National Health Accounts (NHA) and country case studies as well as reports from actuarial firms and reinsurance companies. Nevertheless, some of our findings—especially concerning development trends and development potentials—need to be treated with caution due to the lack of reliable time-series data. Given these data constraints, the extent of private health insurance is assumed to be underestimated.

The broad scope of this analysis goes beyond other research in the field. Previous studies either focused on specific types of PHI such as community-based programs (Preker/Carrin 2004) or microinsurance (Dror and Jacquier 1999), or restricted the analysis to countries where the insurance industry is already well established, as in Latin America (Barrientos/Lloyd-Sherlock 2003; Iriart et al. 2001) and Southeast Asia (WHO 2004b). The present analysis tries to fill this gap, giving a systematic and comprehensive overview of market performance of PHI and discussing regulatory aspects as a response to possible incidents of market failure.

The structure of the chapter is as follows. A typology of private health insurance is developed and distinct features of PHI in low- and middle-income countries are identified. An overview of the health insurance industry in different regions of the world is then given, and an inventory of existing schemes is drawn up. This part also considers trends in PHI development, covering market performance issues and presenting areas of market failure. This last aspect is especially important in deriving policy implications and discussing prospects of PHI in the developing world. Conclusions are presented in the final section.

TYPOLOGY OF HEALTH CARE FINANCING

Health care can generally be financed in four different ways, and no two countries have chosen the same system or the same mixture of features.

Systems of Health Care Financing

The four most common financing systems are: social insurance, which is based on tax-like contributions and managed or regulated by the state; a health system, which is completely financed from tax revenues and other government resources; private direct payments (out of pocket); and private health insurance (Mehrotra and Delamonica 2005). The World Health Organization (WHO 2004c) identifies internal donations as a fifth dimension of health care financing, which is not considered in this analysis. These groups are not mutually exclusive; in fact, all health systems are a mixture of various elements. Similarly, the distinction between private and social insurance is not as clear-cut as indicated in this typology; most health insurance systems are somewhere between the extreme ends of either category (Jost 2001). Figure 2.2 gives an overview of the main systems of health care financing and the corresponding flow of financial resources.

FIGURE 2.2 Health Care Financing Systems

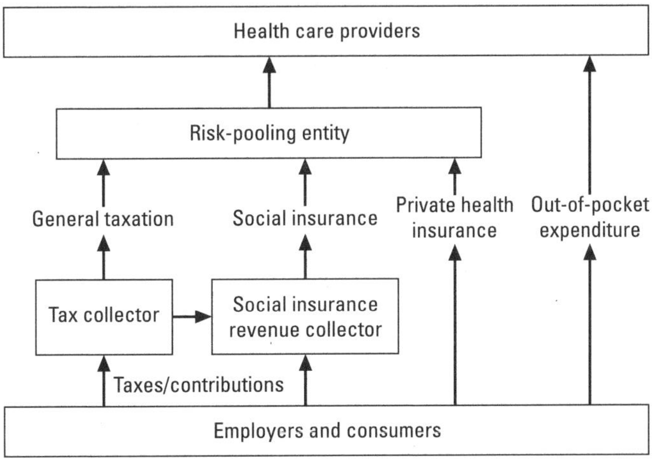

Source: Adapted from Skehri and Savedoff 2005: 128.

Although this chapter focuses mainly on PHI, other forms of health care financing are nevertheless important for the analysis—private health insurance, for instance, may be a tool for eventually achieving universal public insurance. Similarly, PHI-based health systems often contain direct payments and other elements of cost sharing (for example, user fees, copayments, or deductibles) in order to restrain household demand and consumption of health care. Finally, out-of-pocket spending may become the starting point for an insurance-based system if resources are redirected for prepayments. In fact, several studies derive a willingness and ability to pay for health insurance based on the large OOP spending on health in low- and middle-income countries. As argued in the literature, even the poor may be willing to pay for health insurance (Asfaw 2003; Amoako, Feeley, and Winfrey 2002; Asenso-Okyere et al.1997).

Social Insurance

Social insurance is usually compulsory, although people can sometimes choose between various insurance packages or decide whether or not to take additional coverage. Only a few countries (for example, Hong Kong, Mexico[5]) offer public health insurance that is voluntary. Due to this mandated membership, social insurance can spread individual health risks over a large risk pool. This has certain advantages over other forms of health financing. Specifically, premiums can be based on income rather than individual health risks (that is, higher equity), participation is usually nondiscriminatory, and the financial base is large and stable. If schemes are well managed and local circumstances allow easy premium collection, social health insurance can also reduce administrative cost. However, critics claim that social insurance schemes rarely work efficiently. According to some, they neither contain health costs nor prevent premium escalation due to a perceived lack of public oversight. Especially when social insurance separates health financing and provision, health care providers can pass cost increases on to consumers (Savedoff 2004). Furthermore, social insurance often leaves large parts of the population uncovered because premium collection is typically limited to formal sector employment. These aspects may be particularly pronounced in low- and middle-income countries with weak institutional capacities and large informal sectors. As documented in Carrin, Desmet, and Basaza (2001), social health insurance also demands a high degree of consensus among the population. Such consensus may be missing in developing countries that are often torn by internal conflicts and social cleavages.

Tax-Based Financing

Although some countries (for example, Taiwan, China) refer to their tax-funded programs as national insurance, health care directly financed by the state is technically not considered insurance.[6] Funds are raised through general taxation or other government revenues while benefits are usually granted to every citizen (Beveridge model). Health services that are covered can be broad and comprehensive (for example, the United Kingdom and other OECD countries with tax-funded health systems, but also rich oil-producing countries like Saudi Arabia). However, they are often limited to basic treatment or emergency care, especially in low- and middle-income countries with weak tax-raising capability. Frequently, the state not only pays for health care, but also supplies services through public facilities and state employees. This high demand for public oversight and management is rarely free of efficiency loss. Even developed countries like the U.K. have long waiting lines for certain types of medical treatment like nonurgent hospital care. In addition, tax-financed health systems often show low responsiveness to patients' particular needs, which may reduce the quality of care (Mahal 2002: 440).

Out-of-Pocket Spending

Out-of-pocket spending constitutes a large and important source of health care financing in developing countries. Payments are not made beforehand but when care is needed. This can have catastrophic outcomes, especially for low-income families: people may not be able to pay for needed care and thus risk a grave deterioration of their health condition; people may be reluctant to pay for needed care and thus fail to get therapy when it is still effective; or they may pay for needed care by using a large portion of their resources, thus risking impoverishment. Despite these critical perils for both the health situation and the overall economic performance in low- and middle-income countries, OOP is important in the developing world. One in five low-income countries meets more than two thirds of total health care spending through OOP. Furthermore, in roughly 75 percent of all low-income countries OOP accounts for more than a third of total health care spending compared with only 7.9 percent within the high-income category (table 2.1).

TABLE 2.1 OOP Spending in WHO Countries (percent of total health care spending)

	Low-income countries		*Lower-middle-income countries*		*Upper-middle-income countries*		*High-income countries*		*Total*	
Item	*N*	*%*	*N*	*%*	*N*	*%*	*N*	*%*	*N*	*%*
Total	62	100	57	100	35	100	38	100	192	100
OOP < 33% of THE	16	27.4	28	49.1	23	65.6	35	92.1	103	53.6
OOP > 33% of THE	45	72.6	29	50.9	12	34.4	3	7.9	89	46.4
OOP > 50% of THE	27	43.5	14	24.6	6	17.1	2	5.3	49	25.5
OOP > 66% of THE	13	21.0	3	5.3	0	0.0	1	2.6	17	8.9

Source: Authors' calculations based on WHO 2005.
Note: Existence and volume of OOPS are measured as percentage of total health care expenditure in 2002.

Private Health Insurance

Unlike social insurance, PHI is usually voluntary,[7] which may make for a small risk pool. This has certain consequences that may be problematic from a policy maker's point of view. In risk-rated schemes, premiums are based primarily on individual health risks and not on a person's income. In community- or group-rated schemes, the relatively small risk pool makes cross-subsidization between different risk groups more difficult than in social insurance schemes (equity issue). Furthermore, providers of PHI have an incentive to be selective about whom to insure. Beyond raising premiums for bad-risk individuals, providers can simply refuse to insure high-risk/high-treatment patients (discrimination issue). This cream skimming is difficult to prevent. Sometimes, public regulation may even prejudice market outcomes. For example, in the community-rated schemes, general enrollment obligations for insurance providers will attract mainly bad-risk individuals. The ensuing premium escalation further discourages good-risk patients from joining the scheme (adverse selection). Health risks are not shared in a large risk pool, but are spread among few individuals or across time. Without efficient management, PHI may thus court bankruptcy. On the positive side, PHI offers personalized insurance packages[8] and competitive premiums to its clientele, particularly to good-risk individuals. Due to small company sizes and reduced bureaucratic processes, PHI can also work more efficiently than social insurance schemes, although insurers may face higher administrative costs due to product development as well as advertising and distribution activities. Alternative ways of collecting premiums also expand coverage beyond formal sector employment. Especially the nonprofit PHI sector offers room for innovation to include individuals who would otherwise be left outside insurance-based programs. As Ginneken (1999: 29) argues, there is a "need for experimentation" to establish ways of extending health care coverage to the excluded majority in developing countries.

Private Health Insurance in Low- and Middle-Income Countries

Private health insurance in low- and middle-income countries has multiple facets. As defined here, PHI financial resources are channeled directly to the risk-pooling institution with no or little involvement of the state. Specifically, this study allows for public subsidies to a private provider of health insurance. Similarly, "private social insurance schemes" (WHO 2004a) are also considered PHI, although such programs may be managed by a public entity. The main distinction between social and private health insurance consequently stems from the type of contract between the risk-pooling entity and the insured individual or group. Whereas social insurance relies on tax-like contributions, PHI rests upon a private contract between the insurance company and its clientele that sets the insurance premium to be exchanged for a specified benefits coverage. Because participation in these schemes is rarely mandatory, PHI is often referred to as voluntary health insurance (VHI). This analysis nevertheless sticks to the PHI notation.

According to the Organisation for Economic Co-operation and Development (OECD 2004a), health financing through insurance involves both prepayment and risk pooling. Following this general classification, there are several possibilities for financing health care expenditure through private prepaid contributions. The spectrum of PHI in developing countries ranges from large commercial to small nonprofit schemes, which can be run by private entities (including health care providers), nongovernmental organizations (NGOs), or even communities. Furthermore, insurance programs may offer individual contracts or cover particular groups of people, as do employer-based schemes that rarely extend beyond the formal labor market. Finally, in this analysis prepaid medicine programs are considered although their degree of risk pooling is very limited. These schemes also offer insurance-like services, especially when the insurance industry is relatively small or not well developed.

Due to the diversity of existing schemes and the nonexclusivity of particular features it is impossible to derive a strict typology of private risk-sharing arrangements. A classification of schemes may nevertheless consider the type of supplier, the level of compulsion, the extent and type of risk pooling, as well as the form of insurance contract (community, group, or individual). PHI schemes may also be distinguished by the extent of coverage, the type of insurance business (profit vs. nonprofit), and use or nonuse of cost sharing (through copayments, deductibles, and coinsurance). Table 2.2 gives an overview of various dimensions of PHI.

In many OECD countries,[9] for-profit firms are the main supplier of PHI. Such private commercial health insurance has the least significance in low- and middle-income countries. As in Cambodia, commercial PHI in the developing world is usually "restricted to a relatively small population, the so-called better-off, employees of large enterprises and big NGOs" (GTZ 2003: 13). Such observations are confirmed for basically all low- and middle-income countries that in some way rely on PHI in their health care financing. Private commercial health insurance offers both comprehensive and supplementary coverage, where the

TABLE 2.2 Typology of Private Health Insurance in Low- and Middle-Income Countries

Dimension/type of supplier	Public	Parastatal	Private
Level of compulsion	Mandatory	Mandatory, but choice between packages	Voluntary
Extent of risk pooling	Large pool	Small pool	None
Type of risk-pooling arrangement	Community-rated premiums	Group-specific premiums	Risk-rated premiums
Form of insurance contract	Community	Group	Individual
Degree of coverage	Comprehensive	Supplementary	Complementary
Type of cost sharing	Copayments	Deductibles	Coinsurance
Type of insurance business	Profit	Nonprofit	Charity

Source: Authors' compilation.

latter predominantly covers superior treatment or additional services. People with private coverage are generally free to consult the health provider of their choice and get reimbursed according to the specific insurance package they have selected.

The narrow focus of private commercial health insurance on high-income individuals can be attributed to the schemes' specific design, which yields high premiums relative to the disposable income of the majority of the population. Because commercial providers are interested mainly in maximizing profits, they are highly selective about whom to insure. Bad-risk patients with frequent and/or high-cost treatment are not only a menace to the revenue-generating objective of private insurers; they also jeopardize the survival of the firm—especially because the PHI risk pool is typically small, and individual risks cannot as easily be counterbalanced. High-cost patients are often excluded from the schemes, or pay higher premiums to compensate for the financial risks they impose. The outreach of commercial providers is additionally reduced by a lack of information on both the insurer and the consumer side. Potential buyers of PHI are often not aware of the possibility of insuring against health risks through private providers; in some cases, they may not even be familiar with the concept of health insurance (Bennett, Creese, and Monasch 1998: 19; Asfaw and Jütting 2002: 6). However, a lack of reliable data on the health situation in low- and middle-income countries also makes it difficult for insurance providers to offer customized schemes at an affordable price. The U.S. Department of Commerce (2000) estimates, for example, that foreign insurance firms need an average of three to five years to break even. This time span is essential to accumulate all "relevant information about the targeted subsectors of a country's health care system, investment requirements, and cultural attitudes toward health care that will have a bearing on success" (ibid.: 43–46).

EVIDENCE OF PHI IN LOW- AND MIDDLE-INCOME COUNTRIES

This section gives an overview of private prepaid health programs in different regions of the world. The Regions, following a World Bank classification, are PHI markets in Latin America and the Caribbean (LCR), South Asia (SAR), East Asia and the Pacific (EAP), Sub-Saharan Africa (SSA), East European and Central Asian countries in the Bank's Europe and Central Asia (ECA) Region, and the Middle East and North Africa (MENA). Besides illustrating various indicators of market performance, this section also considers areas of market failure, discusses corresponding policy responses, and gives an outlook for PHI development.

Measured as insurance premium income, private risk-sharing markets in low- and middle-income countries are still relatively insignificant. This appraisal is particularly true for private commercial health insurance. Naturally, the role of PHI depends heavily on the government's involvement in this line of business (Swiss Re 2004b: 10). Despite severe shortcomings of other forms of health financing, private health and accident insurance has not yet become a major pillar of the health care system in the developing world. In 2002, insurance penetration amounted to only 0.11 percent in Africa, 0.14 percent in the Middle East, 0.29 percent in Eastern Europe, 0.34 percent in Asia, and 0.40 percent in Latin America (data deducted from Swiss Re 2005). These figures need to be treated with care because premium income from small-scale insurance schemes often goes unrecorded. Figure 2.3 gives a global overview of life and non–life insurance as regards population size and gross domestic product (GDP).

Both life and non–life insurance are still relatively insignificant in low- and middle-income countries. Collectively, all six regions that will be considered in this analysis account for a mere 10 percent of global insurance premium income. This small share is particularly striking considering the fact these regions account for more than 85 percent of the world's population. Furthermore, the low significance of PHI does not necessarily reflect the countries' economic potential as their share of global GDP amounts to around 23 percent.

Figure 2.4 illustrates the regional split of non–life insurance premiums across the developing world, of which PHI is one subcomponent. Evidently, the development of insurance markets is further advanced in some regions like Latin

FIGURE 2.3 Relative Importance of Commercial Insurance Markets, 2003 (percent of global insurance premium income)

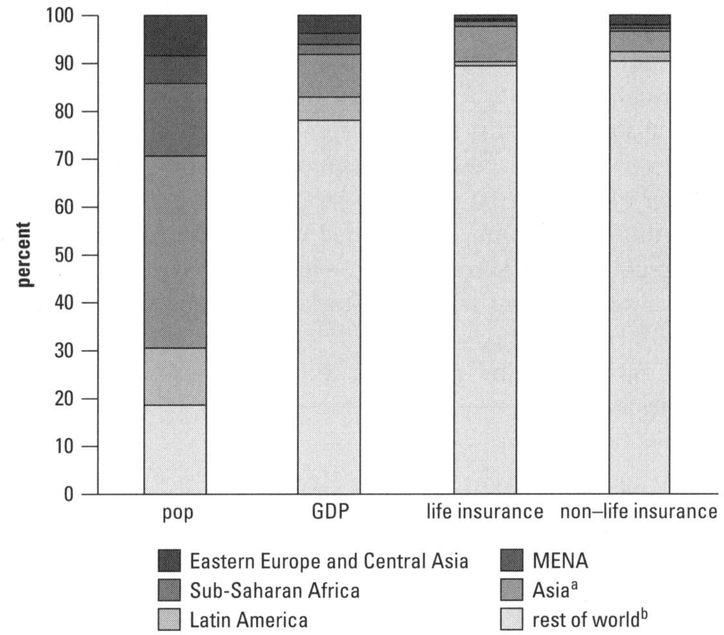

Source: Authors' calculations based on Swiss Re 2005. See annex D, this volume, for numerical values.

a. East Asia and the Pacific excluding Japan.

b. Rest of world, covering mainly OECD countries.

FIGURE 2.4 Regional Split of Non–Life Insurance Premiums in the Developing World (percent of total)

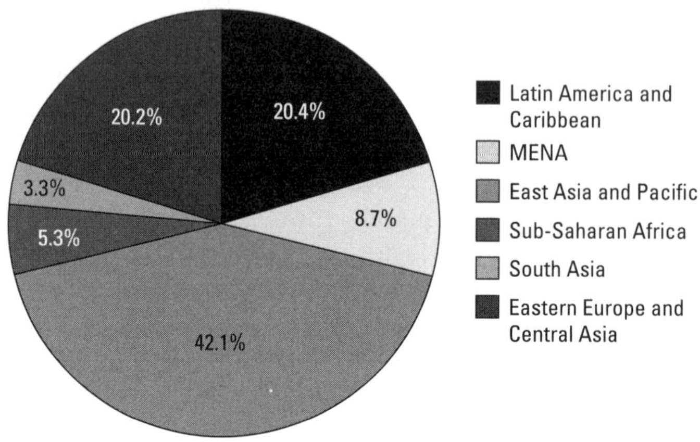

Source: Authors' calculations based on Swiss Re 2005.

America and the East Asian and East European countries. Premium income is particularly low in South Asia and Sub-Saharan Africa.

Several factors seem to influence the development of PHI: a country's economic performance, the institutional capacity of a state to offer health insurance and/or health care, as well as cultural traits that promote or impede the growth of insurance markets. Furthermore, health financing through PHI seems generally more developed in low- and middle-income countries with a high level of income inequality. Private for-profit health insurance does benefit from an unequal distribution of wealth because the rich are more likely than others to buy coverage, even if it is provided through other channels. Countries in which PHI accounts for more then 10 percent of total health expenditure also have an unequal distribution of income, as indicated by high Gini coefficients (table 2.3). Disregarding Uruguay and South Africa, where exceptionally high PHI spending can be explained by other factors (mandated membership in Uruguay), Gini coefficients and PHI spending are strongly correlated with a correlation coefficient of 0.72 (figure 2.5), thus indicating that countries with an unequal distribution of wealth are more likely to have high levels of PHI spending.

Insurance Market and Private Health Insurance in Latin America

The private insurance market in Latin America accounted for 1.4 percent of global insurance premium income (US$42 billion) in 2003. Of this, about 18 percent is attributable to health and personal accident/workmen's compensation insurance. The insurance industry is particularly developed in Argentina, Brazil, Chile, Colombia, Mexico, and República Bolivariana de Venezuela, which account for more than 90 percent of Latin America's total insurance premium income. The volume of

TABLE 2.3 Total Health Expenditure and Gini Coefficient

Country	*Income group*	*Gini coefficient (%)*	*PHI contribution as % of THE*
Argentina	Upper-middle	52.2	15.5
Brazil	Lower-middle	59.1	19.4
Chile	Upper-middle	57.1	28.2
Jamaica	Lower-middle	37.9	13.8
Lebanon	Upper-middle	32.4	12.2
Morocco	Lower-middle	39.5	15.5
Namibia	Lower-middle	70.7	22.4
Philippines	Lower-middle	46.1	10.9
South Africa	Lower-middle	59.3	46.2
Uruguay	Upper-middle	44.6	53.3
Zimbabwe	Low-income	56.8	18.8

Sources: Authors' calculations based on WHO 2005 and UNDP 2004.

FIGURE 2.5 Correlation between Gini Coefficient and PHI Spending

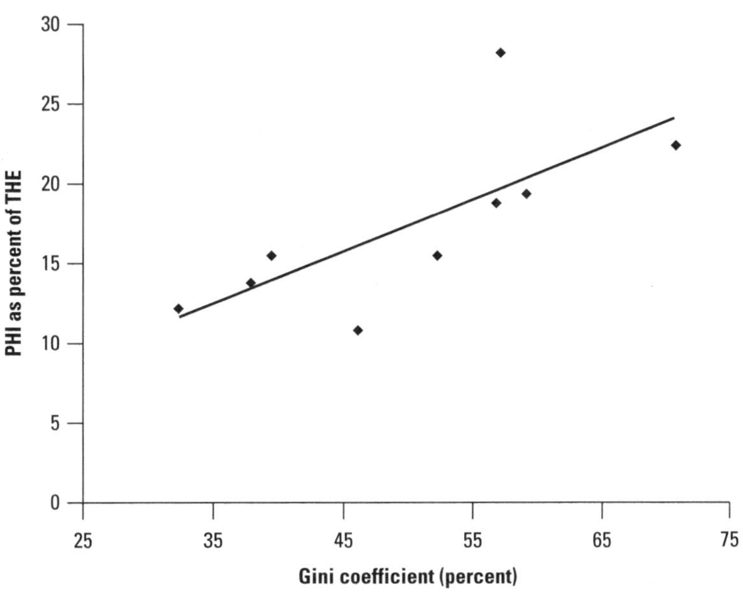

Sources: Authors' calculations based on WHO 2005 and UNDP 2004.

insurance premiums has significantly increased in the past couple of years, following regulatory changes and liberalization efforts in the 1990s, which introduced private and foreign insurers to the national markets. International suppliers cover up to 70 percent of the insurance market in countries such as Chile, Argentina, and Mexico (Swiss Re 2005). Penetration by multinational corporations has also started to increase in Brazil and Ecuador (Iriart, Merhy, and Waitzkin 2001). Beyond the general market liberalization, another driving factor of the private insurance industry might be Latin America's great income inequality, which is particularly pronounced in countries with high insurance penetration, namely Argentina, Brazil, Chile, and Colombia (Gini coefficients above 0.5).

The high inflow of capital and the increased presence of foreign insurance providers in the 1990s have not been met by an equally growing demand for these products. Despite a 5 percent increase in insurance-based transactions, there remains a mismatch of supply and demand. This may have a simple explanation. On one hand, market liberalization in Latin America and the subsequent inflow of foreign providers occurred very rapidly and profoundly: regulations dropped, new licenses were granted, and restrictions on foreign investments fell. On the other hand, consumer preferences usually change more incrementally, especially when per capita income does not increase sufficiently to support a change in consumption (Salazar 1999).

The growth of the insurance industry is due mainly to the development of life insurance. Even though Latin America experienced high growth rates in health and personal accident insurance between 1995 and 2000, the overall non–life insurance sector grew only proportionately to GDP. Furthermore, the comparatively strong 6 percent growth rate in 2001 was driven mainly by higher premiums and rising international prices for property insurance rather than a general business expansion (Swiss Re 2002: 4).

PHI in Latin America

Contrary to what the relatively insignificant volume of private health insurance premiums might suggest, PHI does play a significant role in a number of Latin American countries. It is particularly important in Uruguay, where more than 60 percent of the population is covered through private schemes. This exceptionally high significance of PHI can be explained by Uruguay's particular health care policy. Similarly to public insurance systems, coverage through private entities is mandatory. People (elderly and poor) who cannot afford the premiums are covered through publicly funded programs (Sekhri and Savedoff 2005: 131). PHI is offered through prepaid care associations, membership-based professional cooperatives, or nonprofit health services (PAHO 1999: 6). Although the state exercises some legal and technical control, the autonomy of private health insurance providers in Uruguay is limited; for example, the state sets a price ceiling on monthly premiums.

High coverage is also reached in Colombia where half the population is estimated to have private health insurance (U.S. Department of Commerce

2000: 43–47). Particularly noteworthy is Colombia's significant increase in coverage following health sector reforms in the early 1990s, especially among lower-income groups (Jack 2000: 14). Compared to 1993, insurance coverage had more than doubled in 1997, with 57.2 percent of the population formally insured. Due to special tax benefits for poor households, this increase was particularly large among the lowest-income percentiles. Some authors also argue that the insurance system in Colombia is more focused than elsewhere in Latin America while standard insurance packages for high- and low-income groups allow some redistribution between rich and poor (Jack 2000: 30). After a general deterioration of the country's economy, total spending on health care nevertheless dropped significantly between 1998 and 2002[10] (WHO 2005).

Measured in terms of total expenditure on health care, PHI is also important in Chile and Brazil, largely due to insufficiencies in publicly financed insurance schemes. About one quarter of the population is covered through private health insurance in each country (U.S. Department of Commerce 2000: 43–47). Similar observations apply to Argentina and Jamaica, where PHI spending accounts for around 15 percent of total health expenditure. Though not yet reflected in relative expenditure on private health insurance, PHI has recently also gained significance in Mexico where the industry is experiencing "vigorous growth" (Swiss Re 2002: 35). Still comparatively low, spending on prepaid plans in Mexico increased by more than 50 percent between 1998 and 2002 (WHO 2005). The National Insurance and Securities Commission of Mexico estimates PHI coverage at around 3 percent of the total population. Table 2.4 gives an overview of all Latin American countries in which spending on PHI has been recorded.

TABLE 2.4 Private Health Insurance in LCR Countries

Country	*Importance of PHI*[a]	*Country*	*Importance of PHI*[a]
Argentina	15.5	Jamaica	13.8
Barbados	7.2	Mexico	3.0
Bolivia	3.8	Nicaragua	2.0
Brazil	19.4	Panama	5.2
Chile	28.2	Paraguay	7.1
Colombia	5.4	Peru	8.6
Costa Rica	0.3	Suriname	0.2
Dominican Republic	0.3	Trinidad and Tobago	4.7
Ecuador	1.5	Uruguay	53.3
El Salvador	3.4	Venezuela, República Bolivariana de	2.2
Guatemala	2.7		
Honduras	3.6		

Source: Authors' calculations based on WHO 2005.

a. Expenditure on private prepaid plans as percentage of total expenditure on health in 2002: not including countries without PHI or where data were not available.

Market Indicators and Evidence of Market Failure

Social insurance provided the primary model of health insurance in Latin America before the insurance market was opened for private providers (Mesa-Lago 1991). When PHI emerged in the 1990s (1981 in Chile) most social security programs in the Latin America and Caribbean Region had low coverage, coped with high administrative costs, suffered from inefficiency, corruption, and escalating health care expenses, and faced fiscal imbalances. The entry of private, especially international, insurers led to increased and often predatory competition, characterized by hostile takeovers of local insurers as well as a number of mergers and acquisitions. Multilateral lending agencies, the World Bank in particular, strongly supported the privatization of public services and the entry of foreign corporations. Countries that failed to implement market structures in the health sector according to structural adjustment programs were threatened with cutoffs or drastic reductions in loans, import credits, and food aid (Stocker, Waitzkin, and Iriart 1999).

However, the entry of private insurance providers has not yet resulted in more competitive products such as lower premiums. Although market concentration has recently decreased as some small start-up companies have entered the market, the industry remains uncompetitive and premiums high. Consequently, private health insurance addresses mainly the highest income percentile. Low-income groups remain in the social insurance schemes or are left without any insurance at all. Such inequities have been reported for Argentina, Chile, and Colombia (Barrientos and Lloyd-Sherlock 2003), Brazil (Jack 2000: 26), and Peru (Cruz-Saco 2002: 17). In some cases, the introduction of PHI pushed people out of other forms of prepaid programs (for example, prepaid medicine schemes) and arguably decreased health care coverage (box 2.1).

Frequently, PHI is faced with both the inherent problems of health insurance markets and "the administrative weakness and political conflicts present in the health sector in Latin America" (Barrientos and Lloyd-Sherlock 2003: 189). Previous experience raises concerns about whether the introduction of private schemes will provide a solution for the apparent problems of health care financing in Latin America. In many countries, all relevant indicators of a successful health insurance system have not improved or have deteriorated since the introduction of private schemes. According to Barrientos and Lloyd-Sherlock (2003), private insurance has neither contained health care costs nor promoted equity, nor has it absorbed all risk groups in an undiscriminatory fashion (cream skimming). As noted by the International Labour Organization (ILO), there is a large discrepancy between coverage in urban and rural areas. For the early 1990s, the ILO made out vast disparities between the best- and the worst-served areas in Argentina, Mexico, and Panama (ILO 2000). Small nonprofit schemes may arguably adapt better to local circumstances and cover a higher percentage of people than imported types of insurance that are based largely on the U.S. health maintenance system (Iriart, Merhy, and Waitzkin 2001: 1243). Box 2.2 discusses in more detail managed care, which has become a characteristic feature of the Latin American health care market.

BOX 2.1 PREPAID MEDICINE PROGRAMS IN LATIN AMERICA

In countries where the insurance market is not well developed, prepaid medicine programs offer alternative protection against medical risks. Technically, these plans are not considered insurance because beneficiaries do not buy policies expressly to protect themselves from unexpected expenses. Rather, individuals purchase the right to reduced rates for medical services that they will most likely use in the future. Such programs focus on providing high-quality, simple curative and preventive care. People who know they will need medical services can join the program with the exception of individuals with severe health conditions. For an annual entry fee, people can choose from among various packages offering different degrees of coverage. The annual fee depends on the person's age and medical history, as well as the package chosen.

Prepaid medicine programs have been particularly relevant in such Latin America countries as Argentina, Bolivia, Chile, and Colombia, where such schemes were the only way to insure privately against health risks before PHI was introduced. Similarly to commercial health insurance, prepaid medicine programs cover people mostly from the upper-middle and high-income classes. As a consequence, they rarely extend beyond formally employed workers in urban areas.

Since the introduction of private health insurance, the importance of prepaid programs has decreased. Especially in Argentina, membership declined significantly during 1997 and 2001, also as a consequence of economic crisis that put former beneficiaries out of regular employment. Today, membership is therefore limited even further to the high-income segments of Argentine society. In Bolivia, the decline of membership has been less significant, partly because the public insurance system could not offer sound alternatives. The overall importance of prepaid risk schemes has nevertheless been weak: only 0.86 percent of total resources for health care was channeled through health insurance companies as compared with 1.62 percent to prepaid medical institutions.

Source: PHR 1998.

PHI Regulation in Latin America

Problems connected with the introduction of PHI have been reported for many countries. Due to insufficient regulatory arrangements and lack of public oversight, a large part of the wealthy population in Chile has opted out of the social insurance system, making public health care de facto an insurer of last resort (Barrientos 2000). The Chilean government only gradually responded to these regulatory demands, establishing an official agency (the Superintendencia de ISAPRE) to supervise the private insurance scheme 10 years after the initial reform. Jack (2000) argues that the highly fragmented insurance market in Chile could also have resulted in superfluous insurance for high-income groups—in 1995, 35 private insurance companies offered close to 9,000 distinct insurance programs Although the quality of coverage rises with the premium price (calculated as a percentage of income), this increase may be only marginal for the very rich.

BOX 2.2 MANAGED CARE IN LATIN AMERICA

In the course of liberalizing and privatizing health care, many Latin American countries have adopted private health insurance schemes that are based on the principles of managed care. In this respect, the private insurance market in Latin America is primarily influenced by the U.S.-type health maintenance organization (HMO). HMOs are private, prepaid health programs in which members pay monthly premiums to receive maintenance care (doctors' visits, hospital stays, emergency care). Care is often provided through the organization's own group practice and/or contracted health care providers, which limits consumer choice (exceptions may exist for emergency care). Similarly, it is usually not possible to consult a specialist before seeing a preselected primary care doctor who serves as gatekeeper to all health needs. Other types of managed care include preferred provider organizations (PPOs), which have recently gained importance in the United States.

Managed care can be a way of controlling and limiting health care spending. To some extent, such appraisal may apply to the United States, where managed care dominates the health care industry with a projected share of about 93 percent of patients by 2005 (U.S. Department of Commerce 2000). Due to their combined packages of health insurance and care, HMOs can exert more influence on service delivery than regular insurance providers. Techniques utilized by managed care organization (HMOs, PPOs, and other types) to control costs include a combination of preadmission certification, utilization management, and clinical guidelines. In theory, this should remedy the inherent information problem between insurer and health care entity (principle agent problem) and at the same time limit an overuse of health services (moral hazard). Although their impact on health care provision has not yet led to significant quality improvements (OECD 2004b), managed care may have helped to stabilize and contain the rate of growth in medical costs; from 5.5 percent in 1995 to 4.9 percent in 1996 and 1997, and 4.8 percent in 1998 (U.S. Department of Commerce 2000; Phelps 1997). Recently, double digit growth in health premiums has nevertheless resumed in the United States.

It is doubtful that HMOs will help improve health care delivery and/or contain health care costs in Latin America. Now that the North American market is close to saturated, corporations seek new investment opportunities abroad, which Latin America's growing upper-middle class may offer. In fact, Stocker, Waitzkin, and Iriart (1999: 1132) point out that financial rewards have been the primary motives for foreign HMOs to enter the Latin American market. Other goals traditionally valued by some HMOs in the United States (preventive care or quality control) have only minor relevance. Mandatory copayments have created barriers of access to care and deteriorated health care provision for vulnerable groups. Furthermore, "managed care organizations in Latin America have attracted healthier patients, whereas sicker patients gravitate to the public sector" (ibid.: 1133).

Furthermore, the stop-loss clause of many PHI contracts allows insurance companies to limit the extent of coverage in case of catastrophic health care costs. Because health risks usually increase during a person's lifetime, old people are significantly underrepresented in private schemes: only 6.9 percent of the people older than 65 years are members of an ISAPRE compared with 26.7 percent in the 25 to 54 age group (Jack 2000: 28).

Despite a learning process in Argentina and Colombia, even there the regulatory framework has not yet been completely established. In Argentina, the Superintendencia de Servicios de Salud started to operate in 1997, at first supervising only the public schemes. This situation was extremely beneficial for private health insurers because it did not impose any regulatory requirements on them and at the same time weakened the monopolistic power of public providers. Similarly, the largest of the Entidades de Promoción de Salud in Colombia (competitively operating health insurance schemes) started to participate in the risk-adjustment mechanisms only in 1999. As reported by Jack (2000: 26), "regulation of the private insurance market was virtually nonexistent until 1998" in Brazil—harming not only the equity and efficiency performance of the private insurance industry, but also causing a poor reputation of private prepaid group organizations. Even with an institutional framework in place, regulation is a critical issue, and implementation of adequate legislation is costly—regulation-induced transaction costs are estimated at 30 percent of the total premium revenue in Chile (Kumaranayake 1998: 16). This may be one reason that the costs of administering insurance are estimated to be 10 times higher for PHI than for social insurance (Mahal 2002: 434). Apart from efficiency aspects, the Chilean experience with private health insurance also offers evidence for apparent cream skimming on the side of the insurers. Baeza (1998: 18) reports that the older population of Chile is strongly underrepresented in PHI schemes. Although the share of people over 60 years of age accounts for 9.5 percent of the Chilean population, only 3.2 percent of all people with private insurance belong to this age group.

Trends of PHI in Latin America and the Caribbean

A clear trend for PHI in Latin America and the Caribbean is difficult to derive. After flourishing in the 1990s, in insurance industry activity slowed down (Cruz-Saco 2002). However, measured in terms of spending on private insurance, PHI continues to gain importance relative to other forms of health care financing. Except for Argentina, PHI expenditure increased in all LCR countries in which the industry is already well established (namely, where per capita PHI expenditure exceeds 10 international dollars). Furthermore, this increase was generally larger than the overall development of health care spending. The ratio of PHI spending to total health expenditure decreased in only one LCR country, Barbados (figure 2.6).

The sustained expansion of the health insurance industry may be primarily due to escalating health care costs in the private sector and the consequent increase of PHI premiums. One disadvantage of measuring the importance of

FIGURE 2.6 PHI Spending Relative to Total Health Expenditure in the Latin America and Caribbean Region (percent change, 1998–2002)

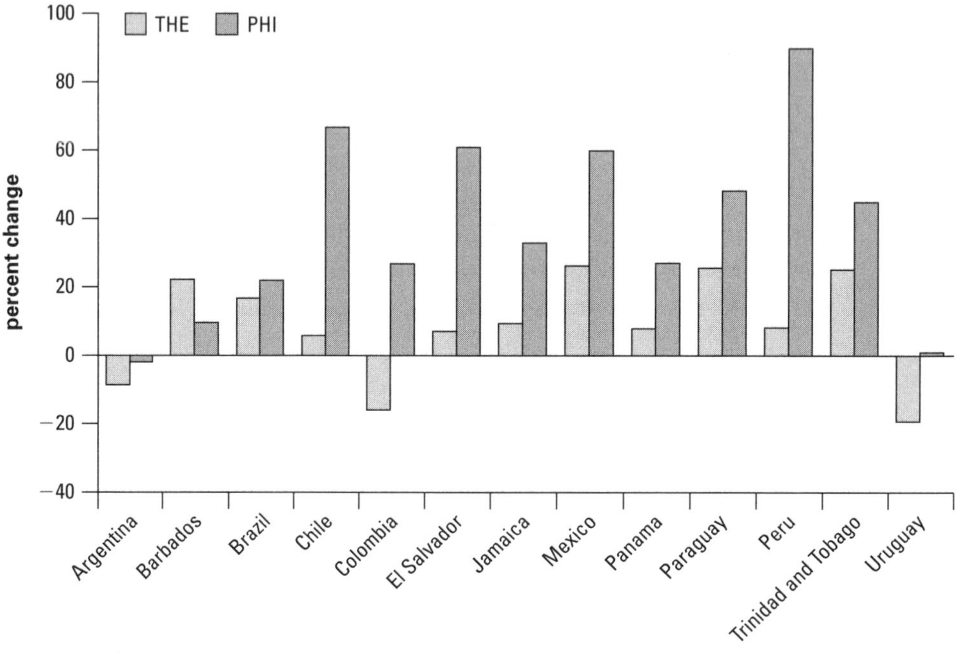

Source: Authors' calculations based on WHO 2005.
Note: Covers only countries in which PHI spending exceeded 10 international dollars in 2002.

private risk-sharing programs in terms of financial flows concerns the inability to derive general conclusions on the industry's performance. Data do not indicate that private insurance schemes significantly increased coverage between 1998 and 2002. It consequently seems reasonable to assume that severe market failures still limit the extent to which PHI provides coverage to the LCR population.

Insurance Market and Private Health Insurance in East Asia and the Pacific

Considering its large population, private insurance is relatively insignificant in the East Asia and the Pacific (EAP) Region. Excluding Japan, the most important insurance markets are in the Republic of Korea, Taiwan (China), Hong Kong (China), Singapore, and Malaysia where insurance penetration reaches between 5 and 7 percent, close to the global average. The insurance industry is also gaining importance in Thailand, Indonesia, Vietnam, and China. China is expected to offer especially significant growth potential in the near future. In 2003, premium income amounted to US$179 billion (US$126 billion life and US$53 billion non–life business respectively), just a little over 6 percent of the world's total premium income.

The positive correlation between insurance premium income and GDP growth seems particularly pronounced in East Asian countries. In the non–life insurance sector, growth has recently regained momentum after a general industry slowdown following the 1998 economic crisis. The severe acute respiratory syndrome (SARS) epidemic of 2003 and its negative consequences on the Asian economy temporarily put another rut in the generally steep growth path of Asian insurance markets. In the long run, SARS may have a positive impact on the non–life insurance sector if it brings home the need to prepare for unexpected health hazards. On average, the non–life insurance industry grew by 6.9 percent across markets in 2002 (Swiss Re 2003: 6).

The presence of foreign insurers is still relatively small. Only 39 percent of all non–life insurance companies are foreign owned. The market share of foreign insurers is particularly strong in Singapore, Indonesia, Malaysia, and the Philippines. In the rest of the continent (including Japan), the foreign market share is below 20 percent. This difference is even more pronounced as regards the relative non–life insurance premium income of foreign insurers. Despite a recent growth of 5.3 percent between 1997 and 2001, foreign insurers account for only 10 percent of premium income in Asia (4 percent, if Japan is excluded).

PHI in East Asia and the Pacific

Like the whole non–life insurance sector, PHI is only gradually evolving in the EAP countries. Private health and accident insurance play a secondary role in health care financing. In many countries, PHI has not yet entered the health care market. This may partly be due to the role of the state in Asian health financing systems, which offers and generally requires public health insurance. Additionally, some countries use medical savings accounts as a form of prepaid health insurance, such as Singapore's Medisave (box 2.3).

Given the EAP Region's high rate of out-of-pocket spending, PHI could nevertheless become an important source of health care financing if resources for direct payments can be channeled to prepaid schemes. Furthermore, high

BOX 2.3 MEDISAVE PROGRAM IN SINGAPORE

The Medisave program is one of the three pillars of Singapore's health care system. Because this program spreads an individual's health risks only over time, Medisave will unlikely cover truly catastrophic health costs in case of severe illness. It is therefore accompanied by an interpersonal risk-pooling entity called Medishield. For the very poor, Singapore provides health care through its third financing pillar, Medifund

Medisave is compulsory for all employees and self-employed who have to pay between 6 and 8 percent of their payroll tax to the Central Provident Fund. Contributions, paid by employers and employees in equal shares, are tax deductible and earn interest. Expenses for hospitalization and surgery can be withdrawn from an account for an individual and his/her family. Patients are free to choose between public or private providers. Public services require a copayment at rates differentiated by the class of care (Mahal 2002: 451).

TABLE 2.5 Private Health Insurance in the East Asia and Pacific Region

Country	*Importance of PHI*[a]	*Country*	*Importance of PHI*[a]
China	0.3	Philippines	10.9
Indonesia	3.3	Thailand	4.3
Malaysia	3.3	Vietnam	3.0
Papua New Guinea	1.1		

Source: Authors' calculations based on WHO 2005.

a. Expenditure on private prepaid plans as percentage of total expenditure on health: not including countries without PHI or where data were not available.

levels of household saving might help underpin the growth of the insurance market (Swiss Re 2004b: 7). Table 2.5 gives an overview of East Asian low- and middle-income countries for which spending on PHI has been documented.

Even in the Philippines, where spending on PHI is relatively significant, most of the population is covered through public health insurance. Specifically, the parastatal Philippines Health Insurance Cooperation extends to both formal and informal employees and covers around 75 percent of the Philippine population (WHO 2004c: 35). Evidently, this situation does not leave much room for PHI development. According to the Institute of Public Health Management, only 2 percent of total health expenditure in the Philippines is channeled to private commercial providers. The remaining 9 percent can be attributed to spending on micro- and community insurance (IPHM 2004).

Market Indicators and Evidence of Market Failure

Private health insurance is mostly a new phenomenon in East Asia and the Pacific, which could nevertheless have a significant impact on the Region's future health financing system. To improve health care coverage, some countries have recently started to shift resources to private risk-sharing programs. This development occurred largely as a response to increased health costs that overburdened existing social security mechanisms. For example, as one option for dealing with the new challenges, the Vietnamese government proposes to expand private commercial and community-based health insurance (ADB 2002). Despite large informal sectors, insurance brokers such as Gras Savoye see significant development potentials of PHI in Vietnam (U.S. Vietnam Trade Council 2003). Another dynamic insurance market is predicted for China (Swiss Re 2004b).

The next part presents preliminary experiences from the promotion of PHI in Indonesia and Thailand. It also discusses initial evidence or projected domains of market failure in both countries. Opportunities and challenges of private health insurance in the EAP Region's biggest market, China, are also considered in this section.

Indonesia

Health insurance is being reorganized in Indonesia. According to the WHO (2004: 101ff), the issue of health care financing has stagnated over the past two decades, leaving large parts of the population uninsured and without equitable access to health care. Census data from 1992 and 2001 (Statistics Indonesia 2001) reveal that hospital care has been barely accessible for the bottom 60 percent of the population.

Existing inequities have multiple sources: a separate insurance scheme for public employees, the possibility of large companies' opting out of the social security scheme, and lack of private nonprofit health insurance. Under current legislation, all private health insurance operating as managed care must be commercial to obtain a license; such U.S.-type HMOs currently cover only 500,000 people. The for-profit nature of managed care is very different from experience in the United States where 96 percent of all HMOs were initially nonprofits. Since legislative reforms in 1992, general and life insurance companies have been selling PHI as riders or separate lines of business, and the market is also open to foreign insurers. Such programs generally address large firms that can afford the high premiums. With 64 insurance companies in 2001, the WHO considers the market for traditional health insurance promising. Recent data indicate that premium income of traditional health insurance is five times higher than in the HMO sector, and coverage is eight times higher.

A 1970s initiative to implement micro and community health care in Indonesia was stopped after the Social Safety Net program was introduced in the late 1990s. At that time, coverage was low, less than 2 percent of the population, and fund members' and nonfund members' access to inpatient care was much different. However, members utilized health centers more often then the uninsured. The difficulties of micro and community schemes in Indonesia stem from multiple sources. First, households exhaust most of their resources buying food and can spend very little of their household income on health (between 2 and 4 percent). Second, health care is highly subsidized for the poor who could often get treatment for less than they had to spend for insurance contributions. Finally, the WHO (2004b: 135) argues that it was unwise to base contributions for the community schemes on consensus among the (mostly low-income) households. This resulted in very low premiums, even for relatively high-income households. While community involvement is usually considered beneficial, it may have had undesired effects in the case of Indonesia.

Thailand

In Thailand, the history of private insurance dates to 1929, although the first private health insurance company started operating only in 1978 (WHO 2004c: 177ff). Coverage from voluntary PHI decreased between 1991 and 1999 from 3.1 percent to 1.4 percent and extended mostly to better-off individuals (reimbursement model). At the same time, contributions to private prepaid programs gained importance in total health expenditure (plus 15 percent between 1998 and 2002; WHO 2005), largely due to the introduction of a health card insurance program (Supakankunti 2000; Nitayarumphong and Pannarunothai 1998).

Since its initiation as a pilot in 1991, this government-promoted, voluntary risk-sharing scheme has attracted 28.2 percent of the Thai population (WHO 2004c: 179). Apart from the fact that half of the insurance premiums are paid from public subsidies, the large expansion of the health card program may also be due to an extensive TV and radio advertising campaign. As argued by the WHO, the card program could therefore pave the way to universal coverage. So far, the initiative is not yet self-sustaining (costs per person exceed revenues plus subsidies) and may attract too many high-risk patients. Because high individual health risks are not reflected in the premiums, such a situation could undermine the program base. To slow the concentration of high-risk individuals in the schemes, individuals now have to qualify for 30 instead of 15 days before being eligible for services.

China

Following massive reforms in 1998 (urban areas) and 2002 (rural areas), the Chinese health care system is being reorganized. Coverage had dropped significantly in the 1980s and 1990s, and by the late 1990s 64 percent of the Chinese population in rural, and 15 percent in urban, areas did not have health or accident insurance (Swiss Re 1998: 21). Particularly challenging are health care costs, which escalated after the trade liberalization and open-market policies of the 1980s. In the reform process, "China has carried out some of the most interesting experiments with new forms of health insurance financing" (Ginneken 1999: 18). At the same time, the government's role in providing medical insurance is declining, making room for increased private involvement (Swiss Re 2003: 24).

With the breakdown of collective economic structures, the once "successful" (WHO 2004c: 60) health care system—which, at its peak in the 1970s, covered up to 98 percent of villages—is still adapting to new market structures. Although the government has started to encourage people to insure privately against health risks, PHI does not yet play a major role in China. According to NHA data, only 3.6 percent of private (0.3 percent of total) spending on health care was channeled to PHI in 2002 (WHO 2004c: 33). Challenges for the private health insurance industry originate from large informal sectors in rural areas and information deficits on individual current health status that make an actuarial calculation and pricing of insurance products difficult. Despite some progress in recent years, a large part of the Chinese population remains without health care coverage.

As reported in Bloom and Shenglan (1999), the recent move toward private risk-sharing arrangements is based upon the belief that people would more readily pay voluntary contributions than accept a tax increase. However, given the low significance of health insurance today, the government's goal of universal coverage by 2010 seems overly ambitious, even if it involves new forms of health care financing. As one initiative, community-based health insurance schemes (CHI) are intended to increase coverage in rural areas and revitalize former commune structures. As argued by the WHO (2004b: 60), the Chinese government should not only promote the development of such schemes but, first and foremost, also try to integrate CHI into the national health insurance framework.

PHI Regulation in East Asia and the Pacific Region

Regulatory requirements for PHI in East Asia vary across countries. Depending on the developmental stage of the economy and particularly the health insurance industry, policies should aim at establishing, consolidating, or regulating the insurance sector. Specifically, policies to open the market for foreign insurers may be a good way for China to import know-how and institutional capacity. Countries where the insurance industry has existed for some time measures have more appropriate ways of increasing coverage. One prominent example would be Thailand's effort to induce higher participation in private plans through its publicly subsidized health card program.

Still, the insurance markets in EAP countries share some common features. Despite some regional variation, PHI is overall a new phenomenon. All countries therefore face a trade-off between promoting a new industry with supportive policies and ensuring ample regulation and consumer protection. As noted by Sekhri, Savedoff, and Tripathi (2004), measures to increase competition among insurers may encourage innovation, efficiency, and responsiveness of private schemes. At the same time, such policies may also "lead to higher administrative costs, small risk pools that are not economically viable and aggressive pricing practices that can create market instability and insolvency" (ibid.: 4). Regulation strategies must therefore find a balanced mix between support and sufficient regulation. Experience from Latin America may serve as a cautionary example of how open-market policies can induce too much competition that does not necessarily result in better products.

Given the large low-income and mostly informal sector in many EAP countries, regulatory requirements will have to deal with equity issues at some point in the industry's development. It is very doubtful that the private commercial insurance industry will cover marginalized individuals without accompanying public regulation. Because private entities rarely opt to cover low-income individuals and high-cost patients, regulation could simply mandate the admission of marginalized individuals or influence the composition of the insured through financial incentives. Specifically, coverage of high-risk and/or low-income patients could be subsidized with public funds, or low-risk individuals could be encouraged to join private schemes by granting tax-benefits. Such policies would increase the PHI risk pool, which would allow some cross-subsidization among the insured. However, whether or not public subsidies do provide a cost-effective way of improving health care coverage depends on a case-by-case analysis.

PHI Trends in East Asia and the Pacific Region

Development potentials of the private health insurance industry in East Asia and the Pacific are subject to a multitude of factors, including the general economic development of the Region as well as the role of international investors. Most important, however, the development of PHI depends upon the future involvement of the state in financing or providing health care. Currently, many social health insurance programs are limited to people employed in the formal sector. Furthermore, insurance coverage is low in small and medium-size firms because insurance requirements often apply only to companies with a certain number of workers. Assuming that these policies will continue, PHI growth potential therefore lies mainly in the informal sector (especially in rural areas) and among unemployed, self-employed, and high-income individuals who might purchase additional coverage. Considering that these groups make up a large part of the population in many countries, development prospects for PHI are significant.

Though small in volume, the private insurance industry in EAP is already on a rise. Measured in international dollars, PHI expenditure augmented in all seven countries, according to WHO data. Prepaid programs are gaining importance as a source of health care spending; their relative share of total health care spending increased in most countries analyzed. This development seems driven primarily by overall economic performance. Except for Papua New Guinea, Indonesia, and the Philippines, economic growth[11] and spending on PHI move in the same direction. Figure 2.7 illustrates the development of PHI spending with respect to total health expenditure between 1998 and 2002. The exceptional growth rate of Papua New Guinea (plus 158 percent) corresponds to an expansion of PHI spending from 0.54 to 1.46 international dollars; it should consequently not be overrated. To reflect the typical expansion of the private health insurance industry, the figure's scale was therefore adjusted accordingly.

In addition to economic performance, the future development of PHI in East Asia crucially depends upon the role of international investors. To a large extent, the optimistic outlook for the development potential of the insurance industry in China, for example, rests upon the country's recent liberalization efforts. The number of foreign insurance companies and investors increased significantly after China opened up markets as part of its drive toward WTO membership. As of March 2004, Swiss Re (2004b: 30) listed 12 large foreign investors that had already entered the Chinese non–life insurance market. Foreign investment and the import of international know-how could become a major pillar of PHI development in East Asia.

Insurance Market and Private Health Insurance in South Asia

Of all Regions studied in this analysis, South Asia represents the smallest and least significant insurance market. Its share of the world's total insurance premium income accounted for a mere 0.6 percent in 2003. This is particularly noteworthy as the Region encompasses 22.7 percent of the world's population and contributes 2.1 percent of the world's GDP. Thus, insurance penetration is

FIGURE 2.7 PHI Spending Relative to Total Health Expenditure in the East Asia and Pacific Region (percent change, 1998–2002)

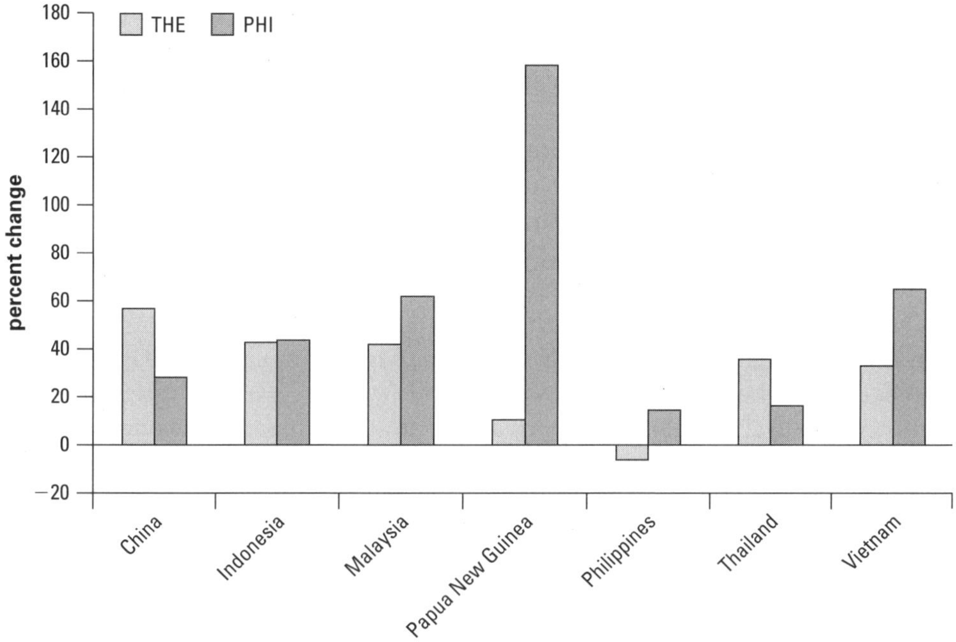

Source: Authors' calculations based on WHO 2005.
Note: Total health expenditure and PHI spending measured in international dollars (percent change between 1998 and 2002).

extremely low in South Asian countries. In 2003, it ranged between 0.57 percent in Bangladesh and 2.89 percent in India as compared with a global average of 8 percent (Pereira 2005).

Extreme poverty obstructs the expansion of private insurance markets. As reported by the World Bank, almost half the world's poor live in South Asia; around 20 percent of the total population lives on less than one international dollar a day. Although progress has been made toward eradicating extreme poverty, South Asian countries often lack a middle-class population that could support PHI development. India, owing to its size and recent economic performance, could become a notable exception in this respect.

However, South Asia's insurance industry has experienced a boom, reaching an astonishing growth rate of 17.6 percent in 2003 (Pereira 2005). This expansion occurred on a very low scale of absolute spending on insurance (average of US$13.43 per capita, compared with a world average of US$470). Nevertheless, remarkably, South Asia's growth rate was almost nine times higher than the expansion of the global insurance market (2 percent). With India, the Region also hosts a large and highly dynamic insurance market that will probably grow significantly in the near future. Total insurance premium income amounted to US$18.7 billion, more than 75 percent (US$14.6 billion) of it in the life insurance segment.

PHI in the South Asia Region

WHO data cover spending on private health insurance in only three countries, Bangladesh, India, and Sri Lanka. The other countries (Afghanistan, Bhutan, Maldives, Nepal, and Pakistan) either did not have PHI when the data were collected, or spending on private programs was too small to be recorded in national statistics. In fact, even Bangladesh, India, and Sri Lanka are basically negligible regarding per capita expenditure on PHI (between 0.01 and 0.17 international dollars in 2002). Yet, these statistics might not reflect more current developments in South Asian insurance markets that leave more room for private companies to expand. Table 2.6 gives an overview of all South Asian countries in which spending on PHI has been recorded.

The insurance industry has been in existence for about 200 years in South Asia but was largely marginalized during a period of nationalization in the 20th century. It has started to recover some of its vigor and vitality as countries begin to reopen their markets for private insurance companies. However, other obstacles like severe "poverty, lack of awareness, and, perhaps, strong belief in fatalism" (Pereira 2005) still prevent the development of private health insurance. To some extent, the low significance of South Asia's insurance industry may also be explained by the region's colonial history. Unlike in East Asia, the influence of the United Kingdom with a long tradition of public health care may have prevented the development of private insurance in South Asia. India, as a relatively developed economy with a strong middle-class population, offers the most promising environment for PHI to evolve. The National Council of Applied Economic Research estimates that 300 million people belong to the middle-class income segment in India, which could become an important demander of private health insurance services.

Unsurprisingly, India is estimated to have the largest PHI market, covering 33 million people, 3.3 percent of its population (Sekhri and Savedoff 2005: 130). These estimates are nevertheless based on 1997 (coverage) and 2001 (PHI spending) data. They consequently do not take into account the dynamic development of private insurance markets that has occurred since then. After progressively privatizing its health sector, the relevance of PHI in India is expected to rise significantly. Furthermore, the fact that India is one of the few Asian countries in which public health insurance is not obligatory could additionally boost the development of PHI.

TABLE 2.6 Private Health Insurance, Selected South Asian Countries

Country	*Importance of PHI*[a]	*Country*	*Importance of PHI*[a]
Bangladesh	0.1	Sri Lanka	0.5
India	0.6		

Source: Authors' calculations based on WHO 2005.

a. Expenditure on private prepaid plans as percentage of total expenditure on health in 2002: not including countries without PHI or where data were not available

In India, the Insurance Regulatory and Development Authority Bill of 1999 opened up the insurance market for foreign investors who can now hold up to 26 percent equity (WHO: 2004c). Such figures should nevertheless belie that this development occurs on a very small scale. As Khetraphal Singh (2002), points out, PHI in India is still in its infancy and many of the problems connected with the introduction of private risk-sharing programs (primarily equity related) have not yet been answered satisfactorily.

Market Indicators and Evidence of Market Failure

Due to the lack of available data, the following section will focus on South Asia's insurance markets in general. Special reference to PHI will be given only in the case of India (box 2.4).

BOX 2.4 PHI IN INDIA

The private health insurance industry in India is still in its infancy. However, PHI can be expected to grow in the near future, especially since legislative reforms that recently introduced the "last phase in the move toward the privatisation of the insurance sector" (Mahal 2002: 412). It is still too early to discuss market indicators for the private health insurance industry or to present evidence of market failure. Nevertheless, an analysis of the current regulatory framework allows some projections about the future performance of PHI in terms of cost and quality of care as well as its influence on equity-related issues.

Mahal (2002: 436) argues that the introduction of PHI will not have cost-increasing effects in the Indian health sector. Similarly, it would equally be unlikely that PHI will deteriorate the quality of health care, which is not to say that it would necessarily lead to improvements either. According to Mahal's analysis, the regulatory framework in India is already sufficiently established or existing gaps could be filled with appropriate legislation to enforce quality and cost standards.

Given the relatively weak legislation on consumer protection and especially the poor enforcement mechanisms in India, Mahal nevertheless believes that the expansion of PHI could have an equity-worsening effect. This could even be amplified if, as Mahal expects, the insurance market remained small for a certain period of time. The establishment of a well-functioning PHI subsector typically requires several years of refining and fine-tuning the system.

Such equity concerns are shared by the WHO (2004b: 97ff). According to their analysis the private sector currently "continues to operate in an almost unhindered manner." In order to gradually advance toward universal coverage (which is still a long way given the fact that currently only 10 percent of the population have some sort of health insurance), policy makers would thus have to implement adequate licensing and regulatory requirements. As PHI will primarily target the middle and upper class population of India, the state would also need to find new and innovative ways to provide health care coverage for the poor.

All major South Asian countries have strengthened the role of private insurance. Bangladesh allowed private insurance companies to operate in 1984 and in 1990 provided greater freedom for market development while at the same time revising capital and deposit requirements. Pakistan opened the formerly nationalized life insurance sector to private providers in the 1990s and left the non–life insurance sector in private hands. In 2000, it improved consumer protection by setting up guidelines of the solvency margin, capital requirements, and the expense ratio. Finally, Sri Lanka converted its state-owned Insurance Corporation into a private company in 1993, set up a regulatory board for the insurance sector in 2000, and permitted foreign companies to own 100 percent of equity in insurance companies in 2002 (Pereira 2005).

Despite these reforms, which resulted largely from pressure from international donor organizations like the World Bank and the Asian Development Bank, the state continues to be the single most important supplier of life and non–life insurance. This is surprising because the reforms introduced a multitude of new players into the market: 61 insurers operate in Bangladesh while 50 companies sell insurance in Pakistan.

Several factors beyond the reasons already outlined may explain the sustained weakness of private insurance in South Asia. Due to the strong marketing networks and immense public supplier infrastructures that were established during their time of monopolistic power, private insurers are reluctant to operate in both labor- and cost-intensive sectors like rural areas. They thus focus their efforts on the few high-income individuals in each country and other niche markets for special products in urban areas. Consequently, the insurance market is very concentrated in many countries. In Pakistan, for example, the top five non–life insurance companies account for 80 percent of the total market premium. The top five non–life insurance companies in India, all state-owned, hold the same share (Pereira 2005).

PHI Regulation in the South Asia Region

The impact of private insurance in South Asian risk markets remains limited. According to available data, just opening markets for private providers did not suffice because previous structures and existing power patterns have prevented efficient development of the private (health) insurance industry. Given the long period of protected and unrestrained operation of public schemes, private insurance in South Asia is still marginalized to a few niche markets. If private insurance is to play a more prominent role, public regulation should aim at reducing entry barriers for new companies and provide adequate room for their market development. Such policies can comprise further privatization of market segments or a clear separation of areas in which private and public companies should operate. In other cases, a positive development of private insurance might simply require more entrepreneurial spirit to explore new market areas and employ innovative insurance instruments (for example, microinsurance, combined insurance packages, group insurance).

From an efficiency point of view, the high market concentration in South Asian insurance markets is particularly worrisome. Market power and market concentration could be tolerated (or, as for a Schumpeterian entrepreneur, could even be a sign of market innovation) if they are a temporary phenomenon in the early development stage of an infant market. In South Asia, however, market power and market concentration stem primarily from preexisting structures, which are unlikely to disappear automatically. As in India, the dominant market actors in the health care industry are still owned by the state, which additionally obstructs the development of a private insurance market.

Trends of PHI in the South Asia Region

With the exception of India, private health insurance will hardly play an important role in South Asian health systems any time soon. Without further reforms and continued political determination to establish a sizeable PHI market—but also economic development and a considerable reduction of poverty—private health insurance will remain a niche-product for a very few, privileged individuals.

For most South Asian countries, privately run microinsurance schemes arguably seem the most promising option to expand coverage to otherwise excluded individuals. The ILO (2000) reports the implementation of such schemes in Bangladesh and India. In Bangladesh, community-based schemes are the country's largest health insurance program (Desmet, Chowdhury, and Islam 1999). Community programs also exist in Nepal (WHO 2004c). They also reach poor regions in some East Asian countries, including the Philippines (ILO 2000), China, and Thailand (WHO 2004c), as well as Lao People's Democratic Republic and Vietnam (WHO 2004b). Microinsurance usually operates on a nonprofit or low-profit basis and is highly subsidized by either the national government or international donors.

Due to the lack of time-series data for South Asian countries, no patterns can be derived for spending behavior on PHI. Bangladesh, India, and Sri Lanka showed a slightly increasing trend of PHI expenditure between 1998 and 2002. However, this expenditure occurred on a very low level (less than 1 international dollar), which prevents any inference about general patterns.

Insurance Market and Private Health Insurance in the Sub-Saharan Africa Region

In 2003, the insurance industry in the Sub-Sahara Africa Region accounted for merely 1 percent of global premium income (US$29.3 billion). This figure is particularly remarkable because almost 90 percent of total insurance premium income can be attributed to South Africa. Though much smaller in volume, important insurance markets also exist in Nigeria, Kenya, and Namibia with a combined market share of about 5 percent. Most of the premiums are traded in the life-insurance segment (US$22.5 billion, 77 percent) while the non–life insurance sector plays a minor role (Swiss Re 2005).

PHI in the Sub-Saharan Africa Region

Similarly to the whole insurance industry, private commercial health insurance is scarcely developed in Sub-Saharan Africa. Nevertheless, private prepaid schemes are a significant source of total health financing in a few countries such as South Africa, Namibia, and Zimbabwe. In South Africa, 46.2 percent of all expenditure on health care was channeled through a private health intermediary in 2002 (WHO 2005). Relative to total health expenditure, PHI also plays a significant role in Namibia and Zimbabwe where, as in South Africa, the importance of private insurance schemes might be explained mainly by their severe income inequalities. While South Africa (0.59) and Zimbabwe (0.57) display Gini coefficients from the top quarter of worldwide inequality, Namibia tops the list with a value of 0.71. Consequently, the high share of PHI spending is not reflected in equally significant coverage rates. In other words, only 8 percent of the population in Zimbabwe is estimated to have private health insurance (Campbell et al. 2000: 2) although PHI expenditure accounts for 19 percent of the country's total health expenditure. Furthermore, Zimbabwe is the only low-income country with PHI spending exceeding 10 percent of THE. Table 2.7 gives an overview of all Sub-Saharan African countries where PHI spending has been recorded.

With rare exceptions, membership, contributions, and coverage under private health insurance are all low. The increasing emergence of community-based health insurance during the past couple of years has been particularly strong in Sub-Saharan African countries (Jütting 2004). Microinsurance schemes were recently implemented in Benin, Burkina Faso, Cameroon, Côte d'Ivoire, Ghana, Guinea, Mali, Nigeria, Senegal, Tanzania, Togo, and Uganda (ILO 2000). The moderate premiums, due to the non- or low-profit nature of these schemes, may explain the low level of expenditure on private prepaid programs. With

TABLE 2.7 Private Health Insurance in Sub-Saharan African Countries

Country	*Importance of PHI*[a]	*Country*	*Importance of PHI*[a]
Benin	5.0	Niger	2.7
Botswana	7.6	Nigeria	5.0
Cape Verde	0.0	Rwanda	0.1
Chad	0.2	Senegal	1.9
Côte d'Ivoire	4.2	South Africa	46.2
Ethiopia	0.2	Swaziland	8.1
Kenya	3.9	Tanzania	2.0
Madagascar	5.0	Togo	2.1
Malawi	1.0	Uganda	0.1
Mozambique	0.2	Zimbabwe	18.8
Namibia	22.4		

Source: Authors' calculations based on WHO 2005.

a. Measured as expenditure on private prepaid plans as percentage of total expenditure on health in 2002; not including countries without PHI or where data were not available.

> **BOX 2.5 PRIVATE HEALTH INSURANCE IN SOUTH AFRICA**
>
> South Africa's strong and significant private health insurance industry is the exception among the continent's general health financing systems. Primarily financed through employer-based private insurance, the South African and the U.S. health financing systems are similar.
>
> Despite the relatively well-developed private insurance market, only foreigners and high- and middle-income residents have private health insurance. Ernst & Young (2003) estimates PHI coverage at 18 percent of South Africa's total population, comparatively little, considering that almost 50 percent of total health expenditure is channeled to private insurance. Eighty percent of the people covered by PHI are in the two highest income quintiles; the lowest income quintile accounts for only 2 percent (Sekhri and Savedoff 2005: 130). The government provides basic health care services to the poor and is committed to achieving universal coverage.

the exception of Botswana, Namibia, South Africa, and Zimbabwe, the average annual per capita expenditure on PHI between 1998 and 2002 did not exceed US$10. During the same period, average spending on private prepaid health insurance across all 21 countries with available data amounted to US$8.06 while South Africa clearly stands out with US$106.25 per capita (box. 2.5).

Information on small and region-specific schemes often is not reported in official data on health care expenditure. Only a few countries have steadily collected and recorded data on their health systems. A comparison of available National Health Accounts from the WHO database reveals that households bear the largest burden of health costs; one third of total health expenditure is out of pocket. Other important sources include the Ministry of Health (MOH), provincial and local governments, and NGOs. Private health insurance plays a minor role, especially bearing in mind that the average value of 5 percent of total health expenditure originates from South Africa's large PHI sector. Figure 2.8 gives an overview of health financing in nine Eastern and Southern African countries.

Market Indicators and Evidence of Market Failure

Among the Sub-Saharan African countries, only South Africa has a strong regulatory environment, built on a long tradition of private insurance. Nevertheless, even there, private coverage is almost exclusively limited to the well-off and the wealthy. Similar observations can be made for Namibia and Zimbabwe where the relatively high spending on PHI stems primarily from formal sector employees. In almost all Sub-Saharan African countries, international donors remain a very important part of the health care system, often providing more than 25 percent of total resources. Again, this number is notably greater for some countries, for example, Mozambique where donor contributions account for 52 percent of total health expenditure, while other countries may not receive any international funding.

FIGURE 2.8 Expenditure for Health Care through Financial Intermediaries in Eastern and Southern Africa, 1997–98 (percent of THE)

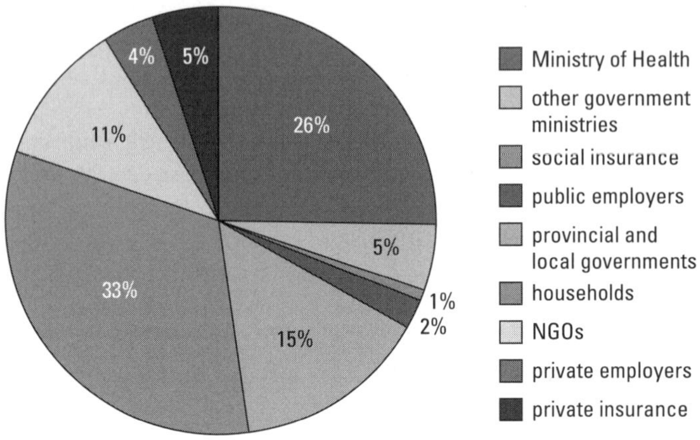

Source: National Health Accounts of respective countries, WHO 1999.
Notes: Countries included: Ethiopia, Kenya, Malawi, Mozambique, Rwanda, South Africa, Tanzania, Uganda, Zambia. Due to rounding, the parts exceed 100 percent.

Thus, private commercial health insurance covers only a small, privileged segment of the Sub-Saharan African population. Due to institutional weaknesses and a lack of public resources, private spending does, however, constitute an important source of health care financing in many countries. Yet, PHI involvement primarily occurs on a non- or low-profit basis, organized by local communities, private associations, or national and international NGOs. Box 2.6 discusses further insights into community-based mutual health insurance (MHI), which could play a prominent role in future health care financing.

Few schemes in Sub-Saharan African countries operate regionally or nationally (table 2.8). About 75 percent of all health insurance programs in Central and Western Africa are either restricted exclusively to a rural or urban environment. The relatively small risk-pool of PHI is also emphasized in table 2.9. More than 70 percent of all insurance schemes describe their target group as smaller than 30,000 people. Considering that the average insurance scheme will probably reach one third of its target group, only a few schemes cover more than 10,000 individuals.

PHI Regulation in the Sub-Saharan Africa Region

Public policies primarily involve the area of mutual health insurance schemes, which may be a small, but possibly important first step toward reaching universal coverage in the long-run. Specifically, policies could initiate and promote the implementation of *mutuelles* or improve the performance of existing programs. This last part may involve policies that support the growth and professionalization of regionally bounded schemes that will become capable of attracting and administering a larger part of the Sub-Saharan African population.

BOX 2.6 MUTUAL HEALTH INSURANCE IN SUB-SAHARAN AFRICAN COUNTRIES

Mutual health insurance is based on "local initiatives of rather small size . . . with voluntary membership" (Wiesmann and Jütting 2000: 195). Programs have been initiated by health care providers (for example, hospitals), nongovernmental organizations, or local associations (Atim 1998; Criel 1998). Schemes are generally limited to a specific region or community and therefore a small number of people. Moreover, insurance packages are not comprehensive, but only offer supplementary coverage for certain medical treatments.

Despite these limitations, MHI is a promising approach for extending health care coverage to otherwise excluded individuals. Specifically, MHI has the potential to integrate a large part of the rural population in Sub-Saharan Africa that would otherwise be left with little or no health care coverage. Although the scope of each scheme is restricted, coverage could still extend to many individuals, depending on the number of MHIs available. A recent survey of health insurance systems in 11 francophone West and Central African countries (Concertation 2004) reveals that 324 MHIs were operating—almost 90 percent of all 366 registered insurance programs considered operational. MHI density is very different across countries, ranging from about 8 schemes per 1 million people in Senegal to just over 0.5 schemes per one million people in Chad. MHIs are also relatively numerous relative to population size in Benin and Guinea.

Mutual health insurance generally operates on a non- or low-profit basis. Besides offering moderate premiums to their clients, MHI has other advantages over other types of prepaid risk-sharing programs. Due to their small size and close ties to the local community, mutual health insurance schemes can better adapt to the specific needs of their clientele. Furthermore, MHIs are often partly or entirely managed by the local community, which again increases program adaptability in each particular environment.

Although health coverage through mutual schemes will typically remain relatively low, recent empirical findings (for example, Jütting 2005) suggest that MHI can under certain conditions increase accessibility to health care and improve household financial protection. In this respect, MHI can serve as an important tool for reducing periodic expense shocks from unanticipated OOP. To serve the health needs of the poor, MHIs should primarily try to keep participation high by adjusting insurance premiums and benefits to the specific needs of individuals, according to other studies (for example, Wiesmann and Jütting 2000). The specific design of community-based health insurance depends on a case-by-case analysis.

As argued by the research group on the development of mutual schemes in Africa (Concertation 2004: 79), one advantage of MHI could also be problematic for its future development. Although their small size ensures mutual schemes sufficient flexibility to adapt to local conditions, it also deprives them of financial stability and consolidation. Nine out of 10 schemes have fewer than 1,000 constituents; 8 out of 10 cover fewer than 1,000 individuals, and half of them cover fewer than 650 individuals, making *mutuelles* truly microinsurance. Though preferable from an organizational and participatory point of view, this situation will hardly be

TABLE 2.8 Types and Characteristics of Health Insurance in Western and Central African Countries

Country	*Pop. (million)*	*PHI (number)*	*MHI relative to PHI (%)*	*Est. number of beneficiaries*	*Beneficiaries relative to pop. (%)*	*Local outreach only (rural/ urban)*	*Regional/ national outreach*
Benin	7.5	43	93.0	43,387	0.58	72.1	27.9
Burkina Faso	13.6	36	77.8	14,580	0.11	88.9	11.1
Cameroon	16.1	22	68.2	10,098	0.06	59.1	40.9
Chad	9.5	7	85.7	2,072	0.02	57.1	42.9
Côte d'Ivoire	17.4	36	88.9	858,348	4.93	75.0	25.0
Guinea	9.3	55	100.0	96,635	1.04	98.1	1.9
Mali	12.0	56	69.6	499,856	4.17	62.5	37.5
Mauretania	3.0	3	100.0	13,056	0.44	100.0	0.0
Niger	11.4	12	91.7	84,372	0.74	16.7	83.3
Senegal	10.9	87	100.0	294,060	2.70	74.7	25.3
Togo	5.6	9	88.9	22,500	0.40	88.9	11.1
Total/average	116.1	366	88.5	1,938,964	1.67	74.8	25.2

Source: Concertation 2004.

TABLE 2.9 MHI Target Groups in Western and Central African Countries

MHI target group[a]	*Number of MHI*	*Relative to total number (%)*	*Cumulative (%)*
< 1,000	52	14.2	14.2
1,000–3,000	43	11.7	26.0
3,000–5,000	32	8.7	34.7
5,000–10,000	61	16.7	51.4
10,000–30,000	74	20.2	71.6
30,000–50,000	17	4.6	76.2
50,000–100,000	20	5.5	81.7
>100,000	31	8.5	90.2
Unknown	36	9.8	100.0
Total	366	100.0	

Source: Concertation 2004: 23.

a. "Own perception of target group," as defined by a microsurvey of African insurance providers.

sustainable. The study therefore recommends more cooperation and possibly partnerships between existing schemes as well as the targeting of more constituents in the development of new programs. Only the expansion of the financial base would ensure growth and long-term stability of mutual schemes in Sub-Saharan Africa. This process is illustrated by the UMASIDA health insurance schemes in Tanzania (Mutual Society for Health Care in the Informal Sector), which resulted from the regrouping of five informal sector associations (Kiwara 1999: 131). Public policies could support this consolidation process, which needs to be based on collective effort by the communities operating the schemes.

For the same reason, MHIs need to start operating in a more professional fashion. Currently, they are limited in both the services they offer and the number of people they cover. They can neither rely on a large risk-pool nor do they have at their disposal security mechanisms like guarantees or reinsurance funds. Professionalization would also include a gradual move from low insurance premiums to contributions that allow both financial stability and a true insurance-based health care coverage. Today, most schemes cover only small risks and rely fundamentally on copayments. Rarely do they cover expenses for specialists or hospital treatment. This situation is particularly regrettable, because the true problem of health care financing often occurs as a result of catastrophic costs for major treatment. Public policies could accompany this process of professionalization by requiring adequate financial standards and security mechanisms.

As for the international donor community, the study on mutual schemes in Africa (Concertation 2004: 76) identifies a negative relationship between the number and functionality of *mutuelles* and the foreign aid received in a particular country. Specifically, the more schemes operate in a country, the less likely is this country to attract financial resources from abroad. Although financial independence should be the long-term goal of health care systems, the current status of MHI in no way approaches universal coverage. In this respect, cutting foreign aid as a response to the initiation of new insurance schemes may give wrong incentives to renounce such initiatives.

PHI Trends in the Sub-Saharan African Region

For most SSA countries, private health insurance is a new phenomenon. Except in some rare cases, health insurance occurs mainly at community level. Many of today's schemes were initiated during the past 15 years. Only a few programs are built on a long tradition of community involvement in health care financing, for example, Senegal and the Republic of Congo (Tine 2000; Criel 1998).

Considering the institutional weakness of many Sub-Saharan African countries and the limited financial resources of the African people (46.5 percent of the population are reported to live below one international dollar a day), PHI will evolve mainly in the nonprofit, community-based insurance segment. Already, almost 9 out of 10 schemes in Central and West Africa are *mutuelles*. Adding to the existing 366 schemes (mutual and others), another 142 are currently being implemented, and 77 are planned for the near future. The regional focus of MHI is on Senegal, Guinea, Burkina Faso, and Togo. Given the limited capacity and outreach of mutual schemes, the development of MHI is not an end in itself but a building block for the future development of health insurance in Sub-Saharan Africa.

Due to the low volume of MHI insurance premiums, this generally positive trend of PHI is not as visible in terms of private spending on prepaid programs.

FIGURE 2.9 PHI Spending Relative to Total Health Expenditure in the Sub-Saharan Africa Region (percent change, 1998–2002)

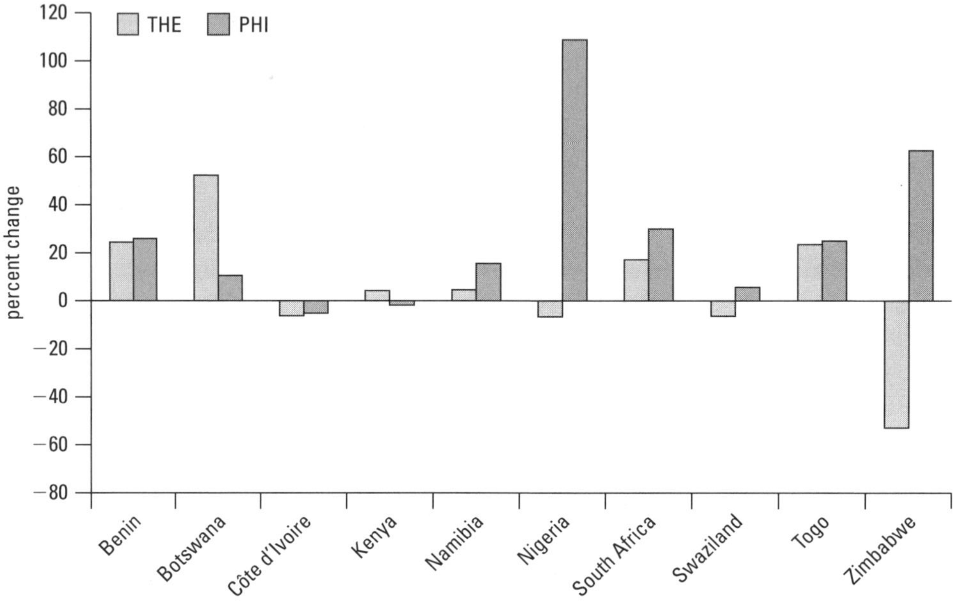

Source: Authors' calculations based on WHO 2005.
Note: Covers only countries in which PHI spending exceeded one international dollar in 2002.

On average, PHI expenditure relative to total health care spending increased by 23.1 percent across all 21 countries, based on available data between 1998 and 2002. This trend is, however, driven partly by significant growth rates in Cape Verde (207 percent), Zimbabwe (173 percent), and Nigeria (120 percent). Figure 2.9 illustrates the development of PHI spending and total health expenditure between 1998 and 2002 for all countries in which PHI spending exceeded one international dollar.

Insurance Market and Private Health Insurance in Eastern Europe and Central Asia

Despite high growth rates in recent years, the insurance industry remains small in Eastern Europe and Central Asia. In 2003, total insurance premium income amounted to US$37.2 billion, about 1.3 percent of global insurance income. Roughly one third of total premium income can be attributed to life insurance (US$11.7 billion); the remaining US$25.5 billion stems from non–life insurance contracts (Swiss Re 2005).

PHI in Eastern Europe and Central Asia

Private health insurance in Eastern Europe and Central Asia is still in its infancy. In many countries, private insurers only recently entered the market as part of the

TABLE 2.10 Private Health Insurance in East European and Central Asian Countries, 2002 (percent of THE)

Country	*Importance of PHI*[a]	*Country*	*Importance of PHI*[a]
Belarus	0.1	Lithuania	0.1
Bulgaria	0.4	Romania	1.9
Estonia	1.0	Russian Federation	6.5
Georgia	0.9	Turkey	4.1
Hungary	0.4	Ukraine	0.7
Latvia	0.4		

Source: Authors' calculations based on WHO 2005.

a. Measured as expenditure on private prepaid plans as percent of total expenditure on health in 2002; does not include countries without PHI or where data were not available.

general reform process toward market-based economic systems. Except in Slovenia, which, as a high-income country, will not be considered in this analysis, PHI does not play a significant role in health care financing. Table 2.10 gives an overview of countries where expenditure for private prepaid programs has been reported.

Market Indicators and Evidence of Market Failure

Despite reform efforts and government-driven PHI pilot programs (for example, in Estonia, Hungary, and Moldova), private health insurance is negligible in Eastern Europe and Central Asia (WHO 2005). Only the Russian Federation and Turkey cover more than 1 percent of total health care spending through private prepaid schemes.

Turkey

Though still small in absolute terms, spending on private health insurance is gradually gaining importance in Turkey. In 1996, the WHO considered PHI the fastest-growing insurance market in the country. Subscribers to private schemes usually acquire higher-quality service in addition to their public coverage. Actually, people can obtain supplementary voluntary health insurance only through private insurers. Ernst & Young (2003) reports that, in the mid-1990s, about 30 institutions offered PHI, covering about 500,000 people. Considering that only 15,000 were covered by PHI in 1990, the industry experienced significant growth in the first half of the decade. Although dissatisfaction with the quality and accessibility of public facilities has raised the popularity of PHI, private risk-sharing programs still do not constitute a major factor in the country's health financing system. According to recent estimates (EOHCS 2002d; Colombo and Tapay 2004), coverage through private providers remains below 1 percent of the total population with approximately 650,000 people insured. Coverage was highest among employees of banks, insurance companies, chambers of commerce, and computer companies (EOHCS 2002d).

Other Countries

The relative insignificance of PHI in Eastern Europe and Central Asia has multiple reasons. As documented in Dixon, Langenbrunner, and Mossialos (2004), many countries experienced problems with private health insurance. In Kazakhstan, most insurance companies went out of business shortly after the market opened up for PHI in the 1990s. The authors identify a lack of public regulation as well as lack of corporate solvency oversight as the main explanation for this failure. Lack of regulation may also be the reason many insurance companies in Russia have not yet been able to snatch a larger market share. Despite liberalization efforts, only 6.5 percent of total health expenditure was channeled through private prepaid schemes in 2002. This figure nevertheless indicates a remarkable expansion of PHI because the share of private prepaid spending increased by more than 200 percent between 1998 and 2002.

In other countries, privatization has not yet been thoroughly accomplished (for example, government joint stock companies sell private health insurance in Uzbekistan) or is limited to certain sectors of the health insurance market (for example, private insurance covers only copayments under the public health insurance regime). Albania opened the market for private health insurance in 1994 but failed to attract PHI suppliers. As of 1999, the only insurance company to enter the market offered private insurance services mostly to people traveling abroad (EOHCS 1999a). The private insurance industry has still not consolidated. Conversely, the country's social health insurance scheme (Health Insurance Institute) is on its way to becoming the primary purchaser of health care services (EOHCS 2002a).

Apart from regulatory deficiencies, the lack of nonprofit or low-profit insurance companies may also contribute to the relative insignificance of PHI. Except for Hungary, all countries with available data rely mainly on private commercial health insurance that much of the population cannot afford. In 1993, Hungary established the legal framework for the establishment of nonprofit PHI, based primarily on the French *mutualité* model. Although few voluntary nonprofit funds have entered the insurance market, public subsidies seem to promote the gradual development of mutual health insurance. Health insurance purchase from mutual funds is subsidized with a 30 percent tax rebate up to a certain limit (EOHCS 2004b: 46). Between 1998 and 2002, the share of PHI relative to total health care spending increased from 0.1 to 0.4 percent, which corresponds to a development of PHI spending from 0.39 to 4.18 international dollars (WHO 2005).

Evidence of market exclusion of the poor is manifold in East European and Central Asian countries. In Azerbaijan, private voluntary health insurance covers about 15,000 people, less than 0.1 percent of Azerbaijan's total population. Insurance premiums vary from US$600 for hospital treatment in insurance-owned facilities up to US$17,000 for medical evacuation to Russia or Turkey, depending on the specific insurance package (EOHCS 2004a). Considering that the average annual per capita income in Azerbaijan amounts to around US$700, it is easy to see why PHI does not cover a larger part of the population.

In fact, insurance companies do not seem to believe "that there is a viable market among the general population" (ibid.: 24). Such observations are confirmed for Belarus (EOHCS 1997), Estonia (EOHCS 2000a), Georgia (EOHCS 2002b), the Russian Federation (EOHCS 2003), and the for-profit market in Hungary (EOHCS 2004b). As in Romania, PHI is often offered by large firms for their employees (primarily multinational organizations), or it is used by residents traveling abroad; such services are not covered through compulsory social insurance (EOHCS 2000b).

PHI Regulation in Eastern Europe and Central Asia

Since its first appearance in the 1990s, PHI has not been able to become a major pillar of the health care financing system in Eastern Europe and Central Asia. As documented for many countries, private risk-sharing programs are either restricted to a small, exclusive part of the population, or the schemes are rudimentary and coverage is limited to very basic services.

Experiences from East European and Central Asian countries underline that successful implementation of PHI demands more than merely opening markets to private providers. Particularly important are sufficient political will and regulatory scrutiny, which is missing in many countries in the Region. Even fairly developed economies like Turkey often do not have legislation on proper risk-sharing or risk-adjustment mechanisms (Colombo and Tapay 2004: 43). At the same time, Turkey lacks strategic planning and policy coordination, which leaves the whole health care sector highly fragmented.

Whether or not PHI should gain a more prominent role is above all a political decision. The determination to actively support the development of PHI varies widely across countries. Whereas the Ministry of Health in Belarus is "broadly in favor of the extension of voluntary [that is, private, DD] health insurance" (EOHCS 1997: 42), Estonia has renounced all attempts to increase the share of PHI. Sometimes, public and private financing mechanisms conflict. Hungary, for example, does not allow private risk-sharing programs to offer the same products covered under the public insurance regime. Equally deterring are policies that do not allow subsidization of public health care coverage through private risk-sharing arrangements. In Moldova, for instance, buyers of PHI are not awarded any tax benefits even though they may not use tax-paid public health care services (EOHCS 2002c: 25).

Given the relatively low incomes in large parts of Eastern Europe and Central Asia, the range of private risk-sharing programs should probably not be limited to the for-profit sector. Legislation that prevents the development of nonprofit or low-profit schemes potentially impedes a wider outreach of PHI among the population. In this respect, Hungary's efforts to establish complementary insurance schemes on a nonprofit basis deserve special attention. Whether its decision to subsidize the purchase of voluntary funds is the most cost-effective public intervention remains uncertain because rent-seeking behavior and other market distortions may undermine such efforts. Alternatively, countries could also consider allowing innovative ways to sell and promote private health insurance. In Georgia, for example, companies sell PHI as packages with other, more prominent, and currently more profitable insurance products (EOHCS 2002b).

Public policies to initiate and support the development of PHI need to be counterbalanced with accompanying measures aiming at more equitable and less discriminatory access to health care coverage. Preliminary experiences from Latvia indicate that the gradual expansion of the private health insurance market could lead to a "two-tier system of health care provision in terms of access and quality of care" (EOHCS 2001: 37). Also, the state often fails to ensure that individuals are sufficiently informed about the pros and cons of private health insurance as well as potential needs to insure privately against health care costs in cases where the state cannot offer sufficient coverage. The move toward market structures and the reorganization of public services and responsibilities has occasionally evoked confusion and uncertainty among the population. As a result of the reform process, many people may no longer be aware of the extent of public health care provision and coverage. Again, experiences from Latvia suggest that private insurers have used public confusion for their own benefit. Such a situation would be extremely harmful for the future development of PHI. Providers would realize a larger producer surplus and block access to PHI for low-income individuals, thus creating market inefficiencies and increasing segregation in health care coverage. More important, insufficient regulation could undermine the fragile trust in private suppliers that has been gradually developing since the region's shift toward market structures. Such trust will be crucial for the success and sustainability of future reforms.

PHI Trends in Eastern Europe and Central Asia

The future development of PHI depends above all on a political decision about the role private risk-sharing arrangements should play in the health care systems of East European and Central Asian countries. If the state continues to provide health care (as before the market reforms) or offers efficient social insurance, PHI will be bought only by people in upper-income brackets who can pay the high premiums. Thus far, private schemes are mostly a supplement to obligatory public health insurance, covering extra services and superior treatment. Many countries have not yet reached a clear political decision about the extent and domain that should be covered by PHI. Naturally, such uncertainties hamper the development of the private insurance industry. In some cases (for example, Estonia), development has been reversed when pilot projects did not have the desired effect on the local health care system. Since Estonia's unsuccessful attempt to promote private insurance for complementary services, there has no been no further "policy attempt to increase the share of private insurance" (EOHCS 2000a: 18).

Another aspect that will influence the development of the health insurance industry in Eastern Europe and Central Asia is each country's general economic performance. Due to the for-profit nature of most insurance schemes, PHI primarily addresses high-income groups and foreign employees. Depending on the general economic development, more people may be able to afford private insurance premiums, or high inflows of foreign employees could drive market demand. In Azerbaijan, for example, the insurance industry might benefit from continued expansion of the oil economy, which would increase the share of wealthy individuals in the local population and similarly increase demand from oil-industry expatriates (Azerbaijan 2004a).

As illustrated by the case of Turkey, the market usually responds to higher demand for private health insurance, when government provides an adequate institutional and regulatory environment for its development. The significant increase of both—insurance companies offering and people having PHI—up to 1998 can be explained primarily by diversification of consumer demand led by increases in per capita income. In fact, the initial increase of PHI was self-reinforcing because it stimulated growth in the private health care sector, which, in turn, made private health insurance more popular. Payments to private health facilities are not covered under the public insurance plan.

However, Turkey also demonstrates that the market does not function perfectly as a substantial increase of premiums has recently slowed down the development of PHI. According to the Turkish Ministry of Finance, coverage in PHI has leveled off at around 600,000 since 1998 (EOHCS 2002d: 53). Between 1994 and 2002, the average annual premium per person increased from US$200 to US$800. Due to limited control over the cost of health care, the private health insurance industry is faced with both fraud and adverse selection as more and more young and healthy individuals opt out of PHI. Increasing premiums and decreasing coverage progressively leave private insurers with older and less healthy people.

As indicated in figure 2.10, the general trend of PHI spending in Eastern Europe and Central Asia is nevertheless positive, although the exceptionally high growth rates in Georgia, Hungary, Lithuania, the Russian Federation, and especially Turkey should not be overrated. The development in Turkey, for example, corresponds to an increase in PHI expenditure from 0.18 to 17.24 international dollars, while total health expenditure amounted to 420 international dollars in 2002. Particularly noteworthy is the significant decrease of PHI spending in Romania combined with a general increase in health expenditure. Compulsory social insurance apparently obstructs consolidation in the private health insurance industry.

Insurance Markets and Private Health Insurance in the Middle East and North Africa Region

The most important insurance markets in the MENA Region are Israel, the Islamic Republic of Iran, Morocco, the United Arab Emirates, Saudi Arabia, Lebanon, and Kuwait. In 2003, total insurance premium income amounted to US$15.2 billion (0.5 percent of global insurance premium income), almost 75 percent of it spent for non–life insurance schemes (US$11 billion); the remaining US$4.2 billion can be attributed to the life insurance sector.

FIGURE 2.10 PHI Spending Relative to Total Health Expenditure in Eastern Europe and Central Asia

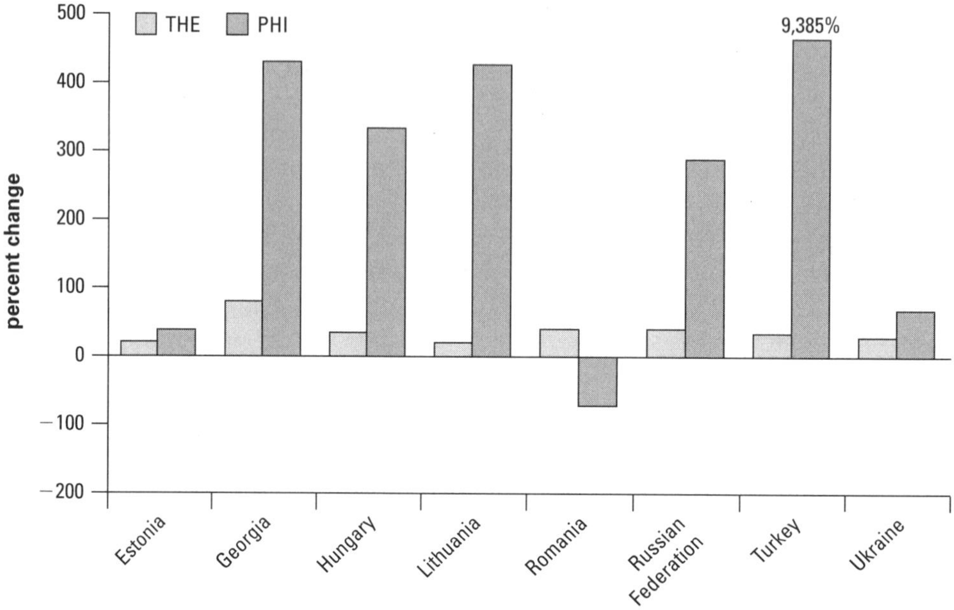

Source: Authors' calculations based on WHO 2005.
Note: Total health expenditure and PHI spending measured in international dollars (percent change between 1998 and 2002; Estonia: 1999–2002).

PHI in the MENA Region

Private expenditure is an important financial source of health care systems in the MENA Region. Nonetheless, PHI is a relatively new phenomenon in most of countries in the Region. Private funds are used chiefly for out-of-pocket expenditure (for example, the Republic of Yemen, where 58.4 percent of total health expenditure was OOP in 2001). Only Morocco, Lebanon, and Saudi Arabia have a sizeable private health insurance industry. Furthermore, in Morocco (23 percent), Oman (48.6 percent), and Saudi Arabia (40.1 percent), a surprisingly large share of private health expenditure is used for prepaid programs. Table 2.11 gives an overview of MENA countries where spending on private insurance has been recorded.

Market Indicators and Evidence of Market Failure

So few countries in the MENA Region have a significant private health insurance market that aspects of PHI will be discussed for each country individually. Based on these observations, the subsequent part will discuss some regulatory issues of PHI and derive development trends in the private health insurance industry for the whole Region.

Morocco

Morocco has a highly diversified health insurance market including private for-profit companies, mutual benefit societies, and various mutual funds for private

TABLE 2.11 Private Health Insurance in MENA Countries

Country	*Importance of PHI* [a]	*Country*	*Importance of PHI* [a]
Algeria	1.2	Morocco	15.5
Egypt, Arab Rep. of	0.4	Oman	8.9
Iran, Islamic Rep. of	1.5	Saudi Arabia	9.2
Jordan	3.8	Tunisia	7.8
Lebanon	12.2		

Source: Authors' calculations based on WHO 2005.
a. Measured as expenditure on private prepaid plans as percent of total expenditure on health in 2002. Does not include countries without PHI or where data were not available.

and public sector companies. The extent of coverage depends on the specific type of scheme. Whereas mutual benefit societies provide broad coverage for major medical risks and vice versa, private companies offer exactly the inverse. All health insurance schemes in Morocco are voluntary and cover a total of approximately 4.5 million beneficiaries, predominantly in urban areas. Public spending on health care from national or local tax sources accounts for only one third of total health expenditure (5 percent of the general state budget), relatively little compared with other countries in the Region (WHO 2005). Although public spending has increased slightly, the MOH budget may still be regarded as "quantitatively insufficient" (NHA Morocco 2001).

A primary concern of Morocco's health financing system is its high level of OOP. According to WHO data (WHO 2005), households bear more than two thirds of total health care costs, mostly in the form of direct payments to health care providers. Only 23 percent of private spending on health care is channeled through insurance schemes, compared with 74 percent for OOP. Other contributions to health insurance schemes originate from public and private enterprises; the former paying 5 percent of total health care cost for company schemes, the latter channeling 5 percent of total health care cost to PHI in the form of employer contributions (Greft Abdeljalil 2002: 35). Health care coverage is almost exclusively limited to high-income individuals, especially public sector employees and their dependants who constitute more than two thirds of the covered population. Low-income families are excluded from the insurance system but can receive treatment at public facilities at very low costs.

In view of the low health care coverage (only 15 percent of the total population), Morocco has been debating the introduction of a mandatory health insurance system for the past 15 years (Greft Abdeljalil 2002: 36). As part of the country's commitment to economic and political opening-up, reforms are underway to liberalize financial services, including health insurance. In 2002 Morocco implemented a new insurance code and reinforced its institutional capacity for insurance supervision (EU Commission 2004). However, regulation still prevents foreign investors from acquiring a majority stake in Moroccan insurance companies. This, and the fact that the state has increased its contribution to total health care spending, may have slowed down the development of PHI in recent years.

Lebanon

Another dynamic insurance market is reported for Lebanon, where private health insurance is already well established, largely due to insufficiencies of public health care institutions. Lebanon also has a highly fragmented health care system, in which private sources account for around 70 percent of total health care spending. Of this, a remarkable 17.5 percent is used for private risk-sharing programs (WHO 2005). Lebanon has a relatively large non–life insurance market with per capita spending of US$84.70 in 2003 (Swiss Re 2005). According to these figures, the country's insurance density is much higher than its gross national income (GNI) would suggest. On a global scale, insurance density puts the country in 48th position while the World Bank GNI index ranks Lebanon in 81st with per capita income of US$4,040 in 2003.

In 1998, some 70 private companies offered comprehensive and supplementary insurance programs that covered, respectively, an estimated 8 percent and 4.6 percent of the total population (NHA Lebanon 2000). Providers of health insurance varied in size and premium income while insurance volumes ranged from below US$1 million to between US$5million and US$50 million. Supply is very competitive, due to the size of the insurance market, which also includes nonprofit providers and mutual insurance funds. Nevertheless, there exists anecdotal evidence that high-risk/high-cost patients are prevented from joining private schemes. It can consequently be assumed that the Ministry of Health is burdened with an extraordinarily large share of bad-risk patients (NHA: 6). The government is also the insurer of last resort for all individuals without any health care coverage.

Saudi Arabia

The high share of PHI expenditure relative to total health expenditure in Saudi Arabia stems mainly from foreign workers (between 5 million and 6 million), who are required to have mandatory private health insurance. Before the reform of 2003, expatriates in Saudi Arabia had been entitled to use public facilities that are now only open to Saudi citizens. Other forces driving the development of the private health insurance industry is a rising population, fast growth of the private sector, the quick pace of industrialization, and high per capita medical expenditure (U.S.-Saudi-Arabia Business Council 2004). This trend materializes in increased PHI spending while total health expenditure declined over the past couple of years. All these factors contribute to the ongoing readjustment of the country's health care system. Due to limited public resources, policy makers in Saudi Arabia are searching for alternative ways of financing health care. The five-stage program that introduced PHI for expatriates will eventually also allow coverage of Saudi nationals (Sekhri, Savedoff, and Tripathi 2004: 8).

Tunisia

Health care coverage in Tunisia is provided through various health insurance schemes, including social security funds, tax-paid public health care, private group insurance, and *mutuelles*. Health insurance provided through social security is compulsory for formal sector employees, covering an estimated 2.2 million households, 85 percent of the Tunisian population. Health care for poor and low-income individuals is provided free of charge or at reduced rates through a tax paid public facilities. Private insurance schemes only supplement other forms of health care financing, covering additional or superior treatment and allowing access to private health care facilities. In 1999, private group insurance schemes, open to both public and private employees, covered 183,000 persons, whereas mutual schemes had 125,000 individuals affiliated (NHA Tunisia 2004). PHI is therefore limited to a very small part of Tunisia's population of 10 million persons.

Tunisia's health care financing system faces various challenges: growing demand for high-quality care (provided mainly by private suppliers), increasing health care costs, efficiency constraints of public health facilities, and an aging society. The Tunisian government has responded to this situation by gradually withdrawing funds from the system, reducing the state's share of total health expenditure from 52.1 percent in 1980 to 34.7 percent in 2000. Given that OOP still constitutes the largest source of health care financing in Tunisia (49.2 percent), this public disengagement is not counterbalanced by other forms of risk pooling and may particularly harm low-income individuals who cannot afford health insurance. So far, contributions to either insurance mechanism have not yet become a major source of health financing. Together, all types of health insurance account for merely 17.7 percent of total health expenditure.

Jordan

In Jordan, 240,000 individuals (5 percent of the population) are reported to have private health care coverage. Another 152,200 people receive coverage through employer-based self-insurance (NHA Jordan 2000). Compared with other forms of health care coverage, the number of privately insured is relatively insignificant: 81 percent of Jordan's population is reported to have some form of health insurance. Private programs do not offer a real alternative to social schemes. Of the 20 companies licensed to sell health insurance, only one offers full coverage. Considering that, in 1997, such packages cost an annual premium of US$866 (about 56 percent of Jordan's average per capita income that year), only a very small portion of the population can afford full coverage through PHI (NHA Jordan 2000; Central Bank of Jordan 1998). Coverage through PHI may equally be limited by the small volume of group insurance sales. Large companies, which would be the primary distribution channels for group insurance schemes, apparently prefer to rely on self-insurance programs. The number of uninsured is estimated at around 30 percent of Jordan's population, while about 20 percent of the insured are reported to have multiple coverage.

Iran

Although official statistics (for example, Medical Service Insurance Organization, Social Security Organization) claim that 90 percent of the Iranian population has health insurance, the number of uninsured is estimated at around 30 percent. This situation may be explained by considerable overlap between certain insurance categories (people who have multiple coverage), which raises concerns about the efficiency of the specific insurance organizations (NHA Iran 1998). Private funds are the most important source of health care financing in Iran. In 1998, households contributed 53 percent of total health expenditure through OOP while 5.5 percent was channeled through different insurance organizations. Apart from specialized insurance companies, PHI is also offered through banks that insure their employees (including dependents) and through the radio and TV networks. Contributions to specialized insurance companies are shared among firms and employees while insurance packages exclusively cover inpatient services in private hospitals. The services covered through bank insurance schemes include physician services, pharmaceuticals, dental and laboratory services, as well as expenses for radiology and imaging. Given the large extent to which people are willing to copay for medical treatment at private hospitals (on average, 65 percent of all medical bills were paid by patients), PHI may be able to mobilize further resources by offering more comprehensive packages.

PHI Regulation in the MENA Region

Regulatory requirements and policy recommendations depend on each country's specific stage of PHI development. Whereas private health insurance companies in Jordan still operate under a general insurance law that lacks regulatory efficiency (NHA Jordan, 2000), other countries in the Middle East and North Africa Region already have a reasonably well-developed and regulated insurance industry. In Lebanon, for example, 17 of the 70 insurance industries use reinsurance mechanisms to prevent financial imbalances (NHA Lebanon 2000).

Overall, however, lack of policy harmonization and institutional accountability seems to be a common feature of insurance markets in the MENA Region. Experience from Jordan suggests that there is little coordination between the Ministry of Industry and Trade, which is responsible for PHI regulation, and the Ministry of Health. In Lebanon, each separate branch of the insurance industry is associated with a distinct supervising ministry. These shared responsibilities impede public oversight, which may lead to overlapping health care coverage, as reported for Jordan and Iran. Under such circumstances, formulating a national strategy for the future development of PHI will also be difficult. Better coordination mechanisms between respective ministries may decrease people's uncertainty about crucial coverage and, as a consequence, improve market outcomes. Similar objectives can be attained by defining the areas in which PHI may support, complement, or substitute other forms of health care coverage. Particularly important is a clear distinction between private and public responsibilities in health care financing.

Without efficient regulatory instruments, it will be difficult to prevent cream skimming, cost and premium escalation, as well as fraud, confirmed for all MENA countries that partly rely on PHI. Equity targets will also be put into jeopardy if the state does not achieve sound administrative and regulatory capacities. In Lebanon, the lack of effective control mechanisms is seen to have contributed to recent cost and premium escalation in the health care sector. As argued in the NHA report, moral hazard behavior led to oversupply of health care coverage and provision, which could partly explain the highly uneven distribution of health care costs. While low-income individuals spend an average of 20 percent of their household income on health care, households in the highest income group spend a mere 8 percent of their resources on health. To respond to these challenges, a flat-rate system was tested for same-day surgical procedures in 1998 (NHA Lebanon 1998: 13). Given the relative success of this program, similar instruments could be implemented for other medical treatments to contain health care costs.

Insufficient public oversight and inappropriate incentive structures also cause inefficiencies in the allocation of resources. Specifically, reimbursement policies in Lebanon have channeled too many resources into the development and prescription of high-tech curative treatment. Primary and preventive care have been neglected by health financing institutions, including PHI. Apart from contributing to the general escalation of health care costs, the focus on curative care may fail to meet the health care needs of the Lebanese people. It would arguably be more advisable to emphasize preventive measures such as vaccination and immunization. PHI schemes also appear to be maladjusted to the health situation in Morocco because they do not take into account the specific needs of low-income families. If PHI were to become a major pillar of Morocco's health financing system, schemes would need to take into account the specific situation of the poor. Their current design, which primarily covers minor health care risks, does not provide sufficient protection against impoverishment because catastrophic health care cost could still arise in the event of major treatment.

PHI Trends in the MENA Region

The MENA Region has experienced a dynamic development of private health insurance in recent years. Measured in expenditure on private risk-sharing programs, the industry expanded particularly quickly in Algeria, Iran, Jordan, and Tunisia. PHI's future development depends on various factors. In systems that rely mainly on public provision of health care, limited fiscal resources will probably intensify the exploration of alternative ways of financing health care, including PHI. In this respect, the introduction of mandatory health insurance for expatriate workers in Saudi Arabia can be regarded as an initial step toward more private involvement in the health care system. Similarly, higher demand for health care and demand for higher-quality treatment may become driving forces of PHI development. Such reasoning applies for a number of countries including Lebanon, Tunisia, and Morocco.

Apart from Saudi Arabia, Sekhri, Savedoff, and Tripathi (2004) identify Bahrain as a country with high PHI development potential in the Middle East.

FIGURE 2.11 PHI Spending Relative to Total Health Expenditure in the Middle East and North Africa Region (percent change, 1998–2002)

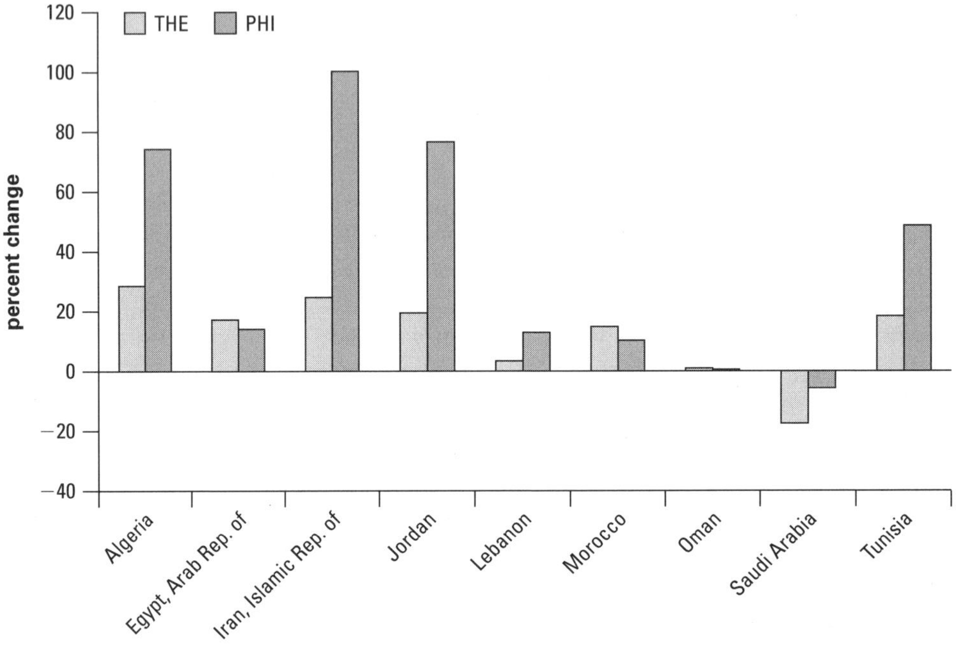

Source: Authors' calculations based on WHO 2005.
Note: Total health expenditure and PHI spending measured in international dollars (percent change between 1998 and 2002).

Driving forces include the need to cope with a large foreign workforce as well as increased demand for health services due to higher incomes. As illustrated in figure 2.11, private prepaid contributions have increased relatively more than total health expenditure in MENA countries between 1998 and 2002. This supports the notion of a generally dynamic insurance market in the Middle East and North Africa Region. Particularly noteworthy is the rapid growth of PHI in Algeria, Iran, Tunisia, and Jordan. In the latter, the number of privately insured individuals multiplied by more than six between 1989 and 1997. As mentioned above, limited insurance packages may, however, restrain the future development of Jordan's health insurance industry.

Lessons Learned: How to Integrate PHI into a Health System?

PHI is gradually gaining importance in low- and middle-income countries but is still a very small part of absolute spending on private insurance. The previous discussion from different countries and regions illustrates that private risk-sharing markets rarely function perfectly. The large inequalities in care access and coverage are especially worrisome from a development point of view. Market failures can occur at various stages of the exchange process and can involve both the supply and the demand sides. Furthermore, failures have different dimensions, including total exclusion of or discrimination against individual patients, financial imbalances of suppliers, premium escalation, and a lack of competition. Private health care markets in low- and middle-income countries are consequently faced with the basic dichotomy of efficiency (for example, adverse selection and premium escalation) and equity (for example, cream skimming). To offer competitive prices, insurers will discriminate against high-risk patients or try to reduce administrative costs by focusing on formal sector employees where premium collection is relatively inexpensive. At the same time, moral hazard behavior induces cost escalation (by offering more insurance or more services than needed) or adverse selection pushes low-risk patients out of private schemes.

How to respond to these market failures and inefficiencies is ultimately a political question. Its answer will in part depend on individuals' preferences about how to weight efficiency and equity as well as the general needs and circumstances in each country. It is nevertheless unlikely that an insurance system can completely renounce control mechanisms to supervise PHI performance. The need for regulation is not fueled only by potentially negative outcomes of the private insurance industry; regulation may be equally important because the introduction of PHI will also affect other forms of health care financing. Specifically, PHI may leave only high-risk patients for public coverage or it may indirectly affect public provision of health care by raising health care costs. Policy makers should thus take into consideration the whole impact of allowing private risk-sharing arrangements into the market. The state needs to be able to respond to the manifold challenges that will arise when PHI is introduced into a health care system. Furthermore, the state should ensure transparency of the system and be clear about public and private responsibilities. This is important for potential consumers of PHI because it allows them to adjust their health expenditure. It is also important for providers of PHI because it enables them to offer adequate insurance packages that take account of the specific needs of their clientele.

An efficient regulatory framework is especially important in low- and middle-income countries because private risk-sharing arrangements may be the only form of health insurance available. At the same time, efficient regulation is often difficult to achieve because these countries rarely have sufficient experience and expertise in dealing with insurance markets. Furthermore, they often lack the institutional capacity to build and maintain a regulatory framework. Setting up a government agency to monitor the insurance sector is just the first step in establishing efficient institutions. Effective supervision has multiple layers and involves many different tasks, various public entities, and requires qualified specialists. Institutional capacity will extend from insurance legislation and licensing requirements to monitoring strategies and corrective control mechanisms. Contributing to the debate on regulatory requirements of PHI in low- and middle-income countries, Sekhri, Savedoff, and Tripathi (2004) propose five key questions to be answered by policy makers who want to establish a regulatory regime:

- Who can sell insurance?
- Who should be covered?
- What should be covered?
- How can prices be set?
- How should providers be paid?

Due to the issue's complexity as well as the large array of possible risk-sharing arrangements and corresponding market-failure and policy-response patterns, the focus here is on selected key issues of PHI in low- and middle-income countries. Particular consideration is given to the question of who and what should be covered through private risk-sharing programs by discussing the desired structure of the schemes. Furthermore, price setting mechanisms are explored by comparing pros and cons of commercial vs. nonprofit schemes. Aspects of premium collection are also analyzed, and advantages of group programs are discussed as regards individual contracts. Finally, advantages and disadvantages of opening insurance markets for international providers are discussed. Although such analysis forcibly entails a high degree of aggregation and generalization, it brings to light some important lessons that have already been learned in dealing with private health insurance in low- and middle-income countries.

Scheme Structure: Comprehensive vs. Supplementary Coverage

Health insurance can be classified according to the extent of coverage it offers, particularly as regards other forms of health care financing. In general, PHI may have a substitutive, complementary, or supplementary role in a country's health care system. As a substitute for other forms of health care financing, PHI offers comprehensive coverage in place of another entity or financial source. Complementary and supplementary coverage close gaps in other forms of health care financing. The former provides coverage for services excluded or not fully covered otherwise; the latter provides coverage for faster access, better quality, and broader consumer choice (Thomson and Mossialos 2004). This analysis combines the last two health insurance types and distinguishes supplementary from comprehensive coverage.

In many low- and middle-income countries, private health insurance is the only available form of risk pooling. More often than in developed countries, private schemes therefore offer comprehensive coverage. Nevertheless, there are only few examples of private comprehensive health insurance that covers a larger percentage of people, one of them Lebanon, where 8 percent of the population was covered in 1998 (NHA Lebanon 2000). Typically, only the highest-income groups can afford comprehensive coverage.

Supplementary insurance can in principle be a valuable tool for extending coverage to otherwise excluded individuals. Experience from Ghana illustrates that supplementary private insurance may be suitable for low-income groups when the respective schemes are adjusted to local conditions (Okello and Feeley 2004). In Ghana, the poor were persuaded by information campaigns to buy only relatively cheap premiums covering inpatient health care. Hospital services are rarely needed, yet pose a severe risk of impoverishment when they occur.

Such a rationale faces a trade-off with other health risks. Specifically, supplementary coverage that is limited to high-cost/low-frequency events may not be the best option when local conditions demand large-scale preventive care (for example, immunization and vaccination campaigns). As in the case of mutual health insurance in Sub-Saharan Africa, limited coverage is furthermore seen to impede the long-run development of PHI (Concertation 2004: 79). Private schemes will become a true alternative to other forms of health financing only if they can expand their services and offer a wider range of coverage. In Sub-Saharan Africa, for example, community-based MHI faces a dichotomy between offering an attractive product and still being affordable. Although low-cost/low-coverage programs may facilitate start-up, MHI eventually needs to develop beyond this stage to attract larger parts of the population and contribute to attaining universal coverage.

Supplementary insurance is often also designed to cover additional or superior treatment, which obviously restricts its outreach to a relatively small group of people willing to pay for such services. In this respect, the role of PHI in low- and middle-income countries is comparable to the present situation in the developed world. Although it is equally difficult to generalize the role of PHI in OECD countries, a basic pattern seems to indicate that private health insurance is no substitute for other forms of prepaid health care financing. In only a few countries and for certain individuals does PHI provide the primary form of insurance and consequently covers a more comprehensive range of services. More important still is PHI's role in providing coverage for "ancillary and supplementary services" because this coverage of "small risks" can be observed for almost all OECD countries (Colombo and Tapay 2004: 16). With the notable exception of the United States, PHI neither accounts for a high share of total health expenditure nor does it offer primary coverage to larger parts of the OECD population. In European countries, for example, PHI primarily covers services that are excluded or not fully covered by the state, for example, in Croatia, Denmark, France, and Slovenia (Thomson and Mossialos 2004).

From a development point of view, such a narrow focus of PHI on high-income individuals could be justified only if other health financing intermediaries (notably social health insurance or tax-paid health care) are compensated for the opting out of good-risk patients. In theory, this could be achieved through financial transfers between public and private suppliers or a clear separation of either domain of health care coverage. Given the limited institutional and regulatory capacity of many low- and middle-income countries, PHI seems to jeopardize rather than support the goal of universal coverage. Private health insurance in the developing world is often either too expensive or the schemes are ill-adjusted to local circumstances to extend to a larger share of the population. At least such assessment seems valid for private commercial schemes. As commercial providers of PHI try mainly to increase profit, their range of adaptability to the needs of the poor is relatively small (Dror and Jacquier 1999). When discussing PHI in the context of low- and middle-income countries, distinguishing carefully between profit and nonprofit schemes is therefore equally important.

Price-Setting Mechanisms: For-Profit vs. Nonprofit Schemes

Health insurance through private commercial providers is generally restricted to upper-income groups that can afford the high premiums (Musgrove, Zeramdini, and Carrin 2002). In fact, "no country [...] uses voluntary private insurance to cover the poor or the elderly" (Sekhri, Savedoff, and Tripathi 2004: 8). Low family income is commonly associated with an increased rate of illness and disease, which seriously impedes any effort to induce insurance companies to offer PHI in poor communities (Sbarbaro 2000: 5). As documented for many countries, commercial schemes therefore rarely extend beyond formally employed workers in urban areas. Such limited outreach of PHI is problematic from a development point of view.

The literature offers many examples and possible explanations for the narrow focus of PHI in low- and middle-income countries. In Thailand, insufficient public oversight is seen to have raised PHI premiums beyond affordability for informal workers (Supakankunti 2000). For Sub-Saharan Africa, Bennett, Creese, and Monasch (1998: 54) find very limited potential for revenue generating by health insurance providers. To reach people outside formal sector employment, the authors therefore propose to focus on nonprofit or highly subsidized schemes that supplement publicly funded health programs. Similar conclusions are reached by the International Labor Organization, which points out significant discrepancies between private health coverage in urban and rural areas in Latin America (ILO 2000).

Dror and Jacquier (1999) argue that a mismatch between supply and demand for PHI in low- and middle-income countries excludes large parts of the population. Specifically, insufficient financial means and a large geographic spread prevent PHI suppliers from interacting efficiently with the demand side. To ensure broader health coverage, the authors propose microinsurance programs, which are essentially "voluntary group self-help schemes for social insurance" (Dror and Jacquier 1999: 6). A key advantage of such programs is their capability to harmonize accumulated reserves with community-specific risk and benefit priorities. Since commercial providers modify benefits packages primarily to increase profit, they are less flexible to respond to particular needs and preferences, which makes them less attractive to low-income groups. The *World Labour Report* reports the existence of microinsurance schemes in Bangladesh, Benin, Burkina Faso, Cameroon, Côte d'Ivoire, Ghana, Guinea, India, Lebanon, Mali, Morocco,

Nigeria, the Philippines, Senegal, Tanzania, Togo, Tunisia, Uganda, and several countries in Latin America (ILO 2000).

Given the narrow outreach of commercial PHI, it therefore seems advisable that policy makers and especially the international donor community ensure ample regulation of private commercial providers or concentrate efforts on developing nonprofit schemes. Nonprofit programs have a wide array of possible structures; they include schemes that are operated by NGOs, communities, voluntary associations, hospitals, large firms or even financial intermediaries like private banks.

The role of NGOs in administering private nonprofit health insurance is manifold. Ron (1999) reports NGO involvement as an intermediary between health providers and a community health insurance scheme in Guatemala (the Association por Salud de Barillas). NGOs often also run and manage insurance programs. For example, community schemes were set up by the Organisation for Educational Resources and Technological Training (ORT) in the Philippines and other developing countries. All ORT schemes try to be self-sustaining while at the same time offering affordable premiums to the target population. NGO involvement in community schemes is also reported for India (Gumber 2001), Lesotho (DeRoeck and Levin 1998), and Cambodia (GTZ 2003). According to the Cambodian study, NGOs are a "leading force in health insurance provision for the informal sector" (ibid.: 29).

Small insurance schemes are occasionally offered by health care providers, including hospitals and local medical centers. Such programs have the advantage of bringing insurance closer to the target population, although evidence from Zaire seems to indicate that they, too, fail to integrate the chronic poor into their coverage (Jütting 2004; Criel, Van der Stuyft, and Van Lergerghe 1999), a perception confirmed for the hospital-based Lacor Health Plan in Uganda (Okello and Feeley 2004). Yet, analyzing a hospital-based scheme in Ghana, the same study also reveals that the poor can be encouraged to join risk-sharing programs through information campaigns, marketing efforts, and insurance packages that are appropriate for the specific needs of low-income groups.

In some cases, even profit-maximizing behavior can lead to the development of low- or nonprofit health insurance schemes, as is indicated by the Grameen Bank health insurance program in Bangladesh. The WHO (2004b) reports that around 140,000 people are covered under this scheme, which was initiated to reduce defaults on the bank's microcredit loans by improving clients' health status (Desmet, Chowdhury, and Islam 1999). Similarly, large companies in Jordan often offer health insurance to their employees, not necessarily as an additional source of income, but to protect the health of their workforce. At the end of the 1990s, almost 100,000 people were reported to have coverage directly through their employer (NHA Jordan 2000).

Premium Collection: Individual vs. Group Coverage

Private health insurance can offer both individual and group coverage, the latter primarily through employer- or community-based schemes. Group affiliation has traditionally been the basis on which small, private risk-sharing schemes developed in many OECD countries, which later became the basis for universal coverage. In 19th century Europe, for example, health insurance was often provided through labor unions, guilds, or employer associations (Sekhri and Savedoff 2005). Because all members of a particular group are usually charged the same premiums—regardless of age, income, or health status—group coverage lacks the customization of an individual scheme. Especially for low-risk patients with small health needs, premiums will probably be less attractive than in an individual PHI because group insurance will always involve some sort of cross-subsidization of bad-risk patients. To include good-risk patients in the schemes, group insurance could be accompanied by mandated participation for all members of a particular firm, association, or community. Good-risk individuals could furthermore be encouraged to join group insurance schemes through information and advertising campaigns. In small groups or within a community, peer-pressure could also increase participation.

Moreover, group insurance schemes may greatly reduce administrative costs, and the savings ideally could be used to lower premiums or improve coverage. Premium collection is enormously simplified if contributions do not vary across individuals. First, the insurance company does not need to calculate premiums for each individual according to risk structure, which limits administrative cost and reduces the information asymmetry between insurer and insured (principle-agent problem). Second, premiums can easily be collected through the management of a firm, the chairman of an association, or the head of a community. Finally, group insurance schemes can also help reduce adverse selection and reinforce the bargaining position of insurance companies vis-à-vis health care suppliers. In this way, group insurance may contain health care costs and improve a country's health care coverage.

Most important, group insurance may often be the only feasible alternative to implement an insurance-based health care system in low- and middle-income countries. Due to information gaps on either side of the market exchange process, suppliers will often not be able to offer customized insurance packages, while buyers may not have sufficient oversight to establish a clear price-benefit structure. Primarily implementing group insurance schemes and focusing efforts on developing better and more efficient ways to collect insurance premiums can thus be an initial step to promote the development of PHI. At a later stage, experience and information from the performance of group insurance can be used to derive more personalized insurance products.

Trade and PHI: International vs. Domestic Provider

With the introduction of PHI into national health care systems, low- and middle-income countries become markets for foreign providers. This development has multiple sources that stem primarily from the ongoing globalization process. Most important, bilateral trade agreements and the expansion of free trade to services have expanded opportunities for international exchange in PHI. Furthermore, multinational firms operating abroad increasingly demand a healthy workforce and either promote the local insurance and health care industry or import respective facilities from abroad.

In general, this development can be acclaimed since low- and middle-income countries import know-how and institutional capacity through increased international exchange. International providers of PHI contribute to the establishment of a functioning insurance market in low- and middle-income countries and possibly activate local providers to start operating in this line of business. They will increase competition in the insurance market that ideally will lead to better services and the development of adequate insurance packages. In the long-run, international providers can therefore help lay the foundation of a functioning insurance system and contribute to the necessary base of information and experience of a national health care system.

Such positive effects are dependent, however, upon the careful integration of foreign providers into local markets. Apart from general rules and regulations in the insurance market, adequate legislation has to ensure that international insurance companies neither exploit a given market nor prevent the development of domestic competitors. Undoubtedly, broad international cooperation can contribute to the development of a functioning insurance market by offering expertise and institutional capacity. However, each health care system requires careful adjustment of insurance products to local needs and conditions. International providers have not always been successful in providing this flexibility. For the case of Latin America, the literature emphasizes that foreign insurance schemes may not be well adapted to local circumstances. Specifically, the gradual implementation of U.S.-type HMOs arguably reflects ideological beliefs in the inevitability of managed care rather than actual needs of the health care system (Iriart, Merhy, and Waitzkin 2001; Stocker, Waitzkin, and Iriart 1999).

OUTLOOK

Private risk-sharing programs are gradually gaining importance in low- and middle-income countries' health care systems. Wisely managed and carefully adapted to local needs and circumstance, they can be an important tool for reaching the "ultimate objective" of universal coverage (Carrin, Desmet, and Basaza 2001: 131). As documented above, prospects for the introduction of PHI are promising in a number of countries, particularly in the sector's nonprofit or low-profit segment. Five crucial factors justify this optimistic outlook: (1) many countries have difficulties with traditional ways of financing health care and look for alternative ways of achieving universal coverage; (2) economic growth leads to higher income and diversified consumer demand in the health care sector that public facilities might not meet; (3) public entities frequently lack people's trust and confidence—because PHI is generally associated with private health care providers it often enjoys wider popularity; (4) globalization and economic opening-up will lead to more trade in the health care sector, which will boost the development of PHI in low- and middle-income countries;

(5) PHI does not require a strong service infrastructure (Sbarbaro 2000: 3) and may thus develop despite a country's institutional weaknesses.

Nevertheless, the introduction of PHI is not an end in itself and demands careful consideration of its impact on a country's health care system. It will neither cure all shortcomings of the previous system nor remain free of possibly negative consequences for existing structures. Private risk-sharing programs are an alternative way to finance health care. As such, they expand a country's options for covering health care costs, lay the foundation for further development toward universal coverage, or both. In this regard, it is particularly important that a country have a clear concept of what role PHI should play in the existing health care system or how it should develop to better serve future health care needs.

As documented above, the immediate effects of allowing PHI to enter a national health care system may occasionally prove disappointing. Potential inequities and discrimination caused by the emergence of PHI are of particular concern and may undermine the objective of universal coverage. First, PHI would directly affect the extent to which people have access to health care because not everybody will be able to afford its services. Case studies indicate that access to the commercial PHI sector in particular will often be limited to high-income individuals. Second, PHI could worsen the quality of public health care by increasing health care cost, taking qualified health care personnel away from public institutions, and leaving public facilities with only bad-risk patients. In this way, the introduction of PHI may have a detrimental effect even on people remaining within existing structures. From a development point of view, a sufficient regulatory framework is therefore fundamental to prevent the gulf between the privileged and underprivileged within a country from widening.

In low- and middle-income countries that are prone to epidemics and infectious diseases, it is equally important to consider the overall effects of PHI on their health indicators. Private risk-sharing programs arguably represent "a threat to the control of, and care for, [the] WHO's ten basic community diseases" (Sbarbaro 2000: 14). Shifting resources from public to private entities may consequently pose additional risks if people are deprived of sufficient preventive health care such as vaccination and immunization (Khaleghian 2004; Scott-Herridge 2002). The state must either continue to provide such services or persuade people through information campaigns to include preventive measures in their private health care coverage. As argued by Sbarbaro (2000: 12), the introduction of PHI may even detract from development potentials as "public health services have the greater effect on a community's economic development." Sustainable economic development could consequently prove more difficult to attain the more a country relies on private insurance.

Despite these risks, the potential for introducing PHI into a country's health care system should not be disregarded. Private risk-sharing arrangements may well contribute to improving health care coverage in low- and middle-income countries if the role of PHI is clearly defined and the impact of its introduction on a country's health care system carefully considered. Schemes need to be adapted to local circumstances, and regulation needs to be in place to correct for possible unintended consequences. The existence of PHI consequently does not discharge the state from responsibilities. On the contrary, it leaves an active role for governments to ensure the optimal performance of insurance markets and the entire health financing system. As illustrated by the case of Brazil, public regulation is not only vital to correct for market failures of PHI (for example, cream skimming, social exclusion, premium escalation). It can equally serve the insurance industry by establishing reputation and creating trust among the population (Jack 2000: 26). PHI is not the only alternative and ultimate solution to address alarming health care challenges in the developing world. But it is an option that warrants—and is receiving—growing consideration by policy makers around the globe. Thus, the question is not whether this tool will be used in the future, but whether it will be applied to its best potential to serve the needs of a country's health care system.

ANNEX 2A WHO DATA ON HEALTH CARE EXPENDITURE BETWEEN 1998 AND 2002

		Prepaid (US$) Change		*Prepaid (int. $) Change*		*Prepaid/THE Change*		*THE (US$) Change*		*THE (int. $) Change*		*THE/GDP Change*	
Country/Region	*Class*	*Level*	*(%)*	*Level*	*(%)*	*Level*	*(%)*	*Level*	*(%)*	*Level*	*(%)*	*Level*	*(%)*
Latin America and Caribbean Region													
Argentina	U-M	85.95	−61.5	157.28	−1.9	14.6	8.1	595.2	−64.8	1,080.80	−8.6	8.90	9.1
Barbados	U-M	46.14	10.8	71.02	9.6	7.7	−11.9	601.6	23.4	926.00	22.2	6.38	14.4
Bolivia	L-M	2.19	35.4	5.57	61.1	3.7	26.5	60.2	19.0	151.80	43.4	6.14	36.7
Brazil	L-M	50.46	−39.0	111.53	21.9	19.6	5.0	258.6	−45.1	568.60	16.7	7.70	6.8
Chile	U-M	68.11	32.7	152.28	66.7	24.8	61.6	279.6	−26.7	612.60	5.8	5.86	−4.9
Colombia	L-M	8.16	−2.8	25.65	26.8	4.6	47.3	182.2	−42.0	563.60	−16.0	8.80	−18.2
Costa Rica	U-M	1.38	−11.3	2.61	−8.0	0.4	−33.0	341.6	23.8	647.80	27.1	8.48	14.3
Dominican Republic	L-M	0.35	58.9	0.65	58.1	0.2	25.5	138.0	32.3	260.00	31.5	5.98	5.4
Ecuador	L-M	2.03	−78.5	4.84	−74.6	2.8	−82.0	74.6	23.6	177.40	17.6	4.56	11.1
El Salvador	L-M	6.10	60.3	12.84	60.9	3.6	56.5	169.0	7.8	355.20	7.1	7.98	−2.3
Guatemala	L-M	2.22	34.0	5.03	33.5	2.7	15.8	83.2	18.2	188.60	16.2	4.70	8.9
Honduras	L-M	1.91	26.1	5.01	18.6	3.5	2.9	54.6	23.5	143.40	15.9	5.92	10.4
Jamaica	L-M	23.69	28.2	30.07	33.0	13.3	22.0	177.2	4.8	224.60	9.4	5.96	3.3
Mexico	U-M	8.08	88.9	12.54	59.9	2.5	31.7	314.0	52.9	492.20	26.2	5.74	12.5
Nicaragua	L	1.45	167.3	4.77	182.0	2.5	155.2	56.8	11.5	186.40	21.4	7.46	8.6
Panama	U-M	16.63	24.5	26.79	27.0	4.9	21.2	339.2	4.8	546.60	7.9	8.64	1.5
Paraguay	L-M	7.49	−4.0	23.59	48.2	7.3	21.0	103.0	−22.4	322.00	25.6	7.78	27.4
Peru	L-M	6.86	66.4	16.00	89.9	7.1	77.9	96.6	−9.1	222.60	8.2	4.62	−1.7
Suriname	L-M	0.62	−56.9	1.14	−43.8	0.4	−71.4	165.4	47.8	311.40	58.3	7.66	49.1
Trinidad and Tobago	U-M	9.85	53.0	16.33	44.9	4.3	18.1	228.2	33.3	379.00	25.1	3.78	−9.7
Uruguay	U-M	286.81	−40.7	458.36	1.0	48.7	21.0	595.8	−57.9	944.20	−19.3	10.50	−5.5

Venezuela, República Bolivariana de	U–M	4.84	−13.2	6.47	−18.2	2.0	4.1	243.8	−8.9	324.00	−17.8	5.44	−5.9
N = 22	Avg.	29.15	17.2	52.29	31.7	8.24	19.2	234.47	2.3	437.67	14.7	6.77	7.8
South Asia Region													
Bangladesh	L	0.00	—[b]	0.01	—[b]	0.0	—[b]	11.0	0.0	50.00	18.8	3.16	0.1
India	L	0.12	109.1	0.36	116.9	0.4	69.6	27.2	33.2	84.20	40.0	5.88	17.0
Sri Lanka	L-M	0.16	16.9	0.62	33.0	0.5	6.1	30.6	10.5	118.00	26.1	3.56	8.6
N = 3	Avg.	0.09	63.0	0.33	74.9	0.32	37.9	22.93	14.6	84.07	28.3	4.20	8.5
East Asia Region													
China	L-M	0.13	33.2	0.57	28.3	0.3	–25.3	47.8	60.6	207.00	56.7	5.40	19.6
Indonesia	L-M	0.91	121.6	4.15	43.9	4.8	4.4	19.4	89.9	89.20	43.3	2.82	25.5
Malaysia	U-M	3.93	63.5	9.21	61.9	3.1	17.6	125.8	43.5	295.20	41.7	3.40	24.9
Papua New Guinea	L	0.23	98.1	1.24	158.1	0.9	129.8	26.0	–26.5	137.80	10.4	4.20	13.0
Philippines	L-M	3.13	11.6	15.91	15.1	9.8	22.1	32.0	–11.5	162.40	–6.0	3.30	–18.1
Thailand	L-M	3.82	6.6	12.83	16.8	5.1	–11.7	75.2	26.8	252.80	36.2	3.82	15.1
Vietnam	L	0.56	58.2	3.53	65.1	2.8	28.6	20.2	26.2	126.60	33.1	5.06	6.2
N = 7	Avg.	1.82	56.1	6.78	55.6	3.83	23.6	49.49	29.9	181.57	30.8	4.00	12.3
Sub-Saharan Africa Region													
Benin	L	0.89	14.8	1.93	25.8	4.9	3.1	18.0	11.4	39.20	24.7	4.60	5.0
Botswana	U-M	13.93	–15.7	27.84	10.8	9.5	–36.3	148.8	23.2	301.20	52.0	5.28	23.2
Cape Verde	L-M	0.05	207.1	0.13	224.2	0.1	207.7	63.4	9.0	170.80	22.1	4.84	−0.8
Chad	L	0.03	5.0	0.10	18.6	0.2	–10.8	12.2	17.4	41.80	30.8	6.32	20.2
Côte d'Ivo re	L	1.93	−17.6	4.63	−5.2	4.2	1.1	46.0	−18.6	110.40	−6.2	6.24	−3.0

(continued)

ANNEX 2A WHO DATA ON HEALTH CARE EXPENDITURE BETWEEN 1998 AND 2002 *(continued)*

		Prepaid (US$) Change		*Prepaid (int. $) Change*		*Prepaid/THE Change*		*THE (US$) Change*		*THE (int. $) Change*		*THE/GDP Change*	
Country/Region	*Class*	*Level*	*(%)*	*Level*	*(%)*	*Level*	*(%)*	*Level*	*(%)*	*Level*	*(%)*	*Level*	*(%)*
Ethiopia	L	0.01	5.6	0.04	42.2	0.2	5.6	5.0	0.0	18.20	35.7	5.28	18.4
Kenya	L	0.72	–4.2	2.75	−1.9	4.0	–3.6	18.0	2.3	69.00	4.1	4.92	1.5
Madagascar	L	0.26	–9.1	0.96	−2.7	5.0	7.8	5.2	−16.7	19.40	−10.3	2.10	−3.5
Malawi	L	0.15	–19.9	0.49	−1.2	1.1	−14.1	13.8	−4.3	44.20	13.9	8.88	15.4
Mozambique	L	0.02	–16.2	0.08	24.8	0.2	−35.8	10.0	21.1	37.60	66.8	5.00	36.4
Namibia	L-M	25.85	–13.9	72.65	15.6	21.7	10.8	119.2	−25.0	334.00	4.6	6.86	−1.4
Niger	L	0.20	–18.0	0.72	−5.7	2.6	−8.2	7.6	−9.7	27.80	4.5	4.24	4.0
Nigeria	L	0.63	137.2	1.46	108.7	3.4	119.9	18.2	12.0	43.60	−6.9	4.90	−13.6
Rwanda	L	0.02	–40.7	0.06	8.1	0.1	−12.5	12.8	−29.2	43.20	21.5	5.42	10.0
Senegal	L	0.34	71.1	0.78	79.8	1.4	45.1	23.8	21.8	54.20	36.4	4.74	20.3
South Africa	L-M	106.25	–10.5	284.24	30.0	44.3	12.0	240.2	−22.6	640.00	16.9	8.60	3.8
Swaziland	L-M	6.25	–24.5	24.13	5.5	7.8	12.3	80.2	−35.6	308.40	−6.2	6.32	−16.2
Tanzania	L	0.27	–8.4	0.60	5.1	2.1	−15.9	12.8	8.9	27.60	27.0	4.82	6.9
Togo	L	0.66	9.5	2.91	24.9	2.1	8.2	31.6	12.7	137.60	23.3	10.34	0.4
Uganda	L	0.02	45.9	0.09	74.2	0.1	15.5	16.8	20.0	62.60	55.5	6.56	33.3
Zimbabwe	L	10.79	216.0	30.76	62.4	17.3	172.6	62.6	124.9	190.00	−52.9	8.72	−23.6
N = 21	Avg.	8.06	24.4	21.78	35.4	6.31	23.1	46.01	5.9	129.56	17.0	5.95	6.5
Eastern Europe and Central Asia													
Belarus	L-M	0.04	n.a.[b]	0.24	n.a.[b]	0.0	n.a.[b]	80.4	10.3	493.20	36.9	6.24	6.8
Bulgaria	L-M	0.13	n.a.[b]	0.46	n.a.[b]	0.1	n.a.[b]	109.0	67.0	386.00	69.7	6.46	39.9
Estonia	U-M	2.30	35.6[a]	5.47	38.4[a]	1.0	28.3[a]	235.0	18.8	550.20	21.0	5.48	–8.2
Georgia	L-M	0.18	387.2	0.88	430.5	0.8	280.7	19.2	58.7	91.40	80.1	3.16	51.7

Hungary	U-M	0.82	337.9	1.94	333.4	0.2	277.9	375.4	44.8	896.20	34.7	7.40	6.9
Latvia	U-M	0.29	n.a.[b]	0.68	n.a.[b]	0.1	n.a.[b]	182.6	25.5	429.40	23.2	5.56	−12.5
Lithuania	U-M	0.15	436.8	0.35	426.8	0.1	377.0	212.2	22.6	500.40	20.4	6.24	−4.6
Romania	L-M	3.33	−71.6	12.17	−71.8	3.3	−101.1	104.0	31.3	390.80	40.6	5.84	20.0
Russian Federation	L-M	4.10	325.8	15.32	288.6	3.2	218.7	112.4	50.9	432.80	40.7	5.84	3.5
Turkey	L-M	5.90	9,012.9	14.20	9,384.6	3.5	7,441.9	166.6	24.9	391.60	34.3	6.16	34.9
Ukraine	L-M	0.22	42.5	1.13	68.5	0.7	42.0	33.6	10.6	171.00	28.9	4.50	−3.0
N = 11	Avg.	1.59	1,313.4	4.80	1,362.4	1.19	1,070.7	148.22	33.2	430.27	39.1	5.72	12.3
Middle East and North Africa Region													
Algeria	L-M	0.62	64.5	1.42	74.4	0.9	37.9	67.0	22.6	151.80	28.9	3.86	13.3
Egypt, Arab Rep. of	L-M	0.24	−9.7	0.69	14.4	0.4	−2.8	63.2	−7.3	180.00	17.6	4.98	−1.9
Iran, Islamic Rep. of	L-M	0.92	149.6	4.96	100.5	1.3	75.4	70.4	73.3	380.60	25.0	5.90	3.7
Jordan	L-M	4.98	70.4	12.38	77.0	3.2	53.9	154.8	13.9	383.60	19.7	9.08	8.0
Lebanon	U-M	67.66	6.1	81.50	13.2	11.7	9.4	577.0	−3.4	694.20	3.5	11.86	−5.7
Morocco	L-M	8.48	−5.6	26.93	10.4	15.6	−4.0	54.4	−1.6	173.00	15.0	4.54	4.7
Oman	U-M	20.92	17.8	32.79	0.6	9.1	0.2	230.6	17.3	362.00	1.1	3.40	−7.3
Saudi Arabia	U-M	31.15	14.3	51.77	−5.5	9.1	18.5	341.6	−1.3	570.40	−17.6	4.38	−12.2
Tunisia	L-M	9.08	28.7	28.25	49.1	7.5	30.3	122.2	0.5	377.20	18.5	5.74	−1.5
N = 9	Avg.	16.01	37.3	26.74	37.1	6.53	24.3	186.80	12.7	363.64	12.4	5.97	0.1

Source: World Health Report 2005, Statistical Annex, Geneva: WHO.
Note: L = low-income, L-M = lower-middle-income, U-M = upper-middle-income.
a. Only 1999–2002.
b. Data cover less than three years.

ANNEX 2B COUNTRY GROUPS ACCORDING TO 2005 WORLD BANK CLASSIFICATION

Low-income (US$765 or less)

Afghanistan
Angola
Bangladesh
Benin
Bhutan
Burkina Faso
Burundi
Cambodia
Cameroon
Central African Republic
Chad
Comoros
Congo, Democratic Republic of
Congo, Republic of
Côte d'Ivoire
Equatorial Guinea
Eritrea
Ethiopia
Gambia, The
Ghana
Guinea
Guinea-Bissau
Haiti
India
Kenya
Korea, Democratic People's Republic of
Kyrgyz Republic
Lao People's Democratic Republic
Lesotho
Liberia
Madagascar
Malawi
Mali
Mauritania
Moldova
Mongolia
Mozambique
Myanmar
Nepal
Nicaragua
Niger
Nigeria
Pakistan
Papua New Guinea
Rwanda
São Tomé and Principe
Senegal
Sierra Leone
Solomon Islands
Somalia
Sudan
Tajikistan
Tanzania
Timor-Leste
Togo
Uganda
Uzbekistan
Vietnam
Yemen, Republic of
Zambia
Zimbabwe

Lower-middle income (US$766 to US$3,035)

Albania
Algeria
Armenia
Azerbaijan
Belarus
Bolivia
Bosnia and Herzegovina
Brazil
Bulgaria
Cape Verde
China
Colombia
Cuba
Djibouti
Dominican Republic
Ecuador
Egypt, Arab Rep. of
El Salvador
Fiji
Georgia
Guatemala
Guyana
Honduras
Indonesia
Iran, Islamic Rep. of
Iraq
Jamaica
Jordan
Kazakhstan
Kiribati
Macedonia, Former Yugoslav Republic of
Maldives
Marshall Islands
Micronesia, Federated States of
Morocco
Namibia
Paraguay
Peru
Philippines
Romania
Russian Federation
Samoa
Serbia and Montenegro
South Africa
Sri Lanka
Suriname
Swaziland
Syrian Arab Republic
Thailand
Tonga
Tunisia
Turkey
Turkmenistan
Ukraine
Vanuatu
West Bank and Gaza

(continued)

ANNEX 2B COUNTRY GROUPS ACCORDING TO 2005 WORLD BANK CLASSIFICATION *(continued)*

Upper-middle income (US$3,036 to US$9,385)

American Samoa	Gabon	Palau
Antigua and Barbuda	Grenada	Panama
Argentina	Hungary	Poland
Barbados	Latvia	Saudi Arabia
Belize	Lebanon	Seychelles
Botswana	Libya	Slovak Republic
Chile	Lithuania	St. Kitts and Nevis
Cook Islands	Malaysia	St. Lucia
Costa Rica	Mauritius	St. Vincent and the Grenadines
Croatia	Mayotte	Trinidad and Tobago
Czech Republic	Mexico	Uruguay
Dominica	Northern Mariana Islands	Venezuela, República Bolivariana de
Estonia	Oman	

High-income (US$9,386 or more)

Andorra	Germany	Netherlands Antilles
Aruba	Greece	New Caledonia
Australia	Greenland	New Zealand
Austria	Guam	Norway
Bahamas, The	Hong Kong, China	Portugal
Bahrain	Iceland	Puerto Rico
Belgium	Ireland	Qatar
Bermuda	Isle of Man	San Marino
Brunei	Israel	Singapore
Canada	Italy	Slovenia
Cayman Islands	Japan	Korea, Republic of
Channel Islands	Kuwait	Spain
Cyprus	Liechtenstein	Sweden
Denmark	Luxembourg	Switzerland
Faeroe Islands	Macau, China	United Arab Emirates
Finland	Malta	United Kingdom
France	Monaco, Principality of	United States
French Polynesia	Netherlands	Virgin Islands (U.S.)

ANNEX 2C PHI SPENDING, BY COUNTRY GROUP

	Low-income countries		Lower-middle-income countries		Upper-middle-income countries		High-income countries		All countries	
Item	*N*	*%*	*N*	*%*	*N*	*%*	*N*	*%*	*N*	*%*
Total	6	100	57	100	35	100	38	100	192	100
Contributions for PHI of up to 5%	21	33.9	34	59.6	18	51.4	30	78.9	103	53.6
Contributions for PHI exceeding 5% of THE	3	4.8	12	35.3	9	25.7	14	36.8	38	19.8
Contributions for PHI exceeding 10% of THE	1	1.6	6	10.5	4	11.4	6	15.8	10	5.2
Contributions for PHI exceeding 20% of THE	0	0.0	2	3.5	2	5.7	2	5.3	6	3.1

Low-income countries where contributions to PHI exceed:

(1) 10 percent of total health care expenditure: Zimbabwe

(2) 5 percent of THE: (1) + Benin, Madagascar

(3) 0 percent of THE: (2) + Bangladesh, Chad, Côte d'Ivoire, Ethiopia, India, Kenya, Malawi, Mozambique, Nicaragua, Niger, Nigeria, Papua New Guinea, Rwanda, Senegal, Tanzania, Togo, Uganda, Vietnam

Lower–middle–income countries where contributions to PHI exceed:

(1) 20 percent of THE: Namibia, South Africa

(2) 10 percent of THE: (1) + Brazil, Jamaica, Morocco, Philippines

(3) 5 percent of THE: (2) + Colombia, Paraguay, Peru, Russian Federation, Swaziland, Tunisia

Upper–middle–income countries where contributions to PHI exceed:

(1) 20 percent of THE: Chile, Uruguay

(2) 10 percent of THE: (1) + Argentina, Lebanon

(3) 5 percent of THE: (2) + Barbados, Botswana, Oman, Panama, Saudi Arabia

ANNEX 2D NON–LIFE AND LIFE INSURANCE AROUND THE WORLD (MEASURED AS PREMIUM INCOME, US$)

Country/Region	*Pop*	*GDP*	*Non–life*	*Life*	*Total*
Latin America and the Caribbean Region					
Brazil	176.6	492.3	8,259	6,306	14,565
Mexico	102.3	626.1	6,737	4,280	11,017
Chile	15.8	72.4	1,225	2,171	3,396
Argentina	38.4	129.7	2,378	921	3,299
Venezuela, República Bolivariana de	25.5	84.8	2,092	65	2,157
Colombia	44.4	77.6	1,449	548	1,997
Peru	27.1	61.0	507	366	873
Trinidad and Tobago	1.3	10.2	216	427	643
Ecuador	13.0	26.9	412	46	458
Jamaica	2.6	7.8	245	148	393
Panama	3.0	12.9	263	127	390
El Salvador	6.5	14.4	246	104	350
Costa Rica	4.0	17.5	290	28	318
Dominican Republic	8.7	15.9	292	26	318
Guatemala	12.3	24.7	222	48	270
Barbados	0.3	2.6	170	83	253
Bahamas	0.3	5.3	94	137	231
Uruguay	3.4	11.2	182	43	225
Other LCR	48.5	40.5	459	175	634
Total	533.9	1728.6	25,738	16,049	41,787
Sub-Saharan Africa Region					
South Africa	45.3	159.9	4,718	21,550	26,268
Nigeria	135.6	50.2	384	87	471
Kenya	31.9	13.8	273	112	385
Namibia	2.0	4.7	111	243	354
Mauritius	1.2	5.2	98	148	246
Zimbabwe	13.1	8.3	104	141	245
Other SSA	473.4	175.2	1,053	254	1,307
Total	702.6	417.3	6,741	22,535	29,276
Middle East and North Africa Region					
Israel	6.7	103.7	3,840	3,052	6,892
Iran, Islamic Rep. of	66.4	208.3	1,428	127	1,555
United Arab Emirates	4.0	71.0	1,093	76	1,169

(continued)

ANNEX 2D NON–LIFE AND LIFE INSURANCE AROUND THE WORLD *(continued)*

Country/Region	*Pop*	*GDP*	*Non–life*	*Life*	*Total*
Middle East and North Africa Region					
Saudi Arabia	22.5	188.5	986	43	1,029
Lebanon	4.5	19.0	381	139	520
Lebanon	4.5	19.0	381	139	520
Kuwait	2.4	35.4	270	61	331
Oman	2.6	20.3	227	36	263
Qatar	0.6	17.5	232	10	242
Jordan	5.3	9.9	212	30	242
Bahrain	0.7	7.7	165	45	210
Morocco	30.1	44.5	927	361	1,288
Egypt, Arab Rep of	13.0	82.4	386	181	567
Tunisia	9.9	24.3	450	38	488
Algeria	31.8	66.0	389	15	404
Other MENA	125.4	13.8	—	—	—
Total	326.1	912.2	10,986	4,214	15,200
East Asia and Pacific Region					
China	1,288.4	1,409.9	14,630	32,237	46,867
Malaysia	24.8	103.2	2,154	3,455	5,609
Thailand	62.0	143.2	2,343	2,587	4,930
Indonesia	214.5	208.3	1,624	1,506	3,130
Philippines	81.5	80.6	491	704	1,195
Vietnam	81.3	39.2	254	419	673
Korea, Republic of	47.9	605.3	17,614	42,524	60,138
Taiwan, China	22.7	287.0	8,641	27,506	36,147
Hong Kong, China	6.8	158.6	2,375	9,917	12,292
Singapore	4.3	91.3	3,054	5,584	8,638
Other EAP	102.1	66.5	108	56	164
Total	1,936.3	3,193.0	53,288.0	126,495.0	179,783.0
Rest of world					
United States	291.0	10,881.6	576,681	481,527	1,058,208
Canada	31.6	834.4	35,863	23,873	59,736
United Kingdom	59.3	1,794.9	93,143	161,220	254,363
Germany	82.6	2,400.7	93,891	76,246	170,137
France	59.7	1,748.0	57,536	103,947	161,483
Italy	57.6	1,465.9	38,881	71,694	110,575
Netherlands	16.2	511.6	24,042	27,994	52,036
Spain	41.1	836.1	26,786	20,182	46,968
Switzerland	7.3	309.5	15,945	23,921	39,866

Belgium	10.3	302.2	12,786	20,302	33,088
Sweden	9.0	300.8	6,742	14,297	21,039
Denmark	5.4	212.4	6,194	10,926	17,120
Ireland	3.9	148.6	8,269	8,005	16,274
Austria	8.1	251.5	8,418	6,469	14,887
Finland	5.2	161.5	3,020	10,763	13,783
Norway	4.6	221.6	5,501	6,030	11,531
Portugal	10.2	149.5	4,809	6,122	10,931
Luxembourg	0.4	26.2	1,143	7,036	8,179
Greece	10.7	173.0	2,048	1,620	3,668
Cyprus	0.8	11.4	290	290	580
Iceland	0.3	10.5	306	32	338
Malta	0.4	3.9	122	125	247
Japan	127.2	4,326.4	100,989	371,831	472,820
Australia	19.9	518.4	20,346	20,845	41,191
New Zealand	4.0	76.3	3,687	1,055	4,742
Others	6.7	252.0	918	198	1,116
Total	873.6	27,928.6	1,148,356	1,476,550	2,624,906
South Asia					
Bangladesh	138.1	51.9	101	192	293
India	1,064.4	599.0	3,707	14,293	18,000
Sri Lanka	19.2	18.5	299	198	250
Pakistan	148.4	68.8	140	110	497
Others	54.6	17.6	—	—	—
Total	1,424.7	755.8	4,146	14,601	18,747
Eastern Europe and Central Asia					
Russia	143.4	433.5	9,257	4,887	14,144
Poland	38.2	209.6	3,946	2,312	6,258
Czech Republic	10.2	85.4	2,297	1,458	3,755
Turkey	70.7	238.0	2,630	685	3,315
Hungary	10.1	82.8	1,466	981	2,447
Ukraine	48.4	49.5	1,699	14	1,713
Slovenia	2.0	26.3	675	344	1,019
Slovakia	5.4	31.9	1,095	463	1,558
Croatia	4.5	28.3	704	201	905
Romania	22.2	60.4	609	187	796
Serbia and Montenegro	8.1	19.2	420	15	435
Bulgaria	7.8	19.9	345	38	383
Lithuania	3.5	18.2	196	70	266
Latvia	2.3	9.7	200	9	209
Other ECA	98.0	108.2	—	—	—
Total	474.7	1,420.8	25,539	11,664	37,203

Source: Swiss Re 2005.
Note: — = not available.

NOTES

1. According to Nitayarumphong and Mills (1998: 3), "universal coverage is defined as a situation where the whole population of a country has access to good quality services (core health services) according to needs and preferences, regardless of income level, social status or residency."

2. Not adjusted for purchasing power parity.

3. In this study, PHI denotes all risk-sharing arrangements for covering health care costs under a private contract between the insurance entity and the insured.

4. In accordance with European Union (EU) and OECD conventions, health and accident insurance is considered to belong to the non–life insurance segment, although some countries or insurance companies may employ a divergent classification (Swiss Re-Insurance Company 2004: 28).

5. In Mexico, a voluntary, publicly financed insurance scheme has recently started to operate. This "*seguro popular*" aims at individuals who are without social security coverage (about 50 percent of the population). This initiative is intended to establish universal coverage by 2010.

6. This distinction is somewhat subtle. Because taxes are not specifically collected to pay for health insurance, this form of health care financing does not involve prepayment (namely, a specific health financing tax—comparable to the taxation of gasoline, tobacco, or liquor—would fall in the insurance category).

7. Switzerland, for example, has a mandatory health insurance system based on private providers.

8. Jack (2000: 27) reports that the 35 private health insurance companies in Chile offered close to 9,000 distinct insurance policies in 1995, "reflecting a near continuum of vertical differentiation."

9. However, in some OECD countries such as Australia and France, private health insurance is offered primarily by nonprofit funds.

10. The significant decrease of total health care spending in Colombia between 1998 and 2002 (–16 percent) may be due to a general "deterioration of [. . . the country's] economic, social, and political situation, aggravated by armed conflict, which has contributed to the most acute crisis in Colombian history" (UNFPA 2003: 230).

11. Data on economic growth are taken from Penn World Tables 6.1; average growth rates between 1997 and 2000 are compared with the respective development of spending on prepaid health insurance.

REFERENCES

ADB (Asian Development Bank). 2002. "Making Health Care More Affordable for the Poor." Technical Assistance Report, TAR 36007, Asian Development Bank, Hanoi and Manila, June 2002. Amoako, Nana, Rich Feeley, and William Winfrey. 2002. "Health Financing in Ghana—Willingness to Pay for Normal Delivery Benefits in a Community-Based Health Insurance Plan." CMS Country Research Series, No. 11, Commercial Market Strategies, Washington, DC.

Asenso-Okyere, W. Kwadwo, Isaac Osei-Akoto, Adote Anum, and Ernest N. Appiah. 1997. "Willingness to Pay for Health Insurance in a Developing Economy—A Pilot Study of the Informal Sector of Ghana Using Contingent Valuation." *Health Policy* 42 (3): 223–37.

Asfaw, Abay. 2003. Costs of Illness, Demand for Medical Care, and the Prospect of Community Health Insurance Schemes in the Rural Areas of Ethiopia, Frankfurt a.M.: Peter Lang Verlag.

Asfaw, Abay and Johannes Jütting. 2002. "Mutual Health Insurance (MHI)—A Viable Solution to Increase Access to Health Care? An Ethiopian Case Study." Center for Development Research (ZEF), Bonn.

Atim, Chris. 1998. "Contribution of Mutual Health Organizations to Financing, Delivery and Access to Health Care: Synthesis of Research in Nine West and Central African Countries." Technical Report 18, Partnerships for Health Reform Project, Bethesda, MD.

Baeza, Christian. 1998. "Tacking Stock of Health Reform in Latin America." Latin American Center for Health Systems Research, Santiago de Chile.

Barrientos, Armando. 2000. "Getting Better after Neo-Liberalism—Shifts and Challenges of Health Policy in Chile." In *Healthcare Reform and Poverty in Latin America,* ed. Peter Lloyd-Sherlock, 94–111. London: Instituto de Estudios Iberoamericanos.

Barrientos, Armando, and Peter Lloyd-Sherlock. 2003. "Health Insurance Reforms in Latin America: Cream Skimming, Equity and Cost Containment," In *Social Policy Reform and Market Governance in Latin America,* ed. Louise Haagh and Camilla T. Helgo, 183–99. London: MacMillan.

Bennett, Sara, and Lucy Gilson. 2001. "Health Financing—Designing and Implementing Pro-Poor Policies." Department for International Development (DFID), Health Systems Resource Centre, London.

Bennett, Sara, Andrew Creese, and Roeland Monasch. 1998. "Health Insurance Schemes for People Outside Formal Sector Employment." ARA Paper 16, World Health Organization, Geneva.

Bloom, Gerald, and Tang Shenglan. 1999. "Rural Health Prepayment Schemes in China: Toward a More Active Role for Government." *Social Science and Medicine* 48:951–60.

Campbell, Paul, Karen Quigley, Pano Yeracaris, and Chaora MacDonald. 2000. "Applying Managed Care Concepts and Tools to Middle- and Lower-Income Countries: The Case of Medical Aid Societies in Zimbabwe." Publication 84, Data for Decision Making Project, School of Public Health, Harvard University, Boston, MA.

Carrin, Guy, Maarten Desmet, Robert Basaza. 2001. "Social Health Insurance Development in Low-Income Developing Countries: New Roles for Government and Nonprofit

Health Insurance Organizations." In *Building Social Security: The Challenge for Privatization,* 125–56. Geneva: International Social Security Association.

Central Bank of Jordan (1998): Annual Economic Report 1998. Amman.

Colombo, Francesca, and Nicole Tapay. 2004. "Private Health Insurance in OECD Countries: The Benefits and Costs for Individuals and Health Systems." OECD Health Working Paper 15, Organisation for Economic Co-operation and Development, Paris.

Concertation. 2004. "Inventaire des système d'assurance maladie en Afrique: Synthèse des travaux de recherche dans 11 pays." Dakar, Senegal: La Concertation.

Criel, Bart. 1998. *District-Based Health Insurance in Sub-Saharan Africa. Part II: Case-Studies.* Studies in Health Services Organization and Policy 10. Antwerp: ITG Press.

Criel, Bart, Patrick Van der Stuyft, and Wim Van Lergerghe. 1999. "The Bwamanda Hospital Insurance Scheme: Effective for Whom? A Study of Its Impact on Hospital Utilization Patterns." *Social Science and Medicine* 48:897–911.

Cruz-Saco, Maria Amparo. 2002. "Global Insurance Companies and the Privatisation of Pensions and Health Care in Latin America: The Case of Peru." Paper presented at the Globalism and Social Policy Programme (GASPP), Seminar 5, Dubrovnik, September 26–28, 2002.

DeRoeck, Denise, and Ann Levin. 1998. "Review of Financing of Immunization Programs in Developing and Transitional Countries." Special Initiatives Report 12, Partnerships for Health Reform (PHR), Bethesda, MD.

Desmet, Maarten, A.Q. Chowdhury, and K. Islam. 1999. "The Potential for Social Mobilisation in Bangladesh: The Organisation and Functioning of Two Health Insurance Schemes." *Social Science and Medicine* 48:925–38.

Dixon, Anna, Jack Lagenbrunner, Elias Mossialos. 2004. "Facing the Challenges of Health Care Financing." In *Health Systems in Transition: Learning from Experience,* ed. European Observatory on Health Systems and Policies. Copenhagen: World Health Organization.

Dror, David M., and Christian Jacquier. 1999. "Micro-Insurance: Extending Health Insurance to the Excluded." *International Social Security Review* 52 (1): 71–97.

Dror, David M., and Alexander S. Preker, eds. 2002. *Social Re-Insurance: A New Approach to Sustainable Community Health Financing.* Washington, DC, and Geneva: World Bank/International Labour Office.

EOHCS (European Observatory on Health Care Systems). 2004a. "Health Care Systems in Transition—Azerbaijan." EOHCS, Brussels.

———. 2004b. "Health Care Systems in Transition—Hungary." EOHCS, Brussels.

———. 2003. "Health Care Systems in Transition—Russian Federation." EOHCS, Brussels.

———. 2002a. "Health Care Systems in Transition—Albania." EOHCS, Brussels.

———. 2002b. "Health Care Systems in Transition—Georgia." EOHCS, Brussels.

———. 2002c. "Health Care Systems in Transition—Republic of Moldova." EOHCS, Brussels.

———. 2002d. "Health Care Systems in Transition—Turkey." EOHCS, Brussels.

———. 2001. "Health Care Systems in Transition—Latvia." EOHCS, Brussels.

———. 2000a. "Health Care Systems in Transition—Estonia." EOHCS, Brussels.

———. 2000b. "Health Care Systems in Transition—Romania." EOHCS, Brussels.

———. 1999a. "Health Care Systems in Transition—Albania." EOHCS, Brussels.

———. 1997. "Health Care Systems in Transition—Belarus." EOHCS, Brussels.

———. 1996. "Health Care Systems in Transition—Republic of Moldova." EOHCS, Brussels.

Ernst & Young. 2003. "Health Care Systems and Health Market Reform in the G-20 Countries." Paper prepared for the World Economic Forum, Geneva.

EU (European Union). 2004. "Country Report: Morocco." Staff Working Paper, COM (2004)373, EU Commission, Brussels.

HSRC (Human Science Research Council of South Africa). 2003. "Botswana." Report, HSCR, Pretoria.

Ginneken, Wouter van. 1999. "Overcoming Social Exclusion." In *Social Security for the Excluded Majority: Case Studies of Developing Countries*, ed. Wouter van Ginneken, 1–36. Geneva: International Labour Organization.

Greft Abdeljalil, Alami. 2002. "Compulsory Health Insurance at the Heart of the Debate in Morocco." Proceedings of the AIM International Conference, "Universalization of Medical Coverage and Action by Mutual Health Insurance Bodies," Marrakech, October 18.

GTZ (German Agency for Technical Cooperation). 2003. "Developing Health Insurance in Cambodia." Report of the Appraisal Mission, Gesellschaft für Technische Zusammenarbeit, Eshborn.

Gumber, Anil. 2001. "Hedging the Health of the Poor: The Case for Community Financing in India." Health Nutrition and Population Working Paper 28875, World Bank, Washington, DC.

Gupta, Sanjeev, Marjin Verhoeven, and Erwin Tiongson. 2001. Public Spending on Health Care and the Poor. IMF Working Paper No. WP/01/127, International Monetary Fund, Washington, DC.

ILO (International Labour Organization). 2000. "Health Care: The Key to Decent Work?" *World Labour Report 2000*. Geneva: ILO.

Iriart, Celia, Emerson Elías Merhy, and Howard Waitzkin. 2001. "Managed Care in Latin America: The New Common Sense in Health Policy Reform." *Social Science and Medicine* 52 (8): 1243–53.

IPHM (2004): An Overview of Private Health Insurance in the Philippines, Institute of Public Health Management, Quezon City, Philippines.

Jack, William. 2000. "The Evolution of Health Insurance Institutions: Theory and Four Examples from Latin America." Background paper for David de Ferranti, Guillermo E. Perry, Indermit S. Gill, Luis Servén (2000): Securing our Future in a Global Economy, Development Economics Research Group, World Bank, Washington, DC.

Jost, Timothy Stolzfus. 2001. "Private or Public Approaches to Insuring the Uninsured: Lessons from International Experience with Private Insurance. *New York University Law Review* 76:419–92.

Jütting, Johannes P. 2005. *Health Insurance for the Poor in Developing Countries. Burlington,* VT: Ashgate.

———. 2004. "Do community based health insurance schemes improve poor people's access to health care? Evidence from rural Senegal." *World Development* 32(2): 273–88.

Khaleghian, Peyvand. 2004. "Decentralization and Public Services: The Case of Immunization." *Social Science and Medicine* 59(1): 163–83.

Khetrapal Singh, Poonam. 2002. "Effective Health Care: The Role of Government, Market and Civil Society." *Regional Health Forum* 6 (1): 7–21 WHO South East Asia Region.

Kiwara, Angwar Denis. 1999. "Health Insurance for the Informal Sector in the Republic of Tanzania." In Ginneken (1999): 117–44.

Kumaranayake, Lilani. 1998. "Effective Regulation of Private Sector Health Service Providers." Working Paper, prepared for the World Bank Mediterranean Development Forum II, Marrakech, September 3–6.

Mahal, Ajay. 2002. "Health Policy Challenges for India: Private Health Insurance and Lessons from the International Experience." In *Trade, Finance and Investment in South Asia*, ed. T.N. Srinivasan, 417–76. New Delhi: Social Science Press.

Mehrotra, Santosh, and Enrique Delamonica. 2005. "Public Spending for the Poor: Getting the Fundamentals Right in Social and Macroeconomic Policy." http://www.gaspp.org/seminars/papers/7/smehrotra.pdf.

Mesa-Lago, Carmelo. 1991. "Social Security in Latin America and the Caribbean: A Comparative Assessment." In *Social Security in Developing Countries*, ed. Ehtisham Ahmad, Jean Dreze, John Hills, and Amartya Sen. 356–94 . London: Oxford University Press.

Musgrove, Philip, Riadh Zeramdini, and Guy Carrin. 2002. "Basic Patterns in National Health Expenditure." Special Theme: Commission on Macroeconomics and Health. *Bulletin of the World Health Organization* 80 (2): 134–46.

NHA Jordan. 2000. Jordan National Health Accounts, Partnerships for Health Reform (PHR) Project, Technical Paper No. 49, PHR, Bethesda, MD.

NHA Iran. 1998. Iran National Health Accounts, World Bank, Washington, DC.

NHA Lebanon. 2000. Lebanon National Health Accounts, World Health Organization / Jordan Ministry of Health /World Bank,Walid Ammar, Hisham Fakha, Rita Freiha Khoury, Charbel Mattar, Maher Halabi, Doried Aoudat, Khaled Srour, A.K. Nandakumar, Abdel Hay Mechbal, WHO, Geneva.

NHA Morocco. 2001. Morocco National Health Accounts 1997/98, Partnerships for Health Reform (PHR) Project, Special Initiatives Report No. 37, various authors, PHR, Bethesda, MD.

NHA Tunisia. 2004. National Health Accounts Tunisia 2000, Arfa Chokri and Achour Noureddine, Ministry of Public Health and National Institute of Public Health, Tunisia.

Nitayarumphong, Sanguan, and Anne Mills. 1998. "Achieving Universal Coverage of Health Care." Bangkok: Office of Health Care Reform, Ministry of Public Health.

Nitayarumphong, Sanguan, and Supasit Pannarunothai. 1998. "Achieving Universal Coverage of Health Care Through Health Insurance: The Thai Situation." In *Achieving Universal Coverage of Health Care*, ed. Sanguan Nitayarumphong and Anne Mills, 258–80. Bangkok: Office of Health Care Reform, Ministry of Public Health,

OECD. 2004a."Proposal for a Taxonomy of Health Insurance." OECD Study on Private Health Insurance, OECD, Paris, June.

OECD. 2004b. "Private Health Insurance in OECD Countries: Policy Brief," *OECD Observer,* September 2004.

Okello, Francis, and Frank Feeley. 2004. "Socioeconomic Characteristics of Enrollees in Community Health Insurance Schemes in Africa." CMS Country Research Series, No. 15, Commercial Market Strategies, Washington DC.

PAHO (Pan American Health Organization). 1999. "Uruguay: Profile of Health Service System." Washington, DC: PAHO, August 30.

Penn World Table 6.1 (2004): Center for International Comparisons at the University of Pennsylvania. http://pwt.econ.upenn.edu/Downloads/pwt61.csv.

Pereira, Joseph Michael. 2005. "Booming South Asian Insurance Market." *DAWN Newspaper*. http://www.dawn.com/2005/03/21/ebr9.htm; accessed March 21.

Phelps, Charles. 1997. *Health Economics*. New York: Addison-Wesley.

PHR (Partnerships for Health Reform). 1998. "National Health Accounts: Summaries of Eight National Studies in Latin America and the Caribbean." Special Initiatives Report 7, PHR, Bethesda, MD.

Preker, Alexander S., and Guy Carrin. 2004. *Health Financing for Poor People: Resource Mobilization and Risk Sharing*. Washington, DC: World Bank.

Preker, Alexander S., Jack Langenbrunner, and Melitta Jakab. 2002. "Rich-Poor Differences in Health Care Financing." In Dror and Preker (2002), 21–36.

Ron, Aviva. 1999. "NGOs in Community Health Insurance Schemes: Examples from Guatemala and the Philippines." *Social Science and Medicine* 48:939–50.

Salazar, Camilo J. 1999. "Foreign Insurance Investors in Latin America: Can They All Survive and Prosper?" *Woodrow Milliman Insurance International* Winter 1999: 5–8.

Savedoff, William. 2004. "Is There a Case For Social Insurance?" *Health Policy and Planning* 19 (3): 183–84.

Sbarbaro, John A. 2000. "Trade Liberalization in Health Insurance: Opportunities and Challenges—The Potential Impact of Introducing or Expanding the Availability of Private Health Insurance within Low- and Middle-Income Countries," CHH Working Paper WG 4:6, Commission on Macroeconomics and Health, WHO, Geneva.

Scott-Herridge, Richard. 2002. "Decentralisation—Does it Deliver Good Governance and Improved Services? The Experience of Uganda." Occasional Paper Series, No. 10, African Studies Centre, Leiden, Netherlands.

Sekhri, Neelam, and William Savedoff. 2005. "Private Health Insurance: Implications for Developing Countries." *Bulletin of the World Health Organization* 83 (2): 127–38.

Sekhri, Neelam, William Savedoff, and Shivani Tripathi. 2004. "Regulating Private Insurance to Serve the Public Interest: Policy Issues for Developing Countries." Paper presented at the Economic Research Forum 11th Annual Conference, Beirut, December 14–16.

Statistics Indonesia. 2001. National Socioeconomic Surveys (Susenas). Jakarta.

Stocker, Karen, Howard Waitzkin, and Celia Iriart. 1999. "The Exportation of Managed Care to Latin America." *New England Journal of Medicine* 340 (14): 1131–36.

Supakankunti, Siripen. 2000. "Future Prospects of Voluntary Health Insurance in Thailand." *Health Policy and Planning* 15 (1): 85–94.

Swiss Re (Swiss Re-Insurance Company). 2005. "World Insurance in 2003: Insurance Industry on the Road to Recovery." Statistical Appendix, update February 2005. *Sigma* 3 (2004).

———. 2004a. "World Insurance in 2003: Insurance Industry on the Road to Recovery." *Sigma* 3 (2004).

———. 2004b. "Exploiting the Growth Potential of Emerging Insurance Markets: China and India in the Spotlight." *Sigma* 5 (2004).

———. 2003. "Asia's Non–life Insurance Markets: Recent Developments and the Evolving Corporate Landscape." *Sigma* 6 (2003).

———. 2002. "Insurance in Latin America: Growth Opportunities and the Challenge to Increase Profitability." *Sigma*. 2 (2002).

———. 1998. "Life and Health Insurance in the Emerging Markets: Assessment, Reforms, and Perspectives." *Sigma*. 1 (1998).

Tine, Justine. 2000. "Les mutuelles de santé rurales de la région de Thiès au Sénégal—des initiatives communautaires pour améliorer l'accès aux soins de santé." Center for Development Research (ZEF), Bonn.

Thomson, Sarah, and Elias Mossialos. 2004. "Private Health Insurance and Access to Health Care in the European Union." *Euro Observer* 6 (1): 1–4.

UNDP (United Nations Development Programme). 2004. *Human Development Report—Cultural Liberty in Today's Diverse World*. New York: UNDP.

UNFPA (United Nations Population Fund). 2003. "Country Profiles for Population and Reproductive Health: Policy Developments and Indicators 2003." UNFPA, New York.

U.S. Department of Commerce. 2000. "Health and Medical Services." In *U.S. Industry & Trade Outlook 2000*, chapter 43. Washington, DC: U.S. Department of Commerce.

U.S.-Saudi-Arabian Business Council. 2004. "The Medical Sector in the Kingdom of Saudi Arabia," Washington, DC.

U.S. Vietnam Trade Council. 2003. "Foreign Broker Breaks Open Local Market." NewsUpdate, June 2–8, 2003, http://www.usvtc.org/News/2003/June%2003/foreign_broker_breaks_open_local.htm.

WHO. 2005. *World Health Report 2005*. Statistical Annex, table 5, "Selected National Health Accounts Indicators: Measured Levels of Expenditure on Health, 1998–2002." Geneva: WHO.

———. 2004a. *World Health Report 2003*. Statistical Annex, table 5, "Selected National Health Accounts Indicators: Measured Levels of Expenditure on Health, 1997–2001." Geneva: WHO.

———. 2004b. "Health Systems Development and Financing." Health Sector Development, online publication, http://www.wpro.who.int/pdf/rcm55/rd/11_HSD_1.pdf.

———. 2004c. "Regional Overview of Social Health Insurance in South East Asia," WHO, New Delhi.

———. 2001a. *Report of Commission on Macroeconomics and Health on Investing in Health for Economic Development*. Geneva: WHO.

———. 2001b. "Expenditures from National Health Accounts, 2001." WHO, Geneva.

———. 2000. *World Health Report 2000*. Geneva: WHO.

———. 1999. National Health Accounts, http://www.who.intnha/en/.

Wiesmann, Doris, and Johannes Jütting. 2000. "The Emerging Movement of Community-Based Health Insurance in Sub-Saharan Africa: Experiences and Lessons Learned." *Afrika Spektrum* 35 (2): 193–210.

Xu, Ke, David Evans, Kei Kawabata, Riadh Zeramdini, Jan Klavus, and Christopher Murray. 2003. "Household Catastrophic Health Expenditure: A Multicountry Analysis." *Lancet* 362 (9378): 111–17.

CHAPTER 3

From Theory to Practice

Peter Zweifel

The economic theory of the demand for insurance was pioneered by Arrow (1965) forty years ago, that of the demand for health insurance, about thirty years ago (Keeler, Newhouse, and Phelps, 1977).[1] However, the reasons for consumers to opt for community-based health insurance or public health insurance (two popular institutional arrangements in lower-income countries) have been much less researched. Moreover, empirical evidence concerning the determinants of health insurance demand has been slow to accumulate outside the United States. Now with all its importance, the demand for insurance coverage is one thing. Whether and to what extent it is met also depends on supply, viz. the behavior of insurers. Here, the gaps in knowledge are even more glaring. The behavior of U.S. for-profit insurers has been studied by Cummins and colleagues (Cummins and Sommer 1996). However, much less is known about for-profit health insurers, let alone not-for-profit, community-based, and public health insurers.[2] Needless to say, empirical evidence is just about nonexistent here.

INTRODUCTION

It was against this background that Pauly and Zweifel (2007, chaps. 2 to 4) were commissioned by the World Bank to lay out the theoretical groundwork for the volume *Private Voluntary Health Insurance in Development: Friend or Foe?* (Preker, Scheffler, and Bassett 2007). They had to draw not only on the received theory of demand for insurance, but in particular of industrial organization (the analysis of phenomena such as cartels, barriers to entry and exit, and mergers and acquisitions that characterize only partially competitive markets) in order to assess the potential of voluntary private health insurance in low-income coutries. Moreover, barriers to entry (as an example) crucially depend on institional detail that varies between countries and about which the authors knew little. For this reason, their theoretical predictions and conclusions were in need of empirical verification.

The objective of this chapter is therefore to check whether the theoretical predictions formulated by Pauly and Zweifel agree with available empirical evidence. This evidence comes from a subset of the country studies contained in the present volume. The countries and areas covered range from Brazil, the Arab Republic of Egypt, on to Sub-Saharan Africa, and the Republic of Korea. This endeavor is motivated by the fact that Pauly (2007, chap. 2) and especially

Zweifel (2007, chap. 3) had to develop theory largely on their own. After all, not much is known about the behavior of insurers, let alone specifically health insurers, and even less about community-based insurers that are prevalent in some African and Asian countries. Therefore, there was a considerable risk of formulating theoretical predictions that would not be confirmed by empirical evidence, creating the risk of providing wrong guidance to policy makers.

When the contributions by Pauly and Zweifel were published in 2007, the country reports had not yet been written. Since then, they have become available, creating the opportunity for testing in this volume. However, this testing necessarily will be partial and incomplete. The country reports emphasize certain features while neglecting others that would have been of theoretical interest. Therefore, not all hypotheses could be confronted with the evidence.

This chapter is structured as follows. First, it contains a review of the theoretical predictions. While this entails a degree of repetition of previously published material, it serves to make the chapter self-contained. Predictions range from the determinants of demand for health insurance (yes/no, amount and premium risk insurance, also known as guaranteed renewability) to the behavior of health insurers who decide about the size of the benefits package, risk-selection effort, and the net price of insurance (the loading). Other dimensions of supply are insurer-driven vertical integration, provider-driven vertical integration, the degree of concentration in the health insurance market, and the intensity of health insurance regulation. A total of 30 hypotheses can be distilled from this theoretical groundwork, paving the way for a juxtaposition of predictions and available evidence from the country studies. No attempt will be made at weighting the favorable and unfavorable outcomes, for example, by the size of the country. Therefore, the evidence from China, for example, will be given the same weight as that coming from small Slovenia. Finally, some conclusions and an outlook pointing out areas of future research are presented.

REVIEW OF THE THEORETICAL PREDICTIONS

This section contains a selection of the hypotheses that were formulated by Pauly and Zweifel. It starts with those relating to the determinants of demand for health insurance under different market conditions (private health insurance in a competitive market, private health insurance in low-income countries, community-based, and public in low-income countries). It then turns to the hypotheses relating to supply, that is, the behavior of health insurers. Finally, a few predictions concerning the factors influencing health insurance regulation are presented.

Demand-Side Factors

A first set of predictions refers to the demand for health insurance. Table 3.1 is based on Pauly (2007, chap. 2). For instance, increased variability of health care expenditure (HCE) is hypothesized to increase the likelihood of purchasing

TABLE 3.1 Factors Affecting Demand for Health Insurance (Yes/No Decision)

Factor	Private insurance (competitive market)	Private insurance (in LICs)	Community-based insurance (CBI)	Public insurance (in LICs)	Hypothesis to be tested
Variability of HCE	+	+ ↑	+ ↓	+ (n.a.)	xx
Risk aversion	+	+ ↑	+	+ (n.a.)	xx
Loading[a]	–	–	–	– (n.a.)	D1
Adverse selection	–	– ↑	– ↑	n.a.	xx
Reserves	+	+	+ ↑	+ (n.a.)	xx
Income[b]	+	+	+ ↓	+/– (n.a.)	D2
Lack of information[c]	–	–	– ↓	– (n.a.)	D3
Distrust of insurers	–	– ↑	– ↑	– (n.a.)	xx
No quid pro quo	–	– ↑	– ↑	– (n.a.)	xx

Source: Pauly 2007, chap. 2.

Note: LICs = low-income countries; HCE = health care expenditure; + = factor increases demand; – = factor decreases demand; ↑ = reinforcement of effect; ↓ = weakening of effect; n.a. = not applicable; xx = not retained for testing

a. The loading is the true price of insurance; see supply factors below.

b. Includes Hyman's hypothesis that income is largely irrelevant if health insurance gives access to life-saving technologies.

c. Includes ambiguity w.r.t. probabilities.

health insurance. This prediction is not applicable (n.a.), however, in the case of public insurance, which is mandatory as a rule.

Hypotheses D1 to D3 are selected for testing in view of their particular relevance. Here, three *dimensions* are distinguished. The first (hypotheses D1 to D3) relates to the yes/no decision of whether to purchase insurance coverage at all. The second (D4 to D5) revolves around the amount of coverage demanded, while the third (D6 to D7) concerns the demand for insuring *premium risk* (the risk of having a permanently lower health status in the future), also known as demand for guaranteed renewability (GR).

Demand Hypothesis 1 (D1)

With an increased loading contained in the premium, consumers are less likely to opt for coverage. The loading being the true price of insurance (note that benefits are paid back to consumers on expectation), a higher loading ultimately results in consumers going without health insurance.

Demand Hypothesis 2 (D2)

With higher income, the likelihood of having health insurance increases. This prediction follows from the fact that with higher income, wealth and assets that need to be protected also increase. In the case of health insurance, the asset is human rather than tangible capital. However, it is still true that higher income reflects a higher stock of health capital, which induces more demand for insurance coverage.

TABLE 3.2 Factors Affecting Demand for Health Insurance (Amount of Coverage)

Factor	*Private insurance (competitive market)*	*Private insurance (in LICs)*	*Community-based insurance (CBI)*	*Public insurance (in LICs)*	*Hypothesis to be tested*
Variability of HCE[a]	+	+ ↑	+	+ (n.a.)	xx
Risk aversion	+	+ ↑	+	+ (n.a.)	xx
Loading[b]	−	−	−	− (n.a.)	D4
Adverse selection	+/−	+/− ↑	− ↑	n.a.	D5
Reserves	+/−	+/− ↑	−	+ (n.a.)	xx
Income[c]	+	+	+	+	xx
Lack of information[d]	−	−	−	− (n.a.) ↓	xx
Distrust of insurers	−	− ↑	− ↓	− (n.a.) ↓	xx
No quid pro quo	−	− ↑	−	− (n.a.)	xx

Source: Pauly 2007, chap. 2.

Note: LICs = low-income countries; HCE = health care expenditure; + = factor increases demand; − = factor decreases demand; ↑ = reinforcement of effect; ↓ = weakening of effect; n.a. = not applicable; xx = not retained for testing.

a. Includes moral hazard, demand- and supply-side cost sharing.

b. The loading is the true price of insurance; see supply factors below.

c. Includes Hyman's hypothesis that income is largely irrelevant if health insurance gives access to life-saving technologies.

d. Includes ambiguity w.r.t. probabilities.

Demand Hypothesis 3 (D3)

With a more marked lack of information, the tendency to sign up for voluntary health insurance decreases. Lack of information (for example, because contracts are not specified sufficiently clearly) amounts to a nonfinancial barrier that consumers must surmount, making the purchase of voluntary health insurance less likely.

Another dimension of health insurance demand is the amount of coverage. As before, table 3.2 distills the arguments proffered by Pauly (2007, chap. 2). Hypotheses D4 and D5 present statements of particular relevance for policy.

Demand Hypothesis 4 (D4)

The higher the loading, the smaller the amount of coverage demanded. Again this is a standard price effect. One way to save on insurance that has become more expensive is to curtail coverage.

Demand Hypothesis 5 (D5)

The more adverse selection effort, the smaller is the amount of coverage. Here, the supplier of insurance indirectly has an influence. When there is substantial risk of adverse selection (that is, insurers are afraid of attracting high risks), consumers have a strong incentive to signal that they are low risk. The literature predicts that one way to send such a signal is to sign up for less complete insurance coverage. Typically, the low risks prefer cost sharing in return for a lower premium.

TABLE 3.3 Factors Affecting Demand for Health Insurance (Guaranteed Renewability)

Factor	*Private insurance (competitive market)*	*Private Insurance (in LICs)*	*Community-based Insurance (CBI)*	*Public Insurance (in LICs)*	*Hypothesis to be tested*
Variability of HCE	+	+	+	n.a.	xx
Risk aversion	+	+	+	n.a.	xx
Loading[a]	+	+	+	n.a.	xx
Adverse selection	+	+	+	n.a.	D6
Reserves	+	+	+	n.a.	xx
Income[b]	+	+	+	n.a.	xx
Lack of information[c]	+	+	+	+ (n.a.)	D7
Distrust of insurers	–	–	–	– (n.a.)	xx
No quid pro quo	–	–	– ↑	– (n.a.) ↑	xx

Source: Pauly 2007, chap. 2.

Note: LICs = low-income countries; HCE = health care expenditure; + = factor increases demand; – = factor decreases demand; ↑ = reinforcement of effect; ↓ = weakening of effect; n.a. = not applicable; xx = not retained for testing.

a. The loading is the true price of insurance; see supply factors below.

b. Includes Hyman's hypothesis that income is largely irrelevant if health insurance gives access to life-saving technologies

c. Includes ambiguity w.r.t. probabilities

However, there may be also a more direct supply influence. Insurers who fear adverse selection seek to limit their financial exposure. Indeed, it is one thing to attract a high risk having full coverage and another, having limited coverage. Therefore insurers seek to limit coverage, in the presence of the data.

One very important aspect of demand is that in voluntary health insurance, there is a *premium risk*, viz. the possibility of someone's becoming a high risk in the future and thus having to pay a higher premium. While a standard health insurance contract does not cover premium risk, in fact many private insurers offer so-called *guaranteed renewability* (GR). Demand for the GR feature, however, also depends on circumstances. Table 3.3 lists the arguments (if any) made in Pauly (2007, chap. 2). The hypotheses retained for testing are the following two.

Demand Hypothesis 6 (D6)

The more there is adverse selection, the greater is demand for guaranteed renewability. This prediction follows from the argument that, when insurers seek to protect themselves against the enrolment of high risks, becoming a high risk in the future poses more of a problem to consumers. Therefore, there is increased willingness-to-pay for GR.

Demand Hypothesis 7 (D7)

The less information a market has, the greater is demand for guaranteed renewability. When contract clauses are opaque, consumers conceive of health insurance as an experience good or even credence good (whose quality may never be learned).

The only chance to find out whether the insurer actually delivers payment as promised is over time. To be able to benefit from this learning effect, it is very important to have GR.

Supply-Side Factors

Five dimensions of supply are considered in this section: the size of the benefits package, the amount of risk-selection effort, the loading, and factors affecting vertical integration (both insurer-driven and provider-driven), and the degree of seller concentration.

Factors Affecting the Size of the Benefits Package

The factors influencing the size of the benefits package are listed in table 3.4, taken from Zweifel, Krey, and Tagli (2007, chap. 3). The following four hypotheses may be of special interest.

Supply Hypothesis 1 (S1)

The more marked the moral hazard effects, the smaller is the size of the benefits package. This hypothesis follows from the consideration that each item in the benefits list induces a change in the insured's behavior. The more such items there are, the greater is the total effect of moral hazard on the insurer.

Supply Hypothesis 2 (S2)

The greater the diversity of preferences, the greater is the size of the benefits package. A competitive health insurer needs to structure products according to the preferences of consumers. Therefore, if consumers have diverse preferences, insurers

TABLE 3.4 Factors Affecting the Size of the Benefits Package

Factor	*Private insurance (competitive market)*	*Private insurance (in LICs)*	*Community-based insurance (CBI)*	*Public insurance (in LICs)*	*Hypothesis to be tested*
Risk aversion of insurer	+/−	+/− ↑	+/− ↓	n.a.	xx
Synergies among benefits	+	+	+ ↓	n.a.	xx
Moral hazard	−	− ↓	− ↓	− ↑	S1
Diversity of preferences	+	+ ↓	+ ↓	+ ↓	S2
Diversity of risks	+	+ ↓	+ ↓	+ ↓	xx
Emergence of new health risks	+	+ ↓	+ ↓	+ ↑	S4
Regulation	+	+	+	+ ↑	S4
Fraud and abuse	−	−	− ↑	− ↓	xx

Source: Zweifel, Krey, and Tagli 2007, chap. 3.

Note: LICs = low-income countries; HCE = health care expenditure; + = factor increases benefits package; − = factor decreases benefits package; ↑ = reinforcement of effect; ↓ = weakening of effect; n.a. = not applicable; xx = not retained for testing.

must offer benefits packages that appeal to a wide enough class of consumers for their business to become financially viable. Hence, diverse consumer preferences cause the benefits package to be more comprehensive. The same argument applies to the diversity of risks. However, it is very difficult to distinguish between diversity of risks and diversity of preferences using market observations. Therefore, risk diversity will not be tested separately.

Supply Hypothesis 3 (S3)

With the emergence of a new health risk, the size of the benefits package is predicted to increase. This is a natural response by any insurer, since new risks mean new business. However, in this context the conditional prediction is of particular interest, viz. that private insurance companies in LICs will have reason to react less markedly to such new business. They simply lack the financial reserves to deal with the new risk unless it diversifies well with existing ones (in that its incidence is negatively correlated with the incidence of already covered risk, a rather rare event).

Supply Hypothesis 4 (S4)

Regulation serves to increase the size of the benefits package. Absent regulation, a voluntary health insurer will carefully consider the extent to which inclusion of a new item in the benefits package has a diversification effect. For example, adding ambulatory coverage to a contract originally limited to hospital care is risky business if the tendency of the insured is to use both ambulatory and hospital care in the course of an illness episode. Conversely, adding ambulatory care may be attractive if it frequently substitutes for hospital care, inducing negative correlation between the two lines of business. Regulation typically aims at bringing more consumers under the purview of health insurance, the ultimate objective of government being to obtain more votes. To achieve this, regulation tends to offer just about everyone something, not least by increasing the size of the benefits package.

Risk-Selection Effort

Here, the argument again follows Zweifel, Krey, and Tagli (2007, chap. 3). In table 3.5, the n.a. entries for both private and public insurance should be noted. In the first case, a truly competitive, unregulated insurer would apply marginal cost pricing. However, the marginal cost of an additional enrollee is nothing but the future expected HCE that must be paid (including a loading for administrative expense, risk bearing, and profit). In this event, a high risk is charged a high premium, whereas a low risk contributes a low premium. There is no incentive for risk selection [see Zweifel and Breuer (2006) for details]. In the second case, public insurance typically is organized as a monopoly, obviating risk-selection issues. The four retained hypotheses concerning the determinants of risk-selection effort exerted by health insurers are listed in table 3.5.

TABLE 3.5 Factors Affecting Risk-Selection Effort

Factor	*Private insurance (competitive market)*	*Private insurance (in LICs)*	*Community-based insurance (CBI)*	*Public insurance (in LICs)*	*Hypothesis to be tested*
Risk aversion of insurer	+ (n.a.)	+ ↑	+ ↑	n.a.	xx
Moral hazard	+ (n.a.)	+ ↓	+ ↓	n.a.	S5
Size of the benefits package	+ (n.a.)	+	+ ↑	n.a.	S6
Diversity of risks	+ (n.a.)	+	+ ↓	n.a.	xx
Access to risk information	+ (n.a.)	+ ↓	+ ↓	n.a.	xx
Sellers' concentration	− (n.a.)	−	− ↑	n.a.	S7
Regulation	+ (n.a.)	+	+	n.a.	S8

Source: Zweifel, Krey, and Tagli 2007, chap. 3.

Note: LICs = low-income countries; HCE = health care expenditure; + = factor increases effort; − = factor decreases effort; ↑ = reinforcement of effect; ↓ = weakening of effect; n.a. = not applicable; xx = not retained for testing.

Supply Hypothesis 5 (S5)

The more marked moral hazard effects, the greater risk-selection effort. The main driver of risk-selection efforts is premium regulation (see below). Given that premiums are not allowed to reflect true risk, however, moral hazard effects put the insurer at greater financial risk because health care expenditure (HCE) to be paid increases. Therefore, in the presence of marked moral hazard effects, risk-selection effort designed to avoid high risks is predicted to be high.

Supply Hypothesis 6 (S6)

The more comprehensive the benefits package, the greater is the risk-selection effort. When the set of medical procedures covered is comprehensive, whether a consumer is a high risk matters more. Therefore risk selection pays off more.

Supply Hypothesis 7 (S7)

The greater seller concentration, the smaller is the risk-selection effort. To see this argument, consider a highly concentrated market consisting of only two health insurance sellers, A and B. Let A successfully stave off high risks. These high risks necessarily end up with B, who is assumed to be unable to grade premiums to risk. Therefore, B must increase premiums across the board to remain financially viable. This in turn makes A even more attractive to low risks, possibly triggering a death spiral. However, when B becomes insolvent in the end, the uninsured risks will return to A. Therefore, provided that the planning horizon of the two insurers is long enough, neither will engage in risk selection. By way of contrast, if the market consists of 100 insurers, each one of them can expect to be able to dump unfavorable risk on the 99 others, causing risk selection to be attractive.

Supply Hypothesis 8 (S8)

With more comprehensive regulation, there will be more risk-selection effort. Absent premium regulation, premiums will reflect risk. As argued above, this is a simple application of the rule that prices most reflect marginal cost; after all, marginal cost in the present context is nothing but the future expected HCE of an additional enrollee. However, as soon as premiums are regulated, and especially if they are uniform, risk selection pays off. Consider a health insurer who need not even be for-profit. It will always have high risks on its books, namely, persons whose HCE exceeds the uniform premium. Absent regulation, that person would pay a high premium, reflecting high future expected HCE. Given regulation, however, the insurer incurs a net loss when enrolling such a person. To make up for it, there absolutely must be low risks in the enrolled population, that is, risks whose HCE falls short of the premium. It only takes the assumption of risk aversion to conclude that more low risks are still better, establishing the incentive to "skim the cream." However, this incentive is regulation-induced.

Loading Contained in the Premium

As argued above, the loading constitutes the net price of insurance coverage. The determinants of the net price of insurance are listed in table 3.6, taken from Zweifel, Krey, and Tagli (2007, chap. 3). The following four hypotheses will be tested.

TABLE 3.6 Factors Affecting the Net Price of Insurance (Loading)

Factor	*Private insurance (competitive market)*	*Private insurance (in LICs)*	*Community-based insurance (CBI)*	*Public insurance (in LICs)*	*Hypothesis to be tested*
Administrative expenses, including capital charge	+	+	+ ↓	+	xx
Reinsurance	+/–	+/– ↑	+/– ↑	n.a.	S9
Pool size	+/–	+/–	+/–	–	xx
Benefits package	+	+	+	+	xx
Share of high-income members	+/–	+/– ↓	+/– ↓	+/–	S10
Copayments and caps	–	–	–	– ↓	S11
Moral hazard	+	+ ↓	+ ↓	+ ↑	xx
Quality and proximity of health care services	+	+ ↑	+	+	xx
Regulation	+/–	+/– ↑	+/– ↓	+/– ↑	S12
Fraud and abuse	+	+ ↑	+ ↓	+ ↑	xx

Source: Zweifel, Krey, and Tagli 2007, chap. 3.

Note: LICs = low-income countries; HCE = health care expenditure; + = factor increases loading; – = factor decreases loading; ↑ = reinforcement of effect; ↓ = weakening of effect; n.a. = not applicable; xx = not retained for testing.

Supply Hypothesis 9 (S9)

The net effect of reinsurance on the loading is ambiguous. The relationship between reinsurance and the net cost of insurance is of great practical interest. On the one hand, the reinsurance premium figures as a cost of business for the direct insurer. Therefore, it is part of the loading. On the other hand, reinsurance permits direct insurers to transfer part of their risk. However, compensation for risk bearing is part of the loading as well. If reinsurance arrangements were fully efficient, they would allow the loading contained in the premium to decrease. However, whether this is the case is an empirical issue to be tested.

Supply Hypothesis 10 (S10)

The impact of a high share of high-income members on the loading is ambiguous. High-income members in voluntary health insurance (and especially in CBI) give rise to ambiguous effects. To the extent that bad debts are an important component of the loading, high-income members contribute to a lowering of administrative expense and hence the loading because they are likely to pay their premiums on time. However, high-income consumers typically exert moral hazard effects. They have a taste for high-tech medicine. Moreover, they usually are urban dwellers who have easy access to hospitals and medical practitioners. Therefore, a health insurer with many high-income members may find its HCE high and rising, which also means more loading for administrative expense. Therefore, the net effect of high-income members on the loading is unclear, constituting a case where empirical evidence is needed to settle the issue.

Supply Hypothesis 11 (S11)

Copayments and a benefits cap on services covered serve to decrease the loading. It is clear that limitations of coverage must go along with a reduced premium. However, the feasible premium reduction exceeds the concomitant lowering of HCE to be borne by the health insurer. Along with HCE, the insurer also has to bear administrative expense for processing claims, and so on. Therefore, the decrease in premium should be more marked than the decrease in HCE, amounting to a reduced loading.

Supply Hypothesis 12 (S12)

Regulation has an ambiguous effect on the loading in health insurance. Again, this is a connection that cannot be sorted out theoretically. On one hand, regulation increases the cost of doing business, causing loadings to rise. On the other hand, quality regulation in particular may increase the size of the market. Therefore, reserves per unit of risk held can be reduced, which permits savings in terms of financial reserves held. This second effect results in lower loadings contained in premiums. The net effect is an open issue to be settled by empirical evidence.

Insurer-Driven Vertical Integration

Managed care (MC) has become quite popular in industrial countries, above all, the United States. The conception is that health insurers initiate vertical integration, meaning that health care providers accept restrictions on their freedom to do business in return for other advantages. For an example outside health, a manufacturer of computers may have on-site inspectors with the suppliers of its chips. By accepting this inspection, the chip manufacturer can possibly count not only on a higher sales price but also on a more lasting business relationship. In the extreme, the computer manufacturer may simply buy up the manufacturer of its chips. In health care, insurers can be seen as purchasers of health care services on behalf of their clientele. MC in particular calls on them to exert more influence on the provision of medical care. In return, they may bear the investment cost for building the practice or guarantee a certain patient flow to participating physicians, who accept restrictions designed to keep the cost of treatment down. The main hypotheses to be tested appear in table 3.7.

Supply Hypothesis 13 (S13)

The more contestable markets for health care services are, the more likely is insurer-driven vertical integration. Vertical integration requires insurers to organize medical manpower and clinics. However, if barriers to entry in health care service markets are high, it is costly to find service providers and hospital units to form a vertically integrated network. Insurers must therefore make do with what is available

TABLE 3.7 Factors Affecting Insurer-Driven Vertical Integration

Factor	*Private insurance (competitive market)*	*Private insurance (in LICs)*	*Community-based insurance (CBI)*	*Public insurance (in LICs)*	*Hypothesis to be tested*
Market power of the insurer	+	+ ↑	+ ↑	+	xx
System efficiency gains to be realized	+	+	+	+ ↓	xx
Management know-how of insurer	+	+	+	+	xx
Contestability of health care markets	+	+ ↓	+ ↓	+ ↓	S13
Potential to increase entry barriers for competitors	+	+	+	n.a.	xx
Contestability of health insurance market	−	− ↓	− ↓	n.a.	S14
Lack of capital of insurer	−	− ↑	− ↑	− ↑	xx
Opportunistic behavior and fraud on the part of insurers	−	− ↑	− ↓	− ↓	S15
Cartelization of service providers	−	−	− ↓	− ↓	xx
Legislation prohibiting vertical restraints	−	− ↓	− ↓	−	xx

Source: Zweifel, Krey, and Tagli 2007, chap. 3.

Note: LICs = low-income countries; HCE = health care expenditure; + = factor enhances integration; − = factor hampers integration; ↑ = reinforcement of effect; ↓ = weakening of effect; n.a. = not applicable; xx = not retained for testing.

on the market rather than being able to rely, for example, on foreign medical graduates or newly created (private) clinics. Conversely, their task is easier if entry barriers are low, that is, if markets for health care services are contestable.

Supply Hypothesis 14 (S14)

The more contestable markets for health insurers are, the less vertical integration will be observed. This prediction is the flip side of the coin. Health care providers are not willing to sign up for a contract limiting their freedom to conduct business as long as there are many competing health insurers with whom to strike contracts. Any one of these insurers runs the risk of their contractual partners' going elsewhere if trying to impose restrictions on providers.

Supply Hypothesis 15 (S15)

The more opportunistic the insurers' behavior, the less likely is vertical integration to succeed. For an insurer to find contractual partners, it must have a good reputation. Health care providers are hesitant to sign up with a partner that has a bad business reputation (for example, for not covering services that were believed to be covered by the insurance policy). Evidence of such opportunistic behavior poses a risk to participating physicians but also clinics in that they cannot be sure that the benefits from accepting vertical integration will materialize.

Provider-Driven Vertical Integration

The hypotheses concerning provider-driven vertical integration are listed in table 3.8, taken once more from Zweifel, Krey, and Tagli (2007, chap. 3). It may be worthwhile to recall that vertical integration historically did not initiate with health insurers but with health care providers. Indeed, BlueCross/BlueShield in the United States was created in the 1930s by hospitals that wanted to avoid bad debts during the depression. The hypotheses of particular interest are the following three.

Supply Hypothesis 16 (S16)

The more contestable markets for health insurance are, the more likely is provider-driven vertical integration. This is the analog to S13. If it is easy to find a newcomer to the market for health insurance, hospitals and possibly networks of physicians can add the insurance function to their service at low cost.

Supply Hypothesis 17 (S17)

The greater the market power of insurers, the less likely to succeed is provider-driven vertical integration. Especially in LICs, insurance markets are rather closed. In this situation, a high degree of market power on the part of health insurers makes it difficult for service providers to initiate vertical integration because the potential contracted partner typically would want to be the leader, in keeping with the first entry in table 3.7.

TABLE 3.8 Factors Affecting Provider-Driven Vertical Integration

Factor	*Private insurance (competitive market)*	*Private insurance (in LICs)*	*Community-based insurance (CBI)*	*Public insurance (in LICs)*	*Hypothesis to be tested*
Market power of service provider	+	+ ↑	+ ↑	n.a.	xx
System efficiency gains to be realized	+	+	+	n.a.	xx
Management know-how of provider	+	+	+	n.a.	xx
Contestability of health insurance markets	+	+ ↓	+ ↓	n.a.	S16
Potential to increase entry barriers to competitors	+	+	+	n.a.	xx
Contestability of health care markets	−	− ↓	− ↓	n.a.	xx
Lack of capital of service providers	−	−	−	n.a.	xx
Market power of insurer	−	− ↑	− ↑	n.a.	S17
Cartelization of insurers	−	− ↓	− ↓	n.a.	S18
Legislation prohibiting vertical restraints	−	−	−	n.a.	xx

Source: Zweifel, Krey, and Tagli 2007, chap. 3.

Note: LICs = low-income countries; HCE = health care expenditure; + = factor enhances integration; − = factor hampers integration; ↑ = reinforcement of effect; ↓ = weakening of effect; n.a. = not applicable; xx = not retained for testing.

Supply Hypothesis 18 (S18)

The higher degree of cartelization of insurers, the less likely to succeed is provider-driven vertical integration. A service provider (such as a clinic) wishing to add the insurance function to its business would have to find among insurers a cartel member willing to cooperate. In the case of LICs, however, control of cartel management over its members is typically less complete, permitting members to "chisel" more easily.

Seller Concentration on Health Insurance Markets

A fifth aspect of the supply of health insurance is the degree of seller concentration. The greater the degree of concentration, the more marked is the danger of monopolization, with concomitant limitations of consumer choice and transaction volume. The main factors affecting the degree of seller concentration are listed in table 3.9, taken from Zweifel, Krey, and Tagli (2007, chap. 3). The following three hypotheses seem particularly relevant for policy in LICs. Note that, in the case of a (monopoly) public health insurance scheme, seller concentration is maximum by definition.

Supply Hypothesis 19 (S19)

The more marked the diversity of preferences, the lower is the degree of seller concentration. When consumers have diverse preferences, competing insurers can seek out

TABLE 3.9 Factors Affecting the Degree of Seller Concentration of Health Insurance

Factor	Private insurance (competitive market)	Private insurance (in LICs)	Community-based insurance (CBI)	Public insurance (in LICs)	Hypothesis to be tested
Diversity of preferences	–	– ↓	–	n.a.	S19
Economies of scale	+/–	+	+	n.a.	xx
Economies of scope	+	+	+	n.a.	xx
Barriers to entry	+	+ ↑	+ ↑	n.a.	S20
Barriers to exit	–	– ↑	– ↑	n.a.	S21
Antitrust policy	–	– ↓	– ↓	n.a.	xx

Source: Zweifel, Krey, and Tagli 2007, chap. 3.

Note: LICs = low-income countries; HCE = health care expenditure; + = increases concentration; – = decreases concentration; ↑ = reinforcement of effect; ↓ = weakening of effect; n.a. = not applicable; xx = not retained for testing.

a market niche at relatively low cost. However, in LICs this effect is likely attenuated because the diversity is mainly in terms of urban versus rural dwellers. In rural areas, typically there are few, if any, competitive insurers.

Supply Hypothesis 20 (S20)

The higher the barriers to entry, the greater is seller concentration in health insurance markets. When barriers to entry are high, it is very costly for any newcomer to enter the market. In LICs, this effect is especially pronounced because the typical newcomer usually does not have much capital and know-how to overcome barriers to entry. The same is true of CBI.

Supply Hypothesis 21 (S21)

The higher the barriers to exit, the lower is the degree of seller concentration. Barriers to exit mean that there are unrecoverable costs associated with leaving a market. For example, an insurer cannot recoup the loss of reputation once it decides to exit from a line of business. If exit costs are high, incumbents fight to remain in the market, causing seller concentration to be low. Again, this effect may be more pronounced in LICs and in the case of CBI. The reason is that consumers left without coverage will have a much harder time finding replacement, causing the loss of reputation with them to be particularly high.

Intensity of Health Insurance Regulation

Usually, regulation is seen as exogenous, predetermined by a country's institutions. To some extent, this may be true; however, regulation can also be traced to the demand and a supply for a service that is treated on an implicit market. Demand originates with consumers but even more importantly with the regulated industry itself (which seeks to capture regulators). Supply comes from politicians in parliament and government as well as public administration. Gleaning from Zweifel and Pauly (2007, chap. 4), table 3.10 lists a few determinants of both demand and supply

TABLE 3.10 Factors Affecting Intensity of Health Insurance Regulation

Factor	*Private insurance (competitive market)*	*Private insurance (in LICs)*	*Community-based insurance (CBI)*	*Public insurance (in LICs)*	*Hypothesis to be tested*
Crises (insolvencies)	+	+ ↑	+ ↑	n.a.	xx
Number of insurers	–	– ↑	–	n.a.	R1
Predominance of domestic companies	+	+ ↑	+	n.a.	R2
Budgetary burden on government	–	– ↑	– ↑	n.a.	xx

Source: Zweifel, Krey, and Tagli 2007, chap. 3.

Note: LICs = low-income countries; HCE = health care expenditure; + = enhances regulation; – = hampers regulation; ↑ = reinforcement of effect; ↓ = weakening of effect; n.a. = not applicable; xx = not retained for testing.

of regulation that result in a higher predicted intensity or comprehensiveness of health insurance regulation. Two hypotheses will be singled out for testing.

Regulation Hypothesis 1 (R1)

The greater the number of insurers, the less intense is health insurance regulation. Demand for regulation importantly originates with the suppliers. If there are few health insurers in the market, they face little cost in organizing a lobby group that can lower the cost for public administration to supply regulation. Conversely, with a greater number of firms, their cost of organization increases. In LICs, this effect is likely more pronounced. Political institutions in LICs are typically weak, permitting a small group of suppliers to exert great influence.

Regulation Hypothesis 2 (R2)

The more predominant domestic insurers, the higher the degree of regulation. Domestic suppliers invariably have an especially close connection to a domestic government. Therefore, if most of a country's insurance companies are domestic, the degree of health insurance regulation will be high, especially in private LIC markets.

EVIDENCE FROM THE COUNTRY STUDIES

In this section, the theoretical predictions are pitted against the evidence gleaned from the country studies. This is a challenging endeavor because the reports were written without having any particular set of hypotheses in mind (except regarding the determinants of demand for health insurance coverage). However, they contain a good deal of material on market structure that may be used to provide some indirect evidence bearing on the theoretical predictions. Since this material is mostly qualitative rather than quantitative, it may be misinterpreted. Moreover, it is easy to simply overlook relevant statements. For these reasons, the findings reported in annex 3A are subject to errors and omissions for which the author apologizes while, of course, assuming responsibility.

Brazil

As noted by Couttolenc and Nicolella (chap. 11, this volume), as many as 25 percent of Brazilians are covered by private voluntary health insurance, making Brazil one of the largest markets for this type of insurance worldwide. While GDP per capita is only some 60 percent that of Chile (see below), it is appropriate to categorize the country as a competitive insurance market of the type approximated in some industrial countries since the section on regulation does not mention any premium regulation (column "PC," table 3.11). The publicly funded National Health Service (Sistema Unificado de Saúde, SUS) offers universal and free coverage to all Brazilians, although the health care services provided are of low quality in some parts of the country. SUS contracts with private providers of health care services, mainly for diagnostic services but also for hospital services. However, the report does not investigate the behavior of SUS management any further, rendering the column "POL" of table 3A.1 irrelevant. Also, there are no community-based schemes (column "CBI," table 3A.1).

Absent premium regulation, loadings likely differ between insurers, creating the possibility of testing for hypothesis D1. However, the influence of price on demand for coverage is not tested for. As to hypothesis D2, income is a crucial predictor of enrolment (annex table 11B.1 of the report). This confirmation of D2 is unambiguous since many other determinants are controlled for statistically. This is probably also due to the fact that both workers and employers can deduct the premium for private health insurance (or out-of-pocket payments to providers) from their taxable income. Given that the tax code is progressive, this statute favors earners of high incomes. Lack of information, though not addressed directly (hypothesis D3), is proxied inversely by education, which has a highly significant positive effect on enrolment. The demand for coverage, given enrolment, is not analyzed in the report, although it likely differs between prepaid plans (HMO-type), indemnity plans, and schemes sponsored by large public and private corporations.

On the supply side, the report contains some discussion of the determinants of the benefits package. Although moral hazard issues are not addressed (hypothesis S1), the fact that there are five main variants of private health insurance (table 11.6 of the report) can be taken as an indirect manifestation of diversity of preferences. Indeed, prior to 1998 legislation, insurers could package benefits in any way they believed to have success on the market. Since 1998, regulation has been cutting down on diversity by allowing only those five variants. The most popular, with a market share of 60 percent, is a plan covering ambulatory and hospital care, while the reference plan (covering also dental care) attains a share of 19 percent. This nicely illustrates the influence of regulation on the benefits package (hypothesis S4). While an important stated objective of the 1998 legislation was to protect consumers from abusive benefit exclusions, this legislation also requires private health plans to reimburse the SUS for health care services delivered to their insured.

The other dimensions of supply are mentioned only cursorily. The authors allude to risk-selection efforts without, however, relating them to reinforcing and mitigating determinants (hypotheses S5 to S8). Determinants of loading, market concentration, and vertical integration (whether insurer- or provider-driven) are not discussed. This last point is noteworthy because the authors describe as contentious the relationship between the SUS and private insurers and providers. This observation could be interpreted as reflecting attempts by the SUS to vertically integrate by acquiring control over private providers. Apparently, providers fear opportunistic behavior on the part of the SUS acting as the insurer. Therefore, this observation provides some (very) indirect evidence supporting hypothesis S15 (column "PUL," table 3A.1). Finally, regulation is viewed as exogenous throughout, obviating tests of hypotheses R1 and R2.

China

The report for China (Hu and Ying, chap. 10) notes that less than 6 percent of the Chinese population had private health insurance in 2004. Still, this share is not negligible compared with the 3 percent covered by public insurance (table 10.10). Another 10 percent have access to "cooperative medical services." Because there is no unregulated private insurance market in China, the "PC" column of table 3A.1 is irrelevant. With regard to the "PUL" column, the authors do mention a price effect in public insurance (likely because of uniform contributions); therefore, hypothesis D1 cannot be tested. They do run a logistic regression relating the decision to have private health insurance coverage to a number of determinants. But again, the regression does not include the premium (or better still, the estimated loading). As to hypothesis D2, the authors find an increase in the odds ratio of holding private insurance with higher income. Moreover, they present experimental evidence on willingness to pay (WTP), with higher income associated with higher WTP for different types of insurance, again confirming D2. However, the report does not discuss the role of lacking information in the demand for insurance coverage, and it does not deal with determinants of the extent of coverage demanded (obviating a test of hypotheses D3 through D7). With regard to supply, the behavior of public and private health insurers is not addressed, making a test of hypotheses S2 to S21 impossible. In passing, moral hazard effects are noted as factors limiting the extent of coverage offered by private health insurers, providing some support for S1. While the share of domestic insurers is noted as being very high, the influence of this fact on the intensity of regulation is not discussed (hypothesis R2). Thus, regulation is viewed as exogenous.

Chile

Health insurance has been deregulated to a sufficient degree to make Chile a case study for private insurance in a competitive market ("PC" column of table 3A.1). Private health insurers can be associated with ISAPREs, while FONASA amounts to a monopolistic public scheme. Community-based insurance does not exist in Chile. Bitrán and Muñoz (chap. 4, this volume) present research (table 4.2) suggesting that the probability of having voluntary private health insurance strongly increases with income, confirming hypothesis D2; however, they do not report on the influence of premiums (or loadings, respectively). Concerning the amount of coverage demanded, the authors use MNC as the dependent variable, which is defined as the amount of income a household still has after having paid the monthly insurance premium plus the value of out-of-pocket health care expenditure. Therefore, MNC can serve as an approximate inverse indicator of the amount of coverage. In a regression (table 4.11), they find that MNC clearly increases with income; therefore, the amount of coverage purchased increases with income, as predicted (D5). The other two determinants of demand for coverage (D6, D7) are not discussed.

The behavior of private of public health insurers is not addressed in the report, obviating a test of hypotheses S1 through S21. Finally, intensity of regulation is viewed as fully exogenous, preventing R1 and R2 from being tested.

Egypt

Although Egypt belongs to the group of low-income countries, its total health care expenditure has been increasing by 13 percent a year since 1996, outpacing general economic growth. Nassar and El-Saharty (chapter 5, this volume) note that there is a National Health Service covering the entire population. Therefore, the entry "PUL" in table 3A.1 is relevant; however, the report does not address the behavior of the managers of this service. In addition, social health insurance covers almost one-half of the population. At the same time, the balance of financing has been shifting from a 50 : 50 split between public and private to a 60 : 40 split in favor of private sources (table 5A.2 of the report). The fact that only 5 percent of the population is covered by private health insurance implies that much of the additional finance must have come out of pocket.

A specialty of Egypt is health insurance provided by professional syndicates. For example, teachers and accountants obtain coverage through such syndicates, with closed enrolment. Although this type of insurance appears to be unique, it has important similarities with the community-based insurance schemes in some African and Asian countries, justifying their entry in the "CBI" column of table 3A.1. First, members of a particular profession constitute a rather homogenous population at risk, comparable to a local community. Second, the syndicate-sponsored schemes are not for profit and impose closed enrolment, which is also typical of CBI schemes.

Turning to health insurance provided by private companies, their categorization in table 3A.1 is difficult. On the one hand, they operate in a low-income country. On the other hand, international companies have entered the Egyptian market. In addition, the authors emphasize the low intensity of regulation, health insurers being simply treated like life insurers. In all, the market very much resembles the competitive model (to a degree that may not even be known in an industrial country), justifying entry in the "PC" column of table 3A.1.

Starting with the "PC" column of table 3A.1, the report provides clear evidence about the influence of higher income on enrolment ("other types of health insurance," table 5A.1), confirming hypothesis D2, while being silent about differences in the loading (hypothesis D1). In addition, table 5A.2 stratifies holders of private insurance by education and occupation. In both cases, those having easier access to information (for example, sales personnel compared with farmers) are more likely to have this type of insurance, weakly confirming hypothesis D3. Although Egyptian private companies likely offer very differentiated products, hypotheses D4 through D7 cannot be tested because the report does not address this aspect.

With regard to the supply side, the report notes that the major private plans are all of the managed care type. This implies that provider choice (and through it, the range of benefits available) are somewhat limited, quite likely in response to moral hazard effects (hypothesis S1). Other determinants of the benefits package and of the loading are not discussed. Risk-selection effort emerges as a topic in the context of the Egyptian International Medical Insurance Company (EIMIC), who does not provide both employee and family coverage within a given employer-based group, presumably in an attempt to limit adverse selection. Since the Egyptian private health insurance market is not concentrated at all, such effort pays off (see hypothesis S7).

EIMIC also owns polyclinics and diagnostic centers, reflecting insurer-driven vertical integration. Such integration is predicted by hypothesis S13 because the Egyptian market for health care providers is highly contestable. Moreover, the market for health insurance is not easily contestable since health insurers must have a license, which requires reserves amounting to US$5 million. The authors decry this as excessive in relation to the typical risks incurred. However, barriers to entry in the health insurance market facilitate insurer-driven vertical integration (hypothesis S13) while hampering provider-driven integration (hypothesis S16). Nevertheless, some provider-driven vertical integration occurs as well (for example, high-care), somewhat contradicting hypothesis S16. With a hardly concentrated insurance market, market power of health insurers is low, however, enabling health care providers to add the insurance function to their activities (hypothesis S17). Finally, the determinants of concentration in the market for health insurance are not discussed, and regulation is viewed entirely as exogenous.

With regard to the "CBI" entry in table 3A.1, a fraction of a page is devoted to the schemes sponsored by professional syndicates. It does point out that premiums are subsidized (likely lowering loadings), which is predicted to encourage enrolment. Although the report does not discuss price and income effects, its table 5A.3. provides evidence that enrolment increases with the wealth index, as predicted by hypothesis D2. The same is true of education and occupation of the head of household, such as clerical and sales, pointing indirectly to the role of (lack of) information in the decision to enroll in voluntary private health insurance (hypothesis D3). However, demand for coverage, given enrolment, is not discussed at all (making a testing of hypotheses D4 through D7 impossible).

Turning to supply-side factors, it is not clear whether the benefits package of a syndicate scheme typically differs from that of private health insurer (say); therefore, hypotheses S1 through S4 cannot be tested. There is no particular mention of risk-selection efforts; however, the homogeneity of the insured population should make adverse selection less of an issue. In particular, the health insurer is predicted to be less concerned about the size of the benefits package. And indeed, coverage is reported to be comprehensive, supporting hypothesis S6. However, copayments are imposed on almost all patient services and a ceiling is placed on annual health care expenditure covered. This may be a reason for low loadings and hence low premiums (hypotheis S11). Yet, the evidence is inconclusive because the schemes receive substantial subsidies from their respective syndicates. Issues such as insurer-driven vertical integration, provider-driven vertical integration, the amount of market concentration, and the possible endogeneity of regulation are not discussed.

The report does not comment much on public health insurance in Egypt (column "PUL," table 3A.1), except to note its inefficiency. This observation can be interpreted as the public scheme's having a high implicit loading, although the determinants are not analyzed. Therefore, hypotheses S9 through S9 cannot be tested. The same is true of insurer-driven vertical integration, whereas provider-driven integration, degree of concentration, and determinants of regulation are not relevant in this context.

India

Although Berman, Ahuja, and Kalavakonda (chap. 12, this volume) do not discuss the general level of regulation of health insurance in India, the country's regulatory tradition is well known, and health insurance is unlikely to constitute an exception to the rule. Therefore, in table 3A.1 the column, "Private competitive health insurance, PC" is marked "not applicable."

However, there is private health insurance in India, for example "Mediclaim," limited to inpatient services. The report is silent about the influence of the loading component on the yes/no decision to purchase health insurance (D1). At the same time, it makes clear that income is a decisive determinant, supporting D2. The influence of lack of information (D3) is not reported at all. This also holds true of supply-side influences (hypotheses S1 through S21) as well as of regulation (R1 and R2).

Korea

Jung (chap. 15, this volume) takes Korea's national health insurance system as the point of departure, which obviates discussion of community-based (CBI) alternatives. The national scheme has been in distress since 2000, resulting in a rapidly expanding private health insurance market. Private coverage is in the main designed as "gap insurance," covering the copayments imposed by public health insurance. From the report, the amount of regulation imposed on private insurers is not clear; however the historical background suggests that the situation comes closer to a competitive market (PC) than to private insurance in a low-income country (PL), which therefore is marked as "not applicable" in table 3A.1.

With regard to demand, Jung estimates a logit regression relating enrolment (yes/no) to income, employment status, size of the family, and density of physician supply. Although results are not shown, the presumption is that income does play a role, as presumably does the level of education (which can be assumed to be negatively correlated with lack of information). Therefore, hypotheses D2 and D3 receive some confirmation.

Turning to the supply side, the fact that people with chronic diseases or injuries are less likely to be in a private plan probably reflects risk-selection effort, which seems to be directed toward high-cost conditions, resulting in special plans (for example, for diabetes and asthma). This provides some support for hypotheses S5 and S6. The authors also examine the impact of private health insurance coverage on HCE to find that consumers with private coverage have a higher likelihood of initiating at least one episode during the year 2002. They also have higher outpatient HCE (but not hospital HCE, see tables 15.10 and 15.11). While this constitutes evidence of both moral hazard and risk-selection effects, the authors do not address the issue of how health insurers (or the national health insurance scheme for that matter) respond to the facts. Therefore, the remaining hypotheses relating to supply (S1 through S4 and S6 through S21) cannot be tested. Finally, health insurance regulation (R1, R2) is seen as entirely exogenous.

Nigeria

Onwujekwe and Velényi (chap. 13, this volume) start by noting that both health status and the health care system of Nigeria are in a bad state, ranking close to the bottom of 191 member states of the World Health Organization. Most private HCE is out-of-pocket, private insurance playing a minimum role. As of 2002, total domestic public HCE is estimated to range somewhere between US$3.65 and US$8.75 per capita. Therefore, there is a modest public health insurance scheme ("PUL" in table 3A.1). However, the report does not revolve around "PUL," focusing instead on (highly regulated) private health insurance ("PL").

The authors perform a WTP experiment in the billing-game format, addressing both consumers and representatives from corporations. Consumers were asked which mode of payment they found particularly easy. Some 60 percent favored national health insurance, 49 percent favored voluntary insurance, and 47 percent favored community-based health insurance. Why exactly national health insurance is preferred does not become clear except that rural dwellers have higher than average WTP for voluntary schemes, whereas urban dwellers have a preference for paying out of pocket. Moreover, the lowest income class has the strongest tendency to enroll in voluntary private health insurance. This constitutes a contradiction of hypothesis D2. However, the contradiction is not strong because other determinants of demand are not controlled for. This also holds for the determinants "adverse selection" and "lack of information" about health insurance (D2, D3).

All supply-side issues are neglected (S1 through S23), and regulation is viewed as exogenous (R1, R2). Concerning representatives of corporations, the report finds that about one-half of the respondents are willing to pay 500 naira monthly to insure their employees (100 naira = US$0.75 as of 2003–04). The average amount they are willing to pay amounts to 398 naira (roughly US$3 per month). However, the authors do not relate this indicator of demand to anything but company size. Therefore, again there is no possibility to test additional hypotheses in the "PL" column of table 3A.1.

South Africa

In South Africa there is no community-based insurance; therefore, the CBI column of table 3A.1 is marked "not applicable." The uninsured majority (about 84 percent of the population) relies on the public health sector without having any insurance coverage (Thiede and Mutyambizi, chap. 6, this volume). Though free, public sector health care is perceived as being of low quality. Until a few years ago, private health insurance in South Africa would have fallen in the competitive market category ("PC" in table 3A.1). With the 1999 Medical Schemes Act, however, community rating has been imposed along with a set of prescribed minimum benefits, suggesting entry in the "PL" column. The "Registered Medical Schemes" fully comply with the requirements of the Act. Bargaining Council Schemes are exempted from certain provisions of the Act, offering only primary health care coverage.

The report does mention high brokerage fees (which are part of the loading) as a factor limiting enrolment, thus conforming with hypothesis D1 and possibly D4. The authors also mention that low-income citizens are less likely to be members of either type of scheme, but basically with regard to the yes/no decision (D1) rather than the extent of coverage (D5). Also mentioned, in passing, is that coverage may be limited by risk-selection efforts on the part of health insurers (D6), whereas lack of information (D7) is not addressed.

With regard to supply, Bargaining Council Schemes are found to limit their benefits package, quite likely to fend off moral hazard effects, as predicted by hypothesis S1. Diversity of preferences is not addressed explicitly but is a likely reason for the diversity of health insurance schemes in South Africa (S2). New health risks (S3) and regulation (S4) are not explicitly cited determinants of the benefits package. The authors seem to think that risk-selection efforts were suppressed by the 1999 Medical Schemes Act. The possibility that covert efforts (induced by premium regulation, S8) occur and are specially marked in response to moral hazard effects (S5) and the size of benefit (S6) is not considered; neither is seller concentration (S7). However, the report does state that the intended cross-subsidization from the healthy to the sick is not successful in all cases, causing the government to consider a risk-equalization scheme. Therefore, S8 receives a measure of indirect confirmation. Reinsurance is explicitly cited as a reason for high loadings in direct insurance (S9). The other hypotheses (S10 to S12) concerning the amount of loading cannot be tested. The report does not touch upon the two types of vertical integration, insurer-driven and provider-driven (hypotheses S19 through S21). It also treats regulation as exogenous (R1, R2).

Slovenia

With the help of their figure 14.1, Tajnikar and Došenovič Bonča give a clear picture of the structure of health insurance in Slovenia. The monopolistic public insurance scheme makes column "PUL" of table 3A.1 relevant. The main purpose of voluntary private health insurance is to cover the cost-sharing provisions of the public scheme; another purpose, to cover extra services (such as a private room in hospital). With the 2005 reform, voluntary health insurance was transformed from capital-funded to pay-as-you-go. This suggests that private insurance does not operate in a competitive market any more but rather falls into the "PL" category of table 3A.1, which stands for heavily regulated insurance typical of low-income countries. Moreover, legislation adopted in 2005 imposed uniform premiums for all insured, regardless of age, gender, and health status, the intention being to prevent premium increases from hitting the elderly population.

The authors do not discuss the determinants of demand, making a test hypotheses D1 through D7 impossible. With the heavy regulation introduced in 2005 in the background, they see no reason to address issues related to supply behavior either (S1 through S21). They do, however, note some adverse effects of the risk-equalization scheme introduced in 2005, which can be interpreted as evidence of regulation's inducing risk-selection efforts (S8).

The authors then turn to the impact of voluntary health insurance on the country's efficiency of primary care providers and take a Data Envelopment Analysis approach to determine an efficient frontier. Their findings suggest that the presence of voluntary health insurance serves to increase inefficiency of both public and private providers. Therefore, in general there does not seem to be much scope for special know-how to facilitate insurer-driven vertical integration. Unfortunately, the role of know-how in vertical integration is not among the retained hypotheses. Provider-driven integration is not considered in the report. Finally, while the reform of 2003 and counter-reform of 2005 are related to developments in the health care sector, regulation is viewed as exogenous, obviating tests of hypotheses R1 and R2.

Thailand

Supakankunti (chap. 7, this volume) starts by noting that, in the wake of the 1997 economic crisis, private hospitals began to rely increasingly on private health insurance for funding. In 2001, the government introduced universal coverage through three major public schemes, which do not, however, seem to be subject to competition. Therefore, the column "PUL" of table 3A.1 is relevant. Figure 7.3 of the report indicates that private health insurers charge risk-based premiums, which suggests a little regulated market ("PC" of table 3A.1).

With respect to demand, the probability of having private health insurance is related to the presence of universal coverage, coverage by social security, income, sickness during the last month preceding the interview, and the cost of inpatient treatment. This cost is insignificant, possibly indicating a lack of information and hence weakly supporting hypothesis D3. The likelihood of enrolment definitely increases with income, confirming D2. The fact that prior sickness does not seem to have an effect might point to an absence of adverse selection, weakly supporting D6 (which in addition relates more to demand for coverage than to the yes/no decision). In a second logistic regression, the dependent variable is a household's possession of a Medical Card, which seems to facilitate access to private providers (no details provided in the report). Interestingly, the premium (reflecting the loading to a considerable extent) has a highly significant negative effect on the probability; constituting evidence in favor of D1.

The author also presents a logit regression suggesting that the probability of at least one visit in the course of a year does not increase with presence of universal coverage but with possession of the Medical Card. They find the associated increase of 28 percent evidence of moral hazard effects or adverse selection (high risks purchasing extra coverage). However, the second explanation is not convincing because individuals with private coverage do not have higher out-of-pocket HCE (which would point to unfavorable health status). Therefore, health insurers have to deal with moral hazard effects that are predicted to limit the benefits package (hypothesis S1), exacerbate risk-selection effort (S5), and call for copayments and caps as countermeasures (S11). This last prediction is not confirmed by table 7.3 of the report, which states that the drug benefit does not have a limit. The other two hypotheses cannot be tested for lack of pertinent information. In passing, the author notes that insurers were willing to respond to consumers' awareness of new health risks such as SARS. This confirms somewhat hypothesis S3, predicting insurer flexibility in this respect especially if not hampered by regulation.

However, it is known that 72 of the 77 non-life companies are domestic, a situation that facilitates regulation (R1, R2). The fact that Thailand has apparently been characterized by a low degree of health insurance regulation therefore constitutes a contradiction. It seems that the government, eager to keep the budgetary cost of its universal coverage scheme low, is quite aware of the (marginal) cost of regulation. The contradiction is therefore deemed partial rather than total.

Turkey

Cederberg Heard and Mahal (chap. 8, this volume) note an increasing reliance on private health care, caused by public sector inefficiencies and low-quality public services, especially in the rural areas of Turkey. The government reacted in

2002 by beginning to provide private insurers with incentives for market entry, which resulted in making private health insurance the fastest growing line of insurance in Turkey. About 60 percent of the privately insured (who make up about 1 percent of the population by 2003) belong to group insurance schemes. The report conveys the impression that private health insurance traditionally has been tightly regulated, suggesting its insertion in the "PL" column of table 3A.1. There is no community-based (CBI) insurance. In addition, the column "PUL" (public health insurance in low-income countries) is relevant. With regard to demand, the authors note that private health insurance has been concentrated among the richer groups, weakly supporting hypothesis D2. The ceteris paribus clause is not satisfied since other demand-side factors are not discussed.

The remainder of the report revolves around estimation of a four-part model, distinguishing the probability of outpatient and inpatient HCE, respectively, from the amount of inpatient and outpatient HCE. Results suggest that coverage by private health insurance does not affect three out of the four parts. However, it is associated with almost a doubling of outpatient HCE. This speaks in favor of moral hazard effects rather than adverse selection effects (which presumably would affect all four parts). However, supply-side issues related to either private or public insurers are absent entirely. Therefore, with the exception of D2, none of the hypotheses retained seem to be amenable to testing in the case of Turkey.

CONCLUSIONS AND OUTLOOK

This chap. is devoted to an attempt to relate a set of hypotheses that can be gleaned from the theoretical groundwork provided by Pauly (2007), Zweifel (2007), and Zweifel, Krey, and Tagli (2007) to the country studies presented in this volume. This attempt was limited from the beginning in two ways. First, only a selection of hypotheses was submitted to the test, with particular emphasis on supply-side hypotheses because it is with regard to the behavior of health insurers that the theoretical literature is little developed or outright lacking. Moreover, it was important to find out whether the empirical evidence contradicts or supports the theoretical predictions. Second, one variant of special interest was community-based insurance (CBI). However, it turned out that none of the countries studied has CBI-type health insurance as it is prevalent in some African and Asian countries. Health insurance offered by Egyptian professional syndicates turned out to be the closest to CBI. In sum, the results of testing displayed in table 3A.1 may be biased and are necessarily incomplete.

Nevertheless, the many entries indicating that a test was not possible ("N" in table 3A.1) are impressive. Almost without exception, the country reports emphasize the determinants of demand for voluntary private health insurance. However, a crucial determinant of demand is the loading contained in the premium, that is, the true price of insurance. Except for the report on Thailand, this determinant never entered the statistical analyses performed. A possible reason is regulation imposing uniformity of premiums, thus obviating tests for price effects.

As far as the demand side is concerned, the little evidence available supports the theoretical groundwork in that demand for private health insurance increases with income. Financial safety in the context of health care thus constitutes a normal good. However, given that there is a demand for private health insurance coverage, the actual quantity that will be transacted crucially depends on the supply side. Apart from the loading (which, in turn, typically varies with the amount of vertical integration, as evidenced, for example, by managed care), the attractiveness of private health insurance increases with the comprehensiveness of benefits and decreases with risk-selection effort undertaken by health insurers. These dimensions of insurance supply have not been sufficiently researched even in industrial countries. Yet they importantly influence the success of a voluntary health insurance option among consumers. The lack of knowledge in this regard weighs especially heavily in countries with governments wanting to encourage private health insurance.

Finally, the development of private health insurance is easily stifled by excessive regulation. For this reason, it is important to recognize that the intensity of insurance regulation is not exogenously given but depends on several factors. However, the country reports studied do not address the endogeneity of regulation. Therefore, a considerable amount of uncertainty remains about the longer-run viability of voluntary private health insurance in low-income countries.

On a more positive final note, this chapter may serve as a chart to a whole new territory of future research. The many gaps noted call for a major research effort. It will be definitely worthwhile to close at least some of them, especially with regard to the behavior of suppliers of private health insurance.

ANNEX 3A OVERVIEW OF HYPOTHESES AND RESULTS OF TESTS

TABLE 3A.1 Overview of Hypotheses and Results of Tests

		Country (chapter)							
	Hypothesis	*Brazil (11)*				*Chile (4)*			
		PC	*PL*	*CBI*	*PUL*	*PC*	*PL*	*CBI*	*PUL*
Demand: Yes/No	D1 Loading	**X**	X	X	**N**	**N**	X	X	N
	D2 Income	**2**	X	X	**N**	**2**	X	X	N
	D3 Lack info.	**1**	X	X	**N**	**1**	X	X	1
Demand: Coverage	D4 Loading	**X**	X	X	**N**	**N**	X	X	N
	D5 Income	**X**	X	X	**N**	**N**	X	X	N
	D6 Adv. select.	**X**	X	X	**N**	**N**	X	X	N
	D7 Lack info.	**X**	X	X	**N**	**N**	X	X	N
Benefits package	S1 Moral hazard	**X**	X	X	**N**	**N**	X	X	N
	S2 Divers. pref.	**1**	X	X	**N**	**N**	X	X	N
	S3 New hlth ri.	**X**	X	X	**N**	**N**	X	X	N
	S4 Regulation	**1**	X	X	**N**	**N**	X	X	N
Risk selection	S5 Moral hazard	**X**	X	X	**N**	**N**	X	X	N
	S6 Size benefits	**X**	X	X	**N**	**N**	X	X	N
	S7 Concentration	**X**	X	X	**N**	**N**	X	X	N
	S8 Regulation	**X**	X	X	**N**	**N**	X	X	N
Loading	S9 Reinsurance	**X**	X	X	**N**	**N**	X	X	N
	S10 High-inc.mbr.	**X**	X	X	**N**	**N**	X	X	N
	S11 Copay, caps	**X**	X	X	**N**	**N**	X	X	N
	S12 Regulation	**X**	X	X	**N**	**N**	X	X	N
Insurance-driven integration	S13 Contest.h.c.m.	**X**	X	X	**N**	**N**	X	X	N
	S14 Contest.h.i.m.	**X**	X	X	**N**	**N**	X	X	N
	S15 Opportunist.b.	**X**	X	X	**1**	**N**	X	X	N
Provider-driven integration	S16 Contest.h.i.m.	**X**	X	X	**N**	**N**	X	X	N
	S17 Mark.pow.ins.	**X**	X	X	**N**	**N**	X	X	N
	S18 Cartelizn.ins.	**X**	X	X	**N**	**N**	X	X	N
Concen-tration	S19 Divers.pref.	**X**	X	X	**N**	**N**	X	X	N
	S20 Barr. to entry	**X**	X	X	**N**	**N**	X	X	N
	S21 Barr. to exit	**X**	X	X	**N**	**N**	X	X	N
Regula-tion	R1 No. insurers	**X**	X	X	**N**	**N**	X	X	N
	R2 Domestic	**X**	X	X	**N**	**N**	X	X	N

(continued)

Sources: Chaps. 4, 5, 6, 7, 8, 10, 11, 12, 13, 14, and 15, this volume.

Note: 2 = clear confirmation of hypothesis; 1 = partial confirmation; X = not applicable; N = not tested; 0 = ambiguous outcome; –1 = partial rejection, –2 = clear rejection of hypothesis;

PC = private insurance (competitive market); PL = private insurance (in LICs); CBI = community-based insurance; PUL = public insurance (in LICs)

TABLE 3A.1 Overview of Hypotheses and Results of Tests *(continued)*

	Hypothesis	*Country (chapter)*							
		China (10)				*Egypt, Arab Rep. of (5)*			
		PC	*PL*	*CBI*	*PUL*	*PC*	*PL*	*CBI*	*PUL*
Demand: Yes/No	D1 Loading	X	**N**	X	X	**N**	X	**N**	**N**
	D2 Income	X	**2**	X	X	**1**	X	**1**	**N**
	D3 Lack info.	X	**N**	X	X	**1**	X	**1**	**N**
Demand: Coverage	D4 Loading	X	**N**	X	X	**N**	X	**N**	**N**
	D5 Income	X	**N**	X	X	**N**	X	**N**	**N**
	D6 Adv. select.	X	**1**	X	X	**N**	X	**N**	**N**
	D7 Lack info.	X	**N**	X	X	**N**	X	**N**	**N**
Benefits package	S1 Moral hazard	X	**N**	X	X	**1**	X	**N**	**N**
	S2 Divers. pref.	X	**N**	X	X	**N**	X	**N**	**N**
	S3 New hlth ri.	X	**N**	X	X	**N**	X	**N**	**N**
	S4 Regulation	X	**N**	X	X	**N**	X	**N**	**N**
Risk selection	S5 Moral hazard	X	**N**	X	X	**N**	X	**N**	**N**
	S6 Size benefits	X	**N**	X	X	**N**	X	**1**	**N**
	S7 Concentration	X	**N**	X	X	**1**	X	**N**	**N**
	S8 Regulation	X	**N**	X	X	**N**	X	**N**	**N**
Loading	S9 Reinsurance	X	**N**	X	X	**N**	**2**	**N**	**N**
	S10 High-inc.mbr.	X	**N**	X	X	**N**	**X**	**N**	**N**
	S11 Copay, caps	X	**N**	X	X	**N**	**X**	**0**	**N**
	S12 Regulation	X	**N**	X	X	**N**	**X**	**N**	**N**
Insurance-driven integration	S13 Contest.h.c.m.	X	**N**	X	X	**1**	X	**N**	**N**
	S14 Contest.h.i.m.	X	**N**	X	X	**N**	X	**N**	**N**
	S15 Opportunist.b.	X	**N**	X	X	**N**	X	**N**	**N**
Provider-driven integration	S16 Contest.h.i.m.	X	**N**	X	X	**−1**	X	**N**	**X**
	S17 Mark.pow.ins.	X	**N**	X	X	**1**	X	**N**	**X**
	S18 Cartelizn.ins.	X	**N**	X	X	**N**	X	**N**	**X**
Concentration	S19 Divers.pref.	X	**N**	X	X	**N**	X	**N**	**X**
	S20 Barr. to entry	X	**N**	X	X	**N**	X	**N**	**X**
	S21 Barr. to exit	X	**N**	X	X	**N**	X	**N**	**X**
Regulation	R1 No. insurers	X	**N**	X	X	**N**	X	**N**	**X**
	R2 Domestic	X	**N**	X	X	**N**	X	**N**	**X**

TABLE 3A.1 Overview of Hypotheses and Results of Tests *(continued)*

	Hypothesis	*Country (chapter)*							
		India				*Korea, Rep. of (15)*			
		PC	*PL*	*CBI*	*PUL*	*PC*	*PL*	*CBI*	*PUL*
Demand: Yes/No	D1 Loading	X	**N**	X	N	**N**	X	X	N
	D2 Income	X	**1**	X	N	**1**	X	X	N
	D3 Lack info.	X	**N**	X	N	**1**	X	X	N
Demand: Coverage	D4 Loading	X	**N**	X	N	**N**	X	X	N
	D5 Income	X	**N**	X	N	**1**	X	X	N
	D6 Adv. select.	X	**N**	X	N	**N**	X	X	N
	D7 Lack info.	X	**N**	X	N	**N**	X	X	N
Benefits package	S1 Moral hazard	X	**N**	X	N	**N**	X	X	N
	S2 Divers. pref.	X	**N**	X	N	**N**	X	X	N
	S3 New hlth ri	X	**N**	X	N	**N**	X	X	N
	S4 Regulation	X	**N**	X	N	**N**	X	X	N
Risk selection	S5 Moral hazard	X	**N**	X	N	**1**	X	X	N
	S6 Size benefits	X	**N**	X	N	**1**	X	X	N
	S7 Concentration	X	**N**	X	N	**N**	X	X	N
	S8 Regulation	X	**N**	X	N	**N**	X	X	N
Loading	S9 Reinsurance	X	**N**	X	N	**N**	X	X	N
	S10 High-inc.mbr.	X	**N**	X	N	**N**	X	X	N
	S11 Copay, caps	X	**N**	X	N	**N**	X	X	N
	S12 Regulation	X	**N**	X	N	**N**	X	X	N
Insurance-driven integration	S13 Contest.h.c.m.	X	**N**	X	X	**N**	X	X	X
	S14 Contest.h.i.m.	X	**N**	X	X	**N**	X	X	X
	S15 Opportunist.b.	X	**N**	X	X	**N**	X	X	X
Provider-driven integration	S16 Contest.h.i.m.	X	**N**	X	X	**N**	X	X	X
	S17 Mark.pow.ins.	X	**N**	X	X	**N**	X	X	X
	S18 Cartelizn.ins.	X	**N**	X	X	**N**	X	X	X
Concen-tration	S19 Divers.pref.	X	**N**	X	X	**N**	X	X	X
	S20 Barr. to entry	X	**N**	X	X	**N**	X	X	X
	S21 Barr. to exit	X	**N**	X	X	**N**	X	X	X
Regula-tion	R1 No. insurers	X	**N**	X	X	**N**	X	X	X
	R2 Domestic	X	**N**	X	X	**N**	X	X	X

(continued)

TABLE 3A.1 Overview of Hypotheses and Results of Tests *(continued)*

	Hypothesis	*Country (chapter)*							
		Nigeria (13)				*South Africa (6)*			
		PC	*PL*	*CBI*	*PUL*	*PC*	*PL*	*CBI*	*PUL*
Demand: Yes/No	D1 Loading	X	**N**	X	N	X	**1**	X	X
	D2 Income	X	**–1**	X	N	X	**1**	X	X
	D3 Lack info.	X	**N**	X	N	X	**1**	X	X
Demand: Coverage	D4 Loading	X	**N**	X	N	X	**1**	X	X
	D5 Income	X	**1**	X	N	X	**N**	X	X
	D6 Adv. select.	X	**N**	X	N	X	**1**	X	X
	D7 Lack info.	X	**N**	X	N	X	**N**	X	X
Benefits package	S1 Moral hazard	X	**N**	X	N	X	**1**	X	X
	S2 Divers. pref.	X	**N**	X	N	X	**1**	X	X
	S3 New hlth ri.	X	**N**	X	N	X	**N**	X	X
	S4 Regulation	X	**N**	X	N	X	**N**	X	X
Risk selection	S5 Moral hazard	X	**N**	X	N	X	**N**	X	X
	S6 Size benefits	X	**N**	X	N	X	**N**	X	X
	S7 Concentration	X	**N**	X	N	X	**N**	X	X
	S8 Regulation	X	**N**	X	N	X	**1**	X	X
Loading	S9 Reinsurance	X	**N**	X	N	X	**1**	X	X
	S10 High-inc.mbr.	X	**N**	X	N	X	**N**	X	X
	S11 Copay, caps	X	**N**	X	N	X	**N**	X	X
	S12 Regulation	X	**N**	X	N	X	**N**	X	X
Insurance-driven integration	S13 Contest.h.c.m.	X	**N**	X	X	X	**N**	X	X
	S14 Contest.h.i.m.	X	**N**	X	X	X	**N**	X	X
	S15 Opportunist.b.	X	**N**	X	X	X	**N**	X	X
Provider-driven integration	S16 Contest.h.i.m.	X	**N**	X	X	X	**N**	X	X
	S17 Mark.pow.ins.	X	**N**	X	X	X	**N**	X	X
	S18 Cartelizn.ins.	X	**N**	X	X	X	**N**	X	X
Concen-tration	S19 Divers.pref.	X	**N**	X	X	X	**N**	X	X
	S20 Barr. to entry	X	**N**	X	X	X	**N**	X	X
	S21 Barr. to exit	X	**N**	X	X	X	**N**	X	X
Regula-tion	R1 No. insurers	X	**N**	X	X	X	**N**	X	X
	R2 Domestic	X	**N**	X	X	X	**N**	X	X

TABLE 3A.1 Overview of Hypotheses and Results of Tests *(continued)*

	Hypothesis	Slovenia (14) PC	Slovenia (14) PL	Slovenia (14) CBI	Slovenia (14) PUL	Thailand (7) PC	Thailand (7) PL	Thailand (7) CBI	Thailand (7) PUL
Demand: Yes/No	D1 Loading	X	**N**	X	**N**	**2**	X	X	**N**
	D2 Income	X	**N**	X	**N**	**2**	X	X	**N**
	D3 Lack info.	X	**N**	X	**N**	**1**	X	X	**N**
Demand: Coverage	D4 Loading	X	**N**	X	**N**	**N**	X	X	**N**
	D5 Income	X	**N**	X	**N**	**N**	X	X	**N**
	D6 Adv. select.	X	**N**	X	**N**	**1**	X	X	**N**
	D7 Lack info.	X	**N**	X	**N**	**N**	X	X	**N**
Benefits package	S1 Moral hazard	X	**N**	X	**N**	**N**	X	X	**N**
	S2 Divers. pref.	X	**N**	X	**N**	**N**	X	X	**N**
	S3 New hlth ri.	X	**N**	X	**N**	**1**	X	X	**N**
	S4 Regulation	X	**N**	X	**N**	**1**	X	X	**N**
Risk selection	S5 Moral hazard	X	**N**	X	**N**	**N**	X	X	**N**
	S6 Size benefits	X	**N**	X	**N**	**N**	X	X	**N**
	S7 Concentration	X	**N**	X	**N**	**N**	X	X	**N**
	S8 Regulation	X	**1**	X	**N**	**N**	X	X	**N**
Loading	S9 Reinsurance	X	**N**	X	**N**	**N**	X	X	**N**
	S10 High-inc.mbr.	X	**N**	X	**N**	**N**	X	X	**N**
	S11 Copay, caps	X	**N**	X	**N**	**–1**	X	X	**N**
	S12 Regulation	X	**N**	X	**N**	**N**	X	X	**N**
Insurance-driven integration	S13 Contest.h.c.m.	X	**N**	X	**X**	**N**	X	X	**X**
	S14 Contest.h.i.m.	X	**N**	X	**X**	**N**	X	X	**X**
	S15 Opportunist.b.	X	**N**	X	**X**	**N**	X	X	**X**
Provider-driven integration	S16 Contest.h.i.m.	X	**N**	X	**X**	**N**	X	X	**X**
	S17 Mark.pow.ins.	X	**N**	X	**X**	**N**	X	X	**X**
	S18 Cartelizn.ins.	X	**N**	X	**X**	**N**	X	X	**X**
Concentration	S19 Divers.pref.	X	**N**	X	**X**	**N**	X	X	**X**
	S20 Barr. to entry	X	**N**	X	**X**	**N**	X	X	**X**
	S21 Barr. to exit	X	**N**	X	**X**	**N**	X	X	**X**
Regulation	R1 No. insurers	X	**N**	X	**X**	**–1**	X	X	**X**
	R2 Domestic	X	**N**	X	**X**	**–1**	X	X	**X**

(continued)

TABLE 3A.1 Overview of Hypotheses and Results of Tests *(continued)*

	Hypothesis	*Country (chapter)*			
		Turkey (8)			
		PC	*PL*	*CBI*	*PUL*
Demand: Yes/No	D1 Loading	X	**N**	X	**X**
	D2 Income	X	**1**	X	**X**
	D3 Lack info.	X	**N**	X	**X**
Demand: Coverage	D4 Loading	X	**N**	X	**X**
	D5 Income	X	**N**	X	**X**
	D6 Adv. select.	X	**N**	X	**X**
	D7 Lack info.	X	**N**	X	**X**
Benefits package	S1 Moral hazard	X	**N**	X	**X**
	S2 Divers. pref.	X	**N**	X	**X**
	S3 New hlth ri.	X	**N**	X	**X**
	S4 Regulation	X	**N**	X	**X**
Risk selection	S5 Moral hazard	X	**N**	X	**X**
	S6 Size benefits	X	**N**	X	**X**
	S7 Concentration	X	**N**	X	**X**
	S8 Regulation	X	**N**	X	**X**
Loading	S9 Reinsurance	X	**N**	X	**X**
	S10 High-inc.mbr.	X	**N**	X	**X**
	S11 Copay, caps	X	**N**	X	**X**
	S12 Regulation	X	**N**	X	**X**
Insurance-driven integration	S13 Contest.h.c.m.	X	**N**	X	**X**
	S14 Contest.h.i.m.	X	**N**	X	**X**
	S15 Opportunist.b.	X	**N**	X	**X**
Provider-driven integration	S16 Contest.h.i.m.	X	**N**	X	**X**
	S17 Mark.pow.ins.	X	**N**	X	**X**
	S18 Cartelizn.ins.	X	**N**	X	**X**
Concen-tration	S19 Divers.pref.	X	**N**	X	**X**
	S20 Barr. to entry	X	**N**	X	**X**
	S21 Barr. to exit	X	**N**	X	**X**
Regula-tion	R1 No. insurers	X	**N**	X	**X**
	R2 Domestic	X	**N**	X	**X**

NOTES

1. For a survey, see Zweifel and Manning (2000).
2. For some theoretical developments, see Zweifel (2007).

REFERENCES

Arrow, K.J. 1965. "Aspects of the Theory of Risk Bearing" Yrjö Johnsson Lectures, Helsinki: Y.J. Säätiö. Reprinted in K.J. Arrow, *Essays in the Theory of Risk Bearing,* Amsterdam: North Holland, 1970.

Berman, P., R. Ahuja, and V. Kalavakonda. 2008. "India." Chap. 12, this volume.

Bitrán, R., and R. Muñoz. 2008. "Chile." Chap. 4, this volume.

Cederberg Heard, A., and A. Mahal. 2008. "Turkey." Chap. 8, this volume.

Cummins, J.D., and D.W. Sommer. 1996. "Capital and Risk in Property-Liability Insurance." *Journal of Banking and Finance* 20:1069–92.

Hu, T.W., and X. Ying. 2008. "China." Chap. 10, this volume.

Jung, K.T. 2008. "Republic of Korea." Chap. 15, this volume.

Keeler, E.B., J.P. Newhouse, and C.E. Phelps. 1977. "Deductibles and the Demand for Medical Services: The Theory of a Consumer Facing a Variable Price Schedule under Uncertainty." *Econometrica* 45 (3): 641–56.

Onwujekwe, O., and E.V. Velényi. 2008. "Nigeria." Chap. 13, this volume.

Pauly, M.V. 2007. "Insights on Demand for Private Voluntary Health Insurance in Less Developed Countries." In *Private Voluntary Health Insurance in Development: Friend or Foe?* ed. A.S. Preker, R.M. Scheffler, and M.C. Bassett, 25–54. Washington, DC.: World Bank.

Supakankunti, S. 2008."Thailand." Chap. 7, this volume.

Tajnikar, M., and P. Došenovič Bonča. 2008. "Slovenia." Chap. 14, this volume.

Thiede, M., and Mutyambizi, V. 2008. "South Africa." Chap. 6, this volume.

Zweifel, P. 2007. "The Theory of Social Health Insurance." *Foundations and Trends in Microeconomics* 3 (3): 183–273.

Zweifel, P., B.B. Krey, and M. Tagli. 2007. "Supply of Private Voluntary Health Insurance in Low-Income Countries." *Private Voluntary Health Insurance in Development: Friend or Foe,* ed. A.S. Preker, R.M. Scheffler, and M.C. Bassett, 55–113. Washington, DC: World Bank.

Zweifel, P., and W.G. Manning. 2000. "Moral Hazard and Consumer Incentives in Health Care." In *Handbook of Health Economics,* ed. A.J. Culyer and J.P. Newhouse, vol. 1, 409–59. Boston, MA: North Holland.

Zweifel, P., and M.V. Pauly. 2007. "Market Outcomes, Regulation, and Policy Recommendations." In *Private Voluntary Health Insurance in Development: Friend or Foe,* ed. A.S. Preker, R.M. Scheffler, and M.C. Bassett, 115–145. Washington, DC: World Bank.

PART 2

Evidence from the Past

CHAPTER 4

Chile

Ricardo A. Bitrán and Rodrigo Muñoz

Voluntary health insurance (VHI) in Chile, focusing on the determinants of enrolment and its impact on access to care and financial protection, is examined in this chapter, based on household data from the CASEN 2000 national socioeconomic survey (MIDEPLAN 2000). The results may help decision makers assess the potential role of VHI in low- and middle-income countries as a policy tool for improving access to services and financial protection. First, the authors examine household VHI enrolment decisions. Second, they evaluate the impact of VHI on access to health services. Third, they use a financial protection indicator based on the stability of nonmedical consumption to evaluate the performance of VHI. The findings show that enrolment in VHI is positively correlated with health risk, income, and education. Also, access to health care is better and financially more equitable among households with mandatory or voluntary health insurance than among uninsured households. What is more, nonmedical consumption appears substantially more stable among insured households. These results highlight the importance of mandatory and VHI schemes in developing countries. A main policy challenge is achieving enrolment for the poor, especially in the informal sector.

INTRODUCTION

In Chile, health insurance has mandatory and voluntary components. By law, formal workers must contribute a health insurance premium, equivalent to 7 percent of their income. However, they can voluntarily affiliate with FONASA (Fondo Nacional de Salud), the state insurer, or with an ISAPRE (Institucione de Salud Previsional), a private insurer. For informal workers, health insurance is entirely voluntary: they are free to choose whether to buy health insurance, and from whom.

The two principal insurer types, FONASA and the ISAPREs, operate in markedly different ways (table 4.1). For example, FONASA offers a mandatory coverage plan, while the ISAPREs offer a set of choices; FONASA provides all its beneficiaries with the same coverage, while the ISAPREs calculate their coverage based on the beneficiaries' premium and health-risk factors.[1] These differences make FONASA preferred by some and the ISAPREs preferred by others.

Product and cost (premium) are possibly the most important determinants of enrolment in one or another type of insurer (amount and quality of coverage). In

TABLE 4.1 Chile: Private and Public Insurance Characteristics

	FONASA	*ISAPREs*
Enrolment	• Individual and indefinite	• Through a private agreement
	• Cannot refuse admission	• ISAPRE reserves the right of admission
Beneficiaries	• Main affiliate and family dependents	• Main affiliate, family and medical dependents[a]
Premium	• Mandatory premium = 7% of income	• Mandatory premium = 7% of income
		• Voluntary premium > 7% possible
Financing	• Through affiliate premium and government subsidy	• Through affiliate premium
Coverage	• Same coverage independent of premium and risk factor	• Depends on premium, number of dependents, and risk factor derived from the age and gender of main affiliate and its dependents

Source: Superintendencia de ISAPREs 2001.
a. Medical dependents are all people that the affiliate includes in his / her health insurance contract.

exchange for the premium, ISAPRE beneficiaries are reimbursed for part of their medical treatment costs. The uncovered part, the copayment, is a percentage of the total costs, up to a ceiling beyond which the ISAPRE does not pay. In 2002, the ISAPREs incorporated catastrophe coverage, a mechanism whereby beneficiaries are fully covered for expenses above a specified threshold (about US$5,000 per event, depending on the ISAPRE).

The percentage of the total costs covered by ISAPREs is proportional to the premium. Because the premium is a percentage of beneficiaries' income, beneficiaries with higher income obtain better coverage than those with lower incomes (figure 4.1). This is inconvenient for lower-income beneficiaries, because their copayments are prohibitively high.

FONASA's coverage, unlike ISAPREs' or other indemnity insurers' coverage, is inversely related to the level of the premium. FONASA groups its beneficiaries in four income categories: A to D. Group A congregates individuals with the lowest income (indigents), and group D congregates the highest-income individuals. Groups B and C fall in between. Beneficiaries in group A pay no premium or copayment. Groups B, C, and D pay a premium of 7 percent of their income, but group B has no copayments, group C has a 10 percent copayment, and group D has a 20 percent copayment. This encourages low-income individuals to enroll in FONASA, because their premium is too low (7 percent of their income) to pay for the equivalent coverage in an ISAPRE. Conversely, higher-income individuals prefer ISAPREs, where they can buy better coverage with their 7 percent premium.

VHI coexists with mandatory health insurance (MHI). For example, formal workers are compelled to buy at least a 7 percent premium (MHI), but also have two components of VHI: choosing between ISAPREs or FONASA (choice 1 in

FIGURE 4.1 Three Modalities of Health Insurance Coverage

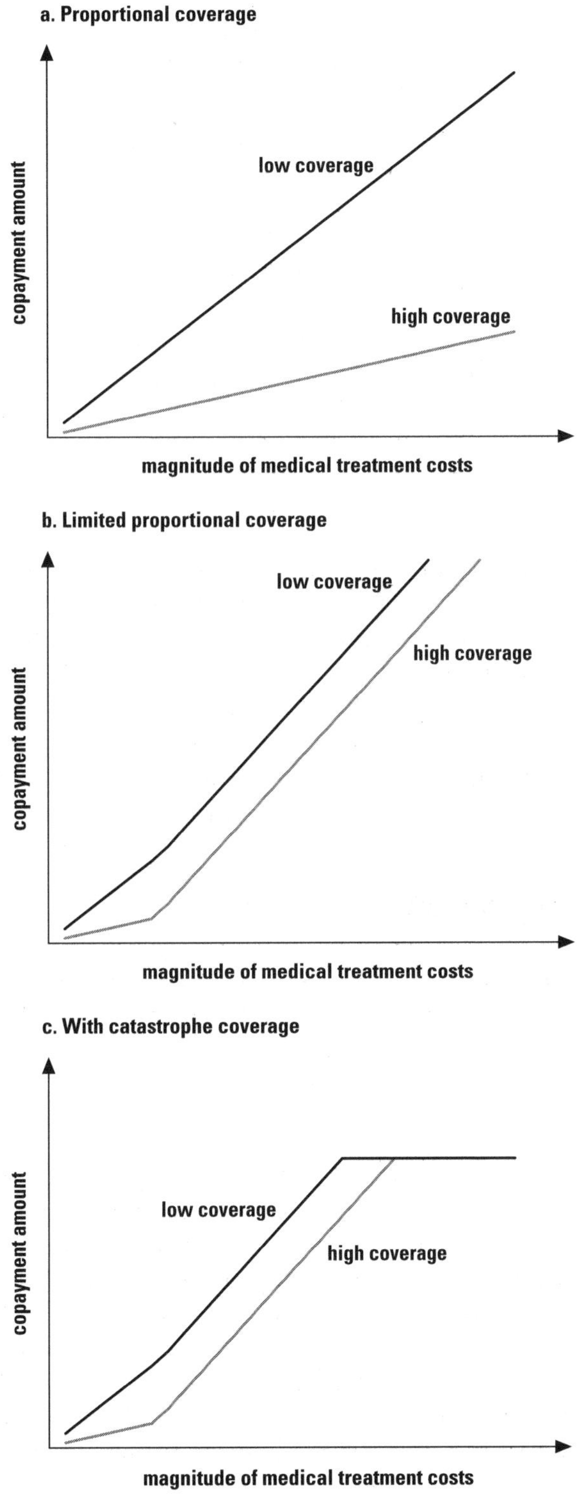

Source: Authors.

FIGURE 4.2 Chile: VHI Components

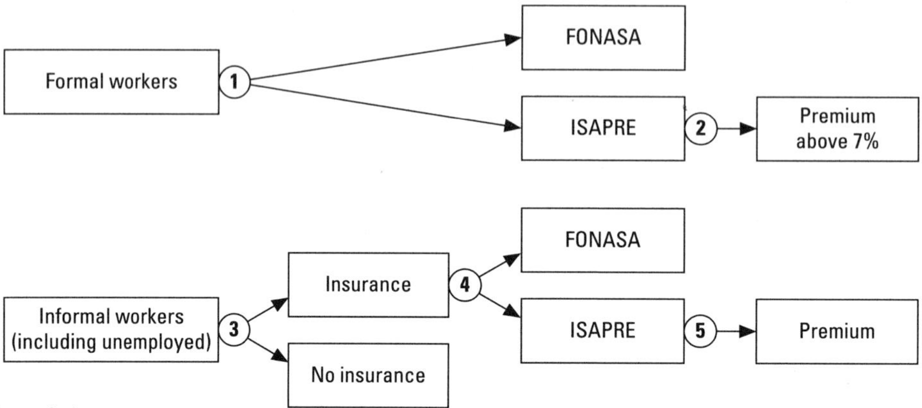

Source: Authors.

figure 4.2); and buying additional coverage above 7 percent in the case of ISAPREs (choice 2). Informal workers, by contrast, have three components of VHI: they may remain uninsured (choice 3); they may choose ISAPREs or FONASA (choice 4); and, when choosing ISAPREs, they may buy any premium they wish (choice 5).

VHI is governed by the laws of supply and demand, and thus determined mostly by the behavior of the individuals buying insurance and by the behavior of the insurers. This study aims at evaluating some aspects of the resulting VHI market.

OBJECTIVES AND METHODOLOGY

The objective of this study is to evaluate VHI in the following aspects: its determinants of enrolment, its impact on access to care, and the financial protection (FP) it confers.

Data

This study uses household data from CASEN 2000, a 65,000 household survey designed to measure a wide variety of social indicators (MIDEPLAN 2000). The relevant topics covered in its health module are: health insurance affiliation and access to health services. These data permit evaluation of the determinants of enrolment in VHI and its impact on access to care. However, the CASEN 2000 is missing two important indicators: out-of-pocket health spending (OOPS) and health insurance premium amounts. This impairs the FP analysis, because any FP measure should take into account the magnitude of the financial health shocks, which is normally measured through OOPS. It also impairs the analysis of choices 2 and 5 (figure 4.2), because the insurance premium is unknown. To allow an FP analysis, OOP health expenses were inferred from other CASEN 2000 variables, using the methodology in Bitrán and Sanhueza (2002).

Unit of Analysis: The Insurance Household

Household surveys have two natural units of analysis: households and individuals. Neither is an appropriate unit for analyzing demand in the VHI market, because VHI is not bought by households or individuals. In Chile, the insurance-buying agent is a group of individuals within a household, composed of the main affiliate and its dependents. This group, which is denominated "insurance household," constitutes a more appropriate unit of analysis.

In a single household, several insurance households may coexist. For example, consider a household with four members: two parents and two children. The mother has been in FONASA since before she was married and had children and has remained in that system. The father, however, has taken charge of his two children under his current ISAPRE health plan. This household is thus composed of two insurance households: (1) the mother, with FONASA, and (2) the father and children, with ISAPRE.

When analyzing FP of insurance households, it is necessary to take into account that they have different premiums, coverage, and OOPS. However, their income is shared with other insurance households in the same household. Therefore, FP depends on both household and insurance household characteristics.

Indicators

This section presents the indicators used for evaluating VHI: (1) determinants of enrolment, (2) impact on access to health care, and (3) financial protection.

Determinants of Enrolment

Several household and individual characteristics influence an insurance household's choice of enrolling or not in a VHI scheme. CASEN 2000 measures some of these, like income, household size and composition, education level, and so on.

To estimate the importance of these determinants, a logit model was created with CASEN 2000 data. The logit model describes the probability of an insurance household's enrolling in VHI, as a function of a set of determinants, as follows:

$$logit\ (Enrolment) = \beta_0 + \beta_1 \cdot X_1 + \beta_2 \cdot X_2 + \ldots + \beta_n \cdot X_n .$$

The logit function is a logarithmic transformation of the odds of enrolling against not enrolling:

$$logit\ (Enrolment) = Ln\ (p/(1 - p)) \qquad (p = Probability\ of\ enrolment).$$

Impact on Access to Health Care

The analysis of the impact on access to health is similar to the analysis of the determinants of enrolment. A logit model can be created with CASEN 2000 data, with the following form:

$$logit\ (Visit) = \beta_0 + \beta_1 \cdot X_1 + \beta_2 \cdot X_2 + \ldots + \beta_n \cdot X_n.$$

This model estimates the probability of health services use when an insurance household member reports a health problem.

Financial Protection

The proposed measure of FP is the inverse of the coefficient of variation of non-medical consumption (NMC):

$$FP = \mu_{NMC} / \sigma_{NMC}.$$

NMC represents the resources a household has left after spending on health. A household that has to pay for an expensive health shock will have few resources left for other uses, a small NMC, and consequently a low FP. Conversely, a healthy household or a household that does not have to pay for an expensive health shock will have more resources left for other uses, a larger NMC, and thus a larger FP.

As a result, population segments with a large average NMC (μ_{NMC}) are better protected against health expenses, and have higher FP, than population segments whose average NMC is low. Also, population segments whose NMC variance (σ_{NMC}) is low have fewer risks of seeing their NMC abruptly altered than population segments whose variance of NMC is high. Thus the former have better FP than the latter. These two behaviors are reflected in the NMC variation coefficient.

According to its definition, NMC represents the resources a household has left after spending on health:

$$NMC = Y - P - OOP,$$

where: *Y* is the household's monthly income;
P is the monthly health insurance premium;
OOP is the value of out-of-pocket health expenses.

OOP, in turn, depends on the magnitude of the health shock and the individual's insurance coverage:

$$OOP = S \cdot (1 - COV)$$

where: *S* is the price of the health shock; and
COV is the percentage of the health treatment cost covered by the insurer.

FIGURE 4.3 Chile: Household Decision Tree regarding Health Insurance

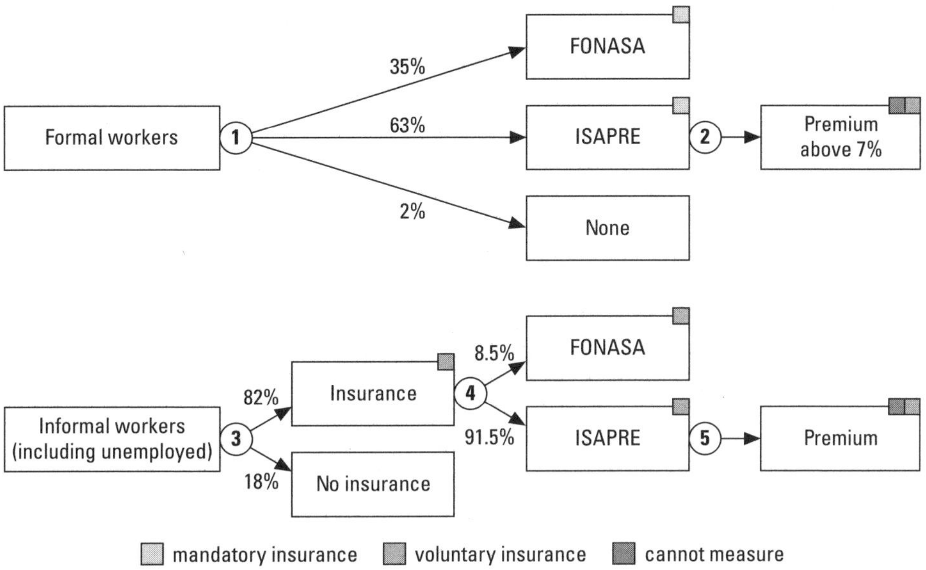

Source: Authors, based on CASEN 2000.

In summary, a household's FP depends on its income, premium, and insurance coverage.

RESULTS

This section presents the results of the study. Some basic VHI statistics describing population coverage in Chile are presented in annex 4A. In this section, the determinants of enrolment are analyzed separately among the informal and formal worker population; the impact of VHI on access to health services is quantified; and descriptive statistics of the FP indicator are presented.

Basic VHI Statistics

The distribution of formal and informal workers in Chile is almost even: 49 percent are formal and 51 percent are informal. Among formal workers, 35 percent choose ISAPRE while 63 percent choose FONASA (choice 1 in figures 4A.1 and 4A.2). The remaining 2 percent were either erroneously surveyed or present an illegal situation. Among informal workers, 18 percent choose to remain uninsured (choice 3) and 7 percent choose ISAPRE over FONASA (choice 4). Choices 2 and 5, however, cannot be measured with CASEN 2000, because insurance premium is unknown.

Determinants of Enrolment

The logit model of the determinant of enrolment in VHI may be applied to choice 3 (informal workers) choice 1 (formal workers) and choice 4 (informal workers). The results of each model are presented next.

Enrolment in VHI among Informal Workers

This model incorporates the following variables as determinants of choice 3: per capita income quintile, level of education, and family risk factor. Table 4A.1 shows that the variables in the model are highly significant (the probability of their coefficients being null is less than 1 percent). However, the model has a low predictive power (low R-square), because most informal workers are insured, making unequal the distribution of outcomes of choice 3.

The resulting logit model may be used to simulate an insurance household's probability of choosing insurance, depending on its income, level of education and risk factor (table 4A.2). The simulation shows that: families with high risk factors have higher probabilities of enrolling; the probability of enrolment is negatively correlated with income; and the probability of enrolment decreases with educational level.

Enrolment in ISAPREs among Informal Workers

This model incorporates the same determinants as in choice 3. Table 4A.3 shows that the variables in the model are highly significant (more than 1 percent). The model has a moderate explanatory power.

The simulation of an informal worker's probability of choosing an ISAPRE over FONASA is shown in table 4A.4: the probability of selecting an ISAPRE increases sharply with education and income, and, as family risk factors become larger, the probability of selecting an ISAPRE decreases.

Enrolment in ISAPREs among Formal Workers

This model incorporates the same determinants as choices 3 and 4. Table 4A.5 shows that the variables in the model are highly significant (more than 1 percent). The model has a high explanatory power.

The simulation of an informal worker's probability of choosing an ISAPRE over FONASA is shown in table 4A.6: the probability increases with the level of education and income and with larger family risk factors. In general, the probability of selecting an ISAPRE is larger among formal than informal workers.

Impact on Access to Health Care

The logit model of VHI impact on access to health care estimates the probability that an insurance household member will use health services when faced with a health problem. Table 4A.7 shows that the variables in the model are highly significant, but the model has a low predictive power. *Exp(β)* is at least 2 for all health insurance dummies. This means that the odds of accessing health care against not doing so are twice as high in households with health insurance than among uninsured households.

The first simulation of the model is shown in table 4A.8. The results show that families with high risk factors have a larger probability of seeking care when faced with a health problem. As with the selection of ISAPREs, access to health care increases with education up to the secondary level. Formal workers are more likely to seek care than informal ones, and income is highly correlated with the probability of access to health care.

The second simulation is shown in table 4A.9. The results show that the probability of seeking care is higher in insured households than uninsured ones; the difference ranges between 12 and 19 percentage points. In addition to increasing access, insurance reduces the inequities between different income quintiles. For example, formal workers in quintiles 1 and 5 have a 0.10 probability difference if enrolled in an ISAPRE, but if uninsured, the difference reaches 0.14. Formal work also contributes to reducing inequities.

Impact on Financial Protection

Using OOP health expenses inferred from other CASEN 2000 variables, NMC may be estimated for each insurance household in the survey. FP may thus be calculated for different segments of the population. Table 4A.10 shows this analysis for informal and formal workers, by type of insurance. In both the informal and formal sector, FONASA A (indigents) and ISAPRES show the largest FP. The uninsured, particularly those in the informal sector, show the lowest FP (high variance of NMC). Thus, one may conclude that VHI increases FP. For example, an informal worker choosing an ISAPRE over staying uninsured almost triples his/her FP.

The second analysis consists of an econometric model of NMC, as a function of individual and household characteristics. A linear regression of the natural logarithm of NMC is shown in table 4A.11. The resulting model is significant and has a high predictive power.

As tables 4A.12 and 4A.13 show, the uninsured have the lowest predicted NMC in comparison to the insured, an expected result. Also, ISAPRE and FONASA B present the highest predicted NMC.

Impact of VHI on FP

As seen in figure 4.4, nonmedical consumption (NMC) decreases as S increases. For a low π (1 percent and 5 percent), NMC has an acute slope, being highest when there is no shock ($S = 0$), and lowest for big shocks. This produces a high variability in NMC, and thus a low FP. For a medium π (7 percent), NMC has a

FIGURE 4.4 Chile: Nonmedical Consumption, Health Shock Magnitude, and Premiums

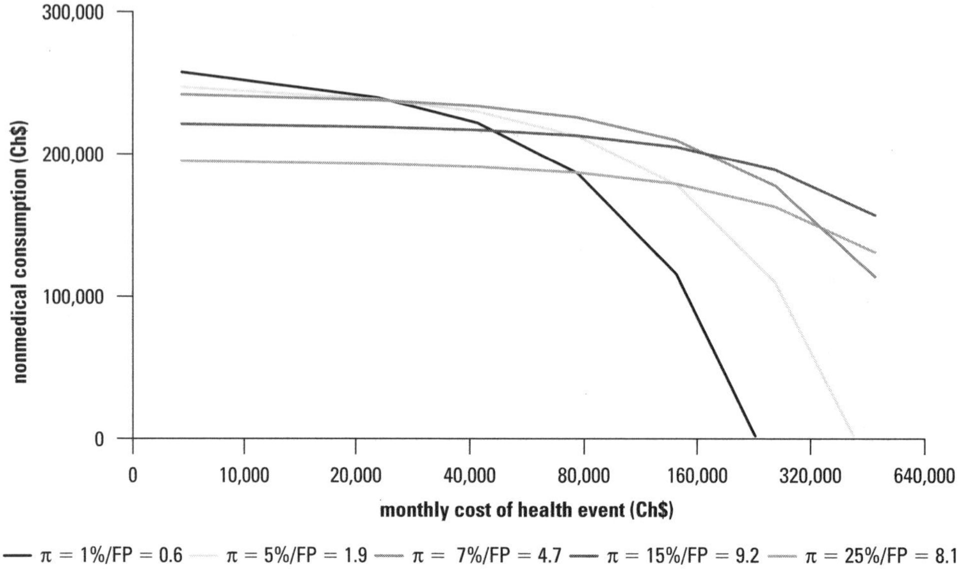

Source: Authors.
Note: Nonmedical consumption (NMC) as function of health shock magnitude (S), for different premiums. (Y = Ch$260.000, RF = 1).

FIGURE 4.5 Chile: Nonmedical Consumption, Health Shock Magnitude, and Income

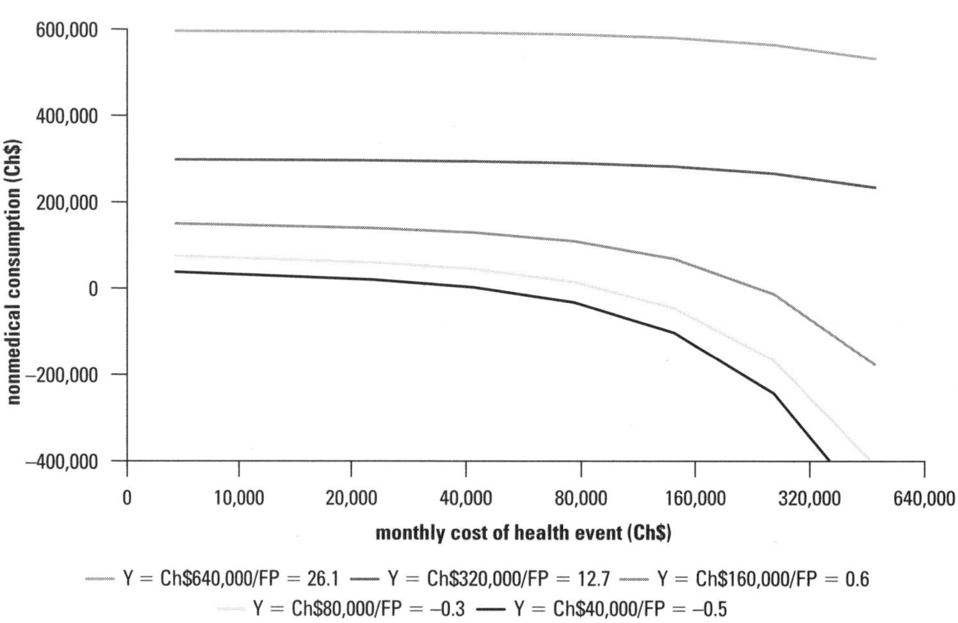

Source: Authors.
Note: Nonmedical consumption (NMC) as a function of health shock magnitude (S), for different income levels. (π = 7%, RF = 1).

FIGURE 4.6 Chile: Nonmedical Consumption, Health Shock Magnitude, and Family Risk Factors

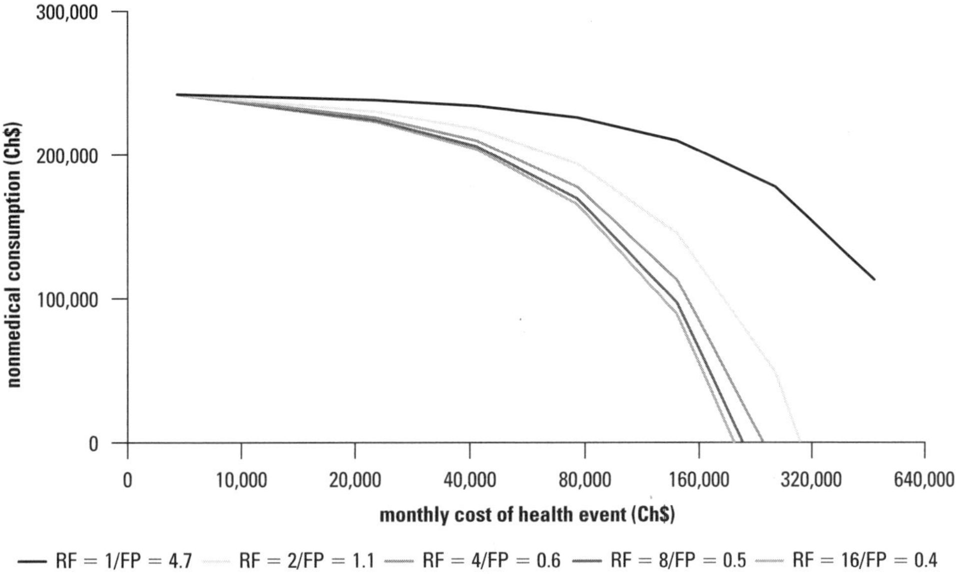

Source: Authors.
Note: Nonmedical consumption (NMC) as a function of health shock magnitude (S), for different family risk factors. (π = 7%, Y = Ch$260,000)

less acute slope, generating a larger FP. For a large π (15 percent and 25 percent), NMC is much less sensitive to shocks (which increases FP due to the lower variability. However, the cost of the premium starts taking on significance, lowering the average of NMC and thus its FP.

Figure 4.5 shows that FP increases with income, for two reasons. First, the average NMC increases with income. Second, NMC is less sensitive to shocks at high income levels (because of the better coverage these household obtain for the same 7 percent premium). FP decreases with a family's risk factor, because, for the same 7 percent premium, coverage decreases with RF (figure 4.6).

CONCLUSIONS

The objective of this study was to evaluate the VHI experience in Chile, focusing on its determinants of enrolment, its impact on access to care, and the financial protection it confers. Using CASEN 2000 household data, the authors examined health insurance enrolment behavior, the impact of health insurance on access to health services, and the financial protection it confers.

The analysis shows that enrolment in VHI is correlated positively with health risk, income, and education. This means that the poor and uneducated have less probability of being insured than the nonpoor and educated. Also, informal workers are at a disadvantage in their choices with respect to formal workers. When their health risk is high, they usually choose FONASA over ISAPREs, while formal workers opt for an ISAPRE. This is probably related to the fact that ISAPREs tend to reject higher-risk individuals, while FONASA is compelled to admit everybody.

Access to health services is also correlated positively with health risk, income, and education. This reflects an expected pattern in a country like Chile: that health insurance and access to health services is not equitable. The poor and the uneducated, who have less access than the rest of the population, are also more likely to be uninsured. This reinforces the finding that access is much more probable in insured than in uninsured households. Summing up, the poor and uneducated are missing a tool that could help them access the health services they need.

In exploring financial protection provided by health insurances, the indicator used was the degree of stability of nonmedical consumption, or, in other words, the probability of having enough resources left after a costly health event. The main finding is that nonmedical consumption appears substantially more stable in insured households. For example, an informal worker insured with an ISAPRE has almost three times as much financial protection as an uninsured individual.

These results have important policy implications. They all point toward the importance of mandatory and VHI schemes in Chile: they are more equitable; they improve access to health services; and they increase financial protection. One of the main challenges remains in enrolling the poor, especially in the informal sector.

ANNEX 4A STATISTICAL TABLES

TABLE 4A.1 Chile: Logit Model of Choice 3

–2 Log likelihood: 6,204,686 *Cox & Snell R-square: 0.081* *Nagelkerke R-square: 0.133*

	B	*S.E.*	*Wald*	*Df*	*Sig.*	*Exp(B)*
Constant	0.407	0.012	1,206	1	0	1.50
Per capita income quintiles						
Quintile 1	0.486	0.004	18,760	1	0	1.63
Quintile 2	0.210	0.003	3,704	1	0	1.23
Quintile 3	0.082	0.003	558	1	0	1.09
Quintile 4	0.034	0.004	95	1	0	1.04
Quintile 5						1.00
Level of education						
None						1.00
Primary	0.071	0.012	37	1	0	1.07
Secondary	–0.598	0.003	37,691	1	0	0.55
College	–0.238	0.003	6,941	1	0	0.79
Family risk factor	0.278	0.000	356,255	1	0	1.32
1						1.00
2						1.32
4						2.30

Source: Authors, based on CASEN 2000.
Note: Shows the probability of choosing insurance over choosing no insurance.

TABLE 4A.2 Chile: Simulation of Choice 3

	Family risk factor				
	1	*2*	*4*	*8*	*16*
Level of education (third quintile)					
None	0.68	0.74	0.83	0.94	0.99
Primary	0.70	0.75	0.84	0.94	0.99
Secondary	0.56	0.63	0.75	0.90	0.99
College	0.50	0.57	0.70	0.88	0.98
Per capita income quintiles (secondary education)					
Quintile 1	0.66	0.72	0.81	0.93	0.99
Quintile 2	0.59	0.66	0.77	0.91	0.99
Quintile 3	0.56	0.63	0.75	0.90	0.99
Quintile 4	0.55	0.62	0.74	0.89	0.99
Quintile 5	0.54	0.61	0.73	0.89	0.99

Source: Authors, based on CASEN 2000.

TABLE 4A.3 Chile: Logit Model of Choice 4

–2 Log likelihood: 2,348,803 *Cox & Snell R-square: 0.159* *Nagelkerke R-square: 0.365*

	B	*S.E.*	*Wald*	*Df*	*Sig.*	*Exp(B)*
Constant	–2.419	0.041	3,557	1	0	0.09
Per capita income quintiles						
Quintile 1	–3.229	0.007	219,792	1	0	0.04
Quintile 2	–3.068	0.007	194,254	1	0	0.05
Quintile 3	–2.083	0.005	165,945	1	0	0.13
Quintile 4	–1.350	0.004	94,449	1	0	0.26
Quintile 5						1.00
Level of education						
None						1.00
Primary	0.185	0.042	20	1	0	1.20
Secondary	1.693	0.010	27,708	1	0	5.44
College	1.033	0.004	77,181	1	0	2.81
Family risk factor	–0.047	0.001	3,912	1	0	0.95
1						1.00
2						0.95
4						0.87

Source: Authors based on CASEN 2000.
Note: Shows the probability of choosing an ISAPRE over FONASA among informal workers.

TABLE 4A.4 Chile: Simulation of Choice 4

	Family risk factor				
	1	*2*	*4*	*8*	*16*
Level of education (third quintile)					
None	0.01	0.01	0.01	0.01	0.01
Primary	0.01	0.01	0.01	0.01	0.01
Secondary	0.06	0.06	0.06	0.05	0.03
College	0.16	0.16	0.14	0.12	0.09
Per capita income quintiles (secondary education)					
Quintile 1	0.02	0.02	0.02	0.02	0.01
Quintile 2	0.03	0.02	0.02	0.02	0.01
Quintile 3	0.06	0.06	0.06	0.05	0.03
Quintile 4	0.13	0.12	0.11	0.09	0.07
Quintile 5	0.36	0.35	0.33	0.29	0.22

Source: Authors, based on CASEN 2000.

TABLE 4A.5 Chile: Logit Model of Choice 1

–2 Log likelihood: 6,860,090		*Cox & Snell R-square: 0.259*			*Nagelkerke R-square: 0.354*	
	B	*S.E.*	*Wald*	*Df*	*Sig.*	*Exp(B)*
Constant	–0.049	0.016	10	1	0.002	0.95
Per capita income quintiles						
Quintile 1	–3.119	0.005	449,470	1	0	0.04
Quintile 2	–2.317	0.003	497,821	1	0	0.10
Quintile 3	–1.483	0.003	259,645	1	0	0.23
Quintile 4	–0.863	0.003	96,492	1	0	0.42
Quintile 5						1.00
Level of education						
None						1.00
Primary	–0.633	0.017	1,469	1	0	0.53
Secondary	1.219	0.006	46,569	1	0	3.39
College	0.825	0.002	135,252	1	0	2.28
Family risk factor	0.014	0.000	1,267	1	0	1.01
1						1.00
2						1.01
4						1.04

Source: Authors, based on CASEN 2000.
Note: Shows the probability of choosing an ISAPRE over FONASA among formal workers.

TABLE 4A.6 Chile: Simulation of Choice 1

	Family risk factor				
	1	*2*	*4*	*8*	*16*
Level of education (third quintile)					
None	0.18	0.18	0.19	0.19	0.21
Primary	0.10	0.11	0.11	0.11	0.13
Secondary	0.28	0.29	0.29	0.30	0.33
College	0.47	0.48	0.48	0.50	0.53
Per capita income quintiles (secondary education)					
Quintile 1	0.07	0.07	0.07	0.08	0.09
Quintile 2	0.15	0.15	0.15	0.16	0.17
Quintile 3	0.28	0.29	0.29	0.30	0.33
Quintile 4	0.42	0.43	0.43	0.45	0.47
Quintile 5	0.63	0.64	0.64	0.66	0.68

Source: Authors, based on CASEN 2000.

TABLE 4A.7 Chile: Logit Model of the Probability of Seeking Care for a Health Problem

–2 Log likelihood: 4,249,481 *Cox & Snell R-square: 0.028* *Nagelkerke R-square: 0.044*

	B	*S.E.*	*Wald*	*Df*	*Sig.*	*Exp(B)*
Constant	0.296	0.003	8,613	1	0	1.34
Per capita income quintiles						
Quintile 1	–0.615	0.005	14,109	1	0	0.54
Quintile 2	–0.375	0.005	5,366	1	0	0.69
Quintile 3	–0.466	0.005	8,785	1	0	0.63
Quintile 4	–0.370	0.005	5,472	1	0	0.69
Quintile 5						1.00
Health insurance						
FONASA A	0.806	0.005	27,848	1	0	2.24
FONASA B	0.729	0.005	20,991	1	0	2.07
FONASA C	0.694	0.006	12,965	1	0	2.00
FONASA D	0.830	0.006	18,739	1	0	2.29
ISAPRE	0.763	0.006	17,376	1	0	2.14
Uninsured						1.00
Level of education						
None						1.00
Primary	–0.052	0.013	16	1	0	0.95
Secondary	0.408	0.003	15,279	1	0	1.50
College	–0.092	0.004	613	1	0	0.91
Family risk factor	0.071	0.001	19,990	1	0	1.07
1						1.00
2						1.07
4						1.24
Occupation	0.191	0.014	185	1	0	1.21
Formal						1.21
Informal						1.00

Source: Authors, based on CASEN 2000.

TABLE 4A.8 Chile: First Simulation of Probability of Seeking Care for a Health Problem

	Family risk factor				
	1	*2*	*4*	*8*	*16*
Level of education (formal worker; third quintile)					
None	0.52	0.54	0.58	0.64	0.76
Primary	0.51	0.53	0.56	0.63	0.75
Secondary	0.61	0.63	0.66	0.72	0.82
College	0.59	0.61	0.64	0.70	0.81
Occupation (secondary education; third quintile)					
Formal	0.61	0.63	0.66	0.72	0.82
Informal	0.56	0.58	0.62	0.68	0.79
Per capita income quintiles (secondary education; formal worker)					
Quintile 1	0.57	0.59	0.63	0.69	0.80
Quintile 2	0.63	0.65	0.68	0.74	0.83
Quintile 3	0.61	0.63	0.66	0.72	0.82
Quintile 4	0.63	0.65	0.68	0.74	0.83
Quintile 5	0.71	0.73	0.76	0.80	0.88

Source: Authors based on CASEN 2000.

TABLE 4A.9 Chile: Second Simulation of Probability of Seeking Care for a Health Problem

	Health insurance					
	FONASA A	*FONASA B*	*FONASA C*	*FONASA D*	*ISAPRE*	*Uninsured*
Per capita income quintiles (secondary education; informal worker; risk factor = 1)						
Quintile 1	0.71	0.70	0.69	0.72	0.70	0.53
Quintile 2	0.76	0.75	0.74	0.76	0.75	0.59
Quintile 3	0.74	0.73	0.72	0.75	0.73	0.56
Quintile 4	0.76	0.75	0.74	0.77	0.75	0.59
Quintile 5	0.82	0.81	0.80	0.83	0.82	0.67
Per capita income quintiles (secondary education; formal worker; risk factor = 1)						
Quintile 1	0.75	0.74	0.73	0.76	0.74	0.57
Quintile 2	0.79	0.78	0.77	0.80	0.79	0.63
Quintile 3	0.78	0.76	0.76	0.78	0.77	0.61
Quintile 4	0.79	0.78	0.46	0.80	0.79	0.63
Quintile 5	0.85	0.84	0.83	0.85	0.84	0.71

Source: Authors, based on CASEN 2000.

TABLE 4A.10 Chile: Financial Protection by Insurance Type in the Formal and Informal Sectors, 2000

	FONASA A	*FONASA B*	*FONASA C*	*FONASA D*	*ISAPRE*	*Uninsured*	*Total*
Informal workers							
Insurance households	3,302,099	1,381,908	329,547	382,671	488,728	1,300,093	7,185,046
Per capita monthly income (Ch$)	49,327	104,952	117,938	182,714	488,436	133,458	115,368
Health problems during last 30 days (%)	36	32	28	27	27	18	31
Sought ambulatory care (%)	77	79	73	78	72	62	75
Hospitalized during last 12 months (%)	24	17	16	16	19	6	18
Monthly OOP (Ch$)	15,425	67,597	101,055	160,458	76,608	186,816	72,264
Monthly premium (Ch$)	15,014	23,675	27,725	42,131	155,216	0	25,527
NMC as a percentage of income (%)	65	56	37	36	67	–12	47
Per capita monthly NMC-mean (Ch$)	36,914	68,132	70,928	111,575	420,471	74,290	81,229
Per capita monthly NMC-std. dev. (Ch$)	63,668	147,362	151,397	205,000	705,964	355,031	273,383
Financial protection	0.58	0.46	0.47	0.54	0.60	0.21	0.30
Formal workers							
Insurance households	319,757	1,688,383	1,016,572	1,221,667	2,477,971	118,086	6,842,436
Per capita monthly income (Ch$)	44,723	71,589	74,959	107,121	241,497	138,737	139,869
Health problems during last 30 days (%)	39	31	30	29	29	18	30
Sought ambulatory care (%)	80	79	82	84	86	69	83
Hospitalized during last 12 months (%)	24	19	17	15	21	8	19
Monthly OOP (Ch$)	25,245	55,385	96,015	142,722	134,182	184,685	106,366
Monthly premium (Ch$)	18,165	21,724	21,624	29,667	79,861	0	43,640
NMC as a percentage of income (%)	75	64	49	42	53	0	53
Per capita monthly NMC-mean (Ch$)	34,441	48,052	40,270	56,853	183,577	85,510	97,547
Per capita monthly NMC-std. dev. (Ch$)	45,263	114,356	91,358	152,085	298,253	229,025	214,622
Financial protection	0.76	0.42	0.44	0.37	0.62	0.37	0.45

Source: Authors based on CASEN 2000.

TABLE 4A.11 Chile: Linear Regression (NMC)

R-squared	*0.692*				
	B	*S.E.*	*Beta*	*t*	*Sig.*
Constant	12.637	0.002		5,495.268	0
Per capita income quintiles					
Quintile 1	–2.785	0.001	–1.038	–3,903.261	0
Quintile 2	–2.025	0.001	–0.748	–2,993.394	0
Quintile 3	–1.577	0.001	–0.549	–2,400.856	0
Quintile 4	–1.107	0.001	–0.369	–1,751.061	0
Quintile 5					
Health insurance					
FONASA A	0.061	0.001	0.024	83.615	0
FONASA B	0.117	0.001	0.043	156.763	0
FONASA C	0.027	0.001	0.007	30.287	0
FONASA D	–0.051	0.001	–0.014	–58.508	0
ISAPRE	0.102	0.001	0.037	123.61	0
Uninsured					
Level of education					
None					
Primary	–0.100	0.002	–0.007	–45.052	0
Secondary	–0.035	0.001	–0.011	–65.065	0
College	0.083	0.001	0.030	158.398	0
Family risk factor	–0.009	0.000	–0.021	–127.123	0
Formal occupation	–0.037	0.000	–0.016	–80.718	0

Source: Authors based on CASEN 2000.

TABLE 4A.12 Chile: NMC Formal Workers with Secondary Education and Risk Factor = 1

	Per capita income quintile				
	1	*2*	*3*	*4*	*5*
Health insurance					
FONASA A	16,859	36,049	56,424	90,278	273,115
FONASA B	17,822	38,108	59,645	95,432	288,707
FONASA C	16,287	34,826	54,509	87,215	263,848
FONASA D	15,072	32,228	50,443	80,708	244,164
ISAPRE	17,556	37,540	58,757	94,011	284,409
Uninsured	15,854	33,900	53,059	84,895	256,829

Source: Authors based on CASEN 2000.

TABLE 4A.13 Chile: NMC Informal Workers with Secondary Education and Risk Factor = 1

	Per capita income quintile				
	1	*2*	*3*	*4*	*5*
Health insurance					
FONASA A	17,501	37,422	58,572	93,714	283,511
FONASA B	18,500	39,558	61,916	99,065	299,697
FONASA C	16,907	36,152	56,584	90,535	273,891
FONASA D	15,646	33,455	52,363	83,781	253,459
ISAPRE	18,225	38,969	60,994	97,590	295,235
Uninsured	16,457	35,190	55,079	88,126	266,606

Source: Authors, based on CASEN 2000..

NOTES

The authors would like to thank Alexander Preker, for his direction and support, and Rafael Cortéz and José Pablo Gómez-Meza for their helpful review of a previous draft of this chapter. They are grateful also to Mark Pauly and the participants at the Wharton Conference on Voluntary Health Insurance in Developing Countries, March 15–16, 2005, for their useful suggestions.

1. A family's health risk factor is a proxy of the probability that one its members suffers a health event. It is used by ISAPREs to define their coverage, and is also a determinant of enrolment. A family's risk factor equals the sum of the individual risk factors of all family members, which depend on their age, gender, and dependency status. The individual risk factors are shown in the table:

Age range (years)	*Male affiliate*	*Female affiliate*	*Male dependent*	*Female dependent*
0–20	0.9	2.0	0.9	0.9
20–49	1.0	2.6	0.6	1.4
50–59	1.7	2.7	1.9	1.9
60 and more	3.0	3.5	3.4	2.8

REFERENCES

Gatica, J., and P. Romaguera. 2005. *El Mercado Laboral en Chile: Nuevos Temas y Desafios*. Geneva: International Labour Organization.

Bitrán, R., and G. Sanhueza. 2002. "The Risk of Poverty from Health Shocks in Chile." Monograph for the World Bank, Washington, DC.

Bitrán, R., and C. Vergara. 2001. *Evolución y Determinantes de los Costos Técnicos de las ISAPRE Abiertas*. Monograph for Salud y Futuro.

Ministerio de Planificación (MIDEPLAN), División Social. 2000. *Encuesta de Caracterización Socioeconómica* (CASEN); accessed at www.mideplan.cl/casen.

Superintendencia de ISAPREs. 2001. *¿Cuáles son los beneficios del Sistema Isapre? Guía del Usuario*. http://alegislativo.bcn.cl/alegislativo/pdf/cat/docs/2981-11/200.pdf; accessed March 25, 2008.

CHAPTER 5

Egypt

Heba Nassar and Sameh El-Saharty

With its significant progress in health status, the Arab Republic of Egypt has caught up with other economically comparable countries. Demand for health services will continue to grow, however, due to Egypt's demographic and health transitions and other challenges confronting the health system. Health expenditure has been outpacing economic growth and is therefore unsustainable, given the modest medium-term economic growth projections. Social health insurance coverage is inequitable, covering less than half the population, and the health spending burden on households has increased. Public expenditures on health are inefficient, as exemplified by the sector's fragmented organization, low bed occupancy rate, and lack of performance-based payments to public providers. The voluntary health insurance (VHI) market is underdeveloped, covering only 5 percent of the population, and is concentrated (96 percent) in the hands of professional syndicates.

This chapter examines the impact of voluntary health insurance on financial protection, consumption smoothing, access to health care, and labor market productivity; and the determinants of enrolment with VHI. According to the econometric analysis presented in this chapter, the authors find VHI could increase workers' financial protection and that people might not object to sharing in its cost for better quality health services and access to them.

INTRODUCTION

By the mid-1990s, the economic reforms of the mid-1980s had brought macroeconomic stability to Egypt and progress on the structural front, particularly in financial and trade liberalization and privatization. However, at the end of the 1990s a combination of external shocks and economic policy failures weighed on overall economic development. Nonetheless, poverty declined from 21 percent to 16.7 percent of the population between 1995/96 and 2000. By 2003 Egypt's economy began to recover, with real growth for fiscal year (FY) 2004 officially estimated at 4.3 percent.

Egypt is a classic example of demographic transition. Most of its population is still young, but as it slowly ages, the structure of the population pyramid will change. A large, young population will enter the labor market, and the elderly population will more than double.

Egypt has made great strides in its health status. Egyptians have a higher life expectancy (68 years) than other countries at the same income level, In the mid-1990s its infant mortality and maternal mortality rates were higher than the other countries, but by 2002 both rates were lowered to the same level of other countries, respectively, 27 percent and 84 per 100,000 live birth.

The Egyptian Constitution guarantees every individual free health care services at government facilities. In practice, the health benefits coverage to the Egyptian population is provided through two systems, both with generous but not formally defined benefits:

- The National Health Services (NHS) system, represented mainly by the Ministry of Health and Population (MOHP), provides a wide range of health services to the entire population.
- A social health insurance (SHI) system, represented by the Health Insurance Organization (HIO), covers about 48 percent of the population.

In 2002, about 10 percent of all Egyptians used outpatient services, mostly from the private sector (56 percent), and about 3.3 percent used inpatient services, mostly from the public sector. Bed occupancy rates are very low. The average length of stay (ALOS) is about 3.4 days.

Egypt's health system is generally fragmented, with many different public and private providers and financing agents (Gericke 2004). The main governmental providers are the MOHP and several other ministries. The MOHP is responsible for overall health policy formulation in terms of execution and implementation in addition to drug policies and licensing for all health-related activities (Loffredo 2004). The governmental health system operates through a network of more than 3,500 rural and urban primary health care units, 161 integrated hospitals, 214 district general hospitals, and more than 209 specialized and teaching hospitals (El-Henawy 2000). The Ministry of Higher Education is responsible for under graduate and post-graduate university education, as well as tertiary-level curative services through about 14 university hospitals.

The public (economic) sector includes the Health Insurance Organization (HIO) and the Curative Care Organization (CCO), and hospitals affiliated with public sector firms. The HIO is Egypt's SHI organization. The CCO is an autonomous public sector provider of health care (El-Henawy 2000).

The private health care sector includes traditional healers and midwives, private pharmacies, private doctors, and private hospitals of all sizes (Gericke 2004). The private sector includes both the private-for-profit and private not-for-profit providers. Most clinics run by nongovernmental organizations (NGOs) are associated with religious institutions, which are registered with the Ministry of Social Affairs (USFCS 2004). Many private voluntary organizations (PVOs) also provide health care, through polyclinics and small hospitals usually affiliated with charitable organizations. Physicians, the most powerful professional group in the health sector, are permitted to work simultaneously for the government and in the private sector (USFCS 2004).

HEALTH FINANCING IN EGYPT

Between 1996 and 2002, total health expenditure (THE) in Egypt increased around 13 percent a year, outpacing overall economic growth during the same period. Total per capita health expenditures increased from US$43.50 to US$79.4 (World Bank 2006).[1] THE increased as a percentage of GDP from 3.8 to almost 6 percent, the same share as in other countries at comparable income.

The composition of health expenditures also changed. In FY 1996 expenditures were divided equally between private and public sources. In FY 2002, 60 percent of total expenditures came from private sources and 40 percent from public funds. In 2002, the largest share of total health expenditures was spent on curative care (52 percent), followed by pharmaceuticals (28 percent). Preventive and public health services constituted about 10 percent of total health expenditures; administrative costs, about 4 percent (MOHP 2005).

Public Expenditures on Health

Between 1996 and 2004, total public expenditures on health increased nearly two and a half times, at an average annual rate of about 6 percent in real terms. During the same period, per capita public expenditures on health increased from 74 to 103 Egyptian pounds (EGP) in real terms. In current U.S. dollars, per capita public expenditures on health increased from US$22 in 1996 to US$35 in 2000, and then in 2004 dropped almost to the 1996 level of US$24 (current dollars). Total public expenditures on health increased as a share of GDP from 1.9 percent in FY 1996 to 2.4 percent in FY 2002, then declined to 2.2 percent in FY 2003 and FY 2004 (figure 5.1). Total public expenditures on health averaged about 3.4 percent[2] of total public spending.

Private Health Expenditures

Private expenditures are predominantly out-of-pocket payment by households with a negligible role for private insurance, NGOs, and professional associations (syndicates). These collectively contributed about 0.6 percent of all private expenditures on health in FY 2002, compared with 0.5 percent in FY 1996 (MOHP 1997). In nominal terms, private expenditures increased from EGP 4.4 billion in FY 1996 to EGP 13.7 billion in FY 2002 (table 5A.1). In real terms, over the six-year period, private expenditures increased to EGP 10.8 billion in constant 1996 Egyptian pounds, a 2.5-fold increase. Per capita out-of-pocket health expenditures increased from EGP 74 in 1996 to EGP 207 in 2002 (El-Zanaty 2004), equivalent to EGP 163 in constant 1996 Egyptian pounds and representing a 1.7-fold increase. As a percentage of total health expenditures in Egypt, private expenditures increased from 50 percent in FY 1996 to 60 percent in FY 2002.

FIGURE 5.1 Egypt: Total Public Expenditures on Health, 1996–2004 (percent of GDP)

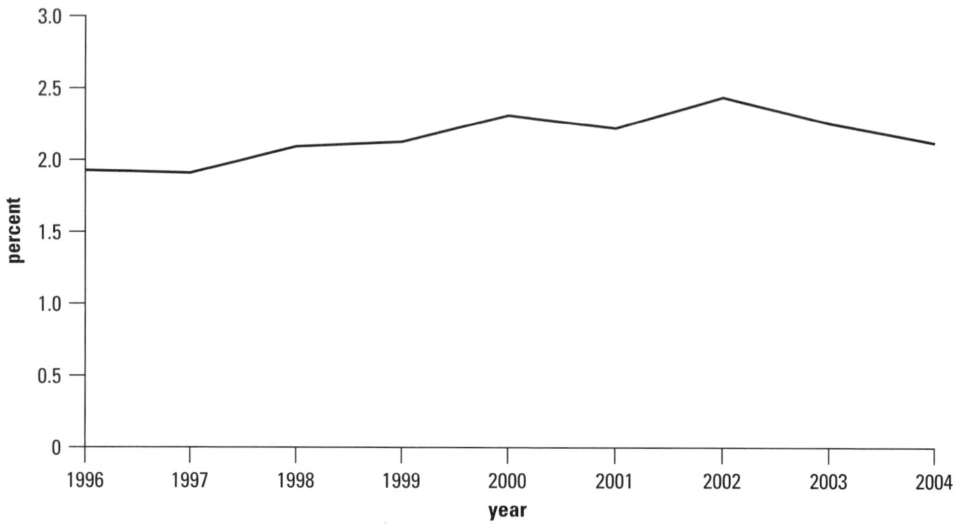

Source: World Bank 2006.

International Comparisons

Compared with countries at similar income levels, Egypt's total health expenditures as percentages of GDP and per capita health expenditures are similar (figure 5.2). However, when factoring in population size, per capita health expenditure is found to be slightly lower (figure 5.3). However, Egypt's total public expenditures on health both as a percentage of GDP and as a percentage of THE were lower than in other countries with comparable income.

STATUS OF HEALTH INSURANCE IN EGYPT

Foreign firms introduced insurance to Egypt in the second half of the 19th century to cover cotton production and export. Only in 1939, however, were the first laws governing the insurance industry enacted. By the 1950s, more than 200 private insurance companies were doing business in Egypt. In 1961, with the nationalization wave, the insurance industry was consolidated into three state-owned insurance companies and one state-owned reinsurance company.

The social security system was established by Law 79 of 1975, which covers civil servants and employees in public and private enterprises. The system was subsequently extended to the self-employed, workers abroad, and casual workers. The system is administered by two separate funds, the Government Fund for government workers and the Public and Private Sector Fund for employees of

FIGURE 5.2 Egypt: Compared with Global Trends in Total Health Expenditures, 2002 (percent of GDP)

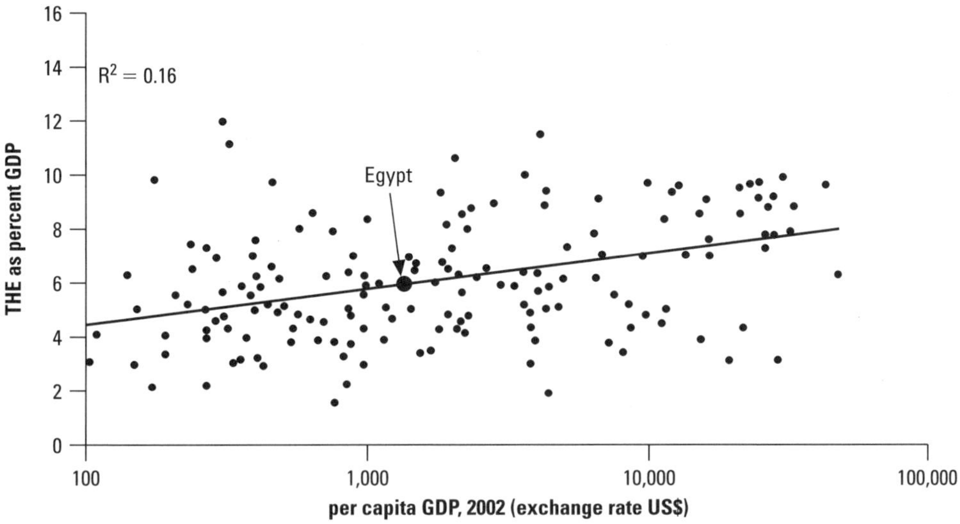

Source: Authors' calculations from WDI 2004.
$R^2 = 0.16$

FIGURE 5.3 Egypt: Compared with Global Trends in per Capita Health Expenditure, 2002

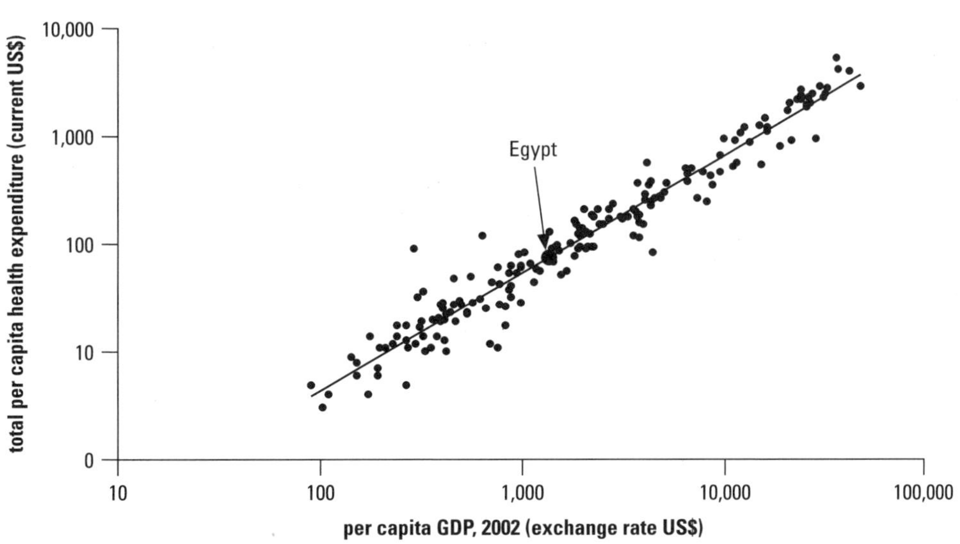

Source: Authors' calculations from WDI 2004.
$y = 1.1x - 1.5$
$R^2 = 0.96$

public and private enterprises, the self-employed, casual workers, and Egyptians working abroad (Loffredo 2004).

Statutory Social Health Insurance

The Egyptian Health Insurance Organization (HIO) was created in 1964. It is a parastatal, government-owned entity under the oversight of the Minister of Health and Population. As a health care provider, the HIO manages 39 hospitals, general practitioner clinics, 7,141 school health clinics, 1,040 specialist clinics, and 49 contracted pharmacies and 51 of its own.

There are four broad classes of HIO beneficiaries: all employees working in the government sector, some public and private sector employees, pensioners, and widows. In February 1993, the Student Health Insurance Program (SHIP) was introduced to cover 15 million students and school age children, thus increasing the total beneficiary population from 5 million in 1992 to 20 million in 1995. Ministerial Decree 380 of 1997 extended coverage to newborns, and by 2003 the eligible beneficiary population had increased to more than 34.8 million, almost 48 percent of the total population (Health Insurance Organization 2004).

HIO is principally funded through a system of premiums and copayments for services rendered. Mandated premiums from covered employees and employers are officially collected by the Social Insurance Organization (SIO), while the Pensions and Insurance Organization (PIO) collects premiums from pensioners. Both are supervised by the Ministry of Insurance and Social Affairs. Payment of premiums is compulsory for all public and private sector employers and employees. All collected premiums are transferred to the HIO. Since 1984, companies have been allowed to waive the employee premium if they purchase comparable care elsewhere. The level of copayments charged for services delivered is extremely low, which often incites overuse.

Voluntary Health Coverage

An estimated 5 percent of Egypt's population was covered by VHI in 2002, predominantly from professional syndicates and to a lesser extent private insurers/health maintenance organizations (HMOs) and state-owned insurers (table 5.1). The

TABLE 5.1 Egypt: Enrolment in VHI Organizations, 2002

VHI organization type	*Enrolment (1,000)*	*Percent of population*
State-owned insurers	22	0.03
Private insurers/HMOs	85	0.13
Syndicates	3163	4.76
Total private coverage	3270	4.92

Source: Calculated by authors from USAID 2002.

Note: Population was estimated at 66.4 million in 2002.

VHI coverage through the professional syndicates is exclusive. The state-owned and most of the private insurance companies offer health insurance together with other insurance products such as property, casualty, or fire insurance. VHI through syndicate and private organizations is more prevalent in urban areas. Moreover, 7.2 percent of the total insured population was found to be covered by VHI (El-Zanaty 2002).

VHI Provided by Public Companies

Al Chark Insurance, the first state–owned company to offer health insurance coverage to employer groups, in 1987, was quickly joined by the other two state-owned insurance companies, National Insurance and Misr Insurance. The three companies dominate the insurance market with a combined market share of 80 percent of all product lines. These three companies offer group health insurance to general insurance clients at below-cost premiums that are cross-subsidized from premiums in other lines of business. These companies are beginning to offer products to individuals as well.

Two main challenges were identified in the sale of individual products. First, marketing and distribution of individual products was difficult due to the inability to use telemarketing and other direct marketing practices effectively. Second, it was difficult for individuals to pay a lump-sum for annual coverage, and the alternative of billing them monthly would raise administrative costs. Al Chark Insurance Company, however, included health insurance with other products that were billed monthly. Companies reported that they subsidize health insurance to obtain the more lucrative lines of business, employ a small number of physicians, and contract with others.

To ensure quality, the National Insurance Company has entered into an arrangement with two other insurers (Mohandes Insurance Company and Delta Insurance Company) to form a company to handle underwriting and claims processing for the three insurance companies.

VHI Provided by Private Organizations

Middle East Medicare was the first HMO established in Egypt, in 1989. It operates a combined staff and preferred provider network. The network spans seven cities and includes 24 hospitals and medical centers, 1,114 consultants and specialists, 100 private clinics, and 15 satellite outreach clinics. Enrolment was estimated at 28,000 in 2000. It relies on the services of primary health care doctors for coordinating referral and ensuring continuity of care between the different service levels. The insured is free to select a service provider. The plan often includes a group coverage option for extending coverage to spouses and children.

Health Care International is an example of an independent practice association model HMO. Since 1997, it has been developing its contracted network of hospitals, physicians, pharmacies, and laboratories for about 5,000 enrollees. Medical examination is required before subscription, and the premium depends on the calculated risk calculation. It does not rely on the family doctor concept and is under the supervision of the Egyptian Insurance Supervision Authority (EISA).

Hi-Care, a physician-based staff model HMO, contracts with other providers. It delivers services at rented offices in hospitals. It owns four clinics and covers about 6,000 beneficiaries. Hi-Care uses specialists to serve as primary care physicians and to provide specialized care.

Other grassroots HMOs began to emerge. Many of these organizations were small groups of physicians serving a local market. The number of these HMOs nationally is estimated between 15 and 30 organizations. The development of HMOs may in part have been an effort by the physician community to generate demand for their services.

The insurance market has also seen the emergence of some commercially oriented companies such as the Egyptian International Medical Insurance Company (EIMIC), the first specialized health insurance company, established in 2000. It owns polyclinics and diagnostic centers and operates a preferred provider network. The network comprises over 1,500 physicians, 150 contracted hospital, and 75 laboratories and radiology centers. The overall enrolment is estimated at 50,000 beneficiaries. To prevent adverse selection, EIMIC provides employee or family coverage, but not both within an employer group.

In general, most private health insurance providers charge affordable subscription fees, ranging between EGP 300 to EGP 400 per enrollee per year for comprehensive coverage. There is usually an annual cap of between EGP 5,000 to EGP 50,000 on benefits per covered beneficiary.

A few health care administration companies have begun to emerge. These companies are agents for insurance companies in contracting service providers, reimbursing insurers, and managing accounts. They manage the insurance programs against a percentage from subscriptions or actual cost of the financing.

The private health insurance market faces a number of challenges. Entry requirements to the private health insurance market are prohibitive and incentives few for the insurance companies to seek a health insurance license. Under the insurance laws, a license requires capital of EGP 30 million (more than US$5 million), an insurmountable obstacle for most entities, and not realistically related to the anticipated risks. Therefore, health insurance often needs to be sold with other insurance products for some cross-subsidization. This is a major barrier to developing a competitive environment. Moreover, *fronting*, the practice of insuring a risk and ceding 100 percent of the risk to another carrier, is prevalent in Egypt, in both legal and illegal arrangements, and raters, underwriters, and other skilled insurance personnel are lacking. At the service delivery level, there is no continuity in medical care, no quality supervision, and insurance policies are subject to modification or cancellation without adequate justification. Finally, the regulatory environment of the private health insurance market is weak (MOHP 2001).

VHI Provided by Professional Syndicates

In Egypt, 21 professional associations ("syndicates") are authorized under the Trade Unions Law (No. 35/1976). A few syndicates offer organized systems of medical assistance in the form of health insurance schemes. About a million professionals and their families—3.2 million beneficiaries—are covered by syndicates.

The oldest of these schemes, established in 1988, is run by the Medical Union, which consists of four syndicates: physicians, dentists, pharmacists, and veterinarians. The Medical Union provides the most far-reaching coverage by extending health insurance coverage to the entire family as an option, including the member's parents. The union relies on a waiting period and a limited open enrolment period to control adverse selection. This arrangement was soon copied by engineers, lawyers and agricultural syndicates, teachers, nurses, and accountants, in FY93. Syndicates provide health insurance coverage exclusively to their members and in some cases their families. All these schemes operate at the national level and are managed by a central financial department except for the commercial syndicate, where each branch of the syndicate arranges its own health insurance scheme. Membership in any of these schemes is voluntary. The majority of the members reside in Cairo (75 percent) and Alexandria (20 percent).

All schemes provide comprehensive benefits, including outpatient and inpatient services with contracted providers at lower premiums than private VHI. The premium paid by beneficiaries varies with age and is higher for relatives of a syndicate member. Copayments are charged for inpatient and almost all outpatient services. Although the annual ceiling on total coverage is relatively low, it increases modestly in certain cases such as treatment in intensive care units. Hospitalizations and major outpatient services are reimbursed only if preapproved by the scheme. Drugs are not covered except for inpatient treatment and cancer chemotherapy. All schemes receive substantial subsidies from their respective syndicates.

Some of the key characteristic of these schemes are that they are not for profit, do not include outpatient drugs, and do not rely on family doctors for referral. Emergency cases, however, are still burdened with administrative procedures, ceilings are limited, and medical files are dispersed among service providers.

Utilization of health insurance and coverage

According to the 2002 Egypt Household Health Utilization and Expenditures Survey (El-Zanaty 2004), about 77 percent of households have at least one member covered by health insurance including around 44 percent covered by one type of insurance, 28 percent by two types of insurance, and 5 percent by three types of insurance. However, 23 percent of households have no health insurance coverage at all. The large percentage of health insurance coverage is due to the introduction of the Student Health Insurance Program (SHIP) in 1991 and the newborn insurance program in 1997.

Educational level is positively associated with health insurance coverage: about 92 percent of households, whose head is highly educated, have at least one member covered by health insurance compared with 66 percent of households, whose head is uneducated. Also, urban households, especially in urban governorates, are more frequently covered by health insurance than rural households. Moreover, the wealth index is positively related to insurance type, in particular the VHI provided by both the private sector and the syndicates.

General Regulatory Environment

Because a formal health insurance industry has not yet fully emerged, there are no specific private market regulations. Health insurance operations are governed by the same regulations as the long-term life insurance industry in terms of reserves (minimum capital requirements are US$ 8.8 million) and solvency requirements. The Egyptian Insurance Supervision Authority, under the Ministry of Investment, has the legal authority to license, regulate, rehabilitate, and liquidate an insurance company.

No Egyptian law or regulation specifically covers the health insurance industry, whether in terms of organizing the provision of services to an insured population under contracts with insurance companies or providing services to HMO members through the HMO's delivery system. Recent changes have permitted foreign ownership of insurance operations in Egypt, which is likely to attract new insurance companies seeking to exploit the market. Moreover, the country is witnessing the unregulated explosion of insurance companies selling subscription-type plans—operating without a license and not subject to any regulation, supervision, or control.

KEY ISSUES AND MAJOR CONSTRAINTS RELATED TO HEALTH CARE FINANCING IN EGYPT

In brief, health sector financing in Egypt is facing a number of challenges:

- *The growth in total health expenditures (13 percent in real terms) is outpacing economic growth* and is therefore unsustainable, given the modest medium-term projections of economic growth.
- *The health expenditure burden on households has increased* as private health expenditures have risen from 50 percent in 1996 to 60 percent of total health care spending in 2002, and almost 98 percent of it is direct out-of-pocket spending (OOPS).
- *Public expenditures on health are low.* Total public expenditures on health constituted 40 percent of total health expenditures and 2.4 percent of GDP in 2002, lower than economically comparable countries.
- *Public expenditures on health are inefficient.* The bed occupancy rate is less than half (43 percent) in large MOHP hospitals and much lower in the smaller hospitals, and operating expenses are low. Moreover, payments to public providers are not linked to performance.

- *SHI coverage is inequitable and covers less than half of the population.* Employees and workers in the formal sector and children attending schools are covered thus leaving out the unemployed, irregular workers, workers in the informal sector and who are out-of-school children, who represent the poorest half of the population.
- *The health care system is highly fragmented;* several organizations have overlapping functions. Moreover, services between different public provider organizations are not differentiated. Furthermore, several organizations combine both the financing and provision of health services.
- *Private health insurance is underdeveloped.* Private health insurance covers about 3.3 million Egyptians, only about 5 percent of the population. The market is dominated by the professional syndicates that cover more than 96 percent of the private insurance market.
- *Entry requirements to the private health insurance market are prohibitive.* Insurance companies have few incentives to seek a health insurance license.
- *The regulatory environment of the private health insurance market is weak.* Egypt is witnessing an unregulated explosion of insurance companies selling subscription-type plans. They are operating without a license and are not subject to regulation, supervision, or control.

ASSESSING THE POTENTIAL FOR VHI

The methodology adopted for assessing different policy options are a result of an econometric model applied to EHHUES 2002 data (El-Zanaty 2004) to analyze the impact of VHI on financial protection, consumption smoothing, access to health care, and labor market productivity, as well as the determinants of enrolment with VHI. The analysis is done twice: once on people insured with a private or state-owned organization, termed *private VHI* and constituting 5.47 percent of the total and once on *syndicate VHI,* the 2.6 percent who hold only syndicate insurance (table 5.2).

Financial Protection Model

The assumption in this model was that protection against high medical expenses is desired both privately and socially. The proposed measure is:

$\wp = \text{NMC}/(\sigma_{\text{NMC}})$ = inverse of coefficient of variation of NMC (nonmedical consumption).

The analysis was done at the household and individual levels, using household module data and data on the household head, a member of any private VHI. Next it was done on household heads who have only syndicate VHI. The main findings of this model follow.

TABLE 5.2 Egypt: Types of Insurance in Egypt Household Health Utilization and Expenditures Survey, 2002

Type of insurance	*All household members*	*Some members*	*One person only*	*School-age children*	*Mother, father of household head*	*Don't know*	*Total number of households*	*Total (%)*[a]	*Total (%)*
Members' work	7.30	13.60	79.20	0.20	0.10	0.00	986	13.00	9.96
Health Insurance Organization	2.30	27.80	73.50	1.30	0.00	0.00	4,103	54.10	41.44
Syndicates	21.00	16.70	62.30	0.00	0.00	0.00	257	3.40	2.60
School	0.00	1.60	1.70	96.40	0.20	0.10	5,217	68.70	52.69
Other types of health insurance	38.90	11.80	50.00	0.00	0.00	0.00	288	3.80	2.91
Private VHI (syndicates and other VHI types)	30.60	14.20	55.20	0.00	0.00	0.00	542	7.10	5.47

Source: Authors' calculations based on data from El Zanaty 2004.

Note: Total percentages are calculated relative to the total number of households with insurance coverage (7,590 households, about 76.7 percent of the total sample (9,901 households).

- Financial protection (FP) in both private and syndicate VHI is similar and relatively high. FP is estimated at 0.86566 (relatively high) for private VHI and 0.865663532 for syndicate VHI calculated for 9,737 households.
- Financial protection and NMC increase as the number of household members covered by public health insurance increases.
- NMC and FP increase as income and educational attainment increase, with one exception. At the highest income level, NMC is declining. This indicates the robust behavior of this category as usually high income levels are not well captured in national household survey; however, the mean of the NMC increases as income increases, even for the highest income category.
- NMC and FP increase with increases in educational attainment, household size, and participation in different insurance schemes, due to a higher degree of awareness of the importance of health insurance and an increase in the number of insured persons.
- NMC and FP decrease if households are located but not urban areas, which is also a result of the number of persons insured in each region. Insurance in Egypt is very much an urban business, because most of the formal workers reside in cities.

Determinants of Enrolment with VHI

To assess the determinants of enrolment with VHI, the suggested model assumes that the choice of whether to enroll is influenced by two main determinants:

(1) individual decisions weighting costs and benefits and (2) household and community characteristics. To estimate the weight of these determinants, a binary logit model was applied, which is described as follows:

$$\text{Prob (enrolment} > 0) = X_1\beta_1 + X_2\beta_2 + \varepsilon.$$

The independent variable takes a value of 1 if the person belongs to a VHI scheme and 0 if he or she does not.

X_1 represents a set of independent variables that are characteristics of the individual and the household. In this case, the following variables were selected: monthly income, public health insurance, educational level, family size, satisfaction with health services, age, gender, and health status.

X_2 represents a set of independent variables that approximate the social values in the communities, which are represented in this study in the location (region) variable. The vectors of coefficient estimates are β_1 and β_2 and ε is the error term.

Control variables also include gender and health status as well as satisfaction with the health services. Satisfaction with the health service was taken in this analysis to reflect the service quality and distance from the health center, which might influence the decision to purchase an insurance scheme.

The following are the main findings.

- The variables found significant in determining the participation in private VHI were: monthly household income, public health insurance, educational level, satisfaction with health services, age of household head and location; household size, region, and health status were insignificant variables.
- In the case of syndicate VHI, household size, location, age of household head, gender and health status were found insignificant variables, while only satisfaction with health services, region, monthly income, membership in health insurance and level of education were found significant as determinants for enrolment in syndicate VHI.
- Increases in income, urbanization, and educational attainment increase the probability of enrolment in both private and syndicate VHI.
- Having at least one family member enrolled in SHI might decrease the likelihood for both private and syndicate VHI enrolment.
- Meanwhile the marginal effect of satisfaction with health services positively affects enrolment in private VHI, while the increase in the age of the head of household has a negative effect, which may be explained by the inadequacy of insurance schemes for elderly people in Egypt. The same can be applied to the analysis of syndicate VHI.

Impact of Voluntary Insurance on Access to Health Care

In this part of the analysis, the model was applied to 33,035 working individuals 16 years and above.

To assess the impact of scheme membership on access to health care, a two-part model was used. The first part of the model analyzes the determinants of using health care services. The second part analyzes the determinants of health care expenditures for individuals who reported any health care use.

Part one of the model is a probit model and can be written as follows:

$$\text{Prob (visit} > 0) = X\beta + \varepsilon.$$

The two variables of primary interest are scheme membership status and income. Other variables were also included in the estimation model to control for the differences in need for health care such as the educational level, family size, VHI, satisfaction with health services, age, gender, health status, region, and work status.

In this part, the last visit for health services is used as a proxy for accessibility due to the dataset. The main findings follow.

Model I: Health Accessibility

- Due to the very limited coverage with private and syndicate VHI, both were found insignificant in this model.
- Other independent variables show that the increase in educational attainment also increases utilization of health services.
- The marginal effect of the age category shows that the percentage change in odds increases by 64 percent with age (the ratio of the probability that an individual will visit a health care provider to the probability that the individual will not visit). An older person is more likely than a younger one to use health services.
- Being a male decreases, and being female increases, the probability of using health services, because females have more reasons to access health services.
- The probability of utilizing health services is decreasing in rural areas in contrast to the urban governorates, particularly rural Upper Egypt, where it is declining.

Despite these findings, participation in both voluntary and public insurance schemes shows a positive impact on use of health services. Having at least one VHI increases the probability of access to health services. However, having public insurance without VHI results in better access to health services than participating in VHI. Having both public health insurance and VHI will bring the probability to accessibility to health services at maximum.

Model 2: Health Accessibility

Part two is a log-linear model that estimates the incurred level of out-of-pocket expenditures, conditioned on positive use of health care services:

$$\text{Log (out-of-pocket expenditure} \mid \text{visit} > 0) = X\gamma + \mu,$$

where

X = a set of individual and household characteristics hypothesized to affect individual patterns of utilization and expenditures

β and γ = vectors of coefficient estimates; and

ε and μ = error terms.

The two variables of primary interest are scheme membership status and income. Other control variables were also included in the estimation model to control for the differences in need for health care are educational level, family size, VHI, satisfaction with health services, age, gender, health status, region, and work status.

- The model shows the median medical expenses for the different categories in comparison to the reference category. Median medical expenses are relatively high for the highest-income category, whereas people with at least public health insurance pay less than those with no public health insurance.
- With the increase in education the median for medical expenses decreases for secondary education assuming that they have a kind of insurance (school age insurance). Also with the increase in the family size the median of medical expenditure will increase relatively in comparison to smaller families.
- VHI and the gender variable were found insignificant in this model. Health status plays a role in determining the median of health expenditure as it decreases, if health status is better, while the median of medical expenses also decreases in comparison with the median health expenditure for not-working people because they have no health insurance of any kind.
- Despite the fact that VHI is insignificant in determining out-of-pocket medical spending (OOPS), in the case of participation in one VHI and no public health insurance, the median OOPS goes down relative to the case, where the person has at least one VHI and at least one kind of public health insurance. Having two kinds of health insurance may increase the median OOPS due to the different installments that should be paid, while having VHI will decrease the median health expenditure relative to total uninsured case. These findings apply in the case of both private VHI and syndicate VHI
- Finally the relationship between age and medical expenses does not show a stable trend like the one in the relationship between health status, type of insurance, and regional location (living in urban governorates) and OOPS.

The same findings as above are applicable to the analysis of syndicate VHI: median medical expense declines if participating in public health insurance, increases with the highest income category, decreases with secondary education (school insurance), decreases with those in better health, increases in rural areas in comparison with urban areas, and finally also decreases with those currently working, because a significant portion of them have some kind of insurance.

Impact of VHI on Household Labor Market Productivity

The hypothesis to be tested is that members, who have access to VHI are more likely to seek care for medical illnesses earlier and therefore require less time off work due to illness than those that do not have access to VHI or other forms of community financing, social insurance, and subsidized care.

Three models were adopted and analyzed. The main findings follow.

Under the first model it is assumed that an insured person seeks health care earlier than an uninsured person and hence might require less time off from work. The dependent variable to be looked for in this model is absenteeism from work due to illness

$$\text{Prob (absenteeism from work} > 0) = X\beta + \varepsilon.$$

- The model was applied for 32,524 working individuals 16 years and above. The independent variables are the monthly income of household head, public health insurance, educational level, VHI, age, gender, health status, and region.
- The model shows that no kind of insurance, voluntary or public, affects an insured person's absenteeism. Only health status and gender were found significant, indicating that the status of health does affect the absenteeism of the insured person and that being female might also lead to more absence.
- Despite the previous finding, if the status of workers 16 years and above is examined with respect to health insurance, it was found that having at least one private or syndicate VHI would reduce their absenteeism even more than having public health insurance with or without VHI.

Under the second model it is assumed that insured persons have better access to drugs as well as appropriate protection schemes to work more productively:

$$\text{Prob (worked hours/man day per given activity} > 0) = X\beta + \varepsilon.$$

Due to the nature of data productivity at work in this analysis, the dependent variable has been measured as: working hours per worker (16 years plus) to the median working hours for each workers' group. Independent variables are the common control variables in addition to health insurance membership.

- In this model all variables are found significant, including private and syndicate VHI.
- Private and syndicate VHI increase productivity as the results of the model show. The productivity of a worker with VHI will increase, when the median number of his working hours and the median number of working hours of this working category are compared.
- The same unexpected relationship can be seen in the educational category. This person's median working hours decreases with the increase in the educational level when compared with the median of the working hours of this working category. This can be a result of the pattern of work performed at each educational level as low educational levels perform informal activities

with irregular working hours. All these results are applicable in the case of both private and syndicate VHI.

- As family size increases, productivity declines. Males show higher productivity than females. Workers in Upper Egypt show lower productivity than workers in other regions, which is a common result of several other studies on employment in Egypt.

The third model assumes a higher probability of hiring-in or hiring-out labor, as households that are better protected against health shocks have a higher probability of joining the labor force.

The dichotomous variable is the household hiring-in or hiring-out labor.

The independent variables are nonmedical income, public health insurance, educational level, VHI, age, gender, region, health status, and family size plus health insurance membership:

$$\text{Prob (hiring labor, in or out} > 0) = X\beta + \varepsilon.$$

In the binary logit model, "hiring workers" is replaced by the work status "currently working" and has never worked due to the absence of the variable hiring or not hiring labor in the data used.

- Private VHI is insignificant, and the data show that the possibility of working is higher with having public health insurance than having private VHI. The results are contradictive because having at least one private VHI will decrease the probability of working if accompanied by public health insurance and increases the probability of working if not accompanied by public health insurance. No logical explanation is found for these results.
- Syndicate VHI is significant, showing that at least one syndicate VHI increases the probability of working. However, participating in public health insurance always increases the probability of working.
- Finally the probability of having worked or currently working is higher for males and is higher for those in better health.

CONCLUSIONS AND RECOMMENDATIONS

Health financing challenges in Egypt are unlikely to be addressed through a single approach. For years, people have expected general taxation to finance government health services and defined contributions to finance its SHI. Due to faster rises in health spending than in economic growth, coupled with poor governance, public financing of the health system faces severe economic constraints. The gravity of this situation is compounded by the increase in OOPS and the weakness of social protection mechanisms for vulnerable populations. In addition, if Egypt's economic situation continues to improve, the middle and upper-middle classes will likely demand better quality and high-end health services.

The government has recently adopted a policy for expanding "social health insurance" coverage under a single payer to cover the uninsured, thus reaching universal coverage in the medium term and merging all health system components.[3] The mandate to expand SHI coverage is likely to further strain public financing, which also has to cover health care for the poor, the fifth of Egypt's population that cannot afford to pay any premiums or copayments.

In the above analysis, however, VHI was found to increase financial protection and contribute to workers' participation in economic activities and enhanced productivity. Moreover, it was found that people might not object to cost participation in VHI to obtain better quality or better access to health services. These findings are important, particularly because they confirm the findings of several analyses of household survey data that people's willingness and ability to pay for health care—even the poor—far exceed the government's capacity to mobilize revenues through taxation.

VHI may therefore be considered a credible policy option for mobilizing additional resources to finance health care, especially for middle-income workers in the informal sector and high-income workers in the public and private sectors. This may significantly contribute to overall health system financing and reduce the upward pressure on public financing if combined with effective risk pooling.

The role of the VHI market must, however, be clearly defined in the context of statutory SHI. Such a role can take one of three forms (Mossialo and Thomson 2003):

- *substitution VHI,* the provision of the same package of health services already covered under the SHI system;
- *complementary VHI,* coverage of the cost of copayments and other cost-sharing elements of the SHI system;
- *supplementary VHI,* coverage of services not covered under the SHI system.

In this context, VHI can be further developed to provide some financial protection against the cost of catastrophic illnesses, expand coverage, and improve access to health care. To this effect, the following recommendations are proposed.

- *Define the role of VHI in the context of SHI.* A critical first step would be to define the benefits package, which will be covered under the expanded SHI, as well as the actuarial and economic studies to determine the potential costs and sources of revenues. These include "demand analysis" to study health needs, revealed preferences, demand for different benefits package, expenditure variance, willingness and ability to pay, insurable and uninsurable risks, degree of risk aversion, moral hazard/free rider, price (loading cost) and transaction costs, access to providers, consumption taxes on insurance, subsidies, and tax exemptions. "Supply analysis" is also needed to understand market structure, competitive environment, choice and coverage, prices transaction costs, expenditure (level, distribution, and variance), adverse selection and cream skimming, and legal and regulatory framework. It is in this context that the role of the VHI could then be defined as substitutive, complementary, or supplementary.

- *Establish effective revenue collection mechanisms.* Among the factors that need to be examined are the level of prepayment compared with direct out-of-pocket spending, and the extent to which contributions are progressive and compulsory compared with voluntary. Moreover, it is critical to ensure adequate revenue pooling and risk sharing, including redistribution from rich to poor, healthy to sick, and gainfully employed to inactive. This implies a strong system of taxation so that tax evasion by the rich and middle classes does not cut their share of the contribution to the overall revenue pool. Without effective revenue pooling and risk sharing, households across a larger income range—not just low-income populations—may be exposed to serious financial hardship at times of illness.
- *Increase advocacy and public awareness of VHI.* VHI is generally perceived as a profit-generating business and as a competitor to the SHI program by both policy makers and the public. This perception has limited the development of VHI, particularly in the presence of a dominant public health sector, prevailing social customs, and low average income. It is therefore critical to have a strategy for advocacy at the level of policy makers and for awareness by the public at large underlining the complementarity of both systems and the need to create an effective public-private partnership to expand health insurance coverage to the entire population.
- *Improve governance and the regulatory environment.* The government has a key stewardship role to ensure good governance within the health care system overall and the achievement of its economic and social development goals. It is therefore equally critical to regulate the system to ensure rational growth of health expenditures and its long-term financial sustainability. The existing laws and regulations need to be revised to remove duplication and inconsistencies and ensure their comprehensiveness but simplicity at the same time. A strong regulatory framework is needed to avoid the health market failures. To this effect, the role of the Egyptian Insurance Supervisory Agency in the regulation of the private medical insurance market should be reinforced, especially in monitoring and assessing new private health insurance products and disseminating information to consumers about their benefits and restrictions. Capital and licensing requirements and procedures for market entry and exit should be made more transparent for both national and international companies that would like to establish private VHI companies.
- *Strengthen health sector organization.* The organizational structure and incentive systems including decision rights, market exposure, financial responsibility, accountability, and coverage of social functions need to be carefully examined. The health sector is highly fragmented and suboptimal.

Reorganization of the sector will require a coherent vision that enlists the strengths of both public and private organizations. This reorganization will entail redefinition of the MOHP role to become more the regulator of the overall system and reducing its role as a provider, the separation of finance from provision in the SHI program, the creation of an independent organization for quality assurance and accreditation, and the development of the capacity of EISA as the regulator of the public and private insurance industry in Egypt. The development of the VHI market should evolve in the context of such vision.

- *Enhance quality assurance, licensing, and accreditation.* The several initiatives and programs to improve the quality of care in both the public and private sectors have not yet had an impact nationally. Two alternative approaches are possible. One would be to have the Medical Syndicate or a medical council develop national standards and guidelines for health service delivery, clinical protocols, and referral guidelines. Alternatively, creating an independent organization to do this may be more pragmatic. This "Egyptian Council for Quality Assurance and Accreditation" would be responsible for developing and updating quality standards and undertaking the appropriate regulatory and licensing mechanisms for relicensing public and private providers and accrediting health facilities. In addition to one-time accreditation of health facilities, a separate key function will be the performance of periodic audits of providers to ensure that standards are maintained. This approach would create both incentives and accountability for the quality of health care. Moreover, it would ensure standardization and benchmarking—both essential for performance standards in the health insurance business. This would be most helpful to the development of VHI.
- *Expand strategic purchasing and contracting.* Many health organizations purchase health services and contract with public and private providers, but the mechanisms used need to be improved. For example, a set of providers' rights and obligations must be defined in accordance with the interests of the overall system, including decent remuneration in return for compliance with certain rules (for example, medical best practice, obligation to share information, prescription of generics, and compliance with a global budget). Furthermore, if these rules are not respected, effective sanctions should be applied, including financial penalties and exclusion of providers from the contractual relationship. This quid pro quo approach is mostly lacking and needs further development.
- *Use effective provider payment mechanisms.* The current provider payment system in the public sector is constrained by the rigid civil service rules and centralized decision-making. Payments to private providers are rarely linked to performance. As such, there are few incentives for both public and private providers for being more efficient and delivering quality health care services.

Different provider payment mechanisms, already used in other countries, may be used in Egypt to link it to performance, accountability, efficiency, and quality of care.

- *Strengthen health information systems.* Several health information system prototypes exist in the public and private sectors. In the health insurance industry, two broadly defined systems are needed. First is the Clinical Information System (CIS) that is primarly linked and with the patient medical history, treatment, and utilization of health services. The second is the Fund Management Information System (FMIS), linking provider and purchaser and including the membership data base of eligible beneficiaries, a provider data base, utilization information, a billing system, and management tools to track revenues and expenditures, as well as asset management. The several CISs now in use need further standardization and harmonization. The combination of the financing and the provision functions in the SHI and the limited development of VHI did not allow for the development of a viable FMIS, which will need to be fully developed.
- *Encourage the development of new private VHI, HMOs, and managed care operations.* The emerging demand for health benefits suggests that a new type of managed health insurance may be attractive. A new entrant may be able to establish an attractive market profile and position as a specialist health insurer offering managed care and high-quality customer service. However, a new operation would be competing with life companies that now offer health insurance as a loss-leading life rider. Therefore, finding an appropriate price for a new initiative may be difficult. The minimum capital requirements for establishing a foreign-owned insurance company in Egypt would be expensive in relation to the small market potential and may discourage other companies from establishing. It may be therefore easier to encourage multiline insurers already doing business to develop a health insurance line. For them, launching a new health insurance line would not be expensive because they have met license and capital requirements, a large part of start-up costs for a new company.

In conclusion, Egypt's health finance faces a number of critical challenges and the prospect of further strains on the state budget in light of the renewed commitment to expand social health insurance coverage to the entire population. This analysis demonstrated that VHI can have positive impact on financial protection and access to health care. Thus, VHI can play a critical role in achieving the health system objectives of increasing health insurance coverage, financial protection, and access to health, as well as relieving upward pressures on public financing.

TABLE 5A.1 Egypt: Total Health Expenditures, Fiscal Years 1996–2004 (EGP)

Item	*1996*	*1997*	*1998*	*1999*	*2000*	*2001*	*2002*	*2003*	*2004*
Health expenditures, nominal (EGP million)									
Public expenditures	4,369.0	5,050.6	5,946.7	6,513.2	7,790.3	7,937.2	9,121.5	9,351.1	10,001.2
Private expenditures	4,373.0	5,935.4	7,497.7	9,060.1	10,622.5	12,184.8	13,747.2	13,791.6	14,034.6
Total expenditures	8,742.0	10,986.0	13,444.4	15,573.3	18,412.8	20,122.0	22,868.7	23,142.7	24,035.8
Change from previous year (%)	n.a.	25.7	22.4	15.8	18.2	9.3	13.7	1.2	3.9
Health expenditures, real (1996 EGP million)									
Public expenditures	4,369	4,560.2	5,171.3	5,577.8	6,390	6,382.7	7173.8	6,922.2	7043
Private expenditures	4,373	5,359.1	6,520.1	7,758.9	,713	9,798.5	10,811.8	10,209.3	9,883.3
Total expenditures	8,742	9,919.3	11,691.4	13,336.7	15,103	16,181.2	17,985.6	17,131.5	16,926.3
Change from previous year (%)	n.a.	13	18	14	13	7	11	–5	–1
Public as percentage of total health expenditures	50	46	44	42	42	39	40	40	41
Per capita expenditures, nominal (EGP)									
Public expenditures	73.7	83.6	96.5	103.7	121.7	121.7	137.4	138.3	145.6
Private expenditures	73.7	98.3	121.7	144.3	166	186.9	207	204	204.3
Total expenditures	147.4	181.9	218.3	248	287.7	308.6	344.4	342.3	349.9
Change from previous year (%)	n.a.	23.40	20.00	13.60	16.00	7.30	11.60	–0.60	2.20
Per capita expenditures, real (1996 EGP million)									
Public expenditures	73.7	75.5	83.9	88.8	99.8	97.9	108	102.4	102.5
Private expenditures	73.7	88.7	105.8	123.5	136.1	150.3	162.8	151	143.9
Total expenditures	147.4	164.2	189.8	212.4	236	248.2	270.9	253.4	246.4

Per capita expenditures, nominal (US$)									
Public expenditures	21.7	24.7	28.4	30.5	35.3	31.6	31.7	27	23.7
Private expenditures	21.8	29	35.8	42.4	48.1	48.5	47.7	39.8	33.2
Total expenditures	43.5	53.7	64.2	72.9	83.4	80.2	79.4	66.7	56.9
Per capita expenditures (PPP$)									
Public expenditures	57.1	61.5	68.5	72.5	83.4	81.2	90.4	—	—
Private expenditures	57.2	72.3	86.3	100.9	113.7	124.6	136.2	—	—
Total expenditures	114.3	133.7	154.8	173.4	197.1	205.7	226.6	—	—
Total health expenditures as percentage of GDP									
Public expenditures	1.9	1.9	2.1	2.1	2.3	2.2	2.4	2.3	2.2
Private expenditures	1.9	2.2	2.6	2.9	3.1	3.4	3.6	3.3	3.1
Total expenditures	3.8	4.1	4.7	5.1	5.4	5.6	6.0	5.6	5.3
Memorandum items									
Exchange rate[a] (EGP/US$)	3.4	3.4	3.4	3.4	3.5	3.9	4.3	5.1	6.2
Exchange rate[a] (EGP/PPP$)	1.3	1.4	1.4	1.4	1.5	1.5	1.5	—	—
GDP deflator (1996 = 100)	100	110.8	115	116.8	121.9	124.4	127.2	135.1	142
Total public spending (EGP million)	—	—	—	—	—	237,642.8	259,541.8	285,819.5	286,479.1
GDP (EGP million)	228,000	265,900	287,400	307,600	340,100	358,700	378,500	415,000	455,000
Population (million)	59.3	60.4	61.6	62.8	64	65.2	66.4	67.6	68.7

Source: World Bank 2006.

Public expenditures for 1996–2002 are all final actual expenditures; those for FY 2003 and FY 2004 are interim actual expenditures. Private expenditures for FY 1996 and 2002 are obtained from the National Health Accounts (NHA) measured for the respective years. Private expenditures for FY 1997–2001 are estimated based on the NHA for 1996 and 2002, assuming a linear trend. Private expenditures for FY 2003 and FY 2004 are based on NHA 2002, assuming the same level of per capita expenditure

Notes: Figures may not add up due to rounding.

— = not available; n.a. not applicable

a. The exchange rate in any fiscal year is the average of exchange rates in the two calendar years.

TABLE 5A.2 Health Insurance Types, by Background Characteristics

	Type of health insurance					
Background characteristics	*Work insurance*	*HIO*	*Syndicate insurance*	*School insurance*	*Other type*	*Number of households*
Residence						
Urban	17.3	65.8	5.6	61	4.7	3,525
Rural	10	56	1.5	75.6	3.1	4,189
Place of residence						
Urban governorates	21.4	58.6	8.6	58	7.1	1,370
Lower Egypt	13	63.1	1.8	68.7	4.1	3,416
Urban	14.7	71.1	2.8	61.9	3.9	1,119
Rural	12.1	59.2	1.4	72	4.2	2,297
Upper Egypt	9	57.9	2.8	74.9	1.9	2,830
Urban	12.5	69.3	5	65.1	2.3	949
Rural	7.3	52.1	1.7	79.9	1.7	1,881
Frontier governorates	36.7	66.3	2	57.1	1	98
Age group						
<5	12.4	80.6	3.4	62.6	3	2,450
5–15	11.7	38.8	2.9	94.3	3.3	2,707
16–29	17.5	61.2	4.4	44.7	5.9	1,238
30–39	22.6	71	5.1	41.5	3.7	217
40–49	14.6	59.5	2.7	55.7	4.3	185
50–59	18.7	72.8	3.7	30.5	7.7	246
60+	10.1	65.1	3.1	61.4	3.4	671
Education, household head						
No education	7.7	45.2	0.8	75.9	1.8	2,493
Primary incomplete	9.4	51.5	1.9	73.3	2.4	1,324
Primary complete/some secondary	13.3	55.9	2.4	68.4	6.9	1,143
Preparatory secondary complete	18.6	76.6	2.5	64.9	4.6	1,380
Higher	22.1	84.1	11.2	56.6	5.4	1,374
Occupation, household head						
Not working	8.4	53.4	2.8	61.7	4.7	738
Professional, technical, and administrative	19.5	77	8.1	61.6	6.6	2,104
Clerical	21.7	88.5	2.4	68.4	1.7	697
Sales	12.9	43.3	2.2	64.6	3.4	178
Farmer	4.1	32	0.4	84.1	1.3	760
Agricultural worker	1.6	33.8	0.2	81.9	0.5	618
Household and domestic worker	0	50	0	50	100	2
Services	14.6	71.4	0.6	67	9.9	700
Manual	12.4	52.2	2.1	70.9	0.9	1,917
Total	13.3	60.4	3.4	69	3.8	7,714

Source: El-Zanaty 2002.

Note: Percentage distribution of households with at least one member covered by health insurance by type of health insurance and background characteristics.

TABLE 5A.3 Health Insurance Types, by Socioeconomic Characteristics

	Type of health insurance					
Socioeconomic characteristic	*Work insurance*	*HIO*	*Syndicate insurance*	*School insurance*	*Other type*	*Number of households*
Gender						
Male	13.6	60.9	3.7	69.9	4	3,627
Female	13	60	3.2	68.1	3.6	4,087
Per capita expenditure						
Quintile 1 (<799)	6	46.8	1.3	81.3	1.2	1,548
Quintile 2 (799–1,170)	9.6	61.4	1.4	78.9	1.7	1,582
Quintile 3 (1,171–1,654)	13.5	59.6	2	72	4.3	1,491
Quintile 4 (1,655–2,551)	18	69.3	2.9	63.3	4.9	1,496
Quintile 5 (>2,551)	19.9	64.8	9.6	50.5	7	1,524
Missing/DK[a]	11	72.6	0	31.5	4.1	73
Wealth index						
1	5.6	38	0.6	81.9	2	1,116
2	8.9	53.2	1.2	78.4	1.6	1,281
3	10.6	59.3	1.5	72.8	3.8	1,403
4	14.6	69.4	2.1	63.5	4	1,755
5	20.6	69.8	8.4	58.6	5.8	2,159
Total	13.3	60.4	3.4	69	3.8	7,714

Source: El-Zanaty 2002.

Note: Percentage distribution of households with at least one member covered by health insurance by type of health insurance and socioeconomic characteristics.

a. No reply or "don't know."

NOTES

The use of the data of the Egypt's Household Health Service Utilization and Expenditure Survey (EHHSUES) would not have been possible without the support of El Zanaty and Associates Team. Our thanks go in particular to Professor Fatma El Zanaty and Noha Ahmed El Ghazali. The authors would like also to thank Mostafa Abdel Aziz and Ahmed Rizk at the Faculty of Economics and Political Science, Cairo University, for support in modeling and data search. The authors also would like to acknowledge the contribution and invaluable research assistance of Sahar Hegazy and Maissa Abdel-Rahmane from the World Bank, Egypt Country Office.

1. See also annex 5A, table 5A.1, this volume.
2. Total public expenditures on health include the expenditures by university hospitals, which represent about 0.4 percent of total public health expenditures.
3. Mubarak, Hosni, President, speech [in Arabic], Sohag, Egypt, *Al-Ahram*, July 7, 2005, n.p.

REFERENCES

El-Henawy, A. 2000. "Current Situation, Progress, and Prospects of Health for All in Egypt." *Eastern Mediterranean Health Journal* 6 (4): 816–21.

El-Zanaty, F. 2004. "Egypt Household Health Service Utilization and Expenditures Survey 2002." Ministry of Health and Population, Cairo, Egypt.

Gericke, C. 2004. "Comparison of Health Care Financing Arrangements in Egypt and Cuba: Lessons for Health Reform in Egypt." Berlin University of Technology, Germany.

HIO (Health Insurance Organization). 2004. *Annual Report for 2002/2003* [in Arabic]. Cairo, Egypt.

Loffredo, L. 2004. "Welfare in the Mediterranean Countries, Arab Republic of Egypt." Centre for Administrative Innovation in the Euro-Mediterranean Region, c/o Formez, Centro Formazione Studi. Arco Felice, Italy. http://unpan1.un.org/intradoc/groups/public/documents/CAIMED/UNPAN019177.pdf.

Mossialos, E., and S. Thomson. 2003. "Voluntary Health Insurance in the European Union: Lessons for Croatia." Report, World Bank, Washington, DC.

MOHP (Ministry of Health and Population). 2005. *National Health Accounts 2002*. Cairo, Egypt.

———. 2001. "Reforming the Insurance Markets." State Information Services, Cairo, Egypt.

———. 1998. "Health Care Utilization and Expenditures in the Arab Republic of Egypt 1994/5." http://www.hsph.harvard.edu/ihsg/publications/pdf/No-52.PDF.

———. 1997. *Egypt National Health Accounts 1994/5*. http://www.hsph.harvard.edu/ihsg/publications/pdf/No-25-1.PDF

USAID (U.S. Agency for International Development). 2002. "Regulation and Supervision of Private Health and Managed Healthcare in Egypt." Unpublished report, USAID, Cairo, Egypt.

USFCS (U.S. Foreign Commercial Services and U.S. Department of State. 2004. "Egypt, Health Care, Industry Sector Analysis." Washington DC.

WDI (World Development Indicators). 2004. Database. World Bank, Washington, DC.

World Bank 2006. Egypt Public Expenditure Review: Policy Note No. 9 on Health. Washington DC.

CHAPTER 6

South Africa

Michael Thiede and Vimbayi Mutyambizi

More than 10 years after the first democratic elections, the provision of health services in South Africa is still characterized by extreme inequities. This chapter focuses on the levels of financial protection in the public and in the private sector of the South African health system and analyzes the determinants of health services utilization. The chapter provides an overview of the context within which the health sector operates. It further sketches the peculiar structure of the private sector, namely the medical schemes environment. The extreme socioeconomic inequality is identified as the main determinant of differences in financial vulnerability through analysis of financial protection and financial vulnerability at different income levels between the public and private sectors (the medical schemes environment) on the basis of a national survey. The chapter examines health services utilization, based on another national household survey. These results reflect the dichotomy of the South African health system and reemphasize the role of socioeconomic status as reflected in education and household wealth. Voluntary health insurance in the form of medical scheme membership is today an option only for the better off. The chapter briefly addresses the government's health reform agenda to conclude that the proposed steps ought to be accompanied by efforts to investigate insurance options for lower socioeconomic strata.

INTRODUCTION

South Africa's first democratic government more than a decade ago inherited a highly fragmented and extremely inequitable health system, rooted in the racially discriminatory economic and social policies of apartheid (Gilson and McIntyre 2001). The health sector today is relatively well developed with health care spending at 8.7 percent of GDP. The health outcomes, however, are considerably worse than in most other middle-income countries. The South African health system is characterized by a two-tier structure, a tax-funded public sector that caters to the majority of the population, and a private system typically serving the better-off households among the formally employed. Since 1994 a number of policy initiatives have attempted to redress inequities and improve redistribution within the system. Yet there is a sharp divide between a highly developed private sector and public health services that struggle to address the health needs of the majority of the population. Over the last decade private sector–oriented policies have hardly addressed the challenges of the health system as a whole, while the public health sector faces a funding crisis. South Africa's voluntary health insurance market does not address the lower-income segments of the population, and there are no initiatives aiming at complementing the private system through insurance initiatives targeted at the poorer half of the population.

This chapter presents an overview of the health system, analyzes the degree of financial protection in both the public and private sectors, and outlines the environment for improving financial protection against the costs of ill-health. It furthermore briefly sketches the opportunities for new forms of voluntary health insurance to develop in a pro-poor context.

SITUATIONAL ANALYSIS OF HEALTH FINANCING IN SOUTH AFRICA

South Africa is classified by the World Bank as a less-indebted upper-middle-income country. The country has entered its second decade of democracy with a population of 46.5 million people (Stats SA 2004a) and a GDP of approximately US$212.8 billion in 2004.

Socioeconomic Context

Since 2000 the South African economy has experienced an average growth rate of 3 percent per annum, fueled mainly by a low interest rate environment, an expansionary fiscal stance by the government, and increased domestic demand (National Treasury 2005). The economic outlook in the medium term is fairly optimistic with expectations that growth rates will rise to a high of 4.4 percent in the period up to 2007 (National Treasury 2005). In 2004 CPIX inflation averaged 4.3 percent and is expected to remain within the 3 to 6 percent inflation targeting range over the medium term and rise to 5.4 percent in 2007 (National Treasury 2005). Despite these moderate growth rates, unemployment remains unacceptably high at 27 percent (using the official definition[1] and 41 percent using the expanded definition) (Stats SA 2004b).

Unlike the labor force structure of most low-and middle-income countries, South Africa's labor force employment is concentrated in the formal sector (figure 6.1). In South Africa high unemployment in respect the formal sector is not countered by a strong informal sector as in most developing countries (Kingdon and Knight 2001).

South Africa has one of the highest income inequalities in the world—the Gini coefficient rose from 0.596 in 1995 to 0.635 in 2001 (UNDP 2003). Table 6.1 reflects the extent of income inequality. The income statistics distinguish between the formal sector, the informal sector, and domestic workers. Approximately 63.9 percent of all employed earn under R 2,500 (about US$381)[2] a month. Income levels in the informal sector and in domestic service are significantly below those in the formal sector.

FIGURE 6.1 South Africa: Employment by Sector, September 2004 (percent)

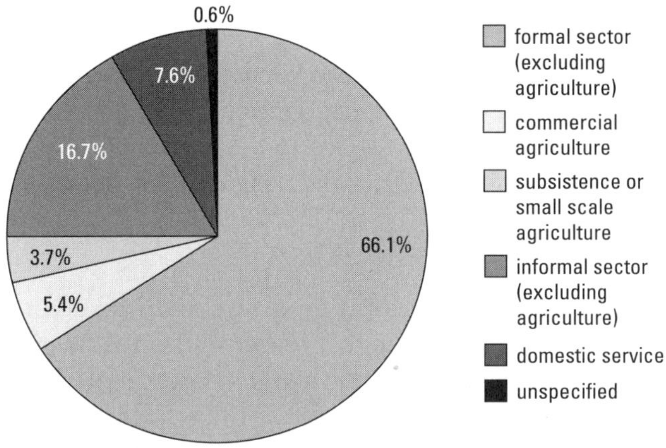

Source: Stats SA 2004b.

The potential for voluntary health insurance to succeed in ensuring equitable access to health care depends to a large extent on employment levels in both the informal and formal sectors of the economy. High unemployment and wide disparities in income pose serious challenges to the success of systemic voluntary health insurance in achieving equitable access to health care.

Health Status Indicators

South Africa spends a significantly greater share of its GDP on financing health care than other upper-middle-income countries.[3] Approximately 8.7 percent of the country's GDP is spent on health care, compared to an average of 6.4 percent for all upper-middle-income countries. The 3.5 percent share of GDP that South Africa spends on public health care services equals the upper-middle-income countries' average. However, in South Africa this represents only 40.6 percent of total health

TABLE 6.1 South Africa: Monthly Employment Income, 2004 (percent)

Monthly income	*Formal sector*	*Informal sector*	*Domestic service*	*Total*
None	0.4	13.8	0.0	3.3
R 1–R 500	4.9	35.8	43.2	14.8
R 501–R 1,000	15.1	22.8	42.9	19.1
R 1,001–R 2,500	31.0	17.7	13.9	26.7
R 2,501–R 8,000	36.1	8.7	0.0	27.2
R 8,001+	12.4	1.3	0.0	8.9

Source: Stats SA 2004b.

care spending—whereas public spending for health care across all upper-middle-income countries averages 55 percent of total health care spending. South Africa's health care spending is thus concentrated in the private sector. The country has an infant mortality rate of 59 per 1,000 live births, and a life expectancy at birth of 55.2 years (Bradshaw et al. 2003). This compares poorly with an average infant mortality rate of 33 and an average life expectancy of 69 for the comparator group of countries. The low life expectancy is due to the high prevalence of HIV/AIDS—estimated at 11 percent—in South Africa (Dorrington et al. 2004).

Overview of South Africa's Health System

South Africa's public health sector aims to serve the uninsured majority (about 84 percent) of the population through a decentralized district health system. Within the public sector, primary health care is free while means-tested user fees apply for hospital services. The private sector offers primary care mainly on a fee-for-service basis. Private hospital services are basically offered by three hospital groups whose shares are traded on the stock exchange.

The private sector is characterized by nonprofit medical schemes, private for-profit health care providers, and for-profit administrators of medical schemes. Regular and comprehensive private health care is accessed mainly by medical scheme members and their dependants. Individuals without medical scheme cover tend to use the public sector. Often, because of a perceived low quality of care in the public sector, they pay out of pocket for private primary health care, if at all affordable. The health sector is characterized by obvious inequities: in 2003/04, medical schemes spent about R 8,800 (US$1,237)[4] per beneficiary, while an average of about R 1,050 (US$148) per person was spent on public sector health services (McIntyre et al. 2005).

Health care funding in the two sectors is markedly different. The public sector is mostly tax-funded, while the private sector is funded mostly through voluntary contributions by medical scheme members and a tax subsidy as a result of the contributions (employer subsidies of medical scheme contributions as well as scheme members' contributions and medical expenses) being tax exempt. The tax subsidy amounts to a sum equivalent to 21 percent of total public sector health care spending. This subsidy is highly regressive, and reforms of the use of this tax break in the system are being discussed.

In South Africa the private and public health systems have a symbiotic relationship, and the two sectors need to function jointly to promote equitable access to health care. For a comprehensive understanding of the factors that affect the private sector schemes, the public sector must be understood.

The public health sector in South Africa is funded principally by general tax revenue. Other sources of revenue include local authority revenue, provincial governments' own revenue, donor funds, and revenue from household user fees. The South African National Health Accounts report (Thomas and Muirhead 2000) identified tax revenue as constituting 94 percent of total public sector health care financing in 1996–99. Revenue from user fees has been unstable. Suggested reasons for the apparent failure of user fees as a sustainable source of finance include: the lack of incentives for collection (no facility-level revenue retention), poor structure of pricing (private patients inappropriately billed), inadequate collection systems, and patient dissatisfaction with the quality of health services. Public hospitals do not have the administrative capacity to consistently apply the exclusions. The user fee system has therefore proved not only inequitable but also inefficient. A system of prepayment has been suggested as a more equitable and effective means of collecting revenue than out-of-pocket payments, which tend to be regressive in nature. A survey of patients' willingness and ability to pay conducted by the Department of Health (DOH) further supports the development of a prepayment system. Respondents indicated that they would be willing to pay a small fee in advance provided that public sector services are improved first (DOH 2001).

Legal Framework

South Africa boasts one of the most progressive constitutions in the world, which promotes the progressive realization of the human rights of the South African citizen. The constitutional mandate to ensure equitable access to health services is the basic premise under which the health system is intended to function. Recognizing the persistent inequities between the two sectors of the health system, the Medical Schemes Act and the National Health Act were instituted to unite the private and public health sector in achieving the goal of progressively realizing equitable access to health care services. The 2003 National Health Act aims to unite the various elements of the South African health system, while also promoting the option of strengthening the public-private mix. The 1998 Medical Schemes Act, which was implemented in 2000, aims to ensure nondiscriminatory access to medical schemes by legislating community rating of premiums, ensuring open enrolment of scheme applicants, and introducing a set of prescribed minimum benefits (PMBs).

THE PRIVATE SECTOR

The private sector consists of a range of key players: medical schemes, medical scheme administrators and reinsurers, managed care organizations and health care providers, brokers who procure members typically for open schemes, and the Council for Medical Schemes (CMS), which regulates the medical scheme environment.

Functioning of the Private Sector

Before detailing the nature of the different types of schemes in South Africa, what is meant by "medical scheme" and "health insurance" in South Africa's private health sector needs clarification.

The term medical scheme in South Africa typically refers to the indemnity nonprofit business of mutual societies where members are reimbursed for actual expenditure on health (McLeod 2003). Medical schemes cover about three quarters of total private health expenditure. Health insurance in South Africa refers to the disability and dread disease insurance products delivered by short-term and life insurers. These products usually offer to pay the insured a specific sum agreed upon in advance in the event of dread disease or disability. Health insurance expenditure in this sense amounts to only 1.4 percent of the total private sector (Cornell et al. 2001).

There are two categories of medical schemes in South Africa—registered medical schemes and bargaining council schemes. Registered medical schemes comply with the requirements of the Medical Schemes Act and are registered with the Registrar of Medical Schemes. The two categories of registered medical schemes are restricted membership and open schemes, serving 28 percent and 68 percent of the medical scheme beneficiaries, respectively (CMS 2004). Restricted membership schemes typically restrict membership by employer or profession, whereas open schemes have open access. Bargaining council schemes (serving only 4 percent of the beneficiaries) do not fully comply with the requirements of the Medical Schemes Act in the type of benefits they offer. These schemes are exempted from certain provisions in the act and generally only offer primary health care coverage. Given the peculiar structure of South African private sector health care, comprehensive voluntary health insurance is really available only to the formally employed.

Even if private health insurance has limited forms in South Africa and low-income groups are basically excluded, it is important to mention in this context two widespread mechanisms of financial protection outside the realm of health care for the less well off. The first is the member-based burial society, which provides funeral insurance to members. About 100,000 of these societies have an estimated 8 million members in South Africa. The other model of financial protection against catastrophic health expenditure for low- and very low-income groups is the *stokvel*, where people save collectively. *Stokvels* are mostly rotating savings and credit associations providing lump-sum benefits to their 2.5 million members on a rotating basis (Bester et al. 2004).

Revenue Collection Mechanisms

Different types of schemes collect contributions in different ways. In open schemes the scheme administrator typically collects contributions, and in restricted membership schemes either an outside administrator is appointed or in-house administration services are used—although this practice is becoming less common (McLeod 2003). The functions of administrators typically include: collecting contributions from members; reimbursing health care providers; and processing beneficiaries' claims. Administration costs have been extremely high and a significant cause for the rise in medical scheme contributions.

An analysis of total administration costs by Doherty and McLeod (2003) (general administration, managed care costs, broker fees, net reinsurance losses/ profits, and bad debts) showed that these costs almost doubled from R 27 per beneficiary per month in 1997 to R 66 in 2001 (in 2001 prices). In the risk-rating environment—before the Medical Schemes Act of 1998 came into effect—administrators made their profits by drawing low-risk members into schemes, then extracting profits through lucrative reinsurance arrangements. In the current community rating environment, profits are being extracted from general administration and managed care costs. The vertical integration between administrators, reinsurers, and managed care organizations also challenges efforts to ensure that the private sector provides better value for money for beneficiaries—the extent of this integration is unknown and needs to be investigated further.

High brokerage fees have also been a characteristic of the private health sector. To control increases in brokerage fees and brokers' practice of moving members between schemes (thus affecting risk pools), regulations set fees at 3 percent of contributions paid (plus 14 percent value-added tax, VAT)—with a maximum of R 50 per member per month (Doherty and McLeod 2003). In addition, these fees are no longer paid on an annual basis in order to prevent brokers from encouraging members to change scheme every year. The revenue collection mechanisms have therefore compromised scheme members' value for money because a significant proportion of their payment goes to pay for profit-centered administration services.

Contributions and Out-of-Pocket Spending

Average contributions per member per month have escalated from R 900 in 1996 to R 1,400 in 2004 (in 2002 rand). Benefits packages have continuously been restructured and, despite the recent introduction of prescribed minimum benefits, coverage of services has decreased for most members. Good risks opt for core packages, and overall medical scheme membership has been stagnant. A number of medical schemes have also introduced medical savings accounts (MSAs)—individualized accounts into which members pay up to 25 percent of their monthly contributions—to meet medical expenses not paid from the pooled fund. Direct out-of-pocket payments paid by beneficiaries over and above the mandatory risk and nonrisk contributions are consistently acknowledged as being difficult to estimate; out-of-pocket expenditure is about 20 percent of expenditure on contributions per beneficiary per annum (Cornell et al. 2001). This outcome is quite concerning because it means beneficiaries have to spend a substantial amount in addition to their already high contributions to meet their health care needs.

In South Africa, all contributions to medical schemes are voluntary. There is no legal obligation for any citizen to join a medical scheme. Membership in restricted schemes is typically a condition of employment but would still be considered "voluntary" as there is no legislated obligation to become a member. The National Department of Health is analyzing policy options for a system of social health insurance that would require all formal sector employees above a certain income level to be members of a medical scheme. Although contributions to medical schemes are voluntary, schemes must cover a minimum set of essential benefits, the prescribed minimum benefits (PMBs), for every scheme member.

Progressivity of Contributions

In the community rating environment, individual contributions depend only on the benefits package chosen. Generally packages are designed so that the more comprehensive the coverage, the more expensive are the contributions. The introduction of PMBs was intended to ensure that beneficiaries, even lower-income members, have access to an essential benefits package, irrespective of the size of their contributions. The PMBs, a package of defined treatments for particular diagnoses, are complemented by a comprehensive care package for a list of 25 specified chronic diseases. One weakness of the PMBs is that they do not include primary health care benefits, implying that many scheme members have to pay for these benefits out of pocket, which is especially problematic for lower-income scheme members. Reforms are underway to correct this situation and include primary health care benefits in PMBs. PMBs must be provided for comprehensively, that is, there is no limit on the benefit that beneficiaries can get related to PMBs. These must also be delivered by one provider (a designated service provider is encouraged) to prevent dumping of patients on the public health system once their care becomes too expensive for schemes. In practice, the wealthy and healthy purchase less expensive and less comprehensive coverage, which limits the extent of cross-subsidization to the less-wealthy and ill scheme members. The scheme members who are less well off and most in need of financial protection from the high costs of ill-health tend to purchase coverage that is more comprehensive in line with their needs. Thus, contributions are essentially regressive. Copayments and levies paid directly by beneficiaries are also regressive in nature. In addition, the tax subsidy for contributions to medical schemes (in the form of income tax exemptions for medical scheme contributions) adds another regressive element, because all taxpayers subsidize health care for members of medical schemes, typically people with better incomes. The larger the contribution a tax payer makes, the larger is the tax subsidy they receive.

Buffers against External Shocks

The buffers against external shocks that are typically used in this environment are the legislated accumulated reserves and reinsurance agreements. Legislation has been enacted to ensure that schemes are financially sound and have reserves to protect them against external shocks. Regulation 29 of the Medical Schemes Act stipulates that schemes must maintain accumulated reserves of 25 percent of gross contributions by December 2004, starting from 10 percent of contributions in 2000. These reserves are intended to be nondistributable and "represent a buffer against unforeseen and adverse fluctuations" (CMS 2004: 65).

Reinsurance agreements are also commonly used to protect small schemes against adverse external shocks. The high level of vertical integration in the medical schemes environment has led to the abuse of such agreements by reinsurers and administrators seeking to profit from these agreements—by reinsuring large schemes with large enough risk pools and accumulated reserves. As a result legislation was implemented stating that all reinsurance agreements could be implemented only after approval by the Council for Medical Schemes. Results to date show that this legislation has been effective in reducing reinsurance costs: "The overall reinsurance deficit was R 123 million at 31 December 2003 compared with a loss of R 297 million in 2002. This represents a decrease of 58.5 percent in net reinsurance losses, and illustrates the continuing positive effect of the changes to the Medical Schemes Act introduced in March 2002." (CMS 2004: 58)

Pooling Revenues and Sharing Risks

In 2003 there were 149 registered medical schemes—composed of 88 restricted membership schemes, 49 open schemes, and 12 bargaining council schemes (table 6.2). The only real change from 2002 was in the number of restricted schemes, which fell from 94 in 2002 to 88 in 2003 as a result of mergers.

Restricted schemes form the largest share of the small schemes (table 6.2). Most of the large schemes are open schemes. Overall most schemes are small., which limits the effectiveness of risk pooling and suggests that there may be too many schemes for the given number of beneficiaries in the current configuration of the private health sector.

Before the institution of the Medical Schemes Act in 2000, schemes were legally permitted to discriminate against the elderly and the chronically ill through risk rating of premiums and the denial of membership to particular

TABLE 6.2 South Africa: Distribution of Medical Schemes, by Type, Size, and Number of Beneficiaries, 2003

Size of medical scheme	*Open*[a]	*Restricted*[a]	*Bargaining Council*[a]	*Consolidated*[a]
Small (<6,000 members)	16 (4)	58 (64)	7 (9)	81 (87)
Medium (>6,000 members but <30,000)	6 (7)	17 (16)	2 (2)	25 (25)
Large (30,000 or more beneficiaries)	27 (28)	13 (14)	3 (3)	43 (45)
Total schemes	49 (49)	88 (94)	12 (14)	149 (157)
Total beneficiaries	4,718,797 (4,731,211)	1,953,004 (1,982,934)	252,885 (249,044)	6,924,686 (6,963,189)

Source: CMS 2004.

a. The figures in parentheses are 2002 data.

applicants (Harrison 2004). These discriminatory practices resulted from the deregulation of the industry in the late 1980s and the 1990s (Harrison 2004). One of the main aims of the Medical Schemes Act was to abolish these discriminatory practices and ensure nondiscriminatory open access to medical scheme coverage through community rating of premiums and open enrolment of applicants in line with the requirements of the type of scheme. In this community rating environment, some cross-subsidization from the healthy to the sick occurs. Practice shows, however, that the degree to which this is the case depends on the type of scheme. Restricted schemes allow for much more redistribution than open schemes because they have more of a mix of high and low-risk members. Restricted schemes tend to have more beneficiaries with high-risk profiles than do open schemes. This is due to the practice of cream-skimming by brokers and risk rating by open schemes prior to 2000, when the Medical Schemes Act was introduced legislating community rating. The result is an environment characterized by distinct high- and low-risk schemes. To promote more cross-subsidy between these two extremes, a risk-equalization system is being implemented (Armstrong et al. 2004).

Many new generation schemes have the option of individualized medical savings accounts, described previously. These accounts can be used to pay for day-to-day expenses so that health expenditure beyond the plan's coverage is taken care off from the accumulated contributions. Any part of the account not used in a year can be rolled over to the next year. The individualized nature of these accounts compromises risk pooling within schemes, and plans for reforms to limit their use are in the pipeline.

Resource Allocation and Purchasing

The categorization of service delivery and payment arrangements in the medical schemes environment is straightforward at a general level, although in detail there may be peculiarities in one or the other setting within the private sector medical schemes.

With a few exceptions the remuneration basis for all service providers is fee for service. In the hospital sector, there has been a trend recently toward global or per diem fees. However, this affects only a small percentage of services offered to medical scheme beneficiaries. The Council for Medical Schemes as the scheme coordinating body, regularly publishes a comprehensive system of reference prices, the National Health Reference Price List (NRPL), against which medical schemes determine benefit levels and providers can determine fees charged to patients. Depending on the design of the chosen benefits package, the medical scheme member can be responsible for certain copayments.

Many of the costs reimbursed for health care services do not resemble market prices. Within the structures of service provision, cross-subsidization between different service areas of one and the same provider is being used as a competitive tool.

TABLE 6.3 South Africa: Medical Scheme Membership, by Expenditure Quintile, 2000 (percent)

	Medical scheme	
Quintile of total annual household expenditure	*Nonmember*	*Member*
1	98.61	1.39
2	98.12	1.88
3	95.47	4.53
4	86.29	13.71
5	41.46	58.54
Total	83.99	16.01

Source: StatsSA Income and Expenditure Survey 2000.

Affordability

Medical scheme membership is currently affordable only for the higher-income groups. This limitation is reflected in table 6.3, which shows the distribution of membership across households in different income quintiles. Membership is concentrated (almost 60 percent) in the top quintile. Even in the wealthiest group, only 13.71 percent belong to medical schemes.

FINANCIAL PROTECTION AND FINANCIAL VULNERABILITY

The aim of any form of health insurance is to protect individuals and households against the negative economic and social consequences of the costs associated with ill-health. The degree of financial protection within a given insurance environment can be measured by the financial protection indicator, the inverse of the coefficient of variation of nonmedical consumption. This measure reflects a set of desired properties, as it rises with increasing insurance coverage. It falls with an increasing variability of spending, but also as paid premiums rise and as income falls.

The financial protection indicator $\wp$ can be presented as:

$$\wp = \overline{\text{NMC}}/(\sigma_{\text{NMC}}) = \text{inverse of coefficient of variation of NMC,}$$

where

$\overline{\text{NMC}}$ = average of nonmedical consumption;
NMC = nonmedical consumption = $Y - (\rho + OOPS)$;
Y = household income;
ρ = premium;
$OOPS$ = out-of-pocket spending; and
σ = standard deviation.

South Africa's dichotomous health system makes it necessary to investigate separately the two "spheres of protection." All calculations in this section are based on analysis of data from the Income and Expenditure Survey 2000, a South African survey of 30,000 households that is representative at the national level and captures households' annual income and expenditure.

In the medical schemes environment the average annual nonmedical consumption per capita amounts to R 100,483.10, with a standard deviation of R 149,467.20. The financial protection indicator for medical scheme members ($\wp_{memb}$) is therefore 0.6723:

$$\overline{NMC}_{memb} = \text{R } 100{,}483.10$$
$$\sigma_{NMCmemb} = \text{R } 149{,}467.20$$
$$\wp_{memb} = \overline{NMC}_{memb}/\sigma_{NMCmemb} = 0.6723.$$

For most South Africans, those outside the medical scheme environment, the financial protection environment is different. In addition to the information on various aspects of living standards discussed above, the financial protection indicator again reflects the persistent inequalities between the segments of South Africa's population. The average annual nonmedical consumption for people in amounts to only R 20,841.48 with a standard deviation of R 48,772.44. The resulting financial protection indicator for nonmember households ($\wp_{nonm}$) is 0.4273:

$$\overline{NMC}_{nonm} = \text{R } 20{,}841.48$$
$$\sigma_{NMCnonm} = \text{R } 48{,}772.44$$
$$\wp_{nonm} = \overline{NMC}_{nonm}/\sigma_{NMCnonm} = 0.4273.$$

Even if the public sector provides comprehensive services for free or at low cost for the population not covered by medical schemes, that financial protection level is significantly lower than in the medical schemes environment. This difference, however, is not fully attributable to health system design alone. The chosen financial protection measure reflects a broader set of socioeconomic factors, but the indicator takes only direct health care costs into account. Particularly for low-income households nonmedical costs associated with ill-health play a critical role. These include the costs of accessing care, for example, transport costs and indirect costs resulting from loss of productive time. Nonmedical costs may exceed direct health care costs and contribute significantly to the economic burden of ill-health (McIntyre et al. 2006).

An alternative approach to analyzing the impact of private voluntary health insurance in providing financial security and buffering risks arising from ill-health is to look at financial vulnerability instead of financial protection. Using the quotient of the standard deviation of households' out-of-pocket expenditure for health care and mean disposable income—that is, the households' gross income less all health-related expenditure (insurance premiums plus out-of-pocket expenditure)—eliminates the effect of premiums in the numerator (Bundorf 2005). The analysis of financial vulnerability across income quintiles yields interesting results.

Figure 6.2 reflects the dimension of the financial vulnerability measure across household income quintiles. The expected result—lower vulnerability of medical scheme members—is apparent only for households belonging to the top income quintile. In the second highest quintile, the vulnerability measure for insured households is only slightly below the value for the uninsured. In the

FIGURE 6.2 South Africa: Financial Vulnerability, by Household Income

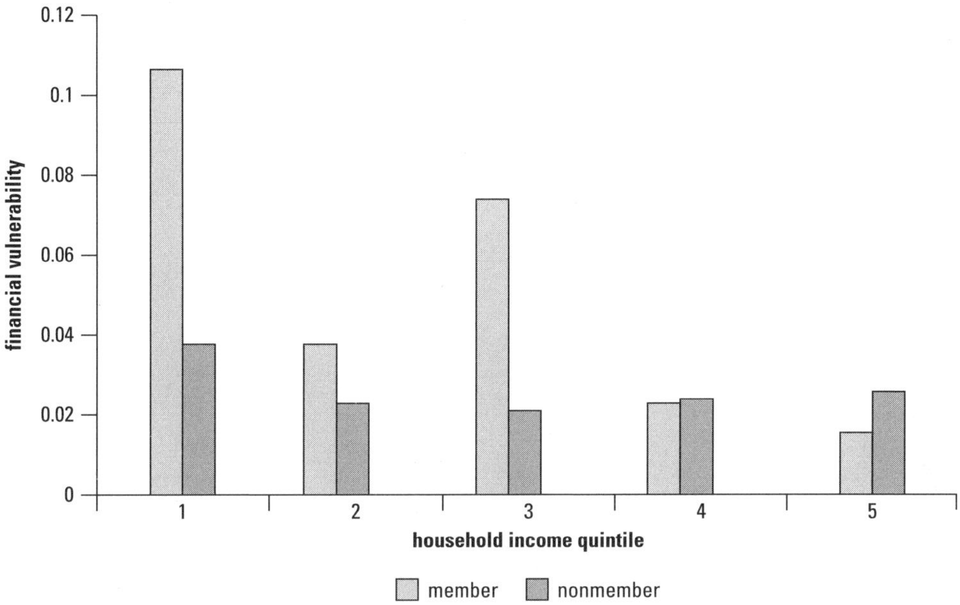

Source: StatsSA Income and Expenditure Survey 2000.

three bottom quintiles, the vulnerability of those who have taken out insurance is considerably higher than for households without medical scheme membership. It is evident from table 6.3, however, that the number of households with medical scheme membership in the lower three income quintiles is insignificant. For the few households in those income segments reporting medical scheme membership, the fluctuation of health-related costs in relation to their disposable income is on average greater than the variation in the economic burden of illness across nonmember households. The results may indicate a preference of those households for private health services, which—in combination with a very limited benefits package—implies relatively high out-of-pocket expenditure. Unfortunately, the dataset does not allow analysis of health provider preference. Given the relative group sizes within the quintiles, however, the results regarding the lower quintiles have to be interpreted cautiously.

The explanation of the counterintuitive results depicted in figure 6.2 becomes clearer when the vulnerability measure is decomposed into its numerator and denominator values, the standard deviation of out-of-pocket expenditure, and the mean disposable income. Although the disproportion in group sizes between members and nonmembers within the quintiles needs to be taken into account, figure 6.3 reflects a steady increase in the standard deviation of expenditure from the lowest to the top income quintile. As implied, the standard deviation of out-of-pocket expenditure in the lower quintiles is higher for member households. In the upper two income quintiles, however, the standard deviation of health-related

FIGURE 6.3 South Africa: Standard Deviation of Out-of-Pocket Health Expenditure, by Household Income Quintile (rand)

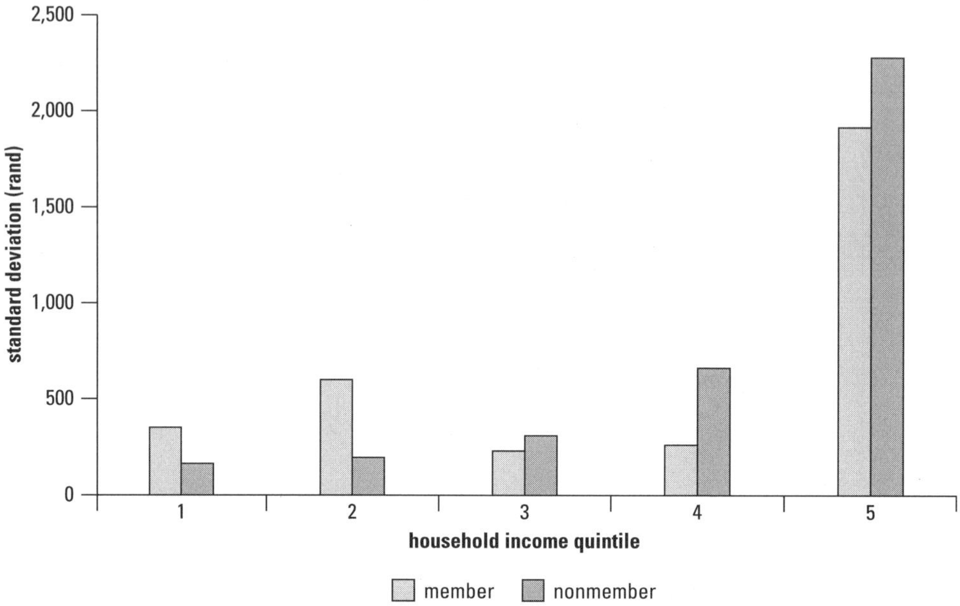

Source: StatsSA Income and Expenditure Survey 2000.

expenditure is higher for households outside the medical schemes environment. These are typically households with a strong preference for private health services who are either not in a socioeconomic position to join a medical scheme (this may apply especially to many households in the second highest quintile) or who are more risk averse and prefer not to belong to any medical scheme.

An analysis of the mean disposable income, net of medical scheme contributions and direct health-related expenditure, exposes the extreme interquintile differences in income, especially with a view to the difference between the top quintile and the second highest quintile (figure 6.4). The highly unequal income distribution within the South African economy becomes visible. Whereas income differences between medical scheme members and nonmembers in the lower four quintiles are not very pronounced, in the highest-income category the 60 percent of households with medical scheme membership have a significantly higher mean disposable income than the nonmember households.

DETERMINANTS OF UTILIZATION

To fully understand the country context and the impact of medical scheme coverage on access to health care, a careful analysis of the determinants of health services utilization is useful. A multinomial logit model has been used to identify

FIGURE 6.4 South Africa: Mean Annual Disposable Income, by Income Quintile (rand)

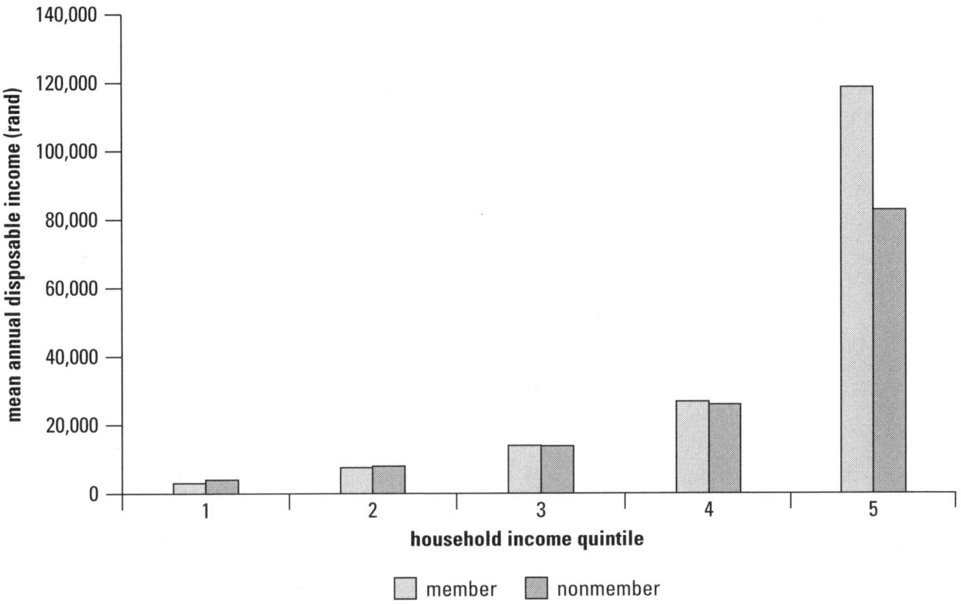

Source: StatsSA Income and Expenditure Survey 2000.

the determinants of utilization of both private and public health services as well as the option of ill household members not seeking care (table 6.4). The analysis uses the South African General Household Survey 2003, with a sample size of 11,454 people who reported illness or injury within the month prior to the interview.

All but two variables used in the model reflect personal characteristics. The wealth quintile and the education of the household head, however, characterize the household background of the individual. The format of income-related variables in the survey unfortunately does not allow the construction of income quintiles. Therefore, a household asset index was created to reflect the socioeconomic status of the respondent. Household assets incorporated in the index include different kinds of household durables (for example, bicycle, car, watch, telephone) as well as access to electricity, the household's main source of drinking water, the type of toilet facility and the wall and roof materials of the house. On the basis of the asset index, wealth quintiles were constructed. The education of the household head was found to be more relevant to an individual's treatment seeking than the ill person's own education level. The choice of the household head's education over the ill person's furthermore excludes the effect of the ill person's age on education.

The results of the multinomial logit model for utilization are presented in table 6.4. The explanatory power (Pseudo R^2) of the model is 0.147 (Prob $>$ $chi^2 = 0.000$). The

TABLE 6.4 South Africa: Determinants of Health Care–Seeking Behavior (Multinomial Logit Model)

Item	*Relative risk ratio*	*Coefficient*	*Significance*
No formal care vs. public			
Medical scheme membership (no member)[a]	2.3409	0.851	0.000
Gender (male)	1.1720	0.159	0.019
Ethnic group (African)			
Coloured	0.6251	–0.470	0.000
Indian	0.5232	–0.648	0.047
White	1.5783	0.456	0.015
Education of household head (no formal education)			
Primary	0.9293	–0.073	0.392
Secondary	0.9196	–0.084	0.367
Post-secondary technical or diploma	1.0821	0.079	0.687
University	1.9670	0.677	0.009
Wealth quintile (lowest quintile)			
Second lowest	0.8663	–0.143	0.140
Medium	1.0181	0.018	0.859
Second highest	1.0966	0.092	0.400
Highest	1.6563	0.505	0.000
Age category (0–14 years)			
15–24 years	2.0589	0.722	0.000
25–34 years	1.3812	0.323	0.004
35–44 years	1.3250	0.281	0.011
45–54 years	1.0717	0.069	0.555
55 years and above	1.1148	0.109	0.282
Constant	n.a.	–1.432	0.000
Private vs. public			
Medical scheme membership (no member)	10.1700	2.319	0.000
Gender (male)	1.0930	0.089	0.143
Ethnic group (African)			
Coloured	0.6450	–0.439	0.000
Indian	0.3841	–0.957	0.000
White	1.2653	0.235	0.137
Education of household head (no formal education)			
Primary	0.9437	–0.058	0.491
Secondary	1.2359	0.212	0.014
Post-secondary technical or diploma	2.0078	0.697	0.000
University	2.8463	1.046	0.000

Item	*Relative risk ratio*	*Coefficient*	*Significance*
Wealth quintile (lowest quintile)			
Second lowest	1.1514	0.141	0.156
Medium	1.6202	0.483	0.000
Second highest	1.8567	0.619	0.000
Highest	4.0894	1.408	0.000
Age category (0–14 years)			
15–24 years	1.0176	0.017	0.870
25–34 years	1.1480	0.138	0.179
35–44 years	1.2404	0.215	0.026
45–54 years	1.0370	0.036	0.710
55 years and above	1.0513	0.050	0.583
Constant	n.a.	−1.527	0.000

Source: Authors.
Note: Wald chi2 (36) = 1620.28; Prob > chi2 = 0.0000; Pseudo R2 = 0.147.

first part of the table looks at the choice of "no formal care" in the case of illness or injury over the comparison group "public sector providers." The most striking result is the highly significant role of medical scheme membership. Medical scheme members' probability of not seeking any formal health care rather than utilize public facilities is more than twice as high as for nonmembers. This corresponds with the results for university graduates and individuals in the highest-income category. Female patients are slightly more inclined to choose no care over public care, and the "Coloured" and the "Indian" populations are more likely to choose public care over the no-care option than the African ethnic group. Patients under 45 years of age have a tendency to choose no care over public services (decreasing with age). The results for the age groups 45 years of age and upward are not significant.

Of higher relevance to the discussion are the results that reflect choices between private health care and public sector services. The probability of a medical scheme member visiting a private provider is 10 times that of a nonmember. Interestingly, gender does not seem to influence the choice between public and private providers. For both the Coloured and Indian population groups there is a lower tendency to choose a private over a public provider as compared to the African population group.[5] There is a clear increase in the odds of choosing a private over a public provider with increasing level of education. Patients with a university degree are nearly three times more likely to seek private health care as opposed to public care than patients with no formal education.

Household wealth turns out to be a highly significant predictor of the public-private choice. The chance of selecting a private provider increases with wealth quintile (the coefficients not being significant for the second lowest quintile).

Patients in the top wealth quintile were found to be four times more likely to consult a private provider than those in the lowest quintile. With the exception of a slight preference for private services in the 35 to 44 age group, the coefficients are insignificant across age categories.

The results of this analysis once more reflect the dichotomy apparent in the South African health system. The higher quality of care of private sector services is accessible only to the better-off, characterized by comparatively high educational level and wealth. Medical scheme membership not only provides a higher degree of financial protection for the better off, but also turns out to be a key predictor of private health care use.

HEALTH REFORM IN SOUTH AFRICA

Different conclusions can be drawn from the findings of this study. If the main focus is on guaranteeing equitable access to quality health care, there seems to be a policy choice between strengthening the public sector, thereby turning public health care into a more attractive choice across all segments of the South African population, and making private sector services more accessible. If, however, the spotlight is on protecting all socioeconomic groups from the economic risks associated with ill-health, there is a clear case for extending the insurance option to the lower-income segments of South African society. Here, the main barrier—and this becomes clear from the foregoing discussion—is unaffordability of the comprehensive benefits packages for the largest part of the population.

The South African government has taken steps to address the system-inherent inequities. A set of initiatives addresses the need for changes in private sector structures to enable steps toward social health insurance. The integration of the public sector and private medical schemes in a universal contributory system is a declared long-term objective of the South African government.

In short, the following important steps have been taken:

- Risk equalization between the medical schemes has been initialized. Since January 2005, a shadow process has been in place.
- The design of a basic benefits package is being discussed.
- The issue of income-related cross-subsidies in the current environment (tax expenditure subsidy) has been tabled, and alternative solutions have been sketched. Mandatory contributions have been suggested for those earning above a certain level.
- An immediate step to increase the number of people covered by medical schemes is the introduction of a medical scheme for public sector employees.
- There are initiatives to design a framework for expanding medical scheme coverage to lower-income groups.

CHALLENGES

Low-income groups and the poor must be offered more efficient ways than those now available to them to reduce and manage their health risks. Some problems inhibiting the extension of coverage to the low-income groups go beyond the affordability issue. Other barriers to entry into the health insurance market are closely linked to distributional issues. Within the target groups, household economic structures are less clear-cut than in high-income environments. Family structures and associated health care needs are complex. To date there is no coherent framework for effectively addressing the complex informal socioeconomic environment in South Africa through an insurance model. Currently, the environment does not appear conducive to radical change in the system. It seems therefore that the low-income environment needs to be addressed outside the existing reform framework, which basically reflects a top-down approach toward broadening insurance coverage. Additional initiatives could address the feasibility of implementing financial protection mechanisms by directly addressing the needs of the poorer and poorest segments of the South African population. Introduction of community-based schemes to protect the economically vulnerable against ill-health associated financial risks is one option that bears investigation.

NOTES

The authors thank the editors and reviewers for their useful comments and support for this review.

1. The official definition of unemployment excludes people who have not taken active steps to obtain employment or start some form of self-employment in the four weeks prior to the interview.
2. The average exchange rate for September 2004 (30 days), the month in which the Labour Force Survey was conducted, was US$1 = R 6.55826.
3. The statistics in this section (unless otherwise stated) are for 2002 and were sourced from the World Bank *HNP stats* Web site (http:// devdata.worldbank.org/hnpstats).
4. The average exchange rate for fiscal year 2003/04 was US$1 = R 7.11187.
5. The use of the terms "African," "White," "Coloured," and "Indian" reflects a statutory stratification of the South African population in terms of the former Population Registration Act. The use of these terms in the analysis does not imply the legitimacy of this racist terminology. In this study "ethnic group" is analyzed as a potential determinant of health-seeking behavior as socioeconomic status is still skewed across the different groups.

REFERENCES

Armstrong, J., J. Deeble, D. Dror, N. Rice, M. Thiede, and W. van de Ven. 2004. *International Review Panel Report to the South African Risk Equalisation Fund Task Group*, Cape Town, South Africa.

Bester, H., D. Chamberlain, R. Hawthorne, S. Malherbe, and R. Walker. 2004. *Making Insurance Markets Work for the Poor in South Africa.* Johannesburg: FinMark Trust/Genesis [www.finmarktrust.org.za/documents/2004/FEBRUARY/InsuranceScoingSA.pdf].

Bradshaw, D., P. Groenewald, R. Laubscher, N. Nanaan, B. Nojilana, R. Norman, D. Pieterse, and M. Scheider. 2003. *Initial Burden of Disease, 2000.* Cape Town: South African Medical Research Council.

Bundorf, K. 2005. *Measuring the Financial Protection from Health Insurance in the U.S.* Paper presented at the conference "Private Health Insurance in Developing Countries," Wharton School, University of Pennsylvania, Philadelphia PA, March 15–16, 2005.

Cornell, J., J. Goudge, D. McIntyre, and S. Mbatsha. 2001. *South African National Health Accounts: The Private Sector.* Pretoria: National Health Accounts Research Team and National Department of Health.

CMS (Council for Medical Schemes). 2004. *Annual Report of the Registrar of Medical Schemes 2003–04.* Pretoria: CMS.

DOH (Department of Health). 2001. *Consultation Document into the Various Social Security Aspects of the South African Health System.* Pretoria: DOH.

Doherty, J., and H. McLeod. 2003. "Medical Schemes." In *South African Health Review 2002,* ed. P. Ijumba, C. Day, and A. Ntuli, 41–66. Durban: Health Systems Trust.

Dorrington, R., D. Bradshaw, L. Johnson, and D. Budlender. 2004. *The Demographic Impact of HIV/AIDS in South Africa. National Indicators for 2004.* Cape Town: Centre for Actuarial Research, Medical Research Council, and Actuarial Society of South Africa.

Gilson, L., and D. McIntyre. 2001. "Experiences from South Africa: Dealing with a Poor Health Legacy of Apartheid." In *Challenging Inequities in Health: From Ethics to Action,* ed. M. Whitehead, T. Evans, F. Diderichsen, and A. Bhuiya. New York, NY: Oxford University Press.

Harrison S. 2004. "Medical Schemes." In *South African Health Review 2003/04,* ed.. Ijumba, P., C. Day, and A. Ntuli, 291–298. Durban: Health Systems Trust.

Kingdon, G., and J. Knight. 2001. *Why High Unemployment and Small Informal Sector in South Africa?* Oxford: Centre for the Study of African Economies, Department of Economics, University of Oxford.

McIntyre, D., H. McLeod, and M. Thiede. 2005. *Comments on the National Treasury Discussion Document on the Proposed Tax Reforms Relating to Medical Scheme Contributions and Medical Expenses.* Health Economics Unit, University of Cape Town.

McIntyre, D., M. Thiede, G. Dahlgren, and M. Whitehead. 2006. "What are the economic consequences for households of illness and of paying for health care in low- and middle-income country contexts?" *Social Science and Medicine* 62:858–865.

McLeod, H., 2003. *An Introduction to Medical Schemes and Social Health Insurance in South Africa.* Cape Town Centre for Actuarial Research, University of Cape Town.

National Treasury 2005. *National Budget Overview.* Pretoria: National Treasury.

StatsSA 2004a. *Mid-year Population Estimates, South Africa 2004.* Statistical Release P0302. Pretoria: Statistics South Africa.

StatsSA 2004b. *Labour Force Survey—September 2004*. Statistical release P0210. Pretoria: Statistics South Africa.

Thomas, S., and D. Muirhead. 2000. *The Public Sector Report*. National Health Accounts Project. Health Economics Unit, University of Cape Town, and Centre for Health Policy, University of the Witwatersrand.

UNDP (United Nations Development Programme). 2003. *South Africa Human Development Report 2003*. Cape Town: Oxford University Press.

CHAPTER 7

Thailand

Siripen Supakankunti

Universal health care coverage began in Thailand late in 2002, so its full effects are not yet known. The analyses done for this study confirm that private health insurance (PHI) can improve access to health care for the insured. However, services are unlikely to cost less. The coexistence of universal coverage heavily influences a person's decision to apply for voluntary private health insurance, it was also found. As a supplementary scheme, private health insurance looks attractive to some Thais, mainly the better off. Unless PHI becomes widely affordable, its impact on the kingdom as a whole does not seem promising.

This chapter examines the roles of private health insurance that affect access to health care of people in Thailand. It starts with descriptive review on the relative importance of voluntary private health insurance vis-à-vis the public scheme. The second part covers quantitative aspects. It was found that private health insurance still has a promising future as the Thai economy prospers even though its share in the whole industry is relatively small especially under the present circumstances of the implementation of the Universal Coverage (UC) scheme, both for the status of private health insurance as a supplementary scheme, and the impacts of the scheme.

INTRODUCTION

Thailand is a low-middle-income country with a population of 64 million. Thailand has made great strides in its health status, along with its economic development. A simple look at progress in life expectancy demonstrates this point. In 1964, life expectancy at birth was a mere 55.9 years for men and 62.0 years for women. Today, those figures have risen to an impressive 69.4 and 74.1 years, respectively. The infant mortality rate was 26.1 per 1,000 live births in 1996, and the maternal mortality rate dropped dramatically, from 374.3 in 1962, to 12.9 per 100,000 live births. These figures show the significant progress Thailand has made in its people's health.

Today the health care system in Thailand consists of many levels of service, from private clinics or public health centers, to regional or university hospitals. The uneven distribution of these services, however, means that some parts of the country are worse-off than others. There is an exceptional disparity in hospitals and hospital patient beds across different regions of the country. Overall, patient hospital beds in Thailand numbered 135,000, an average of one bed per 456 people. In Bangkok, however, this ratio is much greater (1:199) than in the Northeast (1:781). Thus, although the health status has significantly improved, the disparity across the country is still notable.

The distribution of physicians across the country is also uneven, despite some improvements in the past several years. As late as 1996, the disparity was glaring. In Bangkok the doctor per population ratio (1:728) was several times the ratio in the Northeast (1:10,417). The gap has narrowed slightly (Bangkok 1: 761, the Northeast 1: 8,122) but is still wide.

Before universal coverage began in late 2002, the Thai people were covered through several government programs. The four main programs are: the Low-Income Card Scheme, LICS), the Civil Servant Medical Benefit Scheme (CSMBS), the Social Security Scheme (SSS), and the Voluntary Health Card Scheme (VHCS). As late as 1991, government investment and promotion of these health insurance programs was very low—67 percent of the Thai population was not covered by any of these insurance schemes. Over the next decade, however, health insurance became increasingly important to both the Thai government and the Thai people.

This chapter examines the roles of private health insurance that affect access to health care of people in Thailand. It first describes the relative importance of private health insurance (voluntary scheme) and the public scheme. The second part provides quantitative aspects based on Thailand's household social and economic survey.

ON PRIVATE HEALTH INSURANCE

Private health insurance has long played an incidental role in Thailand's health insurance schemes. The advent of universal coverage further weakened its role. The evidence that PHI has an impact on the general public's access to health care is therefore weak.

Health security in Thailand combines two approaches: social insurance, which pools risks and resources in the working population, and public assistance or welfare for the remaining population. Thailand's current health insurance and health welfare schemes may be categorized into four main groups:

- the UC scheme, providing public assistance for the general population such as the uninsured, the indigent (the poor, the elderly, children;
- health benefits for government employees;
- the social security scheme of compulsory health insurance for formal sector employees;
- voluntary health insurance.

The first private insurance business started about 100 years ago, when the East Asiatic Company was the agent for the Equitable Insurance Company of London in Thailand. Supachutikul (1996) argued that the company had not been successful in that the sole agent handled many other businesses, and all sale representatives were foreigners. But most important, it was because most Thai in those days were economically self-sufficient, and buying insurance was a rigid, cumbersome process. Nevertheless, the insurance business stabilized after World War II.

The insurance business in Thailand can be legally categorized into two groups: life and non–life insurance. In Thailand, unlike in other countries, health insurance belongs to the non–life insurance category. However, life insurance companies may offer health insurance as optional plans attached to the main life insurance policies as an accident and injury plan, a health care plan, a cancer and other severe disease plan, or a permanent disability plan. In the early 1990s, only 6 out of the 18 life insurance firms offered health insurance (Kiranandana 1993, cited by Supachutikul 1996).

Relative to other schemes, there has been very little private health insurance in Thailand—only 1.6 percent in 1992 (table 7.1). This situation continues today (table 7.2)

TABLE 7.1 Thailand: Health Benefits Coverage, 1992

Group/scheme	*People covered (million)*	*%*
Health welfare for general population	20.3	35.9
Low-income	11.7	20.7
Aged	3.5	6.2
Primary school children under Ministry of Education	5.1	9.0
Health welfare for state employees	6.4	11.3
Civil Servant Medical Benefit Scheme	5.6	9.9
Public enterprise	0.8	1.4
Compulsory health insurance	2.5	4.4
Social Security Scheme	2.5	4.4
Workmen's Compensation Fund	1.8	3.2
Voluntary health insurance	2.2	3.9
Health Card Project	1.3	2.3
Private insurance	0.9	1.6
Covered	31.4	55.6
Uncovered	25.1	44.4

Source: Supachutikul 1996.

TABLE 7.2 Thailand: Evolution of Private Health Insurance

	Coverage (percent)						
Scheme	*1991*	*1992*	*1995*	*1997*	*1998*	*1999*	*2000*
Voluntary health insurance	2.9	3.9	9.8	15.3	15.9	15.8	17.5
Public	1.7	2.3	7.8	13.3	13.9	13.8	14.2
Private	1.2	1.6	2.0	2.0	2.0	2.0	3.3

Source: Wibulpolprasert 2002.

TABLE 7.3 Thailand: Insurance Coverage, 1998

	Coverage		*Expenditure (baht)*						
Scheme	*Pop. (million)*	*%*	*Billion*	*%NHE*	*Per capita*	*Premium (source of funds)*	*Payment mechanism*	*Health service utilization*	*Drug user*
Social Welfare	27.5	45.1	18.3	6.5	667[a]	Tax	Global budget	Assigned public and referral	Essential drugs
Civil Servant Medical Benefit Scheme	6.6	10.8	16.4	5.8	2,491	Tax	Fee-for-service	Public	Essential drugs
Social Security	5.2	8.5	7.6	2.7	1,468	4.5% payroll[b]	Prepaid capitation	Public and private	Essential drugs
Voluntary public health insurance (Health Card)	8.5	13.9	6.4	2.3	750[a]	500 / family + tax (1,000)	Global budget based on OP&IP	Assigned public and referral	Essential drugs
Voluntary private health insurance	1.2	2.0	3.6	1.3	3,000	Varied	Fee-for-service	Public and private	No limit
Workmen's Compensation Fund	5.2	8.5	1.6	0.6	308	0.2–3.0% payroll[c]	Fee-for-service	Public and private	No limit
Car accident	61.0	100.0	1.5	0.5	—	Private	Fee-for-service	Public and private	—
Total	49.0[d]	80.3[d]	55.4	19.7	1,067[d]	—	—	—	—

Source: Wibulpolprasert 2002.
Note: NHE = National Health Expenditure; OP&IP = outpatient and inpatient.
a. Cross-subsidization added.
b. 1.5 percent of payroll each from employers, employee, and government.
c. Rate according to past history of claims.
d. Excluding Workmen's Compensation Fund and motor vehicle accident insurance.

Most low-income people, urban and rural, use public facilities and are covered by a public insurance scheme, namely, social welfare, health card, and social security. In contrast, medium to high-income people usually use private facilities, and they are the group that can buy private health insurance. In fact, only relatively high-income people hold private insurance (Wibulpolprasert 2002).

Despite the predominance of public insurance, voluntary health insurance coverage has grown. Although private health insurance coverage has stayed at relatively low-constant level of 2.0 percent of the population, coverage expanded. The number rose from 2.0 percent in 1999 to 3.3 percent in 2000, a 65 percent increase. Piravej (2003) claims that lately the number of privately insured has grown by double-digits (to be discussed later).

Circumstantially, these events would seem to improve access to health care, but this is not quite correct. Only the people who buy it are entitled to its benefits, so its impact could be severely limited.

Health facilities in Thailand are either public or private. Public facilities are accessible to everyone, especially those covered by public insurance schemes, because of their low costs. Some private facilities are considered superior in terms of both quality and convenience. Thus, the Thai health system could be said to be market-segmented. Most people are "forced" to go to public providers, putting pressure on service capacity. People who can pay usually opt for higher-quality services.

People who buy private health insurance have an average income of ฿18,000 a month, and most of them have incomes just under ฿30,000 (figure 7.1). Moreover, the cost of the most recent privately insured medical service is high relative to income (figure 7.2). This might imply an ability to financially protect the insured.

FIGURE 7.1 Thailand: Monthly Household Income of the Insured, Quartiles 1 to 3

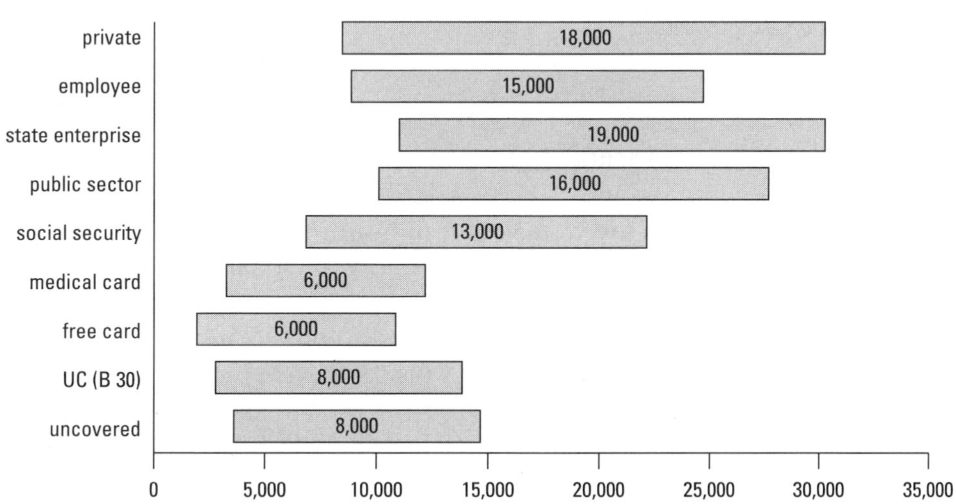

Source: Jariyalerdsak 2004.

FIGURE 7.2 Thailand: Cost of Most Recent Medical Service relative to Household and Individual Income

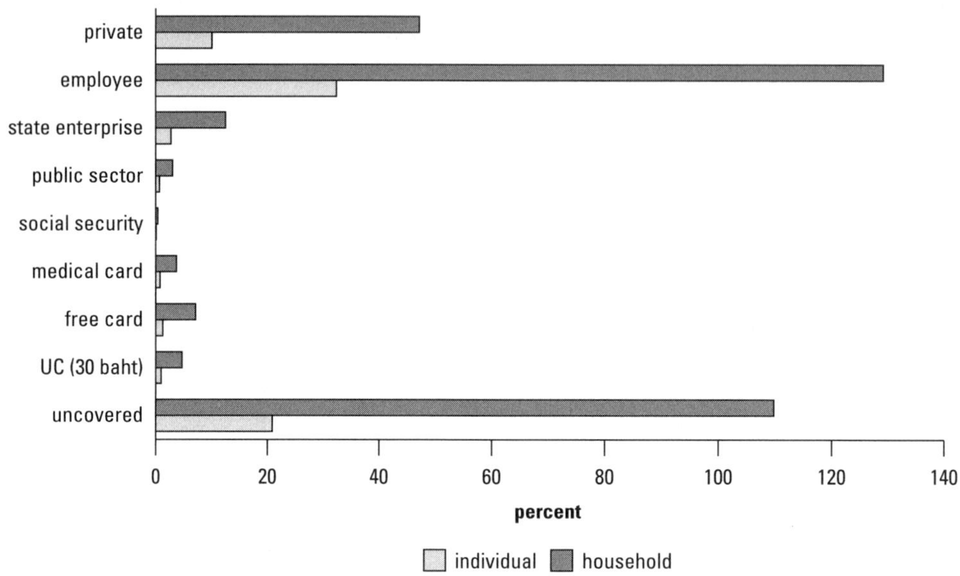

Source: Jariyalerdsak 2004.

In conclusion, the privately insured are decidedly better off than others with respect to both service accessibility and financial hedge against cost. Most people cannot, however, afford private insurance. As a result, unless the government subsidizes the schemes so that the price is lower, its impact on access to health care has to be rated "weak."

SYSTEM, MECHANISM, AND REGULATION

Private insurance is thus is just a small part of health insurance in Thailand, as shown in figure 7.3. The others are Social Security, national health insurance, and Civil Servant Medical Benefit Scheme. Private voluntary insurance is funded by risk-related contributions from enrollees. Those funds are transferred directly to people who need them, the patients, to pay service fees.

Risk management under Thailand's health system is inefficient. The pooling mechanism was found deficient in the work cited by the Health Insurance Research Institute in collaboration with the health insurance office. Most spending on health (65.2 percent) is private out-of-pocket spending (OOPS)

FIGURE 7.3 Thailand: The Health Insurance System

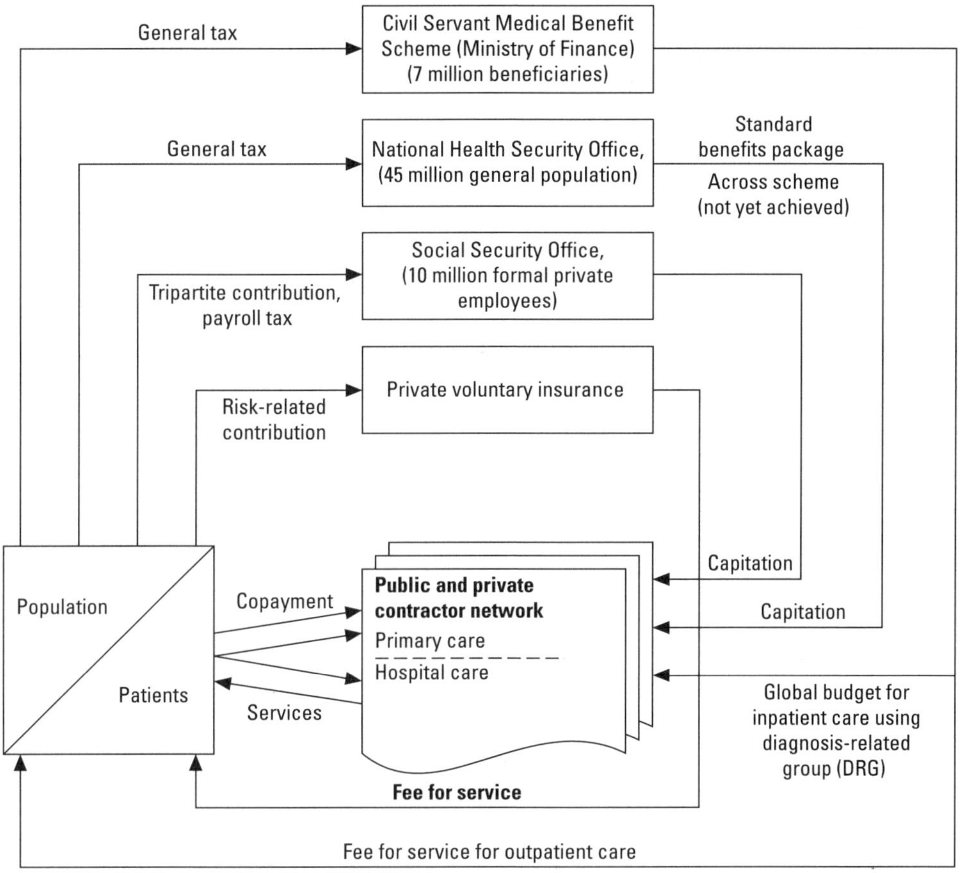

Source: Adapted from Tancharoensathien et al. 2002 (cited by Sein 2005).

(figure 7.4). Only 13.4 percent of the health expenditure is covered by insurance. Private expenditure is mainly on medical supplies[1] and costs of private and public medical facilities. "Many of those who are insured still go to the private pharmacies, private clinics, hospitals, and pay out of pocket or by employers" (Pramualratana and Wibulpolprasert: 18).

Finally, concerning regulation of voluntary health insurance, there are no specific laws or regulations for the business. Health insurance comes under the law for non–life insurance, which does not describe any health-related issues. The life insurance business, however, has laws and regulations of its own. Therefore, most voluntary private health insurance is sold as an option for life insurance with the ambiguity of the laws.

FIGURE 7.4 Thailand: Flow of Health Expenditure, 1998

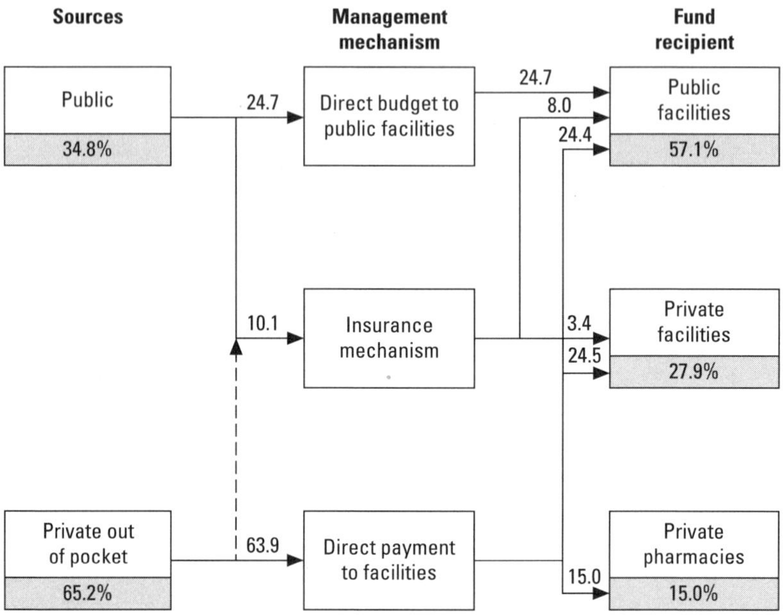

Source: Wibulpolprasert 2002:18.

BUSINESS ENVIRONMENT

Recovery from the economic crisis of 1997 has fueled growth in the insurance business (Piravej 2003). The business is driven mainly by life insurance, which accounts for 90 percent of the market. These insurers were keen to use health as an immediate benefit to promote sale of more complex life insurance policies, until recently. However, the market for private health insurance is still considered small due to lack of direct government promotion or incentive for buying the insurance, limited consumer awareness, and close linkage between and packaging of health and life insurance policies.

In 2002, the entire industry core health premium was around ฿12 billion. Nearly 70 percent of this amount went for direct funding of medical care, mostly in the private delivery systems. The individual ratio was 19 to 1,[2] and about 3.3 million people were covered by private health insurance (Piravej 2003).

As a result of the 1997 economic crisis, many Thai employers cut group health coverage for their employees, and people who still preferred private medical care bought private health insurance individually. Since then, economic growth has had a positive effect on the business. In addition, there was a significant shift toward third-party payment either through the government-sponsored programs including social security or through private health insurance. Meanwhile, private hospitals saw their revenue from private health insurance rise from between 10 and 20 percent to between 30 and 50 percent during the post-crisis period.

Another impact on the private system came from the implementation of the government universal health coverage program (UC) throughout the country in late 2002. Consumers saw the reform as a change from subsidized public health care to guaranteed access to a comprehensive set of covered services via the three major public funding schemes: UC (46 million insured), Social Security (SS, 10 million), and Civil Servant Medical Benefits (CSMBS, 6 million). In terms of financing, the key change was the shift toward the extensive use of at-risk payment methods, namely capitation and prospective payment, from a relatively risk-free fee-for-service environment.

Initially, there was a concern that UC would impede growth of private health insurance. However, since UC implementation, private health insurance has managed double-digit growth. This may stem from continued economic recovery, nonparticipation in UC by most of the leading private hospitals, and the perception of health as a core business by a growing number of insurers. The recent SARS outbreak in the region also created consumer awareness of new health risks, which directly boosts private health insurance sales.

According to the Department of Insurance, Ministry of Commerce, in 2003 77 non–life insurance companies, including 72 domestic companies, were operating under non–life insurance licenses. Sixty-three companies operated in all types of non–life insurance business (including health insurance), and 5 companies sold only health insurance, totaling 68 companies dealing in health insurance. Furthermore, 20,570,172 policies were issued; of which 78,427 were health insurance, an increase of 18.02 percent over the previous year. The direct premiums of the entire non–life insurance business totaled ฿71,160 million, an increase of 13.63 percent. Health insurance premiums, however, accounted for only 1.7 percent.

In a nutshell, from an economic perspective, private health insurance, has a promising future in terms of enlarging its currently small market share in the health insurance "industry" as the economy grows. (See table 7.4 for details.) This could be described as a product of income effect: as people's incomes grow, a policy becomes easier to buy. Nevertheless, this does not mean the whole population will benefit. Only when the majority of people can afford private health insurance can it be interpreted as beneficial.

PROBLEMS AND CONSTRAINTS IN HEALTH CARE FINANCING

Over the past 30 years, the Thai government has implemented and extended its insurance programs to secure for low- and middle-income households of their inherent rights to a healthy life. In its most recent development, the government has guaranteed health care coverage to all Thai citizens, in a program funded

TABLE 7.4 Thailand: Non–life Insurance Business Premiums, 2003 (฿1,000)

		Sum insured		Direct premiums		Net written premiums		Net earned premiums	
Line of business	*Policies*	*Amount*	*%*	*Amount*	*%*	*Amount*	*%*	*Amount*	*%*
Fire	1,864,670	6,889,040,119	25.47	6,981,861	9.81	4,834,195	9.73	4,744,038	10.31
Marine and transportation	604,222.00	4,089,302,428.00	15.11	3,127,221.00	4.39	1,765,468.00	3.55	1,725,159.00	3.75
Automobile	16,435,429	3,590,905,648	13.27	41,601,700	58.46	37,303,733	75.08	34,375,948	74.74
Personal injury	1,058,238	2,221,981,168	8.21	2,676,360	3.76	1,767,244	3.56	1,590,500	3.45
Health	78,429	200,356,062	0.74	1,212,716	1.7	1,103,565	2.22	1,032,240	2.25
Engineering	7,712	795,957,697	2.94	1,662,957	2.34	279,510	0.56	173,026	0.38
Aviation	167	784,167,073	2.90	1,976,511	2.78	(22,780)	(0.05)	40,546	0.09
Crop	0	0	0	0	0	0	0	0	0
Livestock	7	40,292	0.00	1,292	0.00	351	0.00	758	0.00
Other	521,838	8,478,490,153	31.34	11,918,969	16.75	2,651,415	5.34	2,310,763	5.02
Total	20,570,172	27,050,240,640	100.00	71,159,587	100.00	49,682,701	100.00	45,992,978	100.00

Source: Ministry of Commerce 2003.

from general tax revenues (Supakankunti and Siripong 2004). Since 2002, the Thai government has provided health care through the CSMBS, SSS, and UCS.

The CSMBS is provided to all permanent government employees and funded on a fee-for-service basis. Coverage is comprehensive and extends to most of the individual's family as well. Cost escalation is perhaps the most important of the several issues to emerge from this program. The cost has escalated every year since the plan's inception in 1980, a clear result of moral hazard practiced by beneficiaries and their physicians. Only recently has the government restructured its payment scheme to better contain costs.

The SSS, a compulsory scheme, provides health insurance and other benefits to workers in the formal sector. Workers register at their preferred hospital, which receives a capitation payment for each registered patient. Because most workers are healthy, capitation payments often exceed the cost of delivering care to this group of patients. As a result, this program has raised competition among hospitals. Many private hospitals established networks and worked to attract more registrants.

The success of SSS financing dictated the financing of the subsequent UCS, for which the only out-of-pocket payment is a per visit copayment of ฿30 (less than US$1). People register at their preferred local hospital, and the hospital receives a capitation fee in return for providing service to their registered beneficiaries. Although this financing scheme contains costs, it would be too optimistic to expect the same success as in the SSS because the respective beneficiaries' general health statuses are quite different. Two concerns result from this scheme. First, there is concern about the financial sustainability of hospitals and other health care providers. If the capitation is set too low, hospital costs may exceed their revenues, causing some facilities to cut back or close altogether. Second, because cutting back on expenses may compromise service quality, ensuring equity across covered groups remains important.

To supplement publicly provided health coverage, especially the UC, some people buy private insurance, often packaged with some form of life insurance. The private insurance gives them access to "premium" services provided by private facilities while being insured. Purchasers of private insurance, then, are likely to be healthy, middle- and upper-class individuals. This type of health insurance is often reserved for extremely high medical care costs and thus may not be subject to the same kind of financing concerns faced by Thailand's public government schemes or by private health insurance companies in other countries.

QUANTITATIVE ANALYSES

The quantitative analysis was conducted following the "Methodology for Countries Case Studies" (Preker and Jutting 2004: 21–27). Due to data unavailability, some analyses could not be conducted. The data—household and individual—were obtained from the 2002 National Statistical Office household socioeconomic survey. Household records were on (1) characteristics, status, and welfare and benefits and (2) summary expenditure. Individual records were on (1) member characteristics and benefits and (2) morbidity and medical care. In 34,785 households across the country, 118,762 individuals were surveyed. Only 2,137 persons (1.8 percent of respondents) own private insurance. These analyses were carried out on the impact of voluntary insurance on financial protection, access to health care, and the labor market.

Impact of Voluntary Insurance on Financial Protection

Financial protection was defined as an inverse of the variation coefficient of non-medical consumption (NMC), given by

$$\varphi = \overline{NMC} \,/\, \sigma_{NMC}$$
$$NMC = Y - (\rho + OOPS),$$

where

φ = degree of financial protection;
NMC = nonmedical consumption;
Y = household income;
ρ = insurance premium; and
$OOPS$ = out-of-pocket spending.

In the sample families[3] selected, at least one member had a Medical Card, which includes private voluntary insurance. It was found that 17 percent of the sample, (5,918 families) had at least one member with a card. Total monthly income was used to present *Y*. *OOPS* was computed from a sum of expenditures on (1) medical supplies, (2) being an outpatient, and (3) being an inpatient. However, the premium was reported in aggregate form, including premiums for all other insurance (for example, asset insurance, life insurance, and third-party accident insurance). Hence, the proxy of the private insurance premium was computed as 1.7 percent of the total amount, referring to the data presented in table 7.4.

For Thailand, it was found that

$$\varphi = 0.72$$

The average of NMC is about ฿19,902.02 while its standard deviation equals ฿27,754.31. According to the properties of the measure, the value of the statistic rises when insurance coverage increases and falls when premiums rise or incomes drop. At first glance, private insurance in Thailand seems to offer little financial protection because of a large variation in NMC, larger than NMC itself on average.[4]

However, the fact that the variation in NMC was directly affected by the variation in monthly income might (as evident from the definition) invalidate this analysis. Another analysis, consequently, was conducted with the limited sample so as to limit the effect of the high deviation in income in Thailand (that is, the very uneven income distribution). Only households with a monthly income below ฿50,000 were used; 33,660 households met the criterion. The degree of financial protection increased to 1.23, a remarkable increase. This time, the financial protection figure is larger than a unit and may therefore suggest that private health insurance in Thailand helps promote insurance holders' financial protection to some extent.

Impact of Voluntary Insurance on Access to Health Care

Due to unavailability of data about health expenditure at individual level, the analysis was done instead at household level. A two-stage estimating model was used instead of the original Tobin model (1958), for the objective is not really to estimate the propensity of *OOPS*.

The first model estimated was the probability (logit) model of a visit to a health care provider.

$$P(visit > 0) = X\beta + \varepsilon.$$

A "visit" counts if a household had a record of medical services.
Factors entering as independent variables are:

INC = monthly current income (in thousand);
MC = a dummy that takes the value 1 if the household has a Medical Card;
UC = a dummy that takes the value 1 if universal coverage was found; and
SIZE = size of the household is inserted to explain the magnitude of the effect.

The regression result is presented in table 7.5.

The logit model cannot be easily interpreted because the estimated coefficients do not represent the marginal effects as those of the usual regression do. In general, taking the anilog of the *j*th slope coefficient, less 1, and multiplying

TABLE 7.5 Thailand: The Results of Logit Regression Analysis of Voluntary Insurance Impacts on Access to Health Care

Item	*B*	*Standard error*	*Wald*	*df*	*Sig.*	*Exp(B)*
Constant	1.596	.043	1,409.701	1	.000	4.933
Variable						
SIZE	–.219	.007	888.431	1	.000	.804
INC	–.006	.001	85.546	1	.000	.994
MC (1)	.250	.031	64.110	1	.000	1.284
UC (1)	–.009	.028	.101	1	.751	.991

Source: Author.
Cox and Snell $R^2 = 0.036$.
Overall percentage correct = 64.0 percent.

the result by 100, gives the percentage change in the odds for a unit increase in the jth regressor (Gujarati 2003). The odds ratio is given by

$$L_i = \frac{P_i}{1 - P_i}$$

In this context, it is simply a ratio of the probability that a family will visit a health care provider to the probability that a family will not visit a health care provider. The ratio can be interpreted as follows. An increase of 1,000 in household income would decrease the probability ratio of a visit to a health care provider by a seemingly trivial but highly significant 0.6 percent, while every additional member that increases the household's size would lessen the ratio by 19.6 percent. In contrast, if the household is also covered with a Medical Card that includes private health insurance, it appears that the household will increase its chance of visiting the health care provider by a large probability of 28.4 percent, which is very significant. The coefficient of *UC*, though positive, is highly insignificant, so should be ignored.

Therefore, it could be inferred that a private health insurance scheme will, to some extent, promote access to health care in Thailand. However, apart from the fact that *MC* is only a proxy for the scheme, some econometric problems exist. The R^2 is less than 5 percent, which is too low to be acceptable, though in a case of cross-sectional data. Also, the model has predicted the *VISIT* correctly by only 64.0 percent. Thus, the result must be interpreted cautiously.

The second model estimated the log-linear of *OOPS* and other explanatory variables, given that the household had visited health care providers:

$$\log(\text{OOPS} \mid \text{visit} > 0) = \text{Xb} + \varepsilon$$

OOPS, the same as before, is a sum of expenditures for (1) medical supplies, (2) being an outpatient, and (3) being an inpatient.

Selected only "visit" family, the regression can be estimated as shown in table 7.6.

A technical note on this functional form is that a marginal impact of a change in explanatory variable can be computed given the level of the explained

TABLE 7.6 Thailand: The Results of Log-Linear Regression Analysis of Voluntary Insurance Impacts on Access to Health Care

	Unstandardized coefficients		*Standardized coefficients*		
Item	*B*	*Standard error*	*Beta*	*t*	*Sig.*
SIZE	.027	.004	.049	6.905	.000
INC	.000	.000	.001	.197	.844
MC (1)	.023	.015	.010	1.509	.131
UC (1)	.094	.014	.050	6.852	.000
Constant	.558	.015		36.396	.000

Source: Author.
$R^2 = 0.006$.

variable. In other words, the marginal impact of a given explanatory variable is the product of its coefficient and the value of *OOPS* in question.

The coefficients of *SIZE* and *UC* are significant, while those of *INC* and *MC* are not. However, the interpretation could be strange. People who are covered by the *UC* have slightly higher average costs, whereas in reality they should pay only ฿30. This might result from the problem with the fit of the equation. Nevertheless, one thing is certain about the role of private health insurance: the regression results show an insignificant relation between being covered by the scheme and a cost-reduction argument made in the preceding section about the role of UC in Thailand.

According to the regressions, some conclusions can be drawn about the impact of private health insurance on access to health care in Thailand:

- Voluntary health insurance has a significant impact on visits for health care. An insured household will probably make more visits than an uninsured household. Therefore, insurance somehow helps broaden access.
- Costs to insured households are no less than costs to uninsured households—the coefficient for *MC* in the second equation is not significant.

All in all, results for private insurance could be rationalized like this. People with private health insurance visit health care providers relatively less frequently than people with insurance under other schemes. However, these infrequent visits would be for relatively high-cost care and more severe illness. Thus, the private insurance is used as a supplement to the other schemes for payment, resulting in high OOPS despite being covered by the scheme.

Impact of Voluntary Insurance on Labor Market Effects

The impact on labor market could be evaluated on an individual basis because sufficient data were available. The analyses are divided into two parts following the methodology for country case study: effect on labor productivity[5] and labor market effect.

Effect on Labor Productivity of Household Members

The first regression was carried out to test the effect of private health insurance on absenteeism from work. The binary dependent variable is *SICK*. The regression results are presented in table 7.7.

$$P(sick > 0) = X\beta + \varepsilon,$$

where

SICK takes the value of 1 if a person reported sickness that made him/her unable to work in the 30 days before the interview (if not, 0);

GENDER takes the value of 1 if a person is male and 0 female;

SS refers to coverage by social security;

PHI refers to coverage by private health insurance; and

INCOME refers to individual (total) monthly income (in thousand baht).

TABLE 7.7 Thailand: The Results of the Regression Analysis of Labor Productivity of Household Members

Item	*B*	*Standard error*	*Wald*	*df*	*Sig.*	*Exp(B)*
GENDER (1)	–.140	.019	56.958	1	.000	.869
UC (1)	.047	.021	5.128	1	.024	1.048
SS (1)	–.467	.045	109.003	1	.000	.627
PHI (1)	.010	.069	.020	1	.888	1.010
INCOME	.003	.001	15.070	1	.000	1.003
Constant	–2.023	.020	10547.295	1	.000	.132

Source: Author.
Cox and Snell $R^2 = 0.002$.
Overall percentage correct = 88.8 percent.

First, the insignificant coefficient of *PHI* must be pointed out. As a result, it cannot be asserted that "an insured person seeks health care earlier than somebody without insurance and hence might require less time off work." It can be seen that the social security scheme, on the contrary, seems to provide this quality. Its coefficient is negative and significant at less than 5 percent, reducing the probability of being sick by 37.3 percent. The *UC*, on the contrary, coincides with more sickness. This might be indirect causation: most people who use the UC for their medical services tend to be the poor, and the poor might be more vulnerable to being sick, as a result, an observed relation between the UC and being sick. *GENDER* is another variable that can explain the possibility of being sick. Males seem to be hospitalized less frequently than females.

The second regression (table 7.8) examines the relation between insurance coverage and wages. It is hypothesized that a person with coverage should, theoretically, get easier access to health care, so they should work better than a person whose health status is inferiorly treated. Therefore, insurance coverage could be a factor that allows an insured worker to be better paid than an uninsured worker.

The regression is in linear form, and the estimation technique is OLS. The dependent variable is a proportion of wages (and salaries) in monthly income so as to adjust for differences in income level. And the explanatory variables are controlled to be the same as the previous regression, except that *INCOME* was dropped.

Every variable is highly significant in explaining the variations in *WAGE-INCOME* ratio. In addition, the goodness of fit of the equation is acceptable. However, some coefficients take an unexpected value, for example, the coefficient of *PHI*, which contradicts the hypothesis. The coefficient is acceptable if it is true that relatively sick people who have lower productivity, thus lower wages, are more likely to buy insurance. This is not likely to be the case, because of screening by insurance companies. Hence, the equation cannot be interpreted

TABLE 7.8 Thailand: The Results of the Regression Analysis

	Unstandardized coefficients		*Standardized coefficients*		
Item	*B*	*Standard error*	*Beta*	*t*	*Sig.*
GENDER (1)	−.065	.002	−.077	−29.926	.000
UC (1)	−.080	.002	−.090	−33.045	.000
SS (1)	.694	.004	.423	155.419	.000
PHI (1)	−.056	.008	−.018	−6.855	.000
Constant	.356	.004		91.463	.000

Source: Author.
$R^2 = 0.22$

in terms of causation, rather simple correlation—people who buy insurance are likely to have wages as a small fraction of their total income. This makes sense because, as mentioned, higher-income people are the ones who buy private insurance.

In short, according to this empirical analysis, private health insurance seems to have no association with labor productivity of household members. The scheme has no relation to the state of sickness, and the second regression cannot substantiate the impact on wage payment.

Labor Market Effects

To test for the assumptions made about the impact of insurance on labor markets, it is more appropriate to employ a cross-tabulation. Unfortunately, due to the usual data unavailability, the sole assumption that can be tested is the one on labor force participation.

The original work status is classified into nine categories: employer, self-employed worker, unpaid family worker, government employee, state enterprise employee, private employee, member of a cooperative, economically inactive, no occupation, and looking for work. The "economically inactive" and "no occupation" groups were then reckoned as not participating in the labor force (economically "inactive"), leaving the rest as participating (economically "active"). The cross-tabulation is shown in table 7.9.

Among the insured, the proportions of economically inactive and economically active seem not to differ between the groups. However, according to the formal chi-square test of independence, the computed Pearson Chi-Square taking the value of 5.194 is significant at less-than-5 percent level. The Phi correlation, which measures how strong the relation is, is also significant at the 5 percent level. However, it indicates a very weak relationship between insurance status and economic status; the statistic takes the value of 0.08, and it ranges from 0, the weakest, to 1, the strongest.

Contrary to expectations, people who are covered by insurance seem to be more economically active than those who are not. This is because private health

TABLE 7.9 Thailand: Cross-Tabulation of Labor Force Participation and PHI Status

		PHI		
Economic status		*No*	*Yes*	*Total*
Inactive	Number	23,416	367	23,783
	Percent within economic status	98.5	1.5	100.0
	Adjusted residual	2.3	–2.3	
Active	Number	64,844	1,166	66,010
	Percent within economic status	98.2	1.8	100.0
	Adjusted residual	–2.3	2.3	
Total	Number	88,260	1,533	89,793
	Percent within economic status	98.3	1.7	100.0

Source: Author.

insurance in Thailand is not subsidized, so it does not involve the moral hazard problem in the labor market making people participate in the labor force. The insured are wealthier than the uninsured. Therefore, to pay for insurance, they must have been economically active.

Determinants of Enrolment with Voluntary Health Insurance

This part assesses determinants of enrolment within a voluntary insurance scheme. The variables belong to the individual's environment such as income and another type of insurance coverage. The community environment was neglected because of data unavailability. However, to ensure the results, another set of data at household level was tested with the same model. This confirmed cohesion between the results.

The model used for individual data was:

$$P(enrollment > 0) = X\beta + \varepsilon,$$

where PHI is for "enrolment > 0."

The explanatory variables were: *UC, SS, INCOME* (in thousand baht), *SICK*, and the new variable, *COST* of being an inpatient (in thousand baht). The regression results are shown in table 7.10.

Other insurance schemes have significantly negative impacts on enrolment in private insurance. *UC* and SS have considerable impacts on the odds ratio of enrolment by the high probability of 66.8 percent and 47.8 percent, respectively. Every 1,000 baht increase in income raises the ratio by 0.524 percent. Nevertheless, neither *SICK* nor *COST* explains the enrolment in a scheme.

Therefore, at the individual level, determinants of enrolment in voluntary private insurance can be divided in to two groups:

- The encouraging variable is an individual's income. The higher the income, the more likely is an individual to buy insurance.

TABLE 7.10 Thailand: The Results of the Regression Analysis of the Determinants of Enrolment with Voluntary Health Insurance at Individual Level

	B	*Standard error*	*Wald*	*df*	*Sig.*	*Exp(B)*
UC (1)	−1.102	.046	576.487	1	.000	.332
SS (1)	−.649	.088	54.924	1	.000	.522
INCOME	.012	.001	132.057	1	.000	1.012
SICK (1)	.014	.069	.041	1	.840	1.014
COST	.002	.002	.586	1	.444	1.002
Constant	−3.427	.032	11,122.123	1	.000	.032

Source: Author.
Cox and Snell $R^2 = 0.006$.
Overall percentage correct = 98.2 percent.

- The discouraging variables for private insurance are other existing insurance schemes. A person covered by UC or SS is less likely to buy additional, private insurance.

The second model was estimated at household level to confirm this point. The model is again binary. The dependent variable is a binary *MC*, which shows whether any member of the household has a Medical Card that includes private insurance.

The explanatory variables are:

UC = whether any member has a health coverage card (฿30);
INCOME = household income (in thousand baht);
SIZE = size of household;
VISIT = whether any member has a record of using health services;
OOPS = out-of-pocket spending composed of cost of medical supplies, inpatient care, and outpatient care (in thousand baht); and
PREM = insurance premiums other than saving insurance (in thousand baht).

The results shown in table 7.11 are similar to those of the preceding regression. *UC* coverage reduces a family's chances of enrolling in voluntary health insurance by as much as 52.8 percent. Insurance premiums, being only a proxy for the cost of private health insurance, unsurprisingly decrease a family's probability of enrolment by 25.7 percent. *VISIT* is another factor that supports the enrolment; this is not completely surprising. This chance is strengthened by higher income. If the family income expands by ฿1,000, its chance of enrolling is 1.5 percent greater than of not enrolling. Health care costs (*OOPS*) do not play an important role in the determination of enrolling with the insurance.

In conclusion, the factors that seem to determine enrolment with voluntary health insurance at household level are: (1) other insurance coverage, (2) household income, (3) health status (whether any member uses health services), and (4) insurance premiums.

TABLE 7.11 Thailand: The Results of the Regression Analysis of the Determinants of Enrolment with Voluntary Health Insurance at Household Level

	B	*Standard error*	*Wald*	*df*	*Sig.*	*Exp(B)*
UC (1)	–.750	.033	516.990	1	.000	.472
INCOME	.015	.001	279.568	1	.000	1.015
SIZE	.145	.009	256.860	1	.000	1.157
VISIT (1)	.249	.032	59.540	1	.000	1.283
OOPS	.004	.012	.126	1	.723	1.004
PREMIUM	–.297	.041	52.214	1	.000	.743
Constant	–1.916	.046	1,731.933	1	.000	.147

Source: Author.
Cox and Snell $R^2 = 0.036$
Overall percentage correct = 82.9 percent.

INTERPRETATION OF THE RESULTS AND CONCLUSIONS

Voluntary private health insurance generally has a positive impact on both health care access and financial protection. However, unless PHI is made widely affordable, its impact on the kingdom as a whole does not seem promising.

Quantitative analyses show that the benefit of private insurance coverage is not negligible. After adjusting for differences in income, the "financial protection" statistic stays at 1.23. PHI coverage can have substantial effects on access to health care, but it is unlikely to reduce OOPS. No association was found between PHI and labor market effects.

Under the present circumstances, no PHI plan is likely to ensure enrolment of the poor. Few Thais have sufficient income to buy it. The UC theoretically could have an adverse impact on the private health insurance business because some people might prefer to use public facilities over private ones due to lower expenses. However, this substitution effect could be roughly estimated to be less than the income effect. The fact that private insurance coverage has managed to grow fast confirms this proposition and also that private providers serve an elite niche market.

Finally, the poor themselves are unlikely to buy a PHI policy. Although sickness, income, and premiums play an important role in the decision, the coexistence of insurance schemes has even greater effects on both a family and an individual. Therefore, in Thailand where the UC scheme is part of the national health agenda, it is not likely that common folks will buy supplementary private insurance.

LIMITATIONS AND SUGGESTIONS

Data unavailability was the one and only limitation of this study. Analyses were conducted using the NSO Household Socioeconomic Survey 2002. Although the sample size was large enough to achieve desirable statistical properties, it did not have health-related issues as the main focus.

In addition, in the context of Thailand where UC is functioning, it is even harder to distinguish the impact of the private insurance from that of the UC. The analyses could not be based on the Household Socioeconomic Survey of 2000, the year before the UC began operating, for it did not survey any information about private insurance.

A survey of private health insurance is therefore suggested. Not only can it focus only on the issue of private health insurance, but it can also allow researchers to distinguish the effect of UC from that of private insurance. As a result, a more concise and precise outcome could be attained.

NOTES

The author is grateful for comments received from reviewers who attended the Wharton Conference in March 2005 and subsequent feedback received on the paper at the time of the July 2005 meeting of the International Health Economics Association (iHEA).

1. In Thailand, no doctor's prescription is needed for a person to buy medicine to treat his or her own illness.
2. The figure equals 5.3 percent while that in 2000 stayed at 3.3 percent (Pramualratana, and Wibulpolprasert (2002). This is plausible given the trend and the expanding economy.
3. The family-level data were used due to the lack of information for premiums at the individual level.
4. Put another way, this might mean that the actual NMC could be varied to a level below the average NMC, thus the risk of negative NMC (debt).
5. The effect on "a higher probability of hiring in/out labor" and "taking on more risky jobs," cannot be analyzed because data are unavailable. The Labor Survey data must be used; nevertheless, they are not linked with the household survey data currently employed.

REFERENCES

Preker, A.S., and J. Jütting. 2004. "Impact Evaluation of Voluntary Health Insurance in Selected Countries. Concept note, October, World Bank, Washington, DC.

Gujarati, Damodar N. *Basic Econometrics*. 2003. New York, NY: McGraw Hill.

Jariyalerdsak, Suwat, Siripen Supakankunti, Ratana Panpanich, Penprapa Siviroj, Krerksak Bunyapong, Wattana Janjaroen, Yupin Angsuroj, Pirus Pradithavanij, Wongsaa Laohasiriwong, Patara Sanchaisuriya, Karnjana Jansung, Sompon Tasaniyom, Korpchut Tayakkanan, and Vipada Prutkitti. 2004. "Monitoring and Evaluating Health Care" [in Thai]. Health Systems Research Institute, Nontaburi, Thailand.

Ministry of Commerce, Thailand, Insurance Promotion and Information Division, Department of Insurance. 2003. http://www.oic.or.th/stat_data/eng-version/eStat_of_Non-Life_Yearly.htm

Piravej, Nipit. 2003. "Private Health Insurance and Healthcare Financing Reform in Thailand." Paper presented at the conference on Asia Health Care and Insurance, organized by IBC Asia (S) Pte Ltd., June 26–27, 2003, Bangkok, Thailand.

Pramualratana, Phromporn, and Swit Wibulpolprasert, eds. 2002. *Health Insurance Systems in Thailand.* Nonthaburi: Health Systems Research Institute.

Sein, U Than. 2005. "Health Financing: Regional Overview." Paper presented at the Biregional meeting on health care financing, March 7–9, 2005, WHO-WPRO (Western Pacific Regional Office), Manila.

Supachutikul, Anuwat. 1996. "Situation Analysis on Health Insurance and Future Development." Health Systems Research Institute, Nonthaburi, Thailand.

Supakankunti, Siripen. 2003. "Healthcare and Health Insurance Systems in Thailand." Working draft, the Centre for Health Economics, Chulalongkorn University.

Supakankunti, Siripen, and Nalyn Siripong. 2001. "Macroeconomics and Health: Thailand." Working draft, Centre for Health Economics, Chulalongkorn University.

Thammatatarri, Jaded, ed. 2001. "The Health Insurance System in Thailand" [in Thai]. Nontaburi: Health Systems Research Institute (HSRI), Nonthaburi, Thailand.

Wibulpolprasert, Suwit. 2002. "Health Care Systems in Thailand" in Health Insurance Systems in Thailand. Health Systems Research Institute, Nonthaburi, Thailand.

CHAPTER 8

Turkey

Anna Cederberg Heard and Ajay Mahal

Private health insurance coverage in Turkey, though still small, has been growing rapidly. This growth has occurred in an environment where, despite significant coverage by social insurance schemes, government financing and insurance for the poor, between 10 percent and 30 percent of the population is uninsured. Out-of-pocket (OOP) payments account for 28 percent of all spending on health.

In this chapter, the role of private insurance in influencing access to health and OOP health spending is examined. Using data from a large household health care utilization and expenditure survey for Turkey, a two-part model (see, for example, Yip and Berman 2001) is estimated to assess the impact of private health insurance on health care utilization and expenditures. The main finding is that private health insurance has increased utilization of outpatient care, and possibly inpatient care, controlling for other confounders. However, private insurance is associated with increased spending on outpatient care, indicating that it has done more to increase access to high-end private care than to provide protection against the financial risk from illness. The chapter concludes with policy implications and highlights potential areas where an expansion of private insurance may contribute to enhanced utilization and financial risk protection against catastrophic illness.

INTRODUCTION

Turkey is a middle-income country with a per capita GDP of about US$5,521 in 2006 (World Bank 2008).[1] Its real GDP per capita has grown at an annual average rate of about 2.0 percent over the last decade, and the future outlook for the economy is bright, considering the high levels of human capital and savings rates hovering at around 18 percent of GDP. Inflation has also slowed, with annual price increases a more manageable 8 to 10 percent a year during 2005 and 2006 compared with annual increases of more than 100 percent in the mid-1990s.

Demographics and Health Status

Turkey is undergoing a demographic transition in which the share of working age groups (15 to 64 years) in total population is growing rapidly and is expected to grow to nearly 72 percent by 2025, before beginning a slow decline (United States

TABLE 8.1 Turkey: Health and Economic Indicators

Indicator	*Magnitude*
Health	
Life expectancy at birth (years), 2005[e]	71
Infant mortality rate (infant deaths per 1,000 live births), 2005[e]	26
Child mortality rate (deaths per 1,000 children under age 5), 2005[e]	29
Maternal mortality rate (deaths per 100,000 live births), 2000[b]	70
Total fertility rate (lifetime births per woman), 2006[e]	2.2
Population under age 15 (%), 2006[a]	29
Population over age 65 (%), 2007[a]	6
Economic	
Share of urban residents in total population, 2005 (%)[b]	66.8
GDP, (US$ billion), 2006[f]	402.1
Annual GDP growth, (%), 1996–2006[f]	3.5
Labor force participation, female, 2006[c]	27.7
Labor force participation, male, 2006[c]	76.2
Labor force participation, all, 2006[c]	52.0
Unemployment, 2005[c]	10.3
Health services	
Hospitalizations (per 1,000 people), 2003[d]	77
Outpatient visits (per 1,000 people), 2003[d]	4,239
Preventive care visits (per 1,000 people), 2003[d]	296
Physicians per 100,000 people, 2005[e]	130
Public share of total health expenditure (%), 2005[e]	72.3
Private share of total health expenditure (%), 2005[e]	27.7

Sources: a. PRB 2007; b. World Bank 2007a; c. ILO 2007; d. Berman, Toros and Sahin 2003; e. World Bank 2007b; f. World Bank 2008.

Bureau of the Census 2005). In this sense, Turkey is likely to enjoy a demographic boost to its economy in the coming decades (Bloom and Williamson 1998). However, unemployment has been creeping up slowly as well and was in excess of 10 percent in 2006, the most recent year for which data are available (table 8.1) (World Bank 2006) suggesting that Turkey has not fully utilized the opportunities offered by its demographic transition.

Demographic transitions are accompanied by health transitions, and Turkey is no exception. The health status of its population has substantially improved, and an average Turk born today can expect to live for 71 years (table 8.1), compared to 48 years for his counterpart in 1960. Nonetheless, Turkey is likely to face new health policy challenges as its population ages. With still high infant mortality rates (26 per 1,000 live births), Turkish health policy makers confront a dual burden of disease, with rising health care needs among both the very young and the elderly (World Bank 2008). With increasing urbanization—nearly 66 percent of Turkey's population currently lives in urban areas (United Nations

Economic Commission for Europe 2005)—the awareness of and the demand for high-quality health services will likely expand as well.

The Health System

Table 8.1 also presents information on health services available to Turkey's population, in addition to general information on its economy and the health of its population. Much of Turkey's inpatient care is provided by Ministry of Health (MOH) hospitals, which also include facilities formerly owned by the social security agency (the Sosyal Sigortalar Kurumu, SSK), but transferred to the MOH under the SSK Hospital Bill of 2005. The private sector in inpatient care, though relatively small (7 percent of hospital beds, 20 percent of hospitals), grew rapidly during the 1990s. Private hospitals are located mainly in the three largest cities, Ankara, Istanbul, and Izmir, with half of them in Istanbul. A significant number of private specialty hospitals have been opened, especially in Istanbul, subsidized by government credits (World Bank 2003).

The private sector plays a considerably greater role in the provision of outpatient services than inpatient services. About 15 percent of all physicians are exclusively in private practice, and 60 percent of physicians employed in the public sector have private practices (World Bank 2003). Health care utilization by the Turkish population is comparable to that of similarly placed countries (table 8.1).

Private Voluntary Health Insurance

Turkey has supported the goal of a socialized health care system since 1961 with the associated commitment to a program of national health services. However, public expectations of free to partly free care and widespread access to health services in a governmental system have not been fulfilled. Underfunding and rapid expansion have led to understaffing and squeezed operating funds, and access to services has been unsatisfactory, particularly in rural areas and in the East (World Bank 2003). More and more people are looking to private health care and buying private insurance to pay for it. Indeed, though emphasizing development of a general, compulsory insurance scheme covering all citizens, the Turkish government's recent health policy strategy has also included the provision of incentives to private insurers (Morlock et al. 2005: 30).

Private health insurance is the fastest growing form of insurance in Turkey—having grown from US$70 million in premium revenues in 1996 to more than US$1 billion in 2007. By the end of 2007, nearly 1.28 million people were privately insured by 33 firms, a big jump from only 25,000 in 1991 (Association of the Insurance and Reinsurance Companies of Turkey 2008, Morlock et al. 2005). About three-fifths of all privately insured people belong to group insurance schemes and two thirds of premium contributions to private insurance are made by employers, the remainder being household contributions (Berman and Tatar 2003).

Private insurance packages in Turkey cover many of the same services that the more common social insurance health plans cover: drugs, medical supplies, outpatient and inpatient care, surgery, birth delivery, and diagnostic lab and imaging tests. Some private plans also cover dental care, eyeglasses, and ambulatory check-ups. Copays are generally similar as well, in the between 10 and 20 percent of total expenditures. Private insurance companies have been exploring opportunities to insure OOP expenditures incurred as part of copayments of various social insurance and government financed schemes (Morlock et al. 2005). As that happens, increased private sector coverage will likely be associated with increased utilization of public services, increasing the financial burden on social insurance schemes.

Despite its recent rapid growth, private insurance plays a comparatively small role in health financing in Turkey, covering barely 1 percent of the population. Moreover, the privately insured are mainly higher-income citydwellers (Berman and Tatar 2003). Expenditures supported by private health insurance amounted to no more than 3.6 percent of national health spending in 2006 (World Bank 2008; Association of the Insurance and Reinsurance Companies of Turkey 2008; OECD 2007).

Other Sources of Financing

Apart from private insurance, health care in Turkey is financed from: employer/ employee contributions to social security programs such as the SSK (which compulsorily covers private sector employees and blue collar workers in the public sector); Bag-Kur (which covers self-employed workers and is voluntary in nature); GERF (government employees retirement fund); the "Green Card" program (a fully government-subsidized scheme for the identified poor); direct Ministry of Finance support for current government employees; and OOP spending by households. The government also subsidizes many of the social insurance schemes in addition to providing subsidies to Ministry of Health (MOH) hospitals that are often used by the insured under various insurance plans. The MOH also financially supports primary health care through its own network of facilities.

By way of comparison with private insurance, social insurance schemes such as SSK, Bag-Kur and GERF supported more than 35 percent of total spending. In addition, 27.5 percent of total spending took the form of OOPS by households, with another 28.2 percent spent directly by the governments at the central and local levels on health providers (Berman and Tatar 2003).

Challenges Facing the Health Financing System

Turkey spent nearly 7.7 percent of its GDP on health in 2005, which, though small in relation to the average for OECD countries, is higher than in many other middle-income countries (World Bank 2007b). In per capita terms (US$325 in 2005), the amount spent on health care in Turkey is on the low side, even

TABLE 8.2 Turkey: Insurance Coverage, Two Sets of Estimates, end-2000

Insurance type	*Number of observations*	*Share of population covered (%)* Survey[a]	*World Bank (2003)*
No health insurance	14,961	32.8	n.a.
Sosyal Sigortalar Kurumu (SSK), covering active private sector and public blue collar workers	8,285	21.8	n.a.
Sosyal Sigortalar Kurumu (SSK), covering retired private sector and public blue collar workers	4,528	11.7	46.53
Bag-Kur, covering active self-employed and agricultural workers	3,252	8.0	n.a.
Bag-Kur, covering retired self-employed and agricultural workers	1,505	3.7	22.36
Emekli Sendegi, covering retired civil servants	1,953	5.1	n.a.
Ministry of Finance, covering active civil servants	3,062	7.4	16.13
Green Card, covering poor individuals	4,263	8.6	14.92
Private insurance[b]	215	0.7	0.5
Other	236	0.5	n.a.
Total	42,177	100	100

Sources: Authors' estimates using Turkey National Household Health Expenditure Survey 2002–03 data.

a. Estimates were constructed using sample weights.

b. Includes individuals holding supplemental private insurance.

n.a. = not available.

when compared with middle-income countries such as Poland, the Republic of Korea, and Mexico (OECD 2007). One possible explanation for this state of affairs is the population's lack of access to health insurance. A third of Turkey's population may be without insurance of any kind (table 8.2). That nearly 27.5 percent of all health spending comes out of pocket further highlights the lack of adequate insurance coverage.

How far the Turkish system protects the poor from the direct costs of medical care is a major challenge. Evidence suggests that government health expenditures are not well directed, with the poorer eastern region receiving less funding than less-poor areas. Moreover, public health facilities located in rural and remote areas where the poor live suffer from a lack of medical personnel and poor service quality. These same deficits have already impaired delivery of primary and preventive care in these areas, which are not the major focus of any of the social insurance schemes in operation and are essentially a Turkish government responsibility. Government subsidies to insurance programs such as Bag-Kur, directed toward the self-employed and agricultural workers, have not proven particularly equitable. One recent analysis suggests that only about 20 percent of Bag-Kur participants have chosen to buy health insurance offered under social security (Morlock et al. 2005).

Finally, private health insurance has been disproportionately concentrated among richer groups. Data from a recently conducted household survey on health care utilization and financing suggest that nearly seven times more individuals in the top income quintile than in the rest of the population had private insurance. Not surprisingly, the better off are concentrated in urban areas, especially the three major metropolitan regions.

Additional problems of concern to policy makers are related to inefficiency and service quality. The coming together of MOH and SSK facilities under the auspices of the MOH is likely to have addressed at least some of inefficiency associated with service duplication by two sets of hospitals. However, MOH allocations to the hospitals it operates are poorly matched to the scale of services each provides.

The compulsory nature of SSK contributions complicates the decision to buy private insurance to access care in the private sector because that means paying two premiums. During 2004, a committee set up with MOH support looked into the enactment of supplementary health insurance legislation. As proposed, the private health insurance sector would attend to supplementary health insurance and a general health insurance scheme (some consolidation of Bag-Kur, SSK, Green Card, and GERF) would provide a basic package of services (communication with Dr. Haluk Ozsari, March 2005). A bill on social security and general health insurance (Bill no. 5510) that brought this about was passed by the Turkish parliament in mid-2006 but was vetoed by the president in 2006 and later turned back by the Constitutional court in Turkey (Ardar 2007). It now appears that it might go into force later in 2008.

Reform and the Investment Environment

During the late 1990s, several health reform proposals were introduced in Turkey, ranging from a compulsory insurance scheme to making hospitals autonomous, to introducing capitation fee payment of primary care providers. However, many of these proposals fell through on account of the political uncertainty at the time. Since around 2006, a new momentum for these changes seems to have been forming. Obviously, continued economic and political stability is necessary for these developments to bear fruit. Turkey appears to have worked its way out of a currency and banking crisis in the early 2000s, and its current economic and financial indicators are generally much improved since that time (World Bank 2008). But new political conflicts between the ruling party and the opposition have appeared on the horizon.

DATA AND METHODOLOGY

This section focuses on the data and the methodology used to assess the impact of private health insurance on access to health care in Turkey. Unfortunately, the household survey data for Turkey were inadequate for directly assessing the impact of private insurance on a measure of protection from the financial risks associated with ill-health.

Data

The data used in this paper are based on a nationally and regionally representative survey of households carried out in 2002–03. Information on 9,805 households (42,177 individuals) was collected using a multistage stratified cluster sampling strategy (for additional details, see Berman and Tatar 2003).

Data were collected on socioeconomic and demographic characteristics including, age, gender, household size, position in household (for example, head), residence (rural, urban, or metropolitan, and also region), income, expenditure, assets, education, and employment status. Information was also collected on an individual's self-reported health (including daily living activities), morbidity in the two weeks preceding the survey, the associated treatment, and hospitalization in the preceding six months. The survey also obtained household data on OOP spending from individual members (related to any recent illness) and from the household head, reporting on all spending, including health. Finally, the survey also obtained information about the insurance status of individuals under both social and private insurance schemes, and any premiums paid for private insurance.

Tables 8.3 and 8.4 summarize some of the major socioeconomic features and health care utilization and expenditure patterns of the sampled households.

Annual per capita expenditure reported for the sample was TL 1,550 million, about US$1,100 at 2002–03 exchange rates (table 8.3). This is a little less than half the per capita GDP of Turkey reported at the beginning of this chapter. Some of this difference can be accounted for by household savings, tax revenues raised by government and undistributed corporate profits. The remainder is likely the result of either the underreporting of spending/income by survey respondents, or the inclusion of poorer than average households among the sample households.

Table 8.4 provides information on health care use and expenditures. The data in Table 8.4 clearly point to higher rates of outpatient and preventive care utilization by households living in urban (and metropolitan) areas. Inpatient care

TABLE 8.3 Turkey: Economic Status of Surveyed Population, by Rural, Urban, and Metropolitan Areas

Residence	*Survey population*	*Population share[a] (%)*	*Mean income[a] (TL million)*	*Mean expenditure[a] (TL million)*
Rural	15,458	32.0	1,170	1,120
Other urban[b]	17,831	40.7	1,400	1,510
Metropolitan	8,888	27.3	2,180	2,130
Total	42,177	100.0	1,540	1,550

Source: Authors' estimates using Turkey National Household Health Expenditure Survey 2002–03 data.

a. Constructed using sample weights from the household survey.

b. Excludes metropolitan areas.

TABLE 8.4 Turkey: Health Care Utilization and Expenditure, by Care Type and Region, 2002–03

Residence/service	*Expenditure per person (TL million)*	*Utilization rate (per capita)*	*Expenditure per visit (TL million)*
Inpatient stays			
Rural	15.6	0.076	199
Other urban[a]	10.4	0.078	134
Metropolitan	23.3	0.077	291
All regions	15.6	0.077	197
Outpatient visits			
Rural	79.5	1.978	35.3
Other urban[a]	80.8	2.592	25.8
Metropolitan	111.0	2.510	36.1
All regions	88.8	2.373	31.2
Preventive visits			
Rural	7.95	0.245	31.4
Other urban[a]	13.7	0.307	46.1
Metropolitan	20.7	0.338	61.8
All regions	13.8	0.296	47.4

Source: Authors' estimates using Turkey National Household Health Expenditure Survey 2002–03 data, using sample weights.

a. Excludes metropolitan areas.

utilization rates are roughly similar across residential categories. However, OOP spending per visit (or per person) does not follow the same pattern. Urban residents living outside the metropolitan regions spend less on average per person (and per outpatient visit and per hospitalization) than rural residents, suggesting that city dwellers may have better financial coverage for curative health services than rural residents. This view is supported by data on expenditures on preventive services (often not covered by the major social insurance schemes). Individuals in urban areas (including metropolitan areas) unambiguously spend more per person and per visit than rural individuals.

Table 8.5 provides information on health care use and expenditures by insurance status. Both are higher among the insured than among the uninsured for inpatient care and outpatient visits. Moreover, with few exceptions, the uninsured spend more out of pocket per visit than the insured civil servants (both active and retired) and appear to enjoy better illness-related financial risk protection than individuals covered by other forms of insurance.

Methodology

To assess the impact of private health insurance on health care utilization and spending, an equation of the form was estimated:

$$(1)\quad O_i = \beta X_i + \alpha I_i + \varepsilon_i.$$

TABLE 8.5 Turkey: Utilization Rates and OOP Expenditure per Visit/Stay, by Insurance Status and Service Type, 2002–03

Insurance status	Mean age (years)	*Inpatient stays* Utilization per capita	Cost/stay (TL million)	*Outpatient visits* Utilization per capita	Cost/visit (TL million)
No insurance	31.9	0.043	315	1.302	57
SSK, active workers	27.7	0.078	208	2.409	37
SSK, retired workers	46.4	0.102	150	3.406	26
Bag-Kur, active self-employed	30.5	0.068	393	2.448	34
Bag-Kur, retired self-employed	57.1	0.153	183	4.158	16
Emekli Sendegi, retired civil servants	48.6	0.104	144	4.379	15
Ministry of Finance, active civil servants	30.6	0.074	70	3.308	11
Green Card	29.3	0.133	98	2.051	22
Other	30.7	0.143	54	1.270	28
Private only	37.6	0.074	6	3.464	25
Private and SSK, active	25.9	0.107	120	5.989	33
Private and SSK, retired	55.3	0.000	0	1.260	75
Private and Bag-Kur, active	26.0	0.000	0	5.665	20
Private and Emekeli Sendegi	47.5	0.000	0	3.172	100
Private and civil servant	32.8	0.000	0	8.755	0
All	34.1	0.077	197	2.374	31

Source: Authors' estimates using Turkey National Household Health Expenditure Survey 2002–03 data, using sample weights.

In equation (1), O_i refers to OOP spending on health care. Here, X_i is a vector of explanatory variables other than private insurance, including health status, income, demographic data, and publicly provided insurance. The indicator variable I_i captures private health insurance status. The last term ε_i is the stochastic error term. The subscript "i" refers to an individual observation in the cross-sectional data.

Observations on variable O_i in equation (1) are truncated at zero. This is because not every individual gets sick (typically only a small proportion does) and not every sick individual obtains treatment or incurs OOP treatment expenses. Thus, OLS is inappropriate as an estimation method. Instead, the empirical health literature relies on an alternative procedure, referred to as the "two-part" estimator (Yip and Berman 2001). This method, along with a variant (noted below), is the one used in this chapter. Specifically, the first part involves estimating equation (2):

$$(2)\quad Z_i = X_i\beta + \alpha I_i + \omega_i \qquad Z_i = 1, \text{(if } O_i > 0\text{) and } Z_i = 0, \text{(if } O_i = 0\text{)}.$$

The second part involves estimating equation (3) for only observations with expenditure exceeding zero:

$$(3)\quad \text{n}\,O_i = X_i\theta_1 + \theta_2 I_i + \omega_i \qquad [\text{Vi} = 1].$$

Provided that the private health insurance variable is uncorrelated with the error terms in (2) and (3), the two-part estimator yields consistent estimates of the parameters of interest. The issue of correlation between the error term and the private health insurance variable (endogeneity) is explored below.

Because the dichotomous variable Z takes the value of 1 only for cases where utilization results in some expenditure, the two-part model, it is not fully able to capture the impacts of insurance on improved utilization when no payment is incurred at all for services received, or if payment is sufficiently small as to be neglected in household survey responses. Thus, a version of the probit model is also estimated separately, in (2), where the dichotomous variable took the value 1 whenever a health service was utilized, 0 otherwise.

The above estimation procedure is subject to one important caveat. Individuals usually choose between insuring and not insuring. Conditional on one's own or family members' job status, it is probably reasonable to think that public (health) insurance is compulsory and, therefore, a given. Although this assumption may be reasonable in itself, it is not reasonable to assume this for one's private health insurance status. In Turkey, about a third of individuals who have private insurance also have another form of insurance. Employers often add private insurance to supplement the government-mandated social insurance. The data collected do not permit a distinction between employer-supplied and individually purchased private insurance. If the choice of buying private insurance depends on observable and unobservable factors that influence an individual's future likelihood of incurring health spending (or income losses) that are not included as explanatory variables in the regression equation, the private insurance variable will be correlated with the error terms in (2) and (3). Inconsistent estimates may result if this endogeneity is not adequately addressed: in particular, the estimation of (2) and (3) would yield coefficient estimates of private health insurance that are biased toward statistical insignificance. Thus, estimation procedures that fail to take endogeneity into account are perhaps best viewed as lower bounds for the estimated effects of private health insurance on health spending/utilization in Turkey.

In the context of the two-part model outlined in (2) and (3), the proper way to account for endogeneity is instrumental variable estimation in both parts. Unfortunately, it is not straightforward to arrive at instruments for this purpose, and there were none available in the household survey that could be satisfactorily used for the purposes of this chapter. An attempt was made to use household heads' reported job characteristics as instruments in estimation of equations (2) and (3). Unfortunately, the maximum likelihood estimation procedures devised for this purpose did not converge, presumably reflecting the unsuitability of the job characteristics variable as an instrument.

The regression was limited to the adult population, ages 15 and over. Two types of health expenditures and utilization were examined separately: hospitalization over the previous six months and outpatient curative care over the previous two weeks, reflecting the time frame of the survey questions. In each case, the following explanatory variables were used: an indicator variable for private insurance status (includes all people with private insurance, regardless of whether they have other coverage), other insurance statuses (taken separately as indicator variables), log of yearly household per capita expenditure, indicator variables for broad age groups (15 to 39, 40 to 64, and 65 and more), years of education, gender, self-reported health (dichotomized as bad or very bad versus same or better), region (west, east, central, north, south/southeast), type of residence (metropolitan, urban, rural), and whether they were part of the summer or winter survey cycle, to capture seasonal differences. In this connection, although private insurance status is likely to be positively correlated with household economic status, the estimated coefficient of log household per capita per expenditure reflects the direct effect of economic status on utilization and OOP spending, excluding any indirect effects of income that work via insurance.

RESULTS

Table 8.6 presents the results of the two-part model estimation described by equations (2) and (3) for two types of health services: hospital-based care and outpatient services.

TABLE 8.6 Turkey: Regression Results from Estimation of Two-Part Model

Item	*Probit inpatient expense*	*Log of inpatient expenses*	*Probit outpatient expense*	*Log of outpatient expenses*
Observations (number)	26,960	614	26,960	2,098
Indicator variable for private insurance	–0.233	–0.999	0.143	0.925[a]
	(0.244)	(0.829)	(0.157)	(0.346)
Indicator variable for other types of insurance ("0" if No insurance)				
SSK (social insurance) active	0.052	–1.064	0.095*	–0.606**
	(0.060)	(0.575)	(0.042)	(0.128)
SSK (social insurance) retired	0.048	–1.116**	0.223**	–0.927**
	(0.064)	(0.409)	(0.050)	(0.140)
Bag-kur (self-employed) active	0.161*	–0.017	0.224**	–0.538**
	(0.081)	(0.423)	(0.057)	(0.153)
Bag-kur (self-employed) retired	0.178*	–0.643	0.261**	–1.267**
	(0.084)	(0.508)	(0.067)	(0.171)
GERF (retired civil servant)	–0.006	–0.558	–0.062	–0.680**
	(0.089)	(0.586)	(0.070)	(0.196)
Active civil servant	–0.162	–2.486*	–0.027	–0.428*
	(0.093)	(1.117)	(0.068)	(0.176)
Green Card (poor)	0.414**	–0.288	0.098	–0.204
	(0.065)	(0.372)	(0.053)	(0.168)
Other	0.215	–3.441	0.035	–1.133**
	(0.193)	(3.476)	(0.157)	(0.436)

(*continued overleaf*)

TABLE 8.6 Turkey: Regression Results from Estimation of Two-Part Model (*continued*)

Item	*Probit inpatient expense*	*Log of inpatient expenses*	*Probit outpatient expense*	*Log of outpatient expenses*
Economic status				
Natural log of per capita household income	0.052*	0.243	0.058**	–0.036
	(0.023)	(0.225)	(0.016)	(0.046)
Age indicator variables (reference: 15–39 years)				
Age group 40–64 years	0.058	0.176	0.253**	0.153
	(0.045)	(0.308)	(0.033)	(0.090)
Age group 65+ years	0.295**	–0.202	0.200**	0.030
	(0.069)	(0.413)	(0.054)	(0.152)
Education, gender, health status				
Education (years)	–0.003	0.013	–0.016**	0.011
	(0.005)	(0.034)	(0.004)	(0.009)
Male = 1, 0 if female	–0.192**	0.149	–0.249**	–0.130
	(0.037)	(0.259)	(0.024)	(0.077)
Bad or Very bad = 1, 0 otherwise (same, or better health)	0.574**	–0.610	0.588**	0.422**
	(0.058)	(0.401)	(0.048)	(0.100)
Region indicators (reference group: west)				
South = 1, 0 otherwise	0.030	–1.342	–0.071	0.093
	(0.063)	(0.719)	(0.048)	(0.126)
Central = 1, 0 otherwise	–0.012	–0.249	0.002	–0.270*
	(0.054)	(0.385)	(0.043)	(0.106)
North = 1, 0 otherwise	0.071	–0.172	–0.105	–0.346*
	(0.066)	(0.375)	(0.058)	(0.171)
East = 1, 0 otherwise	0.037	–0.045	–0.151**	0.082
	(0.057)	(0.454)	(0.048)	(0.135)
Residence indicators (reference group: rural)				
Metropolitan = 1, 0 otherwise	0.044	0.223	0.045	0.013
	(0.059)	(0.319)	(0.047)	(0.135)
Other urban[a] = 1, 0 otherwise	0.052	–0.555	0.082*	–0.210
	(0.045)	(0.335)	(0.038)	(0.109)
Survey round				
Summer = 1, 0 otherwise	0.107**	–0.080	0.049	–0.083
	(0.038)	(0.253)	(0.032)	(0.082)
Constant	–3.245**	13.976	–2.662**	17.718**
	(0.467)	(4.481)	(0.329)	(0.933)

Source: Authors' estimates using Turkey National Household Health Expenditure Survey 2002–03 data.

Note: Standard errors are reported in parentheses.

*Significant at 0.05 level.

**Significant at 0.10 level.

a. Excludes metropolitan areas.

Column (2) of table 8.6 presents the results from estimating the probit equation in the two-part model for hospitalization expenses. The estimates suggest that, although the coefficient on the private insurance variable is large relative to other insurance status indicators, it is not enough to be statistically indistinguishable from zero. In other words, an individual who has private insurance is no more likely to be *observed paying* for inpatient care than an individual who does not have such insurance, all else the same. Column (4) of table 8.6 reports the analogous results for the probit regression on expenses for outpatient care.

However, note that these findings *do not imply* that insured individuals do not use more care. Indeed, spending on care depends both on whether individuals actually use services of health providers and then actually pay for them. This aspect is clarified by table 8.7, presenting the results of a probit model regression linking the decision to seek care (or not) with the same set of explanatory variables as in the two-part model.

The results in table 8.7 show that being insured (under some type of insurance scheme) is associated with increased use of outpatient care. Moreover, the coefficient on the private insurance is typically smaller in magnitude than other types of insurance, so that being privately insured has a smaller effect on outpatient care utilization than other types of insurance. Moreover, in the case of inpatient care, the coefficient on the indicator variable for private insurance is statistically indistinguishable from zero. In other words, there is no association between private insurance status and use of inpatient care.

Combining the results in table 8.7 with estimates reported in columns (2) and (4) of table 8.6 relating to part one of the two-part model yields interesting insights. First, both SSK insurance and private insurance increase access to care, without increasing the likelihood of paying for services received. In the case of GERF, the likelihood of payments actually falls relative to the uninsured. However, for holders of Green Card and Bag-Kur insurance, the likelihood of payment increases relative to the uninsured case, but this comes along with increased utilization of health services, both inpatient and outpatient, as seen in table 8.7.

TABLE 8.7 Turkey: Probit Regressions on Utilization of Inpatient and Outpatient Services

Item	*Inpatient stay*	*Outpatient visit*
Observations (number)	26,960	26,960
1 Private insurance, 0 otherwise	0.143	0.312**
	(0.204)	(0.150)
1 SSK active, 0 otherwise	0.260*	0.324*
	(0.047)	(0.041)
1 SSK retired, 0 otherwise	0.197*	0.381*
	(0.054)	(0.047)
1 Bag-Kur active, 0 otherwise	0.212*	0.337*
	(0.070)	(0.059)

(*continued overleaf*)

TABLE 8.7 Turkey: Probit Regressions on Utilization of Inpatient and Outpatient Services (*cont.*)

Item	*Inpatient stay*	*Outpatient visit*
1 Bag-Kur retired, 0 otherwise	0.301*	0.475*
	(0.075)	(0.055)
1 Emekeli Sendegi, 0 otherwise	0.220*	0.553*
	(0.068)	(0.057)
1 Active civil servant, 0 otherwise	0.191*	0.505*
	(0.070)	(0.055)
1 Green Card, 0 otherwise	0.523*	0.313*
	(0.060)	(0.057)
1 Other, 0 otherwise	0.392**	0.070
	(0.152)	(0.154)
Economic status		
Log of household per capita income	0.037	0.043*
	(0.019)	(0.016)
Age, education, gender, health		
1 Age 40–64 years, 0 otherwise	0.086**	0.241*
	(0.038)	(0.032)
1 Age 65+ years, 0 otherwise	0.415*	0.226*
	(0.058)	(0.050)
Education (completed years)	–0.006	–0.012*
	(0.004)	(0.003)
1 Male, 0 otherwise	–0.173*	–0.272*
	(0.033)	(0.026)
1 Bad or Very bad health, 0 otherwise	0.612*	0.538*
	(0.051)	(0.047)
Residence and survey round		
1 South, 0 otherwise	–0.000	–0.034
	(0.050)	(0.045)
1 Central, 0 otherwise	–0.039	0.085**
	(0.046)	(0.041)
1 North, 0 otherwise	0.047	–0.081
	(0.052)	(0.049)
1 East, 0 otherwise	–0.001	–0.056
	(0.055)	(0.042)
1 Metropolitan, 0 otherwise	0.038	–0.027
	(0.047)	(0.044)
1 Other urban[a], 0 otherwise	0.049	0.080**
	(0.037)	(0.034)
1 Summer, 0 otherwise	0.028	–0.003
	(0.031)	(0.029)
Constant	–2.793*	–2.511*
	(0.389)	(0.312)

Source: Authors' estimates using Turkey National Household Health Expenditure Survey 2002–03 data.

Note: Standard errors are reported in parentheses.

*Significant at 0.05 level.

**Significant at 0.10 level.

a. Excludes metropolitan areas.

In columns (3) and (5) of table 8.6, results are presented from the estimation of part two of the two-part model, equation (3). The most striking observation here, notwithstanding the relatively high standard errors in some cases, is that, with only one exception, the coefficients on the indicator variables for the different types of insurance have a negative sign. Therefore, conditional on some non-zero spending for health care, the overall spending on health actually falls with insurance status.

Many of the estimated coefficients of the equation in part two are statistically insignificant, particularly for inpatient care. Even taking this into account, combining this finding with the results of the probit equation on utilization in table 8.7, the results suggest that: relative to being uninsured, at the very least an insured sick person is unlikely to be observed spending more, while at the same time using greater amounts of health care. In the case of outpatient visits, with one notable exception, being insured is likely to be associated with both increased utilization and lowered expenditures. Individuals with SSK and active civil servants (who are recipient of subsidies from the Ministry of Finance) are likely to be observed with both greater utilization of inpatient care as well as lowered spending relative to being uninsured. Other categories of insured are more likely to be associated with increased inpatient care utilization, even if out of pocket expenditures are unchanged relative to being uninsured.

The one exception to this discussion is the effect of being privately insured, which requires special comment. Whereas the coefficient on private insurance in the estimated part two for inpatient expenses is of the "right" sign (private insurance is associated with lower inpatient expenses), that is not the case for outpatient care. Indeed, for outpatient care, the sign of the coefficient is opposite that of the insurance variables (is positive) and is statistically different from zero as well. Why might being privately insured be associated with increased expenditures? Relative to not being insured, being privately insured results in greater utilization of outpatient visits, comparable to holders of other types of insurance (this follows from table 8.8). If overall expenditures for outpatient visits are also higher, a natural explanation appears to be that being privately insured offers better access to higher perceived quality (not necessarily the same as clinical quality) among private health service providers.

Table 8.8 shows that private insurance holders use more outpatient private care than holders of other types of insurance. For instance, Green Card members use private providers 10.8 percent of the time, and those enrolled with Bag-Kur (active) 24.5 percent, whereas holders solely of private insurance utilize private providers 37 percent of the time. Holders solely of SSK insurance use private outpatient services 24.1 percent of the time, but those who additionally hold private insurance, do so 84.7 percent of the time. From this perspective, private insurance in Turkey functions less as a device to provide protection against financial risk from catastrophic illness than as a means of enhancing access to more expensive private care.

TABLE 8.8 Share of Private Providers in Total Outpatient Care Utilization, by Insurance Status

Insurance status	*Private provider share (%)* *Outpatient visits*
No health insurance	39.4
SSK, active	24.1
SSK, retired	14.4
Bag-Kur, active	24.5
Bag-Kur, retired	13.3
Emekeli Sendegi	16.7
Civil servant, active	12.0
Green Card	10.8
Other	73.6
Private insurance only	36.8
Private and SSK, active	84.7
Private and SSK, retired	100.0
Private and Bag-Kur, active	100.0
Private and Emekeli Sendegi	100.0
Private and civil servant	0

Source: Authors' estimates.

In table 8.9, the results from tables 8.6 and 8.7 are used for a hypothetical exercise to project the impact of an expansion of private health insurance to Turks in different population groups, relative to a situation where none are privately insured. Admittedly crude, because the statistical insignificance of some of the coefficients is downplayed, the results suggest that expanding private health insurance to cover the entire Turkish population (columns 2 and 3) would increase inpatient care utilization by nearly 30 percent, and outpatient care utilization by nearly 64 percent, relative to a situation where none have access to it (comparing rows A and B of table 8.9). The expansion of private insurance to the entire Turkish population would decrease by nearly 44 percent the likelihood of people's paying for inpatient care and increase by 25 percent the likelihood of payment for outpatient care (comparing rows C and D of table 8.9).

The above exercise assumes that all individuals are potential candidates for purchasing private health insurance. If only a small subset of the total population is able to do so, the overall effects will be much smaller. Thus, focusing only on the richest 20 percent of the population (columns 6 and 7, corresponding to rows A and B in table 8.9), gives a large proportionate increase in inpatient and outpatient service utilization by this group—33 percent and 62 percent, respectively—but the overall effect on the likelihood of service utilization for the country as a whole will be on the order of 7 percent and 13 percent, respectively. Again, although the likelihood of incurring some expenditure on inpatient and

TABLE 8.9 Predictions of Outcomes due to Expansion of Private Insurance

Item	*Total population*		*Privately insured*		*Top income quintile*	
Likelihood of visit	*Hospital stays*	*Outpatient visits*	*Hospital stays*	*Outpatient visits*	*Hospital stays*	*Outpatient visits*
Probability of visit if all have private insurance (A)	0.053	0.143	0.042	0.108	0.057	0.166
Probability of a visit if no private insurance (B)	0.040	0.087	0.031	0.062	0.043	0.103
Change in probability of visit (A – B)	0.013	0.056	0.011	0.046	0.014	0.063
Likelihood of positive expenditure						
Probability of expenditure if all individuals have private insurance (C)	0.013	0.101	0.013	0.092	0.014	0.112
Probability of expenditure if none have private insurance (D)	0.023	0.079	0.022	0.071	0.024	0.088
Change in probability of expenditure (C – D)	–0.010	0.022	–0.010	0.021	–0.010	0.024
Amount of expenditure						
Conditional predicted log of expenditure (if everyone has private insurance) (E)	17.110	17.344	17.956	17.548	17.247	17.222
Conditional predicted log of expenditure (if none have private insurance) (F)	18.109	16.419	18.955	16.623	18.247	16.297
Conditional difference in log of expenditure (E – F)	–0.999	0.925	–0.999	0.925	–0.999	0.925
Unconditional expenditure						
Unconditional predicted log of expenditure (if everyone has private insurance) (G)	0.229	1.752	0.228	1.610	0.239	1.927
Unconditional predicted log of expenditure (if none have private insurance) (H)	0.421	1.298	0.422	1.181	0.440	1.436
Unconditional difference in log expenditure (G – H)	–0.192	0.454	–0.194	0.429	–0.200	0.491

Source: Authors' estimates using Turkey National Household Health Expenditure Survey 2002–03 data.

outpatient care with private insurance does go up, by 40 percent and 25 percent, respectively, the overall population effect is much smaller.

Rows E and F describe the effect of private insurance on the log of OOP spending, conditional on having incurred some expenditure. These suggest small declines in the log of inpatient spending and rising log of outpatient spending, irrespective of the population group considered. Finally rows G and H show the unconditional OOP spending impact of private insurance, or the change in likelihood of utilization *times* the change in log of OOP spending. Unconditional log OOP spending on inpatient care declines by as much as 45 percent, irrespective of the population group, with expected OOP spending rising by 35 percent, on account of private insurance.

In other analyses not reported in this chapter, the authors also experimented with using other explanatory variables, such as daily living activities (as a proxy for health status), per capita household incomes instead per capita household spending, dummies for education instead of years of schooling, and others. None of these efforts yielded estimates that would affect the findings reported above. As noted in the methodology section, this analysis does not take account of the potential endogeneity of the private insurance variable. For this reason, our estimates of the private insurance coefficient results are perhaps best treated as lower bounds to the true population estimates.

CONCLUSIONS AND POLICY IMPLICATIONS

The discussion and the empirical analysis in the preceding sections suggests conservatively that thus far the role of private insurance has been less to provide the Turkish population with protection against financial risk associated with illness than to increase its access to private care. With coverage concentrated in upper-income groups comprising less than 1 percent of the population, this is to be expected.

Despite the limited role of private health insurance thus far, there may be some room for it in Turkey. For instance, properly regulated, it could cover some of the large proportion (perhaps as much as a third) of the Turkish population that is not covered by any kind of insurance. Private insurance could also help cover copayments incurred by many of the insured—under both SSK and Bag-Kur. One or perhaps both factors–the large number of uninsured and copayments under social insurance—explain the relatively large share of OOP spending in total health spending in Turkey. This would suggest a potentially significant market for private insurance—both as a supplement to social/government insurance and as primary insurance for individuals left out of the public programs. Whether the proliferation of supplementary insurance is desirable on health policy grounds needs some careful discussion, however. Some experts may be justifiably concerned that such insurance may increase frivolous use of public health services by the insured, raising both the financial burden on social insurance schemes and causing inefficiency in health care use.

As Turkey takes steps toward a national insurance system, private insurance could potentially be tapped to serve as another pillar in the general health insurance system. Even if one were to disagree about the efficacy of private insurers in providing supplementary insurance to social insurance programs, some gains can still be had from broadening the choice given richer members of public programs. Moreover, involving private insurers in accessing hard-to-reach poor populations might be useful. Given the low coverage rates achieved by the government-run Green Card scheme for the poor, this may well be worth considering as the government continues its policy discussions toward a national, universal insurance system. Regulations, incentives, or both may have potential for enhancing private insurance coverage of poor individuals and individuals uncovered by social insurance. The analysis presented in table 8.9 points to the potentially significant increases in utilization that can result from such efforts.

NOTE

The authors thank Alex Preker and Peter Berman for encouraging us to undertake this work and the World Bank for providing financial support for the study. The authors are also grateful to participants at the conference on voluntary health insurance at the Wharton School on March 15–16, 2005, for their useful comments; and to Mukesh Chawla, Haluk Ozsari, and Mehtap Tatar for excellent and constructive comments that greatly helped improve this work.

1. US$9,060 adjusted for purchasing power parity (World Bank 2007a).

REFERENCES

Ardar, Sinem. 2007. "Turkey: Reform in Social Security." *Journal of European Social Policy* 17 (2): 167–68.

Association of the Insurance and Reinsurance Companies of Turkey. 2008. http://www.tsrsb.org.tr/tsrsb_eng/Publications/; accessed March 27, 2008.

Berman, Peter, and Mehtap Tatar. 2003. *National Health Accounts 1999–2000: Final Report.* Ankara, Turkey: Ministry of Health.

Berman, Peter, Aykut Toros and Ismet Sahin. 2003. Turkey National Household Health Expenditure Survey 2002–03. Unpublished Report. Ankara, Turkey: Ministry of Health, Government of Turkey.

Bloom, David and Jeffrey Williamson. 1998. "Demographic Transitions and Economic Miracles in Emerging Asia." *World Bank Economic Review* 12 (3): 419–55.

ILO (International Labour Organization). 2003. "Key Indicators of the Labour Market." http://www.ilo.org/kilm and http://www.ilo.org/public/english/employment/gems/eeo/download/turkey.pdf; accessed June 21, 2005.

Morlock, Laura, Hugh Waters, Alan Lyles, Haluk Ozsari, and Goksenin Aktulay. 2005. *Charting the Way Forward: Health Care Reform in Turkey*. Istanbul, Turkey: Turkish Industrialists and Businessmen's Association.

OECD (Organisation for Economic Co-operation and Development). 2007. OECD Health Data 2007. http://www.oecd.org/dataoecd/46/5/38980477.pdf; accessed March 27, 2008.

PRB (Population Reference Bureau). 2005. *2005 Women of Our World*. Washington DC: Population Reference Bureau.

United States Bureau of the Census. 2005. International Database. http://www.census.gov/ipc/www/idbsprd.html; accessed August 15, 2005.

United Nations Economic Commission for Europe (UNECE). 2005. *The Statistical Yearbook of the Economic Commission for Europe 2005*. http://www.unece.org/stats/trends2005/Sources/103_Population%20in%20urban%20areas.pdf; accessed March 27, 2008.

World Bank. 2008. http://devdata.worldbank.org/AAG/tur_aag.pdf; accessed March 27, 2008.

World Bank. 2007a. *World Development Report 2008*. Washington, DC: World Bank.

World Bank 2007b. *World Development Indicators Database 2007*. Washington, DC: World Bank.

World Bank. 2006. *Turkey Labor Market Study*. Report #33254-TR. World Bank, Washington, DC.

———. 2005. *World Development Report 2005: A Better Investment Climate for Everyone*. Washington, DC: World Bank.

———. 2003. "Turkey: Reforming the Health Sector for Improved Access and Efficiency." World Bank, Washington, DC.

Yip, Winnie, and Peter Berman. 2001. "Targeted Health Insurance in a Low-Income Country and Its Impact on Access and Equity in Access: Egypt's School Health Insurance." *Health Economics* 10:207–20.

CHAPTER 9

United States

M. Kate Bundorf and Mark V. Pauly

Protection from the financial risk associated with uncertain future spending on health care is an important theoretical rationale for the purchase of health insurance, but relatively little empirical research has been devoted to this benefit. In this chapter, the relationship between the purchase of private health insurance (PHI) and variation in out-of-pocket (OOP) spending on health care in the United States is examined. The estimates presented suggest that an important benefit of private health insurance is the extent to which it provides protection from financial risk, particularly for low-income individuals. In a country where a significant part of the population still does not have full access to health insurance and basic care, the results of this study have significant policy implications.

INTRODUCTION

Although the theoretical rationale for the purchase of insurance is that it provides protection from financial risk, most research on the effects of private health insurance has focused not on its impact on financial risk, but on its effect on access to health care and health outcomes (Medicine 2001; Medicine 2002). In theory, however, demand for health insurance arises from people's desire to reduce their exposure to risk in the form of uncertain future spending on medical care. In other words, health insurance is a financial instrument that allows consumers to exchange a known payment in the present for a reduction in the variation of future consumption. Thus, an important benefit—not only of the voluntary purchase of private health insurance, but also of any policy that extends insurance coverage to a broader population—is the extent to which health insurance provides consumers with protection from the financial risk associated with uncertain future medical spending.

The impact of private health insurance on OOP expenditures for health care is examined in this chapter. Focus is on the United States because it is unique among developed countries in its reliance on voluntary purchase of coverage in private health insurance markets for primary coverage. In addition, the United States is characterized by a relatively large uninsured population. Thus, it provides an interesting case study of potential measures of financial risk and the association between private health insurance coverage and OOP expenditures on health care.

METHODS

The data source for the analysis is the 1996–2002 Medical Expenditure Panel Survey (MEPS), a nationally representative survey of the U.S. civilian noninstitutionalized population produced by the U.S. Agency for Healthcare Research and Quality. The important features of the survey for our purposes are that the sample is large and nationally representative and that it includes detailed data on both insurance status and OOP spending for health care.

In the United States, people obtain health insurance through a variety of sources. For the 65 and over population, the publicly funded Medicare program provides nearly universal coverage, while the majority of the under-65 obtain coverage in the private market, primarily through employers. State Medicaid programs, for which certain segments of the low-income population are eligible, cover approximately 10 percent of adults 19 to 64 years of age. Because the objective of this analysis is to determine how much protection from financial risk private health insurance provides relative to being uninsured, the study includes adults 19 to 64 who were either covered by private employer-sponsored health insurance or uninsured during the entire survey year. In other words, the publicly insured and individuals who changed their source of coverage during the year are dropped.

Because insurance coverage decisions may be made individually and health care expenditures can be attributed to individuals, the analyses are conducted at individual, rather than family or household, level. Developing corresponding measures of income, however, requires making assumptions regarding the allocation of family income across members. Adjustments are made for family size and composition by adopting the OECD equivalence scale, which weights a single adult in the family as 1.0, each additional adult in a family at 0.7, and each child at 0.5 when calculating family size. Individual income is calculated by dividing family income by family size, calculated in this manner.

Both gross and disposable income are calculated for each individual. First reported person-level income is aggregated to the family level.[1] The components of income collected in the MEPS include wages and/or salaries, business income, unemployment compensation, workers' compensation, interest, dividends, pensions, social security, trust/rental income, veteran's income, IRA income, alimony, child support, other regular cash contributions, social security insurance (SSI) and public assistance, and other income. Because individuals are assumed to bear the cost of employer-sponsored coverage in the form of forgone wages, an estimate of the premium for employer-sponsored coverage is added for each individual with employer-sponsored coverage within the family unit.[2] Individual gross income as family income is then calculated, adjusted for the availability of employer-sponsored coverage, divided by the number of people in the household calculated using the equivalence scale. *Disposable income* is defined as gross income less expenditures for health insurance and health care, calculated by subtracting from gross income the estimated premium for individual coverage and individual OOP expenditures for health care. All dollar values are inflated to 2002 U.S. dollars using the U.S. Bureau of Labor Statistics annual Consumer Price Index for all urban consumers.

Three measures of the financial impact of OOP health expenditures are calculated. The first is average out-of-pocket health expenditures as a portion of gross income. This measures the level of OOP spending relative to gross income or resources. The second is the coefficient of variation of disposable income. This has the advantage of accounting for variation in disposable income caused by variation in OOP expenditures. Ideally, this variability would be measured for a population homogenous with respect to income. However, when a subpopulation is selected in the data chosen for measuring variation in spending, income may also vary within that subpopulation. Thus, the empirical measure may also capture variation in gross income that is independent of OOP expenditures on health care. To address this, a third measure is calculated, variation in OOP health expenditures (standard deviation) for the subpopulation divided by average disposable income in the subpopulation. This is intended to proxy the variation in disposable income attributable to variation in OOP health expenditures for a population truly similar in terms of gross income.

These measures are presented as well as the mean of gross income, disposable income, and OOP health expenditures and the coefficient of variation of gross income and OOP health expenditures to demonstrate the sources of differences between the insured and uninsured in these measures of financial impact. These variables are calculated by insurance status as well as insurance status interacted separately with income and demographic groups. Individuals are divided into low-, medium-, and high-income groups, based on terciles of the gross income distribution of the study sample. The age groups in this analysis are 19 to 34, 35 to 54, and 55 to 64, presented separately, by gender. All results are weighted to be nationally representative.

RESULTS

Each measure of the financial impact of OOP expenditures demonstrates that the uninsured are exposed to greater financial risk than the privately insured (table 9.1). The standard deviation of OOP expenditures represents a higher proportion of disposable income for the uninsured (0.054) than the privately insured (0.021) in the population as a whole. This is both because variation in OOP spending, as measured by the coefficient of variation, is greater among the uninsured than the privately insured (2.95 vs. 2.06) and because average gross income is lower among the uninsured than the privately insured (US$22,206 vs. US$46,482). Although the uninsured spend a greater proportion of their net income on OOP health expenditures (1.8 percent) relative to the uninsured (1.0 percent), this is primarily due to lower income rather than higher spending on health care. The mean level of OOP health expenditure is similar between the privately insured (US$442) and the uninsured (US$401). In summary, the uninsured appear to be exposed to greater financial risk than the privately insured both because their OOP health expenditures are more variable and because their average net income is lower.

TABLE 9.1 United States: Out-of-Pocket Spending on Health Care by the Privately Insured and the Uninsured Overall, and by Income

		Mean			*Measures of variation*		*Measures of financial impact*		
Insurance status	*N*	*Gross income*	*Disposable income*	*OOPS*	*CV of gross income*	*CV of OOPS*	*OOPS/gross household income*	*CV of disposable income*	*SD of OOP/mean disposable income*
Pooled									
Privately insured	59,065	46,482	43,402	442	0.58	2.06	0.010	0.625	0.021
Uninsured	20,458	22,206	21,805	401	0.86	2.95	0.018	0.877	0.054
Low income									
Privately insured	16,171	20,105	17,111	376	0.30	2.57	0.019	0.358	0.057
Uninsured	16,356	13,658	13,279	379	0.52	3.13	0.028	0.547	0.089
Medium income									
Privately insured	22,249	36,760	33,724	403	0.14	1.92	0.011	0.158	0.023
Uninsured	2,773	35,026	34,612	414	0.14	2.81	0.012	0.150	0.034
High income									
Privately insured	20,645	71,000	67,827	518	0.38	1.92	0.007	0.399	0.015
Uninsured	1,329	68,051	67,504	547	0.35	2.12	0.008	0.357	0.017

Source: 1996–2002 Medical Expenditure Panel Survey.

Note: Measure of Household Income: per capita household income calculated using OECD Household Equivalence Scale. Income categories are based on terciles of gross income in the study sample. The sample consists of individuals 19 to 64 years of age who are uninsured or privately insured for the entire year. SD = standard deviation; CV = coefficient of variation.

While the coefficient of variation of disposable income is also greater among the uninsured than the insured, the difference between the two groups in this measure is driven by differences in variation in gross income as well as variation in OOP spending on health insurance. In other words, even if variation in OOP spending and mean disposable income were similar between the two groups, this measure could indicate that the uninsured are more financially vulnerable because of differences between the two groups in gross income variation. As a result in the remainder of the discussion, focus is put on the measure of exposure to financial risk that is based on the standard deviation of OOP expenditures divided by disposable income.

Out-of-pocket health expenditures represent a greater financial risk to low-income than to high-income individuals, regardless of insurance status. Variation in OOP spending on health care represents 8.9 percent of disposable income for privately insured, low-income individuals compared with 1.7 percent for uninsured, high-income individuals. Within each income category, however, the uninsured are exposed to greater financial risk than the insured based on this measure, although the extent to which insurance is associated with protection from financial risk declines as income increases. Insurance provides the most protection from financial risk for individuals in low-income families. Variation in OOP spending represents 8.9 percent of net income for uninsured individuals in low-income families relative to 5.7 percent for insured individuals in low-income families. This difference between the insured and uninsured is much smaller for high-income individuals (0.015 vs. 0.017). This is because both variation in OOP spending (as measured by the coefficient of variation) and average disposable income become more similar between the privately insured and the uninsured moving from the lowest to the highest income tercile.

Differences between the uninsured and the privately insured in the level and variation in OOP health expenditures may be influenced by the selection of individuals into insurance coverage. In theory, holding the premium constant, demand for health insurance will be greater among individuals with higher and more variable expected health expenditures. In this case, the level of and variation in OOP spending among the insured would be biased upward by the selection of individuals into insurance. Thus, this analysis, which does not control for selection, likely underestimates the effect of insurance on both the level and variation in OOP spending.

The possibility of selection into insurance is partially addressed by stratifying based on age and gender to make the groups more similar based on their underlying health (table 9.2). Of course, selection into insurance based on the presence of unmeasured health conditions may still exist. Still, variation in OOP spending on medical care generally remains greater among the uninsured than the insured. Although the differences between the uninsured and the insured in the coefficient of variation in OOP expenditures are somewhat smaller than those observed when stratifying based on income, variation is greater for the uninsured than the insured within each demographic group, with the exception

TABLE 9.2 United States: Out-of-Pocket Spending on Health Care by the Privately Insured and the Uninsured Overall, by Age and Gender

		Mean			Measures of variation		Measures of financial impact		
Insurance status	*N*	*Gross income*	*Disposable income*	*OOPS*	*CV of gross income*	*CV of OOPS*	*OOPS/ gross household income*	*CV of disposable income*	*SD. of OOP/mean disposable income*
Male 19–34									
Privately insured	7,953	42,466	39,623	213	0.56	4.31	0.005	0.599	0.023
Uninsured	5,533	22,708	22,543	165	0.80	3.77	0.007	0.810	0.028
Male 35–54									
Privately insured	15,877	48,743	45,769	339	0.57	2.32	0.007	0.609	0.017
Uninsured	4,158	24,467	24,115	352	0.84	2.96	0.014	0.850	0.043
Male 55–64									
Privately insured	4,435	52,109	48,827	617	0.61	1.65	0.012	0.655	0.021
Uninsured	986	25,553	24,845	708	0.93	2.35	0.028	0.956	0.067
Female 19–34									
Privately insured	8,553	40,899	37,883	389	0.56	1.94	0.010	0.603	0.020
Uninsured	4,180	19,196	18,832	364	0.87	3.53	0.019	0.884	0.068
Female 35–54									
Privately insured	17,585	47,474	44,292	544	0.58	1.75	0.011	0.621	0.021
Uninsured	4,333	21,537	20,950	586	0.86	2.39	0.027	0.880	0.067
Female 55–64									
Privately insured	4,662	47,138	43,666	808	0.62	1.41	0.017	0.672	0.026
Uninsured	1,268	21,606	20,573	1,033	0.96	1.66	0.048	1.010	0.084

Source: 1996–2002 Medical Expenditure Panel Survey.

Note: Measure of Household Income: per capita household income calculated using OECD Household Equivalence Scale. Income categories are based on terciles of gross income in the study sample. Sample consists of individuals 19 to 64 years of age, uninsured or privately insured for the entire year. SD = standard deviation; CV = coefficient of variation.

of young men. For this group, however, the greater variation in OOP expenditures among the insured is driven by a single outlier within the insured group that had very high OOP expenditures. In addition, the uninsured within each demographic group are characterized by lower average disposable income than the insured. Thus, variation in OOP health expenditures represents a higher proportion of average disposable income for the uninsured than the insured within each demographic group.

CONCLUSIONS

These estimates suggest that an important benefit of private health insurance is the extent to which it provides protection from financial risk. Private health insurance is associated with a reduction in variation in OOP spending on health care relative to being uninsured. This protection is particularly valuable to low-income individuals for whom variation in OOP spending is high relative to income. An implication of this finding is that simple comparisons between the insured and the uninsured of the level of OOP spending may underestimate the value of private health insurance. In particular, although levels of OOP spending are similar between the two groups, variation in OOP spending is quite different. If people are risk averse, they will value the reduction in the uncertainty of future spending that insurance provides.

Interestingly, the level of OOP spending was found to be similar between the privately insured and the uninsured. If insurance provides protection from financial risk, OOP health expenditures would be expected to be greater among the uninsured than the insured. Three factors potentially explain the similar levels of OOP expenditures among the privately insured and the uninsured. First, because the purchase of coverage is voluntary in the United States, individuals purchasing health insurance may have higher expected expenditures on average than those not purchasing coverage. Thus, in the absence of insurance, those who actually purchased coverage would have had higher OOP expenditures than those who were uninsured due to either worse underlying health or greater demand for health care conditional on health status. Second, the purchase of insurance may increase consumption of medical care among the insured. In other words, the higher spending of the privately insured reflects the cost sharing associated with a much greater quantity of services, holding health constant. Finally, the uninsured in the United States generally pay for only a fraction of the health care they consume (Herring 2005). Because access to uncompensated care functions as an imperfect source of insurance for many of the uninsured, OOP expenditures for the uninsured are lower than they would be in the absence of this informal safety net.

In summary, this analysis indicates that variation in out-of-pocket spending on medical care is lower among the privately insured than the uninsured. This reduction in variation in out-of-pocket expenditures is particularly valuable for low-income individuals for whom the variation represents a greater proportion of disposable income. Issues for future research include the extent to which selection and moral hazard in the private insurance markets affect the extent to which private health insurance provides protection from financial risk.

NOTES

The authors thank Donna MacIsaac for excellent research assistance and participants from the Wharton Impact Conference, Voluntary Health Insurance in Developing Countries, March 15–16, 2005, for helpful suggestions.

1. A *family* is defined as adults, their spouses, including self-identified spouses, and their unmarried natural/adoptive children age 18 and under.
2. For each adult, the value of employer-sponsored coverage is imputed, based on the average monthly premium for single coverage in private establishments in the United States multiplied by the number of months the individual was covered. For children, the assumed value of this coverage, adjusted for months of coverage, is the corresponding average family premium less two times the single premium. The data source for the estimates of the premiums for employer-sponsored coverage is the MEPS Insurance Component, a nationally representative employer-level survey.

REFERENCES

Herring, B. 2005. "The Effect of Availability of Charity Care to the Uninsured on the Demand for Private Health Insurance." *Journal of Health Economics* 24 (2): 225–52.

Medicine, I. o. 2002. *Care without Coverage: Too Little, Too Late.* Washington, DC: National Academy Press.

———. 2001. *Coverage Matters: Insurance and Health Care.* Washington, DC: National Academy Press.

PART 3

Opportunities for the Future

CHAPTER 10

China

Teh-wei Hu and Xiao-hua Ying

Despite China's rapid economic growth during the past decade, health insurance coverage has not improved in either urban or rural areas. Between 1993 and 2003, the proportion of urban residents without health insurance rose from 27 percent to 50 percent. In rural areas, 79 percent of the population did not have health insurance in 2003. The Chinese government has not been able to play a major role in providing public health insurance. While the Chinese government has recently increased some public funding for health care services, private health insurance may also play an important role in China's health care financing. Private health insurance may be able to allot private financial resources for health care services. In the coming few years, at least an additional 2.6 million urban individuals are projected to enroll in China's private health insurance. Since China's entry into the World Trade Organization (WTO) in 2001, foreign insurance companies have been very active in exploring the Chinese private health insurance market. The Chinese government needs to develop an effective regulatory system to insure that private financial resources will be used efficiently to achieve the intended goal of health insurance coverage for all.

INTRODUCTION

Since the early 1980s, China has experienced rapid economic growth, due largely to the Chinese government's economic reform, which changed the country from a socialist economy to a market economy. Between 1980 and 2000, GDP went from RMB 452 billion (US$57.4 billion) to RMB 8,940 billion (US$1,087 billion), an increase of about 20 times. In real terms, adjusted for inflation, GDP grew about 5.5 times. Chinese national health care expenditures also increased, from 2.9 percent of GDP in 1999 to about 5.3 percent of GDP in 2000 (table 10.1).

Health services utilization in China, however, has contracted. Between 1993 and 2003, the percentage of individuals reporting outpatient visits in the previous two weeks dropped from 19.9 per 100 persons to 11.8 per 100 persons in urban areas, and from 16.0 per 100 persons to 13.9 per 100 persons in rural areas (Center for Health Statistics and Information of MOH 1994, 2004). About 57.0 percent of urban residents and 45.8 percent of rural residents reported being unhealthy but did not see a doctor in 2003. In 1993, the rate of residents not seeing a doctor was 42.4 percent in urban areas and 33.7 percent in rural areas.

TABLE 10.1 China: Socioeconomic Background, 1980–2000

Indicator	*1980*	*1990*	*2000*
GDP (billion RMB)	452	1,855	8,940
GDP (1980 prices)	452	916	2,204
Population (million)	987	1,143	1,266
Urban (%)	19	26	36
Health expenditure as share of GDP (%)	3	4	5
Per capita health expenditure (RMB)	13	65	376

Source: National Bureau of Statistics of China 2003.
Note: US$1 = RMB 8.23

Low use of health services was related to the high price of health care and increased health care cost. The annual per capita health expenditure rose from RMB 13 in 1980 to RMB 476 in 2000. The cost per doctor visit increased from RMB 14 to RMB 120 between 1993 and 2003, which accounted for 19 percent and 43 percent of per capita monthly income, respectively (Center for Health Statistics and Information of MOH 1994, 2004; National Bureau of Statistics of China, 2003). Most of the health expenditure was out of pocket. During the past 20 years, the role of the Chinese government in financing health care has been declining. In 1980, government spending accounted for 36 percent of national health care expenditures, 24 percent of personal health care expenditure, and 40 percent of public insurance. By 2000, the government's share had been reduced to only 15 percent, while that of individuals had increased to 60 percent (table 10.2). In the face of this drastic decline in government financing of health care and the increased burden for individual expenditure, recently the Chinese government has recognized its deficiency in health care financing and has begun to devote more resources to the health care sector.

Low health insurance coverage is another crucial aspect of low health service utilization (table 10.3). In 2003, 225 million people in urban areas and 67.2 million in rural areas had health insurance, but 202 million urban residents

TABLE 10.2 China: National Health Expenditures, 1980–2000

Expenditure	*1980*	*1990*	*2000*
National health expenditures (billion RMB)	13	74	476
National health expenditures (1980 prices)	13	37	117
Government (%)	36	25	15
Social insurance (%)	40	38	25
Personal (%)	24	37	60

Sources: China National Institute of Health Economics 2004; China National Health Economics Institute 2004.

TABLE 10.3 China: Health Insurance Coverage Distribution, 2003

Insurance type	*Urban (%)*	*Rural (%)*
Public insurance	43.0	3.1
Cooperative medical services	6.6	9.5
Private insurance	5.6	8.3
No insurance	44.8	79.1
Estimated private insurance enrolment and uninsured (RMB million)		
Private insurance	22.5	67.2
No insurance	202.2	640.9

Sources: Center for Health Statistics and Information of the Ministry of Health, 2004.

and 641 million rural residents had none (Center for Health Statistics and Information of MOH 2004; National Bureau of Statistics of China 2003).

Health insurance is one of the most effective means of risk pooling and risk sharing, and it can affect health care utilization and health care financing (Doorslaer et al. 1999; Gao et al. 2001). Because current public health insurance in China provides less coverage and benefits, private insurance could fill a supplemental role in several areas (Medical Insurance Department of Ministry of Labor and Social Security and Digna 2000). First, private insurance provides supplementary insurance for those enrolled in public insurance programs. Second, it provides primary insurance to the uninsured (Ellis and McGuire 1993). The role of private insurance differs depending on the country's wealth and institutional development (Liu and Chen 2002). As in many other lower- and middle-income countries, private insurance could be an important means of providing primary health coverage for most people in urban areas in China (Sekhri and Savedoff 2005).

One of the key arguments for promoting private health insurance in low- and middle-income countries is that, given limited government resources, private insurance is a useful option for people who can afford to pay the premium. Resources then are freed up for the government to provide health insurance for low-income individuals. Private health insurance could also be used to protect against major financial loss as a result of illness.

This chapter describes and analyzes the role of private health insurance in China and projects its potential there. It describes the background of China's health care financing system and the current status of its private health insurance industry. The description includes the structure of the private health insurance industry, the insurance products and their financial flow, and the role of the Chinese government in regulating the private health insurance industry. Key health care financing issues in China are discussed. Based on household survey data, the determinants of private health insurance enrolment are analyzed, and, using the willingness to pay (contingent valuation) method, demand for private health insurance is studied to arrive at an estimate of the potential market size. The final section presents policy options and conclusions.

BACKGROUND OF CHINA'S HEALTH CARE FINANCING SYSTEM

To understand the status and role of private health insurance in China, it would be important to first describe the background of China's overall health care financing system. Within China, there are essentially two separate health care financing systems between urban and rural areas. Furthermore, the rapid economic development during the past 20 years led to a wide economic disparity between urban and rural regions. This section attempts to describe the effects of private health insurance development in China.

Urban Health Insurance

Driven largely by cost containment needs and increased demand for better access to health care between 1980 and 2000, China experimented with reforming its urban health insurance system (Hsiao 1984; Liu et al. 2004; Liu et al. 2002; Liu 2002). The urban system of medical insurance, initiated in the early 1950s, consisted of two parts: the Labor Insurance Scheme (LIS), and the Government Insurance Scheme (GIS). LIS covered state-run enterprises (owned and managed by central or provincial governments) and collective-run enterprises (owned by local or district governments). The beneficiaries of LIS included its workers, retirees, and workers' dependents. In 1952, the Government Insurance Scheme (GIS) was launched. Beneficiaries included not only workers, workers' dependents, and government retirees, but also university students, teachers, and soldiers. GIS was financed by government funds. For the past 40 years, LIS and GIS have been the two essential health insurance programs for urban Chinese workers (Hsiao 1984). Each organization under the original GIS and LIS system is self-insured.

Since economic reforms began in 1980, several major developments have affected Chinese enterprises and their beneficiaries (Hu et al. 1999). First, state-run and collective-run enterprises faced market competition and lost government subsidies. Thus, many enterprises were no longer able to guarantee full health insurance coverage, and their medical benefits varied according to the enterprises' profit (Hsiao 1995). Second, the cost of health insurance rose rapidly. The increase in the cost of medical care made it difficult for enterprises to continue health insurance coverage. Third, the number of self-owned or foreign joint venture enterprises increased rapidly in urban areas. Many workers in these enterprises do not receive medical benefits.

To expand the number of people covered by health insurance and to rectify the inequity in access, the State Council established a public insurance program, Medical Savings Account (MSA) and Social Risk Pool fund (SRP), for urban workers in 1998 (Central Party Committee and State Council 1997; State Council 1998). This new system replaced LIS and GIS in cities and provided a basic benefits package to all urban workers, including employees of both public and private enterprises. Both employers and employees contribute to the insurance premium: employers contribute 6 percent of their employee payroll; employees, 2 percent of their payroll. MSA covered 109 million people by the end of 2003, only 24 percent of the total population. The amount of the public health insurance fund was RMB 89 billion (US$1 = RMB 8.23) in 2003, about 0.7 percent of GDP (Ministry of Labor and Social Security. PRC and National Bureau of Statistics of China 2004; National Bureau of Statistics of China 2004). According to the National Health Service Surveys, the proportion of urban residents without health insurance rose from 27 percent to 50 percent between 1993 and 2003 (Center for Health Statistics and Information of MOH 2004).

Compared with the old system of GIS and LIS, the benefits structure under the new system has two gaps in coverage. First, urban workers' dependents are not entitled to coverage. Second, the insured amount of individual medical expenditures has a cap (equivalent to four times the average wage in the region). It is estimated that the current premium can cover only about 70 percent of the total outlay under the old systems (Medical Insurance Department of Ministry of Labor and Social Security and Digna 2000), which means that the new system may offer less benefits for the insured.

While China's urban health insurance system has received some attention, most of the literature has focused on experiences and lessons of LIS and GIS (Hsiao 1984; Liu 2002). Other research has focused on the inequity and cost-containment in Chinese health care (Hu et al. 1999; Liu et al. 2002). To date, few published studies have looked at coverage and demand for private health insurance in urban areas.

Rural Health Insurance

Between 1966 and 1980, China implemented a cooperative medical service (CMS) in rural areas. CMS was a decentralized system that relied on local primary health care workers with local financing through a health/welfare fund at the village level and a small contribution from individuals as a membership fee. CMS was an established medical system that served the rural areas and provided treatment and disease prevention, immunization, family planning, and maternal and child health care services. Experience before 1980 suggested that CMS benefited the peasants in rural China (Hu 1981). Following the 1980s' economic reforms, CMS underwent major changes. In some places, CMS stations evolved into various other types of medical and health care systems; in other places, CMS stations ceased operations altogether (Chen, Hu, and Lin 1993).

During the past 20 years, numerous rural health insurance experiments have been launched to restore the cooperative medical system of the early 1960s, with support from UNICEF, WHO, the World Bank, and other international organizations. For several reasons, virtually none of these systems was sustained after the experiments ended (Hu 2004). Since 2003, the Chinese government has made a major effort to increase health insurance coverage among the rural population with the New Cooperative Medical Services (NCMS). The central government and local government each contribute RMB 10 per individual to supplement each individual's RMB 10 contribution, for a total premium of RMB 30. This NCMS program has been actively implemented in several low-income provinces. According to the preliminary results, however, major financial barriers and shortcomings in benefits coverage remain to be resolved.

PRIVATE HEALTH INSURANCE IN CHINA TODAY

Until the mid-1990s, China had no private health insurance companies. Like most developing countries, the health insurance business in China started from life insurance companies. Having a life insurance business (1) enables the company to build a marketing base, (2) reduces the risk of adverse selection among health insurance buyers, (3) provides needed actuarial expertise on setting health insurance premiums, and (4) provides insurance capital or a reinsurance fund for health insurance operations. All of the Chinese private health insurance companies today were a part of Chinese life insurance companies before 2005. Since 2005, there have been three or four companies focused solely on health insurance.

In 1999–2004, China's health insurance industry revenue increased sevenfold, from RMB 3.65 billion (US$443.5 million) to RMB 25.98 billion (US$3.2 billion). Nonetheless, health insurance is still a minor portion of the entire life insurance industry (table 10.4). Thus, although the private health insurance industry still has a relatively small role in China's health care sector, it has been growing rapidly.

The China Life Insurance Company (CLIC) was originally a government-run organization that focused mainly on life insurance business. In the mid-1990s, retired officials from the Ministry of Health joined the company and decided to expand its business to health insurance. The original intent of their business was to provide primary health insurance for people without public insurance coverage. As of 2004,

TABLE 10.4 China: Health/Life Insurance Industry Revenue, 1999–2004

Year	*Revenue (RMB billion)*	*% revenue increase from baseline (1999 base)*	*Health insurance revenue/ total insurance revenue (%)*	*Health insurance revenue/national health care expenditures (%)*
1999	3.65	—	2.6	0.90
2000	6.55	179	4.1	1.43
2001	6.16	169	2.9	1.23
2002	12.24	335	4.0	2.15
2003	24.19	663	6.2	—
2004	25.98	712	6.0	—

Sources: China Insurance Regulation Commission (CIRC) 2004. http://www.circ.gov.
Note: — = not available.

TABLE 10.5 China: Market Share of Life/Health Insurance Industry, 2004

Domestic	*Market share (%)*	*Foreign*	*Market share (%)*
China Life Insurance Company	54.70	AIA Life Insurance	1.49
Pin An (Peace) Life Insurance	17.00	Pacific Aetna Life Insurance	0.20
Pacific Life Insurance	10.68	Manulife-Sinochen Life Insurance	0.19
Other (5 companies)	14.06	Other (16 companies)	0.81
Subtotal (8 companies)	96.31	Subtotal (19 companies)	2.69
Memorandum item: Total (domestic and foreign) = 100.00%.			

Sources: China Insurance Regulation Commission (CIRC) 2004. http://www.circ.gov.

CLIC was the largest semi-official private life/health insurer in China with almost 55 percent of the market share, measured in terms of total insurance revenue.

According to the China Insurance Regulation Commission (CIRC), at least 27 life insurance companies were engaged in life/health insurance business in 2004 (table 10.5). Although there were twice as many foreign-owned as domestic companies, in terms of total insurance revenue, the 8 domestic companies had 96.3 percent of the market. The top three life/health insurance companies were China Life Insurance Company (54.47 percent), PinAn (Peace) Life Insurance (17 percent), and Pacific Life Insurance (10.68 percent). Together, these three companies had about 80 percent of the total market share. The largest foreign-owned life/health insurance company was American International Assurance (AIA) (1.49 percent), while the rest represented less than 1 percent of the total market share. These statistics indicate that foreign-owned companies are very much interested in the Chinese private health insurance industry but still play a very minor role in the sector because of the government's regulation of foreign insurance companies.

Foreign companies were not allowed into the Chinese market until 2001 when China joined the WTO. The Chinese government passed the Foreign Insurance Company Regulatory Law in 2002, which allowed joint ventures of only up to 50 percent foreign ownership before 2004, and up to 51 percent beginning in 2004. The minimum total assets should be more than US$5 billion. An insurance broker is required to have total assets of over $500 million, and foreign insurance companies must have more than 30 years of established experience in a WTO member country.

A successful private health insurance operation requires reliable health care expenditure profiles and actuarial statistics. This information is lacking in China. Thus, reimbursements often are based on a fixed proportion of the insurance premium (for example, RMB 10,000 reimbursement for an RMB 800 premium, or RMB 20,000 reimbursement for an RMB 1,600 premium) or per patient day reimbursement (for example, RMB 250 per day for 30 days). An individual is allowed to buy the same private health insurance program multiple times, in order to raise the reimbursement if suffering from a disease.

Chinese private health insurance serves as primary health insurance for people who have no health insurance or as supplementary insurance for people covered by public health insurance. The main type of health insurance product is inpatient coverage. Special types of insurance also are available for particular illnesses, for example, cancer, or for a special population, for example, child health insurance or child immunization insurance.

Since 2004, to reduce the financial risk to insurance companies, most private health insurance enrollees have had to buy life insurance first. Health insurance is considered supplementary to life insurance. Also, health insurance is limited to ages below 60 or 65. Waiting periods range from 90 to 180 days before making a claim for reimbursement. Furthermore, a reimbursement ceiling stops loss on the part of insurance companies. Finally, companies discontinue the renewal of health insurance in the year following reimbursement of a major claim. Most health insurances cover catastrophic diseases, such as cancer. Patients with these diseases cannot recover and will be permanently revoked by this program. In essence, these insurance products and benefits packages fully reflect that the Chinese private health insurance industry is avoiding adverse selection. In fact, Chinese consumers have an unfavorable image of the private health insurance industry. They believe the industry does not really protect them against major financial loss when a major illness occurs or remove financial barriers for patients seeking health care services.

The financial statistics of the Chinese private health insurance industry are shown in table 10.6. Chinese private health insurance expenditures (reimbursement to claims) as a percent of total revenue varied between 1999 and 2004, ranging from a low of 19 percent in 2000 to a high of 54 percent in 2001 and around 30 percent in 1999, 2003, and 2004. No actual private health insurance management/operating expenses have been reported. The CIRC provides only the overall operating expenses of each life/health insurance company. These expenses ranged from a low of 9 percent in 2003 to a high of 14 percent in 2000, and averaged about 11 percent. Marketing expenses and management expenses for health insurance operations may cost more than life insurance management. Together with

TABLE 10.6 China: Health Insurance Industry

Year	*Revenue (RMB billion)*	*Reimbursement (RMB billion)*	*% revenue increase from baseline (1999 base)*	*Reimbursement/ revenue*	*Operation expenditures/ revenue*	*Estimated net revenue*
1999	3.65	1.10	-	0.30	0.13	0.57
2000	6.55	1.29	117	0.19	0.14	0.67
2001	6.16	3.35	305	0.54	0.12	0.34
2002	12.24	4.99	454	0.41	0.10	0.49
2003	24.19	6.99	635	0.29	0.09	0.62
2004	25.98	8.91	810	0.34	0.10	0.56

Sources: China Insurance Regulation Commission (CIRC) 2004. http://www.circ.gov.

reimbursement payment, the total private health insurance industry has had a net income of at least 55 percent of total revenue on average; in its worst year (2001), net income was about 34 percent.

Considering the nature of Chinese private health insurance products and financial structures, China's private health insurance is in its infancy. While the government established a law regulating foreign insurance companies in 2002, the People's Congress enacted the Insurance Management and Regulation Act on June 15, 2002. It has seven major sections: (1) approval review (including minimum capital), (2) financial and risk supervision, (3) premium rate setting, (4) benefits package/product offering, (5) consumer rights protection, (6) auditing, and (7) dispute-settlement procedures. The objective of this regulation act is to ensure a financially sound private health insurance industry and consumer benefits protection. In June 2004, a Health Insurance Supervising and Management Commission was established to implement these regulations.

KEY ISSUES OF HEALTH CARE FINANCING IN CHINA

Several recent reviews and reports[1] have identified four key health care financing issues in China. They are as follows.

- China has both a large uninsured and a large underinsured population. The 2003 Ministry of Health National Health Services Survey found at least 45 percent of urbanites and 80 percent of the rural population in China did not have health insurance. In addition, insurance reimbursement rates are relatively low, and most insurance provides less than 50 percent coverage.
- Government funding for health care services is inadequate. In 2003, the government funded only 15 percent of total national health care expenditures. This low contribution by the government is one reason for China's large uninsured and underinsured population.
- Inequities exist in health care financing. These inequities exist not only between urban and rural areas, but also between high and low income households. Public funding has been allocated largely to government insurance and labor insurance programs. Only recently has the government reinitiated the New Cooperative Medical Services (NCMS). However, the government subsidy level to NCMS is relatively low, serving only a small portion of "catastrophe" patients.
- China's health care delivery system is inefficient. Under the fee-for-services system with its lack of appropriate government regulation and monitoring, patients have been overbilled, they overuse medication, and they have acquired a heavy financial burden.

Therefore, the key issues with respect to health care financing in China involve how to (1) increase and improve health insurance coverage, (2) increase funding by the public sector, (3) improve the equity of health care services, and (4) improve health care efficiency in the Chinese health care delivery systems.

The World Bank's AAA Briefing Notes (2004–05) and the State Council's Development Research Center (DRC 2005) call for a much stronger role for the Chinese government both in terms of additional funding and more proactive government regulation. However, because of China's large population and the structure of its current public finance system, the Chinese government alone may not be able to resolve these key issues in the near future. Given the current magnitude of out-of-pocket health care expenditures (about 60 percent), there is room to mobilize these private expenditures to develop a private risk-pooling financing mechanism, such as establishing private health insurance institutions. In fact, the DRC report also suggests encouragement of a commercial health insurance scheme in addition to increasing the role of public financing.

This chapter explores the potential for private health insurance in China. The next two sections look at factors that influence individuals enrolled in private health insurance and estimate the price elasticities of demand for private health insurance (willingness to pay) and household ability to pay for private health insurance. Using these empirical findings, a preliminary projection of the potential private health insurance market in China can be estimated.

DETERMINANTS OF PRIVATE HEALTH INSURANCE ENROLMENT

The Chinese private health insurance industry is in its infancy. Only 5.6 percent of the urban population and 8.3 percent of the rural population have enrolled in private health insurance, as shown in table 10.3. To gauge the possibility for further growth in private health insurance, it would be very useful to study the various determinants of current enrollees. This information will be useful for policymakers interested in expanding private health insurance in China. The data can also be used to predict the probability and potential magnitude of private health insurance enrolment.

A number of sociodemographic and key economic factors influence individual enrolment in private health insurance. These include age, gender, education, employment status, location, income, and health status. A person can also have public health insurance and purchase private health insurance as supplemental insurance. Currently, no national survey data are available on this information in relation to individuals' health status. This chapter is based on data obtained from a household survey conducted in four cities in two Chinese provinces, Sichuan in the Southwest and Shandong in the Northwest.

Each city's population density is over 2,500 people per square kilometer. This study includes three smaller cities, each having 30,000 to 60,000 residents, and one large city with 110,000 residents. One district was sampled in each smaller city, and two districts in the large city. Within each district, about 550 households were randomly selected to interview. Respondents were approximately 7,854 individuals aged 15 years and above from 2,671 households. The survey gathered personal information, such as age, gender, marital status, income, and highest educational level, as well as information about the status of employment, health insurance, health, and health care utilization.

The variables in this analysis are defined in table 10.7. Public health insurance includes urban employee basic insurance programs and CMS. Independent variables include region, gender, age, employment status, education, health status, and income.

TABLE 10.7 China: Definition of Variables

Variable	*Definition*
Dependent variable	
Private insurance	Dummy variable = 1 if individual has private health insurance; 0 otherwise
Independent variable	
Public insurance	Dummy variable = 1 if individual has public health insurance; 0 otherwise
Sichuan	Dummy variable = 1 if the individual lives in Sichuan province; 0 otherwise
Male	Dummy variable = 1 if individual is male; 0 otherwise
Age	
15–39	Dummy variable = 1 if person's age is in this range; 0 otherwise
40–59	Dummy variable = 1 if person's age is in this range; 0 otherwise
	(person older than 59 is default variable)
Employment status	
Government or state-run	Dummy variable = 1 if employed by government, national enterprises, or collective enterprises; 0 otherwise
Privately run or self-employed	Dummy variable = 1 if employed by private enterprises or self-employed; 0 otherwise
	Default variable = unemployed
Educational status	
High school	Dummy variable = 1 if household leader finished high school; 0 otherwise
College and above	Dummy variable = 1 if household leader finished college and above; 0 otherwise
	Default variable = primary school and below
Health status	
Normal health	Binary variable = 1 if self-reported health is normal; 0 otherwise
Good health	Binary variable = 1 if self-reported health is good; 0 otherwise
	Default variable = self-report of poor health
Family income	
Middle 25%	Dummy variable = 1 if person's income is middle 25%; 0 otherwise
Higher 25%	Dummy variable = 1 if person's income is higher 25%; 0 otherwise
Highest 25%	Dummy variable = 1 if person's income is highest 25%; 0 otherwise
	Default variable = lowest 25% first quartile

Source: Authors' household survey in Sichuan province and Shandong province.

TABLE 10.8 China: Individual Characteristics, by Health Insurance Group

Group	*Pub (%)* *(N = 1,550) (20%)*	*PRI (%)* *(N = 861) (11%)*	*No ins. (%)* *(N = 5,623) (72%)*	*Total (%)* *(N = 7,854)*
Region				
Sichuan province	46	47	35	38
Shandong province	54	53	65	62
Gender				
Male	55	49	47	49
Female	45	51	53	51
Age				
15–39	51	63	56	56
40–59	36	34	32	33
60 and above	13	3	12	11
Employment status				
Government and state-run	31	13	9	13
Privately run or self-employed	33	54	46	45
Unemployed	36	33	45	42
Educational status				
Junior or less	22	15	29	27
High school	68	76	67	68
College or higher	10	9	4	5
Health status				
Chronic disease	13	8	8	9
No chronic disease	87	92	92	91
Acute disease	9	9	9	9
No acute disease	91	91	91	91
Per capita monthly income (RMB)				
Mean	430.4	504.9	382.9	409.6
SD	408.2	455.4	386.3	396.7

Source: Authors' household survey in Sichuan province and Shandong province.

Table 10.8 indicates that about 1,550 respondents (20 percent) had public health insurance, 861 respondents (11 percent) had private health insurance, and 5,623 residents (72 percent) did not have health insurance. The percent of individuals with private insurance in the study sample was higher than the national average. Although more male respondents had public health insurance (55 percent), more females bought private health insurance (51 percent). More than half of the respondents covered by public health insurance or private health insurance were younger than 40 years old. Among the three employment status groups, government and state-run enterprise employees accounted for 31 percent of the respondents with public health insurance, but only 13 percent of those with private health insurance. About 54 percent of private health insurance purchasers were employed by private enterprises or were self-employed. Those with health insurance were associated with high school or higher levels of education. About 5 percent of the total sample had at least a college education but accounted for 10 percent of the people covered by public health insurance and 9 percent of the privately insured. The average income of the privately insured was RMB 505 per month, higher than the RMB 430 income of individuals with public health insurance or the RMB 383 income of the uninsured. These data are helpful in understanding the general characteristics of individuals covered by different health insurance programs.

Table 10.9 presents health insurance coverage by individual characteristics. Since the percentage of the population with both public health insurance and private health insurance is just 2.3 percent, the analysis is concerned with public health insurance coverage, private health insurance coverage, and no health insurance coverage.

Health insurance coverage differed between people living in Sichuan and in Shandong. Both public health insurance coverage and private health insurance coverage were higher in Sichuan than in Shandong. Males were more likely to be insured than females. About half of the people insured by public health insurance or private health insurance were younger than 40 years old. The likelihood of having public health insurance enrolment appears to increase with age, and private coverage shrinks for older respondents.

A higher percentage of individuals employed by government and state-run enterprises had public health insurance than the unemployed or in the privately employed. The share of the best-educated respondents covered by public health insurance was nearly twice as high as the share of the people with the lowest educational educational attainment. The pattern was similar for private health insurance coverage. As expected, the largest proportion of individuals owning either public insurance or private health insurance was also found among in the higher income brackets.

Although these descriptions are helpful in understanding the magnitude and disparity in the health insurance coverage rates among small city residents in China, the interrelations among these factors in determining enrolment in private health insurance must also be addressed. Whether the individual has private health insurance is the dependent variable. Because it is a binary variable, a logistic regression model was used to analyze health insurance coverage:

$$\text{Log}\,[P_i/(1 - P_i)] = \alpha + \beta_1 X_1 + \ldots + \beta_n X_n + \mu,$$

where

P_i = the probability of being enrolled in private health insurance;
X_n = the explanatory variables; and
μ = the error term.

TABLE 10.9 China: Health Insurance Coverage Rate, by Group

Group	*Pub (%) (N = 1,370) (17.4%)*	*PRI (%) (N = 681) (8.7%)*	*Pub + pri (%) (N = 180) (2.3%)*	*No ins. (%) (N = 5,623) (71.6%)*
Region				
Sichuan province	20.3	10.1	3.6	66.0
Shandong province	15.7	7.8	1.5	75.0
Gender				
Male	19.7	8.7	2.5	69.1
Female	15.3	8.7	2.3	73.7
Age				
15–39	15.8	10.1	2.2	71.9
40–59	18.8	8.4	3.0	69.8
60 and above	21.4	2.5	1.0	75.1
Employment status				
Government and state-run	40.7	5.7	4.6	49.0
Privately run or self-employed	12.4	11.0	2.4	74.2
Unemployed	15.3	7.2	1.5	76.0
Educational status				
Junior or less	14.9	5.1	1.4	78.6
High school	17.2	9.8	2.4	70.6
College or higher	32.8	11.6	6.1	49.5
Health status				
Chronic disease	25.4	7.2	2.6	64.8
No chronic disease	16.6	8.9	2.2	72.3
Acute disease	17.2	8.4	1.9	72.5
No acute disease	17.5	8.7	2.3	71.5
Average income				
Lowest 25%	15.2	6.6	1.5	76.7
Middle 25%	17.6	7.2	1.2	74.0
Higher 25%	16.8	8.6	3.1	71.5
Highest 25	20.1	12.3	3.4	64.2

Source: Authors' household survey in Sichuan province and Shandong province.

Note: Under table 10.9, the range of income quintiles is defined as follows: annual income less than RMB 2,333 is the first quintile, between RMB 2,333 and RMB 3,750 is the second quintile, between RMB 3,750 and RMB 6,000 is the third quintile, and above 6,000 is the fourth quintile. The mean of the quintiles for the lowest monthly income was RMB 134, the second lowest was RMB 261, third lowest was RMB 403, and the top income was RMB 883.

The logistic results in table 10.10 indicate that individuals in Sichuan province had a higher probability of having private health insurance. No difference was found between males and females in terms of private health insurance enrolment. Among the different age groups, the comparison group is age 60 and above. As indicated earlier, most Chinese private health insurance does not cover individuals

TABLE 10.10 China: Random Effects Logistic Regression of Private Health Insurance Coverage

Group	*Coeff*	*Odds ratio*	*Chi-square*	*P*
Intercept	−3.592**	0.220	266.963	<.0001
Sichuan	0.536**	1.709	45.653	<.0001
Male	0.034	1.035	0.213	0.6444
Age				
15–39	1.181**	3.259	36.122	<.0001
40–59	1.190**	3.288	35.737	<.0001
Employment status				
Government or state-run	−0.086	0.918	0.420	0.5171
Privately run or self-employed	0.320**	1.377	13.249	0.0003
Educational status				
High school	0.226*	1.254	5.263	0.0218
College or higher	0.988**	2.686	37.044	<.0001
Health status				
Normal health	−0.091	0.913	0.860	0.3536
Good health	−0.311	0.732	3.333	0.0679
Average income				
First quartile to second quartile	−0.232*	0.793	4.439	0.0351
Second quartile to third quartile	−0.158	0.854	2.327	0.1271
Third quartile to fourth quartile	0.208*	1.231	4.755	0.0292
Have public health insurance	0.068	1.071	0.520	0.4708
Married	−0.217*	0.805	4.740	0.0295
Chi-square	202.950**			

Source: Authors' household survey in Sichuan province and Shandong province.

*Denotes significance at 5% level with two-tailed test.

**Denotes significance at 1% level with two-tailed test.

age 60 and above. Individuals in the 15 to 39 age group or the 40 to 59 age group had a higher probability (odds ratios between 3.26 and 3.29) than the elderly population of having private health insurance. Married individuals might be expected to have a stronger interest than the unmarried in purchasing private insurance, but the results indicate that married individuals were less likely to enroll.

Workers employed in government or state-run institutions were covered mostly by public insurance, and thus had no statistically significant effect on private health insurance enrolment. In fact, these workers were less likely to purchase private health insurance, as shown by the negative sign of the coefficient of government/state-run variables. Self-employed individuals or private sector employees had a positive association with private health insurance enrolment (odds ratio of 1.377).

Education had a positive effect on private health insurance enrolment. Individuals with less than a high school education are the comparison group in the model. The results indicate that individuals with a college education had an odds ratio of 2.686 of buying private health insurance, while individuals with a high school education had an odds ratio of 1.254.

Compared with individuals in poor health, healthy individuals were less likely to buy private health insurance (odds ratio of 0.732). Fair health, unlike poor health, was not statistically significant, although its coefficient was negative, which implies a possible adverse selection bias. In other words, individuals in poor health may have had a higher probability of enrolling in private health insurance.

As expected, high-income individuals (fourth quartile) had a higher possibility of being enrolled in private health insurance (odds ratio of 1.231), than those in the first quartile. In fact, the results indicate that only the top income quartile was statistically significant in predicting private health insurance enrolment. The rest of the population (75 percent) was less likely to purchase private health insurance.

Finally, there is the issue of whether individuals with public health insurance would purchase private health insurance. The coefficient of the public health insurance ownership variable was not statistically significant. In other words, purchasing private health insurance as supplemental insurance for those with public health insurance was not a statistically significant occurrence. It is quite possible that employment in the government/state-run institutions and the variable of public health insurance ownership are correlated. A separate equation that omitted the government/state-run variable was estimated. The coefficient of the public health insurance ownership variable was still not statistically significant. In other words, private health insurance in China is not a supplement to public health insurance. It exercises a primary health insurance function because its benefits are designed mainly for inpatient services.

DEMAND FOR PRIVATE HEALTH INSURANCE: WILLINGNESS TO PAY AND ABILITY TO PAY

The concept of willingness to pay (WTP) has often been used as a measuring tool to solicit public views on the value of life, health, health services, or environmental concerns (Hanemann 1994; Joneslee, Hammerton, and Philips 1985; Wagner et al. 2000). To estimate the demand for private health insurance in the absence of actual premium data, and particularly for the large majority of the population without private health insurance, the WTP method can be used to estimate the possible relationship between enrolment in private health insurance and the premium amount, that is, the price elasticity of demand for private health insurance. Table 10.11 presents definitions of variables for WTP analysis.

The contingent valuation method (CVM) has been widely used to elicit respondents' willingness to pay. CVM provides a set of specific choices with specific scenarios developed for a range of reasonable choices as opposed to open-ended questions (Johansson 1987; Welsh and Poe 1998). This method is easier to analyze and more informative for respondents. Few studies on health insurance in developing

TABLE 10.11 China: Definitions of Variables (Logistic Model for WTP)

Variable	*Definition*
Dependent variable	
WTP for major catastrophic disease insurance	Binary variable = 1 if household leader is willing to buy major catastrophic disease insurance
WTP for inpatient expenditure insurance	Binary variable = 1 if household leader is willing to buy inpatient expenditure insurance
WTP for outpatient expenditure insurance	Binary variable = 1 if household leader is willing to buy outpatient expenditure insurance
Independent variables	
Price of health insurance	Ordinal variable
Public health insurance (PHI)	Dummy variable = 1 if individual has bought PHI
Married	Dummy variable = 1 if individual is currently married
Sichuan	Dummy variable = 1 if individual lives in Sichuan
Male	Dummy Variable = 1 if individual is male
Age	
>=39	Dummy variable = 1 if person's age is in this range
40–59	Dummy variable = 1 if person's age is in this range
	Default variable = person older than 59
Employment status	
Government or state-run	Dummy variable = 1 if employed by government, national enterprises, or collective enterprises
Private-run or self-employed	Dummy variable = 1 if employed by private enterprises or self-employed
	Default variable = unemployed
Educational status	
High school	Dummy variable = 1 if person finished high school
College or above	Dummy variable = 1 if person finished college
	Default variable = primary school and below
Health status	
Chronic disease	Dummy variable = 1 if individual suffered from chronic disease in last three months
Acute disease	Dummy variable = 1 if person suffered from acute disease in last two weeks
Average income	
Middle 25%	Dummy variable = 1 if person's income is middle 25%
Higher 25%	Dummy variable = 1 if person's income is high 25%
Highest 25%	Dummy variable = 1 if person's income is highest 25%
	Default variable = lowest 25% first quartile

Source: Authors' household survey in Sichuan province and Shandong province.

countries have been done using CVM. To date, only one study on supplementary health insurance has been conducted in China using CVM, and no research on WTP for private health insurance has been carried out (Chen et al. 2002).

The research for the current study was based on data obtained from the same household survey conducted on the determinants of private health insurance, described above. The heads of 2,671 households were asked about their willingness to pay for three different insurance programs: (1) major catastrophic disease insurance (MCDI), (2) inpatient expenses insurance (IEI), and (3) outpatient expenses insurance (OEI). Catastrophic disease refers to cancer, end-stage renal disease, leukemia, and so forth. The questionnaire for WTP for three health insurance programs was developed through qualitative research and pretesting. MCDI was a program reimbursing 80 percent of health expenditure to the insured if they suffered from catastrophic disease. IEI would cover 100 percent of enrollee's health expenditure on inpatient health services, and OEI would cover 60 percent of health expenditure on outpatient health services. The benefits covered by each program were first explained to the respondents, then the WTP questions were asked. Respondents were free to make multiple choices. Table 10.12 indicates that almost half (48 percent) of respondents would choose inpatient services insurance, followed by catastrophe insurance (43 percent), and then outpatient services (24 percent).

The probability of choosing any of the three insurance products depends on the annual premium. The mean monthly premium that respondents were willing to pay was RMB 68.1 for inpatient insurance, RMB 42.9 for catastrophe insurance, and RMB 37.8 for outpatient insurance.

Given the possible correlation with the response to multiple contingent valuations, a random effect logistic model was used to estimate three separate choices: catastrophe insurance, inpatient insurance, and outpatient insurance. These estimated results are shown in table 10.13.

The logistic regression results show that the price of insurance was negative and statistically significant for all three types of health insurance. The estimated price elasticity of demand for catastrophic disease insurance was –0.271. The estimated price elasticity for inpatient insurance was –0.342, and the estimated price elasticity for the demand for outpatient insurance was –0.412. All these estimated price elasticities were inelastic. Furthermore, the magnitude for estimated elasticity for outpatients was more elastic than for the other two types of health insurance. Inpatient insurance price elasticity was more elastic than catastrophe health insurance.

The results indicate that individuals who already have public health insurance may purchase inpatient health insurance, perhaps because their public health insurance has a high deductible and copayment. Married individuals are more likely to buy health insurance—IEI more than other types of health insurance. Those between the ages of 15–40 are more likely than elderly individuals to purchase health insurance.

As expected, individuals employed in government or state-run enterprises are more likely to have public health insurance and less likely to buy private health insurance, while employees of private enterprises are more likely to purchase private

TABLE 10.12 Means and Standard Deviations of Variables

Variable	*Mean*	*SD*
Dependent variable		
Percent willing to buy MCDI	43.02	0.50
Percent willing to buy IEI	48.53	0.50
Percent willing to buy OEI	24.45	0.43
Independent variable		
Premium of MCDI (RMB)	42.88	74.12
Premium of IEI (RMB)	68.07	78.20
Premium of OEI (RMB)	37.86	59.97
Health insurance status		
Public health insurance (PHI)	0.40	0.76
Non-PHI	0.60	0.93
Marital status		
Married	0.92	0.26
Unmarried	0.08	0.06
Province		
Sichuan	0.38	0.49
Shangdong	0.62	0.70
Gender		
Male	0.75	0.43
Female	0.25	0.15
Age		
≤39	0.52	0.50
40–59	0.40	0.49
≥60	0.08	0.23
Employment status		
Government or state-run	0.17	0.38
Privately run or self-employed	0.56	0.50
Unemployed	0.27	0.25
Educational status		
Primary school or below	0.25	0.25
High school	0.69	0.44
College	0.06	0.23
Health status		
No chronic disease in last three months	0.89	0.64
Had chronic disease in last three months	0.11	0.31
No acute disease in last two weeks	0.89	0.68
Had acute disease in last two weeks	0.11	0.32
Per capita monthly income (RMB)		
Lowest 25%	134.12	49.42
Middle 25%	260.56	35.85
Higher 25%	403.68	54.97
Highest 25%	883.18	614.66

Source: Author's household survey in Sichuan province and Shandong province.

TABLE 10.13 China: Random Effects Logistic Regression of WTP for Each Program

	MCDI		*IEI*		*OEI*	
Variable	*Coefficient*	*Marginal effect*	*Coefficient*	*Marginal effect*	*Coefficient*	*Marginal effect*
Intercept	−1.2216**	—	−1.0121**	—	−1.1156**	—
Price	−0.0111**	−0.0027	−0.0101**	−0.0025	−0.0154**	−0.0028
Public health insurance	0.0010	0.0002	0.0776**	0.0194	−0.0602	−0.0111
Married	−0.0431	−0.0106	0.2066**	0.0516	0.0435	0.0080
Sichuan province	0.8462**	0.2074	0.4693**	0.1172	0.5073**	0.0937
Male	0.1657**	0.0406	0.1059*	0.0265	0.1270*	0.0235
Age						
15–39	0.6120**	0.1500	0.6718**	0.1678	0.3458**	0.0639
40–59	0.2955**	0.0724	0.3034**	0.0758	0.1679	0.0310
Employment status						
Government or state-run	0.1236	0.0303	−0.0162	−0.0040	0.2481**	0.0458
Private-run or self-employed	0.1549**	0.0380	0.1223*	0.0305	0.1759**	0.0325
Educational status						
High school	0.4314**	0.1057	0.4048**	0.1011	0.3977**	0.0735
College school	0.9763**	0.2393	0.8535**	0.2132	0.8285**	0.1530
Health status						
Had chronic disease in last three months	0.0803	0.0197	0.0795	0.0199	0.2192**	0.0405
Had acute disease in last two weeks	0.0460	0.0113	0.0655	0.0164	−0.0252	−0.0047
Average income						
Middle 25%	0.2896**	0.0710	0.2068**	0.0517	0.0793	0.0146
Higher 25%	0.4567**	0.1119	0.4038**	0.1009	0.3032**	0.0560
Highest 25%	0.7250**	0.1777	0.6472**	0.1617	0.6099**	0.1127
Chi square	287.65**		367.56**		423.85**	
Median WTP (RMB)	110.1		100.2		72.4	
Price elasticity	−0.2712		−0.3416		0.4166	

Source: Authors' household survey in Sichuan province and Shandong province.

*Denotes significance at 5% level with two-tailed test.

**Denotes significance at 1% level with two-tailed test.

health insurance. Better educated and wealthier individuals are more likely to purchase health insurance, based on the magnitude of the coefficients or estimated odds ratio.

The chronically ill are more likely to purchase OEI, not MCDI, while having an acute disease has no influence on the health insurance purchase. One important finding is that more individuals would like to buy MCDI and IEI than OEI. In addition, individuals would pay more for MCDI and IEI than for OEI. As explained above under "Urban Health Insurance," public health insurance in urban China is composed of the Medical Saving Account and Social Risk Pool fund. As compulsory health insurance, public health insurance covers not only outpatient health services, but also inpatient health services and catastrophic diseases. Public health insurance is difficult to expand quickly because some enterprises with a deficit or smaller financial reserve would find it difficult to pay health insurance premiums for their employees. Private health insurance should play an important role in providing flexible health insurance programs with low premiums. This research indicates that MCDI and IEI would be the priority coverage under private health insurance.

The average price elasticity of OEI is higher than those for MCDI and IEI. Compared with MCDI and IEI, OEI is more a luxury good for people in urban areas in China. This finding provides additional evidence for setting MCDI and IEI as priority programs for private health insurance. MCDI and IEI cover the health expenditures for catastrophic disease and inpatient health services, which have lower probabilities of occurring. But CIEI and IEI protect insurance enrollees against higher financial risks than does OEI. WTP would be sensitive to risk perceptions (Lee et al. 1998).

Finally, some of the demand determinants for private health insurance are similar to the determinants of having three private health insurance programs. Employment by private enterprises or self-employment, aged under 40, a college education, and higher income were several of the most important determinants. This finding will be useful in estimating the potential enrolment for private health insurance. As expected, income was positively correlated with WTP, a result also found in several other studies (Chestnut et al. 1996; Chiu et al. 1998; Chiu et al. 1999; Kartman, Andersson, and Johannesson 1996). Economists often view this as a validity check (Ryan 1997).

Table 10.12 indicates that over 40 percent of respondents are willing to purchase either catastrophic disease insurance (MCDI) or inpatient expenses insurance (IEI). The mean values of willingness to pay for these two premiums are RMB 43 a month for MCDI and RMB 68 for IEI. The monthly health premium for MCDI is about 5 percent of the income for the top income quintile; the IEI premium represents almost 8 percent of income for the same group. In contrast, for the lowest income quintile, the same monthly health insurance premium for MCDI would take up to 30 percent of income, and the IEI premium would represent about 50 percent. The financial burden is still quite high for the middle-income quintile. Therefore, under the current scenario, it appears that the top income quintile should be able to afford the private health insurance premium.

The China 2003 National Health Survey (Center for Health Statistics and Information, MOH 2004) indicates that the average health insurance premium was about RMB 20 a month for the rural population and RMB 85 a month for the urban population. The annual household income during 2003 was RMB 6,565 for rural individuals and RMB 19,000 for urbanites. Thus, the insurance premium represented about 3 percent of household income for rural households and 5 percent for urban households. Under the same national survey, total health care expenditures were about 13 percent for rural households and 9 percent for urban households. In other words, the health insurance premium is much smaller than health care expenditures as a proportion of income. In fact, for an enrollee in a health insurance program, the expected out-of-pocket health care expenditures would be less than the premium.

POTENTIAL PRIVATE HEALTH INSURANCE MARKET

According to the 2003 statistics, 202 million individuals in urban areas and 641 million in rural areas in China were uninsured. The econometric model indicated that the key determinants of enrolling in private health insurance were age, employment in the private sector, education, and income (top quartile). One approach to projecting the potential private health insurance market is to first estimate the conditional probability of having private health insurance from the estimated econometric model (table 10.10).

The estimated conditional magnitude of the probability of having private health insurance between those employed in the private sector and those employed in the public sector or unemployed is very large. Other factors held constant, the predicted probability of having private health insurance is only 2.8 percent for males and 2.7 percent for females for those not employed in the private sector. Among those employed in the private sector, 11.8 percent of males and 11.7 percent of females have private health insurance; however, this difference is not statistically significant. Because employment status is the key determinant of private insurance ownership, a set of conditional probabilities of having private health insurance was estimated from those employed in the private sector.

Table 10.14 presents the estimated conditional probabilities for private health insurance coverage for those employed in the private sector, by age, income, and education. The predicted difference between age and gender is small (0.1 percent). However, the income difference is between 2.5 percent and 5 percent and skewed toward the top quartile. The most significant difference in the magnitude of probability is in educational: those with higher education are about twice as likely as those without to have private health insurance.

Since the predicted differences among ages are minimal in terms of the probability of having private health insurance, predicting the potential market for

TABLE 10.14 China: Predicted Probability for Private Insurance Coverage in Private Sector, by Age, Education, and Income (%)

	Age					
	15–39			*40–59*		
Education / *Income*	*Primary school*	*High school*	*College or higher*	*Primary school*	*High school*	*College or higher*
First quartile	11.00	13.42	24.93	11.09	13.53	25.09
Second quartile	8.93	10.95	20.84	9.00	11.04	20.99
Third quartile	9.55	11.69	22.09	9.63	11.78	22.24
Fourth quartile	13.21	16.03	29.01	13.31	16.15	29.20

Source: Authors' household survey in Sichuan province and Shandong province.

TABLE 10.15 China: Predicted Probabilities for Private Insurance Coverage of Private Sector Employees, by Education and Income (%)

Income \ *Education*	*Primary school*	*High school*	*College or higher*
First quartile	11.04	13.47	25.00
Second quartile	8.96	10.99	20.91
Third quartile	9.58	11.73	22.16
Fourth quartile	13.25	16.08	29.09

Source: Authors' household survey in Sichuan province and Shandong province.

private health insurance relies mainly on three key factors: employment in the private sector, income, and education.

Table 10.15 shows the estimated conditional probability of having private health insurance among these three key factors. The Chinese Statistical Yearbook contains data on the size of the population employed in the private sector, but data on their educational attainment is difficult to obtain. Income is divided into four quartiles; thus, even without actual income distribution, the quartile can be used as a predicting tool.

Table 10.16 shows employment status since 1999. The urban population employed in the public sector declined by about 5 million each year, from 85.7 million in 1999 to 71.6 million in 2002, while the number of people employed in the private sector increased from 10.5 million in 1999 to 20.0 million in 2002. Therefore, the main base for predicting potential private health insurance enrollees would be the additional number of employees in the private sector in future years,

TABLE 10.16 China: Urban Employment, 2002 (million)

Employed units	*1999*	*2000*	*2001*	*2002*
Urban areas				
State-owned Units	85.7	81.0	76.4	71.6
Urban collective-owned units	17.1	15.0	12.9	11.2
Cooperative units	1.3	1.6	1.5	1.6
Joint ownership units	0.5	0.4	0.5	0.5
Limited liability corporations	6.0	6.9	8.4	10.8
Share-holding corporations ltd.	4.2	4.6	4.8	5.4
Units with funds from Hong Kong, Macao, and Taiwan, China	3.1	3.1	3.3	3.7
Foreign-funded units	3.1	3.3	3.5	3.9
Self-employed individuals	24.1	21.4	21.3	22.7
Employed by others	68.5	81.5	91.5	96.4
Private enterprises	10.5	12.7	15.3	20.0
Total	224.1	231.5	239.4	247.8

Source: National Bureau of Statistics of China 2003.

TABLE 10.17 China: Sample Distribution between Education and Income, Privately Employed Subsample

Average income \ Education	Primary school and below (%)	High school (%)	College and above (%)	Total (%)
Lowest 25%	0.044	0.155	0	0.199
Middle 25%	0.044	0.193	0	0.237
Higher 25%	0.038	0.219	0.010	0.267
Highest 25%	0.039	0.241	0.010	0.290
Total	0.165	0.808	0.020	1.000

Source: Authors' household survey in Sichuan province and Shandong province.

for example, an additional 5 million or 10 million, up to an additional 20 million in the next four years.

No official statistics are available on the educational and income distribution for private employees. Thus, the predictions based on educational and income distribution rely on the sample statistics obtained for this study. Table 10.17 shows distribution based on the study samples used to predict the private health insurance population for four different scenarios.

Multiplying the additional population to be employed in the private sector, such as 5 million, by the sample distribution in table 10.17, produces the estimated population distribution among four income levels and three educational levels (table 10.18). Multiplying these data by the conditional probability distribution for private health insurance enrolment results in the predicted additional private health insurance enrolment for 2003—646,318 individuals (table 10.19). With an additional 5 million annual employees, by 2006 the private health insurance

TABLE 10.18 China: Estimated Population Distribution between Income and Education

Population	Average income \ Education	Primary school and below (%)	High school (%)	College and above (%)
5 million	Lowest 25%	220,000	775,000	0
	Middle 25%	220,000	965,000	0
	Higher 25%	190,000	1,095,000	50,000
	Highest 25%	195,000	1,205,000	50,000
10 million	Lowest 25%	440,000	1,550,000	0
	Middle 25%	440,000	1,930,000	0
	Higher 25%	380,000	2,190,000	100,000
	Highest 25%	390,000	2,410,000	100,000
15 million	Lowest 25%	660,000	2,325,000	0
	Middle 25%	660,000	2,895,000	0
	Higher 25%	570,000	3,285,000	150,000
	Highest 25%	585,000	3,615,000	150,000

Source: Authors' household survey in Sichuan province and Shandong province.

TABLE 10.19 China: Predicted Private Health Insurance Enrolment, When Additional 5 Million Individuals Join Employment Sector

Income \ *Education*	*Primary school*	*High school*	*College and above*	*Total*
First quartile	24,288	104,393	0	128,681
Second quartile	19,712	106,054	0	125,766
Third quartile	18,202	128,444	11,080	157,726
Fourth quartile	25,838	193,764	14,545	234,147
Total	88,040	532,654	25,625	646,318

Source: Authors' household survey in Sichuan province and Shandong province.

program should have had 2.6 million additional enrolments. This estimate is based on projected private employment in urban areas.

The above prediction—a very low estimate—is based on an employed urban population with different education and income levels. There are about 200 million uninsured urbanites. Assuming people in the top income quintile can pay the health insurance premium and, according to table 10.12, 40 percent are interested in enrolling in MCDI or IEI programs, an additional 20 million new private health insurance enrollees could be expected. This figure is close to the one predicted using information from table 10.16. Using the 200 million urbanites in the top two income quintiles as the projection basis, an additional 40 million people in China could be insured.

Predicting the determinants in the private health insurance model does not consider the effect of premium magnitude, the price elasticity of demand for health insurance. The WTP model has provided a number of price elasticities. Because inpatient health insurance is the most popular insurance product, this product can be used to simulate the effect of differences in insurance premiums on demand for private health insurance in the near future. Using the RMB 160 average inpatient expenditure by individuals willing to buy private health insurance, plus the loading cost of 20 percent, the annual inpatient health insurance premium would be RMB 200. Table 10.20 shows that the magnitude of probability

TABLE 10.20 China: Predicted Probabilities for Private Insurance Coverage, by Education and Income, for Private Employees (%)

Income \ *Education*	*Primary school*	*High school*	*College and above*
First quartile	8.44	12.12	17.74
Second quartile	10.17	14.49	20.95
Third quartile	12.11	17.10	24.38
Fourth quartile	14.94	20.81	29.10

Source: Authors' household survey in Sichuan province and Shandong province.

Note: Premium = RMB 200.

TABLE 10.21 China: Predicted Probabilities for Private Insurance Coverage, by Education and Income, for Private Employees (%)

Income \ *Education*	*Primary school*	*High school*	*College and above*
First quartile	20.13	27.38	37.05
Second quartile	23.64	31.64	41.95
Third quartile	27.36	36.01	46.76
Fourth quartile	32.40	41.74	52.79

Source: Authors' household survey in Sichuan province and Shandong province.

Note: Premium = RMB 100.

of private health insurance enrolment is lower than that shown on table 10.14. However, if the premium were reduced to RMB 100, table 10.21 shows that the probability of purchasing insurance would be much higher, almost double the probability for college-educated individuals and more than double for those with high school education. The magnitude of probability of private health insurance enrolment would be higher than those estimated probabilities in table 10.14. Therefore, the size of future private health insurance enrolment will depend not only on the number of employees in the private sector, income level, and educational level, but also on the magnitude of the premium for private health insurance.

These prediction results are based on a limited household survey in four cities in two provinces in China. A much larger national, representative sample would be more useful in predicting the size of future private health insurance enrolment. The Chinese Ministry of Health completed a national health services survey in 2003. It is hoped that additional work on this topic can be done when the Chinese Ministry of Health releases its survey of this research to the public.

POLICY OPTIONS AND CONCLUSIONS

China still has about 843 million uninsured individuals, 65 percent of its 1.3 billion people. In recent years, the Chinese government has made great efforts to provide public insurance to both urban localities and rural villages. The government's health care budget competes with other public expenditures. It may not be possible to rely on public financing to cover such a large uninsured population in the near future. The Chinese government is unlikely to willingly reform its taxation system and raise its financing for health care insurance. One proposed option would be to raise the tobacco tax to earmark a portion of the revenue for the health insurance fund, especially for the poor or rural populations (Hu and Mao 2002). Other health care systems use earmarked taxes to finance health care. Without drastic public financing reform, mobilizing private resources to increase health insurance coverage may be another option.

Given the current magnitude of out-of-pocket medical expenditures and the amount of private insurance premium payments, it is quite possible that individuals at the middle and upper income levels would enroll in private health insurance, as long as the benefits coverage is attractive and governmental regulations are implemented to ensure the reliability and credibility of the private health insurance system. The public funding currently used for the upper income groups could then be reallocated to the lower income groups.

Private health insurance is suitable for middle- and upper-income groups but may also work for low-income groups. The government could provide insurance premium subsidies to low-income groups, or provide assistance according to ability to pay, thereby encouraging low-income individuals to enroll in private health insurance. In fact, the current rural NCMS program is a government subsidy for individuals who voluntarily join the program. The Chinese government has now invited some commercial health insurance companies to manage its NCMS.

The private health insurance program can be a mix of public and private funding. To avoid potential adverse selection under voluntary private health insurance, either group insurance (for example, schools, factories, large enterprises) is encouraged to increase risk pooling or prior physical examinations or a waiting period before reimbursement are required.

One potential source of private health insurance enrolment comes from the private employment sector. Public sector employment is declining, and private employment is increasing. This study has found that most private insurance enrollees are employed in the private sector. Three key predictors for purchasing private health insurance are (1) private sector employment, (2) higher education, and (3) higher income. The willingness-to-pay analysis revealed that, with respect to price elasticity, demand for catastrophic disease insurance and for inpatient insurance is more inelastic than demand for outpatient insurance coverage. Therefore, new private health insurance programs to provide catastrophic disease insurance or inpatient insurance are top priorities. Opportunities for private health insurance programs most likely will be in urban areas where large private enterprises and joint venture employers are located.

On the supply side of the private health industry, to avoid adverse selection and to protect companies' financial reserves, the benefits design leaves consumers limited chance to avoid large financial loss when major illness occurs. The private health insurance companies provide only limited indemnity or disease-specific products. Moreover, the requirement to purchase a life insurance policy in order to buy health insurance has limited the health insurance market. Health insurance companies need to abandon the life insurance requirement and provide major financial risk protection. Furthermore, private health insurance practices lack close government supervision and monitoring. The government should take a more active role in monitoring benefits package design and financial auditing. China's private health insurance is in its infancy. With China's entry into the WTO, foreign investment companies have been very active in establishing their insurance practices in China. Although their market share is minimal, their number is growing. Joint ventures between Chinese and foreign insurance companies would help the Chinese industry gain management experience and design good insurance business models.

The current insurance reimbursement practice in China is for patients to pay the bill and then apply to insurance companies for partial reimbursement. Patients do not have leverage to bargain or negotiate with providers. Cost containment is one of the insurance companies' objectives. Developing networks between insurance companies and providers to contain costs and monitor quality would be useful. When providers bill insurance companies directly, the company can exercise its power to monitor costs and service quality.

Finally, to promote private health insurance in China, urgent needs include training additional actuarial personnel and insurance management professionals and developing computerized information systems. Educating consumers about health insurance also is an important task. These are immediate challenges facing the Chinese insurance sector.

NOTES

The authors are grateful to Alexander S. Preker, and Vijay Kalavakonda of the World Bank, Zhengzhong Mao of Sichuan University, May Cheng of Princeton University, and Xinzhu Liu of Abt Associates for their helpful comments and suggestions. All views expressed by this paper, however, are those of the authors alone, and do not represent the views of the funding agency or reviewers.

1. These reports include a review of current health care financing and the recent assessment of health care delivery systems in China by the World Bank China Rural Health Analytical and Advisory Activities (AAA) (World Bank, Briefing Note Series 2005) and a report prepared by the Development Research Center (DRC) Team of the State Council (funded by the WHO China office and U.K. Department of Foreign International Development).

REFERENCES

Center for Health Statistics and Information of the Ministry of Health (MOH). 2004. *The Main Outcome of Third National Health Service Survey.* Beijing: Xie He Medical University Press.

Center for Health Statistics and Information of the Ministry of Health (MOH). 1994. *The Main Outcome of Third National Health Service Survey.* Beijing: Xie He Medical University Press.

Central Party Committee and State Council. 1997. "Decisions on Health Sector Reform and Development." Document released by Central Party Committee and State Council, Beijing.

Chen, W., X. Ying, S. Hu, L. Luo, and G. Sun. 2002. "Demand for Supplementary Health Insurance." *Chinese Health Economics* 21 (12): 17–21.

Chen, X.M., T.W. Hu, and Z. Lin. 1993. "The Rise and Decline of the Cooperative Medical System in Rural China." *International Journal of Health Services* 23 (4), 731–42.

Chestnut, L.G., L.R. Keller, W.E. Lambert, and R.D. Rowe. 1996. "Measuring Heart Patients' Willingness to Pay for Changes in Angina Symptoms." *Medical Decision Making* 16 (1): 65–77.

China National Health Economics Institute. 2004. *China National Health Accounts Report.* Beijing

Chiu, L., K.Y. Tang, Y.H. Liu, W.C. Shyu, and T.P. Chang. 1998. "Willingness of Families Caring for Victims of Dementia to Pay for Nursing Home Care: Results of a Pilot Study in Taiwan." *Journal of Management in Medicine* 12 (6): 349–360, 321.

Chiu, L., K.Y. Tang, W.C. Shyu, and T.P. Chang. 1999. "The Willingness of Families Caring for Victims of Stroke to Pay for In-Home Respite Care—Results of a Pilot Study in Taiwan." *Health Policy* 46 (3): 239–54.

Doorslaer, V., A. Wagstaff, H. van der Burg, T. Christiansen, G. Citoni, R. Di Biase, U.G. Gerdtham, M. Gerfin, L. Gross, U. Hakinnen, J. John, P. Johnson, J. Klavus, C. Lachaud, J. Lauritsen, R. Leu, B. Nolan, J. Pereira, C. Propper, F. Puffer, L. Rochaix, M. Schellhorn, G. Sundberg, O. Winkelhake, et al. 1999. "The Redistributive Effect of Health Care Finance in Twelve OECD Countries." *Journal of Health Economics* 18 (3): 291–313.

Ellis, R.P., and T.G. McGuire. 1993. "Supply-Side and Demand-Side Cost Sharing in Health Care." *Journal of Economic Perspectives* 7 (4): 135–51.

Gao, J., S. Tang, R. Tolhurst, and K Rao. 2001. "Changing Access to Health Services in Urban China: Implications for Equity." *Health Policy and Planning* 16 (3): 302–12.

Hanemann, W.M. 1994. "Valuing the Environment through Contingent Valuation." *Journal of Economic Perspectives* 8 (4): 19–43.

Hsiao, W.C. 1995. "The Chinese Health Care System: Lessons for Other Nations." *Social Science and Medicine* 41 (8): 1047–55.

———. 1984. "Transformation of Health Care in China." *New England Journal of Medicine* 310 (14): 932–36.

Hu, T.W. 2004. "Financing and Organization of China's Health Care. Bulletin of the World Health Organization 82 (7): 480.

———. 1981. "Issues of Health Care Financing in the People's Republic of China." *Social Science and Medicine* 15C: 233–37.

Hu, T.W., M. Ong, Z.H. Lin, and E. Li. 1999. "The Effects of Economic Reform on Health Insurance and the Financial Burden for Urban Workers in China." *Health Economics* 8 (4): 309–21.

Hu, T.W., and Z. Mao. 2002. "Effects of Cigarette Tax on Cigarette Consumption and the Chinese Economy. *Tobacco Control* 11 (2): 105–08.

Johansson, P.O. 1987. *The Economic Theory and Measurement of Environmental Benefits.* Cambridge: Cambridge University Press.

Joneslee, M.W., M. Hammerton, and P.R. Philips. 1985. "The Value of Safety—Results of a National Sample Survey." *Economic Journal* 95 (377): 49–72.

Kartman, B., F. Andersson, and M. Johannesson. 1996. "Willingness to Pay for Reductions in Angina Pectoris Attacks." *Medical Decision Making* 16 (3): 248–53.

Lee, S.J., B. Liljas, P.J. Neumann, M.C. Weinstein, and M. Johannesson. 1998. "The Impact of Risk Information on Patients' Willingness to Pay for Autologous Blood Donation." *Medical Care* 36 (8): 1162–73.

Liu, G.G., Z. Zhao, R. Cai, Tetsuji Yamada, and Tadashi Yamada. 2002. "Equity in Health Care Access: Assessing the Urban Health Insurance Reform in China." *Social Science and Medicine* 55 (10): 1779–94.

Liu, G.G., Poyang, T.W. Hu, L. Li, and X. Liu. 2004. "Urban Health Insurance Reform: What can we learn from the pilot experiments?" In *Urbanization and Social Welfare in China,* ed. A. Chen, G.G. Liu, and K. Zhang , 39–61. Hants, U.K.: Ashgate Publishing Limited.

Liu, T.C., and C.S. Chen. 2002. "An Analysis of Private Health Insurance Purchasing Decisions with National Health Insurance in Taiwan." *Social Science and Medicine* 55 (5): 755–74.

Liu, Y. 2002. "Reforming China's Urban Health Insurance System." *Health Policy* 60 (2): 133–50.

Medical Insurance Department of Ministry of Labor and Social Security and Digna. 2000. "The Policy Options for Supplementary Medical Insurance in China." Beijing.

Ministry of Health. 2004. China National Health Services Survey. Beijing.

Ministry of Labor and Social Security. National Bureau of Statistics of China. 2004. "Statistical Communiqué on Labor and Social Security Development in 2003." Beijing.

National Bureau of Statistics of China. 2004. "Statistical Communiqué on the 2003 National Economic and Social Development." Beijing.

———. 2003. *China Statistical Yearbook.* Beijing: China Statistics Press.

Ryan, M. 1997. "Should government fund assisted reproductive techniques? A study using willingness to pay." *Applied Economics* 29 (7): 841–49.

Sekhri, N., and W. Savedoff. 2005. "Private Health Insurance: Implications for Developing Countries. *Bulletin of the World Health Organization* 83 (2): 127–34.

State Council. 1998. "Decisions on Establishing the Basic Medical Insurance System for the Urban Workers. Beijing: State Council. A document released by the State Council, Beijing.

State Council, Development Research Center (DRC). 2005. "A Framework Design for Chinese Medical at Health Care System Reform" [in Chinese]. Beijing, China.

Wagner, T.H., T.W. Hu, G.V. Duenas, and R.J. Pasick. 2000. "Willingness to Pay for Mammography: Item Development and Testing among Five Ethnic Groups. *Health Policy* 53 (2): 105–21.

Welsh, M.P., and G.L. Poe. 1998. "Elicitation Effects in Contingent Valuation: Comparisons to a Multiple Bounded Discrete Choice Approach. *Journal of Environmental Economics and Management,* 36(2): 170–85.

World Bank. 2004–05. "Rural Health in China." Briefing Notes Series, Notes 1–6 (October 2004–May 2005), Washington DC.

CHAPTER 11

Brazil

Bernard F. Couttolenc and Alexandre C. Nicolella

Voluntary health insurance (VHI) has been a feature of the Brazilian health system for many years. It covers more than 40 million people through a diversified set of contractual and coverage arrangements. The private health care sector expanded rapidly in the 1980s and early 1990s while the public sector was undergoing reform to ensure free access to care for all. Macroeconomic difficulties and restrictive legislation passed at the end of the 1990s reduced the growth rate and the prospects of the VHI sector in recent years.

This chapter assesses the impact of VHI on the financial protection of households against disease, on access to health care, and on the labor market, as well as the long-run prospects of the sector under different scenarios. VHI sustainability and expansion is shown to depend in a major way on economic growth through its impact on employers' revenue, household income, and employment (especially in the formal sector), and on a relaxation of some restrictive legislation.

INTRODUCTION

The establishment of the current Brazilian health system occurred with the 1988 Constitution, which created the Unified Health System (Sistema Unificado de Saúde, SUS) as the result of a 10-year reform process. SUS basic principles are: universal access free of charge, equity and comprehensiveness of care, and a hierarchical and decentralized system where municipalities are the main public providers of health services. Although all Brazilians have free access to SUS services by constitutional right, the voluntary health insurance system holds a considerable market share, covering 20 to 25 percent of the population overall but up to 50 percent in some states.

THE BRAZILIAN CONTEXT

Though covering only 20 to 25 percent of the population, the voluntary health insurance sector in Brazil is one of the world's largest: it is the main source of care for nearly 40 million people. Brazil's system developed from two major factors: government incentives for expanding health insurance coverage, and as a preferred alternative for corporations and individuals dissatisfied with the quality of the public system. However, the tenor of complaints in the media and from consumer protection organizations suggests that financial protection by VHI may not be as important as expected.

Macroeconomic Environment

VHI trends in the last two decades indicate that the macroeconomic environment is a major determinant of these trends. This section examines the main macroeconomic factors affecting the growth and sustainability of VHI in Brazil.

Socioeconomic Factors

Brazil is a middle-income country with a GDP per capita of US$2,780 and a PPP value of US$7,510 in 2003 (World Bank 2005). For most of the 20th century, it was one of the world's fastest-growing economies, but successive economic crises with hyperinflation resulted overall in low economic growth since the 1980s. After the adoption of the Real Plan in 1994, the inflation rate was drastically reduced from 916 percent in 1994 to 7.6 percent in 2004. This macroeconomic adjustment was based on a high interest rate, a huge increase in government debt (69 percent from 1994 to 2004), and overvaluation of the real. It forced the government to tighten the budget and restrict production and private consumption. This adjustment also produced a 56 percent increase in unemployment (table 11.1). Nonetheless, the number of the poor decreased by 19 percent (but remains high at 31 percent), and the minimum wage increased by 12 percent in real terms. This economic environment imposes considerable restrictions on public budgets and household consumption and has had a considerable impact on voluntary health insurance. However, in 1999 the overvaluation of the real could not be sustained, and a devaluation ensued.

TABLE 11.1 Brazil: 10-Year Trend in Socioeconomic Indicators

	Year		
Variable	*1993[a]/94[b]*	*2003[a]/04[b]*	*Variation (%)*
GDP (US$ billion)	438.3[a]	492.3[a]	12
GDP per capita (US$)	2,830[a]	2,780[a]	–2
Minimum wage (US$)	77.6[b]	86.61[b]	12
Inflation rate	916.5[b]	7.6[b]	–99
Unemployment rate	6.2[a]	9.7[a]	56
Proportion of poor	38.2[a]	31.1[a]	–19
Public debt (%GDP)	32.5[b]	54.9[b]	69

Sources: World Bank 2005; IPEA 2005.

Note: IPEA = Instituto de Pesquisa Econômica Aplicada (Institute for Applied Economic Research).

a. Data are for 1993 and 2003.

b. Data are for 1994 and 2004.

TABLE 11.2 Brazil: Health and Socioeconomic Indicators, 2003

Indicator	*Brazil*	*Argentina*	*Chile*	*Mexico*	*Colombia*
GDP per capita (US$)	2,780	3,524	4,590	6,120	1,764
Infant mortality rate	33	17	8	23	18
Life expectancy (years)	69	74	76	74	72
Human development index	0.775[a]	0.853[a]	0.839[a]	0.802[a]	0.773[a]
Physicians per 10,000 people	2.1[b]	3.0[c]	1.2[c]	1.5	1.4[a]
Health expenditure per capita US$	206[a]	238[a]	246[a]	379	151[a]

Sources: World Bank 2005; UNDP 2005.

a. Data are for 2002 or earlier. b. 2000. c. 1998.

Health Status

Brazil's health indicators are generally worse than those for other middle-income countries, despite significant improvements in recent years. Table 11.2 presents a few health indicators for Brazil and other middle-income Latin American countries. Brazil has gone in the last 30 years through a rapid process of demographic transition, with its population growth rate dropping from nearly 3 percent to the current 1.3 percent. This, and the concurrent epidemiological transition, has changed the pattern of health services demanded and needed to address the country's health problems. The main causes of mortality now include circulatory diseases (33 percent of all deaths), injuries (16 percent), cancer (14 percent), and infectious diseases (11 percent) (Ministry of Health/Datasus 2005). This mortality profile is now closer to those of developed countries than those of poorer countries.

Brazil also exhibits important regional inequalities in health indicators. Generally, states in the South and Southern regions have better indicators than those in the Northeast. But these disparities have as much to do with general socioeconomic inequities as with the performance and equity of the health system itself.

Unlike income and other economic indicators, most of the health indicators experienced a significant improvement over the last two decades. This performance contrasts sharply with the preceding period, when high economic growth was accompanied by stagnant or slowly improving health indicators. Life expectancy reached 69.3 in 2003 and the infant mortality rate dropped from 31.9 in 1997 to 27.4 in 2001 (table 11.3). At the same time fertility decreased 21 percent in the period (and 63 percent from 1970); Brazil is experiencing one of the fastest demographic transitions among developing countries, with rapidly growing numbers of elderly people stretching the provision of health care services and health budgets alike. The population with access to water supply increased 19 percent covering almost 81 percent, while coverage by public sanitation increased 21 percent covering 60 percent of population. Maternal and infant mortality rates decreased in 1997–2001 due to improved water and sanitation

TABLE 11.3 Brazil: Trends in Health Indicators

	Year				Variation
Index	*1991*	*1996[b]–97*	*2000[c]–01*	*2002[d]–03*	*(%)*
Water supply (%)	68.1	—	—	81.1	19.17
Sanitation (%)	48.8	—	—	59.1	21.00
Life expectancy (years)	66.0	—	—	69.3	4.91
Population aging index[a]	21.0	—	—	35.4	68.57
Fertility (number of children)	2.7	—	—	2.1[d]	−21.25
Maternal mortality (100,000)	—	47.9[b]	47.4[c]	—	−1.21
Infant mortality rate	—	31.9	27.4	—	−14.11
Early neonatal mortality rate	—	15.6	14.0	—	−10.26
Delayed neonatal mortality rate	—	4.2	3.8	—	−21.25
Cesarean rate (%)	—	38.0[b]	39.3	—	3.39

Source: MOH/Datasus (Informações de Saúde).

Note: — = not available.

a. The number of elderly individuals per 100 young individuals.

b. Data are for 1996. c. Data are for 2000. d. Data are for 2002.

and outreach primary care services. However, health services are still faced with quality and effectiveness issues, such as high cesarean rates (almost 40 percent in 2001), poor referral systems and quality assurance, and overall modest health indicators compared with its neighbors.

Health Services

The Brazilian health sector includes two separate systems: the publicly funded SUS and the privately funded and run system, which covers between 40 million and 45 million people. The SUS offers universal and free coverage to all Brazilians for a complete range of health services, but quality is unequal. It is structured according to the three levels of governments—federal, state, and municipal, each with its own role in the system. Health reform decentralized a major part of public care provision to municipalities, but some overlap persists.

Brazil's network of health facilities is extensive and diversified (table 11.4). There are three main subsystems: public facilities, nearly all of them part of the SUS; private facilities providing health services for the SUS under diverse contractual arrangements; and purely private facilities providing services to private health plans and patients paying out of pocket. In actuality, this distinction is not clear-cut, because many facilities provide services to more than one payer system. Most of the ambulatory facilities are run by municipal governments (72 percent), followed by the private sector not under an SUS contract (21 percent). Diagnostic facilities are mostly private (94 percent), and only 32 percent work for the SUS. The hospital network shows a more balanced composition, with 64 percent private, of which 45 percent provide services to SUS patients.

TABLE 11.4 Brazil: Health Facility Network

Level	*Ambulatory*	*Diagnostic*	*Hospital*	*Total*
Federal	483	22	147	652
State	856	134	610	1,600
Municipal	33,747	517	1,831	36,095
Private-SUS	1,619	3,699	3,357	8,675
Private non-SUS	9,723	7,146	1,452	18,321
Total	46,428	11,518	7,397	65,343

Source: IBGE 2002.

Note: IBGE's AMS 2002 is a health facility survey that collected data for 2001 and covered 65,343 facilities throughout the country.

After a 23 percent increase in the number of hospital beds between 1976 (443,888) and 1992 (544,357), the number decreased to 471,171 in 2002 (figure 11.1). Although public beds increased significantly, the number of private beds, and particularly SUS private beds, was considerably cut. Some migration occurred from private SUS beds to purely private beds (that is, in hospitals caring for patients from private health plans and paying out of pocket), due to the deterioration in SUS payment levels over the period.

Twenty million patients were admitted to Brazilian hospitals in 2002 (0.12 admissions per capita); 346 million emergency procedures[1] (2.0 per capita) and

FIGURE 11.1 Brazil: Long-Term Trends in the Number of Public and Private Beds

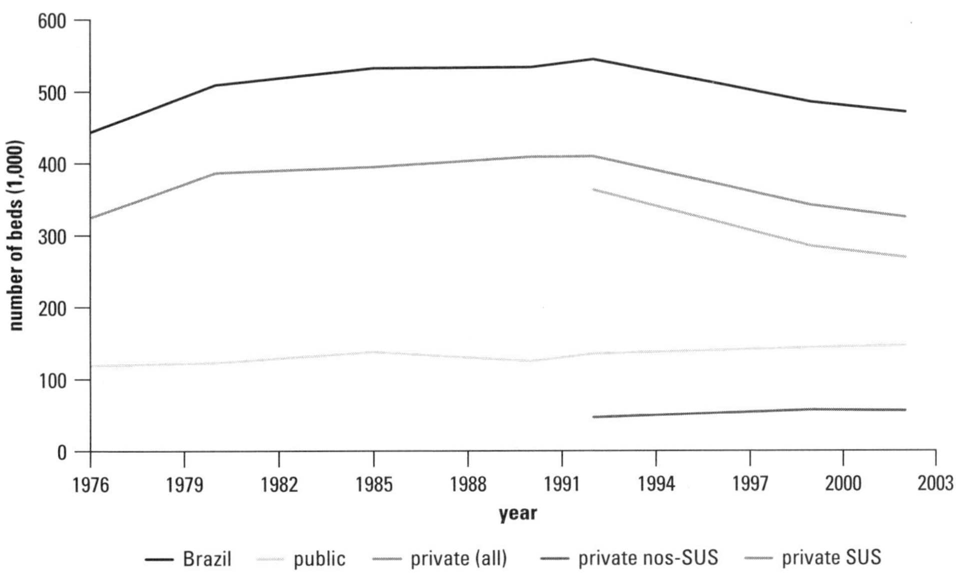

Sources: IBGE 2002; MOH/Datasus (Informações de Saúde).

FIGURE 11.2 Brazil: Production of Health Services by Type of Facility and Clientele

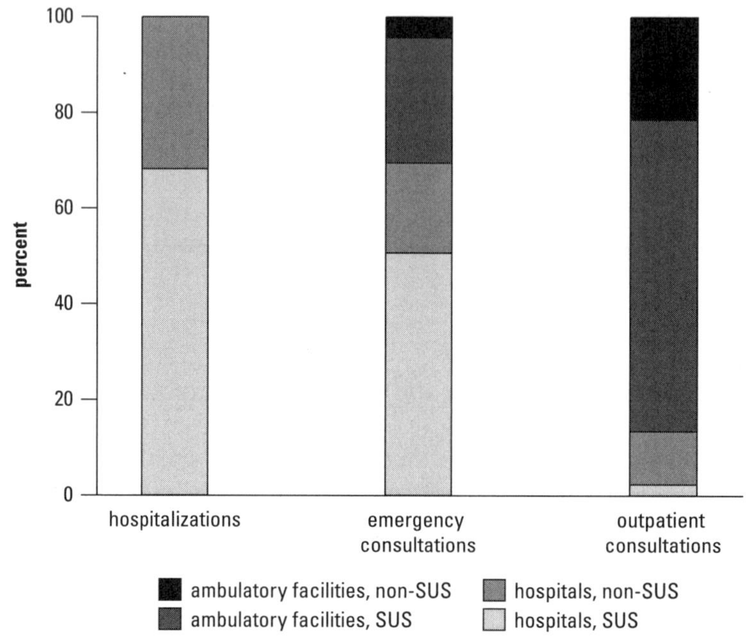

Source: Authors' estimates based on IBGE 2002.

590 million outpatient consultations (3.4 per capita (figure 11.2) were performed. Overall, SUS finances between two thirds and three quarters of ambulatory and hospital services. Hospitals produce a significant part of health services, including 69.5 percent of emergency care, 27.1 percent of outpatient medical consultations, and a significant part of diagnostic services.[2]

Current Status of Private Voluntary Health Insurance

To clarify the context of voluntary health insurance in Brazil, three main groups of people can be identified with respect to their health insurance status:

- people who make the mandatory insurance contribution—through general taxes or social contributions—but seek care outside the public system (SUS), which by law offers all necessary care free of cost. Every citizen is covered , but only 50 to 60 percent of the insured use the SUS as their sole or main source of care. Buying private health insurance does not exempt people from contributing to the public system.
- people who receive insurance from their employer. Around two thirds of the people covered by private insurance receive it through their employer. Whether such insurance is truly voluntary is debatable.

TABLE 11.5 Brazil: Voluntary Health Insurance Coverage, by Income Group, 1998

	Total (%)		*Covered by health plan (%)*		
				Through employment	
Income quintile	*No plan coverage*	*Plan coverage*	*Directly by households*	*Public*	*Private*
1	96.83	3.17	33.22	37.20	29.58
2	92.21	7.79	20.22	36.16	43.62
3	83.54	16.46	22.56	29.24	48.20
4	68.23	31.77	26.38	29.96	43.66
5	37.59	62.41	38.52	26.49	34.98

Source: Viegas 2004; IBGE 2000.

- people who buy insurance themselves. A number of Brazilian households and individuals buy individual or family coverage directly and pay the monthly premiums directly.

In this study, VHI designates private insurance schemes—as opposed to the public universal system—whether acquired through an employer or directly.

VHI in Brazil dates to the 1930s and consists of a variety of organizational and financial arrangements. It covers nearly 25 percent of the population (IBGE 2000, 2004c), mostly employees in the modern sectors of the economy. Overall, over two thirds of private insurance coverage is through employers (private and public), and a third is purchased directly by households. It is also strongly correlated with income (table 11.5). Five main arrangements can be identified (table 11.6):

- Private Group Medicine plans (Medicina de Grupo) are based on the prepayment of a fixed monthly per capita premium and are similar to the health maintenance organizations (HMOs) common in the United States. Most of

TABLE 11.6 Brazil: Private Health Plans, 2003

Classification	*Firms (number)*	*Enrollees (million)*	*Consultations (million per year)*	*Hospitalizations (million per year)*	*Revenue (R$ billlion)*
Group medicine (HMOs)	1,174	16.55	95.50	2.0	10.07
Medical cooperatives	535	11.05	42.00	1.2	8.70
Self-insurance	325	5.35	22.50	0.3	6.94
Indemnity plans	14	4.72	27.60	0.9	6.60
Nonprofit plans	107	1.31	—	—	0.91
Total	2,155	38.99[a]	187.6	6.2	33.22

Sources: ANS 2005a; ABRAMGE 2003.

Note: — = not available; R$ = Brazilian real.

a. Incomplete coverage.

these plan carriers operate a network of preferred providers that are paid according to a negotiated fee schedule. Many plans also have their own services (staff health professionals and/or hospitals).

- Medical cooperatives (Cooperativas Médicas) operate a different type of prepayment plan in which physicians are organized in local or regional cooperatives. But these work more and more like other prepayment plans.
- Health indemnity plans (Seguro saúde), traditionally offered by financial and insurance institutions, are based on the reimbursement of patients' medical and hospital expenses. In recent years they have evolved toward the prepayment model, while the provider choice/reimbursement model is increasingly restricted to high-end plans.
- Many large public and private corporations operate their own plans (self-insurance) to cover their employees (Autogestão or Planos próprios de empresas). Some have their own providers (staff physicians and hospitals), some contract out services with independent private providers; some do both; and some contract out the management of their plan (Unidas 2004).
- A number of nonprofit hospitals offer their own health plans as a fund-raising strategy, but these are minor players in the market.

This historical classification is based on plan ownership and management: for-profit health care corporations (group medicine/HMOs), nonprofit cooperatives, insurance companies, or private/public nonhealth corporations (Médici 1991). In fact, in a trend similar to that observed in the United States, the differences between these arrangements have blurred over time, with the same organization offering different arrangements to different publics. However, the way health plan organizations are structured and contract with providers (on staff or contracted), payment arrangements (prepayment or reimbursement) and the extent of provider choice are more important in characterizing the health plan organizations (box 11.1), but these also have evolved toward mixed or hybrid arrangements (Almeida 1998). The staff model hospitals and preferred provider model are the most common, but these models are increasingly characteristic of a health plan targeted to a particular public, rather than a characteristic of the health plan organization.

Benefits packages used to vary widely depending on the plan type and level. Both packages and provider choice increased with the plan's level and price. This allowed extensive market segmentation and flexibility on the part of health plan organizations, but also led to abuse.

VHI Coverage increased rapidly in the 1980s and early 1990s (from 27 million in 1987 to 36 million in 1995) but has expanded much more slowly in recent years—only 12 percent from 1999 to 2004. This relative stagnation can be attributed to macroeconomic difficulties and a restrictive regulation passed in 1998 (Law 9656, Brasil 1998). Insurance plans and medical cooperatives have been the most dynamic arrangements over the period (1987 to 2003) in terms of revenue

BOX 11.1 BRAZIL: TYPICAL MODELS OF HEALTH PLAN ORGANIZATIONS

Some Brazilian health plan models are similar in many ways to the common U.S. models. The most common are:

- *Staff model/own network.* Physicians are employed by the health plan organization and hospitals are owned by the organization.
- *Exclusive provider model.* The organization selects and contracts with a list of providers-professionals and hospitals, and beneficiaries can seek care only from a listed provider. The health plan pays the provider directly.
- *Preferred provider model.* The organization proposes a list of preferred providers—with which the direct payment arrangement applies—but allows beneficiaries to obtain care with nonlisted providers, in which case the beneficiary must pay the provider and request reimbursement from the organization.
- *Cooperative model.* The Brazilian medical cooperative model has some similarities with the U.S. group model, but in Brazil the physician cooperative is the HMO itself; some of them also employ staff physicians.

Sources: Kongstvedt 1993; ANS 2005a.

(with real increases of 2,412 percent and 390 percent, respectively) and coverage (increases of 786 percent and 142 percent, respectively).

The VHI market in Brazil, though large and diversified, is very fragmented. More than 2,000 organizations cover an average of 18,000 people, resulting in too few insured for effective risk pooling in many plans. Of all plan carriers, 2.8 percent have more than 100,000 enrollees, covering 51.9 percent of the total. At the other end, 73.5 percent of plans, with fewer than 10,000 enrollees, cover only 8.6 percent of enrollees (ANS 2005d). It is very likely that most of the smaller plans will not survive.

Revenue in the VHI sector, after increasing steadily until the mid-1990s, has stagnated or decreased in constant terms since 1999, reflecting economic and regulatory limitations. Total revenue reached a peak in 1999 and since then has been stagnating in real terms at between US$12 billion and US$13 billion (at 2004 exchange rate). Coverage is concentrated in a few states (especially São Paulo, with a 44.7 percent coverage and 44.5 percent of all people covered), larger state capitals (five cities with coverage of around or more than 50 percent), and metropolitan areas in general.

The percentage of individuals covered by a health plan is closely correlated with income (figure 11.3). In the first quintile, 7 percent of the individuals are covered; in the last, 61.7 percent. Coverage also increases with education and varies with employment status. It is highest among the formally employed and lowest among informal workers (figure 11.4).

FIGURE 11.3 Brazil: VHI Coverage, by Income Group

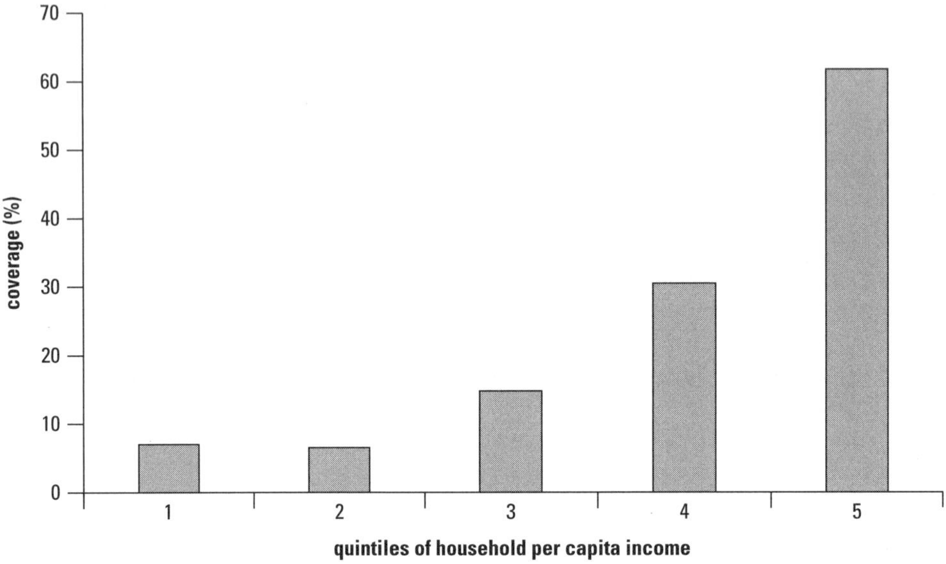

Source: IBGE 2000.

FIGURE 11.4 VHI Coverage, by Employment Status

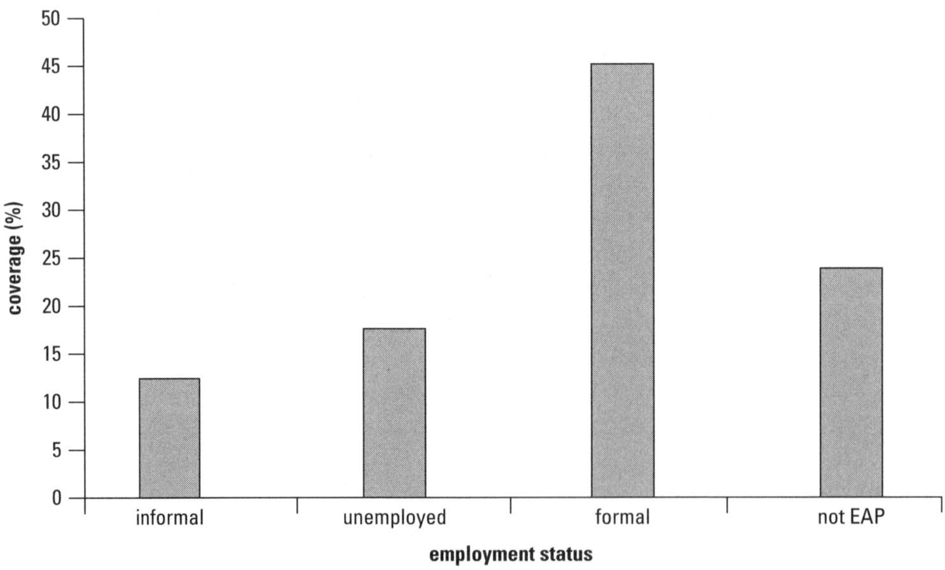

Source: IBGE 2000.
Note: not EAP = not economically active, includes dependents of the formally employed.

In addition to these formal arrangements, an important proportion of health spending is paid out of pocket for the purchase of drugs and other medical goods and, to a lesser extent, payments to health professionals or hospitals. The importance of direct payment for health services decreased consistently in the last 20 years, as the formal insurance schemes—both public and private—expanded to cover nearly all the population (with the exception of dental care and a few other services, which remain mostly financed through out-of-pocket payments). However, household expenditure on health is increasing due to expanding payments for drugs (usually not covered by the SUS or private plans for outpatient care) and, increasingly, the payment of individual or family insurance/health plans.

VHI Regulation

Until the 1998 legislation, every plan carrier could offer a plan covering any package of benefits, from exclusively dental care to full coverage including organ transplants and AIDS. The absence of regulation allowed distortions and abuse. For instance, health plan carriers often denied specific care—especially expensive procedures—and "dumped" expensive cases into the SUS system, on the basis of unclear contract clauses or misinformation of enrollees. Premium increases were arbitrary and sometimes unjustified, because it was easier to pass on cost increases and inefficiency costs to consumers than to improve cost and quality control. High-risk individuals or groups were often denied coverage.

The 1998 legislation was the first comprehensive effort at regulating the private health insurance sector. It attempted to correct market failures such as information asymmetry, risk selection, and abusive benefits exclusions; protect consumers; and ensure financial solvency of organizations offering health plans. An additional feature was to require health plans to reimburse the SUS for care delivered by SUS providers to health plan patients. An independent regulatory body, the National Agency for Private Health ["Supplementary"] Insurance (Agência Nacional de Saúde Suplementar, ANS) was created to take over regulatory and supervisory functions. The new legislation requires all health plans to provide comprehensive benefits packages. Typical new packages are limited to: a reference plan covering all services except dental care (19 percent); a package covering ambulatory care only (4 percent) or hospital care only (1 percent) or both (60 percent); and a dental care–only benefit plan (16 percent). Health plans have had to adapt to the new regulation, in a slow, still ongoing process: in December 2004, 47 percent of enrollees were still covered under "old" plans (ANS 2005c). Implementation and initial regulatory activities in a sector unregulated for 40 years were confronted with strong resistance and challenged by more than 1,800 lawsuits between 2000 and 2002.

KEY ISSUES RELATED TO HEALTH CARE FINANCING

Brazil's total health expenditure amounted to R$140 billions in 2003 (US$47.8 billion at 2004 exchange rate), a 13 percent increase in real terms over 1995. Public sources contributed 43 percent; private sources, 57 percent (figure 11.5). Despite SUS universal coverage and considerable coverage by private insurance schemes, out-of-pocket spending (OOPS) still represents more than a quarter of the total, distributed between the purchase of drugs and other medical goods (57 percent) and direct payments for health services (health professionals, hospitals, diagnostic tests—43 percent). Purchase of health goods has remained stable as a proportion of household expenditure on health, and direct payment for services has seen a consistent reduction along the years, as both the SUS and VHI increased their coverage.

Current Problems in Health Care Financing

The financing flows in the Brazilian health sector, summarized in annex 11A, are complex because of the dual health insurance system (public-private). Several issues threaten its performance, including problems related to sustainability, efficiency, equity, and institutions.

Financing sustainability

The health sector as a whole faces important and increasing difficulties related to the level of financing, inefficient allocation and use of resources, and rising health care costs. Due to the macroeconomic stringencies, public budgets have had trouble keeping up with financial needs, despite important increases in

FIGURE 11.5 Health Expenditure Financing Sources, 2002

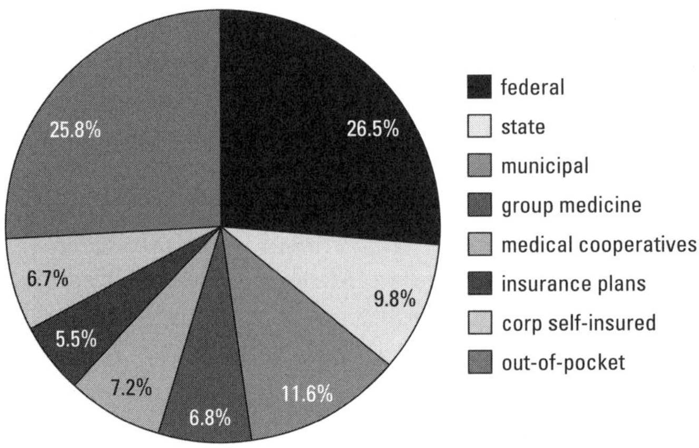

Source: Authors' estimates.

public spending since the inception of the Real plan in 1994. Recent legislation (Constitutional Amendment 29[3]) addressed this issue by requiring that every level of government allocate a minimum proportion of its budget to health (15 percent for municipalities, 12 percent for states), but compliance has been uneven, and many states and municipalities spend much less than specified in the amendment.

Efficiency

Although much of the financing debate has focused on the amount of resources available, allocation and efficiency issues contribute considerably to the problem. Poor cost control associated with inadequate payment mechanisms are the main factors in cost increases, both in the SUS and in the private insurance market. Especially for hospital services, payment mechanisms offer distorted incentives that encourage providers to specialize in high-cost procedures while low- and medium-complexity care is neglected. Resource utilization rates are low, as seen in the mean bed occupancy rate of between 35 and 40 percent. The density of high-complexity services and equipment is irrational from both efficiency and equity aspects: it is very high in large metropolitan areas and several small municipalities. Ensuring access to these services in sparsely populated areas only partially explains this distribution pattern. The lack of integration between the public and private systems results in redundancies and waste.

Equity

The finance burden is distributed unequally among socioeconomic groups. First, an important proportion of public funding comes from indirect taxes and payroll contributions (with the exception of a financial contribution on financial transactions), most of which are regressive. Second, household health expenditure falls disproportionately on the poor; expenditure on drugs, which are insufficiently covered by the SUS and private plans alike, represent as much as 10 percent of poor households' budget and constitute the main equity issue in health financing.

Because medication is the main treatment item neglected by both by the SUS and private insurers, access to drugs has grown into a major concern because of equity issues—the poor have the most difficulty obtaining them—as well as efficiency and quality-of-care issues: many patients do not complete their treatment because they have no money to buy the needed drug. Both SUS authorities and private plans have devised strategies for offering coverage for medication, but still to a very insufficient degree.

An important—and inequitable—government subsidy that has stimulated the growth of private plans has been the possibility for individuals and employers alike to deduct the amount paid for private health insurance (or out-of-pocket payments to providers) from taxable revenue, a practice known in Brazil as *fiscal abdication.* This indirect subsidy represented R$2.4 billion in 2002, or an additional 10 percent of direct federal spending on health (Ministerio da Fazenda/SPE 2003). From an equity perspective, this tax deduction accorded to the 10 percent of Brazilians who pay an income tax implies that this sizeable subsidy is pro-rich.

Institutional

Low managerial qualifications, insufficient cost-control mechanisms, and little analysis of service use data are common characteristics of most private insurers (Malta n.d.). Most private health plans have been established and are run by physicians with little or no managerial training. Most plans use only traditional cost-control mechanisms, such as usage limits and prior authorizations for using certain services. Modern managed care techniques are limited to a few larger plans.

Major Constraints

Macroeconomic instability and stringencies as well as regulatory rigidity constitute significant difficulties in the sustainability and expansion of the VHI sector in Brazil despite its size and importance.

Macroeconomic Conditions

Brazil has experienced significant instability in terms of both health policies and macroeconomic situation and performance. The economy went through several adjustment programs during the 1980s and early 1990s, following divergent and often conflicting orientations, with little success in controlling inflation and stabilizing economic fundamentals. The Real Plan of 1994 brought some stability and reduced inflation to tolerable levels, but at the cost of low economic growth produced by very high interest rates and a large increase in public debt.

Labor Regulation

Labor market legislation, in both the public and private sectors, is complex and rigid, greatly limiting employers' flexibility in labor management, especially in hiring and firing personnel. Additionally, mean wages are low by international standards, and an important proportion of the population live in poverty, while for employers the cost of hiring labor is quite high (due to a number of payroll-based taxes and contributions). These factors are not conducive to labor mobility or employment, and help explain the relative stagnation of employer-based VHI.

Private Insurance Regulation

Private health insurance carriers have traditionally based their growth strategy on covering workers in the urban formal sector of the economy, mostly through an employment benefit. More than 45 percent of the formal labor market is covered, but coverage is much lower among informal workers, the unemployed, and people outside the labor force (12.8 percent, 17.0 percent, and 25.7 percent, respectively). Slow economic growth, falling formal employment, and growing unemployment have limited growth of private insurance by reducing household income and employers' ability to fund it. As a result, coverage has stagnated in the last decade. Throughout most of the 1990s, the sector targeted low-income households for growth, but the restrictive new regulation passed in 1998 aborted this strategy by mandating the comprehensive benefits packages (see above). In the absence of stronger economic growth or more flexible regulation, growth prospects are poor.

To respond to consumers' criticism of the quality of care under VHI, ANS recently issued a policy and methodology for assessing and improving the quality of VHI, using a set of health care quality and financial indicators that VHI carriers will have to meet within a given time frame (ANS 2005c). Despite the need to stimulate quality, this ambitious program has not been well received because of the demanding data requirements and the lack of VHI-carrier participation in its design.

In summary, the main criticism ANS has received is of producing excessive and rigid regulation that most VHI carriers are not capable of meeting and which threatens the sector's growth. Many of the smaller health plan organizations are expected to disappear by shutting down or consolidation. Consolidation is welcome in a sector with too many small insurers but, by forbidding limited benefits packages, the legislation limited the ability of private insurance to diversify its range of services and reduced its growth potential. Overall, the Brazilian regulatory experience shows the difficulty of finding the appropriate balance between consumers rights and market forces.

Public-Private Issues

A major issue in the private insurance sector relates to the constitutional right of every Brazilian to use SUS services for free and the unclear role and relationship between the public and private sectors. This implies the ability for consumers holding private health insurance to use SUS services when they choose to, or when their private plan restricts use of certain services. This has historically led to abuses from private plans, which direct some of their clients to the SUS, especially for expensive procedures. Although current regulation mandates private plans to reimburse the SUS for the cost of treating these patients, this has generated a great deal of debate, and few reimbursements have actually been settled. ANS data up to December 2004 indicate that, out of a total of 574,000 VHI enrollees who have been hospitalized in SUS facilities, 78 percent of the reimbursement claims have been challenged, and only 8 percent have been paid (ANS 2005b).

Finally, an ideological divide has traditionally separated the public SUS system and the private VHI sector. Authorities see the other as an unavoidable but unwelcome player. In this contentious environment, there is little cooperation between public health authorities (including the regulatory agency that is closely associated to the Ministry of Health) and VHI trade associations and managers. Although the importance of this issue is gradually diminishing, it is still very much present.

POLICY OPTIONS

This section analyzes the impact of VHI on three key policy variables: financial protection, access to health care, and labor market productivity. It also examines the determinants of enrolment in VHI.

Methodology for Assessing VHI Impact

The impact of VHI was assessed using the 1998 national household survey (Pesquisa Nacional por Amostragem de Domicílios, PNAD) undertaken by the National Geography and Statistics Institute (Instituto Brasileiro de Geografia e Estatística, IBGE). Similar surveys have been conducted yearly since 1967, with the goal of collecting basic information on demographic characteristics, socioeconomic status, employment and income, based on a large national representative sample. Every few years, the survey includes a supplement on health status and/or health care use. It covers Brazil's five regions except the rural areas in the North region. The sampling, stratified by regions, states, municipalities, and census areas, covers more than 65,000 households with 300,000 persons. Regarding health expenditure, data were collected for the two weeks before the survey and then annualized.

Impact on Financial Protection and Consumption Smoothing

Households that carry health insurance are less likely than those that do not to suffer the financial threat associated with unpredictable and potentially high health expenditures. In that sense, they are protected. Financial protection can be described as follows:

$$\gamma = \frac{\overline{OOPS}}{\sigma_{OOPS}},$$

where γ is the degree of financial protection; and *OOPS* is out-of-pocket spending, including direct payments on medical and other health professional consultations, hospitalizations, home care, diagnostic tests, drugs, dental treatment, glasses, and other goods and services. This approach was preferred to defining financial protection as nonmedical consumption (that is, income *minus* OOPS) because in the latter specification γ can be strongly affected by income.

Through two approaches, γ is estimated. One uses the household as the unit of analysis, in order to take into account possible reallocation of resources among members. The second focuses on the individual as the unit of analysis and uses per capita household expenditure.

Since all Brazilians are covered by the SUS, the "uninsured" category in the present context means those not covered by VHI. Individuals in the sample enrolled in a VHI plan include those covered by a private plan and employees in a public institution or enterprise running a self-insured plan; in some analyses this distinction is made.

Impact on Access to Health Care

To analyze how VHI membership may influence access to care, a selection bias problem has to be taken into account, namely that individuals spending on health care must have chosen to seek care. A Heckman model was used, similar to the two-part model proposed by Duan and others (1983) and Manning and others (1987). In the first step of the Heckman procedure, the probability of seeking care in the last two weeks before the survey was estimated using a Probit model, as follows:

$$
\begin{aligned}
Prob(visit_i{*}) &= \gamma w_i + u_{i.} \\
visit_i &= 1 \quad \text{if} \quad visit_i{*} > 0 \\
visit_i &= 0 \quad \text{if} \quad visit_i{*} \leqslant 0.
\end{aligned}
$$

In the second step of the Heckman procedure, an OLS regression analysis was performed to estimate household expenditure, with the estimated probability of seeking care (resulting from the first step estimation) and other factors as independent variables:

$$OOPS_i = \beta x_i + \varepsilon_i.$$

The independent variables used in this and the following models include:

- *Socioeconomic variables*. Gender (male or female); age (only individuals 21 years of age or older were included in the analysis); education (individual years of study); family per capita income; employment status (formal, informal, and unemployed); race (categorized in the traditional Brazilian way as white, black, mixed, Asian, and indigenous).
- *Regional dummies*: include region (South, Southeast, Central-west, Northeast, and North)[4] and sector (urban and rural).
- *Health status*. Measured by three alternative variables: subjective (assessed by respondents and then grouped as good/very good and fair/bad/very bad); the presence of chronic diseases[5]; and mobility (defined as the individual's ability to perform different daily activities and movements).

Impact on Labor Market Productivity

To assess the impact of VHI on labor productivity, the following were tested: the hypothesis that a person with voluntary health insurance will look for health care earlier than the uninsured, before a disease becomes acute, and will consequently lose fewer days of work. Due to the count characteristic of the dependent variable, the analysis was done using the Poisson regression model. The formulation can be described as follows:

$$\Pr ob(Y_i = y_i) = \frac{e^{-\lambda_i}\lambda_i^{y_i}}{y_i!} \quad y_i = 0, 1, 2, \ldots \text{ and } \ln \lambda_i = \beta x_i,$$

where y is the number of days lost (from normal activities) due to illness,[6] λ is the parameter of the Poisson distribution, and x_i is the independent variable. This formulation can be easily estimated using maximum likelihood approach with the model:

$$\ln E\text{ [days lost]} = \beta x_{i.}$$

Determinants of Enrolment

The factors determining the individual enrolment in a health plan were identified by applying a Probit regression model with VHI membership as a binary dependent variable and individual and household characteristics such as income, age, gender, and race, as the independent variables. The model can be analytically described as:

$$\Pr(enrollment > 0) = \beta x_i,$$

where enrolment is 0 for those without a health plan and 1 for those enrolled in a voluntary health plan. The variable x_i stands for a set of independent variables that affect enrolment.

Feasibility Study

The feasibility study used existing data from several sources to simulate different scenarios for 2005 to 2015, where macroeconomic performance and changes in sector policies and the regulatory framework are the major influence over VHI evolution, financial sustainability, impact on financial protection, access to care, and the labor market. Three main scenarios were defined according to the behavior of these major determinants in relation to the base-line period 1995–2003:

- *Base case.* Most of the variables continue to follow the trend observed in 1995–2003, except when this trend would be unlikely to continue.
- *Best case.* Macroeconomic performance will improve, and the VHI regulatory framework will evolve in a more favorable direction.
- *Worst case.* Macroeconomic performance is expected to deteriorate and the regulatory framework to remain restrictive.

A few variables are assumed as given or as evolving in a given pattern and thus do not affect the different scenarios. This is the case for population growth and its composition, general inflation rate (all financial values are calculated in constant 2004 reais), and health service utilization rates.

FIGURE 11.6 Brazil: Main Determinants of VHI Enrolment and Health Spending

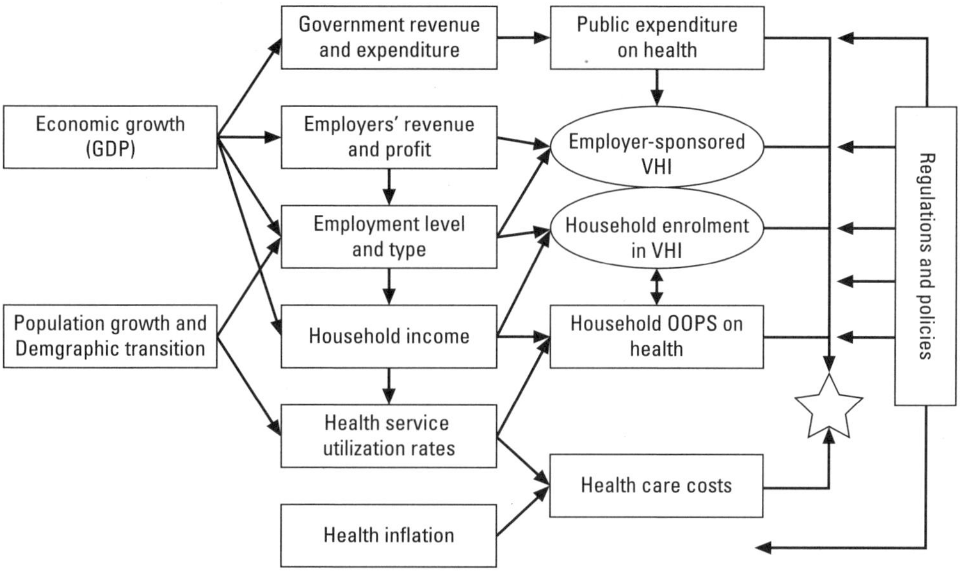

Source: Authors.

Because the SUS is funded through a variety of general taxes and specific contributions whose mix varies year by year, it is not possible to assume a given contribution rate, as other models have done. The same is true for private VHI, whose diversified financial and organizational arrangements cannot be summarized in one single proportional contribution. The mean premium (or expenditure) by enrollee is used as a proxy.

The variables assumed in this simulation to affect VHI enrolment and financial stability are summarized in figure 11.6. GDP is the main driver, affecting government revenue and spending, employers' revenue, employment and household income. Population growth and the demographic transition under way—assumed as given—influence both health needs and the labor force. VHI enrolment depends on employment—and especially formal employment—employers' capacity and willingness to spend on their workers' health (for simplicity, assumed to be mostly driven by GDP) and household income. Public policies can affect VHI in a number of ways: indirectly by stimulating economic growth, defining direct government health expenditure—whose level can encourage or crowd out VHI—or directly subsidizing or stimulating VHI.

Main Findings from the Impact Study

The results from estimating the impact on financial protection, access and labor productivity are presented in turn.

TABLE 11.7 Brazil: Financial Protection—Results for Household OOPS

Sample, households	*Observations*	*Mean of OOPS (household)*	*Standard deviation*	*Financial protection*
All observations	98,618	44.98	156.81	0.2868
Household with no coverage (0%)	66,873	27.11	81.13	0.3341
Household with coverage (1% to 50%)	7,320	65.68	145.80	0.4505
Household with coverage (>50% to 75%)	3,597	83.46	167.54	0.4981
Household with coverage (>75% to 99%)	1,124	96.35	160.69	0.5996
Household with total coverage (100%)	19,704	87.97	287.65	0.3058

Source: Calculated by the authors based on IBGE 2000.

Impact on Financial Protection

At the household level, financial protection was found to be positively related to the proportion of household members covered by VHI (table 11.7). In other words, financial protection increases with the degree of household coverage. The exception is for fully covered households, which have lower mean OOPS but higher variance.

The analysis at the individual level yields similar but weaker results: VHI insured have a higher level of financial protection than those not enrolled in a health plan. However, those holding a public employer health plan (that is, public servants covered by VHI) achieve a higher degree of financial protection than those with a "private" health plan (table 11.8). This is likely to be due to the generally more generous coverage offered by insurance plans held through public employers. The data used here are from 1998, before the regulation enforcing a minimal set of services and procedures to be covered was in place, and many private health plans used to offer limited coverage, excluding many procedures and diseases.

When the analysis is broken down by income quintile (to control for income effects), financial protection provided by VHI membership appears to be higher among the lowest income groups (table 11.9). However, the results do not hold for the third and fifth quintiles.

TABLE 11.8 Brazil: Financial Protection—Results for Individual OOPS

Sample, individuals	*Observations*	*Mean of individual OOPS*	*Standard deviation*	*Financial protection*
All observations	344,975	12.86	80.87	0.1590
No health insurance	260,556	8.12	43.84	0.1852
Health insurance	84,419	27.47	143.21	0.1918
Private health insurance	60,195	28.59	158.04	0.1809
Government health insurance	24,224	24.69	96.91	0.2548

Source: Calculated by authors based on IBGE 2000.

TABLE 11.9 Brazil: Financial Protection—Results by Income Quintile

Quintile	*Income range*[a]	*Sample, individuals*	*Observations*	*Mean of individual OOPS*	*Standard deviation*	*Financial protection*
0–20%	<46.7	All observations	55,962	2.13	6.50	0.3272
		No health insurance	54,386	2.04	6.15	0.3314
		Health insurance	1,576	5.21	13.65	0.3815
20–40%	46.7 to 91.7	All observations	68,457	4.73	14.04	0.3366
		No health insurance	63,114	4.49	13.45	0.3336
		Health insurance	5,343	7.53	19.46	0.3869
40–60%	91.7 to 157.5	All observations	69,354	8.74	23.27	0.3757
		No health insurance	58,062	8.36	21.37	0.3910
		Health insurance	11,292	10.75	31.22	0.3443
60–80%	157.5 to 312.5	All observations	68,904	13.45	28.04	0.4796
		No health insurance	47,011	12.62	26.97	0.4680
		Health insurance	21,893	15.22	30.12	0.5052
80–100%	>312.5	All observations	68,927	34.42	113.22	0.3040
		No health insurance	26,234	26.84	61.27	0.4380
		Health insurance	42,693	39.08	135.40	0.2886

Source: Calculated by the authors based on IBGE 2000.

a. Monthly per capita income in reais.

Impact on Access

The regression results of the Heckman procedure are presented in annex B (columns 2 and 3). All coefficients are statistically significant at the 5 percent level and with the expected sign. Being enrolled in a health plan increases significantly both the probability of seeking care and OOPS, even after controlling for income. Age and years of study also increase medical expenditure but have little effect on the probability of seeking care. Higher income increases both the probability of seeking care and the amount of health expenditure. OOPS is higher among women than men. Informal job holders and the unemployed have larger OOPS than the formally employed. As expected, healthy individuals spend much less than the unhealthy.

Impact on Labor Productivity

Analyzing specifically those individuals in the labor market with a Poisson regression (annex B, column 4), the coefficients have the expected sign but some are not statistically significant. The effect of VHI membership is positive, indicating that insured workers spend more days away from work and their daily activities, but this result is not statistically significant. This result does not corroborate the initial hypothesis that having health insurance reduces absenteeism. Men and older individuals lose more days of activity from disease. The years of study and income have no significant effect. Formally employed individuals lose more days than the informally employed. This probably occurs due to the law protecting the formally employed. Good health status reduces the number of days lost.

Enrolment Factors

The factors determining enrolment in a VHI plan are presented in the last column of annex B. Most coefficients have the expected sign and are significant at the 1 percent level. Women have a 5.5 percent higher probability of joining a health plan than men. Age, years of study, and per capita income all increase the probability of enrolment. Informal employment, economic inactivity, and unemployment decrease the probability by 18.3 percent, 10.1 percent, and 14.8 percent, respectively. This great reduction is probably due to the benefits that formal workers receive, which often include a private health plan. The regional dummies confirm that the great majority of health plans enrollees are in the Southeast. One interesting result is that healthy people have a higher probability of having a health plan than the unhealthy, which may be an indication that private insurers practice cream skimming by targeting low-risk population groups.

Main Findings from the Feasibility Study

This section presents the findings of the feasibility study, which looked at the prospects of VHI for the years to come, with a focus on the potential for expansion and on the sector's sustainability. Three scenarios are considered—base case, best case, and worst case, as indicated in the methodological section—based on factors relating to demographics, the labor market, macroeconomic variables, and VHI regulation.

Demographic and Labor Market Context—Base Case

The Brazilian population grew at an average, but declining, rate of 1.58 percent a year in the base period (1995–2003), and was projected to slow down to 1.5 percent in 2004–2015 (table 11.10). The demographic transition has gradually altered the demographic profile. As the transition continues, although the young population (under 15) is expected to grow little, the elderly population (65 and over) is expected to grow more than 4 percent a year. As a result of the increase in labor-age population and women's increasing labor participation, the economically active population will grow at nearly twice (2.70 percent) the rate of the general population. But employment has been growing much more slowly, at a rate close to the GDP, and is expected to continue to grow at that pace (2.15 percent) under the base-case scenario, without any new employment policy. As a result of poor economic performance, unemployment doubled between 1995 and 2003, but has eased off since. In the base-case scenario, it is assumed to stay at the current level of 11.5 percent in the projection period.

TABLE 11.10 Brazil: Demographic and Labor Trends, Base Case

Item	*1995*	*2003*	*2015*	*Growth 1995–03*	*Projected growth*
Population[a]	158,875	178,985	208,468	1.58	1.35
Population age 10–64	116,966	134,190	157,043	1.84	1.41
Population age 0–14	52,081	51,044	53,566	– 0.26	0.47
Population age >65	7,830	10,461	15,730	4.14	4.02
Economically active population[b]	70,539	87,788	120,859	3.26	2.70
Employment[b]	69,439	79,251	98,170	2.10	2.15
Formal workers[c]	33,749	35,092	40,630	1.01	1.23
Formal employment[c] (%)	48.47	44.28	39.72	– 0.92	– 0.85
Unemployment (%)	6.10	12.32	11.35	11.64	0

Sources: a. IBGE 2004b; b. IMF 2005; c. IBGE 2004c. Projections to 2015 by the authors.

The different proxies used in Brazil for formal and informal employment[7] indicate the same order of magnitude for informal employment. The proportion of workers with a legal employment document (a work book) in metropolitan areas, a better indicator of recent trend in the labor market, has decreased from 48.5 percent to 44.3 percent, but appears to have stabilized since 2000. Its continued decrease is assumed, in the absence of stronger economic growth or specific employment policy, throughout the projected period under the base-case scenario.

Macroeconomic Factors—Base Case

GDP growth, around 2.15 percent a year in the baseline period, is expected to continue in the projected period under the base-case scenario (table 11.11).

TABLE 11.11 Brazil: Macroeconomic Trends—Base Case

Item	*1995*	*2003*	*2015*	*Growth 1995–2003 (%)*	*Projected growth (%)*
GDP (current R$)[a]	646,192	1,556,182	—	15.95	—
GDP (2004 R$)[b]	1,452,195	1,683,518	2,232,366	2.13	2.15
GDP (2004 US$)[c]	496,307	575,365	762,941	2.02	2.15
Household consumption/GDP[a]	59.88	56,74	57.0	–0.87	0.12
Household consumption (2004 R$)[c]	869,507	955,233	1,272,449	1.06	2.60
Price index (IGP-DI)[e]	117.492	285.074	690.99	16.19	6,75
Exchange Rate (R$/US$)[f]	0,918	3.078	4.750	31.96	4.50
Government consumption (% GDP)[d]	19.60	19.90	19.20	—	—
Public primary expenditure[g]	514,291	606,067	821,131	3.11	2.35
Primary expenditure as % of GDP[g]	35.41	36.00	36.78	—	—

Sources: a. IBGE 2005; World Bank 2005; b. IPEA/IPEADATA; c. Calculated by the authors; d. World Bank 2005; e. FGV 2005; f. Banco Central do Brasil 2005; g. IBGE 2005.

Note: Projections to 2015 by the authors. — = not available or not calculated.

While GNI per capita in current terms reached US$2,710, measured in PPP, it was US$7,480, nearly three times higher. As a proportion of GDP, household consumption has been stable around 61 percent for most of the 1990s, dropping to 56.7 percent in 2003, and 55.2 percent in 2004. It is assumed to stabilize at 57 percent in the projected period. The price index (as measured by the IGP-DI index) is assumed to stay at the target inflation level of recent years, 6.75 percent. Exchange rate to the dollar, strongly affected by the 1998–99 devaluation, has stabilized in the last three years at around 3.0 and is assumed to increase at a moderate pace of 4.5 percent a year. Government consumption remained nearly constant between 19 and 20 percent during the base period, as a proportion of GDP, and is assumed to remain at a similar level in the future. Public expenditure—in the primary expenditure (that is, nonfinancial) concept[8]—kept at an average 35.8 percent of GDP over the baseline period and is assumed to increase slightly to 36.8 percent in 2015.

Health Expenditure—Base Case

Public expenditure on health[9] increased 1.55 percent a year in real terms between 1995 and 2003 (table 11.12). That was significantly lower than the growth of public expenditure as a whole and GDP, and its proportion in both respects dropped. In the base-case scenario, it was assumed that the states would maintain their rate of growth, municipalities would reduce theirs, which had been

TABLE 11.12 Brazil: Health Expenditure Trends—Base Case

Expenditure	*1995*	*2003*	*2015*	*Growth 1995–2003 (%)*	*Projected growth (%)*
Federal health expenditure (R$)	35,138	32,116	37,209	0.26	0.40
States health expenditure (R$)	11,296	13,374	17,361	2.32	2.35
Municipal health expenditure (R$)	10,040	15,555	24,078	5.20	4.00
Public health expenditure (R$)	56,474	61,045	78.648	1.55	1.96
Percentage of public expenditure	10.98	10.07	9.58	—	—
Percentage of GDP	3.89	3.63	3.52	—	—
Private health expenditure (R$)	67,312	78,830	101.993	2.07	2.13
Percentage of GDP	4.64	4.68	4.57	—	—
Household health expenditure (R$)	53,909	66,657	83,246	1.43	2.86
Percentage of household consumption	6.20	6.35	6.54	0.32	0.32
Total health expenditure (R$)	123,785	139,874	180,641	1.83	2.12
Percentage of GDP	8.52	8.31	8.09	—	—
Percentage of private health spending	54.38	56.36	56.46	—	—
Percentage of public health spending	45.62	43.64	43.54	—	—

Sources: Ministry of Health (SIOPS); IBGE 2000.

Note: — = not available or not calculated.

quite high in the base period, and the federal government would increase its rate to 0.4 percent. As a result, public expenditure on health would accelerate to 1.96 percent, still lower than the GDP rate.

Private expenditure accounts for between 55 and 56 percent of the Brazil's health expenditure and 4.6 percent of GDP. But its two main components grew at quite different paces in 1995–2003. Household expenditure, which accounts for the larger part, grew at only 1.4 percent during the base period because of the fall in the participation of household consumption in GDP. Given the assumption that its share would stabilize at 57 percent of GDP from 2005 on and the trend for the share of health expenditure would continue to increase at a 0.3 percent a year, household health expenditure is expected to increase significantly in the medium term, at more than 3 percent a year.

Total health expenditure in the country, after growing at 1.83 percent a year in 1995–2003, is expected to accelerate to a rate similar to GDP. Over the full period, it would oscillate between 8 and 8.5 percent of GDP.

Voluntary Health Insurance—Base Case

After a rapid expansion (more than 4 percent a year) in the 1980s and early 1990s, the growth of voluntary private health insurance enrolment slowed to 1.5 percent a year after 1998, reaching nearly a quarter of the population (table 11.13). Employer-based VHI—nearly 60 percent of the total—has grown little in the last decade, while VHI purchased by households grew somewhat faster, especially before 1998. The former is assumed to grow at a rate equal to formal employment in the base-case scenario (1.23 percent), while household enrolment is assumed to grow proportionally to household health expenditure (2.4 percent). The resulting total expected rate is 1.89 percent.

Because people purchasing insurance directly are higher users of health services and pay higher premiums, they represent a larger proportion of revenue (more than 50 percent) than of enrolment. Health insurance expenditures represented

TABLE 11.13 Brazil: VHI Trends—Base Case

VHI	*1995*	*2003*	*2015*	*Growth 1995–2003*	*Projected growth*
VHI coverage, total (1,000)	36,156	43,203	53,059	2.10	1.89
Percentage of population	22.75	24.55	25.45	—	—
Mean revenue/person/year (R$)	741.48	841.27	962.63	2.17	0.75
VHI revenue, total (R$)	26,586	36,049	51,269	4.77	2.95
VHI revenue, corporate, (R$)	13,550	18,373	24,342	4.77	2.20
VHI revenue, household, (R$)	13,036	17,675	26,927	4.77	3.73
VHI revenue as percentage of private expenditure	41.94	44.98	42.32	—	—

Sources: ANS 2005a; ABRAMGE 2000.

TABLE 11.14 Brazil: Total Health Care Costs—Base Case

Item	*2003–04 (R$)*	*2015 (R$)*	*Projected growth (%)*
Ambulatory care, SUS	6,942	8,063	—
Inpatient care, SUS	22,009	25,789	—
Total SUS[a]	57,794	73,366	2.45
Ambulatory care, VHI	4,712	5,865	—
Inpatient care, VHI	12,869	16,157	—
Total VHI[a]	33,335	45,330	3.26
Services, OOPS	13,389	14,896	1.48
Drugs, etc., OOPS	25,278	40,804	5.40
Total OOPS[a]	13,389	55,700	—
Grand total[a]	129,796	174,396	3.13

Sources: Couttolenc et al. 2005; Ministry of Health 2005.

a. Includes diagnostic and other health services, as well as a share for administration and an adjustment for health real inflation, assumed at 0.75 percent a year.

between 40 and 45 percent of private health expenditure in the baseline period and are expected to stay within that range.

Health Care Utilization and Costs—Base Case

Health care utilization rates by age group and gender are assumed to remain constant at the 2003 level throughout the projected period. The two factors determining utilization trend are population growth and the demographic transition. Health care costs are thus the result of changing utilization patterns, due to demographic transition, and real inflation in the health sector, which is assumed in the base-case scenario to remain at the recent level of 0.75 percent a year. The resulting total costs are predicted to increase 34 percent in 2004–15 (table 11.14). OOPS on drugs and VHI premiums are expected to show the biggest increases; OOPS on services, the least.

Best- and Worst-Case Scenarios

The best-case scenario assumes GDP will grow 4.5 percent a year, a feasible rate, given Brazil's performance in good years (table 11.15). Discounting productivity gains, total employment will grow 4.05 percent, and formal employment will increase as a share of total employment, growing 5.06 percent. As a result of this favorable macroeconomic condition, VHI enrolment, which depends in part on formal employment, is expected to increase at this same rate, reaching 78 million people in 2015. Expenditure on VHI will expand even faster due to health real inflation. Public health expenditure will also grow fast, though at a lower rate, due to economic expansion and the possibility of increased government spending. Household OOPS is likely to decrease as a consequence of expanding public and VHI funding.

In the worst-case scenario, shown in table 11.15, GDP, the main driver in the simulation, is assumed to grow only 1.5 percent a year. This will make

TABLE 11.15 Brazil: Best- and Worst-Case Scenarios

	Best-case scenario		*Worst-case scenario*	
Item	*Growth (%)*	*2015 (R$)*	*Growth (%)*	*2015 (R$)*
GDP	4.50	2,855,047	1.50	2,012,845
Employment	4.05	127,617	1.35	93,087
Formal employment	5.06	63,472	0.68	38,043
VHI enrolment	5.06	78,142	0.88	47,978
Public health expenditure	3.50	94,490	1.50	76,211
VHI expenditure	5.81	72,013	1.63	46,199
OOPS	−1.00	39,956	2.00	55,488
Total health expenditure	3.58	206,459	1.84	177,898

Sources: Calculated by authors.

government revenue and spending, private consumption and employment, and consequently VHI enrolment, grow quite slowly. The only component to grow relatively faster is household OOPS, to compensate for the stagnation of government and employer health spending.

The exercise highlights that a major source of financial risk and inequity is medication consumption, but this has hardly been covered by either SUS or VHI schemes. Households pay for drugs mostly out of pocket, and this spending constitutes a great part of OOPS, nearly 9 percent of poor households' budget. Both SUS and VHI plans have begun to address the issue by covering some essential drugs. In the best-case scenario, the issue could be greatly reduced by using part of the additional funding available to increase drug coverage. In the worst-case scenario, it would become much more severe and likely account for an increased proportion of total health expenditure.

CONCLUSIONS

Brazil is a special case among developing countries, because it has simultaneously one of the largest social security systems and the second largest private insurance market in the world. The size and long history of the private market provide useful experience to draw from for developing countries looking to introduce or expand voluntary health insurance.

However, the results of the impact assessment of VHI in Brazil are less clear-cut than might be expected. Households and individuals enrolled in VHI are shown to have some limited protection against the costs of disease for several reasons. First, the fact that every Brazilian is entitled to free care through the public social security system (SUS) implies that most Brazilians have a significant protection irrespective of VHI. Second, medications, eye glasses, and other medical goods are insufficiently covered, which keeps out-of-pocket expenditure an important item in household budgets. Third, health insurance plans up to the time of the PNAD survey (1998) and before enforcement of the 1998 regulation, varied greatly in coverage and quality, leaving many enrollees with limited actual financial protection. This has changed since the new regulation; a new household survey, undertaken in 2003 but not yet available at the time of this study, could indicate the effect of the regulatory changes introduced by the new legislation. Finally, the traditional focus of VHI on workers employed in the urban formal sector of the economy, which tend to present lower risk of disease than the general population, may reduce the potential protective impact of VHI.

The study showed that individuals covered by private insurance do consume more health goods and services, but this can be interpreted either as improved access to health care as a result of VHI or as an indication of moral hazard. The impact of VHI on labor market participation and productivity was not significant. This could be explained by the fact that workers covered by a health insurance plan, because they are in the formal sector, have more legal protection in the case of disease, in contrast with informal workers who cannot afford to interrupt their work and other daily activities.

The simulation exercise confirmed that two main issues have hampered growth and financial sustainability of VHI in Brazil. First, economic growth, coupled with the absence of employment-stimulating policies, has been insufficient to expand employment enough, especially in the formal sector, to stimulate health insurance. Second, the 1998 regulation, though necessary to introduce some discipline into the sector and protect consumers, has been too restrictive and has limited the sector's growth opportunities. Addressing these two issues through general economic and employment policies and easing up and better focusing existing regulation will be needed for the VHI sector to grow to its full potential and ensure its financial stability.

Future research should focus on three main areas: (1) explore analytically the large amount of data on VHI accumulated by the regulatory agency since its inception, in order to better characterize the VHI-covered population and its health care use behavior; (2) analyze VHI carriers' managerial and organizational practices in order to better characterize their strengths and weaknesses, and areas needing improvement; (3) assess systematically the successes and limitations of Brazil's recent, ambitious VHI regulation, so as to better focus this regulation and correct its distortions.

ANNEX 11A FINANCIAL FLOWS IN THE BRAZILIAN HEALTH SECTOR

FIGURE 11A.1 Financial Flows in the Brazilian Health Sector

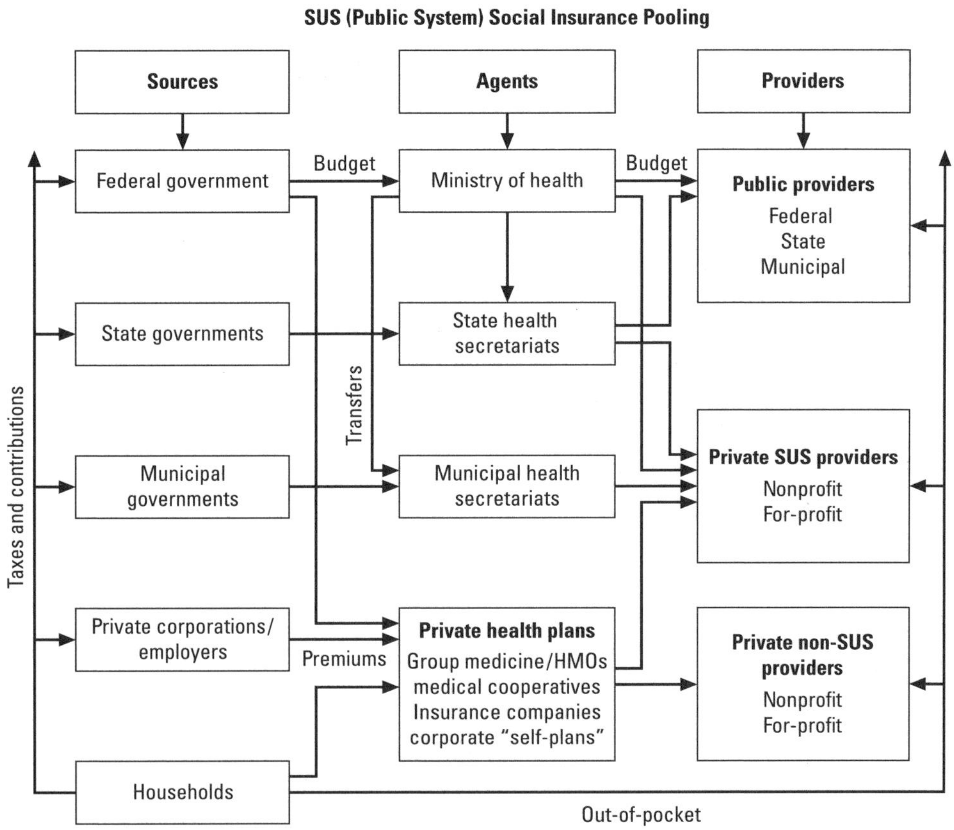

Source: Authors.

ANNEX 11B REGRESSION RESULTS

TABLE 11B.1 Regression Results for Access, Labor Productivity, and Enrolment

Dependent variable / Independent variable	*Access*		*Labor productivity*	*Enrolment*
	Prob. seek care (Step I)	*OOPS (Step II)*	*Days inactivity*	*With health plan*
	Heckman		*Poisson*	*Probit*
Enrolled in health plan[D]	0.328646*	250.3421*	0.043	—
	(47.24)	(4.37)	(1.50)	—
Male[D]	−0.2158364*	−133.7778*	0.094*	−0.055*
	(−37.02)	(−3.52)	(4.79)	(−22.69)
Age	−0.0002854**	1.182338**	0.006*	0.004*
	(−1.81)	(7.06)	(9.15)	(44.55)
Years of study	−0.0009898	2.679951*	0.001	0.031*
	(−1.21)	(3.15)	(0.36)	(82.47)
Per capita HH income	0.0000788*	0.1155516*	−0.0000127	0.0002*
	(14.63)	(7.94)	(−0.40)	(27.7)
Informal employment/formal[D]	−0.0574126*	−55.28007*	—	−0.183*
	(−6.16)	(−3.94)	—	(−67.16)
Not econ active/formal[D]	0.0694613*	49.93843*	—	−0.101*
	(7.92)	(3.37)	—	(−33.33)
Unemployed/formal[D]	0.0039299	−19.06774	—	−0.148*
	(0.26)	(−1.22)	—	(−34.61)
Formal employment[D]	—	−40.65194***	0.102[a]	—
	—	(−2.19)	(4.27)	—
North/southeast[D]	−0.0566525*	−39.5983*	0.003	−0.1*
	(−3.73)	(−4.04)	(0.07)	(−18.49)
Northeast/southeast[D]	−0.0367166*	37.05123*	0.012	−0.083*
	(−5.12)	(3.02)	(0.47)	(−30.95)
South/southeast[D]	0.0512277*	25.07192***	−0.056**	−0.047*
	(6.22)	(2.23)	(−1.93)	(−15.59)
Centralwest/southeast[D]	0.0295002*	98.46738*	−0.005	−0.056*
	(3.04)	(3.99)	(−0.18)	(−15.81)
Urban[D]	0.1312115*	−522.5615*	−0.016	0.116*
	(15.96)	(−4.45)	(−0.68)	(32.69)
Good health status[D]	−0.6811331*	−44.78447*	−0.102*	0.009*
	(−98.24)	(−3.1)	(−4.50)	(3.19)
Black/white[D]	−0.0381901*	−121.3607***	0.065	−0.056*
	(−3.05)	(−2.35)	(1.55)	(−12.23)
Yellow/white[D]	−0.132448*	−40.08981*	−0.022	0.061*
	(−2.95)	(−4.04)	(−0.12)	(3.6)

TABLE 11B.1 (*continued*)

	Access		*Labor productivity*	*Enrolment*
Dependent variable / *Independent variable*	*Prob. seek care (Step I)*	*OOPS (Step II)*	*Days inactivity*	*With health plan*
	Heckman		*Poisson*	*Probit*
Mestiço/white^D	−0.0421938*	127.1727***	0.011	−0.046*
	(−6.53)	(2.00)	(0.50)	(−17.54)
Indigenous/white^D	0.1955634*	−1,263.447*	0.171	−0.016
	(3.65)	(−4.38)	(1.31)	(−0.64)
Constant	−0.7372024*	250.3421*	1.345*	—
	(−47.31)	(4.37)	(28.84)	—
Number of obs		343,456	8671	195,824
Wald chi^2 or F		18,018.04	208.89	32,756.5
Prob > chi^2 or Prob > F		0.000	0	0
Pseudo R^2 or R-squared				0.2778
rho		1		
sigma		1,869.241		
lambda		1,869.241*		
Deviance Goodness-of-fit chi^2			12,600,000	
Prob > chi^2(8654)			0	
Pearson Goodness-of-fit chi^2			13,700,000	
Prob > chi^2(8654)			0	

Source: Authors.

Note: Standard errors are shown in parenthesis. D = dummy variable.

Significant at *1 percent level; **10 percent level; ***5 percent level.

NOTES

This study was funded by the World Bank as part of the project Voluntary Health Insurance in Development: Review of Role in the Africa Region and Other Selected Developing Countries' Experience.

1. Including medical consultations and other procedures.
2. There are no readily available consolidated figures on the volume of such services rendered in a hospital setting, although the information exists for individual hospitals.
3. The amendment was adopted gradually starting in 2000 and as of 2008 is still subject to confirmation and further regulation in congress.
4. Except the rural areas of the latter.
5. Including: back pain, arthritis or rheumatism, cancer, diabetes, bronchitis or asthma, hypertension, heart disease, renal disease, depression, tuberculosis, tendonitis , and cirrhosis.
6. The PNAD dataset recorded only the number of days in which the individual had to interrupt her/his normal activities, without distinguishing work from other daily activities.

7. Several operational definitions of formal/informal employment have been used in Brazil, some of which attempt to apply international methodological standards such as ILO's: employees with a mandated work book, workers effectively contributing to social security, and a combination of these two criteria (this approach has been used in this chapter). All three give a similar order of magnitude, between 45 and 50 percent. A different approach, based on the concept of informal sector (mostly urban enterprises with fewer than five employees) produces a much lower estimate, in the order of 27 percent.
8. Primary expenditure is defined as government final consumption plus transfers, subsidies, and gross capital formation; it excludes any debt-related payment.
9. Defined according to the concept of public expenditure on health services, it excludes spending on pensions and retirement of public servants, debt-related spending, and health care for public servants but includes an additional estimate for federal university hospitals.

REFERENCES

ABRAMGE (Associação Brasileira de Medicina de Grupo). 2003. "Dados e Números da Medicina de Grupo," Informe de Imprensa. São Paulo.

———. 2000. "Dados e Números da Medicina de Grupo." Informe de Imprensa, São Paulo.

Almeida, C. 1998. "O mercado privado de serviços de saúde no Brasil: panorama atual e tendências da assistência médica suplementar." Texto para Discussão no. 599. Instituto de Pesquisa Econômica Aplicada, Brasilia, November.

ANS (Agência Nacional de Saúde Suplementar). 2005a. "Caderno de Informações em Saúde Suplementar-Beneficiários, Operadoras e Planos: Dados do Setor," ANS, Rio de Janeiro.

———. 2005b. "Caderno de Informações ao Gestor, Fevereiro 2005," ANS, Rio de Janeiro.

———. 2005c. "Programa de Qualificação da Saúde Suplementar, Abril 2005," ANS, Rio de Janeiro.

———. 2005d. "Caderno de Informações em Saúde Suplementar-Beneficiários, Operadoras e Planos: Dados do Setor," Junho 2005, ANS, Rio de Janeiro.

———. 2001–04. Boletim Estatístico 2001 a 2004, ANS, Rio de Janeiro.

Banco Central do Brasil. 2005. Série de taxas de câmbio, in IPEA/IPEADATA, www.ipeadata.gov.br.

Brazil. 1998. Lei 9.656. Presidência da República, Brasilia, June 3, 1998.

Cohen, M.M. 2003. "Análise do Modelo de Fiscalização: a efetividade do atual padrão sancionador da ANS sobre a situação das operadoras." http://www.ans.gov.br/portal/upload/forum_saude/objeto_regulacao/AA1.pdf#page=40.

Couttolenc, B.F., A.C. Nicolella, C.A. Machado, P.A. Zapparoli, and L.H.C.S. Dias. 2005. "Estudo sobre Gasto Hospitalar no Brasil." Consultant report, Interhealth Ltda, São Paulo, February.

Duan, N., W.G. Manning, C. Morris, and J.P. Newhouse. 1983 "A Comparison of Alternative Models of the Demand for Medical Care." *Journal of Business and Economic Statistics* 1 (2): 115–26.

FGV (Fundação Getúlio Vargas). 2005. "Índices de preços ao consumidor—IGP." IPEA/IPEADATA. www.ipeadata.gov.br.

Kongstvedt, P.R. 1993. *The Managed Health Care Handbook*. 2d ed. Gaithesburg, MD: Aspen Publishers.

IBGE (Instituto Brasileiro de Geografia e Estatística). 2005. "Sistema de Contas Nacionais." Série SCN_PIBN. In IPEA/IPEADATA (www.ipeadata.gov.br).

———. 2004a *Pesquisa de Orçamentos Familiares 2002–03*. Rio de Janeiro: IBGE.

———. 2004b. "Projeção da População do Brasil por Sexo e Idade para o Período 1980–2050, Revisão 2004." Rio de Janeiro: IBGE.

———. 2004c. *Pesquisa Nacional por Amostragem de Domicílios 2003*. Rio de Janeiro: IBGE.

———. 2002. *Assistência Médico-Sanitária 2002*. Rio de Janeiro: IBGE.

———. 2000. *Pesquisa Nacional por Amostragem de Domicílios 1998*. Rio de Janeiro: IBGE.

———. 1999. *Pesquisa de Orçamentos Familiares 1996–97*. Rio de Janeiro: IBGE.

IMF (International Monetary Fund). 2005. Database. http://www.imfstatistics.org/imf/; accessed October 20, 2005.

IPEA (Instituto de Pesquisa em Economia Aplicada). 2005. IPEADATA, database. www.ipeadata.gov.br.

Malta, D.C. n.d. "Saúde Suplementar e Modelos Assistenciais." http://www.ans.gov.br/portal/upload/biblioteca/TT_AS_14_DCarvalhoMalta_ModelosAssistenciais.pdf.

Manning, W.G., J.P. Newhouse, N. Duan, E.B. Keeler, A. Leibowitz, and M.S. Marquis. 1987. "Health Insurance and the Demand for Medical Care: Evidence from a Randomized Experiment." *American Economic Review* 77 (3): 251–77.

Médici, A.C. 1991. *A medicina de grupo no Brasil*. Brasília: Pan American Health Organization.

Ministério da Fazenda/SPE. 2003. "Gasto Social do Governo Central 2001–2002." Brasilia, November 2003.

Ministério da Fazenda/Secretaria do Tesouro Nacional. 2004. "Balanço Geral da União 2003." Brasília.

Ministério da Fazenda/Secretaria do Tesouro Nacional. 2004. "Perfil e Evolução das Finanças Municipais 1998–2003." Brasília, August.

Ministry of Health. 2005. Public Health Budgets Database (Sistema de Informações de Orçamentos em Saúde, SIOPS), 1995–2003. www.datasus.saude.gov.br.

Ministry of Health/Datasus: Mortality Database (Sistema de Informações sobre Mortalidade, SIM). http://tabnet.datasus.gov.br/cgi/deftohtm.exe?sim/cnv/obtuf.def

Ministry of Health/Datasus: Health Database (Informações de Saúde) http://w3.datasus.gov.br/datasus/datasus.php?area=359A1B0C0D0E0F359G3HIJd1L2M0N&VInclude=../site/texto.php.

Unidas (União Nacional das Instituições de Autogestão em Saúde): "Pesquisa Nacional 2003–2004." São Paulo: Unidas.

UNDP (United Nations Development Programme). 2005. *Human Development Report 2005*. New York: UNDP.

Viegas M. 2004. "Financiamento do Setor de Saúde Suplementar no Brasil: uma investigação empírica a partir dos dados da PNAD /98." In MS/ANS, *Regulação e Saúde*, Vol.3, Tomo 1. Documentos Técnicos de apoio ao Forum de Saúde Suplementar 2003. Rio de Janeiro, 2004.

World Bank, 2005: *World Development Indicators 2005*. Washington DC: World Bank.

CHAPTER 12

India

Peter A. Berman, Rajeev Ahuja, and Vijaysekar Kalavakonda

The private voluntary health insurance market in India is large and growing. If barriers to the development of this market are removed and the estimated potential is tapped, private health insurance can finance a much higher part of India's total health care spending by 2016. Realization of this potential will, however, bring risks as well as benefits, and success will depend on appropriate government activities and policies.

INTRODUCTION

India, with its population of over a billion,[1] could be home to one of the largest health insurance programs anywhere in the world. However, this potential is constrained by a number of factors. Some of them are related to the current stage of development. For example, more than a quarter of India's population is officially below poverty line (Tenth Five Year Plan 2002–07), and around 62 percent of its 400 million workforce is engaged in agriculture (Economic Survey 2003–04), a harder-to-reach segment. Communicable and infectious diseases still account for 4 out of 10 deaths in India. Quality health care services, both public or private, are still thin. Affordability and timely accessibility of health services is a major issue for much of the population. Equally constraining are factors such as unstructured and unregulated delivery of health care services, lack of measures for promotion of dedicated health insurance providers, and absence of health statistics. These, and other constraints, can be quickly addressed through public policies.

With a national literacy rate of 64.8 percent, life expectancy at birth of 66 years, an infant mortality rate of 68 per 1,000 live births, and a child malnutrition rate of 47 (percentage of children under 5 years), India's human development indicators are below average compared with countries at a similar stage of development, although there is considerable variation within the country. For example, the infant mortality rate varies from 14 in Kerala to 97 in Orissa. Similarly, the national maternal mortality rate is 408 but varies from 87 in Kerala to 707 in Bihar and Uttar Pradesh (Peters et al. 2002).

Health insurance, one of the more equitable forms of health care financing, is quite limited in India. All organized health financing arrangements cover around 110 million workers, 21 million of them covered under private voluntary health insurance (PVHI). This number is expected to grow in coming years, reflecting a large untapped market as well as growth in income as a result of faster GDP growth (around 7 or 8 percent a year). Health insurance premium revenue has been growing at the rate of 20 to 25 percent a year. With prospects for robust economic growth, growth in the health insurance business can be easily sustained, and indeed surpassed, if some of the barriers now holding back the development of health insurance market can be removed.

Private voluntary health insurance in India is the focus of this chapter. Estimates of the significant and growing size of the private health insurance market are based on a health insurance claims dataset pertaining to 4.6 million insured individuals for the period January 2003 to November 2004. This study is the first of its kind to have used such a large, representative dataset for India. The authors find significant and growing potential for a private voluntary health insurance market in India. If the estimated potential is tapped—which is possible if the current barriers to the development of health insurance market are removed—private health insurance can finance a significantly higher share (than at present) of total health care spending by 2016. However, if this significantly higher share of total health financing from PVHI could be attained, it would carry with it significant risks as well as possible benefits, which would depend on appropriate government activities and policies. These and some other interesting findings emerge from the analysis carried out in this chapter.

This chapter is organized as follows. After a brief overview of the issues and the problems in health care financing in India, the current PVHI situation is reviewed. Estimates of the potential size of the PVHI market in the current environment are then provided and projections made for health insurance and health care costs for 2006, 2011, and 2016 under alternate scenarios of medical inflation. Based on these findings, some broad conclusions and policy implications are drawn.

OVERVIEW

Health care spending in India is low, somewhere around US$30 per capita in absolute terms. According to one recent national estimate, India spends 4.8 percent of national income on health care, but some other estimates have been higher. As a share of national income, India's health spending is above average in comparison with other low- and lower-middle income Asian countries. Private spending, largely out of pocket (OOPS), is overwhelmingly the largest component of health system financing in India, accounting for at least 70 percent of the total in recent estimates, and higher in some estimates. Government spending accounts for a quarter or less of total spending (Rao et al. 2005). Most of this spending is by state (provincial) governments, although state budgets are in turn financed by both federal grants and states' own revenues. Several other forms of health financing account for the rest. These include formally organized health insurance and self-financing of health benefits by firms.

Public funding for health care has been historically low in India, fluctuating around 1 percent of GDP. In the last decade, the trend of public sector health expenditure has declined. Moreover, this low public health spending is skewed toward curative care that benefits mainly the better off, while preventive health services, benefiting mainly the poor, take a back seat. It is estimated that government spends about one half to two thirds of public expenditure on secondary and tertiary care whereas public health programs, education and research (26 percent), and primary care (12 percent) account for the remaining third. The bulk of public spending on primary health care has been spread too thinly to be fully effective,[2] resulting in the weakening of the referral linkages to secondary care. Public spending on curative services is also inequitable. For every Re 1 spent on the poorest 20 percent, the government spends an estimated Rs 3 on the richest 20 percent of the population (figure 12.1).

The large share of private spending, mainly OOPS, often discourages poorer households from purchasing health care, especially curative care, or forces them into poverty. Across India, those above the poverty line have more than twice the

FIGURE 12.1 India: Public Expenditures on Curative Care, by Income Quintile

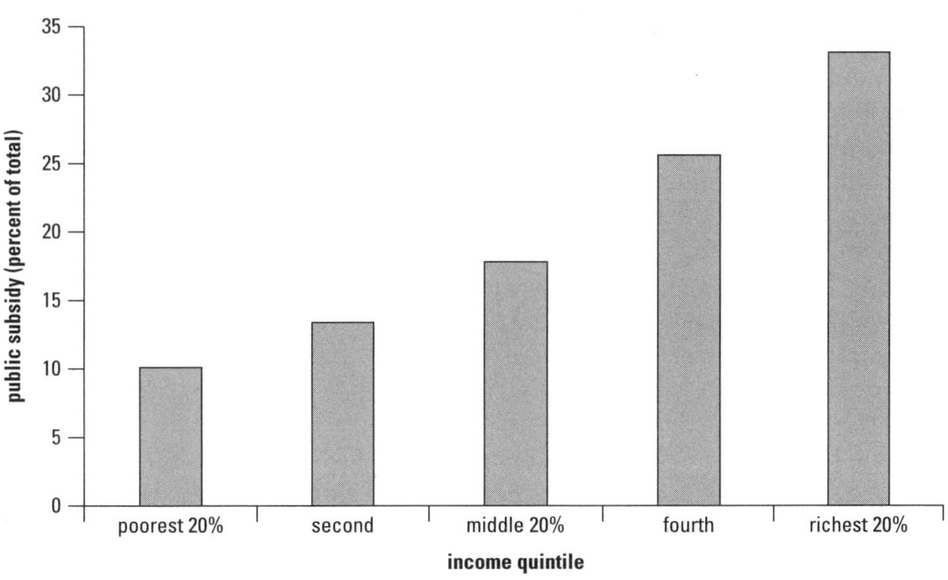

Source: Peters et al. 2002.

hospitalization rates of the poor. Similarly, it is estimated that the amounts spent by hospitalized Indians equal more than half (58 percent) of their total annual expenditures and that more than 40 percent of those hospitalized borrow money or sell assets to cover expenses (Peters et al. 2002). According to one conservative estimate, after meeting hospitalization expenses, a quarter (25 percent) of those hospitalized fall below the poverty line in terms of their remaining consumption expenditure levels. A few microlevel studies corroborate these findings. For example, the baseline survey carried out by the Centre for Population Dynamics in two districts in Karnataka in 2002, found that people in those two districts faced significant financial barriers in seeking medical care as loans constituted the single largest source for meeting illness and hospitalization costs, followed by sale of livestock (Karuna Trust 2004).[3] Such a high percentage is also noted by some micro finance institutions in the utilization pattern of loans advanced by them (see SHEPHERD 2003, for example[4]). Hence, any prepaid health financing arrangement designed especially for the low-income people would have a considerable positive impact on their welfare.

Some of the other important but lesser-known facts about private health care spending are: (1) 61 percent of private spending is on outpatient care, including drug purchases; (2) 57 percent of outpatient spending is on acute infectious diseases[5]; (3) 85 percent of inpatient spending is in five areas: cardio (14 percent), cancer (13 percent), accidents (19 percent), acute infections (22 percent), and obstetrics and gynecology (17 percent); and (4) urban Indians and the rich account for a disproportionate share of the spending.[6]

Formal prepaid, risk-pooling arrangements, typically a more equitable form of health spending, currently account for less than 5 percent of total health spending in India. These arrangements are organized by various agencies such as government at different levels, semigovernmental organizations, private organizations, insurance companies, communities, and health care providers. A wide variety of risk-pooling schemes exists in India, including social insurance schemes such as the Central Government Health Scheme (CGHS) and Employee State Insurance Scheme (ESIS), health schemes of public sector enterprises and private corporate sector, schemes for the unorganized sector (including government schemes for the well-identified groups of unorganized sector workers), health insurance schemes of formal insurance companies (including their microinsurance portfolio) registered with the insurance regulator (IRDA), and self-managed schemes of employers and health care providers. Around 11 percent of the Indian population is formally covered through these prepayment schemes.

These schemes can be better understood with the aid of table 12.1. From top to bottom, the various schemes are listed by organizing agency: government and semigovernmental organizations (both at federal and provisional level), private organizations, informally organized groups, and individuals.[7] Reading from left to right reveals the nature of schemes, that is, whether mandatory or voluntary, contributory or noncontributory.

TABLE 12.1 India: Typology of Risk-Pooling Schemes

			Voluntary		
	Mandatory contribution[a]	*Noncontributory*	*Contribution*	*Noncontributory*	*Number of employees, March 2002 (million)*
Public sector employees[b]					
Government[c]	CGHS	EHS[d]			10.76
Other departments [e]		EHS[d]			3.62
Quasi-governmental[f]				EHS [d]	6.02
Private sector employees[g]					
Low-income[h]	ESIS	EHS[d]			7.90[d]
Others			INS[i]	EHS, [d] INS[i]	
Government initiatives for unorganized					
Social Security Scheme			INS[i]		
Universal Health Insurance			INS[i]		
Central welfare funds				EHS[d]	4.20
State welfare funds			EHS	EHS[d]	
CBHI schemes	INS[i]		INS[i]	INS.	5.00
Individuals			INS[i]		11.00
Total	9.10	13.18	18.60	10.22	51.10

Source: Berman and Ahuja 2005.

a. Contributory schemes may or may not include copayments during sickness. A *contributory system* is one in which beneficiaries make explicit contributions.

b. No information is available on retired employees (excluding those retired from the Defence and the central government) who benefit from the scheme.

c. *Quasi-governmental* refers to public bodies formed statutorily or through executive order and also includes public sector undertakings/enterprises. Quasi-governmental organizations are owned and/or funded but not directly controlled by government..

d. EHS implies entitlement to health services.

e. Includes employees in Railways, Post and Telegraph, and Defence personnel.

f. Includes all three levels of government: central (federal), state (provincial), and local.

g. Private sector includes nonagricultural establishments employing 10 or more persons.

h. Covers all ESIS-insured persons/family units as of March 2004.

i. *Insurance* here refers to a prepaid risk-pooling mechanism.

With a few exceptions, all central government employees are members of the CGHS, which is mandatory as well as contributory. A few notable exceptions are the Railways, the Post and Telegraph, and the Defence personnel. The Railways and the Post and Telegraph have their own medical facilities. Accordingly, government employees in these two departments are entitled to the medical benefit under their respective noncontributory medical scheme. In case of the Defence, only civilian personnel appear in the list of central government employees and therefore come under CGHS. For Defence personnel (noncivilians), however, the Defence has its own health care facilities. These exceptions to CGHS are captured in "Other departments" in table 12.1.[8]

At the state level, state government employees as well as the employees in semigovernmental organizations are entitled to free medical care. It is generally a noncontributory benefit included in their service contract.[9] However, quasi-governmental organizations at state level are free to offer whatever benefits they deem appropriate. Government officials in local bodies, too, are entitled to some medical benefits.

Almost all central quasi-governmental organizations provide medical benefits in some form for their employees and their dependents. With a few exceptions, each central semigovernmental organization has its own medical scheme.[10] This is generally a noncontributory benefit included in the service contract of employees.

For private organizations, there is no statutory requirement to provide employees with medical benefits except for employees earning less than a certain income threshold. For these blue collar employees of private companies of a certain size, enrolment in the Employee State Insurance Scheme is mandatory, and both employer and employee must contribute. State governments also contribute, indirectly. Providing other employees in the private sector with medical benefits is not mandatory, but most private organizations do offer some medical benefits to attract and retain good employees and to take advantage of tax concessions. The level of benefits varies considerably across organizations.

For unorganized workers, government (both at central and state levels) has certain schemes such as social security, universal health insurance, welfare funds, and so forth. These schemes are generally voluntary and contributory. For certain occupationally identified workers in the unorganized sector, government (central and state) has set up welfare boards that provide several social security benefits—chief among them, medical benefits. All the workers registered with these boards are entitled to such benefits. In so far as the workers are free to register, the scheme is nonmandatory. The central welfare board schemes are noncontributory while those of the state government are mostly contributory (Ministry of Labour 2004–05).[11]

Many community-based health insurance (CBHI) schemes are voluntary and contributory. However, in some communities, whether or not to have a scheme is optional but, once opted for, becomes mandatory for each member. Some CBHI schemes are noncontributory because they are funded by donors—government or nongovernmental agencies.

For individuals, health insurance is optional. They can buy an individual/family scheme from an insurance company, join a CBHI scheme if one is available, or do both. The option of buying health insurance is open to everybody, even people insured under a mandatory system. It is not uncommon for a retired organized sector worker to buy health insurance privately from an insurance company.

Thus, almost all organized sector employees, whether in public or private sector, are covered under some health financing scheme or the other. Only a very small percentage of workers in the unorganized sector—which constitutes almost 90 percent of the labor force—is covered under any of these schemes. The number of individuals covered under contributory scheme is somewhat higher than under noncontributory scheme. Similarly, the number of individuals covered under voluntary schemes is somewhat higher than under mandatory schemes (table 12.2).

Neither table 12.1 nor 12.2 indicates the *number of beneficiaries* under different schemes. Beneficiaries, in the case of organized sector workers, include the employee's family members. There are around 30 million workers in the organized sector. With the scaling-up factor of three, the number of beneficiaries would be 90 million. Adding to this number the health insurance schemes of the unorganized sector workers and individuals (around 20 million) gives 110 million beneficiaries, about 11 percent of India's population.

Table 12.3 shows both the type and the level of benefits available under different insurance arrangements. Generally, benefits are better for organized sector workers than for unorganized sector workers, but vary within these broad classifications. For example, these benefits are generally less, moving down the scale from central government employees to employees of state government (and local bodies) (not shown in the table).

Private voluntary health insurance, largely urban-based, is limited in both the number of individuals covered and the extent of financing involved. PVHI covers around 21 million individuals. All types of organized health financing arrangements (including health insurance) cover only around 110 million individuals (11 percent of the population).

With total health insurance premiums of Rs 13 billion[12] in 2003–04, private voluntary health insurance contributes a small percentage (8 percent) of total non–life insurance premiums in India (IRDA 2004a). On the health care financing side, too, health insurance constitutes a small share (less than 5 percent) of total health spending.

TABLE 12.2 India: Employees Covered under Different Systems (number in millions)

	Contributory	*Noncontributory*	*Total*
Mandatory	9.1	13.18	22.28
Voluntary	18.6	10.22	28.82
Total	27.7	23.40	51.1

Source: Berman and Ahuja 2005.

TABLE 12.3 India: Types of Medical Benefits Provided for Different Insured Groups

	Diagnostics	*Outpatient*	*Inpatient*	*Preventive and promotive care*	*Wage loss*
Public sector employees					
Government	X-XXX	X-XXX	X-XXX		X
Quasi-government	X-XXX	X-XXX	XX-XXX	X-XXX	X
Other departments	XXX	XXX	XXX		X
Private sector employees					
Low-income	XX-XXX	XX-XXX	XX-XXX	XX	
Others	XX-XXX	XX-XXX	XX-XXX	XXX	
Government initiatives for unorganized workers					
Social Security Scheme			XX		X
Universal Health Insurance			XX		X
Central Welfare Funds	XX-XXX	XX-XXX	XX-XXX		
State Welfare Funds	X-XX	X-XX	X-XX		
CBHI Schemes	X-XX	X-XXX	XX-XXX	X-XXX	XX
Individuals	XX		X-XXX		

Source: Berman and Ahuja 2005.
Note: X = covers some costs; XX = covers most costs; XXX = covers entire cost; X-XXX = coverage ranges from some to all costs.

India opened its insurance sector to competition from private players in 2000. As a result, eight private insurers entered the non–life insurance business. Despite growing competition from private players, the health insurance business is still dominated by the four incumbent public insurance companies.[13] Much of the health insurance market (around 90 percent both in terms of health premiums and number of lives) is captured by a single product, called Mediclaim,[14] offered by the public insurers. In addition, life insurance companies offer health riders to their life insurance products. However, health coverage offered through these riders is only a tiny percentage of total health coverage.[15] Other private health insurance initiatives for the unorganized sector workers in the low-income category cover anywhere from 5 million to 10 million individuals.[16]

Although interest in health insurance as a health financing mechanism has been growing, overall coverage is still low. Despite efforts to encourage the health insurance market to develop, even among relatively well-off urban populations the persistent low levels of activity in health insurance can be attributed to regulatory and systemic barriers that have been difficult to address. For example, there is no separate set of rules that would promote companies selling only health insurance, health care supply is at best loosely regulated, there is no database, interdepartmental coordination is lacking, and the subsidized health insurance product of the public insurance companies discourages market development. Table 12.4 summarizes these barriers.

TABLE 12.4 India: Barriers to Health Insurance Development

Barriers	*Key issues*	*Implications*
Regulatory		
Capital requirement[a]	High capital requirement is burdensome	• High premium needed to compensate for investment but volumes will be lower due to price sensitivities • Need to grow very rapidly to break even
Systemic		
Customer attitude	No habit of prepayment	• High marketing cost to educate customers about insurance • High transaction costs for distribution (more than 72 percent of population live in rural areas)
	High level of fraud	• Claims ratio higher for existing products
Competitive scenario	Low premium	• Unrealistic standards and expectations caused by excessively low pricing of Mediclaim products[b] relative to benefits
Provider unpreparedness	Providers not standardized	• No standardization of treatment protocols and quality, either through registration or accreditation • No way of controlling claims as prices vary (fee for service is main type of provider payment) • No information technology infrastructure • Rapid networking limited by huge base of small practices (average size of hospitals is about 22 beds) • Easier for providers to perpetrate fraud
Payer unpreparedness	No socioeconomic health data	• Unable to design profitable schemes due to lack of comprehensive data on health requirements and usage patterns of different socioeconomic segments

Source: CII–McKinsey&Company 2002.

a. The minimum capital requirement to get an insurance company license to operate is Rs 1.0 billion (US$22.22 million at the exchange rate of US$1 = Rs 45).

b. Major insurers sell Mediclaim at less than the cost of the risks insured to attract other profitable lines of insurance business.

FINANCIAL FEASIBILITY OF PVHI

The main purpose of this chapter is to develop an exploratory analysis of the financial feasibility of large-scale private voluntary health insurance in India. At present, PVHI coverage extends to only a small fraction of the population and accounts for a similarly small share of total health spending.

In December 1999 the government passed new legislation to help organize and develop the private health insurance market in India. Since that time, despite much public and professional discussion about the potential for rapid growth in health insurance, progress on the ground has been slow. As shown in table 12.3, reasons for that slow growth are related to regulation of both the insurance and provider sectors. Uncertainty about the financial feasibility of schemes is another reason. Information is lacking to help potential investors estimate the costs of providing different benefits packages and, therefore, the premiums they would need to set to prevent losses.

However, some data for estimating the costs of claims have recently become available from some largely urban-based PVHI schemes.[17] In this section, an attempt is made to link these cost estimates to other population-based data on consumption expenditures to estimate the size of the potential market for PVHI in India, always assuming that the other constraints on market development could be addressed.

To gauge the current and emerging size of private voluntary health insurance market in India, two estimates are needed: (1) the cost of providing health insurance and (2) the size of population that can buy health insurance. The cost estimates are based on a health insurance claims dataset pertaining to 4.62 million insured individuals for the period January 2003 to November 2004. The estimates of the population that could afford to buy insurance are based on National Sample Survey Organisation consumption expenditure data (NSSO 2001), NCAER Market Information Survey of Households 2002 data, (NCAER 2002), data on organized sector workers, and a few pieces of information on the Indian labor market. The datasets used, the assumptions made, and the methodology adopted in estimating medical costs/expenditure and size of health insurance market are discussed below.

Estimated Costs of Providing Health Insurance

First, the two well-known summary indicators are estimated: claims frequency and average claim size. Sixty-three out of every 1,000 insured persons make claims, and the average claim size is Rs 16,810.

The available information on the number of claims made by 4.62 million insured individuals is broadly categorized into 30 disease types, and the frequency of claims for each type of disease is computed. The available sample is large as well as random, which allows disease frequencies to be generalized for the entire population. Because information is also available for the total claims amount paid for each of the 30 different types of illnesses, the average claim amount can also be calculated. The average claim amount serves as a good proxy for the cost of treatment for each type of disease. These costs and disease frequencies are used to work out treatment cost per individual across cities and the country as a whole.

Treatment cost per individual comes out to Rs 1,369, Rs 1,149, Rs 907, and Rs 1,053 for four major metro cities, all metros, nonmetros, and for India as a whole, respectively.[18] These per capita costs pertain to 2003 and are unadjusted for the transaction costs involved in running an insurance program. Transaction costs are generally higher for individual business than for group business[19] and also higher in nonmetros than in metros. However, transaction costs are assumed to be 20 percent of the treatment costs. After adjustments, average treatment cost per individual at national level comes to around Rs 1,044 in 2001, the reference year for this analysis.[20]

A question now arises: how representative are these cost estimates? Below, the available dataset is shown to be fairly representative of the population.

In terms of the geographical spread, of the 4.62 million insured persons, around 27 percent is located in four major metro cities, around 33 percent in "other" metro cities, and the balance of 40 percent in nonmetro cities (figure 12.2), although there is considerable variation within these geographical subgroups.

FIGURE 12.2 India: Distribution of the Insured

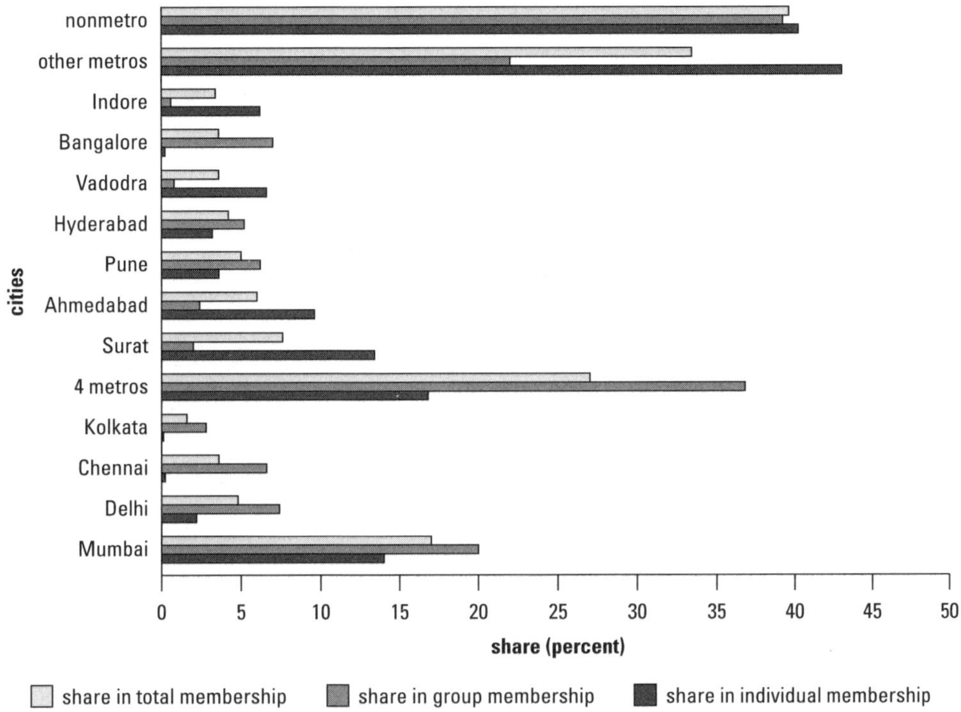

Source: Authors' own construction using the health insurance dataset.

Likewise, the dataset is fairly representative of the type of business (individual and group). Around 51 percent of the insured are in group business, and 49 percent in individual business. In four metro cities, group business is almost double the individual business. This is as expected because organizations are concentrated in metro cities. In "other" metro cities, the converse is true: group business is lower than individual business, by almost half.

On the claims side, total claims are distributed in nearly the same proportion as the number of insured individuals in the three broad geographical groupings. For every 1,000 insured, around 63 individuals made claims.[21] The claims frequency is higher for group business (67 out of every 1,000 persons) than for individual business (59 per 1,000 persons). But the average claim amount for group business (Rs 15,510) is lower than for individual business (Rs 18,325). This difference could perhaps stem from closer screening of group claims to prevent moral hazard.

The gender aspect is also well captured in the dataset. Women make up 45 percent of all insured individuals but file 47 percent of total claims. Accordingly, females have a higher claims ratio than males: for every 1,000 insured females, 65 females make claims compared with 59 for every 1,000 insured males. However, the average claim amount for females is lower (Rs 15,594) than for males

FIGURE 12.3 India: Distribution of Members and Claims, by Age

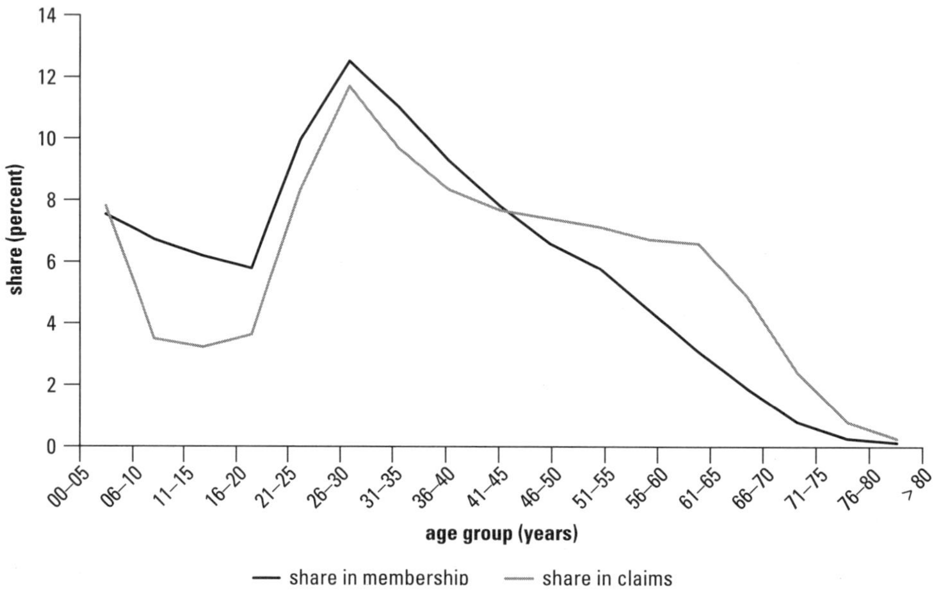

Source: Authors' own construction using the health insurance dataset.

(Rs 18,178). With total claims by individual and group business disaggregated, the female claims ratio is lower than that for males in individual business but higher in group business. This trend is true in all three geographical groupings: metros, other metros, and nonmetros. This could perhaps be due to a stronger female voice/power profile when women are insured as a part of a group rather than as individuals. The average claim amount for both females and males is lower in group business than in individual business.

In terms of age distribution, too, the dataset is fairly representative. Around 77 percent of all insured individuals belong to the age group 0 to 45, but they file only 64 percent of total claims (figure 12.3), implying cross-subsidy from younger to older members. Furthermore, group members are younger than individual members.

In terms of the cost of treating various illnesses, the dataset is well represented. Claims information is disaggregated into 30 types of the most important illnesses and covers both treatment costs and frequencies. Figure 12.4 shows the costs of the 10 most expensive treatments, which account for about 16.4 percent of total claims—about 10 out of every 63 claims per 1,000 members.

The treatment cost varies considerably across cities. This is well-captured in the dataset, as shown in figure 12.5. For example, treatment cost is highest in Mumbai and nearly half as costly in Surat.

FIGURE 12.4 India: The 10 Most Expensive Treatments

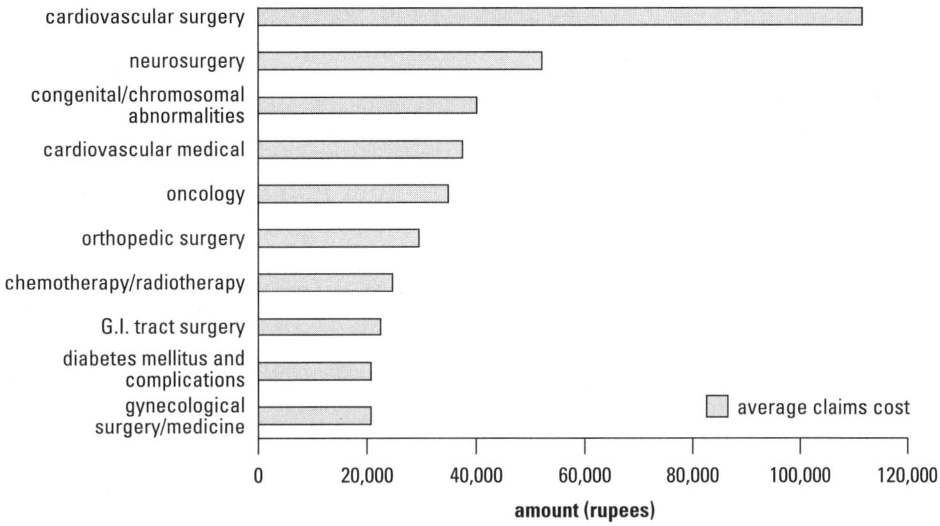

Source: Authors' own construction using the health insurance dataset.

FIGURE 12.5 India: Treatment Cost per Individual, by City

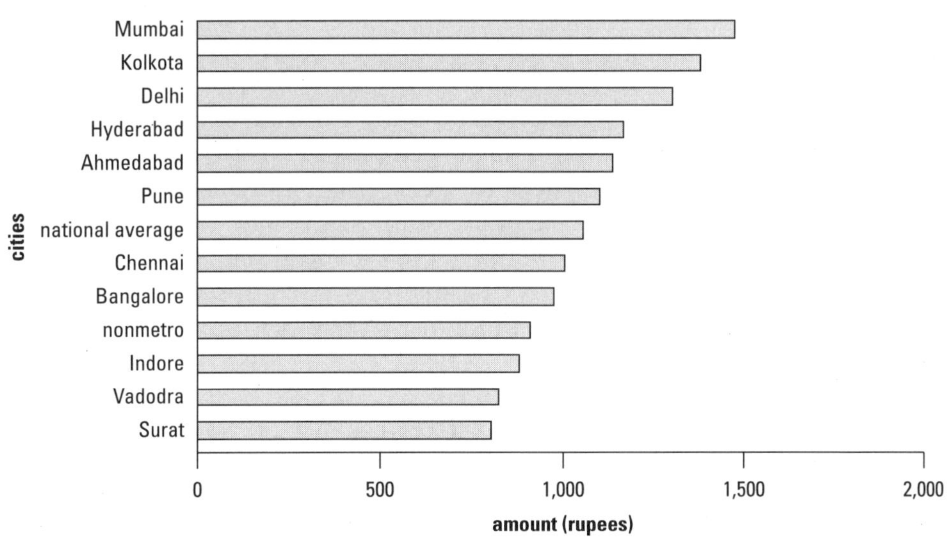

Source: Authors' own construction using the health insurance dataset.

Estimating Customer Base and Health Insurance Market Size

NSS consumption expenditure data for 1999–2000 (NSSO 2001) are used to see what part of India's total population can afford to buy health insurance. The NSS consumption expenditure dataset reports per capita consumption expenditure across deciles. Per capita expenditure data are reported for various consumption items, including expenditure on medical care, broadly categorized into institutional and noninstitutional medical care for rural and urban population. To find out medical expenditure at the national level, the weighted average of the number of urban and rural households surveyed in each decile is used. For the top expenditure decile, per capita medical expenditure comes to around Rs 1,448 a year, of which Rs 480 is institutional medical expenditure. Although institutional and noninstitutional medical care broadly corresponds to inpatient and outpatient care, respectively, an insurance program for inpatient care would typically cover some portion of noninstitutional care as well. Moreover, medical costs in NSS data are somewhat underrepresented because they do not include medical benefits provided directly by employers. In estimating the potential size of the market that could have paid the annual insurance premium of Rs 1044 per individual, it is reasonable to assume that the top expenditure decile could have afforded it in 2001. This assumption seems all the more probable, recognizing the limitations of NSS data and the fact that the data actually pertain to 1999–2000 while the price figure pertains to 2001.[22]

At the turn of the century, India's population numbered around 1 billion. The top expenditure decile would cover about 100 million individuals. To arrive at the untapped market potential in the top decile, individuals who already belong to some health financing arrangement must be excluded. Currently, all organized sector workers belong to some health financing arrangement. In March 2000, India had 28.11 million organized sector workers. But not all these workers (and their family members) belong to the top expenditure decile. It is reasonable to assume that 25 percent of organized sector workers and their family members belong to the top expenditure decile.[23] Assuming an average family size of four and adjusting for the fact that both husband and wife are employed in the organized sector in some families,[24] the untapped market potential was around 72.4 million individuals in 2001 (table 12.4). Had this market potential been fully tapped, at an average premium of Rs 1,044 per individual, it would have amounted to Rs 75.58 billion.

Projecting the Future Health Insurance Market

Two aspects of the future health insurance market were examined: potential growth in the size of the population able to afford PVHI and the possible inflationary effects of increased insurance coverage on the overall cost of health insurance.

The size of the current potential market for PVHI was considered by estimating the population able to pay an actuarially fair premium plus administrative costs based on the current experience of PVHI. For the future, if incomes growth outpaces these costs, the size of the potential PVHI market would be expected to grow. This future market potential was estimated using population projections, an assumption about the expenditure decile that can afford to pay for insurance, and an assumption about the population segment represented by organized sector workers. Population projections are made by the office of the Registrar General of India. About the expenditure deciles who can pay for insurance, the top 15 percent, 20 percent, and 30 percent of population were assumed to be able to pay for insurance by 2006, 2011, and 2016 respectively. From market size figures, the population segment represented by organized sector workers had to be deducted because they are already covered under some health financing arrangement. For this, organized sector employment was assumed to grow at 0.5 percent a year.[25] After making some reasonable assumptions spelled out in table 12.5, the size of population is estimated, represented by a percentage of organized sector workers. That figure is subtracted from the market size to estimate the untapped market: 120 million, 184 million, and 303 million for 2006, 2011, and 2016 respectively (table 12.5).

The possible effects of health care cost inflation on total premium value are also examined. Health care costs under insurance could increase for a variety of reasons. For example, exogenous price increases could outpace the general rate of inflation. Other factors could also affect future health care costs under insurance, such as increased demand for care paid for by insurance, supply- and demand-side moral hazard, and the potential for insurers to improve efficiency

TABLE 12.5 India: Projecting the Size of the Health Insurance Market (million)

	2001	2006	2011	2016
Population[a]	1,027	1,114	1,197	1,275
Organized sector employment[b]	27.8	28.5	29.2	29.9
Total market size[c]	102.7	167.1	239.4	382.5
Less organized sector population[d]	26.4	40.6	55.5	79.61
Untapped market[e]	72.4	119.51	183.9	302.9

a. Projections made by the Office of Registrar General, Delhi.
b. Assuming average annual growth rate of 0.5 percent.
c. Assuming market consisting of top 10 percent, 15 percent, 20 percent, and 30 percent of the population in 2001, 2006, 2011, and 2016, respectively.
d. Assuming 25 percent, 25 percent, and 20 percent of organized sector workers distributed in first, second, and third expenditure deciles, respectively; multiplying 90 percent of workers in top three deciles by a factor of four, and remaining 10 percent by a factor of two (to correct for husband and wife working in the organized sector) to obtain size of population constituted by organized workers.
e. After deducting 3.9 million and 7 million individuals insured by private insurance companies, since private companies' group insurance business is already included in organized sector.

TABLE 12.6 India: Health Financing through Insurance

Years	Insurable population (billion)	Rs billion Scenario 1 5%	Scenario 2 10%	Scenario 3 15%
2006	0.12	174.82	201.00	229.67
2011	0.18	343.37	498.18	710.94
2016	0.30	721.70	1,321.31	2,354.89

Sources: Authors' own calculations.

through care management. Lacking any empirical basis for estimating these factors, these projections are incomplete and simply illustrate the potential for growth in PVHI-related expenditures.

In table 12.6, the potential market for PVHI is estimated under three inflation scenarios showing the increased costs of providing coverage at 5, 10, and 15 percent annual inflation in medical costs.

These projections show that the size of the PVHI market in financial terms is sensitive to assumptions about medical inflation. For example, in 2016 the funds mobilized through health insurance are around Rs 722 billion, Rs 1,321 billion, and Rs 2,355 billion at, respectively, 5 percent, 10 percent, and 15 percent inflation rates. Thus, PVHI has potential as a significant method of health care financing in the 10-year period considered. Development of the health insurance market, by enabling the intended population segment to switch from ex post OOP payments to a prepaid risk-pooling mechanism, can benefit people who enroll in a health insurance program. At the same time, it may also alter the overall composition of health care financing in India in ways difficult to predict at this time. Some possible outcomes may be welfare-enhancing overall, and some not.

SOME POLICY ISSUES AND CONCERNS

In the development of the health insurance market, government has an important role to play, not only because of its strong presence in health care delivery, but also because of the strong stewardship needed to bring about coordination among multiple institutions and actors. Why should government care at all? There are two important reasons. First, if PVHI finances not just private health facilities but also public facilities, it can help build accountability in the management of these facilities, thereby positively influencing the quality of care in the public sector. Second, although development of PVHI may benefit primarily the already better-off segments of society who can pay, the way in which PVHI is developed can have significant consequences for financing other parts of the health care system.

For example, PVHI can replace public resources now being spent on the better-off. Mahal et al. (2002) finds that public health subsidies are disproportionately distributed in favor of richer segments of society. According to the study, around

46.5 percent of public spending is on hospitals.[26] Of this, around 36 percent benefits the top quintile, and only 8.1 percent goes to the bottom quintile. Applying the same percentages to public health spending of Rs 280 billion in 2000–01, of the Rs 130.2 billion spent on hospitals, around Rs 47 billion benefits the top quintile while around Rs 10.5 billion benefits the bottom quintile. If the untapped insurance potential of 72.4 million persons in 2001 had been fully met, the amount of public resources that would have been released for alternate uses, such as benefiting poorer segments of society, would have been Rs 17 billion (almost three times the resources going to the bottom *decile*). If government providers could capture this amount, development of PVHI in India could make it possible for government to reallocate its health spending toward the poor. But in reality the risk runs both ways: government subsidies to the richer segments may increase or decrease (or stay the same), since the population segment that is expected to benefit from the development of the insurance market wields a strong influence on the government decision-making process. If public subsidies to better-off segments increase, the funding may come from an increase in overall public health care spending or from the withdrawal of subsidies from the worse-off segments of society. Conversely, if public subsidies to the better-off go down, government could shift more spending to health care needs of the poorer. The effect depends on the government's stance and on its ability to formulate and implement appropriate policies.

There may also be concerns about whether expansion of PVHI for the upper-income segment would result in a large increase in national health spending, for example, due to demand-driven medical care inflation and increased demand. Alternatively, it could largely substitute for the currently high OOPS spending, creating a more orderly market with little overall expenditure increase. To explore this question, the NSS household consumption expenditure data 1999–2000 were used to work out the cost of inpatient care for the top expenditure decile.[27] The total amount came to Rs 109 billion in 2001–02. Earlier in the chapter, the average cost of providing insurance was estimated at Rs 1,044 per person in 2001, suggesting an expenditure of Rs 104 billion to provide health insurance to everybody (100 million) in the top decile. Comparing these two different methods of financing suggests only a marginal increase in health care spending on inpatient care if everybody in the top decile received insurance coverage. This is encouraging because it suggests the potential for top-end market restructuring with limited systemic side effects.

CONCLUSIONS

Almost four fifths of health care spending in India today is met through private out-of-pocket spending, which is highly regressive. Organized financing is barely developed. Hospitalization costs place a huge burden on Indian families, causing many to fall into poverty. Compared with income, overall spending is high for a poor country like India, but outcomes are below average. The need and the demand for health care financing reform in India are urgent and strong.

This chapter explores the potential for private voluntary health insurance in India, by estimating the potential costs of insurance coverage and the possible market for voluntary purchasing of insurance based on ability to pay. Some recently available data were used to develop this simple feasibility study. The purpose was not to argue for or against this mode of health financing, but simply to ask "what if . . ."?

Using health insurance claims data for around 4.6 million insured people, mostly in urban India, the cost was estimated for a significant package of hospitalization benefits. At current prices, such a package would cost about Rs 1,000 a person a year for a population approximating the general age distribution in India's population.

Private voluntary health insurance schemes sold by formal insurance companies cover only about 2.2 percent of total population, and about 11 percent of population is part of one or another type of organized health care financing arrangement. The potential market for private voluntary health insurance estimated by this study is about 72 million people.

Present coverage falls far short of this potential. Achieving this potential requires eliminating the barriers confronting the insurance industry. It entails streamlining the health care provision side, encouraging dedicated health insurance companies by promulgating a different set of norms for such companies, and enabling sound insurance cost and revenue estimates so that insurance providers can expand their offerings within tolerable risk levels.

Extrapolating from these estimated costs and market size, the estimates suggest that private voluntary health insurance could capture a significant share of out-of-pocket spending in India. OOPS spending thus might be cut from 80 percent to just over 50 percent of total spending.

There are both risks and potential benefits to expanding PVHI. A well-managed and regulated effort could provide significant health and financial protection benefits to India's better-off and urban populations while also helping to finance both government and private sector urban health services, including costly government hospitals at secondary and tertiary levels. A poorly managed effort could allow significant medical inflation and further drain limited public funds. Guessing which way India would go if PVHI were significantly developed is beyond the scope of this chapter. What can be said is that potential is there for important coverage at a cost that India's better off could afford. Under the right policy conditions, PVHI could contribute significantly to better organized health financing.

NOTES

The authors acknowledge with thanks the helpful suggestions and insights of Agnes Couffinhal, who reviewed the initial draft of the paper.

1. Sixty percent of the total population is of working age, and a relatively small part (7 percent) is 60 years and above, according to the latest 2001 census of India.

2. In addition, it is estimated that recurring expenses such as staff salary constitutes more than 85 percent of all primary care budget in a substantial number of the states.
3. Around 52 percent of the cost of illness and 43 percent of hospitalization expenses were met through loans. Similarly, around 13 percent of illness cost and 17 percent of hospitalization expenses were met through sale of livestock.
4. SHEPHERD (2003) found that 40 percent of its internal loans were used by the borrowers for curative purposes.
5. Fevers, diarrhea, gastro, coughs, and so on.
6. CII–McKinsey&Company (2002).
7. Information on government and semigovenment organizations and private organizations is taken from Ministry of Labour (2003a and 2003–04).
8. Although central reserve police appear in the list of central government employees, many employees are entitled to medical benefits provided by their own medical facilities (some personnel, however, are linked to CGHS). Since the number of central reserve police outside CGHS cannot be ascertained, they are included under CGHS.
9. In some states, government employees may make some contribution either a nominal amount toward health care benefits provided by the state government and/or copayments for certain kinds of treatments and services.
10. A few organizations are a part of CGHS.
11. For more information on state welfare schemes, see John (2004).
12. US$1 = Rs 45 in November 2004.
13. Health insurance schemes of these companies cover around 11 million lives (10 million lives by public insurers and 1 million lives by private insurers). For more information on the insurance market in general and health insurance in particular (see IRDA 2003–04, IRDA 2004, and Rao 2004).
14. Mediclaim, the most popular private health insurance product, has more than 95 percent of PHI market share. It is primarily a hospitalization and surgical insurance product.
15. In 2003–04, the total premiums collected on account of health riders constituted less than 1 percent of health insurance premiums of non–life insurance companies.
16. The share of public insurance companies in total health insurance premiums is higher (90.4 percent) than its total share in non–life insurance premiums (83 percent).
17. These schemes are largely those following India's "Mediclaim" product. Mediclaim covers only inpatient services and involves a number of exclusions such as preexisting conditions and others. No outpatient services are covered. For further details, see Berman and Ahuja (2005); also see Rao (2005).
18. The four major metro cities are: Delhi, Mumbai, Chennai, and Kolkata. "Other" metro cities are: Surat, Ahmedabad, Pune, Hyderabad, Vadodra, Bangalore, Indore.
19. *Group business* refers to purchases of group insurance policies, usually by companies and organizations. *Individual business* refers policy purchases by individuals and families.
20. An interesting question to ask here is: what would it cost to cover the entire population of India? For the 1.027 billion population in 2001, it would have cost around Rs 1,072.5 billion. Assumed in this estimate is that the age structure of the insured population is the same as that of the total population, which is certainly not the case. Comparison with the age distribution of the total population, the insured population has a bias toward a higher age group. This fact, coupled with the fact that average

medical costs are lower for younger than higher age groups, implies that the cost of insuring the entire population is likely to be lower than the above estimate. Correcting for the difference in the age structure of the total population and the insured population, the cost of insuring the entire population becomes around Rs 1,011 billion in 2001, Rs 984 per capita (about US$22). This is about equal to estimates of India's total per capita national health expenditure at that time. It is also about five times total government health expenditure. Inpatient services in India account for about a third of total national health spending. Extrapolating from this admittedly nonrepresentative figure suggests that universal coverage with hospitalization insurance could double national health spending from its current level, assuming no other changes.

21. The dataset covers 22 months. Whether all members were covered for the whole period is not known, although this is unlikely. The claims rate of about 6 percent works out to between 3 and 4 percent annually, which is within the range of reported hospital admission rates for India. Various factors might be expected to account for deviations from this average in both positive and negative directions. For example, the insured population is mainly urban and more affluent, which could increase demand. It is also less likely to include the elderly, which could reduce demand. The overall claims level seems plausible and does not present any strong indication of systematic underuse of insurance.

22. And also the fact organized sector workers who actually benefit from employers' medical spending are excluded from these calculations. This therefore increases the average medical expenditure of the individuals included from the top decile.

23. The percentages of organized sector workers belonging to the top expenditure decile come from two sources: (1) Ministry of Labour (2003b) for the distribution of central government employees, on a different pay scale from the census of central government employees and (2) the NCAER Market Information Survey of Households (NCAER 2002) (data pertaining to 1998–99) for the percentage of households belonging to five principal income groups. This information yields the following distribution of central government employees as per expenditure deciles: 25 percent, 25 percent, 20 percent, 15 percent, and 15 percent in the top five expenditure deciles (in descending order). This distribution is applied to all organized sector employees. As per this distribution, 25 percent of organized sector employees and their family members have to be deducted from the 100 million to deduce untapped market potential in 2001.

24. In 1999, women constituted 17 percent of the total employment in the organized sector, up from 13.8 percent in 1990. Five percent of men and 5 percent women in the organized sector are assumed to belong to same family. Thus, to estimate their family size, 10 percent of organized sector workers is multiplied by two.

25. Organized sector employment grew at average annual rate of 0.53 percent in 1994–2000, down from 1.2 percent in 1983–94.

26. The balance goes to primary health centers, subcenters, and immunizations.

27. NSS household consumption expenditure data were used to work out the shares of the top expenditure decile in total inpatient (institutional) care in rural and urban areas for 1999–2000. These shares and total household health expenditure on inpatient care in both urban and rural areas were used to work out total household expenditure on inpatient care in each of these areas by the top decile. This expenditure level comes to Rs 31.37 billion in urban areas and Rs 54.14 billion in rural areas, which yields total household expenditure of Rs 85.50 billion in 2001–02 by the top decile on inpatient care in both rural and urban areas. Public subsidies to hospitals that benefited the top income decile amounted to Rs 23.5 billion in 2001.

REFERENCES

Berman, Peter, and Rajeev Ahuja. 2005. *The Insurance Scene in India: A Brief Guide.* Unpublished. [A copy can be obtained upon request from the authors. <pberman@worldbank.org> or <rahuja@worldbank.org>.

CII–McKinsey & Company. 2002. *Health Care in India: The Road Ahead.* A Report. New Delhi.

IRDA (Insurance Regulatory and Development Authority). 2003-04. *Annual Report.* Hyderabad. www.irdaindia.org.

———. 2004. "Health Insurance." *IRDA Journal* 2 (11): entire issue. http://www.irdaonline.org/irdacontent/journals/irda_oct04.pdf.

Rao, G.V. 2004. "Customer-Driven Business Spurt in 2003–04." *IRDA Journal* 2 (11): 41–43. http://www.irdaonline.org/irdacontent/journals/irda_oct04.pdf.

John, C.P. 2004. "Social Security and Labour Welfare with Special Reference to Construction Workers in Kerala." Discussion Paper 65, Centre for Development Studies, Thiruvananthapuram, Kerala.

Karuna Trust. 2004. "A Draft Report on Community Health Insurance: Karnataka Experience," Mysore, Karnataka.

NCAER (National Council for Applied Economic Research). 2002. "Market Information Survey of Households," New Delhi.

NSSO (National Sample Survey Organisation). 2001. *Consumption of Some Important Commodities in India, 1999–2000.* National Sample Survey 55th Round. Government of India, Report 461(55/1.0/4), New Delhi.

Peters, David. H., A.S. Yazbeck, R.R. Sharma, G.N.V. Ramana, L.H. Pritchett, and A. Wagstaff. 2002. "Raising the Sights: Better Health Systems for India's Poor: Overview." World Bank, Health, Nutrition, Population Sector Unit, Washington, DC.

Mahal, Ajay, J. Singh, V. Lamba, A. Gumber, and V. Selvaraju. 2002. "Who Benefits from Public Health Spending in India? Results of a Benefit Incidence Analysis for India." National Council for Applied Economic Research, New Delhi, October.

Ministry of Labour. 2003a. *Quarterly Employment Review, January–March 2002.* Directorate General of Employment and Training, Government of India, New Delhi.

———. 2003b. *Census of Central Government Employees as of 31st March 2001.* Directorate General of Employment and Training, Government of India, New Delhi. http://dget.gov.in/publications/ccge/census2001.pdf.

———. 2004–05. *Annual Report.* Government of India, New Delhi.

Ministry of Finance. 2003–04. *Economic Survey.* Government of India, New Delhi. http://indiabudget.nic.in/es2004–05/esmain.htm.

Planning Commission. 2002–07. *Tenth Five-Year Plan.* Government of India, New Delhi. www.planningcommission.nic.in.

Rao, Sujatha. K. 2005. "Health Insurance in India." In *Background Papers on Financing and Delivery of Health Care Services in India,* National Commission on Macroeconomics and Health, Ministry of Health and Family Welfare, 275–95. New Delhi.

Rao, Sujatha K., S. Selvaraju, Somil Nagpal, and S. Sakthivel. 2005. "Financing of Health in India." In *Background Papers on Financing and Delivery of Health Care Services in India*, National Commission on Macroeconomics, Ministry of Health and Family Welfare, 239–55. New Delhi.

SHEPHERD (Self-Help Promotion for Health and Rural Development). 2003. *Insurance—A Safety Net to Poor*. Trichy, Tamil Nadu.

CHAPTER 13

Nigeria

Obinna Onwujekwe and Edit V. Velényi

The feasibility of private voluntary health insurance (PVHI) was assessed in southeast Nigeria, using a pretested questionnaire to find out whether households and companies would be willing to pay for it. Most said they would, but budget constraint differences are marked. Smaller firms, rural dwellers, and poorer socioeconomic status (SES) groups are less willing than bigger firms, urbanites, and better-off socioeconomic groups. PVHI appears to be a feasible method of paying for health care in southeast Nigeria. However, PVHI could fail if equity issues are not addressed. Preliminary results from a more recent experience with subsidizing the premiums of the poor in Niger suggest that such a program would confer considerable benefits to the poor in terms of both financial protection and improved access to quality health services.

INTRODUCTION

Like many countries around the world, Nigeria is struggling to improve its health financing system and cope with the spiraling cost of health care (James et al. 2006). Its National Health Policy and National Health Financing Policy articulate funding of the health sector from budgetary sources and recognize additional avenues of revenue such as health insurance schemes and direct employer/employee financing (FMOH 2004, 2006). The Nigerian Health Financing Policy notes that improvements will depend on the availability of equitable and efficient revenue-generation mechanisms, pooling and management of financial risks, protection of vulnerable groups, and efficient health care purchasing arrangements.

Many health financing mechanisms operate in Nigeria, but the predominant one is out-of-pocket spending (OOPS), which was also a major response to the introduction of user fees for health services. Users of health services in most Sub-Saharan African (SSA) countries are required to pay fees at point of service (Gilson and McIntyre 2005). Nigeria introduced user fees for public health services as an additional mode of financing government health services within the framework of the Bamako Initiative revolving drug funds (Ogunbekun et al. 1996; Uzochukwu, Onwujekwe, and Akpala 2002). The poor and other vulnerable groups rely heavily on user fees and other OOPS on health, which are both impoverishing and pose a financial barrier to care (James et al. 2006).

Households and individuals make many inappropriate payments for health care, mostly through out-of-pocket payments (Onwujekwe and Uzochukwu 2005). Public expenditures in Nigeria account for between 20 and 30 percent of total health expenditures, which leaves between 70 and 80 percent of the expenditures uncontrolled for in terms of value for money and their potential to generate health gains (Soyibo 2004). Hence, private expenditures account for between 70 and 80 percent of the expenditures, and the dominant private payment method is OOPS, amounting to about US$22.50 per capita and accounting for 9 percent of total household expenditures (FOS 2004a). Half of the people who cannot access care are prevented from doing so by the out-of-pocket costs (FOS 2004b). The reliance on this nonpooled financing instrument and the related absence of risk sharing puts the largest financing burden on the poor. Moreover, the absence of exemption mechanisms and prepaid instruments is largely responsible for impoverishing health expenditures (Preker 2005).

The real challenge of health care financing in Nigeria, as in many SSA countries, lies not primarily in the acute scarcity of resources, but in the absence of intermediation and insurance mechanisms to manage risk, and in inefficient resource allocation and purchasing practices (Soyibo 2004). Hence, the National Health Policy as well as the National Health Financing Policy articulate that, in addition to improving the efficiency of public expenditures, additional sources of pooled revenue are needed besides annual tax revenue and that these additional sources should urgently include various forms of health insurance (FMOH 2004, 2006).

One strategy for improving revenue mobilization and purchasing of cost-effective services is the National Health Insurance Scheme (NHIS), launched in 2005. The NHIS has the goal of providing universal coverage to the population in 15 to 20 years. This scheme is unique and innovative in that it is government driven but operated by private health maintenance organizations (HMOs). In Phase I of the scheme, the NHIS operates the formal sector health insurance program; coverage is limited to federal government civil servants. The NHIS is contributory, and the annual premium is 15 percent of an employee's basic salary (10 percent from the employer, 5 percent from the employee). The scheme for civil servants is obligatory. The employee contributions cover health benefits for the employee and five dependants (a spouse and four children below the age of 18 years) (NHIS 2005). A surcharge applies for any additional dependents. However, the contributions of two working spouses cover the two spouses and four children only. The benefits package covers all outpatient care (including consumables), emergency care, and essential health care services.

In addition to the NHIS, the government has increased support for the introduction and expansion of private voluntary health insurance (PVHI) offered by private insurers and HMOs, targeting the formal private sector labor market as one strategy for ensuring universal health care coverage in the country. Also, the NHIS intends to initiate other health insurance schemes in Nigeria so as to ensure universal health insurance coverage. These schemes include community health insurance, permanent disability health insurance, and social health insurance for prison inmates (NHIS 2005).

Hence, if PVHI is to be increasingly used to improve efficiency and equity in health care financing in Nigeria, it is important to understand the willingness of corporate bodies and households to enroll and pay for PVHI, as well as determine the factors, such as socioeconomic status, that determine peoples' willingness to pay for PVHI. However, the value of PVHI is disputed. First, PVHI has been vulnerable to increasing health care costs (Ogunbekun, Ogunbekun, and Orobaton 1999; Alubo 2001). The increasing costs are associated with the typical insurance market failures, moral hazard, and adverse selection. Second, for unknown reasons, use of PVHI has been limited in Nigeria, especially among medium and small firms. Third, PVHI is criticized for catering to higher-end market segments and, consequently, for jeopardizing equitable access to care because it has been posited that equal access to health services is an objective for any health reform (Ruiz, Amaya, and Venegas 2007).

There is little data-based empirical evidence to guide health financing policy decisions in many SSA countries such as Nigeria. Thus, many important questions are unanswered: particularly whether PVHI: (1) is financially and fiscally sustainable; (2) improves risk sharing; (3) introduces incentives for more efficient allocation of resources and strategic purchasing of health care; and (4) improves or undermines the equity of financing and access to care. In addition, the determinants of PVHI enrolment as well as willingness to pay for PVHI and issues of equity are important information for developing and implementing feasible, equitable, and viable PVHI schemes. Hence, in SSA countries, research is required to understand the determinants of private and social health insurance and the willingness and ability to pay for various health insurance schemes (Dong et al. 2003; Kirigia et al. 2005). For instance, Kirigia and others (2005) found that area of residence and income explained health insurance ownership among South African women.

This study attempts to generate new policy-relevant knowledge by determining the desirability and feasibility of PVHI in paying for health care from the point of view of individual households as well as from corporate bodies and their willingness to pay for PVHI. This is because the ultimate effect of health insurance on the population is the major determinant for society's valuation of the scheme (Ruiz et al. 2007). Beyond assessing the value of PVHI for corporate entities and households, understanding the equity characteristics of PVHI are crucial for scheme design and for social welfare–enhancing and informed health care financing choices by policy makers.

RESEARCH METHODOLOGY

The study was conducted in an urban area (Enugu, the state capital) and a rural area (Ugwuoba) in Enugu State, located in southeast Nigeria. The data were generated by the authors from a random sample of respondents from Enugu state,

Southeast Nigeria. All calculations (variables of interest) in this chapter are based on this dataset. Though land-locked, Enugu state, with a population of 3.2 million people, is close to coastal cities with major shipping ports and trading centers in Nigeria (Enugu State Government 2000). The city is within five hours' drive from Abuja, the capital of Nigeria, and seven hours from Lagos, Nigeria's administrative and commercial headquarters (Enugu State Government 2000). The rural community Ugwuoba, with an estimated population of 45,000 people, is in Oji-river local government area, 45 kilometers from Enugu. The people in both areas are mostly Igbo, the third largest ethnic group in Nigeria, with a population above 20 million people.

Study Tools and Sampling

A pretested, interviewer-administered questionnaire was used to collect data from a random sample of households in Enugu and Ugwuoba. Another pretested, interviewer-administered questionnaire was used to collect data from a purposive sample of corporate bodies. The interviewers were trained for three weeks to ensure their mastery of the questionnaire and health insurance issues. Random sampling was used to select 200 households from the rural area and 250 households from the urban area. Thirty corporate bodies were interviewed, belonging to three categories, based on staff size. Ten corporate bodies had fewer than 10 employees, 10 had between 10 and 20 employees, and the rest had more than 20 employees. Enugu state is not very industrialized, and Enugu is mainly a civil service city with a large informal sector, which explains why there were so few firms to interview.

To provide a framework for the feasibility of PVHI in Nigeria, the survey data collected includes ranking and rating of the various financing modalities and insurance mechanisms, and elicitation of willingness to pay. Contingent valuation method (CVM) was used to elicit willingness to pay, using the bidding game question format (Mitchell and Carson 1989; Onwujekwe 2004). Before eliciting willingness to pay, a scenario was presented to the respondents describing PVHI, its potential benefits, benefits package, and payment vehicle. All the respondents were read an introductory explanation (in the local language) about PVHI and the CVM scenario.

Operational Definitions of Voluntary Insurance Schemes in the Study

Three operational definitions were used:

- *Private voluntary health insurance* is financial protection offered to individuals or groups by a nongovernmental organization and purchased by the insured without any obligation to do so.
- *Voluntary health insurance offered by government* is financial protection offered to individuals or groups by the public sector and purchased by the insured without any obligation to do so.

- *Retainership* is a situation in which an organization enrolls its employees with a number of health care providers and also directly pays the providers for defined services rendered to employees. The employees usually do not contribute to the payment.

Determining the Level of Acceptability of Health Insurance

The ranking of preferences was determined before willingness to pay was elicited. A brief introductory explanation about health insurance was provided to all the respondents before determining their levels of preferences and acceptability of the scheme. After having been read the descriptions of the different health insurance models, the respondents were asked to rank the three different models from 1 (least preferred) to 3 (most preferred).

To rate the benefits of health insurance, the respondents were asked to draw on either their experience or understanding to rate the potential of health insurance to: (1) offer financial protection against the cost of illness; (2) give households access to affordable health care; (3) improve labor market functioning by ensuring better health, enhanced productivity, and greater job stability; (4) improve household health consumption patterns by reducing individuals' direct health care costs. In the four cases, the ratings were 0 for none, 1 for low, 2 for medium, and 3 for high.

A PVHI scenario was presented to the household respondents before eliciting their willingness to pay. A different scenario was presented to respondents from corporate bodies. The scenario explained the benefits package and the fact that the premiums are to be paid before service utilization and that HMOs are responsible for providing health care. The benefits package described to the respondents was similar to the one offered to federal civil servants under the NHIS, which is geared toward both routine care and mitigation of catastrophic expenses. Hence, the benefits package in the proposed insurance plan covers selected preventive, curative, and health promotion services. They include: (1) outpatient care, including necessary consumables; (2) essential drugs and essential diagnostic tests; (3) maternity care for up to four live births; (4) preventive care such as immunization, health education, family planning, antenatal, and postnatal care; (5) consultation with specialists such as physicians, pediatricians, obstetricians, gynecologists, general surgeons, orthopedic surgeons, ENT surgeons, dental surgeons, radiologists, psychiatrists, ophthalmologists, and physiotherapists; (6) hospital care in a standard ward for up 45 days a year; (7) eye examination and care excluding provision of spectacles and contact lenses; (8) a range of prostheses (limited to artificial limbs produced in Nigeria); and (9) preventive dental care and pain relief.

In the case of consumers, the respondent's willingness to pay was elicited before that of other household members. The bidding game iteration was used to elicit willingness to pay for individuals and corporate bodies. The iterations are presented below as I and II.

I. Bidding Game Iteration for Eliciting Consumers' Willingness to Pay for PVHI from individuals

1. The price of a monthly insurance premium (contribution) per person is 500 naira (120 naira = US$1.00). Are you willing to pay? 1 = Yes (Q2) 0 = No (Q3) Do not know (Q4)

2. What if the premium is 600 naira, will you be willing to pay? 1 = yes (Q4) 0 = No (Q4)

3. What if the premium is 400 naira, will you be willing to pay? 1 = yes (Q4) 0 = No (Q4)

4. What is the maximum amount you are willing to pay for the PVHI premium, bearing in mind your average household income and money that it spends on various items?

II. Bidding Game Iteration for Eliciting Consumers' Willingness to Pay for PVHI from corporate bodies

1. The price of a monthly insurance premium is 500 naira. Are you willing to pay this amount of money per staff member? 1 = Yes (Q2) 0 = No (Q3)

2. What if the monthly premium per person is 600 naira, will you be willing to pay? 1 = yes 0 = No (Interviewer: no matter the answer, go to Q4).

3. What if the monthly premium per person is 400 naira, will you be willing to pay? 1 = yes (Interviewer: no matter the answer, go to Q4).

4. What is the maximum amount you are very certain to pay per staff member, bearing in mind your organizations' average monthly income and money that it spends on various items?

Data Analysis

Tabulations and bivariate and multivariate analyses were the data analytical tools. In the case of consumers, the data were examined for links between SES, geographic location, and occupation with the insurance-related variables. For analyzing the socioeconomic equity implications for consumers, an asset-based SES index was created, using principal components analysis (Onwujekwe and Uzochukwu 2005; Filmer and Pritchett 2001). The first principal component was used to derive weights for the SES index. The SES index was used to divide the households into quartiles, and chi-square analysis was used to determine the statistical significance of the differentiation of the dependent variables into SES quartiles.

The SES index and the urban-rural differences were used to examine both socioeconomic and geographic differentials of the key dependent variables. In the case of data from corporate bodies, the relationships between organization size (small, medium, and large) and the insurance-related variables were examined. Chi-square tests were used to determine whether the trends of the major responses were statistically significant. In addition, ordinary least squares (OLS) multiple regression analyses were undertaken to investigate the relationship of elicited willingness to pay for PVHI with explanatory factors.

RESULTS

In this section, the results from corporate bodies are first presented before those from consumers.

Corporate Bodies

Most of the respondents were decision makers in their organizations. Due to difficulty of finding organizations with more than 20 employees in Enugu, only 8 out of the total sample size of 30 had more than 20 employees, while 11 organizations had fewer than 10 employees and 10 to 20 employees, respectively. Since providing medical benefits is not mandatory for firms with more than 10 employees, few corporate bodies provided their staff with any medical benefit. Companies that did provide medical benefits did so through retainerships with hospitals. Such retainerships covered both ambulatory and inpatient services for the employees and a specified number of their family members, up to variety of monetary ceilings. Two of the organizations had reimbursements, one had an in-house health facility, and none had health insurance. Twenty-three companies (76.7 percent) had no medical benefits for their employees. The monthly health care expenditures reported by the seven organizations that provide medical benefits ranged from 3,000 naira to 180,000 naira.

In general, the firms rated the four benefit indicators of PVHI as mostly medium and high. The indicators were: financial protection offered by health insurance; improved access to affordable services; labor market improvement; and stable household consumption patterns.

Of the 33 respondents, 28 (93.3 percent) stated that health insurance was acceptable to their organizations as a strategy for paying for health care. However, in ranking their preferences for different health insurance models, PVHI was mostly preferred followed by community-based health insurance. Compulsory health insurance was the least preferred model (table 13.1).

Most respondents preferred a health insurance plan with a comprehensive benefits package, but some preferred a benefits package that would cover only emergencies. The majority of respondents stated that their organizations would be willing to enroll their staff members in a PVHI scheme (table 13.2). However, only half of the respondents would be willing to pay an insurance premium of 500 naira per staff member per month. The average willingness-to-pay amount was 397.8 naira; the median was 500 naira.

TABLE 13.1 Nigeria: Preferences for Different Health Insurance Strategies

Ranking of different health insurance strategies	*Least preferred N (%)*	*Middle N (%)*	*Most preferred N (%)*	*Mean (SD)*	*Median*
Private voluntary health insurance	5 (16.7)	3 (10.0)	22 (73.3)	2.5 (1.0)	3
Compulsory health insurance	20 (66.7)	7 (23.3)	3 (10.0)	1.3 (.50)	1
Community-based health insurance	5 (16.7)	20 (66.7)	5 (16.7)	2.3 (.50)	2

Source: The data were generated by the authors from a random sample of respondents from Enugu state, Southeast Nigeria. All calculations (variables of interest) in this chapter are based on this dataset.
Note: N = number; SD = standard deviation.

TABLE 13.2 Nigeria: Willingness to Join and Pay for Employees' PVHI

Willingness to enroll staff members in PVHI [number (%)]	19 (63.3%)
Willingness to pay a premium of 500 naira monthly per staff member [number (%)]	15 (50%)
Willingness-to-pay amount	
Mean (SD)	397.8 (311.4)
95% confidence interval	261.6–534.0
Median	500
Minimum–maximum	0–1,000

Source: See table 13.1.
Note: US$1 = 133 naira.

Many of the variables of interest varied by size of the organizations. No organization with fewer than 10 employees had any staff medical benefits, while it was mostly organizations with more than 20 employees that had such benefits. Most of the differences in types of medical benefits offered to staff members were statistically significant. The organizations with more than 20 employees had the highest health care costs, but the differences were not statistically significant. Although most organizations stated that health insurance was an acceptable method of paying for health care, not all of them were willing to enroll in a health insurance scheme (table 13.3). Organizations with more than 20 employees were most willing to enroll their staff members. The differences in the number of organizations that were willing to enroll their staff members were statistically significant ($p < 0.05$).

The rating of perceptions about the benefits of health insurance, rating of preferences for different health insurance strategies, as well as the rating of different benefits packages did not vary by organizational size. However, there were some differences in perceptions, preferences, and acceptability of the different insurance strategies and benefits packages within each size category. The preferences for different health insurance strategies did not differ by size with the exception of compulsory health insurance, which was mostly preferred by organizations with fewer than 10 employees.

TABLE 13.3 Nigeria: Acceptability and Willingness to Enroll in Health Insurance, by Size of Organization

Response	*<10 employees*	*10 to 20 employees*	*>20 employees*	*Chi-square (p-value)*
Acceptable	10	11	7	.033 (.86)
Willing to enroll	5	6	8	5.35 (.021)
Wiling to pay 500 naira	3	6	5	0.15 (.70)

Source: See table 13.1.

The mean willingness to pay for health insurance was 306.3 naira, 375.0 naira and 528.6 naira, respectively, for firms with fewer than 10 employees, 10 to 20 employees, and more than 20 employees, although the difference was not statistically significant across the three groups ($p > .05$). It was statistically significant ($p < .05$) between firms with fewer than 10 employees and 10 to 20 employees with those with more than 20 employees, respectively.

Consumer Study

There were 247 and 199 usable questionnaires (total of 446) for analysis in the urban and rural areas, respectively. Most of the respondents were household heads, married, male, middle-aged, with some formal education, and working as subsistence farmers. The most common household assets were radio sets, electric fans, and television sets. Of household nonfood expenditures, educational expenses were the highest, followed distantly by expenditures on rent and clothing. The average weekly household cost of food was 3,486.2 naira, and the weekly per capita cost of food was 704.3 naira.

OOPS was perceived to be the most difficult means of paying for health care; the NHIS, the easiest. A total of 48.9 percent of the respondents felt that PVHI presented an easy means of paying for health care. However, 60.3 percent, 47.1 percent, and 13.2 percent of the respondents stated that the NHIS, community-based health insurance, and other community-based health financing schemes were easy means of paying for health care.

In the month preceding the survey, households spent an average of 1,615.7 naira on respondents that were ill, and 2,434.1 naira on other ill household members (US$1 = 133 naira). OOPS was the major health care financing strategy in the study, and people usually paid out of pocket using their own money (table 13.4). Health insurance (of any kind) was rarely used to pay for health care.

Preferences and Acceptability of Health Insurance

Consumers rated their perceptions about the benefits of health insurance from none to high. They were mostly of the opinion that health insurance would be beneficial in offering financial protection against paying for health care and

TABLE 13.4 Nigeria: Mechanisms Used to Pay and Cope with Health Care Payments

Payment	*Respondents* *N* = *256* *n (%)*	*Other household members* *N* = *250* *n (%)*
Out-of-pocket spending	206 (63.1)	203 (79.3)
Health insurance	1 (0.4)	1 (0.4)
Installment	29 (11.3)	28 (11.2)
In-kind	3 (1.2)	3 (1.2)
Others	17 (6.6)	15 (6.0)
	N = *247*	*N* = *239*
Coping	*n (%)*	*n (%)*
Own money	214 (86.6)	203 (0.5)
Borrowed money	9 .6)	11 (4.6)
Sold household movable assets	2 (0.8)	5 (2.1)
Sold family land	1 (0.4)	1 (0.4)
Subsidy from government	1 (0.4)	3 (1.3)
Community solidarity/altruism	8 (3.2)	6 (2.5)
Exemption	4 (1.6)	6 (2.5)
Others	8 (3.2)	5 (2.1)

Source: See table 13.1.

would ultimately stabilize household consumption patterns (table 13.5). The rating of perceived benefits of health insurance showed an increasing monotonic trend from none to high, with the majority of the respondents rating them high in both urban and rural areas. However, the mean rating in the rural area was generally more than that in the urban area for the four indicators of perceived benefits ($p < .01$).

Consumers preferred PVHI and community-based health insurance over compulsory health insurance (table 13.6). However, voluntary health insurance offered by the government had a higher rating than PVHI. Similarly to corporate bodies, consumers preferred that the benefits package not be limited. A benefits package covering only emergencies received the lowest ranking.

Most of the respondents were personally willing to enroll in a PVHI scheme (table 13.7). The respondents also expressed a similar opinion with regard to other household members. Most of the respondents were willing to pay a monthly premium of 500 naira for themselves; a minority was willing to pay the same amount of money for other household members. So that the poorest people in their communities would benefit from health insurance, 226 (53.2 percent) were willing to contribute some money. The median monthly willingness to pay for a personal premium was 500 naira, but 200 naira per person for other household members. The median monthly altruistic willingness-to-pay amount was 33.3 naira.

TABLE 13.5 Nigeria: Rating of Perceptions about Use of Health Insurance to Improve Payment for Health Care

Rating of indicators of perceptions	*None N (%)*	*Low N (%)*	*Medium N (%)*	*High N (%)*	*Mean (SD)*
Financial protection offered by health insurance	24 (5.5)	46 (10.5)	118 (26.9)	250 (57.1)	2.4 (.87)
Improved access to affordable care by households	13 (3.0)	53 (12.1)	153 (34.9)	219 (50.0)	2.3 (.80)
Improvement of labor markets	10 (2.3)	33 (7.7)	99 (23.0)	289 (67.1)	2.5 (.74)
Stabilize household consumption patterns	7 (1.6)	33 (7.7)	109 (24.8)	290 (66.1)	2.6 (.70)
Rating of perceptions of benefits of health insurance in urban and rural areas					
Financial protection	None	Low	Medium	High	Mean (SD)
Urban (N = 243)	21	31	81	110	2.2 (.95)
Rural (N = 195)	3	15	37	140	2.6 (.70)
Chi-square (p-value)					31.5 (.0001)
Improved access to affordable health care					
Urban (N = 244)	12	40	80	112	2.2 (.89)
Rural (N = 195)	1	13	73	107	2.5 (.65)
Chi-square (p-value)					13.4 (.0001)
Improvement of labor markets					
Urban (N = 239)	9	25	64	141	2.4 (.83)
Rural (N = 192)	1	8	35	148	2.7 (.56)
Chi-square (p-value)					19.6 (.0001)
Improved household consumption patterns					
Urban (N =244)	7	27	70	140	2.4 (.80)
Rural (N = 195)	0	6	39	150	2.7 (.51)
Chi-square (p-value)					25.6 (.0001)

Source: See table 13.1.

TABLE 13.6 Nigeria: Preferences for Different Health Insurance Strategies

Ranking of different health insurance strategies	*Least preferred N (%)*	*Fairly preferred N (%)*	*Highly preferred N (%)*	*Most preferred N (%)*	*Mean (SD)*
Private voluntary health insurance	102 (23.2)	110 (25.0)	118 (26.5)	110 (25.0)	2.5 (1.1)
Voluntary health insurance offered by government	23 (5.2)	78 (17.7)	108 (24.5)	231 (52.5)	3.3 (.93)
Compulsory health insurance	205 (46.5)	129 (29.3)	62 (14.1)	45 (10.2)	1.9 (1.0)
Community-based health insurance	109 (24.8)	126 (28.6)	148 (33.6)	57 (12.9)	2.4 (1.0)

Source: See table 13.1.

Differences in Some Dependent Variables, by Geographical Area and Socioeconomic Status

The amount of money people spent on health care in the month before the interview on both treatment and transportation was not statistically significantly different between the urban and the rural areas. Although OOPS was the

TABLE 13.7 Nigeria: Willingness to Enroll and Pay for PVHI

Willingness-to-pay variables	*Measurement*
Willingness to personally enroll in PVHI [N (%)]	380 (86.0%)
Willingness to enroll other household members in PVHI [N (%)]	377 (85.7%)
Willingness to pay 500 naira monthly for self as a premium [N (%)]	220 (52.1%)
Willingness to pay 500 naira monthly for other household members as a premium [N (%)]	98 (23.6%)
Willingness to pay for the poorest to benefit from PVHI [N (%)]	226 (53.15%)
Willingness-to-pay amount (respondents)	
Mean (SD)	395.8 (304.8)
95% confidence interval	368.6–428.8
Median	500
Minimum–maximum	0–2000
Willingness-to-pay amount (other household members)	
Mean (SD)	260.8 (247.3)
95% confidence interval	240.5–291.9
Median	200
Minimum–maximum	0–2,000

Source: See table 13.1.

most common payment strategy for health care in both urban and rural areas, it was used more in the urban area. The difference was statistically significantly different only in paying for other household members ($p < .05$). Conversely, installment payment was used more in the rural area than in the urban area to pay for health care for both the respondent and other household members ($p < .05$). The reasons given by the two people who used health insurance were for financial protection and for access to affordable and good quality health care services.

The use of own money to cope with the burden of payment was about the same in the two areas for both respondents and other household members. However, in the rural areas, more people borrowed money and sold household assets to pay for health care. For respondents' payments 70.8 percent and 53.1 percent ($p < 0.05$), and for other household members 52.5 percent and 38.6 percent, found that it was easy to use OOPS to pay for health care in urban and rural areas, respectively. More urban than rural dwellers stated that it was easy to use OOPS to pay for health care. The majority of rural dwellers, unlike their urban counterparts, felt that all types of health insurance were an easy means of paying for health care.

Similar patterns in rural-urban differences were seen in both ranking of preferences and scoring of acceptability of different health insurance mechanisms. Health insurance was generally more acceptable in the rural area and the chi-square for urban-rural differences is 10.5 ($p = .001$). PVHI was preferred in the urban area, while voluntary health insurance offered by the government was

TABLE 13.8 Nigeria: Geographic Differences in Willingness to Enroll and to Pay for PVHI

Whether willing to enroll and to pay in urban and rural areas

	Willingness to enroll self in PVHI	*Willing to enroll other household member in PVHI*	*Willing to pay (self)*	*Willing to pay (other household members)*
Urban	192 (77.7%)	191 (77.3%)	145 (58.7%)	63 (25.5%)
Rural	188 (96.4%)	186 (95.4%)	75 (38.5%)	35 (17.9)
Chi-square (p-value)	31.5 (.0001)	29.3 (.0001)	16.9 (.0001)	3.2 (.047)
	Mean (SD) Willingness to pay for self	*Median Willingness to pay for self*	*Mean (SD) Willingness to pay for other householders*	*Median Willingness to pay for other householders*
Urban	459.1 (342.8)	500	292.4 (265.3)	200
Rural	314.6 (221.6)	200	218.7 (215.7)	100
Chi-square (p-value)	24.4 (.0001)	18.6 (.0001)	9.2 (.003)	9.1 (.003)

Source: See table 13.1.

preferred in the rural area. Community-health insurance was more acceptable in the rural area but the urban-rural difference was only marginally statistically significant ($p < 0.10$). Compulsory health insurance was also preferred in the rural area ($p < .01$). There were similar preference ratings for benefits packages in both rural and urban areas, with the exception of coverage of only outpatient services, which was rated higher in the rural area and coverage of only emergencies which was rated higher in the urban area.

A larger share of rural respondents was willing to enroll in PVHI but a larger share of urbanites ($p < .05$) was willing to pay (table 13.8). The levels of willingness to pay for PVHI were also higher in urban areas ($p < .05$). This likely reflects the higher socioeconomic status of the urbanites.

While OOPS was used more by the better-off households to pay for health care for other household members, the converse was true for paying for the respondents ($p < .05$). However, installment payment was used most by the poorest SES groups. In the only three instances where health insurance was used, it was by the least-poor SES group. The use of own money to cope with the burden of payment was mostly undertaken by the least-poor SES group ($p < .05$). More people in the most-poor SES borrowed money and sold household assets to pay for health care.

Table 13.9 shows that perceptions of health insurance benefits increases, though not always monotonically, moving from the least-poor to most-poor SES groups. Hence, the poorer the SES group, the higher the perception of the benefits of health insurance. In scoring the levels of acceptability, that of PVHI offered by the government as well as compulsory health insurance and community-based health insurance increased, moving from the least- to the most-poor SES groups ($p < .05$).

TABLE 13.9 Nigeria: SES Differences in Rating of Perceived Benefits of Health Insurance

Perceived benefits	*Mean (SD)*
Financial protection	
Q1 = Most poor	2.7 (.60)
Q2 = Very poor	2.4 (.90)
Q3 = Poor	2.3 (.88)
Q4 = Least poor	2.0 (.96)
Chi-square (p-value)	11.9 (.0001)
Improved access to affordable health care	
Q1 = Most poor	2.6 (.58)
Q2 = Very poor	2.3 (.77)
Q3 = Poor	2.4 (.87)
Q4 = Least poor	2.1 (.88)
Chi-square (p-value)	7.9 (.0001)
Improvement of labor markets	
Q1 = Most poor	2.8 (.53)
Q2 = Very poor	2.6 (.73)
Q3 = Poor	2.5 (.72)
Q4 = Least poor	2.3 (.86)
Chi-square (p-value)	7.5 (.0001)
Improved household consumption patterns	
Q1 = Most poor	2.8 (.46)
Q2 = Very poor	2.6 (.69)
Q3 = Poor	2.5 (.74)
Q4 = Least poor	2.3 (.81)
Chi-square (p-value)	7.7 (.0001)

Source: See table 13.1.

All SES groups preferred a benefits package covering everything. However, while the worse-off SES groups showed greater preference for benefits packages that covered at least basic disease control and outpatient services, the better-off SES groups had higher preferences for benefits packages covering only emergencies. Table 13.10 shows that the more better off the SES group, the more willing the people were to enroll themselves and other householders, and to pay for PVHI offered by private firms ($p < .01$). Table 13.10 shows that as SES increases so does the level of willingness to pay for PVHI.

Differences in Willingness to Enroll and to Pay for PVHI, by Occupation

Farmers, petty traders, and the unemployed consistently rated the benefits of all aspects of health insurance higher than the other occupational groups. In general, more than 50 percent of the respondents belonging to all occupational groups were willing to enroll both themselves and other household members in

TABLE 13.10 Nigeria: SES Differences in Willingness to Enroll and to Pay for PVHI

Item	*Q1 = Most poor N = 109*	*Q2 = Very poor N = 109*	*Q3 = Least poor N = 109*	*Q4 = Least poor N = 109*	*Chi-square (p-value)*
Willing to enroll self in PVHI	104	99	86	88	14.6 (.0001)
Willing to enroll other household members in PVHI	104	97	84	89	12.2 (.0001)
Willing to pay (self)	38	53	58	70	18.2 (.0001)
Willing to pay (other household members)	17	17	28	36	12.3 (.0001)
Altruistic willingness to pay	21	48	74	82	78.4 (.0001)
Mean (SD) willingness to pay for self	287.3 (203.3)	394.3 (271.2)	395.3 (249.6)	515.5 (410.2)	10.4 (.0001)
Mean (SD) willingness to pay for other household members	203.8 (216.5)	244.2 (205.9)	283.8 (240.2)	318.3(304.4)	4.2 (.006)

Source: See table 13.1.

TABLE 13.11 Nigeria: Level of Willingness to Pay, by Occupation

Occupation	*Mean (SD) willingness to pay for self*	*Mean (SD) willingness to pay for other householders*
Unemployed	309.4 (213.1)	256.7 (209.5)
Farmer	300.6 (213.7)	217.1 (218.7)
Petty trader	420.5 (275.0)	295.4 (256.1)
Government employee	457.1 (307.5)	298.8 (258.3)
Private sector employee	476.5 (272.8)	370.6 (248.8)
Big business	573.2 (606.0)	276.7 (470.5)
Self-employed professional	428.2 (309.7)	258.6 (208.7)
Others	366.7 (282.5)	209.3 (168.2)
Aggregate	395.8 (304.8)	260.3 (247.3)
Chi-square (p-value)	4.1 (.0001)	1.7 (.12)

Source: See table 13.1.

a PVHI scheme offered by private firms. However, less than 50 percent of farmers, government workers, and self-employed professionals were willing to pay a premium of 500 naira per month. The majority of private sector employees and big business people were willing to pay 500 naira monthly. However, less than 50 percent of all occupational groups were willing to pay a premium of 500 naira monthly for other household members. Apart from farmers, 75 percent of all other occupational groups were willing to pay for the poor to benefit from PVHI. The highest mean willingness to pay for self was elicited from big business people at 573 naira monthly, while the least was elicited from farmers at 301 naira monthly. Private sector employees were willing to pay the highest amount (308 naira) for other household members; farmers, the least amount (217 naira).

Multiple Regression Analyses

The reduced models of willingness to pay for PVHI for self and for other household members showed that willingness to pay for only the positive cases was positively related to acceptability of health insurance and the household's socioeconomic status. The coefficients and standard errors for acceptability of health insurance and socioeconomic status were respectively 166.4 (53.4) and 48.7 (8.6). The regression models were statistically significant ($p < 0.01$).

DISCUSSION

The results show that private voluntary health insurance is a feasible strategy for financing health care in the study area. The results also indicate that PVHI was more preferred over compulsory health insurance and that even government workers were willing to pay for PVHI. The results imply that private sector–led PVHI could be more acceptable and hence more sustainable than public sector–led NHIS, even for public servants. Since the results showed that PVHI was preferred over the NHIS currently being implemented in Nigeria, the NHIS has a lot of convincing to do before many corporate bodies would agree to join the scheme. Conversely, the result implies that there is a potential untapped market for private sector PVHI in the country. However, issues regarding the effects of corporate bodies' size, as well as socioeconomic and geographic inequity, should be addressed.

The low corporate-level provision of medical benefits for employees implies that there is a potentially huge unmet need for health care within firms, which well-designed and packaged PVHI schemes should be able to satisfy. The higher the number of employees, the more medical benefits are offered to the employees. The fact that many of the firms' responses depended on the size of their staff implies that the size of firms should be taken into consideration in the design of PVHI so that benefits packages and premiums are tailored to firms' income and other peculiarities. For instance, firms with less income could be allowed to pay smaller premiums than larger companies. Also, extensive information, education, and communication campaigns have to be undertaken with firms with fewer than 21 employees to increase their willingness to enroll and to pay for health insurance for their employees.

The finding that subsistence farmers, petty traders, and the unemployed consistently rated the benefits of all aspects of health insurance higher than the other occupational groups could be an income effect. This is because these people earn low incomes and may not have enough money to pay for health care when ill. Thus, the biting effects of lack of money when ill could have led them to appreciate the need to protect against health-related income shocks through insurance. Kirigia et al. (2005) reported similar finding with respect to insurance ownership by women in South Africa where high incomes, white collar occupations, and gainful employment were significant predictors of health insurance ownership. Government workers may be less willing to pay because they already enjoy some medical benefits and thus did not highly appreciate the marginal benefits of PVHI.

Although many people were desirous of enrolling in PVHI, especially those in the lower socioeconomic groups that rated its benefits higher, they were limited by their budgetary constraints. As a result, rural dwellers and poorer SES groups stated smaller willingness-to-pay amounts than the urban and better-off SES groups. Similarly, in South Africa, it was found that people living in formal urban settlements or rural white-owned farms had higher odds of owning a health insurance policy than people living in informal urban settlements of former rural homelands—a reflection of economic well-being (Kirigia et al. 2005). This situation reflects the constraining effect of poverty on enrolment and payment of insurance premiums for PVHI. This finding calls for government intervention in the PVHI market to increase coverage and provide enough clientele for the insurers to remain in business.

All in all, PVHI appears to be a feasible and acceptable method of paying for health care in southeast Nigeria, although this assertion is tempered by the possible replicability of the finding in other parts of Nigeria since health care expenditure and health-seeking patterns differ. The study has also shown that few or no medical benefits are currently available to workers of most firms but that the firms were willing to enroll their workers in PVHI and also pay part of their premium for them. However, the study is limited by the small number of firms, a result of the low number of firms in the study site.

Most consumers were willing to enroll in PVHI but this is limited by geographic, socioeconomic, and occupational equity issues, because the rural dwellers, poor people, and farmers stated the smallest willingness-to-pay amounts for PVHI. Hence, the PVHI market could fail if these equity issues are not tackled. Altruistic contributions at the community level are one way of raising funds for equity, but more sustainable grants from governments and donors would be needed to support PVHI in Nigeria.

NOTE

The authors are grateful to the World Bank for providing them with the opportunity to contribute to this worthwhile project.

REFERENCES

Alubo, O. 2001. "The Promise and Limits of Private Medicine: Health Policy Dilemmas in Nigeria." *Health Policy Plan* 16 (3): 313–21.

Dong, H., B. Kouyate, J. Cairns, F. Mugisha, and R. Sauerborn. 2003. "Willingness to Pay for Community-Based Insurance in Burkina Faso." *Health Economics* 12 (10): 849–62.

FMOH (Federal Ministry of Health). 2006. *The Nigerian Health Financing Policy*. FMOH, Abuja.

———. 2004. *Health Sector Reform Program—Strategic Thrusts with Logical Framework and Plan of Action 2004–2007*. FMOH, Abuja.

Filmer, D., and L.H. Pritchett. 2001. "Estimating Wealth Effects without Expenditure Data—or Tears: An Application to Educational Enrolments in States of India." *Demography* 38:115–32.

FOS (Federal Office of Statistics). 2004a. Core Welfare Indicators Questionnaire Survey: Combined Six-States Main Report. Abuja, FOS, State Statistical Agencies of Abia, Cross River, Gombe, Kebbi, Osun, and Plateau: p. 16–20. Federal Office of Statistics, Abuja.

———. 2004b. Nigeria Living Standard Survey (NLSS) 2003/2004. Abuja, FOS, European Union, World Bank, Department of International Development, UNDP: 35–39. Federal Office of Statistics, Abuja.

Gilson, L. and D. McIntyre. 2005. "Removing User Fees for Primary Care in Africa: The Need for Careful Action." *British Medical Journal* 331:762–65.

James, C.D., K. Hanson, B. McPake, D. Balabanova, D. Gwatkin, I. Hopwood, C. Kirunga, R. Knippenberg, B. Meessen, S.S. Morris, A. Preker, Y. Souteyrand, A. Tibouti, P. Villeneuve, and K. Xu. 2006. "To Retain or Remove User Fees? Reflections on the Current Debate in Low- and Middle- Income Countries." *Applied Health Economics and Health Policy.* 5 (3):137–53.

Kirigia, M.J., L.G. Sambo, B. Nganda, G.M. Mwabu, R. Chatora, and T. Mwase. 2005. "Determinants of Health Insurance Ownership among South African Women." *BMC Health Services Research* 5:17.

Lambo, E. 2004. "Memorandum from the Honorable Minister of Health on a Blueprint for the Accelerated Implementation of National Health Insurance in Nigeria." Federal Ministry of Health, Abuja.

Mitchell, R.C., and R.T. Carson. 1989. "An Experiment in Determining Willingness to Pay National Water Quality Improvements." Draft report to the U.S. Environmental Protection Agency, Washington, DC.

NHIS (National Health Insurance Scheme). 2005. *Operational Guidelines*. Abuja: NHIS.

Ogunbekun, I., A. Ogunbekun, and N. Orobaton. 1999. "Private Health Care in Nigeria: Walking the Tightrope." *Health Policy and Planning* 14 (2): 174–181.

Ogunbekun, I., O. Adeyi, A. Wouters, and R. Morrow. 1996. "Cost and Financing of Improvements in the Quality of Maternal Health Services through the Bamako Initiative in Nigeria." *Health Policy and Planning,* 11(4): 369–384.

Onwujekwe, O.E. 2004. "Criterion and Content Validity of a Novel Structured Haggling Contingent Valuation Question Format versus the Bidding Game and Binary with Follow-up Questions. *Social Science and Medicine* 58 (3): 525–37.

Onwujekwe, O.E. and B.S.C. Uzochukwu. 2005. "Socioeconomic and Geographic Differentials in Costs and Payment Strategies for Primary Health Care Services in Southeast Nigeria." *Health Policy* 71 (3): 383–97.

Preker, A. S. 2005. "Feasibility of Mandatory Health Insurance—Challenges in Health Care Financing." World Bank, Abuja Flagship Course, Abuja.

———. 2004. "Private Voluntary Health Insurance in Development. Review of Role in Africa Region and Other Selected Country Experiences." Concept Note. World Bank. Washington, DC.

Ruiz, F., L. Amaya, and S. Venegas. 2007. "Progressive Segmented Health Insurance: Colombian Health Reform and Access to Health Services." *Health Economics* 16:3–18.

Soyibo, A. 2004. "National Health Accounts of Nigeria 1998–2002." Research report. University of Ibadan, Ibadan.

Enugu State Government. 2001. *Enugu State of Nigeria—The Story of Untapped Potentials*. Information booklet. Enugu State Government, Enugu, Nigeria.

Uzochukwu, B.S.C., O.E. Onwujekwe, and C.O. Akpala. 2002. "Effect of the Bamako-Initiative Drug Revolving Fund on Availability and Rational Use of Essential Drugs in Primary Health Care Facilities in Southeast Nigeria." *Health Policy and Planning* 17 (4): 378–83.

CHAPTER 14

Slovenia

Maks Tajnikar and Petra Došenović Bonča

The scope and size of the voluntary health insurance market (VHI) in the Republic of Slovenia is largely determined by the features of the compulsory health insurance, which provides near-universal coverage and comprehensive benefits. Because the system does not cover the full price of health care services, copayments of between 5 and 75 percent of the price of a service are also required. To provide full coverage of the copayment, the predominant form of VHI was introduced, in 1992. Since then, this type of voluntary health insurance has undergone changes. In 2003, its role was seriously debated, and proposals were made for its elimination and the transfer of premiums paid for full copayment coverage to compulsory health insurance. In 2005, it was eventually decided not to change the general system of health insurance and to reform VHI for full copayment coverage according to the principle of intergenerational mutuality, to declare it in the public interest of Slovenia, and to implement a system of risk-equalization schemes.

INTRODUCTION

The role, emergence, and development of voluntary health insurance within Slovenia's health care system are examined in this chapter. In the early 1990s, financial problems led to the institution of copayments, and hence what became the predominant form of VHI, for full copayment coverage. Developments since then were also attempts to resolve problems with financing the sector from compulsory health insurance revenue and problems in delivering health care. This chapter attempts to show that such a path of development led to a type of voluntary health insurance that could not solve those problems and thus proved unable to reach the goal for which it was introduced. It also became inconsistent and incomparable with characteristics of VHI in other developed countries. The above-mentioned problems with this type of VHI led to the adoption of risk equalization within VHI, which has affected the functioning of the VHI market. In addition, Slovenia's VHI does not function appropriately from the viewpoint of the insured population: it has little effect on rationality of consumer-patient behavior. By empirically analyzing the efficiency of Slovenia's primary care, the authors do, however, demonstrate that the existing funding arrangements affect the provision of health care.

This chapter begins with a brief outline of Slovenia's macroeconomic environment, the health status of its population, and the general characteristics of the health care system and describes the characteristics of the VHI that has developed. The analysis of VHI in this chapter derives from a study of its evolution. Close attention is given to the issue of how VHI in Slovenia affects the relationship between the insured population and the health care providers. Special attention is given to the issue of whether existing organizational features of voluntary health insurance can create appropriate incentives for efficient operation of the VHI market and stimulate increases in efficiency of health care delivery. The chapter concludes by outlining relevant policy options, drawn from negative experiences during the long process of Slovenia's VHI development.

THE SLOVENIAN CONTEXT

To help readers understand the background that determines the features of Slovenia's VHI market, the macroeconomic environment, the population's health status, and the general characteristics of the health care system are first described.

Macroeconomic Environment, Health Status, and Demographic Trends

The GDP of Slovenia has been steadily increasing for a decade (table 14.1). Real GDP growth decreased noticeably after 2000. However, it increased from 2.7 percent to 4.4 percent between 2003 and 2004 and to 5.7 percent in 2006, the highest recorded growth rate since 1999. Compared with 2004, the structure of economic growth has seen an increase in the contribution of international trade in 2005, and external demand has remained a significant factor of economic growth. In the last two years, increased domestic investment by state-owned firms accelerated Slovenia's economic growth. In 2005 domestic final consumption dipped but recovered in the last two years, and economic growth is projected to remain at around 4 percent.

Until 2006 inflation declined steadily in Slovenia (table 14.1), but recently inflation accelerated due to large increases in oil and food prices, and high economic growth. Slovenia has fulfilled the Maastricht price stability criterion of the European Union (EU) and adopted the euro at the beginning of 2007.

Slovenia's labor market performance has also been improving (table 14.1). Employment is rising, and the unemployment rate continues to decline. Both registered and survey unemployment rates are expected to continue their gradual decline.

The health status of Slovenia's people has improved in the last two decades (table 14.2). Infant deaths per 1,000 live births have decreased significantly since the beginning of the 1990s. Life expectancy at birth, increasing for both males and females, amounted to about 80 years for females and 73 years for males in 2000–04.

TABLE 14.1 Slovenia: Basic Macroeconomic Indicators

Indicator	*1996*	*1997*	*1998*	*1999*	*2000*	*2001*	*2002*	*2003*	*2004*	*2005*	*2006*
GDP (€ million, current prices)	11,562	13,140	14,583	16,354	17,945	20,396	22,758	24,716	26,677	28,243	30,448
Population (December 31)	1,986,989	1,984,923	1,978,334	1,987,755	1,990,094	1,994,026	1,995,033	1,996,433	1,997,590	2,003,358	2,010,377
GDP per capita (€, current prices)	8,322	8,914	9,583	10,334	10,701	11,298	12,084	12,695	13,400	14,116	15,167
GDP per capita (US$, current prices)	10,421	10,070	10,744	11,008	9,853	10,108	11,379	14,325	16,638	17,554	19,024
Annual real growth of GDP (%)	3.7	4.8	3.9	5.4	4.1	3.1	3.7	2.8	4.4	4.1	5.7
Export/import ratio (%)	88	89	89	85	86	91	95	92	90	91	91
Annual real growth of goods and services exports (%)	2.7	11.0	7.5	1.6	13.2	6.3	6.7	3.1	12.5	10.1	12.3
Annual real growth of goods and services imports (%)	2.3	11.0	9.6	7.7	7.3	3.0	4.8	6.7	13.2	6.7	12.2
Inflation rate[a] (%)	9.9	8.4	7.9	6.1	8.9	8.4	7.5	5.6	3.6	2.5	2.5
ILO unemployment rate (%)	7.3	7.1	7.7	7.4	7.2	5.9	5.9	6.6	6.1	5.8	5.9
Average gross monthly earnings per person (€)	538.83	601.95	659.61	722.94	799.82	895.35	982.46	1,056.58	1,116.55	1,157.06	1,212.80
Indices of real gross earnings (2003 = 100)	84.8	87.4	88.8	91.6	93.1	96.1	98.2	100.0	102.0	104.2	106.8
Surplus (+) / deficit (–) of the general government (% of GDP)	−1.1	−2.4	−2.4	−3.1	−3.8	−4.0	−2.5	−2.7	−2.3	−1.5	−1.2

Source: SO 2007.

a. Measured by CPI, average of the previous year = 100.

TABLE 14.2 Slovenia: Basic Health Indicators

Indicator	*1985*	*1990*	*Average, 1995–99*	*Average, 2000–06*	*2000*	*2001*	*2002*	*2003*	*2004*	*2005*	*2006*
Deaths per 1,000 inhabitants	10.0	9.3	9.5	9.4	9.3	9.3	9.4	9.7	9.3	9.4	9.1
Infant deaths per 1,000 live births	13.0	8.4	5.0	4.0	4.9	4.2	3.8	4.0	3.7	4.1	3.4
Life expectancy at birth, female	75.52	77.19	78.41	80.50	79.10	79.57	79.87	80.70	81.08	81.30	81.89
Life expectancy at birth, male	67.38	69.38	70.90	73.14	71.94	72.13	72.33	73.15	73.48	74.08	74.84

Source: SO 2007.

Slovenia's population is healthier than those of most new EU member states (table 14.3). Both life expectancy and disability-adjusted life expectancy in Slovenia are highest among the new member states. Infant deaths per 1,000 live births, TB incidence, and the number of clinically diagnosed AIDS cases are among the lowest in new EU member states. However, Slovenia compares less

TABLE 14.3 Slovenia: Health Status Indicators compared with Other New EU Member States, 2003

Country	*Life expectancy*	*Disability-adjusted life expectancy*[a]	*Infant deaths per 1,000 live births*	*TB incidence per 100,000*	*Clinically diagnosed AIDS per 100,000*
Slovenia	76.52	69.50	4.04	13.77	0.3005
Hungary	72.59	64.90	7.29	24.31	0.2567
Czech Republic	75.40	68.40	3.90	10.79	0.0784
Estonia	71.24[a]	64.10	5.69[a]	41.15	0.7388
Slovakia	73.91[a]	66.20	7.63[a]	16.57	0.0370
Poland	74.65[a]	65.80	7.52[a]	25.05	0.4328
Latvia	70.46	62.80	9.44	72.51	2.4900
Lithuania	71.96	63.30	6.73	74.26	0.2606
Malta	79.37	71.00	4.08	4.86	0
Cyprus	78.63	67.6	5.7	1.51	0.5018
EU-15 average	79.06	71.69	4.61[a]	8.65	1.6100
EU-25 average	74.3	65.98	6.63	25.63	0.3842

Source: WHO 2006.

a. Data for 2002.

favorably with health status of old EU member state populations (EU-15). Both life expectancy and disability-adjusted life expectancy in Slovenia are more than two years less than the EU-15 average. However, life expectancy at birth for both genders has been steadily rising and is expected to continue rising.

Slovenia, like other EU countries, faces the consequences of population aging. In Slovenia, the total fertility rate fell from 2 in 1980 to 1.31 children per woman in 2006. According to the estimate obtained using the medium-fertility assumption, total fertility rates are expected to increase to 1.39 by 2020–25. However, the estimates obtained using the constant-fertility assumption project further decreases in total fertility rates (to 1.22 by 2020–25).

One obvious consequence of decreasing total fertility rates and increasing life expectancies for both genders is an increasing proportion of people aged over 65 years. This share, slightly above 15 percent in 2000–06, is projected to exceed 22 percent by 2026 and 26 percent by 2041 (Malačič 2006). The *old-age dependency ratios* (population aged over 65 to population aged 15–64) have also been increasing. The old-age dependency ratio increased from 15 in 1994 to 17.4 in 1994 and to 22.7 in 2006 (SO 2007). It is projected to reach 36 in 2025 (UN 2004). Another important demographic issue is the population decline. According to projections calculated using the assumption of constant fertility, mortality, and migration, Slovenia will have 1.85 million inhabitants by 2026 and 1.61 million by 2041—more than 0.3 million less than in 2004 (Malačič 2006).

General Characteristics of Slovenia's Health Care System

The Slovenian health care system shares some characteristics of the British, German, and Canadian systems. Slovenia's health care system provides universal coverage and almost all health care services are provided within the framework of compulsory health care insurance (MOH 2003: 64, 73).

In Slovenia, the benefits package is not exactly defined, either by type or by number of services. In 1989, a "green paper" was adopted, specifying around 2,600 services based on the example of the World Health Organization (MOH 2003: 102). The benefits package is updated yearly by the compulsory health insurance fund (the Health Insurance Institute of Slovenia) based on negotiations between the insurance fund, Ministry of Health (MOH), the Associations of Health Care Institutes, and other stakeholders. Such a decision-making process enabled a fairly easy inclusion of new benefits in compulsory coverage.

Funds for the compulsory health insurance scheme are collected through contributions made by both employers and employees. Contributions are linked to salaries, not profits. The Health Insurance Institute of Slovenia is independent of the national budget, which funds only 2 percent of total health care costs (MOH 2003: 258). Therefore, it has an independent revenue stream that is not legally bound to the budget and does not have soft budget constraints. The actual practice in dealing with the losses accumulated by the compulsory health care insurance fund and ongoing debates regarding this issue, however, show that the principle of hard budget constraints is not strictly followed. The insurer buys services from the providers which, subject to copayment, are available to the insured, namely all inhabitants. The insurance system in Slovenia is similar to the German one except there is only one insurer, the Health Insurance Institute of Slovenia, for the compulsory insurance scheme. The insurer has only regional offices. The insurance system in Slovenia has also introduced a universal copayment. Copayments are paid either directly by individuals or from voluntary complementary insurance for the full coverage of copayments. Copayments are calculated as a percentage of the service value and can therefore be very high. There are three insurers for this type of voluntary complementary insurance. One operates as a mutual insurance company and two are for-profit commercial insurers. Ninety-four percent of people buying compulsory insurance also buy voluntary complementary insurance for the full coverage of copayments (MOH 2003: 70; Robinson 2002: 173).

In 2006, total health care expenditures in Slovenia amounted to 8.55 percent of GDP. Expenditures funded by the compulsory health care insurance amounted to 6 percent of GDP and all public funds together (compulsory health care insurance, national and local budgets) amounted to 6.5 percent of GDP. Private funds amounted to 2 percent of GDP, 1 percent were direct patient payments (out-of-pocket payments), and 1 percent were funds of the voluntary health care insurance (HII 2008: 15).

Out-of-pocket payments for health care represent 3.5 percent of all household final consumption expenditures (table 14.4). The share of health expenditures in total household final consumption expenditures remained fairly stable in 2000–06 period. The annual volume of health expenditures, decreasing prior to 2004, increased by 7.5 percent in 2005, but in 2006 the increase slowed down.

TABLE 14.4 Slovenia: Household Final Consumption Expenditure, by Purpose

Consumption expenditure, by purpose (%)	*2000*	*2002*	*2004*	*2006*
Food and nonalcoholic beverages	17.0	16.8	15.7	14.4
Alcoholic beverages and tobacco	4.9	4.6	4.9	5.0
Clothing and footwear	6.2	6.3	6.1	5.5
Housing, water, fuel	20.0	19.8	18.7	18.8
Furnishings, household equipment, and maintenance	5.9	6.1	6.0	5.9
Health	3.0	3.2	3.5	3.5
Annual volume changes (%)	*13.9*	*4.8*	*2.5*	*3.1*
Transport	15.8	14.6	15.3	16.2
Communication	2.3	2.8	3.1	3.7
Recreation and culture	9.3	9.4	9.8	9.9
Education	0.9	0.9	1.0	1.2
Hotels, cafes, and restaurants	6.5	6.6	6.8	6.6
Miscellaneous goods and services	8.3	8.9	9.2	9.4

Source: SO 2005, 2007.

In 2006, 51.3 percent of compulsory insurance funds were allocated to the provision of specialist outpatient and hospital services, 19.3 percent to primary health care, 5.4 percent to social security services, 19 percent to services provided by pharmacies and drugs, and 5 percent to spa services, medical aids, conventions, and so forth (HII 2008: 44).

In Slovenia prior to 1992, all health facilities were state owned, and private practice was not allowed. This is why the health care delivery system remains mainly public, with most practitioners employed as salaried employees of the state. Doctors' salaries are determined by the Civil Service Act, and collective contracts and are fixed in the public sector. There is little room for incentive. However, salaries are high, 111 percent above the average earnings in the country, which is more, for example, than in Austria, Finland, and Sweden (Kornai and Eggleston 2001: 167–69).

The private provision of health care services was made possible after 1992. In 1992–95, the first phase of privatization involved mostly dentists and only a small number of physicians who decided to establish their own private practice. In 1996–99, the number of private providers rose significantly. After 2000, privatization moved into basic care as well. Today, more than 50 percent of all dentists and 20 percent of general practitioners have their own private practice. Many private providers have obtained concessions from the local community to provide services (and therefore receive financing) under the compulsory health insurance scheme. This means they are still part of the public health care network. Private health care providers with no concession charge patients directly for services and receive no financing from the public system.

In 2005, there were 236 physicians in Slovenia per 100,000 inhabitants. The number of general practitioners per 100,000 inhabitants was 48, and the number of dentists per 100,000 equaled 60. There were 752 nurses and 45 pharmacists per 100,000 inhabitants. All these figures lag behind the EU-15 average. They compare more favorably with averages for all EU members after May 2004 (EU-25). However, only the number of dentists, nurses, and pharmacists per 100,000 inhabitants exceeds EU-25 average (WHO 2008).

Primary Health Care in Slovenia

In Slovenia, primary care is provided either by health centers, organized as public institutes or private practitioners that can be organized as limited liability companies, sole traders or independent self-employed professionals without a defined legal form. The providers of primary health care, general practitioners, play the role of gatekeepers and are financed up to 92 percent through capitation. In Slovenia, there are 61 health centers, almost a third of them located in the health region of Ljubljana, the capital city. The Health Insurance Institute of Slovenia has 10 regional units, one for each of Slovenia's 10 health regions. In Slovenia, 1,182 private practitioners worked within the public health care network in 2006 (table 14.5).

TABLE 14.5 Slovenia: Number of Private Practitioners with Concessions, 2006

Type of private practitioners	*General practitioners*	*Dentists*	*Specialists*	*Gynecologists*	*Total*
Number	302	556	285	39	1,182
Share of all same type providers (%)	23.43	51.82	17.98	29.54	n.a.

Source: HII 2007.
Note: n.a. = not applicable.

In 2002, 27.5 percent of funds of compulsory and voluntary health insurance were allocated to primary health care in Slovenia (MOH 2003: 101). This type of care is, in terms of the allocated amount of funds, the second most important health care activity. The amount of funds of compulsory and voluntary health insurance allocated to primary health care remains fairly stable.

Hospital Health Care in Slovenia

Hospital care expenditures exceeded 50 percent of all funds of compulsory insurance and voluntary insurance for the full coverage of copayments. The hospital sector in Slovenia has been faced with several changes in the past decade. Their funding mechanisms, for example, have changed several times. The fee-for-service funding of hospitals in place before 1993 was replaced by funding based on number of patient-days. In 2000, case-based funding was implemented, and DRG-based funding was introduced in 2004.

As shown in table 14.6, there were 29 hospitals in Slovenia in 2006. There were 18 general and clinical hospitals, 2 maternity hospitals, 2 hospitals for pulmonary diseases, 4 hospitals for mental diseases, 1 rehabilitation center, and 2 orthopedic hospitals.

Table 14.7 shows data on use of inpatient services and hospital performance in Slovenia as compared with EU-15 and EU-25 countries. All indicators are comparable with European averages. In Slovenia, the number of hospital beds

TABLE 14.6 Slovenia: Basic Hospital Care Indicators

Indicator	*1995*	*2000*	*2004*	*2006*
Number of hospitals	24	27	29	29
Beds	11,411	10,745	9,584	9,567
Admitted patients	310,991	332,601	344,976	357,143
Discharged patients	311,136	332,595	344,596	356,935
Physicians	2,254	2,413	2,860	3,103
State registered nurses	—	—	1,384	1,819

Source: SO 2007.
Note: — = not available.

TABLE 14.7 Slovenia: Use of Inpatient Services and Hospital Performance, 2006

Country	*Hospital beds per 100,000*	*Inpatient care admissions per 100*	*Average length of stay, all hospitals*	*Average length of stay, acute care hospitals only*	*Bed occupancy rate, acute care hospitals only (%)*
Slovenia	476.32	17.78	7.1	5.81	71.62
EU members before May 2004	564.12[a]	17.26[b]	9.55[b]	6.71[b]	—
EU members since May 2004 or 2007	637.18	20.75	7.83	7.76	71.11

Source: WHO 2008.

Note: — = not available.

a. Data for 2005.

b. Data for 2004.

per 100,000 inhabitants, inpatient care admissions per 100 inhabitants and average length of stay are lower than the EU-15 and EU-25 averages, but occupancy rates are on the upper side compared with the EU-25 average.

HEALTH INSURANCE IN SLOVENIA AND THE ADVENT OF VHI

The first major reforms of the Slovenian health insurance system began in the early 1990s when the system experienced serious financial shortage of funds for health care services. These problems, together with the drive toward modernization of the overall social structure, led to the adoption of new health care legislation in 1992. The legislation enacted in 1992 revised the methods of financing, introduced copayments for services covered by compulsory health insurance, implemented changes in the public health network, allowed privatization, reformed the role and organization of primary care, formalized provider contracting processes, and implemented several other changes.

The 1992 legislation defined the roles for both compulsory and voluntary insurance schemes and, although Slovenian health insurance has been changed over the past decade, the general health insurance system remains the same. It is divided into compulsory health insurance, voluntary health insurance for the full coverage of copayments, voluntary health insurance for additional coverage, and voluntary health insurance for services that are not a constituent part of compulsory insurance. The compulsory health insurance system in Slovenia is similar to the German one, except there is only one compulsory health insurance fund (the Health Insurance Institute of Slovenia). Compulsory health insurance in Slovenia operates as a pay-as-you-go system of health care funding in which yearly expenditures are paid for with the income-related contributions of both employees and employers collected in the same year. Due to an overwhelming increase in health care costs, the losses of the compulsory health insurance fund, the Health Insurance Institute of Slovenia, were mounting until 2005. Cost increases are attributed to factors such as cost-increasing technology, aging of the population, supplier-induced demand, escalating health care prices, and inefficiency. In 2004, the accumulated losses amounted to nearly €120 million. In the same year, the accumulated losses were transferred to the national budget. In 2005 and 2006, the revenues of the Health Insurance Institute of Slovenia exceeded the costs due to increases in revenues, cost reduction programs, and a further reduction in the share of health service prices covered by compulsory health insurance.

Considering that increases in contributions are not easily negotiated, private health insurance is used to lighten the public burden. Namely, compulsory health insurance does not ensure the coverage of all costs that arise from treatment. The complete coverage of costs is provided only for children and schoolchildren and for certain diseases and conditions. Most individuals have to pick up the costs not covered by compulsory health insurance. Their copayments are either out of pocket or through their voluntary health insurance. In Slovenia, copayments are calculated as a percentage of service price—anywhere between 5 and 75 percent. Because out-of-pocket payments can involve a large expenditure for an individual, 94 percent of the insured in the compulsory insurance scheme also take out voluntary insurance for the full coverage of copayments (MOH 2003).

That is how one of the most outstanding characteristics of Slovenia's health insurance system emerged, the insurable copayment. It is also the reason the predominant form of voluntary private health insurance in Slovenia is voluntary health insurance for the full coverage of copayments. Offered by three insurance companies, it accounted for 98 percent of all health insurance premiums in 2006 (ISA 2006). Other types of voluntary insurance also exist, but their share is negligible because Slovenia's health care system continues to provide near-universal coverage and almost all health care services are provided within the framework of compulsory health insurance.

The above-mentioned features of voluntary health insurance in Slovenia enabled cutbacks in public health care expenditures in a specific way. Voluntary health insurance expenditures grew from 3 percent of all health care expenditures in the early 1990s to the current 13 percent, not because of exclusion of specific population groups from participating in the compulsory health insurance scheme or the exclusion of certain health care services from compulsory coverage. It happened primarily because of decreases in the percentages of the service and pharmaceutical prices covered by compulsory health insurance and corresponding increases in copayments. As a result, voluntary health insurance for full coverage of copayments became increasingly universal voluntary insurance. Despite the growing role of voluntary health insurance for the full coverage of copayments in funding health care expenditures, insurance organizations providing this type of voluntary insurance do not take part in yearly negotiations determining the benefits package and the size and scope of health programs funded by compulsory health insurance.

In Slovenia, compulsory health insurance and voluntary health insurance for the full coverage of copayments have thus become two complementary universal insurance systems. However, they differ in certain respects. First, contrary to compulsory health insurance contributions, the premiums charged for voluntary health insurance for the full coverage of copayments are not income-related. Second, voluntary health insurance for the full coverage of copayments operated until recently as a capital-funded insurance system. Currently, community rating is used for premium setting. Compulsory health insurance, on the other hand, operates as a pay-as-you-go system of health care funding.

In 2003, the MOH White Paper "Health Reform: Justice, Accessibility, Quality, Efficiency," outlined needed reforms in the Slovenian health care system (MOH 2003). The White Paper proposed the elimination of voluntary health insurance for full copayment coverage. The advocates of this proposal were dissatisfied with the fact that voluntary health insurers generated profits while the compulsory health insurance fund accumulated losses. They also objected to the full copayment coverage premiums' not being income-related. They believed solidarity between people in different income groups should also apply to this type of voluntary health insurance. The proposed reforms were eventually rejected after the 2005 election of a new government that proposed a different reform of full copayments coverage under the voluntary health insurance. The advocates of the new proposals were against the operation of this coverage as capital-funded insurance. This explains why it was transformed back into a pay-as-you-go system of health care funding. They also argued that "intergenerational mutuality" should be strengthened. *Intergenerational mutuality* refers to solidarity that is achieved between different age groups of the population by setting premiums that are not age dependent. Consequently, a community rating was introduced for this type of voluntary health insurance. The former change created the conditions for implementing the risk equalization required to transform a premium-setting model into a community-rating model. Contrary to the White Paper proposal, however, the new legislation did not introduce income-related premiums for this type of voluntary health insurance. These differences and changes highlight the ongoing debates about efficiency and equity issues linked with different premium-setting models.

The outlined changes came as a response to the growing disparity between the available public funds and the expenditures by compulsory health insurance, which continues to provide near-universal coverage of almost all health care services and relies on insurable copayments as a means of alleviating the public burden. However, insurable copayments in Slovenia's general health insurance framework fail to create real demand-side incentives for health care users to rationally use health care services. The widening income-expenditure disparity began to undermine the stability of both compulsory and voluntary health insurance in Slovenia. It also raised a fundamental question: can Slovenia create the conditions in which private health insurance contributes to the efficiency of Slovenia's health care system, improves the population's health and consumer-patient satisfaction, upgrades the quality of health care provision, and achieves a reasonable balance between the two main criteria used to assess the performance of health care systems, namely equity and efficiency?

ISSUES RAISED IN THE DEVELOPMENT OF VHI IN SLOVENIA

Voluntary health insurance in Slovenia was not created to increase systemic efficiency by influencing the behavior of patients or the operation of insurance organizations and health care providers. The fundamental reasons for its implementation were the cumulative losses within the compulsory health insurance system due to the ever-increasing financial unsustainability of universal health care coverage. It can easily be demonstrated that the financial problems were not only the reason for introducing VHI, but they were the driving force behind most of the significant changes made in this sector in the last 15 years. Namely, most changes made in VHI were motivated by the wish to resolve the problem of losses without sacrificing the universality of Slovenia's health care system. However, the changes increasingly prevented voluntary health insurers from operating efficiently and decreased their ability to induce the insured population to behave more rationally. Analysis of Slovenia's experience in developing VHI thus shows that the changes failed to staunch health insurers' losses and resulted in unnecessary increases in state involvement in this sector. The latter consequence is demonstrated in the risk-equalization requirement for all insurers providing VHI to cover the full cost of copayments.

Two Approaches to Stop Insurers' Losses and Maintain Solidarity

The 2003 MOH White Paper first proposed merging the two systems and transferring to compulsory health insurance the premiums paid for full copayment coverage under VHI. This proposal was advocated for two reasons.

First, it would introduce solidarity among income groups. The idea was to substitute VHI premiums for additional compulsory health contributions. It was argued that this reform would augment the solidarity between social classes and ease the pressure on low-income citizens because the additional compulsory health contributions would be linked to the insured's income. This income linkage was a departure from the VHI premiums that did not differ significantly between insured individuals. It was argued that one of the basic principles of health care—equal access to care for all—would thus be better realized.

Second, it was also argued that the proposed change would bolster the health care system as a whole because it would do away with the deficits of the Health Insurance Institute of Slovenia. At that time, VHI for full copayment coverage was creating significant profits. When this reform was proposed, the social insurance fund losses could have been compensated by the VHI surpluses (table 14.8).

However, by the end of 2003, VHI surpluses only slightly exceeded the social insurance fund losses and in 2004, Vzajemna, the largest voluntary insurance company providing full copayment coverage, began losing money and announced plans to increase premiums by 13.5 percent for 383,000 insured individuals over the age of 60. Vzajemna argued this measure was necessary because of its growing losses, mainly from increased copayments and its high proportion

TABLE 14.8 Slovenia: Financial Results of Compulsory and Voluntary Insurance Companies (€)

	Voluntary insurance			*Social insurance*			
Year	*Revenue from premiums (A)*	*Payment of claims processed (B)*	*A–B (E)*	*Revenues (C)*	*Expenditures (D)*	*C – D (F)*	*E + F*
1999	183,589	138,689	44,900	995,626	992,571	3,055	47,955
2000	204,445	165,301	39,144	1,115,856	1,128,552	–12,696	26,448
2001	237,375	202,462	34,912	1,259,032	1,308,088	–49,057	–14,144
2002	273,760	222,984	50,776	1,420,755	1,457,354	–36,598	14,178

Source: MOH 2003: 69.

of pensioners among its insured members compared with its competitors. In addition, it cited the delay in introducing the risk-equalization schemes envisaged by the insurance legislation of 2000 but postponed by the 2003 proposal to eliminate VHI for full copayment coverage. This showed that the first goal of the proposed merger of compulsory health insurance and VHI for full copayment coverage could not be attained without increasing either compulsory health care contributions or VHI premiums.

The proposal to merge compulsory insurance and VHI for full copayment coverage was eventually rejected in 2005 under the new government. The government revised the legislation regulating VHI for full copayment coverage according to the principle of intergenerational mutuality, declaring that this type of voluntary insurance represents Slovenia's public interest, and implementing a system of risk-equalization schemes that equitably neutralize differences in insurers' costs stemming from differences in their individual portfolios in terms of age and gender structures. The new legislation thus introduced unified premiums for all insured individuals regardless of age, gender, and health status for individual insurance companies, implemented a system of risk-equalization schemes, and transformed VHI for full copayment coverage from the capital-funded system into a pay-as-you-go arrangement. The latter change was adopted because the implementation of risk equalization is incompatible with capital-funded insurance. The legislation therefore attempts to resolve the problem of health insurers' cumulative losses by implementing risk equalization and maintains solidarity by introducing the principle of intergenerational mutuality to VHI for full copayment coverage.

Effects of the Selected Premium-Setting Model on VHI

When assessing the proposed and adopted reforms of Slovenia's health insurance system and their impacts on solidarity, it is important to recognize that VHI premiums are rarely income related. In the EU, they are set according to an individual's, a community's, or group's risk. A risk-based premium calculation is the most common method used by EU insurers for setting premiums for complementary and supplementary voluntary health insurance. Under this method, premiums are calculated on risk-based criteria such as age, age at entry, gender, occupation, household size, health status, medical history, family history of disease, and extent of coverage (Mossialos and Thomson 2004). Age and gender are the variables most commonly used for rating premiums. Under such premium-setting models, health insurance distributes the risk among the sick and the healthy within certain age groups of insured males and females.

However, because illness is connected to age and the share of the elderly population is growing, health insurance also often assumes the function of balancing out the risks that emerge due to variations in the population's age structure. This can be achieved in two ways:

- *By implementing intergenerational mutuality at the level of the entire population or a subgroup of subscribers.* Community-rated and group-rated premiums are based on the average risk of a defined community or firm. This implies that premiums are the same for all subscribers or a subgroup of subscribers in a given community or firm. Subscribers thus pay the same premium regardless of their age, gender or health status. In this way, the young and the healthy support the old and the sick.
- *Through capital funding so to avoid premium adjustments arising from age.* Here, premiums are set so that some of the premiums collected are accumulated in a fund that allows no premium adjustment for age. Within such a capital-funded system of insurance, savings are accumulated at younger ages to pay for future health care. This means that, from an intergenerational point of view, each generation finances itself. Health insurance thus balances out the risks that emerge due to population aging at the individual level by creating reserves for old age by paying the same premium over a lifetime.

In Slovenia, the 2005 legislation introduced unified premiums for all insured individuals, regardless of age, gender, and health status for individual insurance companies. This implies that the first of the two approaches was adopted. Following the Irish model, the new legislation thus prescribed community rating with the stated intention of preventing premium increases for the elderly. The new legislation also prescribed open enrolment and risk equalization so that all insurers would share the risks.

Community Rating, Equity, and Efficiency

Under the new legislation, every insurance company providing VHI for full copayment coverage was to introduce unified premiums for all insured individuals, regardless of age, gender, and health status. Premiums set for particular individuals therefore no longer reflect the fact that average health care costs for persons over 65 years of age are 3.5 to 4.5 times higher than for individuals aged between 20 and 40. By introducing a unified premium, the young thus pay in more than they take out, while older individuals cost the insurance companies more than the premiums collected from them. The new legislation therefore introduced intergenerational mutuality within each insurance company.

Bringing about intergenerational mutuality within VHI for full copayment coverage negatively affects the insurer's allocative efficiency, which cannot be achieved because premiums are set without regard to cost within each age group. Such pricing is basically an instrument for income redistribution between population subgroups. In community rating, the young and healthy support the old and the sick. This change achieves the goal of equity improvement, but the price distortions thus created impair efficiency and prevent younger and healthier individuals from maximizing their utility.

The risk-based premium calculation is thus a more allocatively efficient premium-setting model. However, an allocatively efficient premium-setting model requires the identification and classification of risks, which entails access to information that can be used to segregate risks on the basis of certain criteria. In a competitive market, if the insurer could accurately identify healthy and sick people, it would thus offer insurance plans that charge sick people a higher premium. In reality, differences in peoples' propensity to fall ill are not easily observable, and the intrinsic stability of insurance markets can be seriously compromised if the sick buy insurance and the healthy opt out (adverse selection). This is why, in practice, insurers operating in a competitive environment may have strong incentives to lower their costs through risk selection. Thus, on one hand, the premium-setting model selected in Slovenia reduces efficiency in the consumption of health care services and, on the other, it demands a special form of regulation, namely a risk-equalization scheme. However, by implementing community-rated premiums that remain unrelated to income instead of the income-related premiums proposed in 2003 the new legislation prevented through cross-subsidization further reductions in allocative efficiency. Namely, in the case of income-related premiums the young and healthy support the old and the sick, and a further redistribution of income is created because the working population supports the elderly and the sick, and the poor contribute less than the better off to the funding of yearly health expenditures.

From Capital-Funded VHI to a Pay-as-You-Go Funding System

Thus, the function of balancing out risks due to variations in the population's age structure can be achieved at the individual level by creating reserves for old age by paying the same premium over a lifetime. In Slovenia, the 2005 legislation introduced a system of community rating and risk equalization, which is incompatible with and has replaced the VHI for full copayment coverage system that has formed reserves for old age since 2000. In other words, the capital-funded insurance system was transformed into a pay-as-you-go system of health care funding.

This change created two important effects. First, this type of voluntary health insurance, which is complementary to compulsory health insurance, became more compatible with compulsory health insurance, which also functions according to the pay-as-you-go principle. To some extent, this is an acceptable argument for making this change. Second, but more important, the elimination of the capital-funded type of health insurance prevents insurance companies from creating national savings and actively participating in capital markets.

In strong economies with a large enough working and youth population, pay-as-you-go systems are no worse than capital-funded systems. However, pay-as-you-go systems reach their limits with the aging of the population, unemployment, and economic stagnation (Henke and Borchardt 2003). This also limits capital-funded systems. So the question of whether a capital-funded system is needed because of an aging population is, in essence, the question of whether voluntary private insurance companies are truly capable of increasing savings and the investment rate. For capital-funded voluntary health insurance to have an advantage over pay-as-you-go systems, both the savings and investment rates have to raise economic growth based on higher efficiency of the economy, thereby increasing per capita gross domestic product. The increased per capita gross domestic product can then be the source for funding future health care expenditures that are expected to rise as the population ages.

The adopted reform ignored these issues. It also created health insurance companies that are unable to participate in the processes of privatizing and restructuring Slovenia's health care providers. The requirement that insurance companies return the created reserves to insured individuals has also brought about the loss of a significant share of insurance companies' financial revenues in the form of lending and investment income forgone which could, in turn, exert additional pressure on the premiums they charge for insurance.

The Role and Effects of Risk Equalization

As discussed, the predominant form of voluntary health insurance in Slovenia, VHI for full copayment coverage, was developed in the early 1990s due to financial problems in securing funds for health care services only through compulsory health insurance contributions. In 2003 the White Paper attempted to resolve these problems by merging this type of voluntary health insurance with compulsory health insurance. In 2005 the revised legislation implemented risk equalization for the same purpose. In all three cases, the main goal of the advocated changes was to prevent contribution and premium increases.

When the new legislation was adopted, the authors argued that the revised legislation regulating voluntary health insurance in Slovenia would not prevent an increase in VHI premiums for at least two reasons. (1) The introduction of uniform premiums would bring about an increase in premiums charged the younger insured. This price increase could create an incentive for them to terminate their insurance, thereby reducing the main source of risk-equalization funds and, consequently, the effects of the risk-equalization scheme. This adverse effect could thus increase the premiums of all insurance companies providing VHI for full copayment coverage. (2) Additional pressure on the premiums would be created by the loss of a significant share of insurance companies' financial revenues due to the elimination of the capital-funded type of insurance (Tajnikar and Došenovič Bonča 2005). In the three years since the adoption of new legislation, premiums for VHI for full copayment coverage have indeed increased in Slovenia.

It is more important, however, to highlight the effects and role of the risk-equalization scheme in reducing the problem of cumulative losses in Slovenia's health insurance system. Its market structure and efficiency effects must also be analyzed.

The Problem of Health Insurance Losses and Risk Equalization

Risk-equalization schemes create conditions in which several insurance companies providing VHI for full copayment coverage can operate in the market. However, because risk equalization equitably neutralizes differences in the costs arising from age and gender differences in their portfolio structures, they operate as if only one insurance company provided this type of insurance. Risk-equalization schemes enable open enrolment because they eliminate the incentive to cherry pick. For any insurance company, all the benefits of risk selection are compensated for by the payments the insurer has to make to the risk-equalization scheme. Risk-equalization schemes expand the principle of intergenerational mutuality from individual insurance companies to all insurance companies included in the scheme.

Without risk equalization, community rating is distorted because health insurers are encouraged to target young and healthy individuals and reject the old and the sick. In such circumstances, health insurers with young insured can make significant profits, while health insurers with older insured could incur large claims costs and eventually go out of business, destabilizing the health insurance market. Vzajemna, with an 80-percent market share in 2004 and 2005 and the biggest share of pensioners among its insured, began running losses in 2004 and responded by announcing plans to raise its premiums. That was when it became clear that VHI for full copayment coverage had reached its limits in alleviating the burden on compulsory public health insurance. It was precisely with the intention of preventing such instability that new legislation introduced risk equalization to neutralize differences in the costs of different insurance companies arising from age and gender differences in their portfolio structures. An attempt was thus made to enable private voluntary health insurers to continue to provide coverage without premium increases. The Slovenian case demonstrates that risk equalization alone could not attain this objective.

In Slovenia in 2004, the health insurance sector as a whole, not just individual insurance companies, could not break even by increasing the number of insured individuals at the average premium charged for this type of voluntary health insurance in 2004. In that year, the average premium amounted to €200.97. The analysis of the financial statements of Slovenian insurance companies providing VHI for full copayment coverage for 2004 further shows that the break-even point could not be attained despite the fact that the average premium exceeded the average incurred claims costs. In 2004, this claims cost amounted to €176.82. The analysis implied that the average premium for this type of insurance should increase by 3.2 percent for normal conditions to be created in this health insurance sector and for enabling the implemented risk equalization to achieve the expected effects (Tajnikar and Došenovič Bonča 2005).

The analysis based on 2004 data demonstrated that without such an increase in the average premium, the implementation of risk equalization would result in losses for Adriatic, the second largest insurance company providing this type of insurance and paying into the risk-equalization fund. Although Vzajemna was to receive risk-equalization funds, this influx would not remedy its negative business performance. The estimated amount of funds to be paid by Adriatic after the first risk-equalization period amounted to more than €7.5 million, assuming similar conditions for this sector as in 2004. In 2004 Adriatic's profits in this type of VHI amounted to €2.1 million; Vzajemna's losses to €11.2 million (Tajnikar and Došenovič Bonča 2005). This effect was predicted because losses by insurance companies eligible to either pay or receive funds from the risk-equalization fund are not used as a corrective mechanism in calculating the risk-equalization flows. In Slovenia, contrary to the Irish example, matters such as the relative size of insurers, the overall size of the market, the rate of premium inflation, and the effects of payments on insurers' business plans and solvency are not considered when deliberating whether or not risk equalization should be commenced. According to the Slovenian legislation, risk equalization commences when the market-equalization percentage (the ratio of the sum of all the funds to be paid into the risk-equalization fund and the sum of claims costs of all insurance companies included in the risk-equalization scheme) exceeds 1.5 percent. If it is below 1.5 percent, the funds to be paid into the risk-equalization fund are carried over to the next settlement period and added to the amount to be paid in the next settlement period.

In 2006, Vzajemna was indeed the only health insurance company that received risk-equalization payments in the amount €2.3 million (Vzajemna 2007). This amount was smaller than predicted, and Vzajemna concluded the year with profit. However, a 16 percent increase in the average premium compared to 2005 contributed to this result.

This discussion shows that the implementation of risk equalization required an increase in the average premium charged for VHI for full copayment coverage in Slovenia. This example thus demonstrates that risk equalization alone does not resolve the problem of premiums that are not correctly priced and does not improve VHI ability to alleviate the ever-increasing burden on public compulsory health insurance.

Risk Equalization, Community Rating, and Competition

Considering that the purpose of risk equalization is to neutralize differences in insurance companies' costs arising from age and gender differences in their portfolio structure, their average premiums should also no longer reflect cost variations due to those structural differences. It is believed that this will strengthen competition between insurance companies and boost their efficiency. For this purpose and for the purpose of increasing intergenerational solidarity, the legislation envisaged uniform premiums for individual insurance companies. However, pursuant to the law, premiums can vary between different insurance companies. The idea behind this arrangement is that competition between insurance companies providing VHI for full copayment coverage can result in reduced premiums. Namely, more efficient insurers with lower average costs could offer this type of insurance at lower premiums, thereby obtaining new enrollees and encouraging other competitors to lower their premiums.

But competition only works if the market structure is suitable. In Slovenia, the market for VHI for full copayment coverage is a typical monopoly. In 2004, the largest health insurance company offering this type of health insurance insured 80.8 percent of the population holding this type of insurance; it collected 81.8 percent of the premiums and covered 86.7 percent of all claims costs incurred for this type of voluntary insurance (ISA 2004). This monopoly enabled Vzajemna to operate with lower average fixed costs and also reduced its incentives to monitor claims costs. In 2004, Vzajemna's average fixed cost (fixed cost per insured) amounted to €9.32 for its 1,136,715 subscribers to this type of insurance. If in 2004 Vzajemna had been the same size as Adriatic, which insured 273,317 individuals, its average fixed costs would have amounted to €38.78. This implies that Vzajemna was able to operate at average fixed costs that were €29.45 lower than the average fixed costs of Adriatic due to its market monopoly (Tajnikar and Došenovič Bonča 2005). This difference in average fixed costs emerges as a consequence of economies of scale. As a smaller insurance company, Adriatic can to some extent reduce this cost differential by monitoring its claims more closely than Vzajemna. Vzajemna's average claims costs exceeded those of Adriatic by €69 in 2004. It could be argued that this was due to its insured's less favorable age and gender structure. However, Vzajemna's average claims costs exceeded those of Adriatic for all age groups. These differences may well have been the consequence of Vzajemna's reduced incentives to monitor its claims. Also, in 2004 Adriatic had both higher average fixed costs and higher average fixed operating costs. The latter exceeded those of Vzajemna by €10.36 in 2004 (Tajnikar and Došenovič Bonča 2005). This fact further eroded Adriatic's chances of compensating through increased efficiency for the effects of Vzajemna's scale economies.

To ensure normal conditions for effective competition following the introduction of new legislation, it was also necessary to maintain the existing contractual relationships between insurance companies and their insured and adapt them to the proposed changes. The possibility also had to be provided for either an insurance company or insured individuals to end their contractual relationship, thereby creating the necessary mobility of insured. The proposed legislation did provide for such mobility but paid insufficient attention to the consequences of exiting in the case of mutual insurance companies. In Slovenia, the only insurance company that is organized as a mutual insurance company is Vzajemna. For this type of insurance company, the exiting of insured must also be linked with the payout of an equity share because the insured play the dual role of insured and members/ owners. The mass exodus of insured could create capital inadequacy problems for such insurance companies and result in premium increases.

Finally, the implementation of risk equalization is not without market-structure effects. The conditions in which uniform premiums are set for individual insurance companies and those in which premiums can vary between different insurers could have resulted in the increased concentration of Slovenia's VHI market. It is reasonable to hypothesize that an insurance company required to contribute funds to the risk-equalization scheme would attempt to compensate for this outflow through higher premiums. An insurance company eligible to receive funds from the risk-equalization scheme could, however, cut its premiums. Under those competitive conditions, the contributors to risk-equalization schemes would gradually lose their market share while insurance companies receiving risk-equalization funds would expand theirs. In Slovenia, such a process could have led to the creation of a single insurer of full copayment coverage. In Slovenia, there was also a threat that such a process would unfold quickly, considering that only the largest insurance company, Vzajemna, was eligible for payments from the risk-equalization fund. If such circumstances emerged, Vzajemna would benefit even more from its existing scale economies. However, in the two years after the adoption of the new legislation, Vzajemna's market share decreased. Although Vzajemna received additional payments from the risk-equalization scheme, its average premium increased by 16 percent in 2006 over 2005. This increase in average premiums can be explained by the fact that Vzajemna operated below the break-even point with average premiums charged for VHI for full copayment coverage before the changes of legislation were adopted.

Following theoretical predictions and ignoring the case of Slovenia's VHI market, the principle of uniform premiums should be applied not only within an individual insurance company but also for all providers of VHI for full copayment coverage included in a risk-equalization scheme. Setting a uniform premium for all insurance companies would encourage them to form an optimal size in the same way companies would under perfect competition conditions. They would form their optimal size by taking into consideration their operating expenses as well as all their other expenses, including expenditure on health care services provided to the insured and those incurred due to inappropriate supervision of invoices for health services rendered. Implementing a uniform premium for all insurance companies would also put insurance companies in a situation resembling perfect competition. Insurance companies would then have to adapt to the market conditions and their competitors by forming optimal size and scope for their short- and long-term business. For their part, buyers of voluntary insurance would have to make their purchasing decisions without considering the premiums charged, only the additional services offered by VHI providers. This nonprice competition would evolve into a more consumer-oriented approach to the provision of voluntary insurance.

In Slovenia, even though the new legislation envisaged uniform premiums for individual insurance companies and allowed premiums to vary between different insurance companies competition between them significantly reduced premium differences. Currently, the monthly premium charged for VHI for full copayment coverage amounts to about €21 for all insurance companies offering this type of insurance. Mobility of the insured witnessed in the past few years thus demonstrates the strengthening of nonprice competition in Slovenia'a VHI market.

Perverse Effects of the Risk-Equalization Scheme

According to the 2005 legislation regulating health insurance, the amount of funds to be received or paid into the risk-equalization fund by a particular insurance company is calculated as the difference between the sum of actual claims costs for different age groups of insured and the sum of standardized claims costs for different age groups of insured. If the sum of actual claims costs exceeds the sum of standardized claims costs for different age groups, the insurance company is eligible to receive money from the risk-equalization fund. If the opposite were true, the insurance company would have to pay into the risk-equalization fund. The amount of funds actually paid through the risk-equalization scheme equals the smaller of the following two amounts: total contributions to or total claims on the risk-equalization fund. The standardized claims costs of an individual insurance company are calculated as the sum of standardized claims costs for different age groups of this insurance company using the following formula:

$$SC_I = \sum_{A=1}^{n} SC_{IA} = \sum_{A=1}^{n} \left(\frac{C_{IA}}{N_{IA}} \times N_A \times \frac{N_I}{N}\right),$$

where

SC_I = the standardized claims cost of an individual insurance company;
SC_{IA} = the standardized claims cost for different age groups of an individual insurance company;
C_{IA} = actual claims' cost for different age groups of an individual insurance company;
N_{IA} = the number of insured in different age groups of an individual insurance company;
N_A = the total number of insured in different age groups holding this type of voluntary health insurance (the number of insured in all insurance companies);
N_I = the total number of insured of an individual insurance company;
N = the total number of insured holding this type of voluntary health insurance; and
n = the number of age groups.

Calculating risk-equalization flows using this formula can, at least hypothetically, show that no risk equalization is needed despite the fact that insurance companies differ in their age structures.

TABLE 14.9 Slovenia: Risk-Equalization Flows for Two Insurers with the Same Age Structures and the Same Average Claims Cost for the Two Age Groups

	Insurer A			*Insurer B*			*Both insurers*		
Age group	*Claims cost (C)*	*No. of insured (I)*	*C/I*	*Claims cost (C)*	*No. of insured (I)*	*C/I*	*Claims cost (C)*	*No. of insured (I)*	*(C/I)*
Younger	500	50	10	110	11	10	610	61	10
Older	320	32	10	70	7	10	390	39	10
Total	820	82	—	180	18	—	1,000	100	—

Age group	*Standardized costs for insurer A*	*Standardized costs for insurer B*
Younger	500.2	109.8
Older	319.8	70.2
Total	820	180
Calculated risk-equalization flows	0	0
Actual risk-equalization flows	0	0

Source: Authors' calculations.
Note: — = not available.

Table 14.9 depicts a simple hypothetical model of two insurance companies with the same age structure and the same average claims cost for the two age groups. The two insurance companies differ only in their size.

In the above example no risk equalization is needed, considering that the two insurance companies do not differ in their age structures. Examples shown in Tables 14.10 and 14.11, however, show that the amount to be

TABLE 14.10 Slovenia: Risk-Equalization Flows for Two Insurers with Differing Age Structures and the Same Average Claims Cost for the Two Age Groups

	Insurer A			*Insurer B*			*Both insurers*		
Age group	*Claims cost (C)*	*No. of insured (I)*	*C/I*	*Claims cost (C)*	*No. of insured (I)*	*C/I*	*Claims cost (C)*	*No. of insured (I)*	*(C/I)*
Younger	467	47	10	110	11	10	577	58	10
Older	353	35	10	70	7	10	423	42	10
Total	820	82	—	180	18	—	1,000	100	—

Age group	*Standardized costs for insurer A*	*Standardized costs for insurer B*
Younger	473.304	103.896
Older	346.696	76.104
Total	820	180
Calculated risk-equalization flows	0	0
Actual risk-equalization flows	0	0

Source: Authors' calculations.
Notes: Compared with the example in table 14.9, the larger insurer has a higher share of the elderly population. — = not available.

TABLE 14.11 Slovenia: Risk-Equalization Flows for Two Insurers with Differing Age Structures and the Same Average Claims Cost for the Two Age Groups

	Insurer A			*Insurer B*			*Both insurers*		
Age group	*Claims cost (C)*	*No. of insured (I)*	*C/I*	*Claims cost (C)*	*No. of insured (I)*	*C/I*	*Claims cost (C)*	*No. of insured (I)*	*(C/I)*
Younger	467	47	10	142	14	10	610	61	10
Older	353	35	10	38	4	10	390	39	10
Total	820	82	—	180	18	—	1,000	100	—

Age group	*Standardized costs for insurer A*	*Standardized costs for insurer B*
Younger	499.872	109.728
Older	320.128	70.272
Total	820	180
Calculated risk-equalization flows	0	0
Actual risk-equalization flows	0	0

Source: Authors' calculations.

Notes: Compared with the example in table 14.9, the larger insurer has a higher share of the elderly population, and the smaller insurer has a higher share of the young. — = not available.

paid or received from the risk-equalization fund equal zero also if, in the simple model depicted above, only the age structure of insurance companies is altered.

For risk equalization to take place between two insurance companies with differing age structures, the average claims cost of the two age groups should also differ. As shown in table 14.12, the calculated amount to be paid and the calculated amount to be received are the same if average claims cost differs between the two age groups but no differences occur between the two insurance companies in their average claims cost for individual age groups (this conclusion also applies if the average claims cost for individual age groups differs between the two insurance companies but they all differ for the same absolute value).

If the case shown in table 14.12 is altered to hypothesize that the insurance company having to pay into the risk-equalization fund has the same average claims cost in both age groups, the amount to be paid into the risk-equalization fund equals 0. A similar result is obtained if the case in table 14.12 is altered so that the insurance company eligible to receive risk-equalization funds has the same average claims cost in both age groups. In this case, the insurance company is ineligible to receive any money from the risk-equalization fund.

This simple model thus shows that the calculated risk-equalization flows are not only influenced by differences in the age structures of the insurance companies included in risk equalization but they also respond to differences in average claims cost incurred for different age groups of insured.

TABLE 14.12 Slovenia: Risk-Equalization Flows for Two Insurers with Differing Age Structures and Average Claims Cost of the Two Age Groups, but with Same Average Claims Cost for Individual Age Groups

	Insurer A			*Insurer B*			*Both insurers*		
Age group	*Claims cost (C)*	*No. of insured (I)*	*C/I*	*Claims cost (C)*	*No. of insured (I)*	*C/I*	*Claims cost (C)*	*No. of insured (I)*	*(C/I)*
Younger	500	50	10	142	14	10	642	64	10
Older	480	32	15	57	4	15	536	36	15
Total	980	82	—	199	18	—	1,179	100	—

Age group	*Standardized costs for insurer A*	*Standardized costs for insurer B*
Younger	526.768	115.632
Older	439.848	96.552
Total	966.616	212.184
Calculated risk-equalization flows	+13.284	−13.284
Actual risk-equalization flows	+13.284	−13.284

Source: Authors' calculations.

Note: — = not available.

IMPACT OF VHI ON THE EFFICIENCY OF PRIMARY CARE PROVIDERS

Voluntary health insurance for full copayment coverage affects both demand for and supply of health care services. The impact on the demand side is interesting, considering that the predominant form of voluntary health insurance in Slovenia is the one that provides copayment insurance. Uninsured copayments create demand-side incentives for rational use of health care services. Insurance that fully covers copayments therefore dilutes this role of copayments. In Slovenia, there is currently no research analyzing the impacts of VHI for full copayment coverage on demand for health care services and related demand-side moral hazard issues. However, the fast growth of health care expenditures over the past decade implies that copayments have not contributed to rational use of health care resources. Health care expenditures increased by 88 percent in 1992–2002, while GDP increased by 60 percent (MOH 2003: 242).

The increase in health care expenditures also raises the issue of health care provider inefficiency. This issue has been subject to more extensive research, and this is why this chapter looks more closely at the impact of voluntary health insurance on the supply of health care services. Empirical findings regarding the impact of voluntary health insurance on the efficiency of health care provision in Slovenia were obtained by Tajnikar and Došenovič (2004) and Došenovič Bonča (2004) in their research of cost efficiency of primary health care providers. This research revealed that cost inefficiency of primary health care providers is affected by the share of funds received from voluntary health insurance. The lower the share of these funds, the higher is the cost efficiency of public primary health care providers. Apparently a higher share of funds from compulsory insurance enables public primary health care providers to achieve higher degrees of efficiency.

The authors reached this finding by first dividing public primary health care providers into several groups using cluster analysis. Cluster analysis has shown that the most appropriate approach is to split health centers into five clusters according to three characteristics: average costs, inventory turnover, and liquidity. Standardized data were used in the analysis. The analysis of variance was then employed to analyze the characteristics of each cluster and compare clusters against several indicators, one of which is the average share of funds received from compulsory insurance. This approach shows that the source of funding affects health centers' business performance: average shares of funds received from compulsory insurance differ statistically significantly ($P = 0.029$) among the clusters. The correlation coefficient between the average shares of funds received from compulsory insurance and average values of average costs equals –0.59. This implies that public primary care providers with a larger share of funds received from compulsory insurance have lower average costs.

In the second step, the Tajnikar and Došenovič (2004) study is deepened by employing a stochastic cost frontier model. A frontier cost function identifies the minimum costs at a given output level, input price, and existing production technology. All firms are unlikely to operate at the frontier. Failure to attain the cost frontier implies the existence of technical and allocative inefficiency. The stochastic frontier production function was first proposed by Aigner, Lovell and Schmidt (1977) and Meeusen and van den Broeck (1977). The original specification of the model has been used in various empirical applications, but has also been altered and extended in a number of ways, one of them the extension of the methodology to cost functions (Coelli, Rao and Battese 1998). The extension to cost functions is also used in the Tajnikar and Došenovič (2004) study of cost efficiency of Slovenia's primary care providers.

Generally, the model of total cost (TC) can be written as follows (Vitaliano and Toren 1994: 283):

$$TC_i = TC(Q_i, W_i, X_i) + v_i + u_i \qquad u_i \geq 0.$$

In this specification Q measures outputs, W input prices, and X output descriptors at the i-th health care provider. The composed error term is $v_i + u_i$; v_i is a normally distributed random error with zero mean; and u_i is the inefficiency residual which is assumed to be positive (Vitaliano and Toren 1994: 283). In such model specifications, the estimated term u_i is therefore a measure of cost inefficiency. The obtained estimates of the degree of cost inefficiency enable the researcher to find determinants of this inefficiency, thereby identifying the potential sources of cost inefficiency.

The cost function of Slovenia's primary health care providers has a similar form, with total costs as a function of inputs (labor and capital), input prices, and the quantities of output produced. The cost function is estimated in a normalized logarithmic (log-log) form. Data on total costs, inputs, and input prices were obtained from accounting data from original financial statements of individual primary care providers, and data on quantity of services provided were obtained from detailed reports providers must submit to the Health Insurance Institute that finances health care delivery. Input prices were calculated by dividing input costs by the quantity of inputs. Output was calculated as a weighted average of quantities of different types of health care services. In Slovenia, the quantities of different types of health care services are measured in points that can be aggregated, using the per point prices determined by the Health Insurance Institute of Slovenia for different types of health care services. The outlined cost function was used in the estimation of a stochastic cost frontier function that allows estimation of the measures of cost inefficiencies.

The estimation of cost frontier functions of Slovenia's primary health care providers consisted of two parts. In the first part, only public providers, the 57 health centers, were included in the analysis. Data for some health centers are not very reliable. Nevertheless, these were not excluded from the analysis, but this problem was taken into account to the maximum extent possible when interpreting the results. This part of the analysis revealed that the mean cost inefficiency score of health centers equals 1.276 implying that on average actual costs exceed the least-cost level by 27.6 percent. The lowest cost inefficiency score is 1.029, and the highest cost inefficiency score is 3.064. Second stage regression, used to explain the sources of health centers' inefficiency, showed that one of the factors that has a statistically significant effect ($P = 0.063$) on the inefficiency term is the share of funds received from compulsory insurance. This implies that the lower share of voluntary health insurance funds can be linked to higher cost efficiency of public primary care providers. A higher share of funds from compulsory insurance thus enabled health centers to achieve greater efficiency.

In the second part of the analysis, part of the private sector that supplies basic health care services was included. This part of the analysis includes 57 health centers and 23 privately owned providers that are organized as limited liability companies. The estimation of the inefficiency term (u) that is used as a measure of cost inefficiency of both public and private primary health care providers produced the following results. The mean cost inefficiency score of providers is 1.723 implying that on average actual costs exceed the least-cost level by 72.3 percent. The lowest cost inefficiency score is 1.056, and the highest cost inefficiency score is 8.87. Using the second stage regression, the effect of the share of funds from compulsory insurance was again estimated. However, in this part of the analysis the effect of the share of funds from compulsory health insurance was not statistically significant.

The results outlined above show that voluntary health insurance does not contribute to an increased efficiency of either public or private primary health care providers. Surprisingly, in the case of public primary care providers, it even allows less-efficient operation. This supports the conclusions shown earlier in this chapter that VHI for full copayment coverage does not stimulate private health insurers to rationalize the provision of health care.

CONCLUSIONS: THE FUTURE AND THE REFORMS NEEDED IN SLOVENIA'S VOLUNTARY HEALTH INSURANCE

Three important landmarks mark the development of Slovenia's VHI for full copayment coverage: the revised health care legislation of 1992, the 2003 White Paper, and changes to the legislation regulating health insurance adopted in 2005. The three provide very different lessons about the most suitable organization for voluntary health insurance in Slovenia. In every case, the advocated changes have to be assessed bearing in mind the effects of voluntary health insurance on the efficiency of both insurance companies and health care providers.

The reform of the early 1990s shows:

- Reliance on private health expenditures can alleviate the burden on compulsory public health insurance to some extent but that it does not reduce overall health expenditures, which are merely funded from a different source. It also shows that the efficiency of health care providers is affected only if private insurance companies have a greater capacity to monitor the claims filed.
- With voluntary health insurance, solidarity between different income groups can be at least partly abolished because this type of solidarity is guaranteed by compulsory health insurance. Voluntary health insurance, however, also ignores intergenerational solidarity if community-rating is not introduced. However, this model of premium setting reduces allocative efficiency in the consumption of health care.
- Insurers offering voluntary health insurance for full copayment coverage have to be included in risk equalization if this type of insurance is to guarantee intergenerational mutuality, which is incompatible with capital-funded insurance. Capital-funded insurance, however, has positive effects on national savings.

Discussions raised by the White Paper highlighted:

- Private voluntary health insurance has limitations in alleviating the burden on compulsory public health insurance, which makes a merger of the two systems unreasonable. It would not have resolved health insurers' cumulative losses, which stemmed from the universality of compulsory public health insurance and increasing health expenditures.
- The principle of solidarity between income groups should not be extended to voluntary health insurance because premiums would lose their allocative function.
- Merging compulsory and voluntary health insurance for full copayment coverage does not require implementation of risk equalization. Such a merger would only result in a single health insurance company's providing health insurance.

The 2005 changes in the health insurance legislation reveal:

- The alternatives of maintaining capital-funded insurance and implementing risk equalization have to be carefully considered when reforming VHI for full copayment coverage. The capital-funded insurance alternative has important positive macroeconomic effects and enables the flexible and modern operation of health insurers. Conversely, risk equalization involves the development of a complex administrative system that can often have unpredictable repercussions on the voluntary health insurance market.
- The principle of intergenerational mutuality coupled with risk equalization does not necessarily create conditions in which competition works properly. Risk equalization, introduced to an unbalanced market structure, could increase market concentration and decrease competition.
- A risk-equalization scheme alone does not improve voluntary health insurers' ability to alleviate the ever-increasing burden on public compulsory health insurance or their ability to staunch the cumulative losses of compulsory health insurance.
- Risk equalization, if not implemented in the right circumstances, can create unintended effects.

These conclusions also imply that the recently proposed legislation does not comprehensively address the key issue of the inappropriate role and place of voluntary health insurance within Slovenia's health care system. There are two solutions:

- The size and scope of compulsory health insurance have to be changed in order to develop types of private health insurance that are truly voluntary in nature.
- Because the newly proposed legislation does not comprehensively address the issue of the inappropriate role and place of voluntary health insurance, it can be understood only as a transitional arrangement for voluntary health insurance in Slovenia.

Reforming the Size and Scope of Compulsory Health Insurance

To develop types of private health insurance that are truly voluntary in nature, the size and scope of compulsory health insurance have to be changed. This is necessary not only because it opens up new possibilities for the development of voluntary health insurance but also because it is a way to resolve the problem of the losses compulsory health insurance has accumulated in the past. An excessively broad definition of the list of services guaranteed by compulsory health insurance limits possibilities for other types of voluntary health insurance to develop.

The 2005 legislation took an important initial step in redefining the compulsory insurance benefits package. In principle, this is in line with providing the voluntary health insurance market with a new scope and size. It does, however, require more careful consideration of the types of benefits that are being excluded from compulsory coverage. For example, the 2005 legislation reduced cash benefits during a temporary absence from work due to a work-unrelated injury (for example, car accidents, certain types of sports). However, the exclusion of benefits that promote public health or cover losses not caused by the insured individual should not be tolerated.

New services and new technologies in health care, along with the aging of the population, will continue to expand the basket of health care goods and services irrespective of whether the payers are social insurance funds or voluntary insurance providers. The reform in Slovenia will therefore have to take steps toward redefining the compulsory insurance benefits package in a way that guarantees a narrower scope and extent of rights. It will also have to create the conditions in which voluntary insurance companies constitute a normal part of the structure of those paying for health care services in Slovenia. The growth of compulsory health insurance expenditures therefore has to be maintained within reasonable limits by reducing the universality of compulsory coverage, not by fostering a parallel system for funding parts of the health services' prices not covered by the universal compulsory insurance benefits package.

Providing for a New Role for Private Voluntary Health Insurance

Considering that the 2005 legislation does not comprehensively address the issue of the inappropriate role and place of voluntary health insurance, it can be understood only as a transitional arrangement for voluntary health insurance in Slovenia. However, the future calls for a more comprehensive reform of the entire health care system in Slovenia. Figure 14.1 reiterates the main characteristics of the current health insurance system in Slovenia and also proposes future requisite changes. It depicts a redefined compulsory insurance benefits package that guarantees a narrower scope and extent of rights. Copayments for rights covered by compulsory health insurance should not be eliminated but should no longer be insurable and determined as a percentage of the health care service price. Uninsurable copayments should be set in absolute values to create real demand-side incentives for health care users to rationally use health care services. Reforming the role of compulsory health insurance would also open up possibilities for the further development of voluntary health insurance. Voluntary health insurance for full copayment coverage would no longer exist, and voluntary health insurance for services that are not a constituent part of compulsory insurance could be strengthened. Such voluntary insurance should function as capital-funded insurance, thereby also enabling payers to create incentives to improve the efficiency of the entire health care system.

Future reform should therefore focus on redefining the compulsory insurance benefits package so that a narrower scope and extent of rights is guaranteed. This would make compulsory health insurance sustainable by introducing uninsurable

FIGURE 14.1 Slovenia: The Health Insurance System

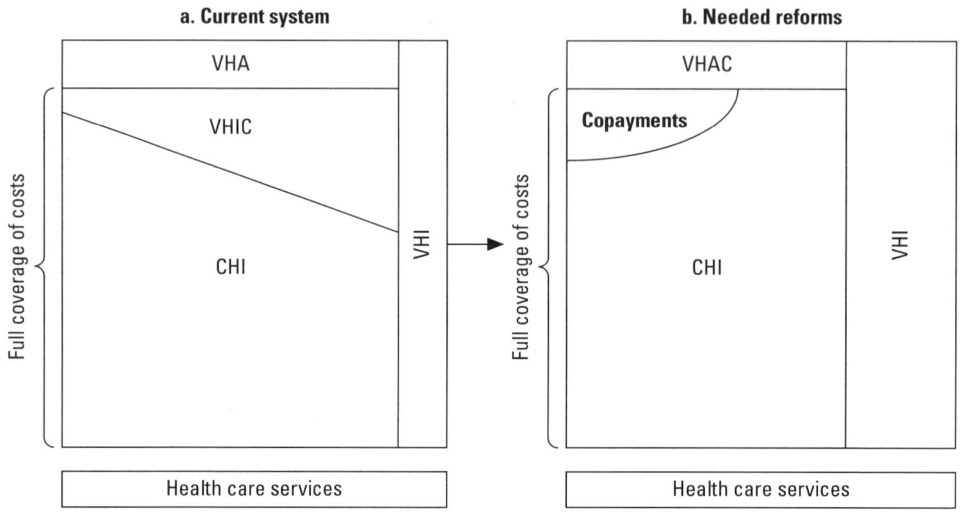

Source: Authors.

Notes: CHI = compulsory health insurance; VHIC = voluntary health insurance for the full coverage of copayments; VHA = voluntary health insurance for additional coverage (for example for above-standard living conditions in hospitals and health spas, for the coverage of costs of more elaborate medical and technical aids, for prescription medicines not listed on positive and intermediate lists, and so on); VHI = voluntary health insurance for services not a constituent part of compulsory insurance; VHAC = voluntary health insurance providing coverage for faster access and increased consumer choice.

copayments that create real incentives for health care users to make rational use of health care services, defining the new role of voluntary health insurance and, most important, making changes that enhance the efficiency of Slovenia's health care system.

NOTE

The authors are grateful to John C. Langenbrunner and Mukesh Chawla of the World Bank for their helpful comments and suggestions. They are also grateful to insurance companies Vzajemna zdravstvena zavarovalnica d.v.z., AdriaticSlovenica zavarovalna družba d.d. and the Ministry of Health of the Republic of Slovenia for their cooperation and financial support of certain parts of the research presented in this chapter. All views expressed in this chapter are, however, those of the authors alone and do not necessarily represent the views of the reviewers or funding organizations.

REFERENCES

Aigner, D.J., C.A.K. Lovell, and P. Schmidt. 1977. "Formulation and Estimation of Stochastic Frontier Production Function Models." *Journal of Econometrics* 6 (1): 21–37.

Coelli, T., D.S.P. Rao, and G.E. Battese. 1998. *An Introduction to Efficiency and Productivity Analysis*. Norwell, MA: Kluwer Academic Publishers Group.

Došenovič Bonča, P. 2004. *Cost Efficiency of Basic Health Care Providers in Slovenia*: Master's Thesis. Ljubljana: University of Ljubljana, Faculty of Economics.

Henke, K-D., and K. Borchardt. 2003. "Reform Proposals for Healthcare Systems." Dice Report. *Journal for International Comparisons* 1 (3): 3–8.

HII (Health Insurance Institute). 2008. *Annual Report of the Health Insurance Institute for 2007*. Ljubljana.

———. 2007. *Annual Report of the Health Insurance Institute for 2006*. Ljubljana.

ISA (Insurance Supervision Agency). 2006. *Report on Business Performance of the Insurance Industry in 2006*. Ljubljana.

———. 2004. *Report on Business Performance of the Insurance Industry in 2004*. Ljubljana.

Kornai, J., and K. Eggleston. 2001. *Welfare, Choice, and Solidarity in Transition*. Cambridge: Cambridge University Press.

Malačič, J. 2006. *Demografija. Teorija, analiza, metode in modeli* [Demography. Theory, analysis, methods and models], 6th edition. Ljubljana: University of Ljubljana, Faculty of Economics.

Meeusen, W., and J. van der Broeck. 1977. "Efficiency Estimation from Cobb-Douglas Production Functions with Composed Error." *International Economic Review* 18 (2): 435–44.

MOH (Ministry of Health). 2003. *Health Reform: Justice, Accessibility, Quality, Efficiency* [Zdravstvena reforma. Pravičnost, dostopnost, kakovost, učinkovitost]. Ljubljana.

Mossialos, E., and S. Thomson. 2004. *Voluntary Health Insurance in the European Union*. London: European Observatory on Health Care Systems and LSE Health and Social Care, London School of Economics and Political Science.

Robinson, R. 2002. "User Charges for Health Care." In *Funding Health Care: Options for Europe,* ed. E. Mossialos, A. Dixon, J. Figueras, and J. Kutzin, 161–84. Buckingham: Open University Press.

SO (Statistical Office of the Republic of Slovenia). 2007. *Statistical Yearbook 2007*. Ljubljana.

———. 2005. *Statistical Yearbook 2005*. Ljubljana.

Tajnikar, M., and P. Došenovič Bonča. 2005. *Analiza vplivov uvedbe izravnalnih shem pri dopolnilnem zdravstvenem zavarovanju v RS na poslovanje zavarovalnice Adriatic d.d. in na razmere na trgu dopolnilnega zdravstvenega zavarovanja* [Analysis of effects created by the implementation of risk equalization to voluntary health insurance for full copayment coverage on the insurance company Adriatic d.d. and on the market for VHI]. Consultant report. Ljubljana: University of Ljubljana, Faculty of Economics.

———. 2004. "Efficiency of Public Primary Care Providers and the Need for Reform of the Health Care System in Slovenia." Paper presented at the Third International Conference on Health, University of Athens, Athens Institute for Education and Research, June 3–5.

UN (United Nations Population Division, Department of Economic and Social Affairs). 2004. "World Population Prospects: The 2004 Revision." http://esa.un.org/unpp; accessed January 31, 2006.

Vitaliano, D.F., and M. Toren. 1994. "Cost Efficiency in Nursing Homes: A Stochastic Frontier Approach." *Journal of Health Economics* 13:281–300.

Vzajemna (Vzajemna zdravstvena zavarovalnica, d.v.z.). 2007. *Annual Report for 2006*. Ljubljana.

WHO (World Health Organization). 2008. "European Health for All Database" (November 2007 update). http://data.euro.who.int/hfadb; accessed March 11, 2008.

———. 2006. "European Health for All Database" (January 2006 update). http://data.euro.who.int/hfadb; accessed January 31, 2006.

CHAPTER 15

Republic of Korea

Kee Taig Jung

Korea's achievement of the national health insurance (NHI) in just 12 years was often cited as a miracle until 2000. Then, the financial distress of the NHI damaged not only the reputation of health services but also the trust of the Korean people in the social security of health care. In response, the private health insurance (PHI) market expanded to 40 percent of the total NHI reimbursements, making it one of the world's largest such markets. It is surprising that Korean insurance market reached to this size without offering any comprehensive major medical coverage. All the PHI products are supplementary or complementary to the national health insurance. The PHI market grew more than 20 percent a year from 1996 to 2004. Most products sold cover specific diseases like cancer or 4 to 10 other critical illnesses and pay fixed amounts instead of covering patient's actual bills.

In this evaluation study, empirical analysis was performed to find factors that affect enrolment in PHI, moral hazard, adverse selection, and financial protection. Age, gender, and chronic illnesses were found to affect enrolment in the PHI. Moral hazard was found in outpatient but not in inpatient care. Having PHI improved financial protection. People with fixed-payment insurance had higher financial protection than those with indemnity type. The success and viability of the Korean health care system will depend on the development of linkages between public and private payers.

INTRODUCTION

The Republic of Korea (hereafter Korea) overcame the economic crisis of 1997 faster than any other nation in Asia, in 2004 it reaching per capita GDP of US$14,000 (NSO 2005). Now numbering 49.2 million, the population has been growing for the last 10 years, but the growth rate has decreased 51 percent (from 1.0 percent in 1994 to 0.5 percent in 2004).

In terms of health indices, Korea has extended life expectancy and reduced infant mortality while spending less than 6 percent of GDP on health. However, the country still faces many challenges to the stability of its health care system. Issues such as an aging population, changing disease patterns, lack of financial resource to expand coverage of the NHI, and debate over the privatization of health care call for systemic changes.

Korea has one of the fastest aging populations in the world. The elderly-to-child ratio (65^+ population/0–14) almost doubled between 1994 and 2004 and will reach 109 in 2020 as a result of the rapidly expanding elderly population and shrinking birth rate. The dependency ratio (population over age 65/15 to 64 year-olds) will increase dramatically in the next two decades. From the 2004 base, it will almost double in 2020 and triple in 2030. Even without considering that the elderly use more health care than other age groups, the fast-growing aging population itself will threaten the financial stability of the Korean health care system.

The changes in disease patterns from acute to chronic and epidemic to cancer are also noteworthy. Among the leading causes of death, cancer accounts for 26.3 percent; cardiovascular diseases, 13.9 percent. A short description of the history and status of the Korean health insurance system sheds some light on current health care financing problems.

THE KOREAN HEALTH CARE SYSTEM

Social security for health care in Korea consists of social health insurance, a Medical Aid program paid by taxation, and long-term care insurance. The bill for long-term care insurance was passed by the Congress in 2005, and the law became effective in 2007.

Discussion in this section focuses on the national health insurance because it covers 96 percent of population (table 15.1). Social insurance for health care has three programs: (1) employer insurance for corporate employees (48 percent of population), (2) employer insurance for government officials and teachers (9.6 percent), and (3) regional insurance for mostly self-employed (38.5 percent).

In 2006, the total contribution for health insurance reached US$22.5 billion, and total benefits paid amounted to US$21.6 billion. Employee insurance accounted for 64 percent of the total contribution and regional insurance covered the rest 36 percent. Of the total benefits, employee insurance paid out 61 percent; regional insurance, 39 percent.

TABLE 15.1 Korea: Classification of Social Health Care Coverage, 2006

		Coverage	
Classification	*Population group*	*Number*	*Percent*
Medical insurance		47,409,600	96.3
Employer insurance	Corporate employees	23,724,134	48.2
National Health Insurance Corporation	Government and private school employees	4,720,889	9.6
	Self-employed	18,964,567	38.5
	Rural	2,038,295	4.1
	Urban	16,926,272	34.4
Medical Aid	Persons without financial means	1,828,627	3.7
TOTAL		49,238,227	100.0

Source: NHIC 2006, http://www.nhic.or.kr/wbm/wbmb/.

TABLE 15.2 Korea: Contributions and Benefits under NHI Programs (US$ million)

		1990	*1995*	*2000*	*2001*	*2002*	*2003*	*2004*	*2005*	*2006*
Total	Contributions	2,219	4,126	8,609	11,322	13,811	17,028	18,956	20,495	22,532
	Benefits	1,946	4,067	9,285	13,195	13,823	14,893	16,265	18,393	21,587
EE subtotal	Contributions	1,281	2,276	4,128	5,240	7,113	9,526	11,186	12,671	14,495
	Benefits	1,071	2,042	4,760	6,892	7,232	7,971	8,986	10,700	13,123
SE subtotal	Contributions	848	1,885	4,480	6,081	6,698	7,501	7,700	7,824	8,037
	Benefits	875	2,024	4,525	6,303	6,590	6,922	7,278	7,692	8,464

Source: NHIC 2006 ; http://www.nhic.or.kr/wbm/wbmb/.

Note: Contributions include subsidies (government budget and public funds). An arbitrary exchange rate of US$1 = 1,000 Korean won (W) was used in calculating contributions and benefits. EE = employee; SE = self-employed.

The contributions shown in table 15.2 include subsidies from government and employers. The results show that the self-employed use more health services than they pay for (NHIC 2006). These results are the opposite of findings by Kwon (2002) that "poor" self-employed individuals subsidize "rich" corporate employees.

History of the Korean Health Care System

In the 1987 presidential election campaign, President Roh Taewoo pledged to achieve universal health insurance coverage. The timing was propitious. In the economic boom of 1985–90, more people, especially the self-employed, could pay for social health insurance.

To administer health insurance, the Korean government chose a familiar model, the health insurance society approach. About 350 health insurance societies were already doing business in Korea. For the self-employed, each regional district had a health insurance society, many of them too small for financial viability. During the health insurance society era (1977–99), each society had incentives to increase its reserves, but this incentive system broke down after the government merged the administrative system into single health insurer in 2000, the National Health Insurance Corporation (NHIC).

The merger made the NHIC a monopsony for all health care providers in Korea. The Korean government did not allow selective contracting for the national health insurance. In this process, the NHIC gained enormous market and political power and was not subject to market pressures. This situation resulted in inefficiency of scale and bureaucratic failure to meet people's needs.

The historical steps in the national health insurance programs are summarized in box 15.1.

The Legal Basis

The national health insurance was developed on four legal levels: the Korean Constitution, the Social Security Act, presidential ordinance, and administrative regulation.

BOX 15.1 KOREA: A CHRONOLOGY OF HEALTH CARE REFORM

1963–77	**The Legal Foundations**
1963	Medical Insurance Act enacted but military government postpones reform to concentrate on economic development.
1977	Targeting social insurance for health care to groups with stable income rather than the poor, mandatory social insurance mandatory health insurance (MHI) for health care is established for companies with more than 500 employees.
1979–81	**Gradual Expansion of MHI**
1979	MHI is established for public servants and teachers and expanded to companies with more than 300 employees.
1981	MHI is expanded to companies with more than 100 employees (voluntary program for companies with more than 16 employees).
1981–98	**Moving toward Universal Coverage**
1981	MHI is launched for self-employed in selected occupations (artists, barbers, and beauticians).
1982	Second phase of regional health insurance is initiated for self-employed in selected regions (Kangwha, Boeun, Mokpo).
1988	Regional health insurance is expanded to uninsured in rural areas.
1989	Regional health insurance is expanded to uninsured self-employed in urban areas.
1990s	Regional health insurance absorbs occupation-based self-employed.
1998 to Present	**Merger of the Programs into the NHIC**
1998	Health insurance for public servants and private school employees and 227 regional health insurance societies of the regional insurance program are merged under NHIC.
2000	In single national program, 139 corporate health insurance societies are merged with NHIC. Health Insurance Review Agency and National Health Insurance Corporation begin operating as separate entities.
2002	Special Act of Financial Stability for National Health Insurance goes into effect January 19, providing the NHIC with a subsidy from general revenues.

Source: NHIC 2006; http://www.nhic.or.kr/wbm/wbmb/.

The Korean government established the National Health Insurance Act to provide people with medical security. The government also began medical security programs in accordance with the Medical Aid Act for those without financial means. The Special Act for Financial Stability of National Health Insurance was enacted to resolve the financial deficit of the NHIC and provide financial stability early in the program. This act established a basis for providing the NHIC with a subsidy from general revenue.

Organizations in the NHI system

The Ministry of Health and Welfare (MOHW) sets major policies and makes decisions in the health care sector. The entities that carry out the government's health insurance operations are the National Health Insurance Corporation (NHIC), Health Insurance Review Agency (HIRA), and medical institutions.

The NHIC: The Insurer

The NHIC acts as the core management for health insurance finance. It oversees the qualification of the insured and their dependents, levies and collects health insurance contributions, drives health promotion, and sets the fees for medical services.

HIRA: Claims Review and Quality Assurance

The HIRA determines the amount of claims that the NHIC must pay for each medical institution by reviewing and assessing the propriety of their medical claims and expenses.

NHI FINANCIAL DISTRESS

The gradual expansion of coverage with low contributions from the insured worked well until 1996, the year before the MOHW changed its policy from "low contribution and low coverage" to "adequate contribution and adequate coverage." To enhance risk pooling and efficiency, Health Minister Cha pursued the merger of 350 health insurance societies into a single health insurer in 2000. Contrary to Minister Cha's intent, the financial distress and bureaucratic inefficiency of the NHI worsened.

Financial Status of the Three Health Insurance Programs

Causes of the NHI deficit, Kim and Jung (2003), Jung (2004) , Kwon (2002), and many others suggest, lie in population aging, NHI coverage expansion, frequent increases in medical fees, increased use of high-technology services, merger of the insurance societies, and the policy of separating drug prescribing and dispensing. It is ironic that the NHI recorded a US$2.2 billion deficit in 2001, right after the major health care reform, which included the separation policy and the insurance societies merger. The same year, both insurance programs for corporate employees and self-employed recorded their highest deficits, respectively, US$1.9 billion and US$294 million.

The merger of insurance societies eliminated each society's incentives to do its best to collect contributions from the self-employed. After the merger, the collection rate plummeted, jeopardizing the financial stability of health insurance for the self-employed (table 15.3).

TABLE 15.3 Korea: Fiscal Status of the National Health Insurance, 1995–2006 (W billion)

Program	*1995*	*1996*	*1997*	*1998*	*1999*	*2000*	*2001*	*2002*	*2003*	*2004*	*2005*	*2006*
All												
Total revenue	5,614	6,631	7,554	8,230	8,892	9,827	11,928	14,305	17,466	19,408	21,091	23,263
Total expense	5,076	6,464	7,795	8,788	9,610	10,744	14,105	14,798	15,972	17,330	20,146	22,944
Industrial workers												
Revenue	2,337	2,704	2,884	3,038	3,123	4,690	5,327	7,223	—	—	—	—
Expenditure	1,992	2,555	3,112	3,425	3,699	5,521	7,211	7,620	—	—	—	—
Surplus	345	149	–228	–387	–576	–831	–1,884	–397	—	—	—	—
Self-employed												
Revenue	2,498	2,983	3,732	4,287	4,552	5,138	6,601	7,082	—	—	—	—
Expenditure	2,365	3,017	3,602	4,161	4,729	5,222	6,895	7,178	—	—	—	—
Surplus	133	–34	130	126	–177	–84	–294	–96	—	—	—	—
Government and school employees												
Revenue	779	944	938	905	1,217	—	—	—	—	—	—	—
Expenditure	719	892	1,080	1,201	1,181	—	—	—	—	—	—	—
Surplus	60	52	–142	–296	36	—	—	—	—	—	—	—
Total surplus	538	167	–241	–558	–718	–917	–2,177	–493	1,494	2,078	945	318
Total accumulated fund	4,119	4,005	3,786	3,228	2,510	1,593	–584	–1,077	417	2,495	3,440	3,758

Sources: NHIC various years.

Note: In 2000, the Government and Employees categories were merged with Industrial workers. In 2003, the three groups (Industrial workers, Self-employed, and Government and school employees were merged into the NHI.

The Burden of Administrative Failure

Chung and Kim (2005) argue that the 2001 deficit was due to the administrative failure of the MOHW, which did not consider the total cost of introducing dispensing fees and the impact of raising medical fees four times that year to appease various interest groups. The evidence can be found in medical fee index trends shown in table 15.4. In 1999–2001, the medical fee index for health care services rose 33.6 points, which is more than half of the increase during the entire decade (1992–2001). The MOHW introduced the prescription fee in 2000 and increased other medical service fees significantly in the three years after 1999.

Since 1988 in various ways, the government has supported the low-income self-employed, especially in rural areas. To resolve the insolvency of the NHI, the government enacted the Special Law of 2002, stipulating that 35 percent of total reimbursement for self-employed insurance will be subsidized from general government revenue and that 15 percent will come from the Special Fund for Health Promotion, financed by the tobacco tax. The amount of subsidy for the NHI grew rapidly, from US$1.2 billion in 1999 to US$3.8 billion in 2004. Forecasts of the government subsidy in 2015 to 2050 will be presented below in the feasibility section. Even without forecasts, however, it is evident that government does not have sufficient resources to cover rapidly increasing health care costs.

TABLE 15.4 Korea: Medical Fee Index and Consumer Price Index, 1990–2005 (2000 = 100)

Year	*CPI*	*MFI (health care)*	*Health services*	*Pharmaceuticals*	*Health-related products*
1990	60.9	64.6	53.2	82.9	75.5
1991	66.6	68.9	55.9	89.3	82.9
1992	70.8	71.9	59.7	90.8	87.9
1993	74.2	73.9	62.8	90.9	90.6
1994	78.8	76.2	64.4	94.7	92.8
1995	82.3	81	68.7	100.9	94.5
1996	86.4	84.8	74	102.2	95.8
1997	90.2	87.8	79.1	102.6	91.9
1998	97	92.3	85.6	103.2	98.4
1999	97.8	93.4	87.8	102.1	101.6
2000	100	100	100	100	100
2001	104.1	112.3	121.4	105	99.1
2002	106.9	111.4	117.3	107.1	100.2
2003	110.7	114.1	119.9	110.2	101
2004	114.7	115.8	123	110.5	101.5
2005	117.8	118.4	127.3	111.8	101.7

Source: Korea National Statistical Office 2005.

EXPANSION OF THE PRIVATE HEALTH INSURANCE MARKET

Korea accomplished the universal health insurance coverage of population in 1989, only 12 years after launching the NHI program. Although this was a remarkable achievement, many individuals are still at significant financial risk from health expenditures due to a high coinsurance rate and lack of NHI coverage for certain services (table 15.5).

Problems of the NHI and Development of Private Health Insurance

Under Korea's NHI, all providers within each type of medical institution are reimbursed the same amount, set by the uniform fee schedule for an insured service, regardless of the provider's reputation or location. Providers complain that the uniform fees are too low. To compensate for the low fees, physicians in certain specialties like pediatrics and internal medicine see more than 100 patients per day. Alternatively, they provide medical services that are not covered by the NHI. As a result, out-of-pocket spending (OOPS) amounts to almost half of total medical costs (Kim and Jung 2003). In 2004, the actual copayment rates were 43.1 percent for outpatient services, 45.1 percent for inpatient services, 27.0 percent for drugs, and 43.6 percent on average (NHIC 2005).

More important, the government did not set a limit for patients' copayments. Many patients with critical illnesses like cancer went bankrupt due to this NHI loophole. After the press took a look at this shortcoming and the financial insolvency of the NHI in 2000, the Korean people became aware of the instability of social security for health care in Korea. The rapidly expanding PHI market reflects Koreans' recognition of the need for protection against the gaps in the NHI. No regulation requires the purchase of PHI, nor is there any tax incentive to buy health insurance (Jung 2003). Thus, PHI in Korea is perfectly voluntary. Yet the market more than quintupled, from US$1.3 billion in 1996 to US$7.5 billion in 2005 (Jung 2005). In 2001, the market recorded its highest growth rate 36.8 percent, up from 26.2 percent in 2000.

The Health Insurance Market and Regulations

Until 1997, the Korean insurance industry market consisted of two markets: life insurance (22 companies) and fire and marine insurance (14 domestic companies).

TABLE 15.5 Korea: NHI Reimbursement and OOPS

			OOPS (%)		
	Total payment	*Insurer payment (%)*	*Subtotal*	*Copayment, covered services*	*OOPS, uncovered services*
Total	100.0	56.4	43.6	23.4	20.2
Inpatient	100.0	54.9	45.1	18.6	26.5
Outpatient	100.0	56.9	43.1	26.4	16.7

Source: NHIC 2005.

Life insurers (L) could sell only fixed payment–type, dread disease insurance, and property insurers (P&L) could sell only indemnity–type accident insurance. In 1997 the Ministry of Finance and Economy (MOFE) established a third sector to lower entry barriers to the health insurance market.

The new PHI products can be classified in two groups by payment method: fixed payment and indemnity of charges incurred. The cancer insurance–type pays predetermined amounts for cancer diagnosis, surgery, and inpatient stays. The indemnity insurance–type, a more recent product, reimburses part of the total copayments.

In the first six years that both life insurers and the fire and marine insurers were allowed to sell the third sector insurance, the market grew more than 20 percent. Competition also increased. As shown in table 15.6, the life insurance companies held 95 percent of the market in 1996 but 84 percent in 2005. In contrast, long-term casualty insurers expanded their share from 3.7 percent in 1996 to 15.1 percent in 2005.

Life insurers won the debate on eliminating the last barrier to their entry to indemnity-type gap insurance in 2004. As of July 2005, the MOFE allowed life insurance companies to sell the indemnity-type gap insurance to the individual market two years after lifting the barrier to the group market in 2003. This regulation is expected to change the dynamics of the health insurance market by shifting all out-of-pocket expenses from limited coverage to comprehensive coverage for critical illnesses and by promoting the development of reimbursement networks among insurers and providers.

This regulatory change encouraged debate among scholars, government officials, insurance companies, providers, and nongovernmental organizations

TABLE 15.6 Korea: Private Health Insurance Market Size

	Life insurance		*Long-term property insurance*		*Property insurance*		*Total*	
Year	*Premiums (W)*	*Percent*	*Premiums (W)*	*Percent*	*Premiums (W)*	*Percent*	*Amount (W)*	*Variation*
1996	1,250,725	94.8	48,180	3.7	20,821	1.6	1,319,726	—
1997	1,498,002	93.9	70,487	4.4	26,064	1.6	1,594,553	20.8
1998	1,767,255	93.7	93,618	5	25,582	1.4	1,886,455	18.3
1999	2,242,596	91.8	156,729	6.4	42,471	1.7	2,441,796	29.4
2000	2,799,958	90.9	249,338	8.1	32,260	1	3,081,556	26.2
2001	3,739,371	90	386,775	9.3	29,239	0.7	4,155,385	34.8
2002	4,486,746	89.4	495,119	9.9	36,419	0.7	5,018,284	20.8
2003	4,840,200	85.2	787,600	13.9	51,100	0.9	5,678,900	13.2
2004	5,515,400	84.6	943,900	14.5	63,500	0.9	6,522,800	14.8
2005	6,294,800	83.9	1,131,200	15.1	78,900	1	7,504,900	15.1

Source: Author's calculation based on internal data of Insurance Development Institute.

(NGOs). NGOs fiercely criticized the expansion of gap insurance as a "real introduction of PHI for the rich."[1] Health care providers began to recognize the significance of PHI because they need to be part of the network under the expanding indemnity-type gap insurance.[2]

Characteristics of Private Health Insurance

Fixed-payment critical illness insurance is the main product in the Korean health insurance market. For patients with critical illness insurance, insurance companies need not deal with hospitals or the national health insurance corporation because they pay predetermined amount directly to patients. The payment limit was predetermined in proportion to the premium, not the medical expense incurred. Thus, fixed-payment health insurance follows the principle of savings instead of guaranteed coverage of losses.

Development Path of PHI

In Korea, the first health care insurance product was provided in 1980 as a cancer rider to life insurance. Cancer insurance products were developed in the early 1980s but did not attract attention until the mid-1990s. In 1988 gap insurance, covering public health insurance copayments was developed. Since the mid-1990s, the life insurance companies have promoted dread disease insurance covering cancer or 4 to 10 critical illnesses. In 1999, the P&L market leader, Samsung, launched comprehensive gap insurance that reimbursed both copayments and OOPS for uncovered services. In 2006, the top three life insurance companies announced their plan to launch comprehensive gap insurance for the individual market.

Major Issues for Public-Private Mix of Health Care Financing

The major issues to be resolved for the development of a public-private mix of health care financing are the lack of linkage among insurers, problems of adverse selection and moral hazard, and installation of an efficient claims processing system.

Lack of Linkage among Insurers

The MOHW announced a roadmap for further expansion of NHI coverage in 2005. The main goal is to broaden NHI coverage from the current 60 percent of the population to 71.5 percent in 2008. Between 2005 and 2008, the MOHW planned to invest US$3.5 billion to provide more complete coverage for 25 major diseases.

So far, there is no link between the NHI and PHI coverage. The government has no information about who has private coverage. Private health insurers are not allowed access to the information about their enrollees' claims on the NHI.

The author's own analysis showed that the MOHW plan resulted in overinsurance for 25 major diseases and underinsurance for all other illnesses (Jung et al. 2006b). The MOHW did not recognize that its roadmap would duplicate the coverage of the most prevalent form of private insurance, cancer and critical illness insurance. In short, the lack of linkage between the government health insurance and PHI would seriously hamper the macro efficiency of Korea's health care financing systems.

Who will coordinate the roles among the NHI, indemnity PHI, and supplementary PHI? This is the most critical challenge to health care financing in Korea at this time.

Adverse Selection and Moral Hazard

Since 1995, there has been a serious conceptual debate about moral hazard and adverse selection of PHI. However, very few empirical studies have been published(Ettner 1997) (Park and Chai 2003) (Sappelli and Bernadita 2003). As major life insurers sell comprehensive gap insurance to the individual market, the issues of information asymmetry will become more important.

How will insurers reduce moral hazard and adverse selection (Jung, Shine, and Kwak 2006a)? How and who will protect the insured from risk selection by insurers (Jung 2006b)? These questions are explored below in the evaluation study section.

Claims Review and Assessment

With indemnity-type gap insurance, a system for filing, reviewing, assessing, and paying claims is a prerequisite. Here, Korea's world-class IT infrastructure is an invaluable asset. More than 90 percent of providers already file NHIC claims through electronic data interchange. Not only hospitals but also public and private insurers will have to join the system or reimbursement network. Otherwise, the providers will have to file claims in the different formats of 40 insurance companies.

There are, however, legal as well as political barriers to the development of a uniform PHI claims processing system. Medical Act forbids sharing a patient's information with others without the patient's consent. Providers and insurers have shown some conflicts over the hegemony of developing the system. Even with these barriers, investing the effort to develop a uniform system and provider-payer networks to implement the system will be worthwhile.

THE EVALUATION STUDY

In this section, factors of enrolling in private health insurance (Vistnes and Banthin 1998) were discussed based on empirical analysis (Kim 2005).

Determinants of Enrolment

The factors determining individual enrolment in a private health plan were identified by applying a logistic regression model among 4,267 households that participated in the fourth Korean Labor and Income Panel Survey (KLIPS) from June to September 2001 (Kim 2005).

Data Description and Model

The model includes binary dependent variable and individual and household characteristics such as age, gender, income, and education as the independent variables (table 15.7).

$$
\begin{aligned}
\text{Logit (enrolment)} = {} & \alpha + \beta 1(\text{age}) + \beta 2(\text{gender}) + \beta 3\ (\text{health status}) \\
& + \beta 4\ (\text{chronic diseases}) + \beta 5\ (\text{health behavior}) \\
& + \beta 6\ (\text{marital status}) + \beta 7\ (\text{income}) + \beta 8\ (\text{employed}) \\
& + \beta 9\ (\text{self-employed}) + \beta 10\ (\text{education}) \\
& + \beta 11(\text{number in household}) + \beta 12\ (\text{disabled}) \\
& + \beta 13\ (\text{number of dependents}) \\
& + \beta 14\ (\text{ratio of physicians to population}) \\
& + \beta 15\ (\text{unemployment rate}) + \varepsilon.
\end{aligned}
$$

TABLE 15.7 Korea: Definitions of Variables, Evaluation Study

Variables			Definitions
Independent variables	Health-related	Age	Individual's age
		Gender	Male (1); female (0)
		Health status	Very bad (1); very good (5)
		Chronic diseases	Yes (1); no (0)
		Disabled	Yes (1); no (0)
		Health-promoting behavior	Yes (1); no (0)
	Socio-economic	Income	Total income
		Employed	Yes (1); no (0)
		Self-employed	Yes (1); no (0)
		Married	Yes (1); no (0)
		Education	Number of years completed if graduated
		Household members	Number of family members living together
		Need care	Household has individual needing care (1); no (0)
		Disabled family	Households has disabled person (1); no (0)
	Supply factor	No. of physicians	Ratio of physicians to population in designated areas, end-2000
	Other factors	No. of dependents	Household has dependents under 19 years(1); no (0)
		Unemployment	Rate in designated areas after July 2001
Dependent variable		Enrolment	Enrolled in private insurance (1); no (0)

Source: Author.

Main Results

People enrolled private insurance comprised 38.14 percent of the total sample. Considering that the sample represents the entire nation, approximately 40 percent of the population is enrolled health insurance. People who bought private coverage were younger than those who did not (mean age of 38.9 and 42.2 years, respectively).

Health Behavior and Self-Recognized Health Status

For health behavior variables, people enrolled in private insurance did more than the unenrolled to stay healthy. In addition, individuals who considered themselves healthy were more likely than others to enroll in private plans. Hypertension was more prevalent among the unenrolled respondents. Furthermore, prevalence of chronic diseases was also higher among the unenrolled: cancer (0.4 percent vs. 1.1 percent), diabetes (1.5 percent vs. 3.2 percent), arthritis (2 percent vs.5.6 percent), and asthma (0.1 percent vs. 0.6 percent). The results are the opposite of selection bias of health insurance.

Average Number of Products and Spending

Private insurance enrollees had 1.58 insurance plans on average and paid about US$77 a month. Male enrollees had more insurance products than females and purchased more expensive plans. People in their 40s paid the highest insurance premium (about US$87); people in their 30s and 50s, the next highest (about US$79). People interested in their health had more insurance plans than the uninterested. However, self-diagnosed health status and chronic illness were not related to the number and premium of private insurance plans.

Health Care Utilization by Private Insurance Enrollees

There was no difference in inpatient admissions by enrolment in a private insurance plan. However, private insurance enrollees visited health care institutions more frequently than the nonenrolled (11.43 visits vs. 7.15). In the survey, health utilization data for the most recent month were considered because respondents may have a memory bias.

Considering the health care utilization and spending statistics, people not enrolled in private insurance plans received more intensive care per visit when using health services, although their frequency of use was lower than those of PHI enrollees. As in the previous study (Jung 1998), the frequency of medical care was substituted by the intensity of care per visit.

Logistic Models Testing Determinants of Enrolment

The logit estimates of testing determinants of PHI plan enrolment are shown in table 15.8. For demographic variables, younger people and females were more likely to enroll in PHI. However, for the health status variables, people diagnosed with chronic diseases or the disabled/injured were less likely to enroll in PHI plans (hypertension, diabetes, and asthma). Also, people who were interested

TABLE 15.8 Logit Model for Testing Determinants of PHI Enrolment

Variable	*Estimate*	*S.E.*	*Wald chi²*	*Pr> chi²*
Intercept	−1.6541	0.2111	61.3714	<.0001
Age	−0.0233	0.00244	91.4856	<.0001
Gender	−0.2567	0.0499	26.4362	<.0001
Health status	0.0389	0.0317	1.5101	0.2191
Hypertension	−0.5015	0.1503	11.1312	0.0008
Diabetes	−0.3098	0.1764	3.0853	0.0790
Cancer	−0.5551	0.3002	3.4190	0.0644
Arthritis	0.0347	0.1465	0.0561	0.8127
Asthma	−1.0523	0.4970	4.4840	0.0342
Disabled/injured	−0.3468	0.1494	5.3835	0.0203
Alcohol/tobacco restricted	−0.0991	0.0926	1.1450	0.2846
Exercise	0.3705	0.0575	41.4551	<.0001
Diet	0.0473	0.0637	0.5525	0.4573
Health nutrient	0.3519	0.1073	10.7538	0.0010
Bath/sauna	0.1610	0.0845	3.6315	0.0567
Other	0.1452	0.1861	0.6086	0.4353
Regular medical exam	0.6374	0.0599	113.3313	<.0001
Marital status	1.1354	0.0742	234.4813	<.0001
Income status	0.000606	0.000048	160.4452	<.0001
Employed	0.7313	0.0553	174.9304	<.0001
Self-employed	0.7805	0.0661	139.5440	<.0001
Education	0.0476	0.00756	39.5690	<.0001
No. of family members	−0.0582	0.0189	9.4941	0.0021
No. of need care	−0.0269	0.1628	0.0272	0.8690
No. of dependents	0.7398	0.0590	157.0918	<.0001
Physician/population	−0.00030	0.000904	0.1135	0.7362
Unemployment rate	−0.0722	0.0366	3.8814	0.0488

Source: Reorganized by author from Kim 2005.

in their health had higher enrolment rates. For economic variables, people with jobs and higher incomes were more likely to enroll in PHI.

Discussion

Using KLIPS data, the determinants of enrolment in PHI plans were identified. The result that people enrolled in the private plan used more health care implied that PHI could increase access to the health care. However, the fact that chronically ill people were less likely to be enrolled in PHI implied that income and education affected PHI enrolment or that insurers selected healthy people by screening (Pourat et al. 2000).

Impact on Access to Health Care

To analyze how NHI membership and private supplemental coverage enrolment affect access to health care, Jung and others (2004, 2006b) explored the impact of private supplemental coverage on publicly financed health expenditure. The difference in medical care utilization was estimated between those who had private supplemental plans and those who did not. In 2002 for the first time in Korea, the NHI claims file was linked with enrolment files of leading private health insurers and medical care use was compared for members and nonmembers of supplemental coverage in 2001. The difference would include the effects of moral hazard, selection, and other omitted variables.

Data Description

The sample consisted of a case group and a control group. The case group was set up by merging data from private insurers and the NHI. In all, 33,342 buyers of health insurance in 2001–03 from two leading insurance companies[3] were matched to NHI claims information in 2002. Case group members filed 620,534 claims in 2002.

Control group samples were stratified by age and gender. The NHI provided data on claims by 66,602 individuals who did not have private coverage in the same period. Control group members filed 225,011 claims in 2002.

Definitions of variables and sample means are shown in table 15.9.

Model

The modified two-part model used earlier (Jung 1998) was again used. The two-part model developed by Manning and others (1981, 1987) assumes that expected annual spending for medical care is the product of episode frequencies and episode expense. Using the two-part model, Manning and colleagues focused on episode utilization. Jung (1998) modified their two-part model in his research to represent two levels of medical care use: probability of medical use during the year and conditional annual spending.

In this study, we excluded first-part analysis (probability of medical use) because we used the claims file of NHI rather than enrolment file in 2002. To analyze the second-part model (conditional annual expense), ordinary least squared model is used. Log transformed measures of annual spending, outpatient visits, and inpatient days made in year 2002 were used as dependent variables. Two variables, whether the person purchased supplemental coverage in 2001 or not (purchase) and whether the person purchased extensive private plans or not (coverage type) were included as test variables.

Main Results

In this section, whether medical utilization is associated with PHI enrolment as well as types of PHI coverage are discussed.

TABLE 15.9 Characteristics of the Sample

Variables		*Control group (N = 66,602)*	*Case group (N = 33,342)*
Gender	Male	27,073 (40.65%)	16,743 (50.2%)
	Female	39,529 (59.35%)	16,599 (49.8%)
Age (standard deviation)		37.2 (13.9)	30.8 (11.4)
Householder	Householder	26,441 (39.7%)	13,719 (41.2%)
	Not householder	40,161 (60.3%)	19,623 (58.8%)
Coverage type	Fixed	—	20,708 (62.1%)
	Indemnity	—	12,634 (37.9%)
Area	Small city	—	3,812 (11.4%)
	Small to medium city	—	10,999 (33.0%)
	Metropolitan area	—	18,531 (55.6%)
Income	Low	—	16,682 (50.0%)
	Middle	—	12,914 (38.7%)
	High	—	3,746 (11.3%)
Number of physicians[a] (per 1,000 population)		—	1.67 (0.60)
Number of beds (per 1,000 population)		—	6.59 (2.35)
Annual outpatient visit days		17.6 (17.8)	28.5 (29.9)
Annual outpatient spending		283,093 (603,772)	386,134 (460,903)
Annual inpatient bed-days		11.9 (22.0)	11.0 (15.8)
Annual inpatient spending		1,359,218 (2,479,514)	1,011,053 (1,860,765)

Source: Author's calculations.

Note: — = not available.

a. The number of physicians per 1,000 population means that the number of physicians worked in the area where individuals in the case group (who purchased private coverage in 2001) lived.

Utilization by whether or not purchasing supplemental coverage

Four measures were used to examine difference in utilization by case and control groups. The case group had more outpatient visit days and higher expenses than the control group. However, the case group had lower inpatient bed days and expenses than the control group. The ordinary least square (OLS) estimates in (table 15.10) indicates that only outpatient case showed the moral hazard and the selection effect in the decision on whether to purchase any type of PHI.

The Effect of Coverage Type on Health Care Spending

Among the individuals who have at least one private health policy, the insured under indemnity-type coverage did not show any significant mean differences in health services utilization from those with fixed-type insurance like cancer.

TABLE 15.10 Korea: OLS Models Testing Moral Hazard and Other Effects, Any Private Coverage

Dependent variable regressors	*Outpatient visit days*	*Log expenditure*	*Inpatient bed days*	*Log expenditure*
Purchasing	0.27*	0.19*	0.006 (0.62)	–0.03*
Age (squared)	0.20*	0.26*	0.12*	0.21*
Gender	0.08*	0.07*	–0.09*	–0.08*
Householder	0.05*	0.05*	0.02 (0.07)	0.04*
N	99,903	99,903	6,866	6,866
F (pr > F)	2,628.8*	2,344.6*	33.2*	88.2*
Adj R-sq	0.10	0.09	0.02	0.05

Source: Author's calculations.
*p<0.01.

Membership in indemnity-type coverage affected only outpatient utilizations. Older people and women used more health care services. People who lived in the larger cities and had higher income used more outpatient medical services.

Discussion

Moral hazard was found to affect the utilization of medical care, especially outpatient services. The results were attributable to the high out-of-pocket payment in government insurance and unique features of services covered by private insurance.

Impact on Financial Protection

Health insurance is expected to protect households from variations in health expenditure. In Korea no one had previously tested this theory empirically. Here, the same datasets used to test moral hazard in the previous section are used to test the following hypotheses:

1. People with health insurance have higher financial protection than people with no health insurance.
2. People with indemnity insurance have higher financial protection than people with cancer insurance.

The measure of financial protection is as follows:

$$\gamma = \frac{Mean(OOPS)}{\sigma_{\text{Oops}}}.$$

TABLE 15.11 Korea: OLS Models Testing Moral Hazard and Other Effects, by Coverage Type

Dependent variable regressors	*Outpatient visit days*	*Log expenditure*	*Inpatient bed days*	*Log expenditure*
Coverage type (indemnity = 1, fixed type = 0)	0.009*	0.008*	−0.005 (0.78)	−0.006 (0.74)
Age (squared)	0.20**	0.22**	0.15**	0.17**
Gender	0.11**	0.12**	−0.08**	−0.08**
Householder	0.02[c]	0.0002 (0.97)	0.02 (0.40)	0.02 (0.46)
Number of physicians (per 1,000 population)	−0.03**	−0.03**	−0.07**	−0.008 (0.77)
Number of beds (per 1,000 population)	0.009 (0.12)	0.005 (0.29)	0.01 (0.62)	−0.005 (0.79)
Area				
Medium city	0.02***	0.03**	0.03 (0.27)	0.04 (0.18)
Metropolitan city	0.04**	0.05**	0.05 (0.18)	0.06 (0.11)
Income				
Middle	−0.08**	−0.07**	0.03 (0.22)	−0.02 (0.44)
High	−0.07**	−0.05**	−0.0002 (0.99)	0.003 (0.88)
N	33,325	33,325	2,606	2,606
F (pr > F)	194.4**	212.6**	8.31**	8.11**
Adj R^2	0.05	0.06	0.03	0.03

Source: Author's calculations.
*p<0.1; **p<0.01; ***p<0.05.

Using the sample of 99,944 observations, γ was calculated. The empirical estimations are given in tables 15.12 and 15.13. People with health insurance had significantly higher financial protection (γ) than those without health insurance (hypothesis 1 supported). But people with indemnity-type health insurance had lower γ than those with fixed-payment, dread disease insurance (hypothesis 2 refuted). This might be partly because the indemnity-type health insurance products sold until 2003 did not provide less-comprehensive coverage than the products that will be introduced in 2008. Among people with

TABLE 15.12 Korea: Financial Protection for the Insured vs. Uninsured

Sample individuals	*Observation*	*Means of individual OOPS*	*Standard deviation (σ)*	*Financial protection (γ)*
All observations	99,944	117,001	230,191	0.508
No health insurance	66,602	110,618	240,773	0.459
Health insurance	33,342	129,753	206,858	0.627

Source: Author's calculation.

TABLE 15.13 Korea: Financial Protection for Insured with Fixed Type vs. Indemnity Type

Sample individuals	*Observation*	*Means of individual OOPS*	*Standard deviation (σ)*	*Financial protection (γ)*
All observations	33,342	129,752	206,858	0.627
Fixed type	20,708	129,273	200,199	0.645
Indemnity type	12,634	130,540	217,339	0.600

Source: Author's calculation.

fixed-payment insurance, income was negatively associated with financial protection. In contrast, a positive association was found among those with indemnity-type insurance (mixed results). Multivariate analysis was used to explain these results in detail.

FEASIBILITY STUDY

Based on Korean Development Institute estimates of health expenditure and government subsidy (KDI 2006), the role of private health insurance in health care financing is examined.

Population and Health Expenditure Forecasts

Korea has the most rapidly aging population in the world. To forecast the medical expenditure, the Korea Development Institute (2006) has been carrying out a multiyear project to forecast the demographics and health expenditure. In this section, the KDI estimates are used to discuss the role of PHI in financing health care in coming decades. The KDI study used a stochastic time series model to estimate birth and death rates for each age cohort. Based on the estimates, the KDI forecast that the Korean population will reach peak of 51 million between 2025 and 2030 and will fall to 47 million by 2050. These results show that the estimates by the National Statistics Office overestimated death rates and therefore underestimated the number of aged population and the maximum expenditure.

Health expenditures per capita for three age groups (0–14, 15–64, 65+) are shown in figure 15.1. The gap in per capita health expenditure between the elderly and other groups was 10 times wider in 2004 than in 1990. This trend reflects that higher intensity of care as well as life expectancy of the elderly are the main drivers of health cost inflation.

Estimation Model

To estimate health expenditure per capita, the KDI study (2006) used the ARIMA model and developed random walk equations for the three age cohorts.

FIGURE 15.1 Korea: Per Capita Health Expenditure, Three Age Cohorts

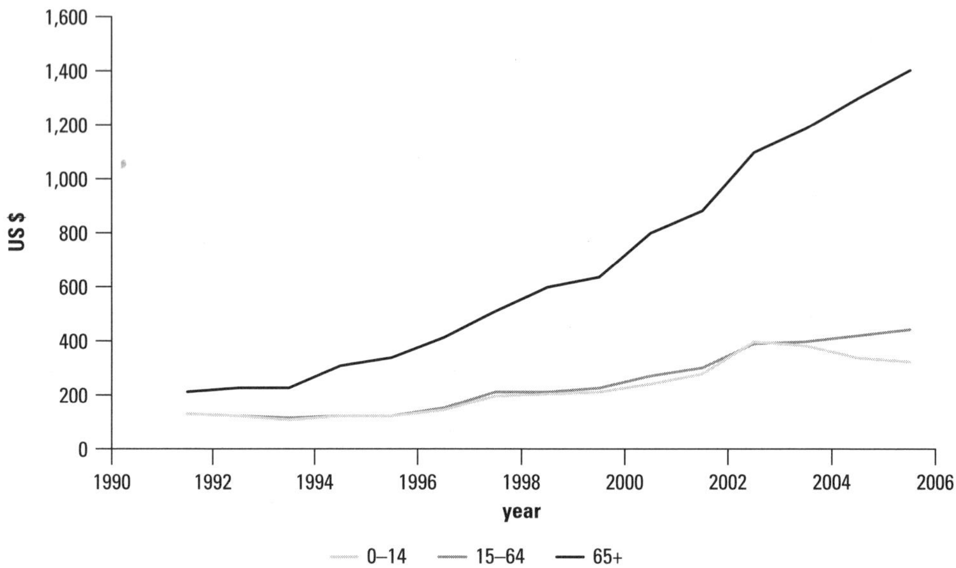

Source: National Statistical Office, National Health Insurance Corporation, all years.

For 0–14 age cohort,

$H^S_{x,t} = H^S_{x,t-1} + 15.607 + e_t.$

For 15–64 age cohort,

$H^S_{x,t} = H^S_{x,t-1} + 17.221 + e_t.$

For 65+ age cohort,

$H^S_{x,t} = H^S_{x,t-1} + 70.950 + e_t.$

From the three equations, the KDI study calculated the growth rate of per capita health expenditure for each age cohort. The growth rate reflects demographic changes, technological innovation, GDP growth, and coverage changes in government health insurance (Getzen 1992; Moon 2002). Based on these growth rates, the KDI estimated health expenditure per capita and the amount of government subsidy required to cover the deficit. Two major assumptions underlie the KDI estimations.

Results

The estimation was based on two population estimates: National Statistics Office and KDI. Growth rates for total health expenditure were calculated in two ways: average growth rate in 1995–2005 (table 15.14, columns 1 and 3), and growth

TABLE 15.14 Korea: Total Health Expenditure, 2010–50 (W billion)

	Based on NSO estimates		*Based on KDI estimates*		*Difference*
Year	*(1)*	*(2)*	*(3)*	*(4)*	*Maximum–minimum*
2010	30.90	32.88	32.73	33.08	2.18
2015	40.21	42.40	43.34	42.68	3.13
2020	50.97	53.21	57.40	53.94	6.43
2025	67.11	65.39	75.62	66.90	10.23
2030	84.78	77.84	98.20	80.78	20.36
2035	103.54	89.46	124.94	94.50	35.48
2040	120.99	99.74	155.90	107.50	56.16
2045	139.21	107.94	191.24	119.08	83.30
2050	157.85	113.57	230.31	128.65	116.74

Source: Reorganized by author from NSO and KDI reports.

rate estimated by the stochastic time series model (table 15.14, columns 2 and 4). The total expenditure in 2015 will range between US$40.21 billion and US$43.34 billion. The range will widen to US$116 billion by 2050.

Total Reimbursement and Subsidy

Based on the estimates of total expenditure, the amount of total reimbursement by the NHI and the government subsidy required to cover the deficit were calculated. The underlying assumptions are as follows. The reimbursement rate (total reimbursement/total contribution) will maintain 71.67 percent, the rate in 2004. The government subsidy rate (government subsidy/total reimbursement) will maintain 21.4 percent, the rate in 2004 and 2003. In 2015, the total reimbursement by the NHI will be between US$31.06 billion and US$28.82 billion, depending on the assumptions on population and growth rate of health expenditure.

By 2015, the subsidy required will be around US$6.5 billion. In 2020, the government will need between US$8 billion and US$8.8 billion to cover the NHI deficit. By 2050, the subsidy required will increase to US$20 billion. If the Korean government does not reform the health insurance benefit and contribution structures, it will consistently incur NHI deficits. The accumulated deficit will put a big burden on the Korean economy.

Role of PHI in Health Care Financing

The market size of PHI has already approached US$8 billion—higher than the US$6.5 billion government subsidy for the NHI required in 2015 (table 15.15). Clearly, the role of the health insurance market cannot be disregarded, considering the relative and absolute market size. If people buying PHI are willing to pay

TABLE 15.15 Korea: Government Subsidy to NHI, 2010–50 (W trillion)

	Based on NSO estimates		*Based on KDI estimates*	
Year	*(1)*	*(2)*	*(3)*	*(4)*
2010	4.74	5.04	5.02	5.07
2015	6.17	6.50	6.65	6.55
2020	7.97	8.16	8.80	8.27
2025	10.29	10.03	11.60	10.26
2030	13.00	11.94	15.06	12.39
2035	15.88	13.72	19.16	14.49
2040	18.56	15.30	23.91	16.49
2045	21.35	16.56	29.33	18.26
2050	24.21	17.42	35.32	19.73

Source: Reorganized by author from NSO and KDI reports.

as large an NHI contribution as they pay for PHI, the NHI deficit or expansion of its coverage will cause no worries.

Two points must, however, be made about future policy. First, the efficiency of the PHI market will have to be increased. The action plans include the standardization of products, which are currently overly complex, and unifying the claims review and payment system. Second, an efficient integration of the NHI and PHI will have to be designed. To achieve this grand goal, the MOHW should update and announce detailed road maps for expanding NHI coverage in advance. Most important, the government must organize a task force or agency to govern PHI policies and regulations, now controlled by more than five ministries, including the MOHW and the MOFE.

CONCLUSIONS

Korea's achievement of the NHI in just 12 years was often cited as a miracle until 2000. At that point, the financial distress of the NHI damaged not only its reputation but also the trust of the Korean people in the social security of health care. Koreans flocked to buy private products that were not designed well enough to provide health care security.

The PHI market expanded to 40 percent of total NHI reimbursements, making Korea one of the world's largest PHI markets. It is surprising that the Korean insurance market could have grown to this size when no insurers sold comprehensive major medical insurance. Unfortunately, most products sold cover specific diseases like cancer or 4 to 10 critical illnesses and pay a fixed amount instead of covering the patient's actual bills. Considering that the average copayment rate is more than 40 percent, the market for gap insurance will grow significantly.

In this evaluation study, factors were empirically explored that affect the enrolment in PHI, moral hazard, adverse selection, and financial protection. Younger people and females were more likely to enroll in PHI. People with chronic diseases (hypertension, diabetes, and asthma) or the disabled were less likely than the healthy to enroll in PHI plans. Moral hazard was found in outpatient but not inpatient care. Having PHI improved financial protection. People with fixed-payment products had higher financial protection than those with indemnity-type products.

The success of the Korean health care system will depend on whether the resources being spent for private coverage can be used to the advantage of the entire system. As suggested by the feasibility study, the PHI market is already larger than the government subsidy that will be needed in 2015. A linkage has to be developed between public and private payers. Policy options suggested for improving the efficiency of the PHI market include forging links between private and public insurers (Pauly 1986) (Jung 2006b), simplifying insurance products, and developing an efficient claims processing system for private insurers and providers.

NOTES

The author is indebted to EunKyu Shin, JunEun Jang and Jeongyoon Kim for their assistance with empirical and institutional analysis. The author is also grateful to Donghyun Kim, Changhwan Kwak, and other staff members at the Healthcare Industry Research Institute for data handling and editorial support.

1. Public hearing organized by Congressman Kang Keejung, National Assembly Hall, Seoul, February 21, 2006.
2. Workshop organized by the Korean Medical Association, KMA Building, Seoul, February 9, 2006.
3. Accounting for 70 percent of the private health insurance market.

REFERENCES

Chung, W., and H.J. Kim. 2005. "Interest Groups' Influence over Drug Pricing Policy Reform in South Korea." *Yonsei Medical Journal* 46(3): 321–30.

Ettner, S. 1997. "Adverse Selection and the Purchase of Medigap Insurance by the Elderly." *Journal of Health Economics* 16: 543–62.

Getzen, T.E. 1992. "Population Aging and the Growth of Health Expenditure." *Journal of Gerontology–Social Sciences* 47(3): 98–104.

Jung, K.T. 2003. "Research for Developing Private Health Insurance." Research Report, Ministry of Finance and Economy, Seoul.

———. 2000. "The Plan for Developing Private Health Insurance." Research Report, Korean Non-Life Insurance, Seoul.

———. 1998. "Influence of the Introduction of a Per-Visit Copayment on Health Care Use and Expenditures: The Korean Experience." *Journal of Risk and Insurance* 65(1): 33–56.

Jung, K.T., U.K. Shine, and C.H. Kwak 2006a. "An Empirical Study on the Relationship between Private Health Insurance and Moral Hazard in Korea." *Korean Journal of Insurance* 4:1–25.

Jung, K.T., J.H. Kim, Y.J. Kwon, U.K. Shine, C.H. Kwak, D.H. Kim, J.H. Kim, K.J. Lee, and S.J. Lee. 2006b. "Policies for Activating Private Health Insurance Market." Research Report, Korea Life Insurance Association and General Insurance Association of Korea, Seoul.

Jung, K.T., and C.H. Kwak. 2005. "Estimation of Private Health Insurance Market Size and Financial Effect." Proceedings of the Scientific Meeting of Korean Insurance Academic Society. Samsung Fire & Marine Insurance Company' International conference room, Seoul, May 13.

Jung, K.T., J.Y. Park, B.H. Choi, B.H., and Y.S. Kim. 2004. "Reforming Governance and Management System of National Health Insurance." Research Report, The Korea Institute of Public Administration, Seoul.

Kim, H.J., K.T. Jung, W.J. Jung, B.I. Kim, E.Y. Kim, S.K. Lee, S.H. Shin, and S.M. Lee. 2003. "Developing a Model for Future National Health Insurance." Research Report, National Congress Committee of Health and Welfare, Seoul.

Kim, S.O. 2005. "Selection and Health Utilization of Enrollment in the Private Health Insurance." Section 4, Issue 2. The Sixth Korean Labor and Income Panel Study Conference. Seoul National University HOAM Faculty House, Seoul, Feb 3.

Korea Development Institute. 2006. "The Second Study on the Effect of Aging Society." Research Report, Seoul.

KOSIS (Korean Statistical Information Service). Department of Korea National Statistical Office. Korea. http://www.kosis.kr/.

Kwon, S.M. 2002. "Health insurance for all: lessons from the Republic of Korea." ESS (Extension of Social Security) Discussion paper, No. 1, International Labor Office, Geneva, Swiss.

Manning, W.G., C.M. Morris, J.P. Newhouse, L.L. Orr, N. Duan, E.B. Keeler, A. Leibowitz, K.H. Marquis, M.S. Marquis, and C.E. Phelps. 1981. "A Two-Part Model of the Demand for Medical Care: Preliminary Results from the Health Insurance Study." In *Health, Economics, and Health Economics,* ed. J. van der Gaag and M. Perlman, 103–123. Amsterdam, Netherlands: North Holland.

Manning, W.G., J.P. Newhouse, N. Duan, E.B. Keeler, A. Leibowitz, and M.S. Marquis. 1987. "Health Insurance and the Demand for Medical Care: Evidence from a Randomized Experiment." *American Economic Review* 77(3): 251–77.

NHIC (National Health Insurance Corporation). 2000–06. *National Health Insurance Statistical Yearbook.* National Health Insurance Corporation. Korea. http://www.nhic.or.kr/.

———. 2005. "Revision of NHI Act." Korea. http://www.nhic.or.kr/wbm/wbmb/wbmb_0100.html.

NSO (National Statistical Office, Korea). 2005. "Population Projection." *National Statistics Annual Report.* Korea National Statistical Office.

OECD. 2007. *OECD Health Data.* Paris: OECD.

———. 2000. *ICHA-HF Classification of Health Care Financing* 11:151–56. Paris: OECD.

Park, J., and H. Chai. 2003. "The Effects of an Increase of Outpatient Co-Insurance Rate on the Financial Status of the National Health Insurance." *Korean Journal of Insurance* 4:109–36.

Pauly, M.V. 1986. "Taxation, Health Insurance, and Market Failure in the Medical Economy." *Journal of Economic Literature* 24: 629–75.

Pourat, N., T. Rice, G. Kominski, and R. Snyder. 2000. "Socioeconomic Differences in Medicare Supplemental Coverage." *Health Affairs* 19(5): 186–96.

Sapelli, Claudio, and Vial Bernardita. 2003. "Self-Selection and Moral Hazard in Chilean Health Insurance." *Journal of Health Economics* 22: 459–47.

Moon, S. 2002. "Forecast of Reimbursement Expenditure of National Health Insurance: Based on the Structural Change of Population." Research Report, Health Insurance Research Center in National Health Insurance Corporation, Seoul.

Vistnes, J., and J. Banthin. 1998. "The Demand for Medicare Supplemental Insurance Benefits: The Role of Attitudes toward Medical Care and Risk." *Inquiry* 34(4): 311–24.

APPENDIX A

Methodology for Reviewing Private Voluntary Health Insurance

Alexander S. Preker, Richard M. Scheffler, and Mark C. Bassett

This appendix presents the methodology used to review the role of private voluntary health insurance (PVHI) in low- and middle-income countries. It includes the methodology for both reviewing the global experience presented in the first volume, *Private Voluntary Health Insurance in Development: Friend or Foe?* (Preker, Scheffler, and Bassett, eds. 2007) and the methodology used for the country case studies in this second volume, *Global Marketplace for Private Health Insurance: Strength in Numbers.*

OBJECTIVES OF THE REVIEWS

Both volumes analyze the strengths, weaknesses, and potential future role of private voluntary health insurance in low- and middle-income countries. They considers the economics of such insurance in terms of supply, demand, market dynamics, and insurance market failure. In addition, they present empirical evidence on the impact of voluntary health insurance on financial protection against the cost of illness, insurance coverage, households' access to affordable health care, labor markets, and household consumption patterns. Finally, they explore the characteristics of voluntary health insurance markets that are emerging in developing countries (current trends in terms of policy framework, organizational structure, institutional environment, and management attributes) and prospects for future business development.

METHODOLOGY USED IN COMPANION VOLUME, *FRIEND OR FOE*

The first set of studies, published in the companion volume, *Friend or Foe,* used a combination of cross-sectional and longitudinal techniques (quantitative and qualitative) to explore the role of private voluntary health insurance in securing wider and better access to health care. Where possible, health financing projection models were used to estimate fiscal implications, labor market effects, and impacts on revenue and expenditure flows in the health sector.

Their analysis built on research in the areas of health insurance (voluntary health microinsurance and government-run mandatory health insurance), user fees, and resource allocation and purchasing. It drew on expertise throughout the World Bank Group: health and social protection, poverty alleviation, public sector management, corruption and fiscal policy, insurance and risk management, and contracting with nongovernmental organizations and the private sector.

Review of the Economics of PVHI at Low Income Levels

Friend or Foe focused on the underlying economics and constraints to private voluntary health insurance found at low-and middle-income levels. These constraints include low household income; low participation in the formal labor market and high participation in the informal labor market; low compliance with contribution requirements in the formal sector; lack of social cohesion; GDP and GDP growth (usually low but sometimes very high); high levels of donor funding; high consumer price index; high medical inflation, morbidity, and mortality; and less use of public health services and more use private health services.

The review of demand-side economic factors focused on health needs, revealed preferences, and demand for health insurance; variations in benefits packages and expenditures; willingness and ability to pay; insurable and noninsurable risks and risk aversion; moral hazard/free rider problems; price (loading cost); and transaction costs. The review of supply-side economic factors focused on market structure; competitive environment; choice and coverage; benefits packages; price (loading cost); transaction costs; expenditure (level, distribution, and variations); adverse selection/cream skimming; legal framework, regulation, and administrative procedures; vertical integration (managed care); and organizational, institutional, and management issues. The review of market equilibrium factors focused on the existence and stability of equilibrium, coverage, market and government failure, performance (efficiency and equity), and the economics of regulatory instruments.

Review of the Empirical Evidence on the Impact of PVHI in Different Regions

The second set of studies presented in the companion volume examined evidence on impact of private voluntary health insurance on selected outcome indicators in different regions across the world. Households in low- and middle-income countries face a variety of covariant and idiosyncratic risks. These risks interact with a household's assets and affect households' risk-management capacity. Risks are transmitted through a change in the value or productivity of assets and affect the reallocation of resources.

Research indicates that illness represents the greatest risk of impoverishment to households. Voluntary health insurance can have an impact on financial protection against the cost of illness, as well as on insurance coverage, nonmedical consumption, access to health care, and labor market productivity, all of which affect household income, nonmedical consumption, saving, and investment behavior. With access to insurance, households might engage in higher-risk activities, but also in more profitable production techniques, which increases their resources

FIGURE A.1 Proximal and Distal Determinants

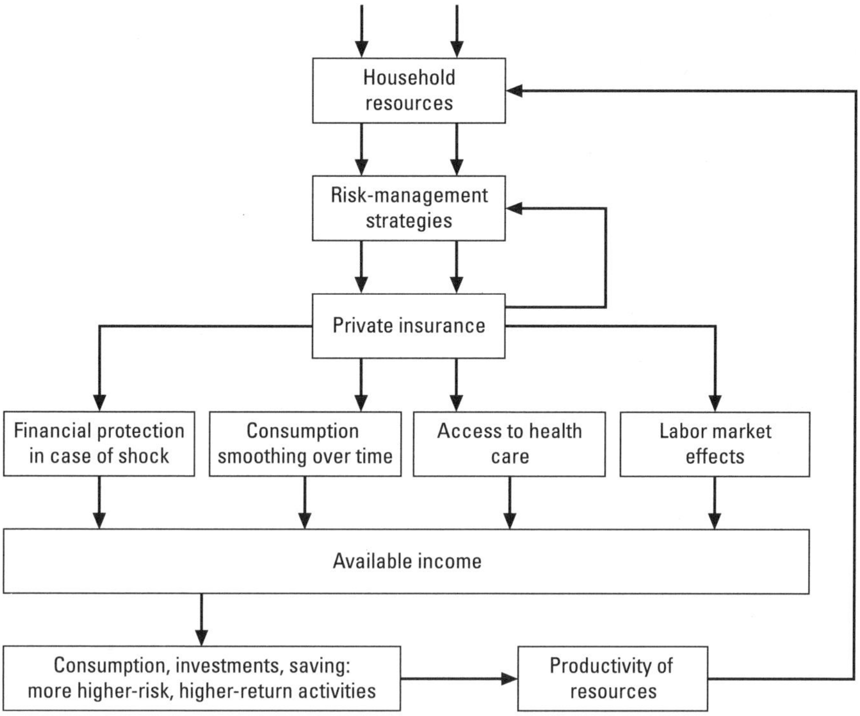

Source: Jütting 2004

and reduces their vulnerability to risks. This process involves a smoothing of household income available for consumption of nonmedical goods and services, saving, and investment (figure A.1).

Review of Opportunities for Expanding PVHI Markets

A third set of studies in the companion volume reviewed the evolution of PVHI markets at the global level, summarizing the prerequisites for good PVHI business practices, and feasibility of expanding voluntary health insurance in countries where market conditions are favorable. They reviewed empirical evidence on the supply, demand, market equilibrium, and market imperfections of voluntary health insurance in developing countries as well as the role and effectiveness of public policy instruments such as regulations, subsidies, and taxes.

Investment Climate

The market analysis examined the investment climate and institutional setting of existing PVHI schemes:

- political orientation (market economy, transition economy, welfare state, or socialist economy)

- economic variables (economic stability and growth, inflation, debt, and competitive environment)
- income levels
- geographic distribution
- labor market participation (urban versus rural, formal versus informal, industrial versus agricultural, employment rate versus unemployment)
- tax structure (level, progressivity, exemptions, payroll taxes, and so on)
- regulatory environment (insurance law, antitrust law, competition law, health legislation),
- social cohesion (tribal, traditional, modern nuclear, and so on)
- corruption
- health sector trends (public versus private)
- health expenditure trends—factor markets (labor, pharmaceuticals, medical equipment, consumables, and so on) and product markets (hospitals, clinics, and diagnostic laboratories).

Supply, Demand, and Market Equilibrium of PVHI

The market analysis also examined the supply and demand side of voluntary health insurance. Data sources include country-level databases (statistical year books), insurance rating agencies (for example, Moody's), actuarial firms (Milliman and Roberts, and so on), and major insurance firms that also deal in health (for example, AIG, AETNA, United, Lloyds, and Munich Re).

On the *supply side*, volume contributors summarized the main characteristics of existing schemes in terms of coverage (full or partial, level of copayments, exclusions), choice (mandatory, compulsory, and so on), and benefits (range and level) and develop a topology for voluntary health insurance on the basis of

- ownership arrangements—private profit (commercial), private nonprofit (nongovernmental organization, NGO), community-based, employer-based, foreign involvement (international versus domestic);
- degree of market concentration—size and distribution; and
- links (particularly when a PVHI scheme is a secondary funder under a mandated national or government system) to other insurance instruments (life, casualty, accident, death, and so on), the overall health financing system (complementary, supplementary, substitutive), and health management organizations (HMOs).

On the *demand side*, the market analysis examined the health needs; preferences as revealed by demand for health insurance; willingness and ability to pay for health care and health insurance, including benefit-incidence analysis;

insurable and noninsurable risks; degree of risk aversion; access to providers; expenditure variance; moral hazard/free rider behavior; consumption taxes on insurance; and subsidies and tax exemptions.

The market analysis also examined the extent to which supply, demand, and competition lead to a functioning voluntary insurance market. Volume contributors assessed the extent to which PVHI schemes in low-income countries are subject to moral hazard, adverse selection, free rider behavior, insurance premium escalation, and so on. They also assessed the extent to which public policy instruments such as taxation, subsidies, tax credits, and exemptions have increased or decreased such market failures.

Development Path for Growth of PVHI

Finally, the market analysis examined the historical context in which PVHI markets have evolved in developed and developing countries. Volume contributors attempted to answer several questions. Is voluntary health insurance part of a critical development path in achieving financial protection against the cost of illness? What were some of the problems encountered in countries with more mature markets today? Which public policy instruments and business strategies—taxation, subsidies, tax credits, exemptions, and so on—were successful in addressing these problems.

Best Business Practice in PVHI

The companion volume reviewed best practices in managing PVHI in four developed countries (Australia, Ireland, New Zealand, and the United Kingdom) and two emerging market economies (Israel and South Africa) and made recommendations that may be relevant to countries in which PVHI schemes are developing. Specifically, they examine:

- Company, sponsors, and management—Who owns, controls, and runs each PVHI company under examination?
- Strategic plan—Where does the company wish to be in 10 years and how does it plan to get there? That is, what are its goals (target markets, customers, cost reduction, repositioning), capital investment strategy, strengths (strategic fit of company mission/skills with potential market), and weaknesses (misalignment of company mission/skills with potential market)?
- Financial performance—What are the company's revenues and main product groups, variable cost structure (expenditures), fixed cost structure (expenditures), capital structure (own and borrowed) and cost, return on capital (own and borrowed), and bottom line (profit or loss)?
- Actuarial balance—What is the company's financial future (solvency and anticipated revenues and expenditures under different scenarios)?

- Management capacity—How capable are the managers to run a health insurance firm?
- Benefits and risks—What are the company's likely opportunities and risks in the future?

On the basis of this information, volume contributors identified the cycle of activity that ensures the sustainability of voluntary health insurers and provided guidelines on setting up regulatory and institutional frameworks for better PVHI business practice in low- and middle-income countries.

The authors of this section of the companion volume also tried to assess the willingness and ability to purchase voluntary health insurance, they examined the affordability and design of benefits packages, they obtained feedback from local officials on the political feasibility of introducing voluntary health insurance, and they identified potential insurance carriers.

In the context of expanding PVHI programs, the contributors explored opportunities for collecting and analyzing data on

- household income distribution, household expenditures distribution (including health/medical care), household health services utilization patterns, and household health insurance participation and premium expenditures;
- the benefit and population coverage, premiums, and organizational structure of public insurance programs;
- inpatient and outpatient distributions of health service providers;
- willingness and ability to pay for voluntary health insurance; and
- potential institutional arrangements and legal regulations for setting up PVHI programs.

Review of PVHI Literature

The annex of the companion volume presents an extensive review of the literature on PVHI in developing countries. The authors emphasized that there was little convincing evidence in the literature on the impact of such insurance on the latter's broad goals, such as increasing health, reducing the risks of impoverishment due to illness, and combating social exclusion. Moreover, little is known about the impact of voluntary health insurance on financial protection against the cost of illness, insurance coverage, nonmedical consumption, access to health care, and labor markets.

Assessment of Studies' Internal and External Validity

The literature review used a meta analysis similar to the approach used in assessing the role of community health financing (Preker and Carrin 2005). Because methodological rigor in research on voluntary health insurance is heavily influenced by researchers' ideological bias, any study that failed to meet high methodological standards was not given serious attention.

Assessment of Overall Performance

Volume contributors examined both the impact and determinants of voluntary health insurance. They assessed the robustness of evidence that such insurance provides financial protection against the cost of illness, expands coverage and includes a wide range of client groups, increases disposable income and household consumption smoothing, increases access to affordable health care, and increases labor market participation.

METHODOLOGY USED IN *GLOBAL MARKETPLACE FOR PRIVATE HEALTH INSURANCE: STRENGTH IN NUMBERS*

Like *Friend or Foe,* this second volume, *Global Marketplace for Private Health Insurance: Strength in Numbers*, used for the country case studies a combination of cross-sectional and longitudinal techniques (quantitative and qualitative) to explore the role of private voluntary health insurance in securing wider and better access to health care. Where possible, health financing projection models were used to estimate fiscal implications, labor market effects, and impacts on revenue and expenditure flows in the health sector.

Methodology Used to Review Empirical and Economic Underpinnings

The studies presented in the Empirical and Economic Underpinnings section of *Global Marketplace* recap some of the central themes from *Friend or Foe.*

The first chapter in this section of the new volume uses the same methodology as the companion volume to review the underlying economics and constraints to private voluntary health insurance found at low-and middle-income levels (see discussion above). The chapter summarizes some of the controversial debates on development paths, supply- and demand-side subsidies, role of regulation, and definition of the benefits package. The authors use institutional analysis to examine the core policy variables, and the management, organizational, and institutional characteristics of health care financing in general (table A.1) Policy actions by governments, civil society, and the private sector are mediated though supply and demand factors that include service delivery systems (product markets), input generation (factor markets), stewardship or government oversight (policy making, coordination, regulation, monitoring, and evaluation), and market pressures.

The second chapter in the *Global Marketplace* volume presents similar but more detailed cross-sectional analysis of the impact of private voluntary health insurance on selected outcome indicators in different regions of the world from the analysis presented in the comparable chapter of *Friend or Foe.* The third chapter tests and validates the theoretical groundwork laid out by Mark V. Pauly

TABLE A.1 Implementation Arrangements for Strategic Purchasing of Health Care

Political economy	Political choice about appropriate role of state Government failure Market failure Stakeholders
Policy design financial flows	**Underlying revenue collection mechanisms** Level of prepayment (full versus partial with some copayment or cost sharing) Degree of progressivity (high versus flat rate) Earmarking (general versus targeted contributions) Choice (mandatory versus voluntary) Enrolment (unrestricted versus restrictions in eligibility, waiting periods, and switching) **Underlying pooling of revenues and sharing risks** Size (small versus large) Number (one versus many) Risk equalization (from rich to poor, healthy to sick, and gainfully employed to inactive) Coverage (primary versus supplementary, substitutive, or duplicative) Risk rating (group or community rating versus individual) **Resource allocation and purchasing (RAP) arrangement** For whom to buy—members, poor, sick, other? What to buy, in which form, and what to exclude? From whom—public, private, nongovernmental organization? How to pay—what payment mechanisms to use? At what price—competitive market price, set prices, subsidized?
Organizational structures	Organizational forms (configuration, scale, and scope of insurance funds?) Incentive regime (from public to private in terms of hierarchies versus agency versus market incentives in decision rights, market exposure, financial responsibility, accountability, and coverage of social functions?) Linkages (extent of horizontal and vertical integration versus purchaser provider split or fragmentation?)
Institutional environment	Legal framework Regulatory instruments Administrative procedures Customs and practices
Management capacity	Management levels (stewardship, governance, line management, client services) Management skills Management incentives Management tools (financial, human resources, health information)

↓ ↓

Possible outcome indicators	*Efficiency*	*Equity (mainly poverty impact)*
Financial protection		
Household consumption		
Access to health care		
Labor market effects		
Coverage		

Source: Adapted from Preker and Langenbrunner, eds., 2005.

and Peter Zweifel in *Friend or Foe* against the empirical evidence from the 12 case studies in the present volume (Pauly 2007; Zweifel, Krey, and Tagli 2007; and Zweifel and Pauly 2007).

Country Case Studies

The case studies use both quantitative analysis of microlevel household survey data and qualitative analysis of key policy, management, organizational, and institutional determinants of good outcomes, using an adapted version of the methodology developed for research on community financing (Preker and Carrin 2005).

The case studies use qualitative techniques to describe insurance schemes' policy, institutional, organizational, and management attributes that may lead to strengths and weaknesses similar to those in the framework used for the review of literature described above and summarized in table A.1. The case studies use quantitative analysis of microlevel household survey techniques to shed light on five possible benefits of voluntary health insurance. Possible market indicators for each of the major benefits are indicated in table A.2.

Volume contributors searched various household budget surveys, Living Standard Measurement Surveys (LSMS), and Demographic and Health Surveys (DHS) for voluntary health insurance data. Most surveys do not allow identification of households with access to voluntary health insurance. Therefore, the subset of countries that can be examined using this methodology is small.

Impact of PVHI on Financial Protection and Consumption Smoothing

To gauge the impact of voluntary health insurance on financial protection and consumption smoothing, a measure with the following properties is needed:

- Given income, premiums, and the distribution of medical spending, the measure *rises* when insurance coverage increases.
- Given income, premiums, and insurance coverage, the measure *falls* when the distribution of spending becomes more variable (higher relative probability of high cost).

TABLE A.2 Market Indicators for Benefits of Voluntary Health Insurance

Dependent variable	*Possible market indicators*	*Independent variables*
Financial protection	Household expenditure	All policy, organizational, institutional, and management variables and factors in PRSP framework
Consumption smoothing	Nonmedical goods and services consumption	
Access to care	Service utilization	
Labor	Labor market and productivity	
Enrolment	Household members	

Source: Preker, Scheffler, and Bassett 2007.

- Given income, insurance coverage, and the distribution of medical expenses, the measure *falls* as paid premiums rise (paid by household).
- Given insurance coverage, premiums, and the distribution of medical expenses, the measure *falls* as income falls.

The proposed measure is

$$\wp = \overline{\text{NMC}} \,/\, (\sigma_{\text{NMC}}) = \text{inverse of coefficient of variation of NMC},$$

where

$$\begin{aligned} \wp &= \text{financial protection;} \\ \overline{\text{NMC}} &= \text{average of nonmedical consumption;} \\ \text{NMC} &= \text{nonmedical consumption;} \\ \text{OOPS} &= \text{out-of-pocket spending;} \\ \rho &= \text{premium;} \\ \sigma &= \text{standard deviation;} \\ \text{Y} &= \text{household income; and} \\ \text{NMC} &= \text{Y} - (\rho + \text{OOPS}). \end{aligned}$$

Definitions:

HEX = health expenditure;
OOPS = out-of-pocket health care expenditure by individuals or households;
Premiums = amount spent by individuals or households;
Income = total revenues of households from formal and informal sector sources;
Insurance coverage = ratio of (total household HEX) – OOPS/total household; and HEX.

Assumptions:

1. Increases in insurance coverage reduce some values of OOPS and so reduce σ_{NMC}.
2. Increases in variance of medical spending increase σ_{NMC}.
3. Increases in paid premiums reduce NMC.
4. Increases in income increase NMC.

Impact of PVHI on Access to Health Care

To assess the impact of scheme membership on access to health care, a two-part model was used.[1] The first part of the model analyzes the determinants of using health care services. The second part of the model analyses the determinants of health care expenditures for those who reported any health care use.

There are several reasons for taking this approach. First, using health expenditure alone as a predictor of financial protection does not allow capture of the lack of financial protection for people who choose not to seek health care because they cannot afford it. As the first part of the model assesses the determinants of utilization, this approach allows us to see whether membership with voluntary health insurance reduces barriers to access to health services. Second, the distribution of health expenditures is typically not a normal distribution. Many nonspenders do not use health care in the recall period. The distribution also has a long tail due to the small number of very high spenders. To address the first cause of non-normality, the study restricted the analysis of health expenditures to those who report any health care use. As the first part of model assesses determinants of use, we will still be able to look into whether scheme membership removes barriers to care. To address the second part of non-normality, a log-linear model specification is used.

Part one of the model is a binary logit model for the Rwanda, Thailand, and India (other countries will also be considered) data sets and a probit model in the Senegal model (other countries will also be considered). The model estimates the probability of an individual's visiting a health care provider. Formally, part one of the model can be written as follows:

(1) $\text{Prob (visit} > 0) = X\beta + \varepsilon.$

Part two is a log-linear model that estimates the incurred level of out-of-pocket expenditures, conditioned on positive use of health care services. Formally, part two of the model can be written as follows:

(2) $\text{Log (out-of-pocket expenditure} \mid \text{visit} > 0) = X\gamma + \mu,$

where X represents a set of individual and household characteristics that are hypothesized to affect individual patterns of utilization and expenditures, β and γ are μ vectors of coefficient estimates, and ε and μ are error terms.

The two variables of primary interest are scheme membership status and income. Other control variables were also included in the estimation model to control for the differences in need for health care (for example, age, gender); differences in preferences toward seeking health care (for example, gender, religion); and differences in the cost (direct and indirect) of seeking health care (for example, distance).

Impact of PVHI on Labor Market Productivity

The assessment of the impact of enrolment with voluntary health insurance on labor market productivity will look at the actual days relative to the total number of days that the person would have worked had he or she not been on leave due to illness.

The hypothesis to be tested is that members who have access to voluntary health insurance are more likely to seek care for medical illnesses earlier and therefore require less time off work due to illness than those that do not have access to voluntary health insurance or other forms of community financing, social insurance, and subsidized care.

Effect on Labor Productivity of Household Members (Household Surveys)

The following assumptions were made about the impact of insurance on labor productivity–related variables:

1. *Insured persons will lose fewer days of work due to illness:* An insured person seeks health care earlier than somebody without insurance and hence might require less time off work. This then has an impact for the sick person as well as for the person who looks after that person.

   Model: Either a binominal model (BMI) or OLS with the same structure

   Dependent variable to be looked for: absenteeism from work due to illness

   Independent variables: the common control variables + health insurance membership

   Prob (absenteeism from work > 0) = $X\beta + \varepsilon$.

2. *Insured persons will be more productive while at work:* One example would be farmers in rural malaria-prone areas. Malaria infections substantially reduce the ability to work and thus lower productivity. We assume that insured persons have better access to drugs as well as appropriate protection schemes (bed nets) and by this effect work more productively in physically demanding agricultural activities. This holds true for other activities as well.

   Model: Either BMI or OLS

   Dependent variable: Income/labor (input, for example, man work days, and so on); alternative BMI

   Independent variables: the common control variables + health insurance membership

   Prob (worked hours/man day per given activity > 0) = $X\beta + \varepsilon$.

3. *Insured persons will have a higher probability of hiring in or hiring out labor:* Evidence from household surveys on cost of illness suggests that households that are better protected against health shocks have a higher probability of joining the labor force. This has an important impact on household welfare as well as on the local economy.

   Dichotomous variable: Household hiring-in or hiring-out of labor

   Independent variable: The common control variables + health insurance membership

   Prob (hiring labor, in or out > 0) = $X\beta + \varepsilon$.

4. *Insured persons will take on riskier jobs:* People having health insurance are willing to take riskier jobs with better pay, but also to invest in more high-risk, high-return activities.

   Dependent variable: The kind of activities a household undertakes (differentiated according to risk profiles and income-earning possibilities)

Labor Market Effects

The following assumptions were made about the impact of insurance on labor markets:[2]

1. *Voluntary health insurance coverage has an impact on wages.* A higher aggregate cost of labor may shift to workers in the form of lower individual wages.
2. *Voluntary health insurance coverage has an impact on labor force participation*: The extension of subsidized health insurance to the nonworking population (for example, married women), led to a decline in their labor market participation (this effect would be most pronounced in low-income households) (Chou and Staiger 2001).
3. *Voluntary health insurance coverage has an impact on employment patterns.* Labor demand may shift toward exempted sectors, primarily low-hour or low-wage sectors.
4. *Voluntary health insurance coverage has an impact on coverage.* Double coverage of dependents might be reduced by discouraging unneeded dependent coverage.

Determinants of Enrolment with PVHI

To assess the determinants of enrolment with PVHI, it is assumed that the choice of whether to enroll is influenced by two main determinants: individual and household characteristics and community characteristics. Individual and household characteristics influence the cost and the benefit calculation of the rational individual decision maker.

This choice is moderated, however, through certain social characteristics of the member households. The individual rational choice model of weighting costs and benefits of joining a prepayment scheme is altered by the social values and ethics of the local culture. For example, two individuals with similar individual and household characteristics (such as income, household size, assets, education, health status) may decide differently about joining or not joining a prepayment scheme depending, for example, on encouragement from community leaders, availability of information, ease of maneuvering unknown processes.

To estimate the weight of these determinants, a binary logit model was applied to four of the data sets and a binary probit was applied to the Senegal data set. The model can be written as follows.

(1) $\text{Prob (enrolment} > 0) = X_1\beta_1 + X_2\beta_2 + \varepsilon.$

The independent variable takes on a value of 1 if the individual belongs to a voluntary health insurance scheme and 0 if he or she does not. X_1 represents a set of independent variables characteristic of the individual and the household such as income, gender, age, or marker on chronic illness or disability. X_2 represents a set of independent variables that approximate the social values in the communities: religion, marker on various communities where appropriate. Other variables specific to the surveys as well as interaction terms were included where appropriate. β_1 and β_2 are vectors of coefficient estimates and ε is the error term.

The two variables of primary interest are income (measure of social inclusion) and a marker for community factors (dummy variable). Control variables also included gender, age, disability or chronic illness, religion, and distance to the health center under the scheme. Some of these variables are important to control for the different probability of health care use (for example, age, health status, distance from provider). These variables also allow us to test the presence and importance of adverse selection to which all voluntary prepayment schemes are subject. Other variables (for example, gender, religion) included control for the different individual and household attitudes toward investment in health at a time when illness is not necessarily present. Literature has shown that the distance to the hospitals and local health centers and existence of outreach programs influence the decision to purchase membership in the scheme.

NOTES

1. This model is similar to the two-part demand model developed as part of the Rand Health Insurance experiment to estimate demand for health care services (Duan et al. 1982; Manning et al. 1987).
2. Labor market effects are more relevant for middle-income countries. For details and methodology, see Thurston 1997.

REFERENCES

Chou, Y. J., and D. Staiger. 2001. "Health Insurance and Female Labour Supply in Taiwan." *Journal of Health Economics* 20 (2): 187–222.

Duan, N., W. Manning, C. Morris, and J.P. Newhouse. 1982. *A Comparison of Alternative Models for the Demand for Medical Care.* Santa Monica: RAND Corporation (Pub. no. R-2754-HHS). Abridged version published in *Journal of Business and Economic Statistics* 1 (April 1983): 115–26.

Jütting, J. 2004. "Do Community-Based Health Insurance Schemes Improve Poor People's Access to Health Care? Evidence from Rural Senegal." *World Development,* February (2): 273–88.

Manning, W. G., J. P. Newhouse, N. Duan, E.B. Keeler, and A. Leibowitz. 1987. *Health Insurance and the Demand for Medical Care: Evidence from a Randomized Experiment.* Santa Monica: RAND Corporation (Pub. no. R-3476-HHS). Abridged version published in *American Economic Review* 77: 251–77.

Pauly, M.V. 2007. "Insights on Demand for Private Voluntary Health Insurance in Less Developed Countries, " In *Private Voluntary Health Insurance in Development: Friend or Foe,* ed. A.S. Preker, R.M. Scheffler, and M.C. Bassett, 23–54. Washington, DC: World Bank.

Preker A. S., and G. Carrin, eds. 2005. *Health Financing for Poor People: Resource Mobilization and Risk Sharing.* Washington, DC: World Bank.

Preker, A.S., and John C. Langenbrunner, eds. 2005. *Spending Wisely: Buying Health Services for the Poor.* Washington, DC: World Bank.

Preker, A.S., R.M. Scheffler, and M.C. Bassett, eds. 2007. *Private Voluntary Health Insurance in Development: Friend or Foe?* Washington, DC: World Bank.

Thurston, N. 1997. "Labor Market Effects of Hawaii's Mandatory Employer-Provided Health Insurance." *Industrial and Labor Relations Review* 51 (1): 117–35.

Zweifel, P., B.B. Krey, and M. Tagli. 2007. "Supply of Private Voluntary Health Insurance in Low-Income Countries." In *Private Voluntary Health Insurance in Development: Friend or Foe,* ed. A.S. Preker, R.M. Scheffler, and M.C. Bassett, 55–113. Washington, DC: World Bank.

Zweifel, P., and M.V. Pauly 2007. "Market Outcomes, Regulation, and Policy Recommendations." In *Private Voluntary Health Insurance in Development: Friend or Foe,* ed. A.S. Preker, R.M. Scheffler, and M.C. Bassett, 115–45. Washington, DC: World Bank.

APPENDIX B

Glossary of Terms

Ability/willingness to pay. Often inappropriately assumed to be equivalent. Willingness to pay is mediated by ability to pay and by individual and cultural aspects that determine the perceived benefit to self and to the community. There are two ways to assess willingness to pay (WTP):

- data on past health care utilization and expenditure;
- contingent valuation methods based on surveys.

Ability to pay (ATP) is largely determined by affordability. ATP for health insurance must be considered in the context of copayments and transaction costs. The concept of fairness may be an important consideration in designing a microinsurance scheme and setting premiums.

Accountability. Result of the process that ensures that decision makers at all levels actually carry out their designated responsibilities and that they are held accountable for their actions.

Actual premium. The premium arrived at by estimating the average benefit payout and adding a safety margin for contingencies.

Actuary. This person compiles statistics on events and works out their probabilities (including joint probabilities) and premiums.

Adverse selection. Problem of asymmetric information that disturbs the operation of the insurance market, resulting in an inequitable transaction. The insured, knowing the likelihood of events, chooses to insure against only those that pose a strong risk. The insurer, having less information, accepts a contract that does not include premiums for low-risk events. The insured gains from the insurer's inability to distinguish "good" and "bad" risks.

Affordability. See Ability to pay.

Agent. Another term for insurer.

Ambulatory care. Outpatient medical care provided in any health care setting except hospitals.

Asymmetrical information. Parties to a transaction have uneven access to relevant information that governs an informed choice. Such asymmetry can result in an inequitable transaction in favor of the party with the most information, or it can result in the abandonment of the exchange.

Balance sheet. Statement showing the financial position at a particular point in time (for example, at the end of the financial year), listing all assets and liabilities at that time.

Bayesian method. A method (originally enunciated in 1763) for revising the probability of an event's occurrence by taking into account data as they come to hand. The usefulness of this approach depends on the relevance and power of the additional data.

Beneficiary or principal. The person designated to receive payouts from the scheme. This is typically the policyholder or a family member, but it may be an employer.

Benefit exclusion. Refusal of access to a specific benefit for an insured. Because this exclusion could be subject to abuse if it is based on arbitrary decisions made at the time of claim rather than as set out in the contract, it tends to be regulated. Reasons for exclusion that are typically allowed include a qualifying period and preexisting illness.

Benefits package or compensation. A list of specific benefits agreed upon in the health insurance contract. While private insurance typically offers modules of benefits from which to choose, microinsurers may offer a standard package for simplicity and fairness.

Beta distribution. Beta is a distribution (first used by Gini, 1911) for a real random variable whose density function is null outside the interval [0, 1] and depends on two strictly real parameters. The shape of this distribution depends on the values of the parameters: it can be U-shaped, or J-shaped, or hat-shaped. For this reason, this distribution is very often used for modeling proportions or probabilities.

Binomial distribution. A statistical method for understanding the probability of events that have only two possible outcomes—"success" or "failure." These probabilities are constant. In insurance, the binomial distribution is applied to estimate the number of persons in a community that will seek (ambulatory) care in a given period.

Bottom-up. See Top-down global strategy.

Broker. An intermediary who sells on behalf of another.

Capacity. Has two meanings:

- Insurers' ability to underwrite a large amount of risk on a single loss exposure or many contracts on one line of event. Reinsurance enables a greater capacity among primary insurers.
- Organizational and individual skills. Organizational capacity implies appropriate systems for information and management and adequate resources for handling operations.

Capacity building. Increasing organizational and individual skills and establishing frameworks for that increase to continue.

Central limit theorem. States that, as the sample size increases, the characteristics of the sample will more closely approximate those of the population from which that sample was drawn. This theorem is valuable in health insurance as it enables estimates of risk in a population to be based on sample data.

Claim load. The amount of benefits paid to the insured in a period. Fluctuations in claim load in the short term are covered by contingency reserves and in the long run by contribution increases.

Coefficient of variation. The ratio of the sample standard deviation to the sample mean. It measures the spread of a set of data as a proportion of its mean. It is often expressed as a percentage. This coefficient enables, for example, estimation and comparison of ranges of likely expenses for various communities.

Coinsurance. Spreads a risk too great for a single insurer over several companies that together act as coinsurers.

Collection rate or compliance rate. The proportion of possible subscriptions from members that the microinsurer collects. Lack of complete compliance can result from cultural as well as economic factors. It may be used as a measure of a microinsurer's efficiency/commercial orientation. Members are more likely to pay contributions if their perceived risk is higher.

Community. A group of people with a common interest. Often implies locality, but can be occupation-, leisure-, or religion-based.

Community financing scheme. See Community-based health insurance.

Community participation. Sharing by citizens in any kind of community in communal decision making processes and definitions of problems.

Community rating. A method for determining insurance rates on the basis of the average cost of providing health services in a specific geographic area. This method ignores the individual's medical history or the likelihood of the individual's using the services.

Community-based health insurance. Community initiatives to generate health care financing through voluntary prepayment schemes.

Compensation. Benefit payout.

Compliance. Payment of contribution owed by members.

Compliance gap. Difference between contributions due and contributions collected.

Compliance rate. The ratio of actual contributions over potential contributions. See collection rate.

Compulsory insurance. Any form of insurance the purchase of which is required by law. Governments typically require the purchase of liability insurance with respect to three types of potential loss-causing activities: those whose severity could be particularly great, with the possibility of large numbers of innocent persons being harmed because of a single event; those whose frequency is sufficiently great to affect large numbers of innocent persons independently; and those judged to be inherently dangerous.

Confidence interval. A range of values that is estimated to contain the population parameter. To be 95 percent confident that a range contains the parameter requires a larger range than to be 90 percent confident. For example, analysis of data from a community might suggest a 90 percent chance that the number of people seeking hospitalization in a year will be between 1,100 and 1,500, but the confidence interval for 95 percent confidence is 978 and 1,747.

Contingency reserves or equalization reserves. Funds held by the insurer that are in excess of expected benefit payouts in order to cover unexpected events (contingencies) that cause fluctuations in benefit payouts. They are typically regulated in order to ensure the insurer's solvency.

Contribution. Payment of an agreed sum of money by a member to a social insurance system in return for specified benefits. The implied assumption is that other sources of income complement members' payments. See also Premium.

Contribution base. The amount that would be available to the insurer if all members contributed fully. This relies on full disclosure of income (disclosure rate).

Contribution rate. The percentage of contribution base actually or expected to be collected.

Cooperative. A group of people who have united voluntarily to realize a common goal, by establishing a democratically run company, providing an equitable quota of the necessary capital, and accepting a fair share of the risks and the profits of this company. Members also take an active part in its operation.

Copayment or cost sharing. The portion of medical expenses paid by a member/beneficiary. This amount is the balance remaining after the insurer has paid its portion.

Cost sharing. See Copayment.

Covariance. A measure of the relationship between two variables. Covariance does not specifically imply a cause-and-effect relationship *(causation),* although it may intuitively be inferred to exist, as can its direction. For example, if health problems vary with housing density, it may be possible to infer that density affects health, but the observed covariance of the frequency of schizophrenia with social status may not have a simple unidirectional explanation.

Covariant risk. When events are not independent, the occurrence of one may affect the occurrence of another. For example, the risk of one family member's catching influenza is covariant with that of another family member. Disasters and shocks are classic cases where proximity influences covariation. When insuring against risk of events, the actuary must consider the covariation between those risks.

Cream skimming (preferred risk selection). An exercise whereby an insurer selects only a part of a larger heterogeneous risk group ("preferred risks") in which all individuals pay an identical risk-adjusted premium. When the insurer reduces its loss ratio compared with the expected average cost that determined the premium, the insurer can retain a profit from cream skimming. This profit depends on the insurer's ability to distinguish several subgroups with different expected costs within the larger group, and to predict the lower future health care expenditure of individuals in the preferred group.

Cross-subsidies. Amounts effectively paid when the wealthy members pay more than poor, or when the healthy pay the same as the sick for lower expected benefits. The poor and the sick are said to receive cross-subsidies from the wealthy and healthy.

Crude birth rate. A summary measurement of the total number of live births in a specified population at the end of a specific time period (generally one year), divided by the midyear total population count. Expressed as the number of births per 1,000 people within that population.

Crude death rate. A summary measurement of the total number of deaths in a specified population at the end of a specific time period (generally one year), divided by the midyear total population count. Expressed as the number of deaths per 1,000 people within that population.

Declaration rate. See Contribution base.

Deductible. A provision requiring the insured to pay part of the loss before the insurer makes any payment under the terms of the policy. Deductibles typically are found in property, health, and automobile insurance contracts. The purpose of establishing deductibles is to eliminate small claims and reduce the average pure premium and administrative costs associated with claims handling. Deductibles can also reduce moral hazard by encouraging persons to be more careful with respect to the protection of their property and prevention of loss. Annual deductibles and waiting periods are the most common forms of deductibles in health insurance contract.

Defined benefit. The amount, usually formula-based, guaranteed to each person who meets defined entitlement conditions. The formula usually takes into account the individual number of contribution or insurance years and the individual amount of earnings during the same period.

Delphi method or nominal group technique. A method of business forecasting that consists of panels of experts expressing their opinions on the future and then revising them in light of their colleagues' views so that bias and extreme opinions can be eliminated.

Demand. The amount of a good or service that consumers seek to buy at a given price. *Solvent demand* implies the ability to pay as well as the willingness to pay. *Elasticity of demand* is a measure of the responsiveness of total spending on a particular good or service to a change in its price. *Elastic demand* implies that as the price goes up the total expenditure falls. Inelastic demand implies that as the price goes up total expenditure goes up also. Necessities typically have inelastic demand (given an adequate income base). For example, the imperative to have an aching tooth removed means that the dentist is in a position of power to charge a high price; such dental services have inelastic demand and it is unlikely that a lower price would attract people not suffering from toothache to have a tooth removed. The concept of "necessity" and therefore of what has an inelastic demand, is cultural. In some cultures prenatal care may not be considered a necessity. Demand for some procedures may be truncated in poor communities. This means that, although the demand for surgery (for example) is inelastic and does not change with price, above a certain price it becomes zero. As half an operation is not an option, the demand is truncated due to poverty.

Dual theory of risk. The theory that describes the attitudes of individuals toward insuring themselves, by weighing on the one hand their wealth and on the other hand their aversion to risk. Two possible modifications could swing the balance in favor of insurance: decreasing the premium, or increasing aversion to risk. Even with identical feelings toward monetary loss, individuals would likely adopt different attitudes toward insurance because their feeling is different toward the probability of monetary loss; the higher that assessment, the more attractive insurance is. Consequently, two individuals sharing the same utility index for certain wealth cannot have a different degree of aversion for risk (and the converse).

Endemic disease. A sickness habitually present in an area or population.

Epidemic. The occurrence of any disease, infectious or chronic, at a frequency greater than expected, based on prior patterns of disease incidence and prevalence.

Epidemiological transition. The changing pattern of health and disease within a specified population from a predominantly infectious disease pattern of low life expectancy and high mortality, to a predominantly chronic disease pattern of high life expectancy with high morbidity. In the intermediate stage of transition, high survival rates from endemic infectious disease combined with high rates of chronic illness in survivors results in a "double burden of disease." The latter is typical of many developing countries.

Epidemiology. The study of any and all health-related issues in specified populations at specified times, including but not limited to: the occurrence and frequency of medical conditions, diseases, or other health-related events; identification of the determinants of medical conditions, diseases, health-related events, and health status; the evaluation of medical procedures and diagnostic tests; the evaluation of a health care system; the evaluation of a population's demand and use of health care services; evaluation of the safety and efficacy of a pharmaceutical product; post-market surveillance of pharmaceuticals to determine product effectiveness and occurrence of side effects or adverse events; the evaluation of quality of life, access to care and health status in general.

Equalization reserves. See Contingency reserves.

Escrow account management. Implies the use of a special account for managing payments of various obligations. For example, a savings account may be set up to establish funds for paying insurance premiums and loan repayments.

Estimation. The process by which sample data are used to indicate the value of an unknown quantity in a population. Results of estimation can be expressed as a single value, known as a point estimate, or a range of values, known as a confidence interval. The outcome of estimation is the *estimator.*

Excluded population or excluded communities. Typically agricultural, self-employed, or poor people who have neither formal employers nor steady wages as the basis for access to government-run or commercial health insurance. They may also be excluded from housing, education, disaster relief, and other social services. They may also be unable to access financial services, or secure formal recognition of property they control or own, including property obtained under traditional (tribal) law.

Experience rating. A system where the insurance company evaluates the risk of individuals or groups by examining their health history.

Externalities. Benefits or costs with an impact beyond the parties to a transaction. That impact is not considered in the buy/sell decision and so is not reflected in the price. Pollution is an example of an external cost; safe waste disposal has external benefits.

Fairness. See Ability to pay.

Fertility rate. A measure of the total number of live births in a specified population during a specific time period (generally one year) in relation to the midyear total number of women in the specified population. Expressed as the number of live births per 1,000 women within that population.

Fiduciary. A person who holds something in trust for another.

First-line insurer. See Insurer.

Formal sector. The part of the economy/society that is registered with authorities and subject to regulations and standards.

Freeriding. Exists in health care when persons can benefit from a health care system without contributing to the system.

Gatekeeper. A primary care physician responsible for overseeing and coordinating all of a patient's medical needs. The gatekeeper must authorize any referral of the patient to a specialist or hospital. Except in cases of emergency, the authorization must be given prior to care.

Government failure. Occurs where government does not provide goods and services or an adequate regulatory or support framework for the private sector to provide them.

Gross domestic product (GDP). The annual total value of goods and services produced in a country for use in that country.

Imperfect competition. Occurs in markets or industries that do not match the criteria for perfect competition. The key characteristics of perfect competition are: a large number of small firms; identical products sold by all firms; freedom of entry into and exit out of the industry; and perfect knowledge of prices and technology. These four criteria are essentially impossible to reach in the real world.

Income effect. A price reduction that gives buyers more real income, or greater purchasing power for their income, even though money or nominal income remains the same. This price reduction can cause changes in the quantity demanded of the good.

Independence. Two events are independent if the occurrence of one of the events gives no information about whether or not the other event will occur; that is, the events have no influence on each other For example, falling ill with measles may be independent of being injured in a cyclone.

Induced demand. Demand created by physicians who face inelastic demand and so can set both the price and the level of care. This ability to determine their own income is difficult to control and has great repercussion on health budgets.

Informal risk-protection mechanism. See Informal sector.

Informal sector. The part of the society/economy that is not registered with authorities and, de jure or de facto, is not subject to public regulation and does not benefit from public services or goods. For example, support given by a family, friends, and members of a community in times of loss or illness effectively forms an informal risk-protection mechanism. Despite the presumption that such care is voluntarily given, in some cases (for example, providing care to foster children), payment may in fact be given.

Inpatient. Individual admitted to a hospital for health care and allocated a bed for the duration of that admission.

Insolvency. Inability to meet current expenses from current income plus reserves, leading, in the long run, to bankruptcy.

Institution. Social constructs that contain "rules of the games" and thereby both constrain behavior and enable behavior within those rules. By enabling the individual and organization to understand and predict behavior, the social constructs facilitate economic and social interaction. Institutions include regulations and policies of organizations and governments. They also include community-based traditional patterns of behavior and those that have developed in the face of modernization.

Insurability. A risk is insurable if it is random, and there is a party willing to accept the risk for an agreed premium and another party is prepared to pay that premium (this means it is solvable). This situation implies that the probability is known, that it is free of moral hazard and adverse selection problems, that it is a legal proposition, and that the premium is affordable. Practical problems associated with information availability may render otherwise insurable risks uninsurable.

Insurance. Insurance is any activity in which a company assumes risk by taking payments (premiums) from individuals or companies and contractually agreeing to pay a stipulated benefit or compensation if certain contingencies (death, accident, illness) occur during a defined period.

Insurance threshold. Insurers typically request that the insured pay the first part of any claim. This cost sharing is a form of deductible, used to simplify administration by reducing the number of small claims.

Insured. Also called *Principal*; the end user contracting with an insurer for insurance coverage.

Insured unit. See Subscription unit.

Insurer (first-line, primary, or ultimate). The company that contracts with the end user for insurance. The first-line insurer may be the ceding insurer if it chooses to reinsure.

Internal rate of return. The discount rate that makes the net present value of an investment project equal to zero. This is a widely used method of investment appraisal as it takes into account the timing of cash flows.

Law of large numbers. The concept that the greater the number of exposures, the more closely will actual results approach the probable results expected from an infinite number of exposures.

Load. The cost of insurance (administration, finance, profit, and so on) as distinct from payouts (benefits). Efficient companies have a low load relative to benefits.

Macroeconomic. Refers to factors that operate at the national and global levels, for example, exchange rates, inflation rates, and interest rates. The origins of any factors operating at the local level are large scale. Macroeconomic shocks are changes in the large-scale factors that affect the economy and society.

Market failure. A condition in which a market does not efficiently allocate resources to achieve the greatest possible consumer satisfaction. The four main market failures are: public good, market control, externality, and imperfect information. In each case, a market acting without any government-imposed direction, does not direct an efficient amount of resources into the production, distribution, or consumption of the good.

Maximum likelihood estimate (MLE). Provides the best estimate of a population value that makes the sample data most likely. For example, given that a survey of 50 households in a community indicates that 5 percent of individuals have tuberculosis, what is the proportion of tuberculosis sufferers in the community that is most likely to have given rise to this statistic? The MLE techniques enable such calculation.

Mean. Average. It is equal to the sum of the observed values divided by the total number of observations

Members. See Subscription unit.

Microfinance institution (MFI). Provides financial services to the poor on a sustained basis. The services include saving and credit societies, agricultural insurance, property insurance schemes and, more recently, health insurance schemes.

Microinsurance. A mechanism for pooling a whole community's risks and resources to protect all its participating members against the financial consequences of mutually determined health risks.

Microinsurance unit (MIU). A very small finance institution specifically designed to offer health insurance to the poor by pooling risks across a community.

Monte Carlo simulation. A statistical technique in which an uncertain value is calculated repeatedly using randomly selected "what-if" scenarios for each calculation. The simulation calculates hundreds and often thousands of scenarios of a model. Uncertain quantities in the model are replaced with fuzzy numbers to see how that uncertainty affects results. Ideally, the simulation aids in choosing the most attractive course of action, providing information about the range of outcomes such as best- and worst-case and the probability of reaching specific targets.

Moral hazard. An insurance-prompted change in behavior that aggravates the probability of an event in order to access benefits, for example, an insured's demanding tests not required on medical grounds. Provider-induced moral hazards include overservicing.

Morbidity. Refers to illness from a specified disease or cause or from all diseases. It is a change in health status from a state of well-being to disease occurrence and thereby a state of illness.

Mortality. Refers to death from a specified disease or cause or from all diseases.

Multilateral utility. See Utility.

Nominal group techniques. See Delphi method.

Nongovernmental organization (NGO). Generally refers to a not-for-profit or community organization.

Normal distribution. Statistically speaking, values of events fall in a pattern around the average value with known frequencies. For instance, if the average stay in hospital after childbirth is three days, the values of each stay would be distributed around three, some more, some less, approximately symmetrically, with greater concentration around three than around any other number. The normal distribution is a particular distribution of this kind that is rigorously defined mathematically and gives the typical bell-shaped curve when graphed. This distribution is very powerful in enabling insurers to calculate costs and utilization.

Outlier. Denotes events that fall outside the norm. For example, in a "review of utilization" a provider who uses far fewer or far more services than the average is called an *outlier.*

Outpatient. Person receiving health care in a hospital without admission to the hospital or accommodation in it. The length of stay is less than 24 hours. It may be a consultation or the carrying out of technical act (diagnosis or therapeutic procedure).

Pandemic. A disease prevalent throughout an extensive region, country, or continent, or throughout the world.

Parameter. A number that describes a characteristic of a population. For example, the life expectancy of men in a community might be 56 years. Health insurance uses statistical techniques to estimate the parameter the estimation of the parameter is called the *statistic.* One sample of 50 men taken from the community might estimate the average age statistic to be 54 years while another sample might estimate it to be 57.5 years.

Pay-as-you-go. Refers to a system of insurance financing under which total expenditure (benefit expenditure plus administrative expenditure) in a given period is met by income (contributions and other sources) from the same period. Pay-as-you-go financed insurance schemes do not accumulate reserves, except contingency reserves; surpluses and deficits translate into increases or decreases in the premium.

Per capita premium. The practice of applying a single premium per head across the population.

Point estimation. An estimate of a parameter of a population that is given by one number.

Poisson distribution. Typically, a Poisson random variable is a count of the number of events that occur in a certain time interval or spatial area. For example, the number of people seeking critical care for malaria in a wet season month in a particular village. The Poisson distribution can sometimes be used to approximate the binomial distribution when the number of observations is large and the probability of success is small (that is, a fairly rare event). This is useful since the computations involved in calculating binomial probabilities are greatly reduced.

Population density. A measure of the size of the population in comparison to the size of a specified geographic area (region, country, province, city). Typically it is a count of the number of residents per square kilometer.

Preferred risk selection. See Cream skimming.

Premium. Fee paid by an insured to an insurance company in return for specified benefits. Under social insurance the premium is called *contribution.* See also Contribution.

Prevalence. The total number of cases or people who have a specified disease, health condition, attribute, or risk factor within a specified population at a specific point in time.

Preventive health care. Medical care directed primarily toward early detection and treatment or prevention of disease or ill health (for example, such as immunizations, prenatal care).

Primary health care. The first level of contact by individuals, families, and communities with the health system, bringing health care as close as possible to where people work and live. The organization of primary health care depends upon the socioeconomic and political characteristics of the country, but should address prevention, curative and rehabilitation services, and include education of the population about major health problems and their prevention and control. Such care may be provided by a variety of health workers, acting together as a team, in partnership with the local community.

Primary insurer. See Insurer

Principal. Denotes the client, in the relationship between an insurer (agent) and the insured (principal). See Insured.

Probability. A quantitative description of the likely occurrence of a particular event. Probability is conventionally expressed on a scale from 0 to 1; a rare event has a probability close to 0, a very common event has a probability close to 1.

Probability distribution. The probability distribution of a discrete random variable is a list of probabilities associated with each of its possible values. It is also sometimes called the *probability function* or the *probability mass function.* For example, the probability of a woman's delivering a single live baby might be 98 percent, twins 1.78 percent, triplets 0.218 percent, more than triplets 0.002 percent.

Providers. Doctors, nurses, hospitals, clinics, laboratories, imaging facilities, pharmacies, and other deliverers of medical services. The insurer or regulating body typically requires that a provider be qualified and/or registered in order to be included in a health insurance scheme.

Public goods. There are two aspects to public goods: it is difficult to prevent nonpayers from consuming them (nonexcludable), and their consumption by one party does not affect their consumption by others (nonrival). Vaccination is an example—those who do not pay and are not vaccinated cannot be excluded from enjoying the lower prevalence of disease; and the fact they are healthy as a result does not affect another's ability to be healthier as a result of the program.

Government usually provides public goods, because private businesses do so profitably.

Pure premium. The pure premium can be defined as the average loss per exposure unit for a specific coverage, or more specifically, the product of the average severity and the average frequency of loss. The result is the amount, which the insurance company should collect to cover all the losses to be met under the predefined types of coverage.

Qualifying conditions. Requirements for acceptance into an insurance plan; also describes the provisions that must be met before a benefit is payable.

Random variable. A function that provides a single numerical value to a particular event or outcome. The value of the random variable will vary from trial to trial as the experiment is repeated. For example, if 10 people visit a hospital as outpatients in a morning, and 7 of them have injuries rather than disease, the random variable for that event is 0.7. Another example: if the life span of a particular baby born 10 weeks premature in a community is 2 days, 4 hours and 7 minutes, the random variable of that event is that duration.

Rating. See Risk rating.

Reciprocating arrangements. Agreements existing between primary insurers to coinsure, the objective being to stabilize funds. These arrangements are sometimes considered an alternative to reinsurance in that they enlarge the pool and reduce risk variance.

Recovery gap. An excess of benefit payouts over income. The gap is not random, when the *compliance gap* is assumed to be zero. The recovery gap is not random and so cannot be solved by reinsurance.

Reinsurance. The transfer of liability from the primary insurer, the company that issued the contract, to another insurer, the reinsurance company. This mechanism allows a diversification of the risk and enlarges the risk-pooling base, thereby reducing the risk of insolvency. However, reinsurance extends only to risk defined in the cession contract (called *Treaty*). For example, a treaty to cede fluctuations in payouts will not cover the primary insurer against the financial risk of insolvency, for example, because of poorly run or unviable insurance.

Reinsurance premium. The amount charged by the reinsurer to accept an agreed amount of risk.

Reinsurance threshold. Reinsurers typically require that the insurer retain the first proportion of risk for any event. That proportion is the threshold as it is equivalent to the deductible or excess borne by the insured when making a claim against property insurance.

Reserves. Funds held either for a possible but unknown event (contingency funds) or because of regulation. A major financial management goal is to minimize reserves and thus maximize funds available for current use.

Risk. The probability or likelihood that a specified health event (for example, the occurrence of a disease or death) will occur to an individual or population group within a specific period of time.

Risk factor. An attribute (for example, a lifestyle factor or a personal characteristic) or an exposure to an environmental factor associated with an increase in the probability that a specified health event (for example, onset of disease) will occur.

Risk pooling. The process by which fluctuations in risk are reduced by averaging the risk over large numbers and heterogeneous memberships. Insurers risk pool through reinsurance.

Risk rating. Calculation of health insurance premiums based on the risk of each client. When the premium is calculated based on the risk not of a single individual but of a group, this is called *community rating* or *group rating.* When the premium is set in relation to the client's income, this is called *income rating.*

Risk segregation. Each individual faces his or her own risks without pooling.

Risk sharing. Individuals agree to split the cost of risky events. Insurers share risk through reciprocal relationships and reinsurance. Loan guarantees and insurance are among the many ways of sharing risks.

Safety coefficient. A measure of the difference between the expected annual result of an insurance scheme and the worst possible loss than can be borne. Information on the safety coefficient enables management to make better decisions about reserve levels.

Self-insurance or self-protection. Refers to all the arrangements made by an individual or group to protect themselves from risk. It includes not only saving and establishing contingency reserves but also changing behavior to diminish or avoid risk.

Simulation. The technique of imitating behavior and events during an experimental process. Typically involves a computer.

Social capital. Refers to the multidimensional "glue" that binds community members together. While concepts of social capital vary from culture to culture, Putnam (1993) defined it as including trust, community involvement, tolerance of diversity, value of life and extent of connectivity (socially and professionally.

Social exclusion. Inadequate or unequal participation in social life, or exclusion from a place in the consumer society, often linked to the social role of employment or work.

Social insurance. An insurance program that is shaped by broader social objectives than just by self-interest of each individual principal or agent, while retaining insurance principles that persons are insured against a definite risk.

Social protection. Policies and programs designed to reduce poverty and financial vulnerability. Social protection policies typically focus on labor market policies, social insurance, social assistance, community-based schemes, and child protection.

Social reinsurance. Reinsurance undertaken in pursuit of social goals rather than profit.

Social utility. The gain to society from, in this case, insurance. Where insurance has zero or negative social utility it may be banned; where it has high social utility but low private utility it may be mandated. The choice of rendering a public utility mandatory or not depends on political will or the power of authorities, including community leaders.

Soft budget. A budget with a flexible limit.

Solidarity principle. Applying rules that spread risks and resources across members of a group in a way that provides both insurance coverage and egalitarian distribution. *Risk solidarity* would imply that high-risk individuals receive a subsidy from low-risk individuals, allowing all risk levels equal access to health care coverage. Solidarity between high- and low-income individuals *(income solidarity)* implies income redistribution through organized transfers. In insurance, the solidarity principle is juxtaposed to the *equivalence principle,* which implies that the insurer has to break even on each insurance contract, by applying *risk rating.*

Solvable. An insurance transaction is said to be solvable if the risk is observable; there is no antiselection *(adverse selection),* and the premium is acceptable to both parties.

Solvent demand. See Demand.

Spot market transaction. The "spot market" implies transactions for immediate delivery of services as distinct from the insurance requirement of prepayment against (possible) future delivery of services. Populations that are excluded from health insurance rely on spot payments (user fees).

Standard deviation. A statistical term for a measure of the variability in a population or sample.

Subscription unit. Refers to the people covered by a single membership. This may be the individual (usually in developed economies) or the household (usually in developing economies).

Target group. Refers to both current and future beneficiaries of the insurance system. The target group can comprise several subgroups of people with similar characteristics (for example, income, economic sector).

Top-down global strategy. Implies that the approach to improving access to health care or health insurance was directed by a powerful global body to national governments and down through the rank and file to the community.

This contrasts with the "bottom up" approach based on the empowerment of communities.

Transaction costs. The costs additional to the price of a good or service, arising, for example, from search costs, travel costs, or transfer of ownership costs.

Ultimate insurer. See Insurer.

Underwriter. A company that receives the premiums and accepts responsibility for the fulfillment of the policy contract; the company employee who decides whether or not the company should assume a particular risk; the agent who sells the policy.

Underwriting. The process by which the insurer decides what risks to cover. The profit objectives may conflict with social obligation. For the reinsurer, underwriting considerations determine the risks of the primary insurer that can be accepted for reinsurance, and which the insurer will retain.

Underwriting assistance. Reinsurance companies gather extensive data on the insured and events. They can share this information with insurers to improve the performance of insurers.

Unilateral utility. See Utility.

Uninsurable. See Insurability.

Unit cost. The average cost of particular health care treatments. These are negotiated between a microinsurance unit and providers. Insurance enables a move away from fee-for-service toward averaging out-of-unit costs.

Universal coverage. Implies that all members of a community have health insurance.

User fees. See Spot market transaction.

Utility. The satisfaction gained from having the desire for goods and services met. Multilateral utility means that several parties benefit from outcomes. This can be a group of insured or the insurer and the insured. Unilateral utility means that only one party gains. The balance between group and individual utility is a delicate component of relations within a community, between insurer/insured, or between insurer/reinsurer.

Utilization. Refers to use patterns of medical services in a location over a period. Data on recent utilization, collected at the national and community levels, is a valuable asset in predicting future patterns.

Variation coefficient. See Coefficient of variation.

Vector-borne infectious disease. Infections caused by human contact with an infectious agent, transmitted from an infected individual by an insect or other live carrier. For example, malaria is biologically transmitted from an infected individual to a noninfected person by the same mosquito (the vector) biting both people.

Working capital. Current assets minus current liabilities. It is the capital available for an organization's short-term financing.

Willingness to pay (WTP). See Ability to pay.

NOTE

This glossary was adapted from "Glossary of Terms," Appendix C in *Social Reinsurance: A New Approach to Sustainable Community Health Financing,* David M. Dror and Alexander S. Preker, eds., 465–485, World Bank, Washington, DC, and International Labour Office, Geneva, Switzerland.

About the Coeditors and Contributors

COEDITORS

Alexander S. Preker is head of Health Investment Policy and lead economist in the Investment Climate Department of the World Bank Group. Previously he served as chief economist for the World Bank's health sector in 2000–03 and lead economist in the Africa Region 2004–08. He coordinated the World Bank team that prepared the Bank's *Sector Strategy for Health, Nutrition, and Population* in 1997 and worked with the World Health Organization (WHO) in 1999–2000 in preparing the World Health Report 2000 *Health Systems: Measuring Performance*. In 2000–2001, he was a member of Working Group 3 of the WHO Commission on Macroeconomics and Health. He was a member of a team of researchers that assisted the WHO African Regional Office in preparing a regional health financing strategy in 2006. In 2007 he contributed to the Global Task Force on Scaling Up the Education of Health Workers. He is currently on the technical advisory committee for a new US$1 billion private sector investment facility for Africa and a member of the Bank's Global Expert Team. Preker has published extensively on topics related to health financing, health economics, and institutional development in the health sector. He is on the Bank's External Operations Editorial Committee and managed the Bank's formal Health, Nutrition, and Population Series as well as several online newsletters and electronic journals. In addition to his work with the World Bank Group, Preker is an adjunct professor of health policy and management in the Mailman School at Columbia University in New York and an adjunct professor of public administration and health at the Wagner Graduate School of Public Service at New York University. He teaches regularly in the Berkeley/Cambridge Health Leadership Forum and at the Faculty of Management at McGill University in Montreal. Preker's formal training includes a PhD in economics from the London School of Economics and Political Science, a fellowship in medicine from University College London, a diploma in medical law and ethics from King's College London, and an MD from the University of British Columbia/McGill.

Peter Zweifel is a professor of economics at the Socioeconomic Institute, University of Zurich. He also serves as coeditor-in-chief (with Mark Pauly, Wharton School) of the *International Journal of Health Care Finance and Economics (IJHFE)*. His main research interests are health economics, insurance economics, energy economics, and regulation. His current research projects deal with the division of labor between private insurance and social insurance, and the relationships between technological change in medicine and health insurance. His published works include *Ein ökonomisches Modell des Arztverhaltens* [An economic model of physician behavior], Lecture Notes in Economics and Mathematical Systems (Springer), *Internationaler*

Handel: Theorie und Empirie [Foreign trade: theory and empirical evidence] (jointly with Robert H. Heller), *Versicherungsökonomie* [Insurance economics] (jointly with Roland Eisen), *Energieökonomie* [Energy economics] (jointly with Georg Erdmann), and *Health Economics* (jointly with Friedrich Breyer), also published in German. (pzweifel@soi.uzh.ch)

Onno P. Schellekens is managing director of the PharmAccess Foundation and founder of the Health Insurance Fund for Africa and the Investment Fund for Health in Africa. PharmAccess is a not-for-profit organization for improving the quality of basic health care and HIV/AIDS treatment and care in Africa. This includes both the medical services and the financial/administrative organization of health care. PharmAccess provides medical, administrative, and financial support to public and private health care providers and health insurers. Before joining PharmAccess, Schellekens worked for 10 years for Solvay Pharmaceuticals, a European chemical and pharmaceutical company. He is author and coauthor of many publications on the HIV/AIDS pandemic, particularly in Africa. He holds a master's degree from the School of Management and Organization at the University Groningen, The Netherlands, and took the INSEAD Asia Executive Course (1996). (o.schellekens@pharmaccess.org)

OTHER CONTRIBUTING AUTHORS

Rajeev Ahuja, PhD, is a health economist in the Health, Nutrition and Population Unit of the World Bank, Delhi office. He has been working on health care financing in India, with special focus on public health spending, risk pooling mechanisms, and demand-side financing. Formerly, he was a senior fellow with the Indian Council for Research on International Economic Relations (ICRIER), New Delhi. At ICRIER, Ahuja did economic policy research, particularly on trade and social and security issues. His recent work has focused on health insurance, especially for low-income people. In April–October 2002, he was a visiting fellow at the Centre for Development Research in Bonn. In 2004 he was also a recipient of a GDN visiting fellowship to the International Monetary Fund, Washington, D.C. He has published articles in several national and international journals and has participated in many conferences and seminars. (ahujaahuja@yahoo.com)

Mark C. Bassett has, since 1998, been head of public policy at the British United Provident Association (BUPA), the United Kingdom's largest independent health care group. From 2003 to 2005, he was seconded to the World Bank as senior health specialist and International Federation of Health Plans fellow. He has worked in the United Kingdom National Health Service in various managerial roles and was seconded to the Department of Health (England), where he was responsible for policy on independent health care. He has a master's in health services management from Manchester University and is a fellow of the Royal Society of Medicine in London.

Peter A. Berman, MSc, PhD, is a health economist with thirty years of experience in research, policy analysis and development, and training and education in global health. He joined the World Bank's New Delhi office as lead economist for health, nutrition, and population in July 2004 from the Harvard School of Public Health, where he had been professor of population and international health economics and director of the International Health Systems Program (IHSP). Berman is the author or editor of five books on global health economics and policy as well as dozens of academic articles and papers. He has led and/or participated in major field programs in all regions of the developing world. Berman's specific areas of technical expertise include analysis of health systems performance and the design of reform strategies; assessment of the supply side of health care delivery and the role of private health care provision in health systems and development of strategies to improve outcomes through public-private sector collaboration; and the use of national health accounts as a policy and planning tool. (pberman@worldbank.org)

Ricardo A. Bitrán is a health economist with more than 25 years of experience in Chile, the United States, and more than 35 developing countries. His areas of expertise include the prioritization of health spending, the economic evaluation of health investment and reform projects, the analysis of equity, efficiency, and financial sustainability, and the formulation and evaluation of health policy. Since 1995, he has been president of Bitrán & Asociados, an international consulting firm based in Santiago, Chile, specializing in health finance and economics. Previously, he worked for Abt Associates Inc. of Cambridge, Mass., and for the Massachusetts Department of Public Health. Over the past 20 years, he has been a consultant to the World Bank, the Inter-American Development Bank, the World Health Organization, and the governments of two dozen developing countries. His academic experience also spans more than 20 years, with teaching posts or assignments in Chile, China, France, the United States, and Zaire and a dozen other developing countries. Since 2000 Dr. Bitrán has been academic director of the Harvard/Bank Flagship Program on Health Sector Reform. He is the author of academic articles, book chapters, and research papers. He received a PhD in economics and an MBA in finance from Boston University, and an MS in industrial engineering from the University of Chile. (ricardo.bitran@bitran.cl)

Petra Došenovič Bonča, MSc, is a teaching and research assistant in the Department of Economic Theory and Policy in the Faculty of Economics at the University of Ljubljana, Slovenia. Her research fields are health economics and public economics. Her current research focuses on efficiency and performance of health care providers in Slovenia and on innovations as factors of efficiency and performance. She is a member of the Statistical Advisory Committee for Health at the Statistical Office of the Republic of Slovenia and participated in the development of the first postgraduate degree program offered in Slovenia in health economics and management. The development of this program was sponsored by the European Union. She has published several papers analyzing and assessing Slovenia's health care system and policy initiatives related to this sector. She participates in reform efforts and is currently involved in two consultancy projects for hospitals in Slovenia. (petra.d.bonca@ef.uni-lj.si)

M. Kate Bundorf is an assistant professor of health research and policy at the Stanford University School of Medicine and a faculty research fellow at the National Bureau of Economic Research. Her research focuses on health insurance markets, including the determinants and effects of individual and purchaser choices, the effects of regulation in insurance markets, the interaction of public and private systems of health insurance, and incentives for insurers to improve health care quality. She received her MBA and MPH from the University of California at Berkeley in 1996 and her PhD from the Wharton School at the University of Pennsylvania in 2000. (bundorf@stanford.edu)

Anna Cederberg Heard is a doctoral student in the Department of Population and International Health in the School of Public Health at Harvard University and holds a Master's degree from the same department. Her current research interests include determining how public-private performance-based contracts can be used to improve health services in developing countries. She is also interested in the roles of social insurance and pharmaceutical companies in improving access to care. (acederbe@hsph.harvard.edu)

Bernard F. Couttolenc is a health economist, a professor at the University of São Paulo School of Public Health, and president of Interhealth Ltda, a consulting company based in São Paulo, Brazil, specializing in economic analysis, health care management, and health reform and policy. He has been a consultant to the World Bank and other international organizations on health sector reform, health sector financing and health insurance, and has accumulated more than 20 years of international experience in developing countries. He has recently coordinated a series of pioneering studies on the hospital sector in Brazil, including hospital efficiency, payment mechanisms, expenditure, and financing. He holds a PhD in health economics from the Johns Hopkins University and an MBA in health service management from Fundação Getúlio Vargas in São Paulo. (bernard@interhealth.com.br)

Denis Drechsler is a policy analyst at the OECD Development Centre where he coordinates work on policy coherence, in particular in the areas of gender equality, migration, and human security. He is the author of several articles and papers on the impact of institutions on development and the initiator of an innovative data platform to exchange information on gender equality (Wikigender). Before joining the Development Centre in September 2004, Drechsler was a member of the Poverty Reduction and Economic Management Group of the World Bank and a visiting fellow at the American Institute for Contemporary German Studies at Johns Hopkins University. His other positions include assistantships at the German Parliament and the European Institute for International Economic Relations. Drechsler completed his graduate studies in political science and economics at Potsdam University, the Institute d'Etudes Politiques de Grenoble, and the University of Wisconsin. (Denis.Drechsler@oecd.org)

Teh-wei Hu is a graduate school professor and professor emeritus of health economics at the University of California, Berkeley. During the past 20 years, he has served as a consultant/adviser to the Ministry of Health in China, the Department of Health in Taiwan (China), and the Bureau of Health and Welfare in Hong Kong (China) on health care financing reform. He has also served as consultant to the World Bank, World Health Organization, U.S. government, and the Rand Corporation. He has published more than 200 articles in leading professional journals. (thu@uclink4.berkeley.edu)

Kee Taig Jung is a professor and chair of health services management programs at Kyung Hee University in Seoul, Republic of Korea. His recent research and consulting work have focused on developing the health care industry for the 21st-century growing economy. He has served as chief adviser to the presidential committee on envisioning the Korean economy, the prime minister's committee for developing a biomedical city, and the deregulation committee in the Ministry of Health. In 2000, he received the best article of the year award from the Korean association for health policy and administration. In 2001, He was awarded the faculty fellowship by the Korean Ministry for sabbatical leave at the Stanford Center for Health Policy. He is an adjunct fellow at the Leonard David Institute of Health Economics at the University of Pennsylvania and the Center for Health Policy and Center for Primary Care Outcomes Research at Stanford University. Jung received his BA from Seoul National University in 1986, his MBA from Cornell University in 1988, and his PhD from the Wharton School at the University of Pennsylvania in 1992. (ktjung@khu.ac.kr)

Johannes P. Jütting is a senior economist at the OECD Development Centre and head of the unit on policy coherence for development and human security. His responsibilities include conceptualizing, managing, and providing leadership in the areas of employment, gender, social protection, and institutions. He has published extensively in peer reviewed journals such as *World Development* and the *Journal of Human Development*. Prior to joining the OECD in 2002, Jütting was a research fellow at the Center for Development Research in Bonn (ZEF) where he directed a research group on poverty (1997–2002). He holds a PhD in agricultural economics from Humboldt-University, Berlin, and received his habilitation in development economics from the University of Bonn. (johannes.jutting@oecd.org)

Vijaysekar Kalavakonda, an insurance specialist with both policy and operations experience, leads health financing and insurance work for the Financial Operations and Policy Department at World Bank headquarters. He has worked on insurance issues in Bangladesh, the Caribbean, Central America, Ghana, India, Mexico, Morocco, Tunisia, Turkey, and Sri Lanka. He has worked in the health division of the Munich Reinsurance Company and for a major health care company in India. His primary focus is private health care financing and insurance. He has a triple Master's degree in biotechnology, business administration and European social insurance. In addition he is a certified Health Insurance Associate (HIA) and Managed Healthcare Professional (MHP) from the America's Health Insurance Plans (USA)/Health Insurance Association of America (HIAA). (vkalavak@worldbank.org)

Marianne Lindner is senior policy adviser of PharmAccess Foundation, a Dutch not-for-profit organization that focuses on increasing access to quality basic health care by building sustainable health systems in Africa. Lindner started her career as an economist with the ABN AMRO Bank (then, AMRO), one of the largest commercial banks in the Netherlands. From there she moved into the field of development. During most of the 1990s she undertook assignments with the United Nations. She worked as an economist in the Africa Bureau of the United Nations Development Programme in New York, focusing on economic policy and programs in Africa. This was followed by various assignments with UNICEF in Africa, where she lived and worked in several countries (Zimbabwe, Senegal, Somalia, and Angola), focusing on socioeconomic policy and social sector program planning, research, monitoring, and evaluation with an emphasis on health. After her return to the Netherlands in 2000 she undertook consultancy assignments with the European Union, bilateral donor agencies, and nongovernmental organizations in the areas of health systems development and socioeconomic policy. She has published in various journals and is currently coediting a book on the scaling up of health insurance in collaboration with the World Bank. She received Master's degrees in economics from the University of Amsterdam and in health policy, planning, and financing from the London School of Economics and the London School of Hygiene and Tropical Medicine (with distinction). (m.lindner@pharmaccess.org)

Ajay Mahal, PhD, is an assistant professor of international health economics in the Department of Population and International Health at the Harvard School of Public Health. Prior to joining Harvard, he was a senior researcher at the National Council of Applied Economic Research in New Delhi. His current and ongoing work encompasses a wide range of topics, including: the growth of the medical education sector in India and migration among India's medical graduates; diffusion of modern medical technology in India and other developing countries; health systems; health and support systems for India's elderly; economic analysis of injecting-drug use behavior; and the impact of HIV/AIDS in Botswana and Nigeria. He has policy experience in the Dominican Republic, India, Jamaica, Nigeria, Palestine, Sri Lanka, Ukraine, and elsewhere. Mahal holds degrees from Columbia University (PhD, 1995) and the University of Delhi (MA, 1985; BA 1983). (amahal@hsph.harvard.edu)

Rodrigo Muñoz is an engineer specializing in social sector studies in low- and middle-income countries. He first did social sector studies as a consultant for the World Bank Living Standards Measurement Studies. He then became a consultant at Bitrán and Associates, where he was hired for his expertise in sampling, fieldwork management, data modeling, information systems, and custom software design in the field of health economics. Now an associate of the firm, Muñoz leads several economic studies in Africa, Asia, and Latin America. (rodrigo.munoz@bitran.cl)

Vimbayi Mutyambizi is a researcher in the Health Economics Unit at the University of Cape Town. She has worked in the Department of Health of Limpopo Province, South Africa, as well as in private sector consulting. Her current research interests include private health care financing and access to quality health care services for low-income, poor, and vulnerable households and communities. She has also done research on the strategies and resources used by poor urban households in coping with HIV/AIDS. Vimbayi has a Master's degree in health economics from the University of Cape Town, South Africa. (vimbayim@yahoo.com)

Heba Nassar, professor of economics, has been head of the Economics Department, Faculty of Economics, Cairo University, since 2007. In 2004–07 she was the vice dean for community development, Faculty of Economics and Political Science (FEPS), Cairo University and vice chair for all academic centers at FEPS. In 1988–2005 she was the director of the Center for Economic and financial Research and Studies. Since 1992 she has also been a research professor at the Social Research Center, American University in Cairo. She serves as adviser to the Economic Committee of the Parliament, a member of the board of the Holding Company of Electricity, a member of the Permanent Scientific Committee for Promotion of Professors in Economics in Egypt, a member of the Health Committee of the National Specialized Councils, a member of the economic committee of the National Council for Women. She is a fellow of the Economic Research Forum and a member of the Steering Committee of the Research Alliance for Development, World Bank Paris. She has published several papers in national and international academic conferences and proceedings on health, population economics and labor market, microfinance, MDGs, structural adjustment, small business, women's economic participation, human resource development, poverty, social protection, and migration. (hebanas@aucegypt.edu)

Alexandre C. Nicolella holds a doctoral degree in economics from the University of São Paulo, Brazil, and is a professor at the same university in the School of Economics, Business, and Accounting at Ribeirão Preto. In recent years he has undertaken research in health economics and has been involved at Interhealth Ltda in several studies on hospital efficiency (applying the DEA and benchmarking techniques), hospital costs, health sector and hospital spending and resource allocation, and health insurance in Brazil. (anicolella@fearp.usp.br)

Obinna Onwujekwe, MD, MSc, PhD (health economics), is a post-doctoral fellow with the Gates Malaria Partnership, London School of Hygiene & Tropical Medicine as well as a senior lecturer in the Department of Health Administration and Management, College of Medicine, University of Nigeria Enugu Campus. He is also the coordinator of the Health Policy Research Group (HPRG) at the University of Nigeria. The HPRG is one of the partners of the Consortium for Research into Equitable Health Systems (CREHS), an initiative funded by the British Department for International Development (DFID). Major research interests and work include the use of context-specific contingent valuation question formats; economics of endemic diseases, especially malaria; equity in health care; health sector reforms, and health care financing. (onwujekwe@yahoo.co.uk)

Mark V. Pauly is Bendheim Professor in the Department of Health Care Systems at the Wharton School, professor of health care systems, insurance and risk management, and business and public policy at the Wharton School, and professor of economics in the School of Arts and Sciences at the University of Pennsylvania. He has made significant contributions to the fields of medical economics and health insurance. His classic study on the economics of moral hazard was the first to describe how health insurance coverage may affect patients' use of medical services. Subsequent work, both theoretical and empirical, has explored the impact of conventional insurance coverage on preventive care, outpatient care, and prescription drug use in managed care. He received his PhD in economics from the University of Virginia. (pauly@wharton.upenn.edu)

Sameh El-Saharty, MD, MPH, is a senior health policy specialist in the Middle East and North Africa Region (MENA) at the World Bank. Before joining the Bank, he held several positions with international donors, academic institutions, and consulting firms, including the U.S. Agency for International Development, Harvard University, the United Nations Population Fund, and Pathfinder International. Dr. El-Saharty has 20 years of experience in medicine, maternal and child health, public health, health systems and management, health insurance and health sector reform programs in several countries in the MENA and Africa Regions and in the United States. He is responsible for leading the Bank's health policy dialog in a number of countries in the MENA Region and for coordinating regional initiatives. Dr. El-Saharty has written several publications, health strategy reports, and analytical studies. He holds a Doctor of Medicine from Cairo University and a Master's degree (MPH) from Harvard University in international health policy and economics. (selsaharty@worldbank.org)

Richard M. Scheffler is distinguished professor of health economics and public policy at the University of California, Berkeley, and holds the university's chair in health care markets and consumer welfare. He is also director of the Global Center for Health Economics and Policy Research at Berkeley. His research is focused on health care markets, health insurance, the health workforce, mental health economics, social capital and health, pharmacoeconomics, and international health systems. He is a former World Bank visiting scholar, Rockefeller scholar, Fulbright scholar, and scholar at the Institute of Medicine at the National Academy of Sciences. He received a senior scientist award from the National Institute of Mental Health and the Carl Taube Award for distinguished contributions to the field of mental health services research. In 2003 he was elected president of the International Health Economics Association. He is the author of *Is There a Doctor in the House? Market Signals and Tomorrow's Supply of Doctors* published by Stanford University Press (2008).

Siripen Supakankunti, PhD, is an associate professor of economics and director of the WHO Collaborating Centre for Health Economics at the Faculty of Economics, Chulalongkorn University, Bangkok, Thailand. Her areas of specialization include: health economics, impacts of structural change on the health sector; the economics of the pharmaceutical industry; and international trade in health services. (ssiripen@chula.ac.th)

Maks Tajnikar, PhD, is a professor of economics in the Faculty of Economics at the University of Ljubljana, Slovenia. He served as Minister of Small Business (1992–93) and Minister for Economic Affairs (1993–96) of the Republic of Slovenia. He was dean of the Faculty of Economics in 2001–07. He has published more than 230 papers, articles in various journals, text books (microeconomics, managerial economics, venture management, post-Keynesian economic theory) and is the author of five books and coauthor of five books. His current research fields are entrepreneurship, public economics, and health economics. He participated in the development of the first postgraduate degree program in health economics and management offered in Slovenia and is currently head of this program. He is also a member of the council of the Trbovlje General Hospital in Slovenia. (maks.tajnikar@ef.uni-lj.si)

Michael Thiede, PhD, is a senior consultant at the IGES Institute, Berlin, Germany, where his current focus is on pharmaceutical markets. Previously he worked as an associate professor for health economics at the University of Cape Town, South Africa, where he was also the director of the Health Economics Unit. He has conducted research on health care inequities, pro-poor strategies in health reform, and the economics of pharmaceutical markets. He received his PhD in economics from the University of Kiel, Germany. (Michael.Thiede@iges.de)

Edit V. Velényi is a consultant with the Development Economics Research Group of the World Bank and affiliated with the Africa Results and Learning Unit.

Her work focuses on impact evaluation of malaria programs in a multicountry comparative design. She has been consulting for the Amsterdam Institute for International Development (AIID) on the design of a multicountry operational research program in Africa to evaluate the impact of interventions enabled by the Health Insurance Fund for Africa. Velényi is a PhD candidate at the Department of Economics, University of York, United Kingdom. Her PhD research focuses on microeconometric modeling of choice and impact of micro health insurance on low-income households in India. Before beginning her doctoral program, Velényi worked as a consultant with the Africa Region's Human Development Technical Unit, and with the Health, Nutrition, and Population Sector Hub of the World Bank. During her consultancy with the World Bank, she coedited the volume *Public Ends, Private Means: Strategic Purchasing of Health Services* (Preker, Liu, Velényi, and Baris 2007). She has been a coauthor of several book chapters on health insurance for World Bank publications. Velényi has an MA with a concentration in international economics and law from the School of Advanced International Studies, Johns Hopkins University, Washington, D.C., and an MA from the University of Economics, Budapest, Hungary. (evelenyi@worldbank.org)

Xiao-hua Ying is associate professor of health economics in the School of Public Health, Fudan University (Former Shanghai Medical University), Shanghai, China. Ying has participated in many research programs as a research member or principal investigator in last 10 years. His research specialties are private health insurance, public health insurance, equity in health services, and cost-effectiveness analysis of health services. He has published more than 40 papers in Chinese journals and top professional journals. He holds a PhD in health economics. (xhying@fudan.edu.cn)

Index

Boxes, figures, notes, and tables are indicated by b, f, n, and t, respectively.

ECO-AUDIT
Environmental Benefits Statement

The World Bank is committed to preserving endangered forests and natural resources. The Office of the Publisher has chosen to print ***Global Marketplace for Private Health Insurance*** on recycled paper with 30 percent postconsumer fiber in accordance with the recommended standards for paper usage set by the Green Press Initiative, a nonprofit program supporting publishers in using fiber that is not sourced from endangered forests. For more information, visit www.greenpressinitiative.org.

Saved:

- 23 trees
- 7 million BTUs of total energy
- 2,155 pounds of CO_2 equivalent greenhouse gases
- 10,378 gallons of waste water
- 630 pounds of solid waste

green press INITIATIVE